A WANDERING ARAMEAN

SOCIETY OF BIBLICAL LITERATURE

MONOGRAPH SERIES

edited by
Leander E. Keck

associate editor
James L. Crenshaw

NUMBER 25

A WANDERING ARAMEAN
Collected Aramaic Essays
by
Joseph A. Fitzmyer, S.J.

JOSEPH A. FITZMYER, S.J.

A WANDERING ARAMEAN
Collected Aramaic Essays

SCHOLARS PRESS

Distributed by
Scholars Press
PO Box 5207
Missoula, Montana 59806

A WANDERING ARAMEAN
Collected Aramaic Essays
by
Joseph A. Fitzmyer, S.J.

Library of Congress Cataloging in Publication Data

Fitzmyer, Joseph A
A wandering Aramean.

(Monograph series - Society of Biblical Literature ; no. 25)
Includes bibliographical references and indexes.
1. Aramaic philology—Addresses, essays, lectures. 2. Aramaic literature—Relation to the New Testament—Addresses, essays, lectures. 3. Bible. N.T.—Criticism, interpretation, etc.—Addresses, essays, lectures. 4. Bible. N.T.—Language, style—Addresses, essays, lectures. I. Title. II. Series: Society of Biblical Literature. Monograph series ; no. 25.
PJ5201.F5 492'.29 77-21379
ISBN 0-89130-150-X
ISBN 0-89130-152-6 pbk.

Printed in the United States of America

1 2 3 4 5

Edwards Brothers, Inc.
Ann Arbor, Michigan 48104

CONTENTS

List of Abbreviations vii

Foreword xv

Chapter 1. The Study of the Aramaic Background of the New Testament 1
- I. Aramaic as a Language of Jesus 6
- II. Aramaic Names, Words, and Phrases Preserved in the New Testament 10
- III. Aramaisms in New Testament Greek 12
- IV. Mistranslations 14
- V. Aramaic Literary Forms in Prose and Poetry 15
- VI. Aramaic and Variant Readings in the New Testament Text-Tradition 17
- VII. Jewish Literary Traditions Found in the New Testament and in Known Aramaic Literature 17
- VIII. Aramaic Epistolography 19

Chapter 2. The Languages of Palestine in the First Century A.D. 29
- I. Latin 30
- II. Greek 32
- III. Aramaic 38
- IV. Hebrew 44

Chapter 3. The Phases of the Aramaic Language 57
- I. Earlier Attempts to Divide the Aramaic Language 58
- II. The Five Phases of Aramaic 60
- III. Reasons for the Phases and Related Problems 63

Chapter 4. The Contribution of Qumran Aramaic to the Study of the New Testament 85
- I. Lexical Matters Supplying a First-Century Palestinian Background to Certain New Testament Problems 87
- II. Jewish Practices or Beliefs that Have Emerged from Qumran Aramaic Texts 96
- III. Qumran Aramaic Literary Parallels to the New Testament 97
- IV. Addendum: Implications of the 4Q "Son of God" Text 102

Chapter 5. The Semitic Background of the New Testament *Kyrios*–Title ... 115
I. The Background of the *Kyrios*–Title ... 115
II. The Original Application of the *Kyrios*–Title to Jesus ... 127
III. The Implication of the *Kyrios*–Title for Jesus ... 130

Chapter 6. The New Testament Title "Son of Man" Philologically Considered ... 143
I. The New Testament Data and Attempts to Translate the Title ... 144
II. The Semitic Data, Hebrew and Aramaic, that Bear upon the Title ... 145
III. The Connotations of the Title in a First–Century Palestinian Context ... 153

Chapter 7. The First-Century Targum of Job from Qumran Cave XI ... 161
I. Job in the Qumran Community ... 162
II. The Qumran Targum of Job ... 163
III. The Qumran Targum of Job and the Second Targum of Job ... 167

Chapter 8. Aramaic Epistolography ... 183
I. The Types, Provenience, and Contents of Aramaic Letters ... 184
II. Some Features of Aramaic Epistolography ... 187
III. Conclusion ... 196

Chapter 9. The Syntax of כל, כלא, "All" in Aramaic Texts from Egypt and in Biblical Aramaic ... 205
I. כל in the Absolute State ... 206
II. כל in the Construct State ... 208
III. The Emphatic State כלא ... 210
IV. The Form כלה ... 214

Chapter 10. The Padua Aramaic Papyrus Letters ... 219

Chapter 11. The Aramaic Letter of King Adon to the Egyptian Pharaoh ... 231

Chapter 12. A Re-Study of an Elephantine Aramaic Marriage Contract (*AP* 15) ... 243

Indexes ... 273
I. Subjects ... 273
II. Modern Scholars ... 278
III. Scripture References ... 285

List of Abbreviations

A	Aḥiqar
AAH	F. Rosenthal (ed.), *An Aramaic Handbook* (Porta linguarum orientalium, ns 10; Wiesbaden: Harrassowitz, 1967)
AB	Anchor Bible
ABL	R. Harper (ed.), *Assyrian and Babylonian Letters*
AC	J. Koopmans, *Aramäische Chrestomathie* (Leiden: Nederlands Instituut voor het Nabije Oosten, 1962)
AD	G. R. Driver, *Aramaic Documents* (see p. 76 below)
ADAJ	*Annual of the Department of Antiquities of Jordan*
AdANdL	*Atti dell'Accademia Nazionale dei Lincei*
AdonL	*Adon Letter* (see p. 242 below)
AfO	*Archiv für Orientforschung*
Ag. Ap.	Josephus, *Against Apion*
AGJU	Arbeiten zur Geschichte des antiken Judentums und des Urchristentums
AION	*Annali dell'istituto orientale di Napoli*
AIPHOS	*Annuaire de l'institut philologique et historique orientale et slave*
AJA	*American Journal of Archaeology*
AJBA	*Australian Journal of Biblical Archaeology*
AJSL	*American Journal of Semitic Languages and Literatures*
AnBib	Analecta biblica
ANET	J. B. Pritchard (ed.), *Ancient Near Eastern Texts*
ANHW	G. Dalmann, *Aramäisches und neuhebräisches Handwörterbuch*
Ant.	Josephus, *Antiquities*
AOS	American Oriental Series
AP	A. Cowley, *Aramaic Papyri of the Fifth Century* (see p. 76 below)

APE	A. Ungnad, *Aramäische Papyri aus Elephantine* (see p. 76 below)
APN	K. L. Tallqvist (ed.), *Assyrian Personal Names*
APO	E. Sachau, *Aramäische Papyrus und Ostraka* (see p. 76 below)
ArDial	G. Dalman, *Aramäische Dialektproben* (see p. 133 below)
ArOr	*Archiv orientální*
ASAE	*Annales du service des antiquités de l'Egypte*
ASOR	American Schools of Oriental Research
AšOst	Aššur Ostracon
ASTI	*Annual of the Swedish Theological Institute*
ATANT	Abhandlungen zur Theologie des Alten und Neuen Testaments
ATR	*Anglican Theological Review*
AUSS	*Andrews University Seminary Studies*
B	Behistun (*or* Bisitun) inscription (see *AP*, pp. 248–71)
BA	*Biblical Archaeologist*
BAG	W. Bauer, *A Greek-English Lexicon of the New Testament* (tr. W. F. Arndt and W. F. Gingrich)
BASOR	*Bulletin of the American Schools of Oriental Research*
BBB	Bonner biblische Beiträge
BDF	F. Blass and A. Debrunner, *A Greek Grammar of the New Testament* (tr. R. W. Funk)
BeO	*Bibbia e oriente*
BETL	Bibliotheca ephemeridum theologicarum lovaniensium
Bib	*Biblica*
BibOr	Biblica et orientalia
BIES	*Bulletin of the Israel Exploration Society*
BJPES	*Bulletin of the Jewish Palestine Exploration Society*
BJRL	*Bulletin of the John Rylands Library*
BKAT	Biblischer Kommentar, Altes Testament

BLA	H. Bauer and P. Leander, *Grammatik des Biblisch-Aramäischen* (see p. 55 below)
B-M	H. Bauer and B. Meissner, "Ein aramäischer Pachtvertrag aus dem 7. Jahre Darius I.,"*SPAW* 72 (1936) 414-24
BMAP	E. G. Kraeling, *Brooklyn Museum Aramaic Papyri* (see p. 75 below)
BMB	*Bulletin du Musée de Beyrouth*
BNTC	Black's New Testament Commentaries
Bodl Aram Inscr	Bodleian Library, Aramaic Inscription(s)
Bowm	R. A. Bowman, "An Aramaic Journal Page,"*AJSL* 58 (1941) 302-13
BSOAS	*Bulletin of the School for Oriental and African Studies*
BTS	*Bible et terre sainte*
BVC	*Bible et vie chrétienne*
BWANT	Beiträge zur Wissenschaft vom Alten und Neuen Testament
BZ	*Biblische Zeitschrift*
BZAW	Beihefte zur *ZAW*
CBQ	*Catholic Biblical Quarterly*
CC	*Corpus Christianorum*
CII	J.-B. Frey, *Corpus inscriptionum iudaicarum*
CIL	*Corpus inscriptionum latinarum*
CIS	*Corpus inscriptionum semiticarum*
CJT	*Canadian Journal of Theology*
Cl-G Ost	Clermont-Ganneau Ostracon
CRAIBL	*Comptes-rendus de l'académie des inscriptions et belles-lettres*
CSEL	Corpus scriptorum ecclesiasticorum latinorum
DBSup	*Dictionnaire de la Bible, Supplément*
DISO	C.-F. Jean and J. Hoftijzer, *Dictionnaire des inscriptions sémitiques de l'ouest*
DJD	Discoveries in the Judaean Desert (of Jordan)

DTT	*Dansk teologisk tidsskrift*
Ephemeris	M. Lidzbarski, *Ephemeris für semitische Epigraphik* (3 vols.; Giessen: Töpelmann, 1900-15)
ESBNT	J. A. Fitzmyer, *Essays on the Semitic Background of the New Testament* (London: Chapman, 1971; reprinted, Missoula: Society of Biblical Literature, 1974)
EstBib	*Estudios bíblicos*
ETL	*Ephemerides theologicae lovanienses*
ETR	*Etudes théologiques et religieuses*
EvT	*Evangelische Theologie*
ExpTim	*Expository Times*
FRLANT	Forschungen zur Religion und Literatur des Alten und Neuen Testaments
Gabba	E. Gabba, *Iscrizioni greche e latine per lo studio della Bibbia* (Turin: Marietti, 1958)
GJPA	G. Dalman, *Grammatik des jüdisch-palästinischen Aramäisch*
GCS	Griechische christliche Schriftsteller
GPL	Z. Harris, *Grammar of the Phoenician Language* (see p. 80 below)
HermWP	Hermopolis West Papyri (see p. 76 below)
5/6Ḥev	Cave 5/6 of Naḥal Ḥever (Wadi Ḫabra)
HeyJ	*Heythrop Journal*
HJPAJC	E. Schürer, *History of the Jewish People in the Age of Jesus Christ* (rev. ed.; Edinburgh: Clark, 1973)
HNT	Handbuch zum Neuen Testament
HTR	*Harvard Theological Review*
HUCA	*Hebrew Union College Annual*
IEJ	*Israel Exploration Journal*
IPN	M. Noth, *Israelitische Personennamen*
IR	R. Hestrin (ed.), *Inscriptions Reveal* (Jerusalem: Israel Museum, 1973)
ITQ	*Irish Theological Quarterly*

J	P. Joüon, "Notes grammaticales, lexicographiques et philologiques sur les papyrus araméens d'Egypte," *MUSJ* 18 (1934) 1-90
JA	*Journal asiatique*
JAOS	*Journal of the American Oriental Society*
JBL	*Journal of Biblical Literature*
JBR	*Journal of Bible and Religion*
JEOL	*Jaarbericht ex oriente lux*
JJS	*Journal of Jewish Studies*
JNES	*Journal of Near Eastern Studies*
JPCI	S. Klein, *Jüdisch-palästinisch Corpus inscriptionum*
JPOS	*Journal of the Palestine Oriental Society*
JQR	*Jewish Quarterly Review*
JRAS	*Journal of the Royal Asiatic Society*
JRS	*Journal of Roman Studies*
JSJ	*Journal for the Study of Judaism in the Persian, Hellenistic and Roman Periods*
JSS	*Journal of Semitic Studies*
JTS	*Journal of Theological Studies*
JW	Josephus, *Jewish War*
KAI	H. Donner and W. Röllig, *Kanaanäische und aramäische Inschriften* (3 vols.; Wiesbaden: Harrassowitz, 1962–64)
KB	L. Koehler and W. Baumgartner, *Lexicon in Veteris Testamenti libros* (Leiden: Brill, 1958)
KlT	Kleine Texte
L	P. Leander, "Laut- und Formenlehre des Ägyptisch-Aramäischen," *Göteborgs Högskolas Årsskrift* 34 (1928) 1-135; reprinted, Hildesheim: G. Olms, 1966.
LCL	Loeb Classical Library
MDOG	Mitteilungen der deutschen Orient-Gesellschaft
MGWJ	*Monatsschrift für Geschichte und Wissenschaft des Judentums*

MPAIBL	*Mémoires présentés à l'académie des inscriptions et belles-lettres*
MPAT	J. A. Fitzmyer and D. J. Harrington, *Manual of Palestinian Aramaic Texts* (BibOr 34; Rome: Biblical Institute, 1978)
MT	Masoretic Text
Mur	Murabbaᶜat texts (see DJD 2)
MUSJ	*Mélanges de l'Université St.-Joseph*
NKGWG	*Nachrichten der königlichen Gesellschaft der Wissenschaften zu Göttingen*
NovT	*Novum Testamentum*
NovTSup	Novum Testamentum, Supplements
NSI	G. A. Cooke, *A Text-Book of North-Semitic Inscriptions* (Oxford: Clarendon, 1903)
NTAbh	Neutestamentliche Abhandlungen
NTB	C. K. Barrett, *The New Testament Background: Selected Documents* (New York: Harper, 1961)
NTS	*New Testament Studies*
NTTS	New Testament Tools and Studies
OGIS	W. Dittenberger, *Orientis graeci inscriptiones selectae*
OLZ	*Orientalische Literaturzeitung*
OrAn	*Oriens antiquus*
Ost	Ostracon
Pad	Padua Aramaic Papyri I–III (see pp. 230 below)
Pan	Panammu (see p. 76 below)
PEFQS	*Palestine Exploration Fund, Quarterly Statement*
PEQ	*Palestine Exploration Quarterly*
PG	J. Migne, *Patrologia graeca*
PJB	*Palästina Jahrbuch*
PPG	J. Friedrich, *Phönizisch-punische Grammatik* (see p. 77 below)

PRU	J. Nougayrol, *Le Palais royal d'Ugarit III* (Mission de Ras Shamra, 6; Paris: Imprimerie Nationale, Geuthner, 1955)
PSBA	*Proceedings of the Society of Biblical Archaeology*
QDAP	*Quarterly of the Department of Antiquities of Palestine*
RA	*Revue d'assyriologie*
RArch	*Revue archéologique*
RB	*Revue biblique*
RE	A. von Pauly and G. Wissowa, *Real-Encyclopädie der classischen Altertumswissenschaft*
RechBib	Recherches bibliques
REJ	*Revue des études juives*
RES	*Répertoire d'épigraphie sémitique*
RevEtSem	*Revue des études sémitiques*
RevScRel	*Revue des sciences religieuses*
RGG	*Religion in Geschichte und Gegenwart* (3d ed.)
RHR	*Revue de l'histoire des religions*
RivB	*Rivista biblica*
RQ	*Revue de Qumran*
RSO	*Rivista degli studi orientali*
RSPT	*Revue des sciences philosophiques et theologiques*
RSR	*Recherches de science religieuse*
RTL	*Revue théologique de Louvain*
SBAW	*Sitzungsberichte der bayerischen Akademie der Wissenschaften*
SBFLA	*Studii biblici franciscani liber annuus*
SBLDS	Society of Biblical Literature Dissertation Series
SBLMS	Society of Biblical Literature Monograph Series
SBLSBS	Society of Biblical Literature Sources for Biblical Study
SBT	Studies in Biblical Theology
SEG	*Supplementum epigraphicum graecum*
Sem	*Semitica*

Sf	Sefire Inscriptions (see p. 76 below)
Shunnar	Papyrus letter published by Z. Shunnar (see p. 198 below)
SNTSMS	Society of New Testament Studies Monograph Series
SPap	*Studia papyrologica*
SPAW	*Sitzungsberichte der preussischen Akademie der Wissenschaften*
SSS	Semitic Study Series
STDJ	Studies on the Texts of the Desert of Judah
SUNT	Studien zur Umwelt des Neuen Testaments
TDNT	G. Kittel and G. Friedrich, *Theological Dictionary of the New Testament*
TGI	K. Galling (ed.), *Textbuch zur Geschichte Israels*
TLZ	*Theologische Literaturzeitung*
TRu	*Theologische Rundschau*
TS	*Theological Studies*
TTKi	*Tidskrift for teologi og kirke*
TWAT	*Theologisches Wörterbuch zum Alten Testament*
TZ	*Theologische Zeitschrift*
UT	C. H. Gordon, *Ugaritic Textbook* (Rome: Biblical Institute, 1965)
VAB	Vorderasiatische Bibliothek
VD	*Verbum domini*
VT	*Vetus Testamentum*
VTSup	Vetus Testamentum, Supplements
WO	*Die Welt des Orients*
ZA	*Zeitschrift für Assyriologie*
ZAW	*Zeitschrift für die alttestamentliche Wissenschaft*
ZDMG	*Zeitschrift der deutschen morgenländischen Gesellschaft*
ZDPV	*Zeitschrift des deutschen Palästina-Vereins*
ZNW	*Zeitschrift für die neutestamentliche Wissenschaft*
ZTK	*Zeitschrift für Theologie und Kirche*

Foreword

Though Aramaic was long known through its biblical, rabbinic, and Syriac forms, the number of texts written in some form of Aramaic that have come to light during the last seventy-five to a hundred years has been extraordinary. By and large, they have given us a good idea of earlier forms of the language and of some of its intermediate stages. Most of the texts have come from Egypt, Palestine, or Syria, even though it is now apparent that during the period of its heyday, when it served as a sort of *lingua franca* for vast areas of the eastern Mediterranean world, it was used in many other countries as well. These new acquisitions have shed light on all sorts of older texts, biblical, ancient Near Eastern, and otherwise.

One of the important areas that the recovery of these ancient Aramaic texts has affected is the study of the New Testament. Even though the writings of this part of the Bible have been composed in Greek, they describe a movement that had its roots in Palestine of the first-century A.D. The fact that Aramaic words are preserved in the Greek has supported the contention that some of its peculiarities are owing to Semitic interference in that language, and in particular to Aramaic interference. Now that Aramaic texts have come to light from Palestine itself and from the period immediately prior to or contemporaneous with the beginning of the Christian religious movement, the question naturally arises to what extent these newly discovered texts bear upon questions with which New Testament students have often wrestled.

But anyone who becomes interested in the Aramaic background of the New Testament soon realizes that it is not limited solely to Palestinian texts, even though they are naturally the most relevant. Interest in Aramaic texts eventually leads one beyond the confines of the problems of the Aramaic background of the New Testament, and this is reflected in the present collection of essays on Aramaic topics.

Even though one or other of the first eight essays in this collection deals with Aramaic matters that go beyond the concerns of a New Testament scholar, they are all of such a nature as to provide a discussion of the wide background of Aramaic with which one has to cope. Essays 9-12 deal with more specific problems in Aramaic texts of an earlier period. They are included here because even in them one finds items that bear at times on various New Testament problems (e.g., the meaning and use of "brother" in the Padua Papyri and its relation to Aramaic texts of the Bar Cochba period and to New Testament ἀδελφός; or the possibility of divorce instituted by a Jewish woman in an Elephantine Aramaic marriage contract).

The first essay is programmatic and seeks to sort out the various aspects of the so-called Aramaic problem of the New Testament; when that generic term is used, it can mean various things, and an effort has been made to sort out at least eight different aspects of the Aramaic problem and indicate some methodological guide-lines for the study of them. The second essay seeks to situate the Aramaic spoken in first-century Palestine against the background of other languages used there at that time (Latin, Greek, and Hebrew). The third essay discusses the various phases of the Aramaic language as they have to be distinguished today in the light of the recent discoveries; the purpose of it is to give some justification to the division that I had proposed earlier and to mark out clearly the sort of Aramaic that one should be considering in the debate about the Aramaic background of the New Testament. The fourth essay seeks to set forth a number of the items that have been brought to light in Qumran Aramaic texts which have a bearing on the study of the New Testament. Of prime importance here is the evidence from such texts that bear upon the study of the New Testament titles such as *κύριος*, *ὁ υἱὸς τοῦ ἀνθρώπου*, *λόγος*, and *ὁ υἱὸς τοῦ θεοῦ*. The fifth essay probes more deeply into the Semitic background of the *Kyrios*-title in the New Testament and explores its application to Jesus and its implications. The sixth essay surveys the philological material that bears on the use of the New Testament title, *ὁ υἱὸς τοῦ ἀνθρώπου*. The seventh essay describes various facets of the new targum of Job from Qumran Cave XI and compares it with the older-known targum in an effort to set forth the differences between a targum from the first-century and that of a later date. The pertinence of this study for the comparison of other targums is easily seen. Finally, the eighth essay attempts to single out the various features of Aramaic epistolography as a contribution to the growing interest in ancient epistolography and the comparable items that one finds in the various New Testament letters. These eight essays, then, all have direct pertinence to various New Testament problems.

The other four essays are concerned with more specifically Aramaic problems or problematic texts. The syntax of the pronoun כל, "all," has created problems in the understanding of various Elephantine texts and biblical Aramaic texts; a study of details of its usage in essay 9 attempts to set forth the major aspects of its syntax. Essays 10–12 are devoted to the re-study of important texts that have either recently come to light or have been affected by new discoveries.

The unity of the twelve collected essays is, admittedly, not perfect. But they reflect the vagaries of my study and research over almost twenty years. The earliest of them (No. 9) was first published in 1957; it was part of a chapter in my doctoral dissertation. But these vagaries in the field of Aramaic also account for the title of the collection, derived from a well-known verse in Deuteronomy, "A wandering Aramean was my father" (26:5).

The essays that have appeared elsewhere have been revised, some more than others. In most instances this has meant the addition of new bibliographical material and reactions to it; on occasion paragraphs have been rewritten or expanded. But the basic theses proposed in these essays have remained substantially the same as in the original publications. In some instances the essay has been given a new title, but the original title and place of publication are indicated in the first (asterisked) footnote.

Two essays appear here for the first time (Nos. 3 and 6); part of the fifth appeared earlier in German in the Conzelmann *Festschrift,* but it now appears here for the first time in English dress. Additional material has been appended to it, as has also been done to the fourth essay. The additional material originally formed part of two lectures given at Oxford University in May 1974 (Speaker's Lectures in Biblical Studies).

Thanks are hereby expressed to the following publishers or editors of journals who have kindly given permission for the use of material which originally appeared in their publications:
Editions J. Duculot for permission to use essay 1;
The Catholic Biblical Association for permission to use essays 2 and 7;
Cambridge University Press for permission to use essay 4;
Prof. Dr. Georg Strecker for permission to present essay 5 here in English;
The Society of Biblical Literature for permission to use essay 8;
The Biblical Institute, Rome for permission to use essays 9 and 11;
The University of Chicago Press for permission to use essay 10;
The Johns Hopkins University Press for permission to use essay 12.

Finally, it is my pleasant duty to thank Prof. Leander E. Keck, the editor of the Monograph Series of the Society of Biblical Literature, for his kind acceptance of this collection into his series.

The production of this book has taken longer than anticipated. The manuscript of it was finished several years ago, before some recent publications. As a result, some statements in it have at, times become outdated, and it has not been possible to remedy this situation at page-proof stage.

Joseph A. Fitzmyer, S.J.
The Catholic University of America
Washington, DC 20064

Chapter 1

The Study of the Aramaic Background of the New Testament*

The discussion of Jesus and the beginnings of Christology sooner or later always comes to grips with the so-called Aramaic substratum of his sayings in the NT. This is not to deny that the person of the historical Jesus of Nazareth is in reality much more significant for those beginnings. What he was and what he did must in the long run be considered more important for the christology of the NT and of the Christian church than merely what he said. But, unfortunately, in the writings of the NT, we have no pipeline to the person or the deeds of the historical Jesus that can be separated from what the early Christian community recounted of him, of his sayings, and of the movement that he began. His sayings, of course, form an important *part* of the written heritage of the early Christian community, which is in its own way part of the norm of Christian belief in every century. Hence the sayings of Jesus bear directly on the question of the beginnings of christological faith.

Because Jesus of Nazareth has normally been regarded as the founder of Christianity and because he was a Palestinian Jew of what we call today the first century, students of the NT have always looked to first-century Palestinian customs and phenomena for an intelligible background of the traditions that have come down to us about him and his early disciples. But the writings of that early phase of Christianity and the sayings of Jesus preserved in them are couched in Greek, in effect, in a translation. Even if we make allowances for sayings that were put on his lips by evangelists or by the tradition before them, we still have to cope with the degree to which the Greek saying might reflect an Aramaic saying that he might have uttered. In effect, the question of the origins of christology cannot dispense with the Aramaic problem—unless, of course, one's hermeneutical approach to the New Testament is dominated by a philosophy in which such a question is *belanglos*.

Claims are sometimes made for the authenticity of Jesus' sayings, based on the Aramaic substratum that is said to shine through the Greek in which they are preserved.[1] Such claims are at least insinuated on all sorts of Aramaic evidence; and anyone who tries to cope with the matter today realizes how complex it is. My purpose is to sort out here a number of generic aspects of the problem of the Aramaic substratum of the sayings of Jesus in the NT and to set forth a programmatic approach to each one on the basis of the new Aramaic evidence that has come to light from the contemporary period. Unravelling the complex strands is not easy, and my remarks in this essay may at times seem rather general; but I shall try to introduce specific examples.

Eight aspects of the problem can be isolated at present, and their diversity calls for a variety of treatment, and hence of methodology. The eight aspects are these: (1) the question of Aramaic as a language of Jesus, or more broadly, as a language in use in first-century Palestine; (2) the question of Aramaic words, names, phrases preserved in NT writings, Josephus, the Mishnaic tradition, etc.; (3) the question of Aramaisms in NT Greek, usually of a lexical or a syntactic nature (this is the question of Aramaic interference); (4) the question of mistranslations; (5) the question of Aramaic literary forms in prose and poetry; (6) the question of Aramaic and variant readings in the NT text tradition; (7) the question of Jewish literary traditions that are found in the NT and in known Aramaic literature of various periods; and (8) the question of Aramaic epistolography. One or other issue may be lacking in this line-up, but the bulk of the problem is made up of these eight aspects.

Before the discussion of these aspects three preliminary remarks are in order about the history of the inquiry into the Aramaic problem, the diversity of the NT writings, and the appeal that is often made to so-called Semitisms.

First, the study of the Aramaic background of the NT has been complicated by the history of the inquiry into it and by the way that history has developed from the time that scholars began to be interested in it. But we have come to a point where a radical break must be made with some of the methods of investigation that have been used and where a more rigorous critique and sorting out of evidence must be undertaken.

It is impossible to survey here all the phases of the inquiry into the Aramaic substratum of the NT and the contributions of all who took part in them. The early phases of the inquiry have been set forth in Arnold Meyer's monograph, *Jesu Muttersprache.*[2] From it I shall cull only a few items that will serve to illustrate my first remark. Though certain patristic writers, such as Eusebius, Epiphanius, Jerome, and Julius Africanus,[3] were, in general, aware of Aramaisms in NT Greek, the history of the inquiry into the Aramaic substratum began only with the Renaissance and the Humanists' return *ad fontes.* The inquiry was thus remotely associated with the study of the Greek text of the NT, and even more closely with the emergence of Syriac literature and of Syriac translations of the Bible in the West.[4] In yet another way, the name of Nicholas of Lyra came to the fore when he began to interest himself in rabbinic lore and its possible relation to the NT.[5] At that time, what we call Aramaisms today were often labelled Syriacisms. In 1555 Johann Albrecht von Widmanstadt translated the Syriac NT and entitled it, *Liber sacrosancti Evangelii de Iesu Christo Domino & Deo nostro—lingua syra Jesu Christi vernacula divino ipsius ore consecrata et a Joanne evangelista hebraica dicta.*[6] From this translation and its title stems the long and well-known tradition of claims that Syriac was the mother-tongue of Jesus. Between 1609 and 1639 the two Buxtorfs (père et fils) published their Chaldaic Lexicon.[7] But it remained for Joseph Justus Scaliger to distinguish Syriac from what he called Chaldaic; he regarded the language of the non-Hebrew chapters of Daniel and Ezra as "Babylonian Chaldee," whereas "Jewish Chaldee" became his name for the Aramaic of the targums. Together, all of these constituted for him "Aramaic."[8] Again, little do we realize today how much Brian Walton's London Polyglot Bible of 1657 contributed to the sorting out of the languages, as he published the OT in the original Hebrew and, besides the usual versions (Latin and Greek), added also the Syriac version and the targums of Onqelos, Jonathan, and the so-called Fragmentary Targum.[9] Walton looked on the language of Onqelos and Jonathan as the Jerusalem dialect of Jesus' day. This historical litany of the names of scholars who contributed to the inquiry into the Aramaic problem could be easily prolonged, especially with those of the last century and of the beginning of this.

However, I have sketched the beginnings of the inquiry merely to indicate the piece-meal fashion in which it was often carried out in the past. This is not meant as a criticism of the scholars who wrestled with one or other aspect of the problem, as they related words or phrases in the New Testament to resemblances in the Syriac Bible, in the "Chaldee" of Daniel or Ezra, or in the various targums that had come to light. Their piece-meal work was determined by what little was known about Aramaic and its various phases at that time. Moreover, most of their knowledge of Aramaic was derived from texts that came into existence after the beginning of the Christian movement and the composition of the Greek NT itself. As is well known, the dates for the translation of the Bible into Syriac and for the composition of the traditional, non-Qumran targums are disputed; but in the form in which we have them today they all postdate the Greek NT, and the evidence derived from them for illustration of the NT poses a real problem.

The recovery of earlier Aramaic from extrabiblical sources has been largely an achievement of this century; and when it comes to Palestinian Aramaic of the first century it is almost a matter of discoveries of the last two decades.[10] As a result, the older material that has been written on the problem of Aramaic and the NT can only be used today *with great caution.* It is part of the material to which the aforementioned rigorous critique must now be applied.

It is, moreover, not simply a question of sorting out Aramaic into various phases or periods[11] or of scrutinizing with rigor the claims made for the dates of various Aramaic texts.[12] This brief and very incomplete sketch of the beginnings of the inquiry into the Aramaic problem has been made for another purpose. For one notes in the course of the history of the inquiry a tendency to compile what had been said earlier by others without a sufficiently critical examination of the evidence or material itself. When Matthew Black first wrote his *Aramaic Approach to the Gospels and Acts,*[13] he criticized indeed Wellhausen, Nestle, Dalman, Torrey and others for their almost exclusive dependence on the late targums, Onqelos for the Pentateuch and Jonathan for the Prophets. He preferred to use instead the so-called Palestinian targums (e.g., the Cairo Genizah texts, alleged to be of earlier vintage), Christian Palestinian Aramaic texts, and the Samaritan targum. Black's attitude was certainly correct, and his work remains the first real attempt to be critical in the matter. But one must note that his own discussion of individual texts depends largely on what others have said.[14] All too frequently he cites would-be Aramaic expressions, culling them from others without sufficient scrutiny so that his book, especially in its third edition, remains a compilation of proposals about Aramaisms in the Gospels and Acts that are good, bad, and indifferent, When he seems to be critical of some proposal or other, it is often not easy to know just where he stands.

The history of the inquiry into the Aramaic background of the NT has thus brought with it a certain determinism which reveals a strange reluctance to sort out what is really valid from claims made in the past. When this is coupled with a reluctance to cope with newer aspects of the problem, then the call for a break with methods of the past can legitimately be raised.

My second preliminary remark concerns the diversity of books in the NT and the difficulty that this diversity causes for the inquiry. How few Aramaisms are claimed for the writings of Paul, despite the fact that he called himself Ἑβραῖος (Phil 3:5; 2 Cor 11:22)[15] and that he it is who has preserved two of the Aramaic expressions normally attributed to Jesus and the early Palestinian Christian church (respectively), *ἀββά* (Gal 4:6; Rom 8:15) and *μαραναθά* (1 Cor 16:22). Most discussions of the Aramaic problem have been limited to the Gospels and Acts, but even there the problem differs, depending on the gospel, whether it is a Synoptic or John; and each of them has problems that are not the same as the Aramaic substratum of Acts, if it exists at all. The idea of Aramaic sources of Acts, once put forth by C. C. Torrey, now seems to be wholly discredited.

But this question of the diversity of the NT books and the varied approach to a possible Aramaic substratum is compounded by the problem of just how many of the Greek NT writings were actually composed in Palestine itself. The vast majority of the Pauline and Deuteropauline literature seems to have been composed elsewhere: 1-2 Thessalonians probably in Corinth; Galatians, Philippians, 1 Corinthians probably in Ephesus; 2 Corinthians probably in Macedonia (in part at least); Philemon, Colossians, Ephesians, possibly in Rome.[16] Only if one were to consider seriously the Caesarean origin of some of the Pauline Captivity Letters would there be a Palestinian origin for them. As for the Gospels, again even though one might agree that they reached their final stage of redaction in places other than Palestine (Mark possibly in Italy; Luke possibly in Greece; Matthew possibly in Syria; John possibly in Ephesus), there is nevertheless a certain proneness to reckon with an underlying tradition that may ultimately have been Palestinian. While the same is possibly to be admitted for the Acts of the Apostles, the extent to which any of the other NT writings comes from a Palestinian locality is indefinite and can be debated. In a highly interesting discussion, entitled *Do You Know Greek?*, J. N. Sevenster raised the question about "How much Greek could the first Jewish Christians have known?"[17] He raised this question specifically about such NT writings as 1 Peter and James and gathered all sorts of material that not only bear indirectly on the attribution of these NT writings to the persons whose names they bear, but even more importantly on the question of the knowledge and use of Greek in Palestine by Jews of the first century.

Today we hear much about the Hellenistic background of the NT writings. The work on the *Corpus hellenisticum* is doing much to elucidate that background with detailed, critical studies that are badly needed. But however important the need is to pursue the study of that background, the need to reckon seriously with the Aramaic background has also to be stressed—and precisely because of the diversity of the books in the NT.

The third preliminary remark concerns so-called Semitisms and the Semitic background of the NT. There are obviously times when one can legitimately discuss matters that are best grouped as pertaining to the Semitic background of the NT.[18] But the word "Semitism" can be abused and can turn out to be a weasel-word. It is obviously legitimate to use it in a generic sense to refer to Jewish or OT traditions or to expressions which are clearly different from classical or Hellenistic Greek, but which are common to both Aramaic and Hebrew. Thus, e.g., a superfluous retrospective personal pronoun turns up in a Greek relative clause which could reflect either a Hebrew or an Aramaic retrospective pronominal suffix in a relative clause, since in both Hebrew and Aramaic the relative pronoun is indeclinable: *ἀλλ᾽ εὐθὺς ἀκούουσα γυνὴ περὶ αὐτοῦ, ἧς εἶχεν τὸ θυγάτριον αὐτῆς πνεῦμα ἀκάθαρτον, ἐλθοῦσα προσέπεσεν πρὸς τοὺς πόδας αὐτοῦ,* "But immediately a woman, whose little daughter was possessed by an unclean spirit, heard of him, and came and fell down at his feet" (Mark 7:25[*RSV*]).[19] But the way in which claims are sometimes made for the Aramaic substratum of the sayings of Jesus, when the evidence is merely "Semitic" in general, or, worse still, derived from some other Semitic language, e.g., Hebrew, should no longer be countenanced.[20] In other words, the discussion of the Aramaic background of the NT should be limited to *Aramaic* evidence, and to Aramaic evidence of the period contemporary with or slightly prior to the composition of the Greek New Testament writings themselves. The ideal period would be from the first century and the beginning of the second up until the revolt of Simon ben Kosiba (132-35). Of course, one can more easily grant the evidence from a still earlier period of Palestinian Aramaic (e.g., from Ezra or Daniel) than from a later period (e.g., from the traditional, non-Qumran targums and rabbinic writings). But in any case it must be Aramaic evidence. So much for the preliminary remarks, which have been judged necessary in a discussion of methodology such as this. We can now turn to the various aspects of the Aramaic problem outlined earlier.

I. *Aramaic as a Language of Jesus*

First of all, concerning Aramaic as a language of Jesus, or more broadly, as a language of first-century Palestine, I need not repeat here the details that I amassed in my presidential address before the Catholic Biblical Association of America in 1970, "The Languages of Palestine in the First Century A.D."[21] I shall rather single out a few elements that call for some further comment and that bear precisely on the question of methodology.

From at least the eighth century B.C. Aramaic had become a *lingua franca* in the ancient Near East; and contrary to the impression that one gets from the ordinary Hebrew Bible, in which (according to Kittel's edition[22]) the Aramaic portions occupy a maximum of 22 pages and a few stray verses in Genesis (31:47) and Jeremiah (10:11)[23] out of a total of 1434 pages, Aramaic was not the less important of the two languages. Hebrew, which as the שפת כנען (Isa 19:18) or even as יהודית (Isa 36:11, 13), was apparently the more indigenous of the two in Palestine. Indeed, it seems never to have disappeared completely in the first millennium B.C. or even in the early centuries of the Christian era, despite the affirmations about its dying out in the postexilic period that are legion in the history of this inquiry.[24] Small pockets of the population (grouped geographically or sociologically?) in that period apparently continued to use a form of the language, often called today "Postbiblical Hebrew," which was related to the Hebrew in Qoheleth, Canticles, and Lamentations, and which eventually developed into what is now called Mishnaic Hebrew. Evidence of such Hebrew is now found in Qumran texts, graffiti, and epitaphs of the early Roman period in Palestine, the Copper Roll, and in the letters and contracts of the caves of Murabbaᶜat, Ḫabra, and Seiyal. But the evidence is not abundant and comes from restricted areas; it has been suggested that it should be ascribed to small groups who deliberately sought to revive the use of Hebrew at the time of the Maccabean movement or similar national reforms.

As for the use of Aramaic in Palestine, it is now attested from the middle of the ninth century B.C. onward.[25] The earliest text is a short inscription on a jar from ᶜEin Gev, dated to the middle of the ninth century by B. Mazar; and likewise from that century comes an inscribed bowl from Tell Dan, published by N. Avigad.[26] From these (currently) earliest attestations of the language right down to roughly A.D. 500 one can trace a line of evidence showing a continuous use of Aramaic in Palestine, which includes the numerous fragments from the Qumran caves,[27] and not a few from various synagogue inscriptions dating from the third to the sixth centuries.[28]

Moreover, the invasion of Aramaisms, Aramaic vocabulary, and Aramaic syntax into the Hebrew of the later books of the Bible and into Post-Biblical Hebrew suggests its predominant use.[29] This is detected in certain Qumran texts, which have been composed in Post-Biblical Hebrew, but which manifest no small amount of Aramaic influence (e.g., 4QTestimonia).[30] There is, moreover, the evidence of the Aramaic form of Tobit, extant now in four fragmentary copies from Qumran Cave IV, which when compared with the one Hebrew copy reveals not only that the Aramaic is the more original, but that the Hebrew version is no little Aramaized. The texts of Tobit still await publication, but Milik has revealed some information on them.[31] Furthermore, the existence of Aramaic targums in written form from Qumran (4QtgJob, 11QtgJob, 4QtgLev) indicates that the practice of translating the Hebrew Scriptures into Aramaic was well under way, and presumably for the usually stated reason, because the original Hebrew text read in the synagogues was no longer so readily and widely understood.[32] (This evidence from pre-Christian times does not, however, permit one to attribute the traditional, non-Qumran targums to this period—or to think that there was only one Palestinian targum). Lastly, the use of Aramaic on tombstones and ossuaries of the first century in and around Jerusalem clearly shows that the language was in popular use, not to mention an Aramaic I.O.U. dated to the second year of Nero Caesar, A.D. 56 (Mur 18).

Such an attestation of the use of Aramaic in Palestine does not, of course, deny the use of Greek there in the first century B.C. or A.D. This is too well attested to deny it, as I have indicated elsewhere.[33]

As a result of the survey of the current evidence for the use of such languages in Palestine in the first century, one can cautiously conclude that "the most commonly used language of Palestine in the first century A.D. was Aramaic, but that many Palestinian Jews, not only those in Hellenistic towns, but farmers and craftsmen of less obviously Hellenistic areas used Greek, at least as a second language," and that "pockets of Palestinian Jews also used Hebrew, even though its use was not widespread."[34] As for the language that Jesus would have used, the evidence seems to point mainly to Aramaic. There is little cogency in the thesis of Harris Birkeland and others who maintain that it was normally Hebrew (which Birkeland regarded as the language of the common people).[35] Presumably, Jesus used Hebrew on occasion. If one could give historical credence to the details of Jesus' visit to Nazareth as depicted in Luke 4:16-20, one would have to conclude that he read Isaiah in the original; but that is a big "if," in view of the Lucan redaction of the passage. That Hebrew was the Semitic language that he regularly used is not yet sufficiently substantiated, despite the attempts of I. Rabinowitz, J. Cantineau, and others to support the thesis of Birkeland in one way or another.[36] S. Segert and others have tellingly criticized the Birkeland thesis.[37] For this reason the consensus of opinion at the moment seems to support Aramaic as the language most commonly used by Jesus and his immediate disciples in Palestine.

But the use of Aramaic in first-century Palestine and by Jesus or his disciples raises a further question. How much of the extant Aramaic language can be considered valid for comparison, when one is studying the substratum of the Greek sayings attributed to Jesus in the NT? Some years ago I proposed a fivefold division of the phases of the Aramaic language,[38] and it has found acceptance with a number of scholars (E. Y. Kutscher,[39] H. L. Ginsberg,[40] E. Vogt,[41] and others). Since the composition of NT writings, and indeed the utterances of Jesus himself, fit into the phase of Middle Aramaic chronologically, it is methodologically correct to look to Aramaic of this phase for the best evidence of the Aramaic substratum. I still think that "Qumran Aramaic, either slightly prior to the NT period or contemporary with at least part of it—and other first-century Aramaic, such as tomb and ossuary inscriptions—must be the latest Aramaic that should be used for philological comparisons of the Aramaic substratum of the Gospels and Acts."[42] J. C. Greenfield has recently stressed the same idea: "Properly speaking, this [Qumran Aramaic] is the only literary Aramaic that we have that is contemporaneous with the Gospels and Acts and theoretically it is with the Aramaic of the Qumran finds that one should begin the examination of a possible *Aramaic approach.*"[43]

However, it has been contended that "if an Aramaic sayings source was written in A.D. 50, it would be closer to rabbinical material of A.D. 150 than to a Qumran document of 100 B.C. In the absence of evidence to the contrary one would suppose that different groups spoke and wrote different dialects; this is normal."[44] Why would it be closer to "rabbinical material of A.D. 150"? This is merely asserted without any evidence. It is conceivable that the content of the sayings may be closer to rabbinical utterances, but it is not evident that the form of the language and the expressions would be such. Moreover, what is this rabbinic *Aramaic* "material of A.D. 150" to which reference is being made? In the absence of clear examples of it, I prefer to stand by the contention set forth above.

As for the supposition that "different groups spoke and wrote different dialects," since "this is normal," something more than mere assertion is needed. Was the Aramaic used in the Qumran group so different from the language spoken or used in the rest of the small country of Palestine? S. Segert, who has been studying various linguistic aspects of Qumran Aramaic texts, has shown that some of them vary slightly and that we should have to allow for earlier and later texts within the phase of Middle Aramaic. I should also admit slight differences between Qumran and Murabbaᶜat texts; but that these differences really constitute a variety of dialects would have to be debated.[45] Segert has noted that Aramaic was not used for the Qumran rule-books, halakah, and pesher interpretations of the OT Prophets and Psalms, or for other sectarian literature; for these Post-Biblical Hebrew was rather employed.[46] By and large, this is correct. In the case of the Aramaic Genesis Apocryphon of Qumran Cave I and of the Targum of Job from Qumran Cave XI, there is not the slightest hint of Essene authorship,[47] so that the content of these scrolls even supports Segert's contention that they were literary productions introduced into the community from outside, composed elsewhere in Palestine, and were representative of Aramaic used on a larger scale than in the small esoteric community of Qumran. While Segert's view has much to commend it, I am not wholly convinced that the Aramaic composition betrays extra-Qumran provenience in all cases, or that Aramaic was not used in the community itself. Recently, J. T. Milik published some fragments from Qumran Cave IV, entitled the Visions of ᶜAmran,[48] and in them one now finds the typically Qumran dualistic vocabulary of the sectarian literature and theology turning up in Aramaic dress: not only the new counterpart of מלכיצדק called מלכירשע, but the contrast of נהורא, "light," and חשוכא, "darkness," and the classic designation of the members of the community, "all the sons of light," [כול בני נהו]רא (partly, but certainly, restored in the context). Consequently, it seems that one cannot exclude the composition of works in Aramaic from the Qumran community. But the similarity in language between these texts and others without the distinctive Essene traits suggests that the language in writings of possibly diverse provenience was not really that much different. So in the long run the bulk of Aramaic texts from Qumran remains the best available material for the study of the Aramaic substratum sayings of Jesus in the Greek NT.

I remain very skeptical about the alleged differences between the literary and spoken forms of Aramaic of this period. While every one knows that the distinction is valid and that it is precisely the spoken form of a language that eventually invades the literary and brings about the development of one dialect or phase of it from another, it is another thing to document this distinction and make it the basis of synchronic datings. A. Díez Macho has tried to insist on this distinction in his effort to maintain a first-century (or even earlier) dating of the Aramaic of the so-called Palestinian targums (e.g., of the Cairo Genizah, or of Neofiti I).[49] But until we get real evidence about the form of the spoken Aramaic of the first century—which is presently more postulated than attested—this mode of argument is wistful. This is especially true since the best instances of the language, which one normally finds in the traditional, non-Qumran targums, are found on the inscriptions from synagogues of the third to the sixth centuries.

As a result, correct methodology would seem to call for the comparison of the sayings of Jesus with Aramaic of the contemporary phase, the Middle Period, in preference to that of the later phases, such as is found in the various classic targumim, Syriac writings, Christian Palestinian Aramaic lectionaries, and so-called Palestinian Jewish Aramaic in general.

There is, however, another angle to this question, which must be considered for a moment. Jesus' words are recorded *in Greek* in the NT. Is it possible that he uttered some of them in Greek? This question has been raised in recent times.[50] It has also been asked in what language Jesus would have conversed with Pilate, and Greek is the likely answer; but I am extremely skeptical about the sayings-tradition in the NT being rooted, even in part, in Greek sayings of Jesus himself.

If one considers the sayings-tradition to be rooted in Aramaic sayings, there is a reason for it—and we shall be coming to that shortly. But a *caveat* must be introduced at this point, which affects the whole question of the origin of the sayings-tradition. It is introduced because it bears directly on the problem of the sayings of Jesus in the NT and their roots in either Aramaic or Greek words on the lips of the historical Jesus. The *caveat* is derived ultimately from other aspects of modern Gospel study, for no discussion of the Aramaic problem of the Gospels can prescind from the issues raised by Synoptic source criticism, form criticism, and redaction criticism. Consequently, in treating of the Aramaic background of the NT, and especially of the sayings of Jesus within it, one has to reckon with (*a*) the well-known refractory process of underlying oral tradition; (*b*) the coloring of the tradition by a later faith-experience of the early Christians; (*c*) likely additions to the traditional collections of sayings, made perhaps in a spirit of a genuine extension of his words or an adaptive reinterpretation of them to new situations; (*d*) words actually put on his lips by early Christians (e.g., in the Johannine discourses); and (*e*) the language of the given evangelist. When due regard is had for these legitimate factors, then the real discussion about the Aramaic substratum of the sayings of Jesus can be undertaken. This *caveat* forms a digression; but it has to be introduced because of the obvious tendency in the question raised about whether Jesus might have uttered some of his sayings in Greek. The possibility of it is always there, but when other factors are taken into consideration, it seems rather unlikely.

II. *Aramaic Names, Words, and Phrases Preserved in the New Testament*

No little part of the evidence for the conclusion that Jesus' words were by and large uttered originally in Aramaic and for the Aramaic substratum of various parts of the New Testament is found in the existence of Aramaic words, names, and phrases in the Greek text itself. Puzzling indeed is the complete loss of Aramaic source material of early Palestinian Christianity; and it is just as puzzling as the lack of reference to Jesus, his disciples, or anything Christian—so far at least—in the documents from Qumran. The tour de force of C. C. Torrey, who tried to translate the Gospels back into Aramaic and to maintain that they were all originally written in Aramaic has convinced no one.[51] It is in reality no proof of the Aramaic substratum itself. Moreover, the Aramaic background to the sayings of Jesus has often been argued on the testimony of Papias' statement about the First Gospel: *Ματθαῖος μὲν οὖν Ἑβραΐδι διαλέκτῳ τὰ λόγια συνετάξατο, ἡρμήνευσεν δ' αὐτὰ ὡς ἦν δυνατὸς ἕκαστος*, "Now Matthew compiled the sayings in a

'Hebrew' dialect, but each person translated (interpreted?) them as best he could" (Eusebius, *Hist. eccl.* 3.39.16). Even granting for the moment that Ἑβραΐδι διαλέκτῳ most likely means "in the Aramaic language,"[52] the collection of logia so written remains an unknown quantity, and the relation of it to the sayings of Jesus in our Greek First Gospel is highly debatable. As a result, Papias' testimony is little more than a red herring drawn across the path of the modern discussion of the Aramaic substratum of the sayings of Jesus.

The classic discussions of the Aramaic words, names, and phrases preserved in the New Testament—by such scholars as G. Dalman, E. Kautzsch, A. Meyer, J. Koopmans, J. Jeremias, and others[53] —need to be updated. What is needed, first of all, is a *complete* catalogue of such items; many of the usual lists merely repeat what was collected earlier, and some items have never been introduced (e.g., *ἄλφα, ἰῶτα, μνᾶ*). Once the list is fully compiled, it will have to be evaluated in the light of the Palestinian Aramaic now known to come from the contemporary period and rigorously distinguished from the material of later targumic or midrashic sources.

Two examples may be cited, for which contemporary evidence can be used in different senses. The Greek word *κορβᾶν* is still explained by M. Black as "a form of solemn prohibition found . . . in the Talmud" (with support drawn from J. Lightfoot's *Horae hebraicae* and J. Levy's references to *Nedarim* 3:2).[54] But the overtones of the talmudic usage have always embarrassed the NT commentator who appealed to them to illustrate the Marcan usage, *κορβᾶν, ὅ ἐστιν δῶρον, ὃ ἐὰν ἐξ ἐμοῦ ὠφεληθῇς,* "any support you might have had from me is *korban*" (i.e., a gift [made to God]), Mark 7:11. And the cryptic Matthean formula (15:5), *δῶρον ὃ ἐὰν ἐξ ἐμοῦ ὠφεληθῇς,* has even less of the overtones. (Indeed, it might be queried whether we would ever have understood the meaning of the Greek text of Matthew, if we did not know of the earlier Marcan form of the episode with its preserved Aramaic word.) The use of the word קרבן on two Palestinian Aramaic inscriptions of the first-century reveals its dedicatory sense, with the connotation of tabu, that is better suited to illustrate the Marcan and Matthean usage of the words *κορβᾶν* and *δῶρον*. One instance of it comes from a Palestinian ossuary published by J. T. Milik some years ago, which reads, כל די אנש מתהנה בחלתה דה קרבן אלה מן דבגוה "All that a man may find to his profit in this ossuary (is) an offering to God from him who is within it."[55] No one will miss the pertinence of the phrase קרבן אלה to the Marcan word, *κορβᾶν*.[56] The other instance is found on a stone jar discovered by B. Mazar in the excavation of Jerusalem south of the Temple area, which again indicates the dedicatory sense of the word.[57] Such evidence, in fact, renders unnecessary the references to later Jewish material from sources such as the Talmud.

On the other hand, the alleged Aramaic background for *μαμωνᾶ* may have to be questioned. Such a background has been illustrated by appeals to the Babylonian Talmud (*Berakoth* 61b), to a Palestinian targum of Gen 34:23

(Kahle's Cairo Genizah text, C—which he dates between 700–900), and to passages in the Palestinian Talmud.[58] But can one pass over the occurrence of the word in the Hebrew text of Sir 31:8 and in Qumran Hebrew (ממון, 1QS 6:2; 1Q27 a ii 5; and even CD 14:20) or over Augustine's testimony to the word as current in the Punic of his day (ממן, *De serm. Dom.*, 2/14.47; *Sermo* 113, ch. 2), or over the un-Aramaic ending *-ôn* that the Greek reflects?[59] Here is an instance where we may have to cease appealing to Aramaic for the explanation of the Greek *μαμωνᾶ* and resort merely to a common Semitic background of the word.

With regard to the forms of some proper names in the NT that have often been puzzling, W. F. Albright was long of the opinion that some of them reflect Aramaic forms, which are preserved in various Syriac versions of the NT. Perhaps a fresh investigation of some of the Syriac variants will shed fresh light on names that still puzzle us. Albright himself made some brief suggestions about them in the Anchor Bible commentary on *Matthew,*[60] but even he did no more than open an area of investigation. The point here is that though the Syriac tradition is obviously secondary and derivative from the Greek, it is not impossible that, in the choice of Syriac forms of names, especially geographical names, that tradition may be closer to some of the native Palestinian names that have become Grecized in the NT text tradition. Personally, I have not yet had the time to investigate this aspect of the problem, but it needs attention.

III. *Aramaisms in New Testament Greek*

Beyond the preservation of Aramaic names, words, and phrases in the NT there is the question of Aramaisms in the Greek text, i.e., Aramaic interference in the lexicon or syntax of the Greek, when Greek words or phrases are used with nuances that reflect Aramaic usage. Again, what is needed, first of all, is a comprehensive listing of these items, and comparison with genuine Aramaic evidence. Several recent works have discussed aspects of this problem, but not from the viewpoint that interests us now. For instance, K. Beyer devoted a volume to *Semitische Syntax im Neuen Testament,*[61] but for all its excellence it does not always specify sufficiently the Semitic data involved. From a different standpoint, D. Hill's monograph, *Greek Words and Hebrew Meanings: Studies in the Semantics of Soteriological Terms,*[62] adopted a clearly theological approach to the words so that the philological approach that the Aramaic problem demands is still wanting.

As an example of a Greek word with an Aramaic nuance, I may be permitted to cite here a form that is now familiar. In Luke 6:7 the evangelist records that the scribes and Pharisees kept watching Jesus to see whether *ἐν τῷ σαββάτῳ θεραπεύει, ἵνα εὕρωσιν κατηγορεῖν αὐτοῦ,* "he would heal on the Sabbath so that they might find an accusation against him" (*RSV*). The use of *εὕρωσιν* with a dependent complementary infinitive (*κατηγορεῖν*) is peculiar. Bauer-Arndt-Gingrich have cited a supposed parallel from an Egyptian papyrus in a Parisian collection, dated 153 B.C., *μὴ εὕρῃ τι κατά σου* ⟨*ε*⟩*ἰπεῖν*, "lest he find anything to say against you."[63] But the parallel is not perfect, because *εὕρῃ* has the object *τι* expressed in the papyrus and the infinitive (*εἰπεῖν*) is epexegetic, not complementary. A propos of this construction in another Lucan passage (13:24), M. Black wrote, "There is no instance hitherto adduced of this verb (*ʾaškaḥ*) in the sense 'to be able' for Palestinian Aramaic; it means 'to find' only; it is in Syriac that it has the two senses 'to find' and 'to be able.'"[64] Though Black is reluctant to call it therefore a Syriacism, he concludes that "our knowledge of Palestinian Aramaic is still far from complete." That conclusion will probably always remain true; but for this specific case the verb אשכח in the sense of "be able" is clearly attested in Palestinian Aramaic, in 1QapGen 21:13: God promises Abram, "I shall make your descendants as numerous as the dust of the earth which no man can number" (די לא ישכח כול בר אנוש למניה).[65] And another example of it seems to be present in Milik's recently published "Book of the Giants" section of Enoch.[66] This makes it plausible that *εὕρωσιν* with its dependent complementary infinitive in Luke 6:7 means simply, "so that they might be able to accuse him." The verb *εὕρωσιν* would reflect Aramaic interference, and the Greek verb *εὑρίσκειν* would have been made to carry the Aramaic nuance of "be able."

Another instance of a Greek phrase that is often said to carry an Aramaic nuance is *ὁ υἱὸς τοῦ ἀνθρώπου* or *υἱὸς ἀνθρώπου* (John 5:27; Rev 1:13; 14:14), being said to reflect בר נשא or בר נש by a literal translation or a mistranslation. In this matter I cannot go into great detail here and must reserve for elsewhere a fuller discussion of this issue.[67] I shall confine myself here to three comments. First, we have in such a view of the matter a good example of the uncritical repetition of phrases from the days of Dalman et al. and of the determinism in the inquiry into the Aramaic problem of which I spoke earlier. This concerns the linguistic feature that is involved in the spelling of the word for "man," *ʾĕnāš* (or in the Hebraized form *ʾĕnōš*), which never seems to occur in any pre-Christian texts or in any Palestinian Aramaic texts of the first century or of the early second century without the initial consonant *ʾaleph*.[68] This fact is now recognized by J. Jeremias.[69] Consequently, the form בר נשא or בר נש immediately reveals its late provenience, and one should therefore be wary of citing texts in which this form of the expression occurs as if they were contemporary with the NT material. Secondly, the form בר אנש or בר אנוש designates the individual belonging to the collectivity (mankind), so that it can mean generically "a human being" (so in 11QtgJob 26:3 [in parallelism with גבר], or some word for "man"; cf. the Hebrew text), or more indefinitely "someone" (or with the negative לא, "no one"; so in 1QapGen 21:13). This generic or indefinite sense, which was once thought to be unattested or unusual in Aramaic,[70] is now clearly in evidence. But what is significant for the first century is that the phrase is still to be found in any of the three following senses: (*a*) as a form of address directed to some person, like the Hebrew בן אדם used of the prophet Ezekiel—and this despite the multiple occurrences of it in that biblical book; (*b*) as a title for an expected or apocalyptic figure—and herein one notes that the Greek phrase applied to Jesus as a title in various senses has no precise Aramaic counterpart; and (*c*) as a surrogate or a circumlocution for "I."[71] The phrase *ὁ υἱὸς τοῦ ἀνθρώπου,* used of Jesus in the NT, is almost certainly intended in each case as a title, and thus we are still looking for the link between the corporate sense given to the phrase in Dan 7:13 and 18 and the NT titular sense. A further question is raised whether Jesus himself might have used בר אנש in the generic or indefinite sense referred to above and whether this might have given rise to a later titular interpretation within the Christian community; but to go into this question here would take us too far astray, important though it is. Thirdly, if J. T. Milik is correct about the form of the Book of Enoch in Palestine of the first century B.C., when the five parts of it were the Book of the Heavenly Luminaries, the Book of the Watchers, the Book of the Giants, the Book of Dreams, and the Letter of Enoch,[72] then we can no longer look to the second part of Enoch, as we now know it in the Ethiopic translation, the so-called Similitudes, for the titular use of "Son of Man." For Milik, the "Similitudes" never formed part of the pre-Christian Book of Enoch; it was substituted for the Book of the Giants in Christian times.[73]

In much of this discussion the evidence from the Aramaic texts of the first century is negative and amounts at most to an argument from silence—or at least it may seem so. But it is enough to warn us in using Aramaic material of a later date too facilely in constructing arguments about the first-century material.

IV. *Mistranslations*

The question of Aramaic interference in the Greek of the NT is related to another problem, on which I can only comment briefly, viz., that of the mistranslation of an Aramaic source. The number of alleged mistranslations is almost legion, and some rigorous assessment has to be found to cope with them. Again, the criteria used must be contemporaneous.

For example, in Matt 7:6 the *RSV* reads, "Do not give dogs what is holy; and do not throw your pearls before swine, lest they trample them under foot and turn to attack you." The parallelism of *τὸ ἅγιον* and *τοὺς μαργαρίτας ὑμῶν* is striking, and from at least 1700 it seems to have been suggested that *τὸ ἅγιον* is a mistranslation of the Aramaic קדשא. It would have been understood as *qudšāʾ*, an abstraction, "what is holy," instead of *qĕdāšāʾ*, "ring." Without going into all the other less plausible suggestions that have been made for alleged mistranslations of the Aramaic in other words of the verse,[74] one can now cite the passage in 11QtgJob 38:8, where the Aramaic word for "ring" has turned up precisely in the form that makes the suggestion plausible: ויהבו לה גבר אמרה חדה וגבר קדש חד די דהב, "and they gave him (Job), each one a lamb and a ring of gold." No matter what one will say about the plausibility of the suggestion in this case, the Aramaic evidence for the parallelism will no longer have to be sought in late Syriac or other texts. Moreover, the parallelism of the "ring" and the "pearls" in a proverbial saying not unlike the Aramaic Wisdom-aphorisms of Aḥiqar now becomes plausible because of a closely contemporary Palestinian Aramaic text.

In discussing this question some years ago, R. M. Grant maintained that the view that some parts of the NT were originally composed in Aramaic, not in Greek, while interesting, could "never be convincing."[75] He claimed that one had to show that the existing Greek is bad Greek, a feature which might not appear in the work of a "really good translator," that the alleged bad Greek could not be accepted as Hellenistic Greek of the time, that the existing Greek did not make sense, and lastly that the passage if retranslated into Aramaic does make sense. He emphasized the difficulty of this process and concluded, "Moreover, experts in Aramaic have a tendency to disagree as to what the original was."[76] Most of what Grant maintained is, in my opinion, correct; for the problem of mistranslation has to be rigorously scrutinized in terms of the items which he has mentioned. But his last comment about the disagreement of Aramaists represents an excuse to flee from a problem. Will Aramaists—or any other group of human beings—ever be unanimous? Perhaps, however, a more rigorous methodology and approach will eliminate some of the disagreement. Moreover, the hypothesis of mistranslations, which has to be seriously entertained because of the possibility of different vocalizations of one consonantal Aramaic text, should not, however, be confused with the question whether parts of the NT were originally composed in Aramaic (Torrey's *tour de force*). This Grant seems to have done.

V. *Aramaic Literary Forms in Prose and Poetry*

The fifth question concerns Aramaic literary forms in prose and poetry. The question may seem idle until one recalls the famous debate between E. J. Goodspeed and A. T. Olmstead, "Could an Aramaic Gospel Be Written?"—i.e., in first-century Palestine. Goodspeed thought that it would have been impossible because there was no "creative Aramaic literary writing" attested in that period.[77] He was thinking of the lacuna that existed between the final redaction of the Book of Daniel and the beginning of the so-called rabbinic Aramaic writings, the *Měgillat Taᶜănīt*, "Scroll of Fasting," which may be dated somewhere between A.D. 66 and 100.[78] This lacuna has since been filled somewhat by the Qumran Aramaic texts, and though they are not abundant, they are extensive enough to show that Aramaic literary compositions were in fact produced. Unfortunately, because of the fragmentary state of so many of the texts we are not able to discern the degree of inventiveness or creativity that was at work in such compositions. Was some new or characteristically Aramaic literary form produced? We know of only the targum as specifically Aramaic, but that is a translation process. Using other considerations, M. Smith has argued for Palestinian "romantic narrative literature about biblical heroes" composed prior to 70, i.e., works in Aramaic produced in Greco-Roman literary forms.[79]

Much more crucial in the discussion of the Aramaic substratum of the sayings of Jesus is the question of Aramaic poetry. Claims have been made for the "formal elements of Aramaic poetry in non-dominical sayings or speeches and in the Gospel dialogue as well as in the sayings of Jesus."[80] M. Black has discussed this aspect of the sayings and dialogue in Part III of his *Aramaic Approach to the Gospels and Acts.*[81] This is one of the areas where the evidence has not been restricted to Aramaic, and refuge has been taken in "Semitic poetic form." Black's discussion builds on C. F. Burney's *Poetry of Our Lord,*[82] and in it he treats of such things as "the formal element of Semitic poetry in the Gospels," i.e., "alliteration, assonance, and paronomasia." He began his chapter with a reference to Burney, who, he said, "has shown that the sayings of Jesus are cast in the form of Semitic poetry, with such characteristic features as parallelism of lines and clauses, rhythmic structure, and possibly even rhyme."[83] Without questioning the validity of such elements as specifically Aramaic, Black proceeded to adduce further instances of them in the non-dominical sayings or in the dialogue of the Gospels (in such passages as the sayings of the Baptist, the sources of the Fourth Gospel, the Lucan hymns, the Beatitudes, and various other dialogues). The subtle shifting back and forth between the adjectives "Aramaic" and "Semitic" in his discussion is revealing, for the question arises whether such formal rhetorical elements as parallelism, rhythm, rhyme, alliteration, assonance, and paronomasia are really the specific elements of *Aramaic* poetry. Such things may not be the usual features of classic Greek poetry and were studied more in connection with rhetoric in classical antiquity than with poetry, and one wonders to what extent Hellenistic poetic forms may not be operative here.[84]

No little part of the hesitation that one has in this question is the scarcity of what may be called Aramaic poetry, which should logically serve as a basis for comparison. As far as I can see, it is quite limited: (1) the Carpentras stele (KAI § 269), a four-line Egyptian Aramaic funerary stele, usually regarded as rhythmic in form and dated to the fourth century B.C.;[85] (2) several passages in the Book of Daniel (2:20-23; 3:31-33; 4:7-13, 31-32; 6:26-28; 7:9-10, 13-14, 23-27);[86]; (3) Tobit 8:5-6, 15-17; 13:1-8, which at present are accessible only in the Greek or Latin forms of the book, but some of which are preserved in the as yet unpublished texts of Qumran Cave IV;[87] (4) 11QtgJob, which may be regarded as poetry *in* Aramaic—but is it really Aramaic poetry?[88] (5) some of the proverbs of *Aḥiqar;*[89] (6) possibly part of the description of Sarai's beauty in the *Genesis Apocryphon* (1QapGen 20:2-7), if M. Black's view be accepted,[90] for some of it is written in parallelism, although it is scarcely well balanced; and finally (7) possibly 4QpsDan^{c}, the so-called Son of God text in Milik's lot, which is composed in a series of paratactic clauses that manifest a certain rhythm.[91] In all of this material, meagre as it is, one has to ask, What are the features of such poetic writing? That question is not easily answered at present. How does it differ from Hebrew poetry? Should it? In this instance the evidence is not such as to present a clear answer, but one should at least pose the question about the evidence for the nature of Aramaic poetry. I am not calling in question the existence of the rhythmic sayings attributed to Jesus in the Greek gospels or even their poetic character. The question is merely whether these elements necessarily indicate an *Aramaic* substratum. I am, moreover, aware of the thrust of the argument, that such formal elements are detected when one retrojects the Greek sayings back into Aramaic and that they are often not detected in the Greek itself. But I am not too sure that the presence of such elements, when thus detected, can be made to bear the weight of the argument that is often constructed upon them.

VI. *Aramaic and Variant Readings in the New Testament Text-Tradition*

This aspect of the Aramaic problem can only be mentioned briefly here, because I have never been able to go deeply into it; and yet it is an area that differs considerably from the others and merits further investigation. Some studies have been devoted to it by others,[92] and one crucial question always seems to emerge in them: Suppose a variant reading—say in Codex Bezae—manifests an Aramaism, whereas other Greek MSS have none of this, does that mean that Codex Bezae has preserved for us an earlier, or even more original, form of the saying or narrative? It has been debated whether the so-called Aramaisms in the Codex Bezae are dependent on some Syriac version.[93] But has the view that the Greek tradition of that MS, which is several centuries younger than the oldest Greek texts on parchment or papyrus, has been somewhat Syriacized been completely ruled out of court? The source of the alleged Aramaic material in Codex Bezae has not been convincingly ferreted out, and since we know so little about the provenience of that NT MS, distinctive and important though it be, one should be reluctant to regard its readings as more primitive simply because they seem to be more Aramaized.

VII. *Jewish Literary Traditions Found in the New Testament and in Known Aramaic Literature*

Another aspect of the Aramaic problem is the question of Jewish literary traditions that are found in the NT and in known Aramaic literature. Here it is not so much a question of Aramaic words or Aramaic interference as of motifs, modes of interpretation of the OT, or additions made to OT passages because of some halakic or haggadic process. A great amount of work has been done in this area in recent years by scholars such P. Grelot, M.-E. Boismard, M. McNamara, R. Le Déaut, B. Malina, et al.,[94] who have turned up paraphrases of OT texts in the targums or other literature that have distinctive motifs, themes, expansions, or expressions that resemble certain NT passages. They seem to suggest that the NT writers were often dependent on a targumic tradition rather than on the OT itself, in either the Hebrew or Greek form. In this matter the question is the extent to which the NT writers are dependent on such targumic traditions; it is, moreover, aggravated by the problematic dates assigned to much of the targumic material and by the multiplicity of so-called Palestinian targums that have come to light.

P. Kahle was apparently responsible for inaugurating a way of speaking about the Palestinian targums, giving one the impression that "the Palestinian targum" had been recovered, i.e., that the multiple copies that have turned up were all copies of *one* Palestinian targum. This mode of reference, "the Palestinian targum," turns up constantly in the writings of some of the scholars just mentioned. Indeed, on one occasion M. McNamara even went so far as to say, "The text of the PT as Paul found it was very apt for the doctrine Paul expresses in Rm 10,6-8."[95] This is obviously an exaggeration. Such targums may indeed preserve a literary tradition that Paul knew or used; but it has to be shown by outside control of some sort (e.g., from Philo or Josephus or some other contemporary source) that the Jewish literary tradition was actually known in the first century. The mere fact that the same tradition appears in Paul and in a non-Qumran, classical targum does not immediately mean that Paul's use of it is derived from such a source, i.e., explicitly or directly from a Palestinian targum.

There is a further aspect of this problem that needs more extensive investigation: What constitutes a "Palestinian" targum? Normally, the adjective "Palestinian" has been applied to Pseudo-Jonathan on the Pentateuch or the Fragmententargum in contrast to Targum Onqelos, which, whether it originated there or was merely given its final form there, at least has been recognized to have some historical connection with Jewish Babylonia. Its official character and its more or less word-for-word version of the Hebrew Pentateuch makes it stand out from Pseudo-Jonathan and the Fragmententargum, which are characterized by paraphrases of the Hebrew text in varying lengths, by significant additions, etc. When P. Kahle discovered the Cairo Genizah targumic texts,[96] they were seen to resemble Pseudo-Jonathan and the Fragmententargum more than Onqelos, and because of their paraphrastic character were labelled "Palestinian." But the language in these Cairo Genizah targumic texts is at times rather peculiar, if they are judged by what we know of first-century Palestinian Aramaic. In some instances at least the language is closer to Syriac or Eastern Aramaic than to Palestinian material.[97] The problem can only be broached here and a fuller investigation of it must really await the publication of critical editions of the so-called Palestinian targums and more extensive studies of the language used in them.

VIII. *Aramaic Epistolography*

In the study of NT epistles a considerable amount of work has been done on the comparison of them with extant extra-biblical letters of various sorts. The studies of A. Deissmann, L. Champion, J. -A. Eschlimann, F. X. J. Exler, E. Fascher, O. Roller, H. Koskenniemi, W. G. Doty, L. Stirewalt, J. L. White, C.-H. Kim, and others have contributed much to the understanding of the Greek letters of the NT.[98] But it has been felt that just as the Hellenistic background of other NT problems does not represent the sole influence on them, so too perhaps one should look into the Semitic background, and specifically the Aramaic background, of NT epistolography. At a consultation on letter-writing in the ancient Near East, held at the 1973 annual meeting of the Society of Biblical Literature in Chicago, I was asked to present a survey of Aramaic epistolography, the text of which appears elsewhere in this volume.[99] There one will find a list of Aramaic letters on skin, papyrus, and ostraca, a brief sketch of the contents, types, and provenience of such letters, as well as of details in the letters such as the names for the Aramaic letter, its *praescriptio,* initial greeting, secondary greetings, concluding formulas, dates, scribes or secretaries, and the exterior addresses.

Several factors lie behind the concern to look into Aramaic epistolography in the study of NT letters. First of all, the fact that Paul who labels himself a "Hebrew" and who preserves two Aramaic words in his letters, writes in Greek. Yet one wonders to what extent Aramaic epistolographic customs have influenced his writing. Is it possible that some distinctively Pauline epistolographic features are derived from Aramaic letter-writing habits? This would only be able to be established if Aramaic epistolography were studied more than it has been. Secondly, if the Caesarean hypothesis of the origin of the Captivity Letters in the Pauline corpus were to prove acceptable,[100] would there be any elements in them that might be related to Palestinian Aramaic letter-writing habits? Though I am personally skeptical about this origin of these letters, this aspect of that hypothesis might deserve some further investigation. Thirdly, we have already referred to J. N. Sevenster's thesis about Greek in Palestine and its relation to the epistles of James and 1 Peter.[101] The further implications of that thesis with regard to epistolography may need some exploration. Finally, among others M. Black has called attention to the Aramaic background of the initial greeting in 1 Pet 1:2, χάρις ὑμῖν καὶ εἰρήνη πληθυνθείη, and compares it with Dan 3:31, שלמכון ישגא.[102] He also wonders whether Aramaic was not the recognized medium of communication with the Diaspora in the first century.[103] Finally, I may mention in passing two letters coming from Palestine of the time of the Bar Cochba revolt, which deal with the same matter, one in Aramaic and the other in Greek. They deal with the requisitioning of materials for the celebration of Succoth,[104] and the similarity of subject-matter and vocabulary, despite the difference of the languages, cannot be missed. Coming from the same situation and revealing an identical concern about religious matters, they illustrate the use of the two languages in epistolary correspondence that makes Aramaic epistolography of some importance for the study of Greek letters from the eastern Mediterranean area.

Even if the study of Aramaic epistolography would have little direct bearing on NT letters, there is still the likelihood that the study of it would shed some comparative light on them, since it represents a form of ancient letter-writing from the eastern Mediterranean area.

Conclusion

An attempt has been made here to gather together some thoughts on the problems involved in the study of the Aramaic substratum of the NT. In some instances the remarks go beyond the question of the Aramaic substratum of the sayings of Jesus, which is the specific topic. But this specific question is part of the larger one that needs new attention. Each aspect of the larger problem discussed above usually bears in some way on the specific question.

Moreover, the remarks have been at times deliberately generic. I am all too aware of the fact that they have not always been supported specifically with as much evidence as they should have. But that is owing in part at least to the limitations of time and space. My intention has been to outline and delimit areas and aspects of the generic problem in view of further research. The paper is programmatic. It has been made such because of the evidence that has become available for the study of Palestinian Aramaic in the first centuries B.C. and A.D. in the last few decades, which is now forcing us to reopen many questions and approach them anew. This has called for the methodological considerations set forth above. I am not persuaded that all of these considerations are of equal value or have been refined as they should be or that they are as definitive as they may appear. But an attempt has at least been made to formulate them.

There are those who will read the above pages and think that I am trying to "gerrymander" the study of the NT. This would obviously be a delusion, if it were so. The study of the Aramaic problem will never dominate NT studies, but it will remain a facet of that study and will continue to intrigue students as long as new Aramaic texts from the contemporary period continue to come to light. Fortunately, it is an aspect or a facet of that study that exposes itself to outside control and that can reflect new gains. Because it reflects such material, it is not *immediately* caught up into the dialectic and hermeneutical cycle of interpretation born of a certain philosophy. The latter have given rise to an introspective hermeneutic—even a certain "hypochondria" or a morbid worry about the state of NT (or biblical) theology. Who knows but that a little more attention paid to the positive aspects of NT study (such as its Aramaic substratum) will enable one to break into the cycle with new evidence.[105]

NOTES TO CHAPTER 1

*A slightly revised form of a lecture delivered at the *Journées bibliques* de Louvain in 1973 and published as "Methodology in the Study of the Aramaic Substratum of Jesus' Sayings in the New Testament," *Jésus aux origines de la christologie* (ed. J. Dupont; BETL 40; Gembloux: Duculot, 1975) 73-102.

[1]See, e.g., B. Fletcher, *The Aramaic Sayings of Jesus* (London: Hodder & Stoughton, 1967).

[2]Subtitle: *Das galiläische Aramäisch in seiner Bedeutung für die Erklärung der Reden Jesu und der Evangelien überhaupt* (Freiburg im B./Leipzig: Mohr, 1896) 1-35.

[3]Eusebius, *Demonstratio evangelica* 3.4.44 (*GCS*, 23. 119); 3.7.10 (*GCS*, 23. 142); Epiphanius, *Panarion* 69.68 (*GCS*, 37. 216); John Chrysostom, *In Matthaeum homilia 88* (*PG*, 58. 776); Jerome, *Comm. in Danielem* 1.2.4 (*CC* ser. lat., 75A. 785); 2.7.28 (*CC* ser. lat., 75A. 850).

[4]See A. Meyer, *Jesu Muttersprache,* 9.

[5]Ibid., 10.

[6]Vienna: M. Cymbermannus (Zimmermann), 1555. Cf. W. Strothmann, *Die Anfänge der syrischen Studien in Europa* (Göttinger Orientforschung, 1/1; Wiesbaden: Harrassowitz, 1971).

[7]J. Buxtorf, *Lexicon chaldaicum talmudicum et rabbinicum . . .* (Basel: L. König, 1640).

[8]See Meyer, *Jesu Muttersprache,* 12.

[9]*Sacrae Scripturae Biblia polyglotta . . .* (6 vols.; London: Thomas Roycroft, 1657).

[10]For a list of Palestinian Aramaic texts and in particular of Qumran Aramaic texts (both published and otherwise known to exist), see pp. 99–102 below.

[11]See p. 57–84 below.

[12]The dating of ancient Aramaic texts is always a problem. But it should be noted that in some cases texts have come to light that are dated (e.g., Mur 18, dated to the second year of Nero, A.D. 55/56; or Mur 19, dated to A.D. 111[?]) and in others archaeological evidence of a different sort bears on the issue of dating. For example, the kind of Aramaic that turns up on inscriptions from synagogues dated archaeologically from the third to the sixth centuries, A.D. This sort of evidence is precious, indeed, and not easy to use, but it cannot be disregarded.

[13]Oxford: Clarendon, 1946. (The second edition appeared in 1954; the third in 1967.)

[14]For instance, in chap. 4 of the third edition.

[15]The meaning of ἑβραῖος is, of course, debated. It may also be questioned whether Paul (Phil 3:5; 2 Cor 11:22) uses it precisely in the same sense as it is used in Acts 6:1. But in any case the most plausible solution to the problem seems to be that proposed by C. F. D. Moule, "Once More, Who Were the Hellenists?" *ExpTim* 60 (1958-59) 100-2: the "Hellenists" were "Jews who spoke *only* Greek," whereas "Hebrews" were "Jews who, while able to speak Greek, knew a Semitic language *also*." For discussions of Aramaisms in Pauline writings, see W. C. van Unnik, "Aramaeismen bij Paulus," *Vox theologica* 14 (1943) 117-26; tr. into English, "Aramaisms in Paul," *Sparsa collecta: The Collected Essays of W. C. van Unnik: Part One, Evangelia, Paulina, Acta* (NovTSup 29; Leiden: Brill, 1973) 129-43; W. F. Albright and C. S. Mann, "Two Texts in I Corinthians," *NTS* 16 (1969-70) 271-76; P. Grelot, "Deux notes critiques sur Philippiens 2,6-11," *Bib* 54 (1973) 169-86.

[16]I am assuming proveniences for these books that are often proposed; if they are not correct or if others are preferred, there is little likelihood of their Palestinian provenience in any case.

[17]This is actually the subtitle of the book (NovTSup 19; Leiden: Brill, 1968).

[18]I am aware that I have used the adjective this way myself, in the title of the first book of my collected essays, *Essays on the Semitic Background of the New Testament* (London: Chapman, 1971; reprinted as paperback, Missoula: Scholars Press, 1974).

[19]See further Luke 3:16; Apoc 3:8; 7:29; 13:8; 20:8; 12:6 (ἐκεῖ, an adverb used similarly); Mark 13:16. See BDF §297, 466; M. Zerwick, *Biblical Greek* (Rome: Biblical Institute, 1963) §201-3.

[20]See further *CBQ* 30 (1968) 422.

[21]See pp. 38–43 below.

[22]*Biblia hebraica* (10th ed.; Stuttgart: Privileg. Würtembergische Bibelanstalt, 1951).

[23]And possibly Prov 30:1, if the suggestion of C. C. Torrey were to prove to be right (see "Proverbs, Chapter 30," *JBL* 73 [1954] 93-96).

[24]See, for example, the opinions of A. Dupont-Sommer and of F. Altheim and R. Stiehl quoted below on p. 55 n. 99.

[25]See p. 99–102 below.

[26]B. Mazar et al., "ᶜEin Gev: Excavations in 1961," *IEJ* 14 (1964) 1-49, esp. pp. 27-29 (+ pl. 13B); N. Avigad, "כתובת ארמית על קערה מתל דן [An Aramaic Inscription on the Tell Dan Bowl]," *Yediot* 30 (1966) 209-12; "An Inscribed Bowl from Dan," *PEQ* 100 (1968) 42-44 (+ pl. XVIII).

[27]For a list of the Qumran texts published so far, see pp. 101–2 below; also *The Genesis Apocryphon of Qumran Cave 1: A Commentary* (BibOr 18A; 2d ed.; Rome: Biblical Institute, 1971) 20 n. 55; 28 n. 67.

[28]For a collection of these inscriptions, see the appendix in J. A. Fitzmyer and D. J. Harrington, *A Manual of Palestinian Aramaic Texts (200 B.C. to A.D. 200)* (BibOr 34; Rome: Biblical Institute, 1978) 151–303 see also p. 54 below.

[29]Cf. M. Wagner, *Die lexikalischen und grammatikalischen Aramaismen im alttestamentlichen Hebräisch* (BZAW 96; Berlin: de Gruyter, 1966); E. F. Kautzsch, *Die Aramaismen im Alten Testament* (Halle a.S.: M. Niemeyer, 1902); A. Hurvitz, "The Chronological Significance of 'Aramaisms' in Biblical Hebrew," *IEJ* 18 (1968) 234-40.

[30]Or 4Q*175* (DJD, 5. 57-60). See also S. Segert, "Aramäische Studien: II. Zur Verbreitung des Aramäischen in Palästina zur Zeit Jesu," *ArOr* 25 (1967) 21-27, esp. pp. 34-35. Further bibliography on this text can be found in my article, "A Bibliographical Aid to the Study of the Qumran Cave IV Texts 158-186," *CBQ* 31 (1969) 59-71, esp. pp. 68-70.

[31]See his article, "La patrie de Tobie," *RB* 73 (1966) 522-30, especially the list of passages in Tobit identified in the four Aramaic texts and the one Hebrew copy (p. 522 n. 3); see also his *Ten Years of Discovery in the Wilderness of Judaea* (SBT 26; Naperville, IL: Allenson, 1959) 31, 139.

[32]The targums from Qumran Cave IV are now published; see J. T. Milik, DJD, 6.86–90; R. Le Déaut, *Introduction à la littérature targumique* (Rome: Biblical Institute, 1966) 64-68. For 11QtgJob, see J. P. M. van der Ploeg and A. S. van der Woude, *Le targum de Job de la grotte XI de Qumrân* (Koninklijke nederlandse Akademie van Wetenschappen; Leiden: Brill, 1971); also pp. 161–82 below for bibliography and comments on this targum.

[33]See p. 32–38 below.

[34]See p. 46 below.

[35]*The Language of Jesus* (Avhandlinger utgitt av det Norske Videnskaps-Akademi i Oslo, II. Hist.-Filos. Kl., 1954/1; Oslo: J. Dybwad, 1954) 1-40, esp. p. 16.

[36]E.g., I. Rabinowitz, "Be Opened = Ἐφφαθά (Mark 7,34): Did Jesus Speak Hebrew?" *ZNW* 53 (1962) 229-38; J. Cantineau, "Quelle langue parlait le peuple en Palestine au 1er siècle de notre ère," *Sem* 5 (1955) 99-101; W. Chomsky, "What Was the Jewish Vernacular during the Second Commonwealth?" *JQR* 42 (1951-52) 193-212; S. Aalen, Review of H. Birkeland, *The Language of Jesus, TTKi* 26 (1955) 45-61; R. Meyer, Review of the same, *OLZ* 52 (1957) 47-50; J. M. Grintz, "Hebrew as the Spoken and Written Language in the Last Days of the Second Temple," *JBL* 79 (1960) 32-47; J. A. Emerton, "Did Jesus Speak Hebrew?" *JTS* 12 (1961) 189-202; "*Maranatha* and *Ephphatha*," *JTS* 18 (1967) 427-31; M. Black, "Ἐφφαθά (Mk. 7.34), [τὰ] πάσχα (Mt. 26.18W), [τὰ] σάββατα (passim), [τα] διδραχμα (Mt. 17.24bis)," *Mélanges bibliques en hommage au R. P. Béda Rigaux* (eds. A. Descamps et A. de Halleux; Gembloux: Duculot, 1970) 57-62; S. Morag, "Ἐφφαθά (Mark vii. 34): Certainly Hebrew, not Aramaic?" *JSS* 17 (1972) 198-202; J. Barr, "Which Language Did Jesus Speak—Some Remarks of a Semitist," *BJRL* 52 (1970) 9-29; J. A. Emerton, "The Problem of Vernacular Hebrew in the First Century A.D. and the Language of Jesus," *JTS* 24 (1973) 1-23; P. Lapide, "Insights from Qumran into the Languages of Jesus," *RQ* 8 (1972-76) 483-501.

[37]S. Segert, "Zur Orthographie und Sprache der aramäischen Texte von Wadi Murrabbaᶜat," *ArOr* 31 (1963) 122-37; A. Díez Macho, "La lengua hablada por Jesucristo," *OrAn* 2 (1963) 95-132, esp. pp. 113-14, 122-23; W. Eiss, *EvT* 16 (1956) 170-81; J. A. Emerton, *JTS* 12 (1961) 189-202.

[38]In my commentary on the *Genesis Apocryphon of Qumran Cave 1* (1st ed., 1966) 19-20; for a slight modification of it, see the 2d ed., pp. 22-23. For an explanation of the divison, see pp. 57–84 below.

[39]In his article, "Aramaic" (*Current Trends in Linguistics 6: Linguistics in South West Asia and North Africa* [The Hague: Mouton, 1971] 347-412), Kutscher presents abundant evidence in support of the divisions of Old and Official Aramaic. Unfortunately, he died before he was able to complete his discussion of the later phases. But he did adopt in principle the division of the phases, as I had proposed them (see pp. 347-48); and coming from an authority in the Semitic languages such as this, it is a welcome recognition.

[40]Private communication.

[41]See *Lexicon linguae aramaicae Veteris Testamenti documentis antiquis illustratum* (Rome: Biblical Institute, 1971) 6*-8*.

[42]See *CBQ* 30 (1968) 420.

[43]In his review of M. Black, *An Aramaic Approach to the Gospels and Acts* (3d ed.; Oxford: Clarendon, 1967), *JNES* 31 (1972) 58-61, esp. p. 60.

[44]M. Smith, in his review of the same edition of Black's book, *JBL* 90 (1971) 247. Smith's comment has been quoted with approval by G. Vermes, *Jesus the Jew: A Historian's Reading of the Gospels* [London: Collins, 1973] 190. He thinks that "the illogicality" of my thesis has been exposed by Smith's "critical acumen." But has it? And is it really illogical? This is a Vermes flight to *obscurum per obscurius*. The problems which this "historian's reading of the Gospels" raises will have to be dealt with elsewhere; they are legion. Meanwhile, see the review of L. E. Keck, *JBL* 95 (1976) 508-9.

[45]"Sprachliche Bemerkungen zu einigen aramäischen Texten von Qumran," *ArOr* 33 (1965) 190-206; and his article cited in n. 37 above.

[46]*ArOr* 33 (1965) 205.

[47]See my commentary on *The Genesis Apocryphon of Qumran Cave I* (2d ed., 1971) 11-14, where I have become a little more open to the Essene composition of 1QapGen in view of the observation made by R. de Vaux; but even that is an extrinsic argument. The Essene composition of 11QtgJob has been proposed by E. W. Tuinstra, *Hermeneutische Aspecten van de Targum van Job uit Grot XI van Qumrân* (Dissertation, Rijksuniversiteit te Groningen, 1970), but the arguments proposed are singularly unconvincing; see below. pp. 166–67.

[48]"4Q Visions de ᶜAmram et une citation d'Origène," *RB* 79 (1972) 77-97.

[49]*El Targum: Introducción a las traducciones aramaicas de la Biblia* (Barcelona: Consejo superior de investigaciones científicas, 1972), esp. pp. 46-54.

[50]See further below, p. 37.

[51]See "The Translations Made from the Original Aramaic Gospels," *Studies in the History of Religions Presented to Crawford Howell Toy* (New York: Macmillan, 1912) 269-317; *The Four Gospels* (New York: Harper, 1933); "The Aramaic Gospels," *Christian Century* 51 (1934) 1338-40; *Our Translated Gospels* (New York: Harper, 1936); *Documents of the Primitive Church* (New York: Harper, 1941).

[52]This meaning is, of course, not certain, but it still remains the best interpretation. See W. Gutbrod, *TDNT* 3 (1965) 374, 388; see below pp. 45–46.

[53]E.g., G. Dalman, *The Words of Jesus Considered in the Light of Post-Biblical Jewish Writings and the Aramaic Language* (tr. D. M. Kay; Edinburgh: Clark, 1902); E. Kautzsch, *Grammatik des Biblisch-aramäischen, mit einer kritischen Erörterung der aramäischen Wörter im Neuen Testament* (Leipzig: F. C. W. Vogel, 1884) 4-21; A. Meyer, *Jesu Muttersprache* (n. 2 above), 47-53; J. Koopmans, *Aramäische Chrestomathie: Ausgewählte Texte (Inschriften, Ostraka und Papyri) bis zum 3. Jahrhundert n. Chr. für das Studium der aramäischen Sprache gesammelt* (Leiden: Nederlands Instituut vor het Nabije Oosten, 1962) §68, pp. 209-12; J. Jeremias, *New Testament Theology: The Proclamation of Jesus* (New York: Scribner, 1971) passim; S. Segert, *Altaramäische Grammatik mit Bibliographie, Chrestomathie und Glossar* (Leipzig: VEB Berlag Enzyklopädie, 1975) 519. Cf. A. Neubauer, "On the Dialects Spoken in

Palestine in the Time of Christ," *Studia biblica: Essays in Biblical Archaeology and Criticism* (Oxford: Clarendon, 1885) 39-74, esp. pp. 55-57, 62.

[54]*Aramaic Approach* (3d ed.), 139.

[55]"Trois tombeaux juifs récemment découverts au Sud-Est de Jérusalem," *SBFLA* 7 (1956-57), esp. pp. 232-39.

[56]I have tried to bring this out in my discussion of the inscription, "The Aramaic Qorban Inscription from Jebel Ḫallet eṭ-Ṭûri and Mark 7 11 / Matt 15 5," *JBL* 78 (1959) 60-65; reprinted with slight revisions in *ESBNT*, 93-101. A query was recently posed about this inscription: Why could not קרבן אלה in this text mean "a qorban, a curse" (from him who is within it)? Then it would be closer to the rabbinic use of קרבן. My interpretation of the phrase was based rather on קרבן יהוה (Num 9:13; 31:50), "an offering to Yahweh," with the divine name changed to Aramaic אלה, hence "an offering to God." However, the question is really whether אלה, which is a good biblical Hebrew word for "curse" (see Gen 24:41; Deut 29:19), is also known in Aramaic. As far as I can see, the only place where it might possibly occur is in the *Panammu* inscription from Zenjirli (line 2). Here A. Dupont-Sommer (*An Aramaic Handbook* [ed. F. Rosenthal; Porta linguarum orientalium, ns 10; Wiesbaden: Harrassowitz, 1967], I/1.7) reads אלה hesitatingly. J. C. L. Gibson (*Textbook of Syrian Semitic Inscriptions, Volume 2: Aramaic Inscriptions Including Inscriptions in the Dialect of Zenjirli* [Oxford: Clarendon, 1975] 78) reads it unhesitatingly, rejecting the meaning "conspiracy" (p. 82) that is sometimes given to it. However, H. Donner and W. Röllig, *KAI* §215:2, read אזה as a fem. rel. pronoun. Given this state of affairs, I am reluctant to consider אלה here as meaning "curse." See, however, the remarks of J. C. Greenfield in a review of my *ESBNT*, *JNES* 35 (1976) 59-61.

[57]"The Excavations in the Old City of Jerusalem," *W. F. Albright Volume* (Eretz-Israel, 9; Jerusalem: Israel Exploration Society, 1969) 168-70 (+ pl. 45, 5).

[58]See M. Black, *Aramaic Approach* (3d ed.), 139-40.

[59]The vocalization of the word is problematic. The Greek suggests the vocalization *māmôn*, and this would be a better Hebrew form (with the lengthened pretonic vowel) than an Aramaic form, despite the Aramaic-like ending on the word (*-a*). I have partially discussed the meaning and form of the word elsewhere (see "The Story of the Dishonest Manager [Lk 16:1-13]," *TS* 25 '1964] 23-41, esp. p. 30; reprinted, *ESBNT*, 161-84, esp. pp. 169-70). The English spelling "mammon" (with two m's) is said to be derived from Latin usage (although the Vulgate has *mamona* in Luke 16:9 [see R. Weber, *Biblia sacra iuxta Vulgatam versionem* (Stuttgart: Württembergische Bibelanstalt, 1969), 2. 1640], where no variant spelling is given). However, in the *Compact Edition of the Oxford English Dictionary* (London / New York: Oxford University, 1971), 1. 1709, the Vulgate spelling is listed as *mam(m)ona*]). The form with two m's would better reflect the Semitic spelling *mammōnā* (< *maʾmôn*). But the English spelling is still problematic.

[60]W. F. Albright and C. S. Mann, *Matthew: Introduction, Translation, and Notes* (AB 26; Garden City: Doubleday, 1971) clxviii-clxxii.

[61]*Band I, Satzlehre Teil 1* (2d ed.; SUNT 1; Göttingen: Vandenhoeck & Ruprecht, 1968).

[62]SNTSMS 5; Cambridge: Cambridge University, 1967.

[63]BAG, 325b.

[64]*Aramaic Approach* (3d ed.), 133.

[65]See my commentary (2d ed., 1971), 150-51.

[66]See "Turfan et Qumran: Livre des Géants juif et manichéen," *Tradition und Glaube: Das frühe Christentum in seiner Umwelt: Festgabe für Karl Georg Kuhn zum 65. Geburtstag* (eds. G. Jeremias et al.; Göttingen: Vandenhoeck & Ruprecht, 1971) 117-27, esp. p. 122: 4QEnGiants[b] 1 ii 13, which Milik reads as follows: [השכחו גבריא לחויא לה[ון]/[חלמא . . .], and translates: "Les géants cherchaient (quelqu'un) qui pût leur expliquer [le songe]," and so they sought out Enoch, "the distinguished scribe" (לספר פרשא). But does השכח ever have the meaning "chercher"? It seems to me rather that one should restore the first lacuna, in part at least, with כדי לא, and then translate: "[since] the giants were [not] able to explain [the dream] for them[selves], . . ." But any certainty in this matter will have to await further discussion of this text. Meanwhile, one can consult *The Books of Enoch* (see p. 112 below, n. 72), 305. In any case,

another clear example of the verb has appeared in 4QEn[a] 1 ii 8: [ולמ]דרך על עפרה ו[ע]ל [כפ]יה לא תשכחון מן / [חמתה], "and you are not able [to tr]ead on the dust or o[n] the [ro]cks because of / [the heat]." See *The Books of Enoch*, 146-47. But שכח in the sense of "to find" is also found: 4QEn[c] 4:50; 4QEnGiants[c] 2:5. Cf. M. Black, "The Fragments of the Aramaic Enoch from Qumran," *La littérature juive entre Tenach et Mischna: Quelques problèmes* (RechBib 9; Leiden: Brill, 1974) 15-28.

[67]See G. Vermes, "The Use of בר נשא / בר נש in Jewish Aramaic," in M. Black, *Aramaic Approach* (3d ed.), 310-28; but cf. my discussion on pp. 143–60 below.

[68]See p. 149 below.

[69]*New Testament Theology*, 260-62 (see n. 53 above).

[70]E.g., see P. Benoit, "La divinité de Jésus," *Exégèse et théologie* (Paris: Cerf, 1961), 1. 134 ("insolite en araméen").

[71]G. Vermes ("The Use," 320) has, in particular, argued strongly for the circumlocutional meaning, even going so far as to say that it "means 'I'" (p. 323). See further *Jesus the Jew*, pp. 188-91. However, J. Jeremias (*New Testament Theology*, 261 n. 1) has also raised his voice against this interpretation and against Vermes' use of the evidence.

[72]See "Problèmes de la littérature hénochique à la lumière des fragments de Qumrân," *HTR* 64 (1971) 333-78, esp. p. 334.

[73]Ibid., 373-78.

[74]E.g., M. Black, *Aramaic Approach* (3d ed.), 200-202.

[75]*A Historical Introduction to the New Testament* (New York: Harper & Row, 1963) 41.

[76]Ibid.

[77]*New Chapters in New Testament Study* (New York: Macmillan, 1937) 127-68, esp. pp. 165-66; A. T. Olmstead, "Could an Aramaic Gospel Be Written?" *JNES* 1 (1942) 41-75; E. J. Goodspeed, "The Possible Aramaic Gospel," ibid., 315-40, esp. p. 328.

[78]For this text, see *MPAT*, 184–87; also my commentary on *The Genesis Apocryphon* (2d ed., 1971), 21 n. 57.

[79]"Aramaic Studies and the Study of the New Testament," *JBR* 26 (1958) 304-13.

[80]*Aramaic Approach* (3d ed.), 184.

[81]Ibid., 143-85.

[82]Oxford: Clarendon, 1925.

[83]*Aramaic Approach* (3d ed.), 143.

[84]I hesitatingly mention this aspect of the problem because I have not yet had the time to investigate it; but it is a legitimate question that must be asked.

[85]See, e.g., [J. J.] Barthélemy, "Explication d'un bas-relief égyptien, et de l'inscription phénicienne [sic] qui l'accompagne," *Mémoires de littérature tiréz des regîtres de l'Académie royale des inscriptions et belles lettres* 32 (1768) 725-38; M. Lanci, *Osservazioni sul basso-rilievo fenico-egizio che si conserva in Carpentrasso* (Rome: F. Bourlié, 1825); A. Merx, "Bemerkungen zur bis jetzt bekannten aramäischen Inschriften," *ZDMG* 22 (1868) 674-99, esp. pp. 697-99; J. Derenbourg, "Notes épigraphiques: V. L'inscription dite de Carpentras," *JA* 6/11 (1868) 277-87; [J.] Lauth, "Aegyptisch-aramäische Inschriften," *SBAW* 1878/2, pp. 97-149, esp. pp. 115-31; C. Clermont-Ganneau, "Origine perse des monuments araméens d'Egypte," *RArch* ns 37 (1879) 21-39, esp. pp. 31-33; K. Schlottmann, "Metrum und Reim auf einer ägyptisch-aramäischen Inschrift," *ZDMG* 32 (1878) 187-97; P. de Lagarde, "Zur Erklärung der aramäischen Inschrift von Carpentras," *NKGWG* 1878, pp. 357-72; E. Ledrain, "Mots égyptiens contenus dans quelques stèles araméennes d'Egypte," *RA* 1 (1884) 18-23, esp. pp. 18-21; S. R. Driver, *Notes on the Hebrew Text and the Topography of the Books of Samuel* (Oxford: Clarendon, 1913) xii-xv; C. C. Torrey, "A Specimen of Old Aramaic Verse," *JAOS* 46 (1926) 241-47; P. Grelot, "Sur la stèle de Carpentras," *Sem* 17 (1967) 73-75; B. Couroyer, "A propos de la stèle de Carpentras," *Sem* 20 (1970) 17-21 (with a postscript by P. Grelot, pp. 21-22).

[86]See W. S. Towner, "The Poetic Passages of Daniel 1-6," *CBQ* 31 (1969) 317-26.

[87]See J. T. Milik, "La patrie de Tobie," *RB* 73 (1966) 522-30, esp. p. 522 n. 3.

[88]See note 32 above.

[89]The litterature on this text is vast and will have to be sought elsewhere; for a recent discussion of the proverbs, see P. Grelot, "Les proverbes d'Ahiqar," *RB* 68 (19 61) 178-94; *Documents araméens d'Egypte* (Litteratures anciennes du Proche-Orient; Paris: Cerf, 1972) 425-52.

[90]*Aramaic Approach* (3d ed.), 41.

[91]See pp. 90–94 below.

[92]E.g., M. Black, *Aramaic Approach* (3d ed.), 244-71, 277-80, 303-4; M.-E. Boismard, "Importance de la critique textuelle pour établir l'origine araméenne du quatrième évangile," *L'évangile de Jean: Etudes et problèmes* (RechBib 3; Bruges: Desclée de Brouwer, 1958) 41-57.

[93]See, e.g., F. H. Chase, *The Old Syriac Element in the Text of Codex Bezae* (London: Macmillan, 1893). This question, however, is far from simple; cf. E. Ferguson, "Qumran and Codex 'D,'" *RQ* 8 (1972-76) 75-80; S. P. Brock, Review of J. D. Yoder, *Concordance to the Distinctive Greek Text of Codex Bezae* (NTTS 2; Leiden: Brill, 1961), *TLZ* 88 (1963) 351-52, esp. col. 352.

[94]E.g., "'De son ventre couleront des fleuves d'eau'—La citation scripturaire de Jean, vii, 38," *RB* 66 (1959) 369-74; "A propos de Jean vii, 38," *RB* 67 (1960) 224-25; M.-E. Boismard, "Les citations targumiques dans le quatrième évangile," *RB* 66 (1959) 374-78; M. McNamara, *The New Testament and the Palestinian Targum to the Pentateuch* (AnBib 27; Rome: Biblical Institute, 1966); *Targum and Testament: Aramaic Paraphrases of the Hebrew Bible: A Light on the New Testament* (Grand Rapids: Eerdmans, 1972); R. Le Déaut, *La nuit pascale* (AnBib 22; Rome: Biblical Institute, 1963); *Liturgie juive et Nouveau Testament* (Rome: Biblical Institute, 1965); B. J. Malina, *The Palestinian Manna Tradition: The Manna Tradition in the Palestinian Targums and Its Relationship to the New Testament Writings* (AGJU 7; Leiden: Brill, 1968). See further P. Nickels, *Targum and New Testament: A Bibliography together with a New Testament Index* (Rome: Biblical Institute, 1967).

[95]*The New Testament and the Palestinian Targum to the Pentateuch,* 77. McNamara (*Targum and Testament,* 14-15) tries to brush aside my criticism of this usage: "Every student of this material is, of course, acutely conscious of the complexity to which Fitzmyer refers." But if so, then why is it better "to abide by the traditional name 'Palestinian Targum'"? One suspects that this is being done because it is more convenient in view of the thesis being propounded. Keep it vague, and no one will question the weakness in the thesis itself!

[96]See *Masoreten des Westens* (Stuttgart: Kohlhammer, 1930; reprinted, Hildesheim: Olms, 1967), 2. 1-62.

[97]See especially Cairo Genizah Text C. This whole area needs further scrutiny.

[98]See, e.g., A. Deissmann, "Prolegomena to the Biblical Letters and Epistles," *Bible Studies: Contributions Chiefly from Papyri and Inscriptions to the History of the Language, the Literature, and the Religion of Hellenistic Judaism and Primitive Christianity* (tr. A. Grieve; Edinburgh: Clark, 1901) 3-59; L. Champion, *Benedictions and Doxologies in the Epistles of Paul* (Oxford: Privately printed Heidelberg dissertation, 1935); J.-A. Eschlimann, "La rédaction des épîtres pauliniennes d'après une comparaison avec les lettres profanes de son temps," *RB* 53 (1946) 185-96; F. X. J. Exler, *The Form of the Ancient Greek Letter: A Study in Greek Epistolography* (Washington: Catholic University, 1923); E. Fascher, "Briefliteratur, urchristliche, formgeschichtlich," *RGG*[3] 1 (1957) 1412-15; O. Roller, *Das Formular der paulinischen Briefen: Ein Beitrag zur Lehre vom antiken Briefe* (BWANT 58; Stuttgart: Kohlhammer, 1933); H. Koskenniemi, *Studien zur Idee und Phraseologie des griechischen Briefes bis 400 n. Chr.* (Suomalaisen Tiedeakatemian Toimituksia: Annales academiae scientiarum fennicae, ser. B, tom. 102/2; Helsinki: Suomalaisen Tiedeakatemia, 1956); W. G. Doty, *Letters in Primitive Christianity* (Guides to Biblical Scholarship, NT series; Philadelphia: Fortress, 1973); J. L. White, *The Form and Function of the Body of the Greek Letter: A Study of the Letter-Body in the Non-Literary Papyri and in Paul the Apostle* (SBLDS 2; Missoula: Scholars Press, 1972); *The Form and Structure of the Official Petition: A Study in Greek Epistolography* (SBLDS 5; Missoula: Society of Biblical Literature, 1972); C.-H. Kim, *Form and*

Structure of the Familiar Greek Letter of Recommendation (SBLDS 4; Missoula: Society of Biblical Literature, 1972).

[99]See p. 183–204 below.

[100]See p. 200 n. 7 below.

[101]See p. 5 above.

[102]*Aramaic Approach* (3d ed.), 300.

[103]Ibid., n. 2.

[104]See pp. 35–36 below.

[105]See further my review of M. Black, *Aramaic Approach* (3d ed.), *CBQ* 30 (1968) 417–28.

Chapter 2

The Languages of Palestine in the First Century A.D.*

With the deportation of Palestinian Jews to Babylonia in the early sixth century B.C. there began a gradual but distinctive shift in the language-habits of the people of Palestine. What had been known as *śĕpat Kĕnaᶜan,* "the language of Canaan" (Isa 19:18) or *Yĕhûdît*, "the language of Judah" (2 Kgs 18:26, 28; Isa 36:11, 13), or what is often called today classical Hebrew of the pre-exilic period, gave way at first to a more Aramaicized form of the language.[1] Though the two languages, Hebrew and Aramaic, had co-existed for several centuries in the Near East before this, Aramaic became the more important of the two, serving as the *lingua franca* during the latter part of the Neo-Assyrian empire and during the Persian period. Hebrew is usually regarded today as the more important of the two languages, because it is the tongue of the bulk of the OT. And yet, historically it was restricted to a small area on the south-eastern coast of the Mediterranean, whereas Official or Imperial Aramaic was used across a major portion of the Near Eastern world, from Egypt to Asia Minor to Pakistan. Indeed, it gradually supplanted Hebrew in most of Palestine itself as the common tongue.[2]

With the conquest of the East by Alexander a new linguistic influence was felt in Palestine. Even prior to the golden age of Greece, its culture had been influencing the eastern Mediterranean world, and Palestine was affected. But the extent to which the Greek language was advancing into the area at an early period is not easy to say. The evidence for the use of Greek in Palestine prior to the third century B.C. is very sparse indeed, the oldest extant Greek inscription dating from only 277 B.C.[3]

Hebrew did not wholly disappear from Palestine, either when Aramaic had become the more common language or when Palestinian Jews gradually began to use Greek. The composition of Daniel and of Ben Sira is an indication of the continued use of it.[4] Though these compositions may point to a learned and literary use of the language, it would be oversimplified to regard it as only that. There were areas or pockets in Palestine, and perhaps even strata of society, where Hebrew continued as a spoken language too. It is often thought that an effort was made to resurrect it (if that is the proper term) at the time of the Maccabean revolt and that the use of Hebrew became a token of one's loyalty to the national effort.[5] If the origins of the Qumran Essene community are rightly related to the aftermath of that revolt, this may explain why the majority of the Qumran texts discovered to date were written in Hebrew and composed at a time when most Palestinian Jews were thought to be speaking Aramaic. These texts, of course, do not tell us how much Hebrew was *spoken* among the Essenes, because they bear witness only to what is called a "neo-classical Hebrew," a form of the language that may be only literary. Since, however, the majority of the sectarian literature was composed in Hebrew, this seems to mean that it was being spoken. But in any case, the use of Hebrew for such compositions did not exclude the use of Aramaic; the latter is also found in the Qumran fragments, but not to the same extent as the Hebrew. A few fragments of an Old Greek translation of the OT were also found in Qumran Cave IV; they suggest that at least some of the community were reading Greek, and possibly speaking it.[6] The relative paucity of the Greek texts in comparison with the Hebrew and Aramaic is noteworthy.

With the advent of the Romans in 63 B.C. and the conquest of Pompey, Latin too was introduced into the area. Again, the evidence for its early use is exceedingly sparse.[7] Yet it must be considered among the languages of Palestine at the beginning of the Christian era.

This very brief historical sketch provides the background for the use of four languages in Palestine about the time when Christianity emerged. The complex linguistic picture that they created is not easy to draw. Yet that complexity bears on a number of problems in the interpretation of the NT and of intertestamental writings. It bears too on the use and interpretation of the targums. My topic is one that has been discussed many times over during the last century and the opinions expressed have often been in favor of one language over another; the topic is vast and my treatment here can only hope to survey it without going into great detail.

In speaking of first-century Palestine, I would like to include the first part of the second century too, up to the time of the Second Revolt against Rome (A.D. 132-135), since this marks a logical cut-off point in the history of Palestine and is often regarded as the end of the NT era. The sources that I shall be using in this discussion will be both literary and epigraphic.

I. *Latin*

I shall begin with the latest language to appear on the scene and work back to the oldest. The evidence of Latin in first-century Palestine indicates that it was used mainly by the Romans who occupied the land and for more or less official purposes. Thus there are dedicatory inscriptions on buildings and aqueducts, funerary inscriptions on tombstones of Roman legionnaires who died in Palestine, milestones on Roman roads with Latin inscriptions,[8] and the ubiquitous Roman terra-cotta tiles stamped with various abbreviations of the Tenth Legion, the *Legio decima fretensis* (LX, LXF, LXFRE, LEXFR, LCXF, LEG X F).[9]

Two of the most interesting Latin inscriptions have only recently come to light and both of them are from Caesarea Maritima, the town rebuilt by Herod the Great between 22 and 9 B.C. in honor of Augustus, which eventually became the seat of the Roman governor. Tacitus called it *caput Iudaeae* (*Hist.* 2.78.10). One of the inscriptions comes from the architrave of a building in Caesarea and partly preserves the name of the Roman colony established by the emperor Vespasian. It reads:[10]

[COLONIAE] PRIMAE FL(aviae) AVG(vstae) [Caesareae?]
[CLEO]PATRA MATER EIVS HOC F(ieri) I(vssit)

The other is the now famous fragment of a dedicatory inscription on a building, the Tiberieum, that Pontius Pilate erected in honor of the emperor Tiberius It reads:[11]

[TI(berio) CAES(are) AVG(vsto) V CO(n)]S(vle) TIBERIEVM
[PO]NTIVS PILATVS
[PRAEF]ECTVS IVDA[EA]E
[ ] ´[ ]

This inscription thus attests the official use of Latin in Palestine, prior to A.D. 36, the year of Pilate's recall to Rome. It also records the historical presence of Pilate in Judea, a fact scarcely doubted,[12] but never before attested epigraphically. Finally, it confirms the suggestion made by Roman historians that Pilate's official title was not *procurator,*[13] but rather *praefectus.*[14]

Such Latin inscriptions as these illustrate the information supplied by Josephus who tells us that prohibitions forbidding non-Jews to enter the inner courts of the Jerusalem temple were erected along the stone balustrades surrounding them, "some in Greek, and some in Latin characters" (*αἱ μὲν ἑλληνικοῖς, αἱ δὲ ῥωμαϊκοῖς γράμμασιν*).[15] Though exemplars of this warning have been found in Greek,[16] none has yet turned up in Latin. Such a prohibition carrying the death penalty would understandably be erected in Greek and Latin to warn foreign visitors little acquainted with the Semitic languages. But one cannot restrict the understanding of them to foreigners alone. Josephus also mentions decrees of Caesar concerning the Jews which were formulated in Latin as well as in Greek.[17]

All of this makes intelligible the action of Pilate recorded in the Fourth Gospel,[18] writing the official title on Jesus' cross *ῥωμαϊστί*, "in Latin," as well as *ἑβραϊστί* and *ἑλληνιστί* (John 19:20).

This evidence points to an official use of Latin in Palestine by Romans which might have been expected. From the period between the two revolts there are four (or five) fragmentary papyrus Latin texts which were found in the caves of Murabbaʿat. Though they are so fragmentary that one cannot be certain about their contents, yet one of them (Mur 158) seems to have been an official, archival copy of a document belonging to the Roman invaders.[19] Part of a Roman name is preserved on it, *C. Iulius R*[ ].

There are also a few funerary inscriptions, one of them marking the burial of a Roman soldier of the Tenth Legion, Lucius Magniu[s] Felix.[20] From the same period come other Latin inscriptions too, e.g., one belonging to a monument, possibly an altar, dedicated to Jupiter Sarapis and found in Jerusalem itself. It is dated to A.D. 116, and invokes Jupiter for the health and victory of the emperor Trajan.[21]

Such evidence is precious, indeed, because it is not abundant. It says, however, little about the amount of Latin that might have been spoken in Palestine by the indigenous population, despite the long time since the Roman occupation began in 63 B.C.[22] But one reason for this is that Greek was still a common means of communication not only between Romans in the provinces, but also between the capital and the provinces. Greek was still more or less the *lingua franca* in the Near East.

II. *Greek*

Greek culture had been increasingly affecting the Jews of Palestine for some time prior to the conquest of Alexander.[23] The influence of this culture continued after his conquest, especially with the Hellenizing efforts of the Lagide and Seleucid kings, and even with the Herods. Greek cities were founded in Palestine and older towns were transformed into *poleis.* Alexander himself ordered the reconstruction of Gaza. The names of some towns of the Decapolis, Pella and Dion, reveal the early Macedonian influence. Under Lagide domination Acco became Ptolemais and Rabbat-Ammon became Philadelphia, another town of the Decapolis. Philoteria was established under the same influence on the western shore of Lake Gennesareth, and Joppa was hellenized. Ancient Beth-shan was conquered by Antiochus III the Great in 218 B.C. and became Scythopolis. The Hellenization continued under Herod the Great, who transformed the ancient town of Strato's Tower into Caesarea Maritima, Samaria into Sebaste, and established a number of other towns and fortresses throughout the country on Greek models (Antipatris, Phasaelis, Antonia at Jerusalem, etc.). Nor did his heirs desist from such activity, because to them is ascribed the founding of such places as Caesarea Philippi, Tiberias, Bethsaida Julias. In all some thirty towns of the area have been counted that were either Greek foundations or transformed *poleis.*[24] These Hellenistic cities dotted the countryside of Palestine for several centuries prior to the first Christian century and were clearly centers from which the Greek language spread to less formally Hellenistic towns, such as Jerusalem, Jericho, or Nazareth. As in the case of the Roman occupiers of the land, the new language was undoubtedly used at first in official texts, decrees, and inscriptions, and from such use it spread to the indigenous population.

However, it is not possible to document the use of Greek in Palestine prior to Alexander or to indicate what influence it might have had then. The earliest Greek text found there is apparently the bilingual Edomite-Greek ostracon dated in the sixth year of Ptolemy II Philadelphus (277 B.C.), discovered in the spring of 1971 at Khirbet el-Kom, along with other ostraca (see n. 3 above). Prior to this discovery the earliest known inscription was that erected by Anaxikles, a priest of the royal cult of Ptolemy IV Philopator, who was installed at Joppa shortly after the Egyptian victory over Antiochus III at Raphia in 217 B.C. It gives clear evidence of the use of the language by foreigners, but says little about the use of it by the indigenous population.

When the Hellenization of Palestine under Antiochus IV Epiphanes began, his efforts were aided by the Jews themselves, as both 1 Maccabees and Josephus make clear.[25] There seems to be little doubt that the use of the Greek language was part of this assistance.[26] Antiochus' reign, however, lasted only a little over a decade, and in its aftermath, the Maccabean revolt, the book of Daniel was reduced to its final form. In the Aramaic stories that form part of that book one finds the first clear instance of Greek invading a Palestinian Aramaic text. In Dan 3:5 the names of three of the musical instruments, "the lyre, the harp, and the bagpipe" (*RSV*—קיתרוס < Gk. *κίθαρις,* פסנתרין < *ψαλτήριον;* סומפניה < *συμφωνία*), are all given in slightly Aramaicized forms of clearly Greek names.[27] Further evidence of Greek influence is seen also in the linguistic problem of the book as a whole; in its protocanonical form it is composed in two languages, Hebrew and Aramaic, but in its deuterocanonical form Greek appears. This influence is further seen in other apocryphal and deuterocanonical compositions in Greek by Jews, such as 1 Esdras, 2 Maccabees, and the additions to Esther (to mention only those writings that are probably of Palestinian origin).

Though the names of a host of Hellenistic Jewish litterateurs who wrote in Greek are known,[28] and some fragments of their writings are preserved in patristic authors such as Clement of Alexandria,[29] or Eusebius of Caesarea,[30] there are only a few whose writings are related to first-century Palestine. The most important of these are Justus of Tiberias and Flavius Josephus, both of whom wrote mainly historical works. The first was the bitter opponent of Josephus in the First Revolt against Rome, a man of Hellenistic education and noted for his eloquence, the author of *Ἱστορία ἡ τοῦ Ἰουδαϊκοῦ πολέμου τοῦ κατὰ Οὐεσπασιάνου.*[31]

Josephus tells us something about his own knowledge of Greek and about his use of it to compose his works. At the end of the *Antiquities,* he says of himself:

> My compatriots admit that in our Jewish learning (*παρ' ἡμῖν παιδείαν*) I far excel them. But I labored hard to steep myself in Greek prose [and poetic learning], after having gained a knowledge of Greek grammar; but the constant use of my native tongue (*πάτριος . . . συνήθεια*) hindered my achieving precision in pronunciation. For our people do not welcome those who have mastered the speech of many nations or adorn

> their style with smoothness of diction, because they consider that such skill is not only common to ordinary freemen but that even slaves acquire it, if they so choose. Rather, they give credit for wisdom to those who acquire an exact knowledge of the Law and can interpret the Holy Scriptures. Consequently, though many have laboriously undertaken this study, scarcely two or three have succeeded (in it) and reaped the fruit of their labors.[32]

Several points should be noted in Josephus' statement. First, his record of a popular boastful attitude that the learning of Greek would be an ordinary achievement for many Palestinians, even for freemen and slaves, if they wanted to do so. The attitude is at least condescending. Secondly, such learning was not so much esteemed as knowledge of the Mosaic Law and the interpretation of Scripture. Thirdly, Josephus testifies about the efforts that he personally made to acquire a good command of Greek. Fourthly, he also gives the impression that few Palestinian Jews of his day could speak Greek well.

From other places in his writings we know that he acted as an interpreter for Titus, speaking "in his native tongue" to the populace toward the end of the war.[33] Titus himself had addressed the Jews of Palestine in Greek, but preferred to have Josephus parley with them *hebraïzōn.* This may suggest that Palestinian Jews did not understand Greek very well, and bear out the comment of Josephus himself cited above. However, J. N. Sevenster has plausibly noted that we do not know how well Titus himself could speak Greek.[34] Hence Josephus' task as interpreter does not necessarily mean that little Greek was actually understood.

Again Josephus informs us that he composed his *Jewish War* originally "in his native tongue" (τῇ πατρίῳ [γλώσσῃ]), destining it for Parthians, Babylonians, the tribes of Arabia, Jews beyond the Euphrates and in Adiabene.[35] This destination almost certainly implies that it was originally written in the *lingua franca*, Aramaic.[36] Josephus subsequently translated this composition into Greek (ἕλλαδι γλώσσῃ μεταβαλών),[37] to provide subjects of the Roman empire with his version of the Palestinian revolt. What a problem this was for him he reveals in the *Antiquities,* where he still looks on Greek as "foreign and unfamiliar."[38] And yet, despite this attitude, the end-product of his efforts has been hailed as "an excellent specimen of the Atticistic Greek of the first century."[39]

But the real difficulty in this testimony of Josephus is that his Greek writings were composed in Rome, not in Palestine; and he frankly admits that he composed the Greek version of the *Jewish War* in the leisure that Rome afforded, "making use of some assistants for the sake of the Greek" (χρησάμενός τισι πρὸς τὴν ἑλληνίδα φωνὴν συνέργοις).[40] Presumably, other Jewish authors in Palestine who might have wanted to write in Greek could have found there comparable assistants. This may seem to have been essential for literary composition, but it says little about the degree of communication between Palestinian Jews in Greek.

If Josephus' testimony leaves the picture of Greek in first-century Palestine unclear, there are many other considerations that persuade us that Greek was widely used at this time and not only in the clearly Hellenized towns, but in many others as well. Indeed, there are some indications that Palestinian Jews in some areas may have used nothing else but Greek. Reasons for considering the matter in this way may now be briefly set forth.

There is first the epigraphic material. Several famous Greek inscriptions are extant from this period. There is the Greek inscription forbidding non-Jews to enter the inner courts of the Jerusalem temple,[41] the Jerusalem synagogue inscription which commemorates its building by Theodotos Vettenos, a priest and leader of the synagogue,[42] the hymn inscribed in the necropolis of Marisa,[43] the edict of Augustus (or some first-century Roman emperor) found at Nazareth concerning the violation of tombs,[44] the Capernaum dedicatory inscription,[45] and the numberless ossuary inscriptions, some written in Greek alone, others in Greek and Hebrew (or Aramaic) from the vicinity of Jerusalem.[46] In several cases the Greek inscriptions on these ossuaries have outnumbered those in Aramaic or Hebrew,[47] and it is unlikely that the language chosen for most of these crudely incised identifications was merely the *lingua franca* of the day. Rather, they bear witness to the widespread and living use of Greek among first-century Palestinian Jews, as does the adoption of Greek and Roman names by many of them in this period. H. J. Leon is undoubtedly right when he writes that such "sepulchral inscriptions . . . best indicate the language of the common people."[48] For they reveal that Greek was not confined merely to official inscriptions. The real question, however, is how widespread it was among the common people.

Information concerning Palestine during the period between the two revolts against Rome has always been sparse, and information about the use of Greek at that time is no exception. Recently, however, some new material has come to light in the Greek papyri from the Murabbaᶜat caves and in copies of Greek letters from the Bar Cochba revolt.

From the Murabbaᶜat caves have come examples of grain transactions (Mur 89-107), IOU's (Mur 114), contracts of marriage and remarriage among Jews (Mur 115-16), fragments of philosophical and literary texts (Mur 108-12), even texts written in a Greek shorthand (Mur 164).[49] The letters from a cave in the Wadi Ḥabra indicate that Greek was also used in a less official kind of writing. From the period just before the Second Revolt there is a batch of letters which are communications between Bar Cochba and his lieutenants, and surprisingly enough written even in Greek.[50]

One letter, in particular, merits some attention because of the special bearing it has on the topic under discussion. It comes from the so-called Cave of Letters in the Wadi Ḥabra and was discovered in 1960. It is written in the name of one *Soumaios*. The editor of the letter, B. Lifshitz, thinks that this is a Greek form of the name of *Šimĕᶜōn ben Kōsibāh,* the real name of Bar

Cochba. If it is not Bar Cochba himself, then it is someone very closely associated with him, who writes to the same two lieutenants to whom Bar Cochba wrote in other letters—and, indeed, about the same matter. Soumaios requests of Jonathan bar Ba^{c}yan and Masabbala that they send wooden-beams (?) and citrons (the $^{\supset}$*etrōgîm*) for the celebration of Succoth or Tabernacles. The text reads:

Σου[μαῖ]ος Ἰωναθῆι	Sou[mai]os to Jonathe,
Βαϊανοῦ καὶ Μα-	(son of) Baianos, and Ma-
[σ]άβαλα χαίρειν.	[s]abbala, greetings!
Ἐ[π]ηδὴ ἔπεμσα πρὸς	S[i]nce I have sent to
ὑμᾶς Ἀ[γ]ρίππαν σπου-	you A[g]rippa, make
δ[άσα]τε πέμσε μοι	h[ast]e to send me
σ[τε]λεοὺ[ς] καὶ κίτρια	b[e]am[s] and citrons.
α[ὐτὰ] δ' ἀνασθήσεται	And furnish th[em]
ἰς [χ]ιτρειαβολὴν Ἰου-	for the [C]itron-celebration of the
δαίων καὶ μὴ ἄλως	Jews; and do not do
ποιήσηται. Ἐγράφη	otherwise. No[w] (this) has been writ-
δ[ὲ] Ἐληνιστὶ διὰ	ten in Greek because
τ[ὸ ὁρ]μὰν μὴ εὑρη-	a [des]ire has not be[en]
θ[ῆ]ναι Ἑβραεστὶ	found to w[ri]te in Hebrew. De[s]patch
γ[ρά]ψασθαι. Αὐτὸν	him quickly
ἀπ[ο]λῦσαι τάχιον	fo[r t]he feast,
δι[ὰ τ]ην Ἑορτὴν	an[d do no]t
κα[ὶ μ]ὴ ἄλλως ποιή-	do otherwise.
ση[τα]ι.	
Σουμαῖος	Soumaios.
ἔρρωσο	Farewell.[51]

Two things are of importance in this letter. First, Bar Cochba's solicitude to have provisions for the celebration of Succoth is again attested; a similar request for citrons and willow-branches is found in one of his Aramaic letters.[52] Secondly, at a time when the nationalist fever of the Jews must have been running high the leader of the revolt—or someone close to him, if Soumaios is not Šimĕ^{c}ōn bar Kōsibāh—frankly prefers to write in Greek, or at least has to write in Greek. He does not find the ὅρμα, "impulse, desire," to compose the letter ἑβραϊστί. The cursive handwriting is not elegant and the spelling leaves much to be desired; if a scribe were employed for the writing of it, then he was not very well trained. In any case, this Palestinian Greek is not much worse than other examples of Greek in the provinces that have been found elsewhere.

A NT problem that bears on this discussion may be introduced at this point. It is the names for Jerusalem Christians recorded in Acts 6:1, the Ἑλληνισταί and the Ἑβραῖοι. I have discussed this matter more fully elsewhere,[53] adopting the interesting suggestion of C. F. D. Moule,[54] which seems to cope best with the data available and seems to be far more plausible than other attempts to explain these names.[55] Moule proposes that these names designate two groups of Palestinian *Jewish* Christians in Jerusalem. The Ἑλληνισταί were not simply Gentile converts who spoke Greek, while the Ἑβραῖοι were Jewish converts who spoke Hebrew (or possibly Aramaic). The Greek-speaking Paul of Tarsus stoutly maintained that he was Ἑβραῖος ἐξ Ἑβραίων (Phil 3:5). Rather, Ἑλληνισταί undoubtedly denotes Jerusalem Jews or Jewish Christians who habitually spoke Greek only (and for that reason were more affected by Hellenistic culture), while the Ἑβραῖοι were those who also spoke a Semitic language. In any case, it can scarcely be maintained that ἑλληνίζειν did not mean "to speak Greek" at all. Moule's distinction fits in very well with the widespread use of Greek in first-century Palestine. It raises a further problem of the determination of what Semitic language would have been commonly used along with it by the Ἑβραῖοι.

Before we approach that problem, however, two final remarks about the use of Greek in first-century Palestine are in order. The first concerns Jesus' use of Greek. This question has been raised from time to time for a variety of reasons, and obviously little can be asserted about it.[56] "Galilee of the Gentiles" (Matt 4:15) has often been said to have been an area of Palestine where the population was more bilingual than in the south, e.g., at Jerusalem. Hence it is argued: Coming from an area such as this, Jesus would have shared this double linguistic heritage. While it must be admitted that there were undoubtedly areas where less Greek was used than others, nevertheless the widespread attestation of Greek material in Palestine would indicate that "Galilee of the Gentiles" did not have a monopoly on it. The general evidence that we have been considering would suggest the likelihood that Jesus did speak Greek. Further, his conversations with Roman officials—Pilate or the centurion, and perhaps even that reflected in John 12—would point in this direction. This question, however, is related to the others about the Semitic language that he used, and I shall return to it later. However, what evidence there is that he used Greek yields at most a probability; if it be used to insist that we might even have in the Gospels some of the *ipsissima verba Iesu graeca,* actually uttered by him as he addressed his bilingual Galilean compatriots,[57] then the evidence is being pressed beyond legitimate bounds.

The other remark concerns the researches and studies of such scholars as S. Krauss, M. Schwabe, S. Liebermann, B. Lifshitz et al., who have done yeoman service in ferreting out the evidence for the Hellenization of Palestinian Jews. In particular, the two books of S. Liebermann, *Greek in Jewish Palestine* and *Hellenism in Jewish Palestine,*[58] are outstanding in this regard; but their subtitles reveal that they are largely based on materials of a much later date than the first century—on the Mishnah, the Talmud, and other rabbinical writings. J. N. Sevenster has frankly stated the difficulty in using this material as an indication of the first-century situation.[59] Moreover, Liebermann has been criticized for neglecting the inscriptional material from the cemetery of Beth-She^{c}arim,[60] and for not using the older Greek materials from Joppa, Capernaum, etc., that have been known for a long time. The materials which these scholars have amassed make it abundantly clear that the Palestinian Jews *of the third and fourth centuries A.D.* were quite hellenized and used Greek widely. This is the sort of situation that the numerous hebraized and aramaicized Greek words that appear in rabbinical literature also suggest.[61] From 200 on it is clear that not only Hellenism but even the Greek language used by the Jews had made heavy inroads into the Aramaic being spoken; it is the same sort of influence that one detects in the Aramaic being spoken in the territory of Palestine's neighbor to the north, in Syriac. This is, by contrast, the advantage of J. N. Sevenster's recent book, *Do You Know Greek?* For he has sought to sift data from literary and epigraphic sources and presents an intriguing thesis on the wide use of Greek in first-century Palestine both among Jews and Christians. Unfortunately, the reader is distracted at times by lengthy discussions of texts from periods prior and posterior to this century.[62]

III. *Aramaic*

If asked what was the language commonly spoken in Palestine in the time of Jesus of Nazareth, most people with some acquaintance of that era and area would almost spontaneously answer Aramaic. To my way of thinking, this is still the correct answer for the *most commonly* used language, but the defense of this thesis must reckon with the growing mass of evidence that both Greek and Hebrew were being used as well. I would, however, hesitate to say with M. Smith that "at least as much Greek as Aramaic was spoken in Palestine."[63] In any case, the evidence for the use of Aramaic has also been growing in recent years.

Evidence for the use of Aramaic toward the end of the first millennium B.C. has never been abundant. A scholar such as W. F. Albright was led by this situation to think that its use was actually on the wane, especially during the Seleucid period. He writes:

> There are no Aramaic literary works extant from the period between the third or second century B.C. and the second or third A.D., a period of over three hundred years. There can be little doubt that there was a real eclipse of Aramaic during the period of the Seleucid Empire (312 B.C. to the early first century B.C.), since scarcely a single Aramaic inscription from this period has been discovered, except in Transjordan and the adjacent parts of Arabia, which were relatively freer from Greek influence than Western Palestine and Syria proper. After this epigraphic hiatus, Palmyrene inscriptions began to appear in the second half of the first century B.C.; recent excavations have brought to light an inscription dating from the year 44 B.C. Inscriptions in Jewish Aramaic first appeared about the middle of the first century B.C., and became more abundant during the reign of Herod the Great, just before the Christian era. . . . They thus help to clarify the actual Aramaic of Jewish Palestine in the time of Jesus and the Apostles. If the Megillat Taᶜanith, or 'Scroll of Fastings,' a list of official Jewish fasts with accompanying historical notations, really precedes the year A.D. 70, as held by some scholars, it belongs to our period, but it is safer to date it in the second century A.D., in accordance with its present chronological content.[64]

Between the final redaction of Daniel (ca. 165 B.C.), in which roughly six chapters are written in Aramaic, and the first of the rabbinical writings, *Mĕgillat Taᶜănît*,[65] dating from the end of the first Christian century, there had never been much evidence of the use of Aramaic in Palestine prior to the discovery of the Qumran scrolls and fragments. Before 1947 numberless ossuary and sepulchral inscriptions had been coming to light.[66] But they were scarcely evidence of what E. J. Goodspeed has called "creative Aramaic literary writing."[67] Except for a few with extended texts, they consist for the most part of proper names, written in the cursive Hebrew-Aramaic script of the time. Indeed, it is often hard to tell whether their inscribers spoke Hebrew or Aramaic. The most important of the extended texts are the Uzziah plaque, commemorating the first-century transfer of the alleged bones of the famous eighth-century king of Judah,[68] an ossuary lid with a *qorban* inscription that illustrates the use of this Aramaic word in Mark 7:11,[69] and a Kidron Valley dipinto.[70] There was also the evidence of Aramaic words preserved in the Greek Gospels and Josephus' writings, as well as the Aramaisms in the syntax of the NT in general.[71] This was more or less the extent of the evidence up to 1947.

Since the discovery of the Qumran material it is now evident that literature was indeed being composed in Aramaic in the last century B.C. and in the first century A.D. The number of extant Aramaic texts of a literary nature is not small, even though the fragments of them found in the various Qumran caves may be. Only a few of these texts have been published so far: the *Genesis Apocryphon,*[72] *the Prayer of Nabonidus, the Description of the New Jerusalem,* the *Elect of God* text; parts of such texts as the *Testament of Levi, Enoch, Pseudo-Daniel,* a *Targum of Job,* and a number of untitled texts to which a number has merely been assigned. Reports have been made on still other Aramaic texts from Caves IV and XI, such as several copies of Tobit, of targums of Job and Leviticus, of a text mentioning "the Son of God" and "the Son of the Most High" in phrases remarkably close to Luke 1:32, 35.[73] All of this points to an extensive Aramaic literary activity and an Aramaic literature, at least used by the Essenes, if not composed by them.

Objection might be made at this point that this evidence points only to a literary use of Aramaic and that it really says little about the current spoken form of the language. True, but then one must beware of exaggerating theoretically the difference between the literary and spoken forms of the language. Contemporary with the Qumran evidence are the ossuary and sepulchral inscriptions already mentioned, many more of which have been coming to light in recent years.[74] Again, an Aramaic IOU, dated in the second year of Nero (i.e., 55-56), came to light in one of the Murabbaᶜat caves, and a letter on an ostracon from Masada.[75] And from a slightly later period comes a batch of legal documents, composed in Aramaic as well as in Greek and Hebrew, from caves in the wadies Murabbaᶜat, Ḫabra, and Seiyâl.[76] Many of these still await publication.

One of them, which has already been published by H. J. Polotsky,[77] merits some attention here because of its unique bilingual character. Discovered in 1961 in the so-called Cave of Letters of the Wadi Ḫabra, it belongs to the family archives of Babatha, daughter of Simeon, who at one time lived in a small Nabatean town called Maḥoz ᶜEglatain (or in Greek, *Maōza*), which since A.D. 106 had become part of *provincia Arabia*. The main part of the text, which is a copy of a receipt given by Babatha to a Jewish guardian of her orphan son, is written in Greek. It is dated to 19 August 132 and acknowledges the payment of six denarii for the boy's food and clothing. The ten lines of Greek text of the receipt are followed by three in Aramaic that summarize the Greek statement. This Aramaic summary, however, is immediately followed by four lines of Greek, written by the same scribe who composed the main text; they give an almost literal translation of the Aramaic and are explicitly introduced by the word ἑρμενίας, "translation." The text ends with Γέρμαν[ος] ᾿Ιούδ[ο]υ ἔγραψα, "I, Germanus, (son) of Judah, have written (this)." Though this receipt was found in the southern part of Palestine, it was actually written in Nabatean country, to the southeast of the Dead Sea. From the same place comes yet another Greek document, a *Doppelurkunde,* with the Greek text written twice, but with the *scriptura exterior* endorsed by two men who write, one in Aramaic, the other in Nabatean.[78] It is dated to 12 Oct. 125. Apparently there are other examples of bilingual or trilingual texts still to be published by Yadin or Polotsky.[79] Here we have in official documents the simultaneous use of Greek, Aramaic, and Nabatean; the problem is to say to what extent this might represent language habits in southern Palestine of roughly the same period.

Given this simultaneous use, the real question is to what extent Greek would be affecting the Aramaic and vice versa. In the case of the receipt from the Babatha archive, the main text written in Greek, with an Aramaic abstract itself rendered again in a Greek translation, obviously attests to the importance of Greek in the area where such documents were composed. The woman was Jewish, and it is scarcely credible that she would have legal and financial documents drawn up for her in a language that she did not understand or read. But the text raises the question to what extent Greek vocabulary and idiom were invading Aramaic. We know that the converse took place. Aramaic certainly affected the Greek used by Jews. The Aramaic words in the Gospels and Josephus, and the Aramaisms in their Greek syntax reveal this. A small Greek fragment from Murabbaᶜat, containing a broken list of proper names, gives one of them as ᾿Ιώσηπος ἀσωφήρ Κητα[ ], "Josephus, the scribe, *Keta* [ ]." Here a Hebrew title, *has-sōphēr,* has simply been transcribed.[80] Even though this is evidence for Hebrew affecting Greek, it serves as an illustration of the sort of data we should expect in Aramaic texts of the period: Greek words transcribed into Aramaic, such as we have in the names of the musical instruments in Dan 3:5.

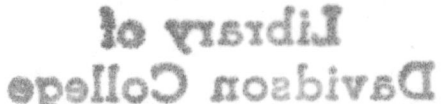

However, this sort of evidence is surprisingly lacking in the first-century Aramaic texts that are extant. This phenomenon is still to be discovered in Qumran Aramaic texts or in the Aramaic IOU of 55/56 (Mur 18). In all of the Aramaic texts of slightly later date from the caves of the wadies Murabba^{c}at and Ḫabra that have either been published so far or reported on with partial publication of texts, I have found to date only four isolated words and one formula that are clearly due to Greek. These are:

כנמסא,	"according to the Law" (Mur 21:11 [a marriage contract with the date missing; Milik would not exclude a first century date])	*νόμος*
באספליא,	"in security" (5/6Ḥev 1 ar:2 [an Aramaic letter of Bar Cochba])	*ἀσφάλεια*
רהומיה,	"Romans" (5/6Ḥev 6 ar:2 [another letter of Bar Cochba])	*Ῥωμαῖοι*
[אפ]טרפא,	"guardian" (5/6Ḥev 27:12 [receipt of payment from Babatha archive, dated 19 August 132; Polotsky's restoration is certain, because *ἐπίτροπος* occurs in the Greek version, line 16]).[81]	*ἐπίτροπος*

A date formula in an Aramaic text was taken over from Greek usage:

על הפטות ליקים קטילים סורם תנינותא ומרקס
אורלים אנתונינס שנת תלת לאוטוקרטור קסר טרינס
הדרינס סבסטס ועל מנין הפרכיה דא בעשרין וארבעה
בתמוז שנת עשר וחמש

"in the consulship of Lucius Catilius Severus for the second time and Marcus Aurelius Antoninus, in the third year of Imperator Caesar Traianus Hadrianus Augustus and according to the era of this province, on the 24th of Tammuz, year 15" (= 13 July 120).[82] The date is given by the consulship, by Hadrian's regnal year, and by the era of *provincia Arabia.* Aside from the proper names, the clear Grecisms are על הפטות for *ἐπὶ ὑπάτων*, לאוטוקרטור for *αὐτοκράτωρ* ("emperor"), קסר for *Καῖσαρ*, סבסטס for *σέβαστος*, ועל מנין הפרכיה דא for *κατὰ τὸν τῆς νέας ἐπαρχίας Ἀραβίας ἄριθμον.*[83] This is a clear example of Greek affecting Aramaic; it is a stereotyped legal formula that was undoubtedly often used and perhaps required in official documents of that province. Again, it is not easy to say to what extent this clear Greek influence was also found in first-century Palestine itself.

In sum, there is precious little evidence for the influence of Greek on Palestinian Aramaic, and none of it certainly from the first century. This is indeed surprising and may be a sheer coincidence; it is purely "negative evidence"[84] at this time. It is an argument from silence that could be proved wrong tomorrow—by the discovery of first-century Palestinian Aramaic texts with abundant examples of borrowed Grecisms. But at the moment we have to await such a discovery.

The reason for making something of all this is the contention of M. Black, A. Díez Macho, and others that the language of the Palestinian targum(s) is that of the first century, and indeed represents spoken Aramaic of that time in contrast to the literary Aramaic of Qumran. Black's main argument for the thesis that "the language of the Palestinian Targum is . . . first-century Aramaic" is this: "The large number of borrowings in it from Greek point to a period for its composition when Palestinian Aramaic was spoken in a hellenistic environment."[85] But, as we have already seen, the Hellenization of Palestine stretched over a long period, from at least the time of Antiochus IV Epiphanes (if not much earlier) well into the first half of the first Christian millennium. And yet what evidence there is for Greek words borrowed into Palestinian Aramaic is very sparse indeed up to A.D. 200. There comes a time, however, *after that* when it is surprisingly abundant, as epigraphic material and the researches of S. Krauss, S. Liebermann, et al. have shown time and again.[86] The same heavy influence of Greek is paralleled in classical Syriac too—a form of Aramaic that emerges toward the beginning of the third century C.E. The fact, then, that the Aramaic of the Palestinian targums contains a "large number of borrowings in it from Greek" could point theoretically to any period from the third century B.C. (at least) to A.D. 500 (at least). But when we look for the first-century evidence, it is certainly negative.

There is no doubt that targums were beginning to be written down in first-century Palestine, as the discovery of fragments of a targum on Job from Qumran caves IV and XI and a targum on Leviticus from Qumran Cave IV illustrate. Until these are fully published and the relation of them to the previously known and existing targums can be assessed, we cannot without further ado assume a genetic relationship between them or believe that they manifest the same degree of Greek influence as the other targums. J. van der Ploeg has already indicated in a preliminary report that 11QtgJob is unrelated to the later, little-known targum on Job, the origin of which is quite obscure.[87] As for 4QtgLev, which is the sole fragment of a targum on the Pentateuch, Milik has already revealed some differences in it.[88] In my opinion, the evidence from the borrowing of Greek words in the Palestinian targums argues for a date after A.D. 200—a date that could be supported by a number of other orthographic, lexical, and grammatical considerations which are absent from Biblical, Qumran, and similar Aramaic texts, but that begin to appear in Murabbaᶜat and Ḫabra texts and become abundant in the targums, in Syriac, and in dated Aramaic inscriptions from Palestinian synagogues from the third to the sixth centuries.[89] A handy catalogue of such synagogues has now been made available by S. J. Saller.[90]

In speaking of the influence of another language on first-century Aramaic we must not restrict our remarks to Greek alone. For the influence of Hebrew on it is also evident. This issue is more difficult to assess because the languages are so closely related. But a number of Hebraisms are clearly evident in the literary Aramaic of the *Genesis Apocryphon*,[91] and in the less literary writings from Murabbaᶜat and Ḫabra. There are masculine plural absolute endings in *-îm* instead of *-în*, the occasional use of the prepositive article (הנכסי, 5/6Ḥev 1 ar:1[92]), the conjunction אם, "if," instead of הן or אן, the apocopated form of the imperfect of the verb "to be," יהי; etc. This Hebraized Aramaic is, of course, not surprising; nor is it confined to the first-century evidence, since it is already found in Ezra and Daniel.[93]

Two last remarks concerning the Aramaic of first-century Palestine. The first deals with the Nabatean dialect; so far I have left it out of consideration for the most part. It is a dialect of Aramaic, which betrays Arabic influence. There is no doubt that it was being used in Petra and in the Nabatean country to the south of Palestine. Was it also being used in the southern part of Palestine as well? In the Daroma? In Idumea? We do not know for certain, and the possibility cannot be excluded. The fragments and documents written in Nabatean and recovered from the Cave of Letters in Wadi Ḫabra were obviously brought there by refugees who hid in the caves of the area. They were written, as we have already indicated, for the most part in Maḥoz ᶜEglatain, a town or village in Nabatea. Yet they speak of relations with En-Gedi and persons who lived on the western shore of the Dead Sea. When these texts are finally published, perhaps it will be possible to establish more definitely the use of this special dialect of Aramaic in first-century southern Palestine as well.

The other remark concerns the name for Aramaic. It is well known that the Aramaic portion of Daniel begins with the adverb ʾ*ărāmît* (Dan 2:4b). This gloss, which at some point in the transmission of the book crept into the text itself, reflects the ancient name of the language attested in the OT and in Elephantine papyrus texts.[94] Greek writers of a later period refer to the language as *συριστί* or *συριακή*.[95] When, however, Greek writers of the first century refer to the native Semitic language of Palestine, they use *ἑβραϊστί*, *ἑβραῒς διάλεκτος*, or *ἑβραΐζων*. As far as I can see, no one has yet found the adverb *aramaïsti*.[96] The adverb *ἑβραϊστί* (and its related expressions) seems to mean "in Hebrew," and it has often been argued that it means this and nothing more.[97] As is well known, it is used at times with words and expressions that are clearly Aramaic. Thus in John 19:13, *ἑβραϊστὶ δὲ Γαββαθᾶ* is given as an explanation of the Lithostrotos, and *γαββαθᾶ* is a Grecized form of the Aramaic word *gabbĕtā*, "raised place."[98] This long-standing, thorny question is still debated; and unfortunately, the Greek letter of Bar Cochba (?) cited earlier does not shed a ray of light on the meaning of *ἑβραϊστί*. We know that the author preferred to write "in Greek" than in it; but both Aramaic and Hebrew letters belong to the same cache of documents and the question still remains unresolved about the precise meaning of *ἑβραϊστί*. In any case, this problem forms a fitting transition to the consideration of the fourth language of first-century Palestine, viz., Hebrew.

IV. *Hebrew*

Hebrew probably was the oldest language still spoken in first-century Palestine. We may speculate about the language that was spoken by the "wandering Aramean" (Deut 26:5) who returned from Egypt at the time of the conquest of Palestine. Was it Old Aramaic of the form known in the early inscriptions from northern Syria? Or had this semi-nomadic people already adopted the *śĕpat Kĕnaᶜan* of the inhabitants who preceded them? The likelihood is that the "nomad" was still speaking the tongue of his forebears (Aḫlamē). In any case, the earliest epigraphic material points heavily in the direction of Hebrew, as a Canaanite dialect, dominating the land. It was never completely supplanted by Aramaic after the exile, when the latter became more commonly used because of its international prominence. It is, however, often asserted that Aramaic was the only Semitic language in use in Palestine at the time of Jesus and the Apostles.[99] But there are clear indications, both epigraphic and literary, that Hebrew continued in use in certain social strata of the people and perhaps also in certain geographical areas. The evidence, however, is not as abundant as it is for Aramaic.

It is true that the number of Qumran texts written in Hebrew far outnumber those in Aramaic, and these bear witness to a lively literary productivity in the language. It is not great literature, no more than the Aramaic literature of the time; even the War Scroll and the Thanksgiving Psalms are scarcely exceptions to this, though they are the most literary pieces in the Qumran scrolls. However, much of this Qumran Hebrew composition dates from the last two centuries B.C. But the *pĕšārîm*, which exist in only one copy of each *pēšer* and were written for the most part in the late Herodian script, may be regarded as first-century compositions.[100] They are literary compositions, reflecting on earlier stages of the sect's history and interpreting the biblical books in the light of that history and of the sect's beliefs. Along with the rest of Qumran Hebrew, the language of these texts represents a slight development beyond that of the late books of the OT. It has been called a "neo-classical Hebrew," lacking in spontaneity and contaminated by the contemporary colloquial dialect.[101]

The evidence for colloquial Hebrew is not abundant. What is surprising is that there is scarcely a Hebrew inscription from Palestine in the first century outside of the Qumran material—the inscription of the *Bĕnê Ḥĕzîr* tomb being almost the sole exception.[102] There are, of course, ossuaries with Semitic names that could have been inscribed by Hebrew-speaking Jews as well as by Aramaic-speaking Jews. The use of *ben* instead of *bar* in the patronymics is no sure indication of a Hebrew proper name, even though it is often used to distinguish Hebrew from Aramaic inscriptions on the ossuaries. This is a recognized convenience and no more. The proper name with *ben* or *bar* could have been used properly in its own language milieu or could easily have been borrowed into the other because of the close relationship of the two; it is even conceivable that the stereotyped character of the *ben or bar* might have been the unique borrowed element.[103] Texts from Murabbaᶜat illustrate this.[104] *Bar* is found in Semitic names in a text written in Hebrew, and *ben* in a text written in Aramaic. The only noteworthy thing in the Murabbaᶜat texts is that *bar* is more frequent in Hebrew texts than *ben* is in Aramaic texts. The evidence, however, is so slight that one could scarcely conclude that this argues for Aramaic as the more common language.

The Copper Roll from Qumran Cave III, which almost certainly had nothing to do with the Essenes themselves, is "the oldest known text to be written in Mishnaic Hebrew,"[105] or perhaps more accurately, in Proto-Mishnaic Hebrew. Texts from the Murabbaᶜat and Ḫabra caves, which consist of letters as well as quasi-official documents, are written in practically the same form of Hebrew. Mishnaic Hebrew, reflecting a still further development of the language, is usually regarded as a literary dialect. But it is now seen to have been a development of the colloquial Hebrew of the first century. All of this points to a clear use of Hebrew in Palestine of that time, but it is really not sufficient to say with J. T. Milik that it proves "beyond reasonable doubt that Mishnaic was the normal language of the Judaean population in the Roman period,"[106] unless one is willing to specify what part of the Roman period is meant. For that must be reckoned as lasting from the Pompeian conquest of Palestine (63 B.C.) until at least the time of Constantine (early fourth century), if not later. While it seems apparent that certain pockets, or perhaps strata, of the population in the early Roman period were using Hebrew and that this language became enshrined in the Mishnah in a still more developed form, as of its codification ca. 200, I find it difficult to think of Hebrew as "the normal language of the Judaean population" in the *whole* Roman period. If it were, one would expect more evidence of it to turn up—especially in the first century and in more widespread locales.

This leads us naturally to the issue raised by H. Birkeland some years ago that Hebrew was actually the language of Jesus, because it had still "remained the language of the common people."[107] Little can actually be said about Jesus' use of Hebrew. That Hebrew was being used in first-century Palestine is beyond doubt, as we have been saying; but this fact is scarcely sufficient evidence for maintaining that Jesus therefore made use of it. We would have to look for further indications of this fact. If Luke 4:16-30 records a historical visit of Jesus to Nazareth with all its details, it might suggest that Jesus opened the scroll to Isaiah 61, found his place there, and read from it, presumably in Hebrew. The Lucan text completely prescinds from any use of a targum. Literalists among commentators on Acts 26:14 have also sought to insist that the risen Jesus, appearing to Paul on the road to Damascus and speaking τῇ ἑβραΐδι διαλέκτῳ, actually spoke in real Hebrew, not Aramaic. A similar suggestion is made that the *logia* that Matthew put together, according to Papias' statement in Eusebius (*HE* 3.39.16), were actually Hebrew, not

Aramaic. And the appeal is made to the extensive literature in Hebrew from Qumran as an indication of the possibility of writing a Hebrew gospel. There is certainly some plausibility in such suggestions; but do they really exceed the bounds of speculation?

Just as we mentioned the influence of other languages on the Greek and Aramaic spoken in Palestine, so too one can detect foreign influence on the non-literary Hebrew of this period. Phoenician or Punic influence has been claimed for the use of *t* as the sign of the accusative (instead of the older, Biblical *ʾet*); Aramaic influence for the frequent use of *-în* instead of *-îm* as the absolute masc. plur. ending (5/6 Ḥev hebr 1:3, 4; 2:1),[108] of the 3d plur. masc. suffix in *-hn* instead of *-hm* (Mur 44:4; 45:7), of the 3d sing. masc. suffix in *-h* instead of *-w* (Mur 44:9; 42:8, 9 [*ktbh*, "wrote it"]). Aramaic influence is clear in the Hebrew text of 4QTestimonia.[109] Is it, again, sheer coincidence that the only Greek word that I have been able to detect in this non-literary Hebrew is הפרנסים, a form that some have explained as derived from Greek *πρόνοος*? An Aramaic lexical expression may be found in Mur 46:7: בשל ש, possibly reflecting the Aramaic בדיל די.[110] In this case, the evidence is truly negative, because there is so little to go on.

By way of conclusion, I should maintain that the most commonly used language of Palestine in the first century A.D. was Aramaic, but that many Palestinian Jews, not only those in Hellenistic towns, but farmers and craftsmen of less obviously Hellenized areas used Greek, at least as a second language. The data collected from Greek inscriptions and literary sources indicate that Greek was widely used. In fact, there is indication, despite Josephus' testimony, that some Palestinians spoke only Greek, the Ἑλληνισταί. But pockets of Palestinian Jews also used Hebrew, even though its use was not widespread. The emergence of the targums supports this. The real problem is the influence of these languages on one another. Grecized Aramaic is still to be attested in the first century. It begins to be attested in the early second century and becomes abundant in the third and fourth centuries. Is it legitimate to appeal to this evidence to postulate the same situation earlier? Latin was really a negligible factor in the language-situation of first-century Palestine, since it was confined for the most part to the Roman occupiers. If Aramaic did go into an eclipse in the Seleucid period, as some maintain, it did not remain there. The first-century evidence points, indeed, to its use as the most common language in Palestine.

NOTES TO CHAPTER 2

*Originally published as the presidential address of the Catholic Biblical Association (21 August 1970) in the *CBQ* 32 (1970) 501-31.

[1]Evidence of this can be found in the Aramaisms in Biblical Hebrew. See p. 22 above, n. 29. See also A. Kropat, *Die Syntax des Autors der Chronik verglichen mit der seiner Quellen* (BZAW 16; Berlin: Töpelmann, 1906); J. Courtenay James, *The Language of Palestine and Adjacent Regions* (Edinburgh: Clark, 1920) [to be used with caution].

[2]Neh 8:8 may be hinting at this situation. The interpretation of the participle מפרש is quite disputed. Does it mean "clearly" (*RSV*)? Or "with interpretation" (*RSV* margin)? Cf. Ezra 4:18, where it occurs in a context suggesting translation; but also Ezra 4:7, which uses מתרגם explicitly for this idea. For a recent discussion of the verse and its meaning, see R. Le Déaut, *Introduction à la littérature targumique* (p. 22 above, n. 32), 29.

[3]See B. Lifshitz, "Beiträge zur palästinischen Epigraphik," *ZDPV* 78 (1962) 64-88, esp. pp. 82-84 (+ pl. 10), for the Raphia inscription of 217 B.C. For an earlier bilingual inscription (Greek and Edomite) on an ostracon, dating from 277 B.C., see the dissertation of L. T. Geraty, *Third Century B.C. Ostraca from Khirbet el-Kom* (dissertation summary in *HTR* 65 [1972] 595-96); also his article, "The Khirbet el-Kom Bilingual Ostracon," *BASOR* 220 (1975) 55-61.

[4]This evidence depends on the usual interpretation of Sir 50:27, that "Yeshua ben Eleazar ben Sira," of Jerusalem composed his book in Palestine ca. 180 B.C. and that the Book of Daniel took its final protocanonical form there within a short time after the Maccabean revolt, ca. 165 B.C. Parts of Daniel, however, especially the Aramaic stories about the hero at the Persian court, may well be older, as some scholars have argued. For an important discussion of this view, see K. A. Kitchen, "The Aramaic of Daniel," *Notes on Some Problems in the Book of Daniel* (London: Tyndale, 1965) 31-79. If this is so, it makes little difference to the issue being discussed here.

[5]See J. T. Milik, *Ten Years* (p. 22 above, n. 31), 130.

[6]See P. W. Skehan, "The Qumran Manuscripts and Textual Criticism," *Volume du congrès, Strasbourg 1956* (VTSup 4; Leiden: Brill, 1957) 148-60, esp. pp. 155-57 (4QLXX Num [3:40-42; 4:6-9]; 4QLXX Lev[a] [26:2-16]). See also the Greek papyrus fragments discovered in Qumran Cave VII, where apparently nothing but Greek texts was found (M. Baillet et al., *Les 'Petites Grottes' de Qumran* [DJD 3; Oxford: Clarendon, 1962] 142-47). They have been dated by C. H. Roberts to ca. 100-50 B.C. 7Q*1* is a fragment of Exod 28:4-7; 7Q*2* is a fragment of the Letter of Jeremy (vv. 43-44). For an attempt to interpret the Greek texts of Qumran Cave VII as Christian, see the writings of J. O'Callaghan cited in my book, *The Dead Sea Scrolls: Major Publications and Tools for Study* (SBLSBS 8; Missoula: Scholars Press, 1975) 119-23. P. W. Skehan informs me that there are also three pieces of non-biblical Greek texts in Cave IV; they are as yet unpublished but are apparently of literary and liturgical character. For the view that the Aramaic texts of Qumran are of non-Essene origin, see pp. 8-9 above.

[7]The earliest Latin texts from Palestine that I have been able to uncover are all dated to the first century A.D. L. Kadman (*The Coins of Caesarea Maritima* [Jerusalem: Schocken, 1957]) lists no coins from Caesarea with Latin inscriptions before the time of Domitian.

[8]M. Avi-Yonah, "The Development of the Roman Road System in Palestine," *IEJ* 1 (1950-51) 54-60. Some of the milestones were erected in both Latin and Greek; see B. Lifshitz, *Latomus* 19 (1960) 111 (+ pl. IV). Cf. *Année épigraphique* 1925, §95; 1927, §151; 1948, §142.

[9]The Tenth Legion was transferred from northern Syria to Palestine (Ptolemais) by Nero, who put it under the command of Vespasian. See D. Barag, "Brick Stamp-Impressions of the *Legio X Fretensis,*" *E. L. Sukenik Memorial Volume (1899-1953)* (Eretz-Israel, 8; Jerusalem: Israel Exploration Society, 1967) 168-82 [Hebrew; English summary, p. 73*]. This article has an ample bibliography on the subject. See further N. Avigad, "Excavations in the Jewish Quarter of the Old City of Jerusalem, 1969/70 (Preliminary Report)," *IEJ* 20 (1970) 1-8, esp. p. 3; B. Mazar, *The Excavations in the Old City of Jerusalem near the Temple Mount: Preliminary Report of the Second and Third Seasons 1969-1970* (Jerusalem: Institute of Archaeology, Hebrew University, 1971) 5 (fig. 6); "Excavations near the Temple Mount," *Qadmoniot* 5 (1972) 74-90, esp. p. 83 (an

inscription mentioning LEG X FR and Lucius Flavius Silva, governor of Judea, A.D. 73-79/80); J. Olami and J. Ringel, "New Inscriptions of the Tenth Legion Fretensis from the High Level Aqueduct of Caesarea," *IEJ* 25 (1975) 148-50; cf. *Qadmoniot* 7 (1974) 44-46; G. B. Sarfatti, "A Fragmentary Roman Inscription in the Turkish Wall of Jerusalem," *IEJ* 25 (1975) 151. Cf. D. Bahat, "A Roof Tile of the Legio VI Ferrata and Pottery Vessels from Ḥorvat Ḥazon," *IEJ* 24 (1974) 160-69. See also *IR* §217.

[10]A. Negev, "Caesarea Maritima," *Christian News from Israel* 11/4 (1960) 17-22; "New Inscriptions from the High Level Aqueduct of Caesarea," *Yediot* 30 (1966) 135-41 [Hebrew]; B. Lifshitz, "Inscriptions latines de Césarée (Caesarea Palestinae)," *Latomus* 22 (1963) 783-84; *Année épigraphique* 1964, §188; cf. K. Zangmeister, "Inschrift der vespasianischen Colonie Caesarea in Palästina," *ZDPV* 13 (1890) 25-30; A. Negev, "Inscriptions hébraïques, grecques et latines de Césarée Maritime," *RB* 78 (1971) 247-63 (+ pls. I-IX); J. Ringel, "Deux nouvelles inscriptions de l'aquéduc de Césarée Maritime," *RB* 81 (1974) 597-600. Cf. M. Gichon and B. H. Isaac, "A Flavian Inscription from Jerusalem," *IEJ* 24 (1974) 117-23.

[11]This fragmentary inscription was found in the northern part of the orchestra of the Roman theatre of Caesarea. In the fourth century the stone was used as part of a small stairway which was then being constructed; the stairway was obviously more important than the memory of the man mentioned on the stone. See A. Frova, "L'iscrizione di Ponzio Pilato a Cesarea," *Rendiconti dell'istituto lombardo, Accademia di scienze e lettere,* cl. di lettere, 95 (1961) 419-34; "Quattro campagne di scavo della missione archeologica milanese a Caesarea Maritima (Israele) 1959-1962," *Atti del convegno La Lombardia e l'Oriente* (Milan: 1963) 175. Also J. Vardaman, "A New Inscription Which Mentions Pilate as 'Prefect,'" *JBL* 81 (1962) 70-71; B. Lifshitz, *Latomus* 22 (1963) 783; J. H. Gauze, *Ecclesia* 174 (1963) 137; A. Calderini, "L'inscription de Ponce Pilate à Césarée," *BTS* 57 (1963) 8-19; A. Degrassi, "Sull'iscrizione di Ponzio Pilato," *ANL Rendiconti,* cl. di sc. morali, 8/19 (1964), fasc. 3-4, 59-65; E. Stauffer, "Die Pilatusinschrift von Caesarea," *Erlangen Universitätsreden* 12 (1965) [Erlangen: Palm und Enke, 1966]; L. A. Yelnitzky, "The Caesarea Inscription of Pontius Pilate and Its Historical Significance," *Vestnik drevnei istorii* 3 (93, 1965) 142-46 [Russian]; C. Brusa Gerra, "Le iscrizioni," *Scavi di Caesarea Maritima* (Milan: Istituto lombardo, 1965) 217-20; A. N. Sherwin-White, Review of A. Frova, "L'iscrizione . . . ," *JRS* 54 (1964) 258-59. H. Volkmann, *Gymnasium* 75 (1968) 124-35; E. Weber, "Zur Inschrift des Pontius Pilatus," *Bonner Jahrbücher* 171 (1971) 194-200; E. Schürer, *HJPAJC* (rev. ed., 1973), 1. 357-59. Cf. L. I. Levine, *Roman Caesarea: An Archaeological-Topographical Study* (Qedem, 2; Jerusalem: Hebrew University, 1975) 19-21.

Various attempts have been made to restore line 1: (a) Frova: [CAESARIEN]S(ibus)—Pilate would have dedicated the Tiberieum to the citizens of Caesarea; (b) Lifshitz: [TIB(erio) CAES(are) AVG(vsto) V? CON]S(vle)—the date of the inscription in Tiberius' fifth(?) consulate; (c) Degrassi: [DIS AVGVSTI]S—Pilate dedicates the building to Augustus and Livia, who were considered *theoi sebastoi* in the east.

The name *Tiberieum* is not attested elsewhere, but it is similar to *Hadrianeum* (*RB* 4 [1895] 75-76), *Kaisareion,* and *Agrippeion* (Josephus, *JW* 1.21.1 §402). The accent in the fourth line was probably over an E (possibly [D]É[DICAVIT] or [D]É[DIT] or [F]É[CIT].

[12]Josephus mentions him (*Ant.* 18.2.2 §35; 18.3.1-3 §55-64; 18.4.1-2 §87-89; 18.6.5 §177), as does also Philo (*Embassy to Gaius* 38, §299-305). Cf. Mark 15:1-44; Matt 27:2-65; Luke 3:1; 13:l; 23:1-52; John 18:29-38; 19:1-38; Acts 3:13; 4:27; 13:28; 1 Tim 6:13. Cf. F. Morison [= A. H. Ross], *And Pilate Said—A New Study of the Roman Procurator* (New York: Scribner, 1940); Paul L. Maier, *Pontius Pilate* (Garden City, NY: Doubleday, 1968).

[13]As Tacitus entitled him proleptically (*Annales* 15.44.2); cf. Tertullian, *Apologeticum* 21:18, "Pontio Pilato Syriam tunc ex parte romana procuranti" (*CSEL* 69.57); Philo, *Embassy to Gaius* 38 §299, Πιλᾶτος ἦν τῶν ὑπάρχων ἐπίτροπος ἀποδεδειγμένος τῆς Ἰουδαίας. Philo's text may well reflect the shift in title that apparently took place about the time of the emperor Claudius (ca. A.D. 46). Latin *praefectus* was usually rendered in Greek as ἔπαρχος, and *procurator* as ἐπίτροπος.

[14]See O. Hirschfeld, *Die kaiserlichen Verwaltungsbeamten bis auf Diocletian* (2d ed.; Berlin: Wiedman, 1905) 382-83; A. N. Sherwin-White, "Procurator Augusti," *Paper of the British School at Rome* 15 (1939) 11-26; *Society and Roman Law in the New Testament* (Sarum Lectures, 1960-61; Oxford: Clarendon, 1963) 6, 12; A. H. M. Jones, "Procurators and Prefects in the Early Principate," *Studies in Roman Government and Law* (Oxford: Blackwell 1960), 115-25; E. Schürer, *A History of the Jewish People in the Time of Jesus Christ* (6 vols.; Edinburgh: T. and T. Clark) 1 / 2 (1905) 45; rev. ed. (1973), 1. 357-59; H. G. Pflaum, *Les procurateurs équestres sous le haut-empire romain* (Paris: Maisonneuve, 1950) 23-25.

[15]"Proceeding across this [open court] towards the second court of the temple, one found it surrounded by a stone balustrade, three cubits high and of exquisite workmanship; in this at regular intervals stood slabs giving warning, some in Greek, others in Latin characters, of the law of purification, to wit that no foreigner was permitted to enter the holy place" (*JW* 5.5.2 §193-94). Cf. *Ant.* 15.11.5 §417; Philo, *Embassy to Gaius,* 31 §212; Acts 21:26-30.

[16]See p. 35.

[17]*Ant.* 14.10.2 §191.

[18]A similar notice is also found in some MSS of Luke 23:38 (S*,C,A,D,W, the Koine tradition, etc.); but it is undoubtedly due to scribal harmonization.

[19]See P. Benoit, J. T. Milik, R. de Vaux, *Les grottes de Murabbaʿât* (DJD 2; Oxford: Clarendon, 1961) 270-74 (Mur 158-63).

[20]*CIL,* 3. 14155:3; Thomsen §178 (cf. G. Jeffery, *PEFQS* 29 [1898] 35).

[21]*CIL,* 2. 13587; Thomsen §1 (cf. F. J. Bliss, *PEFQS* 26 [1895] 25). For other Latin inscriptions of this period, see Thomsen §92, 237; *Année épigraphique* 1927, §151; Z. Vilnay, *PEFQS* 1928, 45-47 (cf. D. Barag, *IEJ* 14 [1964] 250-52), 108-9; A. Negev, *IEJ* 14 (1964) 237-49, esp. pp. 244-48; Y. Yadin, *IEJ* 15 (1965) 1-120, esp. p. 110.

[22]See T. Frankfort, "Présence de Rome en Israël," *Latomus* 19 (1960) 708-23.

[23]D. Auscher, "Les relations entre la Grèce et la Palestine avant la conquête d'Alexandre," *VT* 17 (1967) 8-30. Auscher's evidence consists of three things: (a) the remains of Greek pottery in Palestine; (b) Greek coins and Palestinian imitations of them; (c) the problematic Proto-Ionic pillar capitals. Cf. K. A. Kitchen, "The Aramaic of Daniel" (n. 4 above), 44-50. Kitchen amasses all sorts of evidence for Greek influence in the Near East from the eighth century on: Greek pottery in many places, Greek mercenaries, Greek papyri in fourth-century Egypt, etc. But his evidence is drawn from all over the Near East, and his argumentation about the two or three Greek words in Elephantine Aramaic papyri says nothing about the influence of Greek on Palestinian Aramaic. Cf. W. F. Albright, *The Archaeology of Palestine* (Pelican A199; rev. ed.; Baltimore: Penguin, 1960) 143-44; *From the Stone Age to Christianity* (Baltimore: Johns Hopkins, 1946) 256-61. Clear evidence of Greek (and Roman) arts and mythology in first-century Palestine can now be found in artifacts from the Cave of Letters of Wadi Ḥabra; see Y. Yadin, "Expedition D," *IEJ* 11 (1961) 49-64, esp. p. 52.

See now the monumental treatment of this subject by M. Hengel, *Judaism and Hellenism: Studies in Their Encounter in Palestine during the Early Hellenistic Period* (Philadelphia: Fortress, 1974).

[24]See V. Tcherikover, *Hellenistic Civilization and the Jews* (Philadelphia: Jewish Publication Society of America, 1959) 90-116. Cf. the Ḥepṣiba Slab of 195 B.C. (*IR* §214).

[25]1 Macc 1:11-15; Josephus, *Ant.* 12.5.1 §240 (*τὴν ἐλληνικὴν πολιτείαν ἔχειν*, "adopt the Greek way of life" [R. Marcus, *LCL,* 7. 123]). This Jewish support scarcely substantiates the thesis once proposed by I. Voss that Greek became the only language spoken in Palestine since Alexander.

[26]For further Greek epigraphic material from Palestine in the last two centuries B.C., see the graffiti from Marisa (*SEG,* 8. §247-51; E. Oren, *Archaeology* 18 [1965] 218-24); a dedication to Serapis and Isis from Samaria, probably dating from the end of the third century B.C. (*SEG,* 8. §95); a sepulchral poem from Gaza of the third century B.C. (*SEG,* 8. §269); a Gazara (Gezer) graffito, dated ca. 142 B.C. and bearing on 1 Macc 13:43, 48 (*CII* §1184; Gabba §9); the dedication

to Zeus Soter from Ptolemais, ca. 130-29 B.C. (*SEG*, 19. §904; 20. §413); an inscribed handle of the same period from Joppa (*SEG*, 18. §627; cf. *SEG*, 9. §252-60 [Marisa]); an execration from Marisa, dated before 128 B.C. (*SEG*, 8. §246; Gabba §10); the dedication to Herod the Great on a statue from Bashan, dated ca. 23 B.C. (*OGIS* §415; Gabba §12); the second-century list of priests of the temple of Zeus Olympios at Samaria (*SEG*, 8. §96); a second-century inscription about Antiochus VII Sidetes from Acre (Y. H. Landau, *IEJ* 11 [1961] 118-26; J. Schwartz, *IEJ* 12 [1962] 135-36); the votive offering on an altar to Syrian gods, Hadad and Atargatis, from Ptolemais, probably from the second century B.C. (*SEG*, 18. §622). Y. H. Landau ("A Greek Inscription Found Near Hefzibah," *IEJ* 16 [1966] 54-70) has published an unusual inscription recording orders issued by Antiochus III and his eldest son, the junior king Antiochus, for the benefit of Ptolemaios, the military governor (*στρατηγός*) and high priest (*ἀρχιερεύς*) of Coele-Syria and Phoenicia, along with the memoranda sent by Ptolemaios to the king. The documents come from the time of the Fifth Syrian War, begun by Antiochus III in 202-201, and are variously dated between 202 and 195 B.C. Part of the orders include the royal instruction to record them on stone stelae or white tablets in the villages. The foregoing list scarcely pretends to be exhaustive for this period. See further, Y. Meshorer, "A Stone Weight from the Reign of Herod," *IEJ* 20 (1970) 97-98 (with a Greek inscription dated to the 32d year of Herod, 9 B.C.); K. Treu, "Die Bedeutung des Griechischen für die Juden im römischen Reich," *Kairos* 15 (1973) 124-44.

[27]Part of the evidence that these words are foreign in the Aramaic text is the lack of the distinctive Aramaic ending on them in contrast to the names of other instruments in the same verse. These are the only words of certain Greek origin in Daniel; it is significant that they are the names of musical instruments and were probably borrowed with the importation of the instruments themselves. Since they are isolated instances and technical words, it is difficult to say to what extent they are a gauge of the influence of Greek on the Palestinian Semitic languages. See T. C. Mitchell and R. Joyce, "The Musical Instruments in Nebuchadrezzar's Orchestra," *Notes on Some Problems in the Book of Daniel* (London: Tyndale, 1965) 19-27. Cf. E. M. Yamauchi, "The Greek Words in Daniel in the Light of Greek Influence in the Near East," *New Perspectives on the Old Testament* (ed. J. B. Payne; Waco, TX: Word Books, 1970) 170-200. Other words, which were once thought to be Greek derivatives (e.g., *pitgām* in Dan 3:16, allegedly from either *ἐπίταγμα* or *φθέγμα*), are more correctly recognized today as of Persian origin. See S. Telegdi, "Essai sur la phonétique des emprunts iraniens en araméen talmudique," *JA* 226 (1935) 177-256, esp. p. 253; H. H. Schaeder, *Iranische Beiträge* (Schriften der Königsberger gelehrten Gesellschaft, Geisteswiss. Kl., 6/5; Halle a.S.: M. Niemeyer, 1930) 199-296; reprinted, Darmstadt: Wissenschaftliche Buchgesellschaft, 1972) 272.

[28]A convenient list of them can be found in C. Colpe, "Jüdisch-hellenistische Literatur," *Der kleine Pauly: Lexikon der Antike* (Stuttgart: A. Drückenmüller) 2 (1967) 1507-12; cf. E. J. Goodspeed, *JNES* 1 (1942) 315-28.

[29]*Stromata* 1. 21-23 §141-55 (*GCS*, 15. 87-98).

[30]*Praeparatio evangelica* 9. 22-28 (*GCS*, 43/1. 512-27).

[31]Most of what we know about him comes from the not unbiassed account in Josephus (*Life* §34-41, 65, 88, 175-78, 186, 279, 336-40, 355-60, 390-93, 410). Josephus severely criticized his ability as an historian (§336, 357-58), but openly admitted his good Greek training. Cf. Eusebius, *History of the Church* 3.10.8 (*GCS*, 9/1. 226); F. Jacoby, *PW* 10/2 (1919) 1341-46, S. Krauss, "Justus of Tiberias," *Jewish Encyclopedia* 7 (1904) 398-99; C. Mueller, *Fragmenta historicorum graecorum* (Paris: Didot, 1848-74), 3. 523.

[32]*Ant.* 20.12.1 §263-65. The interpretation of these words of Josephus is notoriously difficult, and the manuscript tradition in this passage is not firm. For a recent discussion of the problems involved in an interpretation largely identical with mine, see J. N. Sevenster, *Do You Know Greek? How Much Greek Could the First Jewish Christians Have Known?* (NovTSup 19; Leiden: Brill, 1968) 65-71.

[33]*τῇ πατρίῳ γλώσσῃ* (*JW* 5.9.2 §361). Cf. 6.2.1 §96; 6.2.5 §129; 6.6.2 §327.

[34]*Do You Know Greek?*, 63-65. Sevenster compares the emperor Claudius' excellent command of Greek with the halting use of it by the emperor Augustus, who was, nevertheless,

greatly interested in it and intensely applied himself to the study of it (see Suetonius, *Vita Claudii* §42; *Vita Augusti* §89).

[35]*JW* 1.1,2 §6.

[36]This is also the opinion of F. Büchsel, "Die griechische Sprache der Juden in der Zeit der Septuaginta und des Neuen Testaments," *ZAW* 60 (1944) 132-49, esp. p. 140. But H. Birkeland (*The Language of Jesus* [p. 22 above, n. 5], 13–14) contests this view: "That Josephus should name Aramaic 'the ancestral language,' when he knows the difference between this language and Hebrew, cannot seriously be maintained." He insists that Josephus was using the common language of Palestine, which was Hebrew.

[37]*JW* 1.1,1 §3.

[38]*Ant.* 1.1.2 §7 (*εἰς ἀλλοδάπην ἡμῖν καὶ ξένην διαλέκτου συνήθειαν*).

[39]H. S. J. Thackeray, *Josephus, the Man and the Historian* (New York: Jewish Institute of Religion, 1929) 104.

[40]*Ag. Ap.* 1.9 §50.

[41]Two exemplars of this inscription have been found; the better preserved is in the Istanbul Museum, the other in the Palestine Archaeological Museum, Jerusalem. See *OGIS*, 2. §598; *SEG*, 8. §169; 20. §477; Thomsen, *ZDPV* 44 (1921) 7-8; *TGI* §52; Gabba §24; Barrett, *NTB* §47. Two modern falsified reproductions of it have also been reported; see W. R. Taylor, *JPOS* 13 [1933] 137-39. See note 15 above for Josephus' description of such inscriptions.

[42]See R. Weill, *REJ* 71 (1920) 30-34; Thomsen, 261; *SEG*, 8. §170; 20. §478; *Année épigraphique* 1922, §117; *CII*, 2. §1404; Gabba §23; *TGI* §54; Barrett, *NTB* §50.

[43]*SEG*, 8. §244; cf. H. W. Garrod, "Locrica," *Classical Review* 37 (1923) 161-62; H. Lamer, "Der Kalypso-Graffito in Marissa (Palästina)," *ZDPV* 54 (1931) 59-67.

[44]This inscription begins *διάταγμα* Καίσαρος; but it is neither certainly attributed to Augustus nor certainly of Nazareth provenience. See F. Cumont, "Un rescrit impérial sur la violation de sépulture," *Revue historique* 163 (1930) 241-66; cf. S. Lösch, *Diatagma Kaisaros: Die Inschrift von Nazareth und das Neue Testament* (Freiburg im B.: Herder, 1936); S. Riccobono, *Fontes iuris romani antejustiniani, pars prima: Leges* (Florence: Barbera, 1941) 414-16; J. Schmitt, *DBSup* 6 (1960) 333-63.

[45]See G. Orfali, "Une nouvelle inscription grecque découverte à Capharnaüm," *JPOS* 6 (1926) 159-63; cf. *SEG*, 8. §4; 17. §774.

[46]What is badly needed is a systematic collection of the Greek, Aramaic, and Hebrew inscriptions on ossuaries from Jerusalem and elsewhere. It is impossible at the moment to give any sort of comprehensive view of this topic. Many of the Aramaic inscriptions can now be found in *MPAT*; see p. 22 above, n. 28. Some examples of Greek inscriptions from Jerusalem can be found in *CII* 2; Thomsen §190-97, 199, 201-5; *SEG*, 8. §179-86, 197, 201, 208-9, 221, 224; 6. §849; 17. §784; 19. §922; 20. §483-92.

[47]M. Smith ("Aramaic Studies and the Study of the New Testament," *JBR* 26 [1958] 310) says, "Of the 168 published in Frey's *Corpus inscriptionum iudaicarum*, 5 are illegible, 32 are in Hebrew or Aramaic or both, 17 are in a Semitic language and Greek, but 114 are in Greek only." But are they all of the first century?

[48]*The Jews of Ancient Rome* (Philadelphia: Jewish Publication Society of America, 1960) 75.

[49]See P. Benoit et al., *Les grottes de Murabbaᶜât* [n. 19 above], 212-33, 243-56, 234-40, 275-79.

[50]B. Lifshitz, "Papyrus grecs du désert de Juda," *Aegyptus* 42 (1962) 240-56 (+ 2 pls.). The first text is apparently the one that Y. Yadin refers to as Ḥev 3 (see *IEJ* 11 [1961] 42-43; *BIES* 25 [1961] 57). Cf. Y. Yadin, "New Discoveries in the Judean Desert," *BA* 24 (1961) 34-50; "More on the Letters of Bar Kochba," ibid., 96-95.

[51]Lifshitz takes Σουμαῖος as a Greek transcription of *Šamay* or *Šemaᶜ*, which he regards as a hypocoristicon of *Šimᶜôn*. In the second papyrus letter that Lifshitz publishes in the same article, the name is written in Greek as Σίμων, with Χώσιβα clearly written above it (between the lines). For a discussion of the name of Bar Cochba, see my article, "The Bar Cochba Period," *The Bible in Current Catholic Thought* [ed. J. L. McKenzie; New York: Herder and Herder, 1962], 133-68, esp. pp. 138-41. Cf. the revised form in *ESBNT*, 305-54, esp. pp. 312-16.

The spelling of certain words in this document is defective: thus ᾿Επηδὴ = ἐπειδὴ; ἔπεμσα = ἔπεμψα; πέμσε = πεμψαι; ἀνασθήσεται = ἀναστήσετε; ἰς = εἰς; ἄλως = ἄλλως; ποιήσηται = ποιήσητε; Ἑληνιστὶ = Ἑλληνιστὶ; Ἑβραεστὶ = Ἑβραϊστὶ. The meaning of στελεούς is not clear; does it refer to "beams" that might be used for huts, or to the "branches" (*lûlāb*)?

The real problem in this letter is the restoration of the word [ ]μαν in line 13, and even the reading of it. Though I originally went along with Lifshitz's reading of [ὁρ]μὰν, I have never been satisfied with it, because it looks like a Doric form of the accusative singular of the feminine noun, which should otherwise be ὁρμήν at this period in Palestine. The same difficulty has been noted by G. Howard and J. C. Shelton ("The Bar-Kokhba Letters and Palestinian Greek," *IEJ* 23 [1973] 101-2), who suggest as "the most obvious possibility" for restoring the lacuna [Ἑρ]μαν, comparing Rom 16:14. But they do not tell us how to construe the rest of the Greek with such a restoration (does the preceding neuter article remain?). Y. Yadin (*Bar-Kokhba: The Rediscovery of the Legendary Hero of the Second Jewish Revolt against Rome* [London: Weinfeld and Nicholson, 1971] 130-31) gives an abbreviated translation of the letter, especially of this crucial part: "'the letter is written in Greek as we have no one who knows Hebrew [or Aramaic].'" Yadin supplies a good photo of the text, but he does not tell us how he reads the text's Greek writing; and it is not possible to puzzle out what in the text could be understood as "no one" in his translation. As a result, I leave the translation and interpretation of the text stand according to the original Lifshitz interpretation until further light is shed on it by someone.

As for the four elements required for Succoth, one should consult Lev 23:40 and Josephus, *Ant.* 3.10.3 §245.

[52]See Y. Yadin, "*Mḥnh* D," *BIES* 25 (1960) 49-64, esp. pp. 60-61; also my article, "The Bar Cochba Period," 155–56; *ESBNT*, 336–37; cf. *MPAT* §60.

[53]"Jewish Christianity in Acts in Light of the Qumran Scrolls," *Studies in Luke-Acts: Essays . . . in Honor of Paul Schubert* (eds. L. E. Keck and J. L. Martyn; Nashville: Abingdon, 1966) 233-57, esp. pp. 237-38; *ESBNT*, 271-303.

[54]"Once More, Who Were the Hellenists?" *ExpTim* 70 (1958-59) 100-102; see also J. N. Sevenster, *Do You Know Greek?* 37; W. G. Kümmel, *RGG*³ 6 (1962) 1189.

[55]Compare the opinion of C. S. Mann (Appendix VI in J. Munck, *The Acts of the Apostles* [AB 31; Garden City: Doubleday, 1967] 301-4); he believes that Ἑβραῖοι refers to Samaritans or Samaritan Christians! Older discussions can be found in H. J. Cadbury, "The Hellenists," *The Beginnings of Christianity* (London: Macmillan), 5 (1933) 59-74; H. Windisch, "*Hellēn*," *TDNT* 2 (1964) 504-15, esp. pp. 511-12. Note the use of Josephus' ἑβραΐζων, meaning "speaking in 'Hebrew'" (*JW* 6.2.1 §96).

[56]For some literature on the subject, see A. Roberts, *Greek the Language of Christ and His Apostles* (London: Longmans, Green, 1888); S. Greijdanus, *Het gebruik van het Grieksch door den Heere en zijne apostelen in Palestine* (Kampen: Kok, 1932); S. M. Patterson, "What Language Did Jesus Speak?" *Classical Outlook* 23 (1946) 65-67; L. Rood, "Heeft Jezus Grieks gesproken?" *Streven* 2 (1949) 1026-35; A. W. Argyle, "Did Jesus Speak Greek?" *ExpTim* 67 (1955-56) 92-93; J. K. Russel (same title), ibid., 246; H. M. Draper (same title), ibid., 317; A. W. Argyle (same title), ibid., 383; R. M. Wilson (same title), *ExpTim* 68 (1956-57) 121-22; R. O. P. Taylor, "Did Jesus Speak Aramaic?" *ExpTim* 56 (1944-45) 95-97; *The Groundwork of the Gospels* (Oxford. Blackwell, 1946) 91-105.

For some older discussions, see also D. Diodati, *De Christo graece loquente exercitatio* (Naples, 1767; reissued, ed. by O. T. Dobbin; London: J. Gladding, 1843); A. Paulus, *Verosimilia de Judaeis palaestinensibus, Jesu atque etiam Apostolis non aramaea dialecto sola, sed graeca quoque aramaizante locutis* (Jena, 1803 [*non vidi*]).

[57]Cf. A. W. Argyle, *ExpTim* 67 (1955-56) 93: "The importance of establishing that Jesus and His disciples sometimes spoke Greek cannot be overestimated. It means that in some cases we may have direct access to the original utterances of our Lord and not only to a translation of them." See also his articles, "'Hypocrites and the Aramaic Theory,' *ExpTim* 75 (1963-64) 113-14; "Greek among the Jews of Palestine in New Testament Times," *NTS* 20 (1973-74) 87-89.

[58]*Greek in Jewish Palestine: Studies in the Life and Manners of Jewish Palestine in the II-IV Centuries C.E.* (2d ed.; New York: P. Feldheim, 1965); *Hellenism in Jewish Palestine: Studies in the Literary Transmission, Beliefs and Manners of Palestine in the I Century B.C.E.—IV Century C.E.* (New York: Jewish Theological Seminary of America, 1950). Though the latter does go back to an earlier date, it is largely devoted to a broader topic than the first book and the issue being treated here.

[59]*Do You Know Greek?*, 38-44.

[60]See G. Alon, *Kirjath Sepher* 20 (1943-44) 76-95; B. Lifshitz, *Aegyptus* 42 (1962) 254-56; "L'hellénisation des Juifs de Palestine: A propos des inscriptions de Besara (Beth-Shearim)," *RB* 72 (1965) 520-38; *"Yĕwānît wîwānût bên Yĕhûdê ᵓereṣ-Yiśrāᵓēl," Eshkoloth* 5 (1966-67) 20-28.

For the important Greek material coming from Beth-Sheᶜarim, see M. Schwabe and B. Lifshitz, *Beth Sheᶜarim: Volume Two: The Greek Inscriptions* (Jerusalem: Israel Exploration Society, 1967). These inscriptions date from the first quarter of the third century A.D., when R. Judah the Prince was buried there. To be buried in the vicinity of this Jewish leader and compiler of the Mishnah was regarded as a privilege and a sizeable necropolis developed there up until A.D. 352, when the city was destroyed by the army of Gallus. These dates are also confirmed by coins found there. See further B. Lifshitz, "Beiträge zur palästinischen Epigraphik," *ZDPV* 78 (1962) 64-88; 82 (1966) 57-63; "Les inscriptions grecques de Beth Sheᶜarim (Besara)," *IEJ* 17 (1967) 194.

For a similar important group of sepulchral inscriptions dated merely to "the Roman period," see B. Lifshitz's articles on the necropolis of Caesarea Maritima: "La nécropole juive de Césarée," *RB* 71 (1964) 384-87; "Inscriptions de Césarée en Palestine," *RB* 72 (1965) 98-107; "Notes d'épigraphie palestinienne," *RB* 73 (1966) 248-57; "Inscriptions de Césarée," *RB* 74 (1967) 50-59.

[61]See the old, but still useful list in S. Krauss, *Griechische und lateinische Lehnwörter im Talmud, Midrasch und Targum* (Berlin: S. Calvary, 1899-1900).

[62]Cf. M. Smith, "Palestinian Judaism in the First Century," *Israel: Its Role in Civilization* (ed. M. Davis; New York: Jewish Theological Seminary of America, 1956) 67-81 (much of the material used as evidence in this article is not derived from the first century).

[63]"Aramaic Studies and the Study of the New Testament," *JBR* 26 (1958) 304-13, esp. p. 310.

[64]*The Archaeology of Palestine* (5th ed.; Pelican A199; Baltimore: Penguin, 1960) 201-2. See also V. Tcherikover, *Corpus papyrorum judaicarum* (Cambridge: Harvard, 1957), 1. 30.

[65]For literature on this text, see my commentary on the *Genesis Apocryphon* (2d ed., 1971), 21 n. 57; also *MPAT* § 150.

[66]For an attempt to gather the Aramaic ossuary inscriptions from Palestine, see *MPAT* § 69-148 (and the literature cited there).

[67]Goodspeed's skepticism about the "possibility of an Aramaic Gospel" was first expressed in his *New Chapters in New Testament Study* (New York: Macmillan, 1937) 127-68, esp. pp. 165-66. A. T. Olmstead sought to answer Goodspeed in an article, "Could an Aramaic Gospel be Written?" *JNES* 1 (1942) 41-75. Goodspeed replied in another, "The Possible Aramaic Gospel," ibid., 315-40 (his words quoted in the text are taken from p. 328 of this reply). The heat of the debate between Olmstead and Goodspeed produced more rhetoric than clarity; some of the new factors that I have been trying to draw together here would change a number of contentions of both of these writers. The limited topic of my discussion does not bear exactly on the point at issue between them.

[68]See E. L. Sukenik, *"Ṣiyyûn ᶜUzziyāhû melek Yĕhûdāh," Tarbiz* 2 (1930-31) 288-92; W. F. Albright, "The Discovery of an Aramaic Inscription Relating to King Uzziah," *BASOR* 44 (1931) 8-10; J. N. Epstein, *"LĕṢiyyûn ᶜUzziyāhû," Tarbiz* 2 (1930-31) 293-94; J. M. van der Ploeg, *JEOL* 11 (1949) pl. XVIII, fg. 29; *TGI* §55.

[69]See pp. 11, 24 above, nn. 55–57. Cf. J. Bligh, "'Qorban,'" *HeyJ* 5 (1964) 192–93; S. Zeitlin, "Korban," *JQR* 53 (1962) 160-63; "Korban: A Gift," *JQR* 59 (1968) 133-35; Z. W. Falk, "Notes and Observations on Talmudic Vows," *HTR* 59 (1966) 309-12.

[70]See E. L. Sukenik, "A Jewish Tomb in the Kidon Valey[sic]," *Tarbiz* 6 (1934-35) 190-96; for the literature on this inscription, see *MPAT* §71.

[71]See p. 23 above, n. 53.

[72]N. Avigad and Y. Yadin, *A Genesis Apocryphon: A Scroll from the Wilderness of Judaea* (Jerusalem: Magnes, 1956); see my commentary on it (2d ed., 1971). The other Qumran Aramaic texts are listed on pp. 101–2 below.

[73]On this text, see pp. 90–94 below.

[74]These too have been gathered together with those referred to in n. 66 above in *MPAT,* §69–148 (see the literature cited there).

[75]See Mur 18 (DJD, 2. 100-104); also Y. Yadin, "The Excavation of Masada—1963/64: Preliminary Report," *IEJ* 15 (1965) 1-120, esp. p. 111.

[76]See Mur 8, 19, 20, 21, 23, 25, 26, 27, 28, 31, 32, 33, 34, 35, 72. Cf. S. Segert, "Zur Orthographie und Sprache der aramäischen Texte von W. Murabbaᶜat (Auf Grund von DJD II)," *ArOr* 31 (1963) 122-37. The material from Wadi Ḫabra is still to be published; for preliminary reports and partial publication of it, see Y. Yadin, "Expedition D," *IEJ* 11 (1961) 36-52; *BIES* 25 (1961) 49-64; "Expedition D—The Cave of Letters," *IEJ* 12 (1962) 227-57. Cf. E. Y. Kutscher, "The Language of the Hebrew and Aramaic Letters of Bar Cochba and His Contemporaries," *Lĕšonénu* 25 (1961) 117-33; 26 (1962) 7-23. From this cave (official siglum 5/6Ḥev) came the Nabatean contract published by J. Starcky, "Un contrat nabatéen sur papyrus," *RB* 61 (1954) 161-81. Yadin (*IEJ* 12 [1962] 229) reveals that he recovered the *scriptura interior* of this "tied deed" and thus established the provenience of the contract. It is also likely that two other Aramaic documents published by J. T. Milik come from the same cave ("Un contrat juif de l'an 134 après J.-C.," *RB* 61 [1954] 182-90; "Deux documents inédits du désert de Juda," *Bib* 38 [1957] 245-68, esp. pp. 255-64). Cf. E. Koffmahn, *Die Doppelurkunden aus der Wüste Juda* (STDJ 5; Leiden: Brill, 1968). See *MPAT,* §38–64.

[77]"Three Greek Documents from the Family Archive of Babatha," *E. L. Sukenik Memorial Volume,* 46-51, esp. p. 50 (document 27); cf. "The Greek Papyri from the Cave of the Letters," *IEJ* 12 (1962) 258-62.

[78]See H. J. Polotsky, "Three Greek Documents," 46-49.

[79]See Y. Yadin, *IEJ* 12 (1962) 246.

[80]Mur 103a 1 (DJD, 2. 232).

[81]See DJD, 2. 115; *Lĕšonénu* 25 (1961) 119, 126; *E. L. Sukenik Memorial Volume,* 50.

[82]See Y. Yadin, *IEJ* 12 (1962) 242; cf. his article, "The Nabatean Kingdom, Provincia Arabia, Petra and En-Geddi in the Documents from Nahal Hever," *JEOL* 17 (1963) 227-41, esp. pp. 232-33.

[83]The last Greek formula is taken from the receipt in the Babatha archive, document 27 (see note 77 above), lines 2-3.

[84]To borrow a phrase from K. A. Kitchen, used in his critique of H. H. Rowley's studies of the Aramaic of Daniel (see note 4 above).

[85]*Aramaic Approach* (p. 23 above, n. 43), 22.

[86]See nn. 58 and 61 above. On early Syriac inscriptions, see p. 71 below.

[87]"Le targum de Job de la grotte 11 de Qumran [11QtgJob]: Première communication," *Mededelingen der koninklijke Nederlandse Akademie van Wetenschappen,* Afd. Letterkunde, n.r. 25/9 (Amsterdam: Noord-Hollandsche Uitgevers M., 1962) 543-57, esp. 552. The full text of the Qumran targum of Job has been published; see J. P. M. van der Ploeg and A. S. van der Woude (avec la collaboration de B. Jongeling), *Le targum de Job de la grotte XI de Qumrân* (Koninklijke nederlandse Akademie van Wetenschappen; Leiden: Brill, 1971). For a comparison of it with the earlier-known targum of Job, see pp. 167–74 below.

[88]*Ten Years* (p. 22 above, n. 31), 31. See further p. 22 above, n. 32.

[89]E.g., the inscriptions from the ᶜAin-Dûq synagogue (see E. L. Sukenik, *Ancient Synagogues in Palestine and Greece* [Schweich Lectures, 1930; London: British Academy, 1934] 73-74 [I], 75-76 [II], 76 [III]), the ᶜAlma synagogue (R. Hestrin, "A New Aramaic Inscription from ᶜAlma," *L. M. Rabinowitz Fund for the Exploration of Ancient Synagogues, Bulletin* 3 [1960] 65-67), the Beth Alpha synagogue (E. L. Sukenik, *The Ancient Synagogue of Beth Alpha* [Jerusalem: University Press, 1932] 43-46), the Beth Gubrin synagogue (E. L. Sukenik, "A Synagogue

Inscription from Beit Jibrin," *JPOS* 10 [1930] 76-78), the Capernaum synagogue (G. Orfali, "Deux inscriptions de Capharnaüm," *Antonianum* 1 [1926] 401-12), the Chorazin synagogue (J. Ory, "An Inscription Newly Found in the Synagogue of Kerazah," *PEFQS* 1927, 51-52), the Fiq synagogue (S. A. Cook, "Hebrew Inscription at Fik," *PEFQS* 1903, 185-86; cf. p. 274), the Gaza synagogue (D. J. Saul, "Von el-ᶜAkabe über Gaza nach Jerusalem," *Mitteilungen des deutschen Palästina-Vereins* 7 [1901] 9-14, esp. 12-13), the Gischala synagogue (G. Dalman, "Die Zeltreise," *PJB* 10 [1914] 47-48), the Hammath-by-Gadara synagogue (E. L. Sukenik, *The Ancient Synagogue of El Hammeh* (Hammath-by-Gadara) [Jerusalem: R. Mass, 1935]), the Hamat-Tiberias synagogue (M. Dothan, "The Aramaic Inscription from the Synagogue of Severus at Hamat-Tiberias," *E. L. Sukenik Memorial Volume*, pp. 183-85), the ᶜIsfiyah synagogue (M. Avi-Yonah, "A Sixth Century Synagogue at ᶜ(Isfiyā," *QDAP* 3 [1933] 119-31), the Khirbet Kanef synagogue (G. Dalman, "Inschriften aus Palästina," *ZDPV* 37 [1914] 138), the Jerash synagogue (J. W. Crowfoot and R. W. Hamilton, "The Discovery of a Synagogue at Jerash," *PEFQS* 1929, 211-19, esp. 218; see E. L. Sukenik, "Note on the Aramaic Inscription at the Synagogue of Gerasa," *PEFQS* 1930, 48-49), the Kafr Birᶜim school inscription (*JPCI* §9), the Kafr Kenna synagogue (C. Clermont-Ganneau, "Mosaïque à inscription hébraïque de Kefr Kenna," *CRAIBL* 1900, pp. 555-57), the Umm el-ᶜAmed synagogue (N. Avigad, "An Aramaic Inscription from the Ancient Synagogue of Umm el-ᶜAmed," *BIES* 19 (1956-57) 183-87. S. Segert once reported (*ArOr* 33 [1965] 196 n. 12) that E. Y. Kutscher was preparing a "zusammenfassende Ausgabe dieser Texte." Since, however, death has taken Kutscher away, one may have to be content with the collection that D. J. Harrington and I have made in *MPAT*, App., § A1-A156.

[90]*A Revised Catalogue of the Ancient Synagogues of the Holy Land* (Publications of the Studium Biblicum Franciscanum, collectio minor, 6; Jerusalem: Franciscan Press, 1969). Cf. B. Lifshitz, *Donateurs et fondateurs dans les synagogues juives: Répertoires des dédicaces grecques relatives à la construction et à la réfection des synagogues* (Cahiers de la RB, 7; Paris: Gabalda, 1967).

[91]See my commentary (2d ed., 1971), 25-26. Cf. E. Y. Kutscher, *Or* 39 (1970) 178-83.

[92]This is an instance of the prepositive article and may have to be discounted, because it is the title of Bar Cochba. It may be part of a stereotyped way of referring to him, even if one spoke or wrote in Aramaic. However, there is another instance of it on a Jerusalem ossuary, *Yhwdh br ʾlᶜzr hswpr* (see *MPAT*, §99). Compare the Greek fragment mentioned above, p. 40.

[93]Cf. F. Rosenthal, *A Grammar of Biblical Aramaic* (Porta linguarum orientalium, ns 5; Wiesbaden: Harrassowitz, 1961), §187; H. Bauer and P. Leander, *Grammatik des Biblisch-Aramäischen* (Halle: Niemeyer, 1927), §1 t-v (p. 10). This reference to Daniel (and even to Ezra) should not be misunderstood. It may seem that such "Hebraisms" were already a living part of Aramaic of an earlier day. This is undoubtedly true; but it does not make them indigenous in Aramaic. They were originally Hebraisms, and they persisted in the language because of the more or less simultaneous use of the languages throughout a long period. Cf. S. Segert, "Sprachliche Bemerkungen zu einigen aramäischen Texten von Qumran," *ArOr* 33 (1965) 190-206.

[94]2 Kgs 18:26; Isa 36:11; Ezra 4:7—cf. Cowley, *AP* 28:4, 6.

[95]Cf. the LXX passages corresponding to the OT passages in the preceding note; also Job 42:17b (*συριακή*) and the *Letter of Aristeas* §11. This Greek name may be reflected in the Hebrew (contemptuous ?) name for Aramaic, לשון סורסי (*b. Soṭah* 49b; *b. B. Qam.* 82b, 83a).

[96]However, *χαλδαϊστί* is added in the LXX of Dan 2:26, corresponding to nothing in the MT.

[97]As it certainly does in the Greek prologue of Ben Sira. This exclusive meaning has been argued for it by H. Birkeland, "The Language of Jesus" (p. 22 above, n. 35), 12-16.

[98]See further G. Dalman, *The Words of Jesus* (p. 23 above, n. 53).

[99]E.g., A. Dupont-Sommer, *Les araméens* [L'orient ancien illustré, 4; Paris: Maisonneuve, 1949] 99 ("L'araméen continua longtemps à se parler et à s'écrire en Palestine. A l'époque du Christ, il était la seule langue courante pour la masse du peuple; c'est l'araméen que parlaient Jésus et les Apôtres"). F. Altheim and R. Stiehl, "Jesus der Galiläer," *Die Araber in der alten Welt* (Berlin: de Gruyter) 3 (1966) 92 ("Das Hebräische war als lebende Sprache seit dem Beginn der hellenistischen Zeit ausgestorben und in Palästina durch Aramäische ersetzt worden.")

[100]See J. T. Milik, *Ten Years* (p. 22 above, n. 31), 41.

[101]Ibid., 130.

[102]See N. Avigad, *Ancient Monuments in the Kidron Valley* (Jerusalem: Bialik, 1954) 59-66. Also the Bethphage ossuary lid may be considered here (R. Dussaud, "Comptes d'ouvriers d'une entreprise funéraire juive," *Syria* 4 [1923] 241-49).

[103]As בר in the Phoenician inscription of Kilamuwa I (*KAI* §24).

[104]For instance, Mur 22:1-9 i 3, 4, 11-12; 29:1, 2, 10, 11-12; 30:1, 4, 6, 9, 10, 11, 17, 26, 32; 36:1, 2, 8; 42:12; 46:10. These examples are scarcely exhaustive.

[105]J. T. Milik, *Ten Years* (p. 22 above, n. 31), 130. Here Milik dates the text to "the middle of the first century A.D."; but in the official publication of this text (DJD, 3. 217) he says, "le document se situe par conséquent au premier siècle de notre ère ou au début du siècle suivant, entre 30 et 130 après J.-C. en chiffres ronds, avec préférence pour la second moitié de cette période." He also cites the date proposed by W. F. Albright, "between cir. 70 and cir. 135 A.D." S. Segert (*ArOr* 33 [1965] 190-206, esp. p. 191) thinks that 3Q*15* was written in Hebrew by a Jew who otherwise spoke Aramaic; but he does not specify how this is revealed in this text.

[106]*Ten Years*, 130.

[107]"The Language of Jesus" (p. 22 above, n. 35), 16. For further negative reactions to Birkeland's thesis, see p. 22 above, n. 37.

[108]M. H. Segal (*A Grammar of Mishnaic Hebrew* [Oxford: Clarendon, 1927] §281, p. 126) is often cited in opposition to this claim: "The termination *-în* [in Mishnaic Hebrew] is not an Aramaism," but rather "a purely Hebraic phenomenon." Yet the fact that "*-n* is common to nearly all Semitic languages" or is "the only one found on the Mešaᶜ stone" or that it occurs "as early as the Song of Deborah" still does not rule out the influence of a dominant language of the area (such as Aramaic was) on Hebrew (or Moabite).

[109]See the analysis of this text by S. Segert, *ArOr* 25 (1967) 34-35. Aramaic orthographic practice seems to be the best explanation of such further forms as [*kwḥ*] *gbwr*ʾ[ ] in 6Q9 45:2 and of [ ]ʾ*ḥt* ᶜ*śr*ʾ[ ] in 6Q9 1:1.

[110]See J. T. Milik, DJD, 2. 166.

Chapter 3

The Phases of the Aramaic Language*

In 1966, as part of a discussion of the language of the *Genesis Apocryphon* from Qumran Cave I, I proposed a five-fold division of the Aramaic language. It was no more than a footnote in the introduction to a commentary on that Qumran scroll.[1] The reasons for the phases and for the proposed division of Aramaic were not explained. This I should like to attempt here, as a background for further discussion of the Aramaic substratum of the NT. One reason for this latter-day explanation is that my proposed phases of Aramaic have been adopted in some quarters and criticized in others. Perhaps the attempt to explain the division will meet some of the objections and also provide the opportunity to utilize further data and some of the material that others have brought to light in support of the division.

Why propose a reclassification of the phases of Aramaic? The answer to such a question is complex. First of all, there was no generally accepted division of the phases of the language. Second, some of the divisions being used were clearly inadequate, because much of the evidence that has come to light in the last two or three decades has called for a reassessment of categories that have become obsolete. Third, there is still no little disagreement about some of the phases, and an attempt is needed to discuss them. It is undoubtedly a pipe-dream to think that there will ever be a universally-accepted view of this matter—any more than of other matters. Yet the *student* who begins to interest him / herself in Aramaic is immediately confronted with scholarly opinions which use labels for phases of the language which are nominally the same, but differ widely in extension. Thus, one is consequently confronted with the task of trying to discover what a given writer means by "Old Aramaic," "Middle Aramaic," and so on. And many of these labels come from a period of the study of Aramaic that is *passé*. Hence it might be well, first of all, to survey various attempts to divide up the Aramaic language and comment on their adequacy or inadequacy. Then, we shall propose the five phases again—this time a little more fully. And finally, the reasons for the division of the phases and their related problems will be discussed.

I. *Earlier Attempts to Divide the Aramaic Language*

In his monumental survey of Aramaic research in 1939,[2] F. Rosenthal included under "Altaramäisch" not only the 9th/8th century inscriptions from North Syria, but Reichsaramäisch, Pahlevi ideograms, Nabatean, and Palmyrene. All of this he distinguished from "Jungaramäisch," by which he meant Jewish Palestinian Aramaic, Samaritan Aramaic, Christian Palestinian Aramaic, and Modern Syrian Aramaic—as well as from "Ostaramäisch," by which he meant Syriac, Babylonian Talmudic Aramaic, Mandaic, and Modern East Aramaic. Thus he began with a chronological division (Altaramäisch—Jungaramäisch) but shifted to a geographical one (Ostaramäisch); and the rationale for the division of the phases is thus not consistent. Moreover, the grouping together of the early inscriptions with such dialects as Nabatean and Palmyrene—to mention only the most obviously disparate elements—as "Altaramäisch" raises all sorts of questions today. But the categories that Rosenthal used were adequate to the survey that he was making; he was not really discussing the specific problem to which this paper addresses itself. Rosenthal was followed, in part at least, by E. G. Kraeling (in his lengthy introducion to the *Brooklyn Museum Aramaic Papyri*),[3] E. Y. Kutscher (in an early article),[4] A. F. Johns,[5] and most recently by S. Segert.[6]

But even earlier than Rosenthal the term "Altaramäisch" had been given a broad range of meaning by G. Bergsträsser in his *Einführung in die semitischen Sprachen*,[7] where he distinguished in it three dialects: Biblical Aramaic (the oldest), Syriac, and Mandaic. He used "Old Aramaic" in a *wide* sense to include forms of the language in pre-Christian centuries (as the aforementioned divisions reveal), but also in a *narrow* sense to include inscriptions and papyri down to about 400 B.C. In his wide sense "Old Aramaic" was obviously being used in contradistinction to present-day, living forms of the language.[8] The inadequacy, however, of such terminology was and is apparent.

In 1948, R. A. Bowman restricted the term "Old Aramaic" to the early inscriptions of North Syria.[9] This was apparently not original with him, but it was indicative of the growing awareness of the need to set apart the phase of the language found in these inscriptions, as more and more of them were gradually coming to light. This restricted sense of "Old Aramaic" has been used by others, such as F. M. Cross and D. N. Freedman,[10] W. Baumgartner,[11] S. Moscati,[12] S. Segert,[13] K. A. Kitchen,[14] K. Beyer,[15] R. Degen,[16] although the number of texts included in this phase varies with the writer. The purpose of the restricting the sense of "Old Aramaic" was to set it off from a vast body of Aramaic texts that emerge from the seventh century B.C. and onwards, representing a form of the language that seems to have been standardized and from which, in fact, we get most of our impressions of what might be called "normal" Aramaic and by which we tend to judge the earlier inscriptions of the "Old Aramaic" period.

The name "Reichsaramäisch" for these texts of the seventh century onward was first coined by an Iranian scholar, Josef Markwart in 1927. He used this label in a footnote to a discussion of a matter quite unrelated; but it was quickly picked up and its use became widespread—and, in fact, is still widely used—despite its inadequacies. It is sometimes translated into English as "Imperial Aramaic," and the empire that Markwart had in mind when he wrote his footnote was Persia: "So nenne ich die aramäische Kanzleisprache der Achaimeniden, in welcher die Mehrzahl, wenn nicht alle, aramäischen Inschriften und sämtliche Papyri der Achaimenidenzeit, sowie die Stücke in den Büchern ᶜEsra und Daniel abgefasst sind."[17] Markwart's label was derived from the period in which this sort of "chancery" Aramaic was widely used; it had the advantage of being a chronological designation. But it seemed to suggest that the use of this sort of Aramaic began in the Persian period, whereas it was obviously in use already in the time of the Neo-Assyrian empire. It was H. L. Ginsberg who pointed out the use of it in pre-Persian times, calling attention to the *rab-šāqeh* episode in 2 Kgs 18:26-28 and Isa 36:11–13 and to the language in the Aššur Ostracon (*KAI* 233), dated ca. 660–50 B.C.[18] As a result, Ginsberg suggested the use of the name "Official Aramaic" for this phase of the language. Later on, E. G. Kraeling, thinking that Ginsberg's view might be somewhat entangled in hypotheses, suggested that it might be better to "speak of 'standard Aramaic.'"[19] One reason to support Kraeling's opinion is the fact that the same form of the language is now found in ostraca from Egypt which record everyday messages between persons who were almost certainly not officials or persons in chancery work. In any case, the names "Imperial Aramaic" or "Official Aramaic" are quite commonly used for this phase of the language today.

The extent of "Imperial Aramaic" or "Official Aramaic" is, however, the problem that is of concern today. For it is differently proposed by various scholars; it is often not demarcated from what seems to be a phase of the language that follows it, in which there is a seemingly direct linear development of it, but also a number of side, local dialects. Even F. Rosenthal, who grouped Reichsaramäisch, Nabatean, and Palmyrene under "Old Aramaic," sensed the need to set off from Reichsaramäisch both Nabatean and Palmyrene.[20] However, W. Baumgartner considered Reichsaramäisch to include not only the Pahlevi ideograms, the Aramaic texts from Egypt,[21] the Arsames correspondence,[22] and Biblical Aramaic, but also Nabatean and Palmyrene. From this huge group of texts Baumgartner distinguished what he called "real local dialects," i.e., Jewish Aramaic, including that of the Babylonian Talmud, the targums, Samaritan texts, and even Christian Palestinian Aramaic.[23] All of these in turn were distinguished by him from Modern Syriac.[24]

To add to the confusion, E. Y. Kutscher seems at one time to have listed under Reichsaramäisch such disparate types as Biblical Aramaic, Targumic Aramaic, and later Western Aramaic (i.e., Galilean, Samaritan, and Christian

Palestinian Aramaic).[25] As one reads on in that early article of Kutscher, one perceives that for him all of this was to be understood in addition to Egyptian Aramaic, the Arsames correspondence, Nabatean, and Palmyrene. All was to be grouped together as Reichsaramäisch and distinguished from "Middle Aramaic," which began for him "about 500 C.E."[26] Somehow, in between this Reichsaramäisch and this Middle Aramaic Kutscher sought to find room for Qumran Aramaic, especially that of the *Genesis Apocryphon.* Admittedly, Kutscher had not proposed these classifications in a well thought out scheme of the phases of the Aramaic language; that was not the purpose of his article. The grouping of texts under Reichsaramäisch according to Kutscher, that we have given above, has been garnered from his valuable article on "The Language of the Genesis Apocryphon," the purpose of which was to situate the Aramaic of that text among the known dialects of the language. It is a basic study that excels in comparative material. As far as I know, no one has contested his fundamental work on the grammar of 1QapGen or his judgment about the kind of Aramaic that it contains, or his dating of it to the first century B.C. or A.D.[27] Though his classification of the phases of the Aramaic language in that article did not invalidate the basic thrust and purpose of the article, it is, nevertheless, problematic. Fortunately, one can use his data and consider their relative value, without always identifying the forms as he did.

Because of problems of this sort which the earlier use of labels for phases of the Aramaic language caused—and still others could be mentioned—I sought to introduce *a purely chronological division* into the discussion of the phases of the Aramaic language. The dominant view of dividing the language would be chronological, i.e., by centuries, even though the labels might not always be immediately indicative of chronology. Within such categories or phases one could allow for local or geographical subdivisions into further dialectal differences (e.g., into eastern and western Aramaic), when necessary. The names that I have used are not ideal, I realize, since that of the second phase is not expressive of time, being still tied to the groping, traditional way of looking at that phase. But it is retained in view of the popularity of the label, and it is done with the conviction that it would be hard to start a new name in this phase. Below, I shall propose an alternative name, but also the problems that attend it.

II. *The Five Phases of Aramaic*

The reclassification of the known phases of the Aramaic language is proposed as follows:

(1) *Old Aramaic,* from roughly 925 B.C. to 700 B.C. This phase is represented by inscriptions on stone and other materials, written in the borrowed Phoenician alphabet[28] and preserving the earliest known forms of the language that we have come to recognize as Aramaic. The evidence for this phase comes not only from Northern Syria and Upper Mesopotamia, as was

known for a long time, but also from Northern Palestine. Included in this phase of the language are the Tell Halaf inscription, the Bir Hadad inscriptions, the ᶜEin Gev jar inscription, the Tell Dan Bowl, the Hazaᵓel Ivory inlay, the Ördek Burnu inscription, the Hamath graffiti, the Zakir inscription, Hadad, Panammu, the Sefire inscriptions, eight Bar Rākib inscriptions, the Hazor sherd, the Calah ostracon, the Nērab inscriptions, and possibly the Luristan Bronzes I-II and the Nineveh Lion Weights.[29] These texts all represent an archaic form of the language, and though two of them have peculiarities that set them apart within this group (i.e., the Hadad and Panammu inscriptions from ancient Yaᵓdi),[30] the general character of the group is sufficiently homogeneous to be recognized as representatives of "Old Aramaic."[31]

(2) *Official Aramaic,* from roughly 700 B.C. to 200 B.C.[32] The Aramaic of this phase, also called Reichsaramäisch, Imperial, or Standard Aramaic, is a form of the language which was not only relatively standardized, but also widespread. "Standardized" may, indeed, be too strong a word for the language of this phase and may seem to fail to reckon with minor local differences that too appear from time to time. But it is used to stress the otherwise striking homogeneity of the language at this period despite the vast range of geographical areas in which it has been found to have been in use. Moreover, it is this form of the language that we normally use to judge whether that of other phases is really related to it or not. In this phase Aramaic is attested in Egypt (chiefly in Upper Egypt at Elephantine and Aswan, but also in Lower Egypt at Saqqarah and Hermopolis West),[33] in Arabia and Palestine, in Syria and in scattered areas of Asia Minor, in Assyria and Babylonia, in Armenia, and in the ancient Indus Valley (what is now Afghanistan and Pakistan). The vast corpus of Official Aramaic texts knows of letters written on papyrus and skin, contracts or deeds of various legal proceedings, literary texts, graffiti, ostraca messages, wooden labels, clay tablets, etc., all of which present a fairly homogeneous form of the language. Local differences have been detected at times, and some have sought to distinguish between eastern and western forms of Official Aramaic.[34] But this is a debatable matter;[35] and if it is valid, it is not simply to be equated with the similar distinction made at a later phase of the language. In any case, to Official Aramaic certainly belongs the Aramaic of Ezra (minus the Masoretic encrustations),[36] and undoubtedly also the Aramaic of Daniel (at the very end of this phase).

(3) *Middle Aramaic*, from roughly 200 B.C. to A.D. 200. Here one notes the development of Official Aramaic and the emergence of "real local dialects."[37] To this phase belong the dialects of (a) *Palestine and Arabia*: Nabatean, Qumran, Murabbaᵓat, that of the inscriptions on Palestinian ossuaries and tombstones, of the Aramaic words preserved in the Greek texts of Josephus and the NT, and some of the texts of early Palestinian rabbinic literature (without their obvious later encrustations); (b) *Syria and*

Mesopotamia: those of Palmyra, Edessa, and Hatra, and perhaps also the beginnings of early Babylonian rabbinic literature.

(4) *Late Aramaic*, roughly A.D. 200 to 700. These Aramaic texts of various areas and dialects have further peculiarities that distance them even more from Official Aramaic than those in the Middle phase. They fall into two large geographic subdivisions: (a) *Western:* the dialects of Jewish Palestinian Aramaic,[38] Samaritan Aramaic, and Christian Syro-Palestinian Aramaic; (b) *Eastern:* the dialects of Syriac (further distinguished into a western [Jacobite] form and an eastern [Nestorian] form), Babylonian Talmudic Aramaic, and Mandaic.

The closing limit of this phase of the language is not easily set. 700 is taken merely as a round number close to the Muhammadan Conquest and the consequent spread of Arabic which put an end to the active use of Aramaic in many areas of the Near East.[39] But it is obvious that neither Aramaic nor Syriac died out at this time. There are, indeed, all sorts of reasons for extending the lower limit of the phase to the end of the 11th century (i.e., to the end of the Gaonic period in Palestine and Babylonia) and even to the end of the 13th century among Syriac writers (Bar Hebraeus, or Abu ᵓl-Faraj Gregory [1226-86], and his contemporaries). The extent of the areas in which Aramaic or Syriac was still spoken was greatly reduced; and the position that it assumed vis-à-vis Arabic even in those areas is problematic. Was it being used only in closed circles (domestic, scholastic, synagogal)? In any case, it is obvious that the language did not die out completely, as the following fifth phase shows, even though it is not easy to trace the line of connection between the Late and the Modern phases.

What is striking in the Late phase of Aramaic is not only the elements that set off its various local dialects (such as imperfects in *neqtol* or *liqtul*, the waning of the absolute and construct states of the noun, the piling up of pronominal forms, the widespread use of the possessive pronoun *dīl-*, etc.), but also the mounting influx of Greek words and constructions into almost all dialects of the language. Though the Hellenization of the eastern Mediterranean areas, such as Palestine and Syria, began much earlier,[40] the sparse incidence of Greek words in Aramaic texts of the Middle phase stands in contrast to that of this phase.

(5) *Modern Aramaic,* still spoken in various areas of northern Syria, Iran, Iraq and related regions. It is found in the West in isolated villages of the Anti-Lebanon region, north of Damascus (Maᶜlūla, Jubbᶜadîn, Baḫᶜa); in the East it is found in several areas (Ṭūr ᶜAbdîn, between the Lakes Urmia and Van [in Kurdistan and Azerbaijan], and north of Mossul [Iraq]).[41] The language spoken in these regions is a remnant of Aramaic or Syriac, heavily influenced, however, by other modern local languages such as Arabic, Kurdish, or Turkish.

In a sense, the reclassification of the phases of the Aramaic language that I have been proposing is nothing more than the distillation of views of scholars that have been emerging with the gradual increase of the documentation of the Aramaic language in the last two or three decades. The major divisions of "Old Aramaic" and "Official Aramaic" were already in use. What I have called "Late Aramaic" was likewise admitted by many scholars before me, even though they did not use this name. The major difference, then, lies in the recognition of the "Middle Aramaic" phase between that of "Official" and "Late" Aramaic. Given the nature of the dialects found in that phase—Palestinian, Nabatean, Edessene, Palmyrene, and Hatran, all of which coexisted more or less simultaneously—I thought that it was necessary to recognize them as a development of "Official Aramaic," but not yet the same as "Late Aramaic."

III. *Reasons for the Phases and Related Problems*

As a result of the discoveries of the last fifty to seventy-five years, we realize that the starting-point for the discussion of the phases of the Aramaic language is the relation of it to the Northwest branch of the Semitic languages. It emerges in history as a language only several centuries after the earliest attestation of the Arameans as a people, and its character is discerned in any given phase from a comparison with other phases of the language and with cognate Northwest Semitic languages.

The Arameans appear explicitly for the first time in the records of the fourth regnal year of the Assyrian king Tiglath-Pileser I (1115-1076 B.C.).[42] As far as we can judge today, the Arameans spoke a language that was apparently derived ultimately from a common Northwest Semitic stock, but that developed separately from cognate Canaanite dialects.[43] The first emergence of the language in the Old Aramaic inscriptions reveals it to be written in the alphabet of the Phoenicians.[44] Though it eventually developed on its own specific forms of some of the letters,[45] it is to be noted that the Arameans adopted the Phoenician alphabet and suited it to their distinctively Aramaic sounds.[46] Whereas Phoenician had already lost some of the original Proto-Semitic sounds by several consonantal shifts (e.g., *ḏ* had already become *z*, *ṯ̣* had already become *ṣ*, as had *ḏ̣*, *ṯ* had already become *š*—so that there were no consonants in the Phoenician alphabet to represent the Proto-Semitic sounds, *ḏ*, *ṯ*, *ḏ̣*, *ṯ̣*), Aramaic still retained the original Proto-Semitic sounds. Hence some adjustment had to be made in the use of the 22 characters of the Phoenician alphabet. Hence Aramaic *ḏ* was written, not with *d*, but with *z*; Aramaic *ṯ* was written, not with *t*, but with *š*; Aramaic *ḏ̣* was written with *q*;[47] and Aramaic *ṯ̣* was written with *ṣ*. This is the question of the treatment of the sibilants and the interdentals in Old Aramaic,[48] which is one of the characteristics of this phase.

A further characteristic of this phase of the Aramaic language is concerned with the orthography. Phoenician itself had not developed a system of writing vocalic sounds, and the diphthongs were usually contracted and represented as zero in the writing. But at an early stage the Arameans developed a system of using certain consonants to represent vocalic sounds. At first this system was confined to final long vowels: *y* was used to write long *i*, *w* to write long *u*, and *h* to write long *a*. Moreover, the diphthongs *ay* and *aw* were normally uncontracted in Aramaic, and these sounds, whether final or medial, were represented respectively as *y* or *w*, but the occasional contraction of *-ay* to *-ê* in a final position was also written with *h*. The thesis of F. M. Cross and D. N. Freedman that it was from the use of *w*, *y*, *h* as final vowel letters that the medial vowel letters were developed in Aramaic (and then spread to other Northwest Semitic languages) is still valid,[49] even though these authors had glossed over some problematic instances in their original dissertation and would now have to admit more exceptions to the occurrence of medial long vowels being written with *w* or *y*, given the further publication of Old Aramaic texts since the dissertation was written.[50] A further detail in their thesis is that *aleph* in these Old Aramaic texts was still treated as a consonant, and was not a vowel-letter. This thesis was proposed as a hypothesis; but, as far as I can see, the evidence that they amassed has been supported by subsequent texts that were published (e.g., Sefire II and III, and the more adequate publication of Sefire I by A. Dupont-Sommer and J. Starcky[51]).

An extensive critique of the thesis of Cross and Freedman has been written by D. W. Goodwin, *Text-Restoration Methods in Contemporary U.S.A. Biblical Scholarship*.[52] But it not only indulges in uncalled-for and arrogant criticism but is fundamentally misconceived; Cross and Freedman were easily able to defend their position and answer the criticism.[53] In spite of the heat engendered, there was, alas, no light. A more serious criticism of their thesis was attempted by L. A. Bange, *A Study of the Use of Vowel-Letters in Alphabetic Consonantal Writing (Inauguraldissertation 1961-62 an der Universität Oxford)*.[54] It was written almost ten years prior to its publication, contains some interesting minor corrections, but in the long run scarcely overthrows the basic thesis of Cross and Freedman.

Their treatment of the vowel-letters was first criticized by G. Garbini,[55] and a number of his points have been repeated by others, so that it merits a reconsideration. Most of his arguments, however, are based on a faulty explanation of the words that he uses as examples of forms with vowel-letters; only one of them, a proper name—which is readily arguable—might be a valid criticism.[56] In a later publication, Garbini returned to the attack and accused Cross and Freedman (and myself) of arguing in a vicious circle and without any real proof in two respects: (a) in treating final *aleph* as a consonant, not a vowel-letter; and (b) in treating most instances of medial *yodh* and *waw* as diphthongal.[57] To many readers it looks as though Cross and Freedman just asserted, for instance, that final *aleph* was consonantal and then proceeded to cite examples of it. But Garbini and their other critics fail to recognize that the hypothesis that Cross and Freedman sought to test by their examples had its starting-point, not in the Aramaic evidence alone, but in Phoenician (and a number of other Canaanite texts), in which in the early contemporary period the writing was wholly consonantal.[58] In agreement with the Phoenician consonantal *aleph,* the Arameans, it was argued, used it likewise—even as a marker of a final *a*-vowel in certain cases; and there is no instance in the Old Aramaic texts, which Cross and Freedman treated or which have subsequently been published,[59] that militates against this thesis. In the case of medial *waw* and *yodh,* their starting-point again was the normal Phoenician zero-writing of the diphthongs, but also the evidence of comparative Northwest Semitic grammar (and other comparative Semitic grammar) which would call for diphthongal usage. Thus, the Cross and Freedman thesis is not dependent on a vicious circle; the only problem with it originally was their reluctance to admit the inceptive use of medial vowel-letters in some Old Aramaic texts, for which the evidence is now clear. But this use is scarcely as abundant or widespread as the evidence in favor of their original position. In a sense, the evidence, such as it is, merely confirms the basic thrust of their original contention.

Criticism of Cross and Freedman's treatment of the Old Aramaic consonantal *aleph* has also been voiced by M. Tsevat[60] and S. Segert,[61] but their affirmation that Cross and Freedman have merely affirmed the consonantal character of *aleph* with no proof is really met only with a parallel affirmation of it as a vowel-letter. No real example of the latter is given that cannot be contested. In support of the Cross and Freedman thesis, one should perhaps recall that the prefixed negative *lā*- is never written in these texts with an *aleph;*[62] it is difficult to explain such a form if *aleph* were a real vowel-letter in this phase, especially in the light of the subsequent development in Aramaic, where it is almost always written separately and with final *aleph,* which has by this time become a vowel-letter (as far as we can judge—at least there is no reason in Official Aramaic texts to treat it any differently than it is in Biblical Aramaic). Moreover, the feminine demonstrative pronoun may seem to be a problem at first sight, in that it is written זא (Sf I A 35, [36], 37, [42]; III 9). But this form is attested in Phoenician both for the masculine[63] and for the feminine demonstrative.[64] This Phoenician evidence argues for the consonantal character of the *aleph (zaʾ);*[65] and the Phoenician origin of the borrowed alphabet would argue in favor of the same character for the *aleph* in such a form in Aramaic.

Besides the foregoing characteristics of Aramaic in this early phase (the widespread preservation of the Proto-Semitic phonemes,[66] and the development of orthographic habits from the initial Phoenician starting-point), one should also consider the following elements that are more or less distinctive of this phase of the language: (a) *morphological:* the use of *ʾnh,* "I," in contrast to *ʾnk* in Phoenician, Ugaritic, and the Zenjirli inscriptions (Hadad 1, Panammu 1); the Peal infinitive without preformative *m*- (e.g., Sf I B 32); Peal passive forms in *yuqtal;*[67] and the prefixed negative *lā-;* the 3d sg. masc. suffix on plural nouns in *-wh;* (b) *syntactic:* the use of the intensifying infinitive, resembling the infinitive absolute in Hebrew (Sf I B 30[?]; II C 8; III 2, 6, 12, 13, 18; Nerab 2:6); the use of the *waw*-consecutive (Zakir a 11). Finally, one should consider here the emergence of the post-positive article, a characteristic of this phase of Aramaic that is now clear (since it appears abundantly in the Sefire inscriptions); it is not as rare as it once seemed. It persists in later phases of the language, of course; but the real problem is to explain its origin. In this I again go along with the highly plausible suggestion made by Cross and Freedman, that it represents the addition of the deictic particle *haᵓ* (often translated "lo, behold") to the noun for emphasis.[68] The problem is to explain why it appears in the postpositive position in this language alone of the Northwest Semitic tongues.

Two problems are related to the attempt to describe the character of Old Aramaic. The first is the number of texts that should be attributed to it; or, perhaps a better way of putting it, the lower limit of the phase. I have suggested 700 B.C. as a cut-off, in dependence on other writers who have proposed this date, which should obviously be understood broadly. Cross and Freedman limited their discussion to the inscriptions from Tell Halaf, Bir-Hadad, Zakir, Sujin (as Sefire I was then called), and Bar-Rakib.[69] They treated the Hadad and Panammu inscriptions from Zenjirli in an appendix, regarding them as Aramaic "with occasional Canaanite borrowing," but in reality a sort of "archaizing Aramaic." [70] S. Segert would prefer to put the lower limit of the phase at 612 B.C.[71] More recently R. Degen, in an excellently conceived and executed comprehensive treatment of some Old Aramaic texts, limited them to Zakir, Bir-Hadad, Hama graffiti, Bar-Rākib I-III, Bar-Rākib fr. I, Sefire I-III, Luristan I, and ᶜEn-Gev Bowl, which he assigned to the tenth-eighth centuries B.C.[72] His study excels in that it is conducted on an admirable syntactic approach, which has enabled him to resolve some of the outstanding problems of phonology and morphology; and his categorization of the texts is significant. He writes, further, that "the monuments from the seventh century on agree with the texts from the fifth century B.C. in phonology, morphology, and syntax. . . . From the seventh century on begins the dissolution of the set word-order, and there begins to appear multiple word-positions that are well-known in later dialects." [73] I agree fully with the first sentence quoted here; and am inclined to go along with the basic thrust of the second.

But I find it difficult to agree with him when he omits certain inscriptions from this Old Aramaic phase; one wonders whether a new Procrustean bed has not been constructed.[74] To cite but one problematic example: I am not happy about the exclusion of the Nērab inscriptions from the phase of Old Aramaic.[75] This is not said because of the supposed presence of Akkadian (or Canaanite?) *š*- at the beginning of these inscriptions, a phenomenon that S. Kaufman has recently disposed of in an obviously enlightened solution.[76] Yet these inscriptions belong to the phase of Old Aramaic because of certain forms that are found in them (*nṣr,* "guard, preserve" [Nērab 1:12-13], instead of *nṭr;* the 3d sg. masc. suffix in *-wh* [*qdmwh,* Nērab 2:2 (cf. *ᵓlwh,* Sf III 8)]; the prefixed negative *l-* (Nērab 2:4, 6, 8) and of the syntactic feature of the intensifying infinitive (*hwm* [Nērab 2:6]). One would have to wait to see what elements in these inscriptions Degen would consider different in syntax from the Old Aramaic word order, before one could agree with the exclusion of them from this phase. These inscriptions are often dated ca. 700 B.C., and they may represent borderline cases.[77] But they contain enough characteristics of the Old Aramaic phase to keep them there. And the same would have to be said about some of the other inscriptions mentioned above in part II.

A second problem of a different sort has been raised by G. Garbini and R. Degen. In my commentary on the Sefire inscriptions I considered the Aramaic of this phase to be "definitely under Canaanite influence."[78] In this judgment I was concurring with that of C. Brockelmann, W. F. Albright, Cross and Freedman, et al.[79] Degen has objected to this characterization of Old Aramaic and called in question its so-called Canaanitisms.[80] Garbini has not spared his scorn of it, when he writes, "'cananeismi' cari agli studiosi ancora legati alla tradizione ottocentesca."[81] Concerning the Canaanitisms, Degen writes:

> Phenomena so described and originally isolated have subsequently often been found in later discovered inscriptions; the correctness of the original name has not yet been demonstrated. In my opinion, they must be regarded as genuine components of Old Aramaic as long as their dependence on "Canaanite" cannot be proven. Since this proof is lacking, one can only say that the phenomenon in question is attested in several of the Semitic languages.[82]

In a footnote Degen discusses the instances of the imperfect with *waw*-consecutive in the Zakir inscription (a 11, [12], 15), which is otherwise attested only in Hebrew, Moabite, and probably in the Aḥiram inscription in Phoenician.[83] This is the only item that Degen discusses at any length, and most of the data used by him taken from South Arabic are irrelevant.

However, when one considers some of the orthographic, morphological, and syntactic elements that I have discussed above as characteristics of Old Aramaic, one would have to consider some sort of Canaanite influence. As for the *waw*-consecutive, it is at home in the three above-mentioned Northwest Semitic languages; it is not found in any of the later phases of Aramaic. Many features of Old Aramaic are found in later phases of the languages, and these may not count as "characteristics" of the Old Aramaic phase. The characteristics are not overly abundant, but they are in the Old phase and do mark it off from what follows. The *yuqtal*-forms, the Peal infinitives without preformative *m-,* the use of the infinitive to intensify a finite verb, the use of the *waw*-consecutive are phenomena that I would consider Canaanite. These phenomena are not known in the later phases of the language and therefore they are not "genuine components" of the language.[84] Moreover, the mere fact that an alleged Canaanitism does turn up at a later stage of the language does not show that it is a "genuine component," because it still has to be shown that it is a *native* element. The element might have been borrowed at any early period and might have persisted in isolated forms in the language or in isolated areas. This is the explanation that I prefer to give for the instances of the Peal infinitive without preformative *m*-, which is found in inscriptions of this period,[85] and even for the stereotyped לאמר which is found in Official Aramaic texts, not only in the early Aššur Ostracon, but in Elephantine texts as well.[86] Merely to point to the occurrence of infinitives without *mem* in a later phase does not prove that it is genuinely Aramaic, since that obscures the question of origin.

It may be that the term Canaanitism should be dropped and an attempt made to specify the Canaanite dialect which is involved. If this is all that Degen means, then I should agree. E. Y. Kutscher used to like to speak of "languages in contact,"[87] and in such a sense the source of the Canaanite interference in this phase of Aramaic should have to be made more specific.

A slightly different attitude toward the problem has been adopted by G. Garbini. He quotes approvingly S. Moscati's view of the "non-existence of the Aramaic-Canaanite subdivision in the 2d millennium B.C."[88] Moreover, he refuses to admit that the known first millennium Northwest Semitic languages can be reduced to the Canaanite-Aramaic "binomial." This is partly because he refuses to see Ugaritic as Canaanite and partly because he prefers to treat so-called Yaʾudic as distinct from Aramaic—if I understand him correctly.[89] He lays great stress on Amorite as the background of an Aramaic-Arabic branch and as having great influence on Canaanite, "Yaʾudic," and Ugaritic. The whole is a process of Amoritization *(amorreizazione)*. The following chart gives a quick view of his theory:[90]

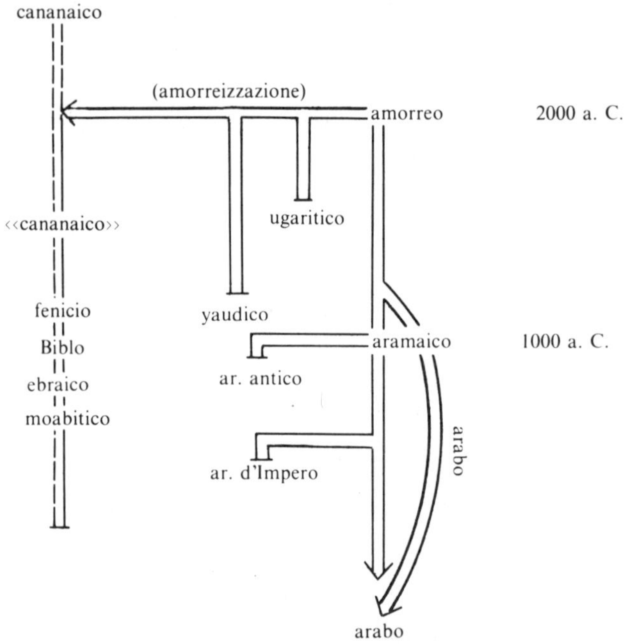

The upshot is that those components of Old Aramaic that are often regarded as (ottocentesque) Canaanitisms really become Amoriticisms, and a direct line of descent from Old Aramaic to Official Aramaic is denied.

Now it may be that the usual division of the Northwest Semitic languages into two branches, Canaanite and Aramaic,[91] is in need of revision and more account should be taken of the Amorite culture and language in Palestine and Syria of the second millennium. However, the evidence for a sweeping revision of the relationships between the Northwest Semitic languages, such as Garbini proposes, is simply non-existent. It is all too speculative. What little we know about the Amorite language is almost wholly confined to proper names,[92] and to use such material to construct a more elaborate explanation of the relation of Northwest Semitic languages in this early period is asking for too much.

The thesis that Garbini is proposing is speculative and far less well-founded than the Cross and Freedman thesis that he otherwise criticizes. Garbini may be right in rejecting the idea of Old Aramaic as a "Mischsprache,"[93] or as "una lingua ibrida, mosaico di elementi cananaici et aramaici," a description that he attributes to me,[94] though I have never so expressed it; nor would I. One has to insist, with him, that Old Aramaic has a well-defined physiognomy; but that does not prevent it from being "under Canaanite influence," especially when one realizes that part of that well-defined physiognomy is a stock of material common to Old Aramaic and Official Aramaic and of other elements that I have tried to isolate above as "characteristics" of Old Aramaic (some of which are legitimate Aramaic developments from Phoenician; others are Canaanite borrowings). However, it has to be noted that much of the well-defined Aramaic physiognomy of Old Aramaic will be verified in the Hadad and Panammu inscriptions of Zenjirli as well, despite the peculiarities that these inscriptions have. Operative in any judgment about the Aramaic character of texts in the Old phase is the use—at least subconscious—of data known to characterize the Official Aramaic texts; they become the prime analogate by which one judges that the Old Aramaic texts belong to the Aramaic family. Details such as these are part of that physiognomy: the post-positive article in *-aʾ*, the masc. pl. emphatic ending in *-ayyāʾ*, the absolute masc. pl. ending in *-īn*, the relative *zy*, the 1st sg. personal pronoun in *ʾnh*, the *br* form of "son," the absence of niphal forms, the 3d sg. masc. sf. on pl. nouns in *-wh* (> *-why*),[95] etc. (the list could be prolonged).

Finally, in the light of the foregoing, the question might be raised whether the first phase of the Aramaic language could not better be called "Proto-Aramaic," and whether "Old Aramaic" might not be a better label for "Official" or "Imperial" Aramaic. This would enable one to use strictly chronological names: Proto-Aramaic, Old Aramaic, Middle Aramaic, Late Aramaic, Modern Aramaic. The main problem is the conventional use to which certain terms have already been put (e.g., "Old Aramaic"), as explained above. There is the further difficulty that "Proto-Aramaic" has already been used to designate a form of the language that some scholars think they can detect in the second millennium B.C.[96] In the light of these difficulties, I think that it is better to stick with the ones proposed above.

So much for the discussion of the Old Aramaic phase and its problems. We now pass to the phase of Official Aramaic.

The first problem that confronts one in the discussion of Official Aramaic texts is whether they may be clearly divided into Eastern and Western dialects. This distinction is well known in the phase that I call Late Aramaic; and J. C. Greenfield has tried to show the evidence for it even in the phase of Old Aramaic.[97] E. Y. Kutscher presents a strong case for the distinction in the phase of Official Aramaic.[98] But he never finished his discussion of it, and hence I hesitate to be too critical of it. On the one hand, his evidence for Eastern Aramaic in this phase depends on the provenience or supposed provenience of certain documents (e.g., the Aššur Ostracon, the Behistun inscription are undoubtedly of historical eastern provenience). But even Kutscher eventually sensed the difficulty that one faces about the origin of Aḥiqar (East? West?); and the "eastern" character of the letter of the Elephantine Jews (*AP* 30) is an issue that must be further investigated, since it is far from clear. On the other hand, Kutscher eventually admitted that he had not taken into consideration a major bulk of this Official Aramaic material. What he did do[99] has to be taken seriously; but that has not closed the matter, and the eight characteristics of so-called eastern Official Aramaic isolated by him need rigorous scrutiny. Judged against the whole corpus of Official Aramaic texts, they evoke no little hesitation. Kutscher had relied on the work of Y. Muffs[100] in part, and appealed to the "difference between deeds, in which the wording does not change too easily, and administrative documents that try to keep as close as possible to the Eastern *OfA* [= Official Aramaic]."[101] This may be, but Kutscher has not presented the evidence that bears him out. Moreover, when at the end of his discussion of Official Aramaic distinctions he says that "it is impossible to deal here with the language of the letters of Cowley and of the ostraca,"[102] then he is saying that the last word in the matter has not yet been spoken. Because of this and because of several hesitations about a number of the eight criteria that Kutscher has proposed, I hesitate to use the distinction of eastern and western Official Aramaic.

I recognize with H. L. Ginsberg that "official Aramaic was never absolutely uniform except in intention."[103] But I have a problem with the rest of his judgment, that ". . . in the course of time, especially after the destruction of the Achaemenian empire, [it] became more and more colored by the spoken languages of the writers." *In se,* I fully agree with what is said here, but it is the coloring of Official Aramaic after the Achaemenian empire that leads me to conclude that a new phase of the language has to be reckoned with, viz., the Middle Aramaic phase. Ginsberg's presupposition, when he wrote that statement, was that Official Aramaic persisted as such, and in this I hesitate. I am not trying to maintain that Official Aramaic was monolithic; I recognize that the division of it into eastern and western is debatable, but it needs more evidence and a better sifting of the data for support.

A more crucial problem is the lower limit of Official Aramaic, or the existence of the phase of Middle Aramaic. Kutscher eventually accepted the phase in the sense in which I had proposed it.[104] I have adopted the suggestion of S. Segert that the cut-off date should be 200 B.C. rather than 300 B.C.[105] The main reason for the distinction of Middle Aramaic from Official Aramaic is the coexistence of a number of local dialects: Palestinian Aramaic (from Jerusalem, Qumran, Murabbaᶜat, Seiyal, etc.),[106] Nabatean, Palmyrene, Hatran, and the early Syriac material. Of these forms of Aramaic the closest to Official Aramaic seems to be that represented in Palestine, and I tend to regard this as the direct lineal descent, with the others as manifestations of local dialects or side developments. I should be ready to consider the distinction between eastern and western forms of the language in this phase; but this has not yet been worked out in detail.

Special note, however, has to be made here of the long neglected early Syriac inscriptions, texts from Edessa, Dura Europos, and their environs. They date from the first to the third centuries in the Christian era, but are almost exclusively written by non-Christians and certainly antedate the rise of Christian Syriac literature. They are important because of certain orthographic, phonetic, and morphological peculiarities which relate them to the Middle phase of Aramaic (because of what K. Beyer has called the *Einschlag* of Official Aramaic still present in them[107]) and set them off from classical Syriac of the Late phase. For instance, the preformative of the 3d masc. sg. and pl. of the imperfect is still *y-* in most instances (and not yet *n-*); the *śīn* of earlier Aramaic, which becomes *samekh* in later Syriac, is represented in these texts by *šīn*; short *o* and *u* are still written defectively (in contrast to the usual full writing of later Syriac).[108]

When one takes cognizance of this early Syriac material along with the growing corpus of Palestinian Aramaic, which must be recognized as existing more or less at the same time as Nabatean, Palmyrene, and Hatran Aramaic, then there is real reason to speak of Aramaic of the Middle phase.

Why make the lower limit of this period A.D. 200? This is a somewhat arbitrary date, adopted mainly because of the beginning of the rabbinic literary tradition that coincides with the codification of the Mishnah by R. Judah the Prince. Moreover, it is not far removed from the beginning of the classical Syriac literary period. With further study and the further acquisition of Aramaic texts, it may be possible to specify the limit better. I have toyed with the date of the Bar Cochba revolt (A.D. 135), but that would cut out later Palmyrene material.

There are, however, some scholars who think that the Aramaic of the last two centuries B.C. and of the first two centuries A.D. should be considered part of Official or Imperial Aramaic. For example, P. Grelot, in his review of the first edition of my commentary on the *Genesis Apocryphon,* wrote that "there are hardly any differences between this language [i.e., that of 1QapGen] and those of Daniel, of the fragments of Enoch (4Q), of the Prayer of Nabonidus, of the Testament of Levi (4Q). The differences of orthography can be explained by the fact that the copy would have been *dictated,* and not read by the scribe from another manuscript. It is a question in all these cases of a literary Aramaic which was able to impose itself on a more developed spoken language, already oriented toward the peculiar forms attested in the Palestinian targum."[109] Similarly, A. Díez Macho writes that "the targum of Job of Qumran Cave XI (11QtgJob) was written in the literary Aramaic called 'imperial' or, with the German designation, 'Reichsaramäisch.'"[110] Or again, "all the Aramaic writings of Qumran or Murabbaᶜat have been written in this type of Aramaic. It is a question of the Aramaic which followed that called 'Old Aramaic,' of which Rainer Degen recently published an excellent grammar. . . . Klaus Beyer, who is preparing a grammar of Imperial Aramaic, situates it between the 5th century B.C. and the 4th century A.D., but warns that since the second century B.C. this Aramaic bears the impress of spoken local dialects."[111]

Aside from the fact that the last half of Díez Macho's last statement merely points up in its own way the very distinction that I have been trying to make, it is obvious that he and Grelot are thinking only of a lineal connection between Official Aramaic, Qumran Aramaic, and the Aramaic of *the* (so-called) Palestinian Targum. The statement attributed to Beyer at least allows for the other dialects that constitute part of the evidence for the Middle phase.

At issue here are several things that often enter the discussion: (1) whether one can speak of the form*s* of Aramaic that are attested between 200 B.C. and A.D. 200 as the same as those which preceded them (from 700–200 B.C.)—all of them, not just Qumram Aramaic; (2) whether the forms of Aramaic that develop after A.D. 200 must not be reckoned as a still further development (with its clear distinction into Eastern and Western Aramaic); and (3) whether the distinction between literary and spoken Aramaic, that has recently been introduced into parts of the discussion, is a tolerable way of clinging to the label of "Official" or "Imperial" Aramaic for all of this. The latter distinction is invoked to establish a synchronic explanation for various forms of so-called Official Aramaic: Qumran Aramaic as "literary" Aramaic, that of the Palestinian targums as "spoken" Aramaic, all of which allegedly comes from the same chronological period.

Involved in this view of Official Aramaic is the claim that is made by Díez Macho and his followers for early dating of the Palestinian targums, and especially of that of Tg. Neofiti 1.[112] I have already set forth my hesitations about the list of arguments presented by Díez Macho for an early dating in the introduction to the volume on Genesis in that targum.[113] More recently, he has returned to the question of the language that is found in that targum, in an article entitled, "Le targum palestinien," in which he seems to follow the opinion of K. Beyer already quoted that Official Aramaic stretched from the fifth century B.C. to the fourth century A.D. and brands my presentation of the phases of Aramaic as "une présentation diachronique simpliste qui ne semble pas tenir suffisament compte des arguments favorisant la solution synchronique du problème. . . . On n'envisage pas sérieusement que l'araméen de Qumrân et celui du TargP soient contemporain, le premier littéraire, le second parlé, populaire."[114] This is Díez Macho's main contention (and is shared by P. Grelot, by implication at least), that the classic (non-Qumran) targums of Palestine date from the first century (or earlier) and have been composed in *spoken* Aramaic, which is somewhat different from the literary Aramaic of the Qumran material. This, of course, allows Díez Macho to claim an early date for the Targum Neofiti 1, which he is publishing, and which he would like to see utilized for all sorts of reasons in NT study.

But before such a distinction, which lays claims to a "synchronic" approach to the matter and, therefore, is not "simplistic," can be admitted, there are a number of factors to be considered: (1) Palestinian Aramaic in the Roman period is not represented solely by the literary texts of Qumran; there are inscriptions on tombstones and ossuaries, letters of Bar Cochba and his colleagues, legal and commercial contracts or deeds, etc.[115] Most of these texts have come to light in the last 25-50 years and they force us to raise the question about what we know of a distinction between literary and spoken Aramaic of this period. (2) How can one draw a distinction between common, spoken, or popular Aramaic and literary Aramaic in an historic period? We all recognize that there is a difference between the spoken and literary form of the language, and that the development of a language begins in the mouths of those who speak it and only after a certain amount of time does it invade the written language itself. It is the spoken form of a language that is alive and developing, and it manifests itself gradually in writing despite the weight of the literary tradition. But when one is dealing with ancient written texts, especially of limited number, and of (in some cases) uncertain provenience, it is a moot question whether one can say that one text is written in a literary form of the language and that another is composed in the spoken or popular form—unless, of course, one has some independent, extrinsic evidence of such a distinction. How do we know what the spoken form of Aramaic was like in first-century Palestine? There is no reason to deny that the targums came into existence as orally translated forms of the Scriptures being read in Hebrew in the synagogues. We may even like to assume that the meturgeman turned the sacred Hebrew text into the currently spoken form of Aramaic so that it would fully correspond to the very purpose of a targum. Moreover, from references in rabbinic literature we know that *written* targums were at one point prohibited. And who has not heard by now of the immuring of a copy of the written targum of Job under R. Gamaliel I during some construction on the site of the Jerusalem temple?[116] But do such reasons (speculative assumptions and unrelated historical data) amount to proof that the Aramaic text in any of the classic non-Qumran targums of Palestinian provenience (Pseudo-Jonathan, the Fragmentary Targum, Neofiti 1—or even Onqelos) preserves a popular, spoken form of Aramaic in contrast to the literary Aramaic of the Qumran texts? Moreover, we must not forget that the targumim are a form of literature, an Aramaic creation. The presumption would be that they are just as much a form of literary Aramaic as that of the Qumran texts. For a synchronic approach to this matter to be valid, one would have to show that the Aramaic of the so-called Palestinian targums is, in fact, contemporary with that of the Qumran literature. In the case of the latter there is archaeological evidence for dating it prior to A.D. 70. The only reasons that are ever given for the first-century dating of the so-called Palestinian targums are philological, based on the assumption that we can identify their language with the spoken, popular form of first-century Palestinian Aramaic. The loud and constant assertion of this thesis evokes only an equally vociferous counter-assertion. (3) It is well known that the Aramaic in the classic, non-Qumran targums abounds in Greek words that have been transliterated and/or slightly Aramaized. This, however, is not necessarily a sign of antiquity or of first-century Palestinian provenience; Greek words in such texts do not necessarily mean that the texts themselves date from the beginning of Hellenization in Palestine.[117] Rather, the closest parallels to the sort of Aramaic in which the non-Qumran targums are written are found in the inscriptions from synagogues and tombs of the Byzantine period in Palestine (roughly from the third to the sixth centuries),[118] and often enough in the literary texts of rabbinical literature and classical Syriac.[119]

But E. Y. Kutscher and J. C. Greenfield have insisted that common or popular Aramaic has been used in *Genesis Rabbah*.[120] This I would not contest. But that writing comes clearly from a period later than the Middle phase of Aramaic; it is usually ascribed (at the earliest) to the first generation of the Palestinian Amoraim.[121]

The debate over the phase of Middle Aramaic will continue until more reliable criteria for dating some of the texts emerge. The biggest problem is the dating of the non-Qumran targums. As far as I am concerned, until proof emerges to establish an earlier date, they are to be reckoned as part of the literature of the Late Aramaic phase, when due allowance is made for their obviously later encrustations at times.

These are the main issues that confront one who is concerned about the phases of the Aramaic language today. Further discussion will obviously clarify a number of the points that I have raised above.

NOTES TO CHAPTER 3

*This essay appears here for the first time; it is a revision of one of the Speaker's Lectures, delivered at Oxford University in May 1974.

[1]*The Genesis Apocryphon of Qumran Cave I: A Commentary* (BibOr 18; Rome: Biblical Institute, 1966) 19–20 n. 60. The second edition (see p. 22 above, n. 27) appeared in 1971, with a slight modification of the phases that will be mentioned below. See also "Ancient Aramaic Language," *New Catholic Encyclopedia* (New York: McGraw-Hill, 1967), 1. 736-37.

[2]*Die aramaistische Forschung seit Theodor Nöldeke's Veroffentlichungen* (Leiden: Brill, 1939; reprinted, 1964) vii-ix, 1, and passim.

[3]*The Brooklyn Museum Aramaic Papyri: New Documents of the Fifth Century B.C. from the Jewish Colony at Elephantine* (New Haven: Yale University, 1953; reprinted, New York: Arno, 1969) 4-7.

[4]"The Language of the Genesis Apocryphon: A Preliminary Study," *Aspects of the Dead Sea Scrolls* (Scripta hierosolymitana, 4; Jerusalem: Magnes, 1958) 1-35, esp. pp. 1-3. Cf. "Aramaic," *Encyclopaedia judaica* (Jerusalem: Keter; New York: Macmillan, 1971), 3. 259-87.

[5]*A Short Grammar of Biblical Aramaic* (Berrien Springs, MI: Andrews University, 1966) 2.

[6]*Altaramäische Grammatik* (p. 23 above, n. 53), 5: "Der so aufgefasste Bereich des Altaramäischen entspricht grundsätzlich der Terminologie von Franz Rosenthal und anderen Semitisten (Nabatäisch und Palmyrenisch sind jedoch nicht einbezogen[!]), während sich die unter demselben Titel (nach Abschluss des vorliegenden Werkes) 1970 erschienene 'Altaramäische Grammatik' von Reinhold [*sic*] Degen nur auf die Texte aus der älteren Periode, d.h. aus 9.-7. Jh. v. u. Z., beschränkt, die in der vorliegenden Grammatik als 'früharamäisch' bezeichnet werden." To be fair to Segert, one has to know that his manuscript was already composed and lay with the publisher in East Germany for many years. It is a wonder that it finally appeared at all; and for that we are grateful to him. The advantage of it is that it stresses the homogeneity of the language in what I should call the "Old Aramaic," "Official Aramaic," and "Middle Aramaic" phases (from the latter phase he includes even Qumran Aramaic texts under "Altaramäisch"). He marks the differences of the dialects, indeed (using sigla such as AA [Altaramäisch], BA [Biblisch-Aramäisch], FA [Früharamäisch], Ja [Jaʾudisch], Q [Qumran-Aramäisch], RA [Reichsaramäisch]); but it is difficult to acquire a good view in this grammar of the nature of any of these dialects. Moreover, see n. 13 below.

[7](Munich: M. Hueber, 1928) 59-80. "Neuaramäisch" includes for him the dialects of Maʿlula and Urmia (pp. 80-95).

[8]This is similarly used by P. Grelot, *RB* 80 (1973) 144.

[9]"Arameans, Aramaic, and the Bible," *JNES* 7 (1948) 65-90, esp. p. 71.

[10]*Early Hebrew Orthography: A Study of the Epigraphic Evidence* (AOS 36; New Haven: American Oriental Society, 1952) 21 n. 1 ("from the tenth to the seventh centuries B.C."). See also F. M. Cross, Jr., "Semitische Epigraphik," *RGG*[3] (ed. K. Galling; Tübingen: Mohr [Siebeck]) 2 (1958) 523-26, esp. col. 523 ("Altaramäisch, 10-8. Jh. v. Chr.").

[11]L. Koehler and W. Baumgartner, *Lexicon in Veteris Testamenti libros* (Leiden: Brill, 1958) xix.

[12]*An Introduction to the Comparative Grammar of the Semitic Languages* (Porta linguarum orientalium, ns 6; Wiesbaden: Harrassowitz, 1964) 11.

[13]"Zur Schrift und Orthographie der altaramäischen Stelen von Sfire," *ArOr* 32 (1964) 110-26, esp. pp. 115-18; see also his review of J. J. Koopmans, *Aramäische Chrestomathie*, ibid., 454; "Aramäische Studien: III. Zum Problem der altaramäischen Dialekte," ibid., 26 (1958) 564.

[14]"The Aramaic of Daniel," *Notes on Some Problems in the Book of Daniel* (London: Tyndale, 1965) 50.

[15]"Der reichsaramäische Einschlag in der ältesten syrischen Literatur," *ZDMG* 116 (1966) 242-54, esp. p. 247 n. 10.

[16]*Altaramäische Grammatik der Inschriften des 10.-8. Jh. v. Chr.* (Abhandlungen für die Kunde des Morgenlandes, 38/3; Wiesbaden: Deutsche morgenländische Gesellschaft, 1969) 1-3.

[17]"Np. *adīna* 'Freitag,'" *Ungarische Jahrbücher* 7 (1927) 89-121, esp. p. 91 n. 1.

[18]"Aramaic Dialect Problems," *AJSL* 50 (1933-34) 1-9; 52 (1935-36) 95-103. E. Y. Kutscher ("New Aramaic Texts," *JAOS* 74 [1954] 233-48, esp. p. 246) and R. A. Bowman ("Arameans, Aramaic, and the Bible," *JNES* 7 [1948] 65-90, esp. p. 76) have further cited the Sheikh Fadl Tomb Inscriptions from a site near Oxyrhynchus in Egypt, which they date to 663 B.C. and take as an indication of the use of this sort of Aramaic in Egypt in the 7th century B.C. However, J. Naveh (*The Development of the Aramaic Script* [Proceedings of the Israel Academy of Sciences and Humanities, 5/1; Jerusalem: Israel Academy, 1970] 41), after a fresh study of the original photographs, has concluded that paleographically "the inscriptions are from approximately the second quarter of the fifth century B.C.E."

[19]*BMAP*, 6 n. 11.

[20]*Die aramaistische Forschung,* 92.

[21]KB, xxxvi-xli. By "Aramaic texts from Egypt," we mean those published by A. H. Sayce and A. E. Cowley, *Aramaic Papyri Discovered at Assuan* (London: A. Moring, 1906); E. Sachau. *Aramäische Papyrus und Ostraka aus einer jüdischen Militär-Kolonie zu Elephantine. Altorientalische Sprachdenkmäler des 5. Jahrhunderts vor Chr.* (Leipzig: Hinrichs, 1911); N. Aimé-Giron, *Textes araméens d'Egypte* (Cairo: Institut français d'archéologie orientale, 1931); "Adversaria semitica," *BIFAO* 38 (1939) 1-63; E. G. Kraeling, *BMAP* (n. 3 above); G. R. Driver, *Aramaic Documents of the Fifth Century B.C.: Transcribed and Edited* (Oxford: Clarendon, 1954; reprinted, Osnabrück: Zeller, 1968); an abridged and revised edition of the same title was subsequently issued [without plates] (Oxford: Clarendon, 1957; further revised [with pages of additions and corrections], 1965); E. Bresciani and M. Kamil, "Le lettere aramaiche di Hermopoli," *Atti della Accademia Nazionale dei Lincei,* Memorie, Classe di scienze morali. . . , 8/12, fasc. 5 (Rome: Accademia Nazionale dei Lincei, 1966) 357-428 (+ pls. I-X). The foregoing list gives the main collections of so-called Egyptian Aramaic texts; many further texts were published singly in various periodicals. Convenient handbook-collections of these texts can be found in the following: A. Cowley, *Aramaic Papyri of the Fifth Century B.C.: Edited with Translation and Notes* (Oxford: Clarendon, 1923; reprinted, Osnabrück: Zeller, 1967); A. Ungnad, *Aramäische Papyrus aus Elephantine: Kleine Ausgabe unter Zugrundelegung von Eduard Sachau's Erstausgabe* (Leipzig: Hinrichs, 1911); B. Porten and J. C. Greenfield, *Jews of Elephantine and Arameans of Syene: Aramaic Texts with Translation* (Jerusalem: Hebrew University, 1974).

[22]This is a commonly used title for the texts published by G. R. Driver (see the preceding note).

[23]KB, xl.

[24]Ibid., xli. Or better, "Modern Aramaic." See n. 41 below.

[25]"Language" (n. 4 above), 1. At least so I read his first paragraph, which is scarcely clear, in the light of what follows in the rest of the article.

[26]Ibid., 3. In a later article ("Aramaic," *Current Trends in Linguistics: 6. Linguistics in South West Asia and North Africa* [The Hague: Mouton, 1971] 347-412, esp. p. 347) he speaks of Rosenthal's division as "the accepted division" (Old Aramaic, Middle Aramaic, Late Aramaic), but then he abandons it in favor of mine.

[27]Now that the Targum of Job from Qumran Cave XI is published and the language of it has been examined, it seems that the *Genesis Apocryphon* represents a stage of Middle Aramaic that is later than that of the targum (see further p. 164 below); hence we may have to date the *Genesis Apocryphon* more specifically to the first century A.D. (without, however, being apodictic about it).

[28]On this problem, see further p. 63 below.

[29]Most of these texts can be found in *KAI* (§201 [Bir Hadad], §202 [Zakir], §203-13 [Hamath graffiti], §214 [Hadad], §215 [Panammu], §216-21 [Bar-Rākib inscriptions], §222-24 [Sefire inscriptions; see further my commentary, *The Aramaic Inscriptions of Sefîre* (BibOr 19; Rome: Biblical Institute, 1967)], 225-26 [Nērab], 231 (Tell Halaf), 232 (Hazaʾel). See further J. C. L. Gibson, *Textbook of Syrian Semitic Inscriptions: Volume II, Aramaic Inscriptions* (p. 24 above, n. 56).

[30]The language of these two inscriptions should not be called "Yaʾudic" (see my commentary on *The Aramaic Inscriptions of Sefîre* [BibOr 19; Rome: Biblical Institute, 1967] 62-63). The peculiarities in them are not sufficient to merit the designation of a "Sondersprache," as J. Friedrich once sought to characterize it (see "Skizze der Sprache von Jaʾudi im nördlichen Syrien (8. Jhd. v. Chr.)," *Phönizisch-punische Grammatik* [AnOr 32; Rome: Biblical Institute, 1951] 153-62; "Zur Stellung des Jaudischen innerhalb der nordwestsemitischen Sprachgeschichte," *Studies in Honor of Benno Landsberger* [Chicago: University of Chicago, 1965] 425-29). See G. Garbini, "Studi aramaici—1-2," *AION* 29 (1969) 1-15, esp. pp. 1-8; "L'Aramaico antico," *Atti della Accademia Nazionale dei Lincei,* Memorie, Classe di scienze morali. . . , 8/7, fasc. 5; Rome: Accademia Nazionale dei Lincei, 1956) 242-43.

R. Degen (*Altaramäische Grammatik* [n. 16 above], 2 n. 17) recognizes that Friedrich's work is "weitgehend überholt," but he still persists in regarding these inscriptions as representatives of a "Sondersprache" and promises a new grammatical treatment of them. To be noted, however, is that Friedrich's *Skizze* has not been included in the new edition of his Phoenician grammar, published in collaboration with W. Röllig, *Phönizisch-punische Grammatik* (AnOr 46; Rome: Biblical Institute, 1970).

J. C. Greenfield ("קווים דיאלקטיים בארמית הקדומה [Dialect Traits in Early Aramaic]," *Lĕšonénu* 32 [1967-68] 359-68) came closer to the truth of the matter in seeing these inscriptions as fundamentally part of "Old Aramaic." A refutation of Friedrich is included in E. Y. Kutscher's article, "Aramaic," *Current Trends* (n. 26 above) 350-51; cf. H. L. Ginsberg, "The Classification of North-West Semitic Languages," *Akten des XXIV. internationalen Orientalisten-Kongresses* (Wiesbaden: Harrassowitz, 1959) 256-57; H. Tadmor, "Azriyau of Yaudi," *Studies in the Bible* (ed. C. Rabin; Scripta hierosolymitana, 8; Jerusalem: Magnes, 1961) 232-71.

[31]For the texts of Palestinian provenience, see the list given on p. 99–100 below. I have not included here the following inscriptions, which may be Ammonite written in Old Aramaic script (at least they are so judged by F. M. Cross): Amman Citadel Inscription (see S. H. Horn, "The Ammān Citadel Inscription," *BASOR* 193 [1969] 2-13; F. M. Cross, "Epigraphic Notes on the Ammān Citadel Inscription," ibid., 13-19); Deir ʿAlla Inscription (see H. J. Franken, "Texts from the Persian Period from Tell Deir ʿAlla," *VT* 17 [1967] 479-81; this text was originally wrongly dated. See further J. Naveh, "The Date of the Deir *ʿAllā Inscription in Aramaic Script,*" *IEJ* 17 [1967] 256-58; F. M. Cross, "Epigraphic Notes," 14 n. 2; "Ammonite Ostraca from Heshbon: Heshbon Ostraca IV-VIII," *AUSS* 13 [1975] 1-20, esp. pp. 11-12). See now J. Hoftijzer and G. van der Kooij, *Aramaic Texts from Deir ʿAlla* (Documenta et monumenta orientis antiqui, 19; Leiden: Brill, 1976); and my review, *CBQ* 40 (1978) 93-95. If one were not to agree with Cross and were to regard these as Aramaic, then they would have to be included in the above list.

[32]Originally, I set the lower limit as 300 B.C. (see *The Genesis Apocryphon of Qumran Cave 1* [1966], 19 n. 60), taking 300 B.C. as a round number shortly after the time of the conquest of the East by Alexander the Great. The waning of Aramaic as a *lingua franca* and the rise of Greek in its place in the eastern Mediterranean world was the main reason for that cut-off point. However, further consideration of a number of texts and of the problem of the Aramaic of Daniel have moved me to set the lower limit at about 200 B.C. But even that should not be pressed too rigidly.

[33]For the texts from Hermopolis West, see those published by E. Bresciani and M. Kamil in n. 21 above. A number of texts have also been found at Saqqarah (e.g., the letter of King Adon to an Egyptian Pharaoh, see pp. 231–42 below), but they have not yet been published. See the preliminary reports on these discoveries in the following articles: J. Leclant, "Fouilles et travaux en Egypte et au Soudan," *Orientalia* 37 (1968) 103 (mentions 51 Aramaic papyri); 38 (1969) 254 (mentions 83 Aramaic papyri); 42 (1973) 400 (". . . plus de 230 fragments de papyri démotiques, grecs et même araméens").

[34]E.g., E. Y. Kutscher, "Aramaic," *Current Trends* (n. 26 above), 361-62; J. C. Greenfield ("Standard Literary Aramaic," *Actes du premier congrès international de linguistique sémitique et chamito-sémitique Paris 16-19 juillet 1969* (The Hague: Mouton, 1974) 280-89.

[35]E.g., A. F. Johns, *Short Grammar* (n. 5 above), 2. He speaks against the division at this early stage.

[36]By "Masoretic encrustations" I mean chiefly the vocalization of Biblical Aramaic in the different later traditions (Tiberian, Palestinian, or Babylonian). At times, especially in the Tiberian system, certain forms have been Hebraized; others have been vocalized according to a pronunciation that was characteristic of later periods (and is attested in Jewish Palestinian Aramaic or in Syriac). The distinctions between *Qĕrê* and *Kĕtîb* is often an example of this (e.g., the Masoretic pronunciation of the 2d sg. masc. pronominal suffix on *plural* nouns as *-āk*, in contrast to the *Kĕtîb* which preserves the *y* [= older *ayk*]; the segholate forms of nouns [like *melek*, instead of *mĕlēk*]; or the occurrence of lengthened vowels in open pretonic syllables [e.g., ᵓ*ābî*, instead of ᵓ*ăbî*]. See further H. H. Powell, *The Supposed Hebraisms in the Grammar of the Biblical Aramaic* (University of California Publications, Semitic Philology, 1; Berkeley: University of California, 1906; F. R. Blake, *A Resurvey of Hebrew Tenses with an Appendix, Hebrew Influence on Biblical Aramaic* (Rome: Biblical Institute, 1951) 81-96.

[37]To use the phrase of W. Baumgartner quoted above, p. 59 (see n. 23).

[38]I retain this name for such Aramaic at this period, along with F. Rosenthal (*A Grammar of Biblical Aramaic* [Porta linguarum orientalium, ns 5; Wiesbaden: Harrassowitz, 1961] 5). Others, e.g., E. Y. Kutscher ("Aramaic," *Encyclopaedia judaica,* 3. 270), have objected to the use of this name, preferring to speak of "Galilean Aramaic." The extent to which this is a better designation is quite debatable.

I would include under this heading not only the so-called Palestinian targums and the usual literary texts of the late Tannaᵓitic and Amoriac periods, but also the inscriptions from numerous synagogues of Palestine (for a list of which, see *MPAT*, App. A1–A56.

[39]See T. Nöldeke, *Compendious Syriac Grammar* (tr. J. A. Crichton; London: Williams & Norgate, 1904) xxxiii.

[40]See further p. 32 above.

[41]In general, see F. Rosenthal, *Die aramaistische Forschung* (note 2 above), 104-5, 160-72, 255-69; H. Fleisch, *Introduction à l'étude des langues sémitiques: Eléments de bibliographie* (Paris: Maisonneuve, 1947) 84-87; J. Friedrich, "Das Neusyrische als Typus einer entarteten semitischen Sprache," *AION* 4 (1962) 95-106; H. Polotsky, "Studies in Modern Syriac," *JSS* 6 (1961) 1-60. On *Maᶜlūla:* G. Bergsträsser, *Glossar des neuaramäischen Dialekts von Maᶜlūla* (Abhandlungen für die Kunde des Morgenlandes, 14/4; Leipzig: Brockhaus, 1921); *Neuaramäische Märchen und andere Texte aus Maᶜlūla* (Abhandlungen für die Kunde des Morgenlandes, 13/2; Leipzig: Brockhaus, 1915); "Neue Texte im neuaramäischen Dialekt von Maᶜlula," *ZA* 32 (1919) 150-70; C. Correll, "Ein Vorschlag zur Erklärung der Negation *ču (ću)* in den neuwestaramäischen Dialekten des Antilibanon," *ZDMG* 124 (1974) 271-85; E. Littmann,"Der neuaramäische Dialekt von Maᶜlūla," *OLZ* 29 (1926) 803-9; H. Müller, "Maᶜlūla vor hundert Jahren: Reisebriefe von Albert Socin aus dem Jahre 1869," *ZDPV* 85 (1969) 1-23; T. Nöldeke, "Beiträge zur Kenntniss der aramäischen Dialecte," *ZDMG* 21 (1867) 183-200; "Texte im aramäischen Dialekt von Maᶜlula," *ZA* 31 (1917-18) 203-30. A. Spitaler, *Grammatik des neuaramäischen Dialekts von Maᶜlūla (Antilibanon)* (Abhandlungen für die Kunde des Morgenlandes, 23/1; Leipzig: Brockhaus, 1938); reprinted, 1966; F. Rosenthal, "Spitalers Grammatik des neuaramäischen Dialekts von Maᶜlula," *Or* 8 (1939) 346-60; A. Spitaler, "Neue Materialen zum aramäischen Dialekt von Maᶜlula," *ZDMG* 107 (1957) 299-339. On *Jubbᶜadîn*: V. Cantarino, *Der neuaramäische Dialekt von Ǧubb Adin (Texte und Übersetzung)* (Chapel Hill, NC: Curriculum in Linguistics of North Carolina, 1961); S. Reich, *Etudes sur les villages araméens de l'Anti-Liban* (Documents d'études orientales, 7; Damascus: Institut français de Damas, 1937). On *Baḫᶜa:* C. Correll, *Materialien zur Kenntnis des neuaramäischen Dialekts von Baḫᶜa* (Munich: University Dissertation, 1969).

On *Tur ᶜAbdin:* H. Anschütz, "Zur Gegenwartslage der syrischen Christen im Tur ᶜAbdin, in Hakkarigebiet und im Iran," *ZDMG* 118 suppl. 1/2 (1969) 483-510; O. Jastrow, *Laut- und Formenlehre des neuaramäischen Dialektes von Mīḏin im Ṭūr ᶜAbdīn* (Bamberg: R. Rodenbusch, 1966; 2d ed.; Bamberg: Bamberger Fotodruck, 1970); H. Ritter, *Ṭūrōyo: Die Volkssprache der syrischen Christen des Ṭūr-ᶜAbdīn* (Orient-Institut der DMG, Beirut; 2 vols.; Wiesbaden: F. Steiner, 1967-69). A. Siegel, *Laut - und Formenlehre des neuaramäischen Dialekts des Tûr Abdîn* (Hanover: Lefaire, 1923). On *Urmia:* A. J. MacLean, *A Dictionary of the Dialects of Vernacular Syriac, as Spoken by the Eastern Syrians of Kurdistan, North-West Persia, and the Plain of Mosul* (Oxford: Clarendon, 1901; reprinted, Amsterdam, 1971); *Grammar of the Dialects of Vernacular Syriac as Spoken by the Eastern Syrians of Kurdistanc, North-West Persia, and the Plain of Mosul—With Notices of the Vernacular of the Jews of Azerbaijan and of Zakhu near Mosul* (Cambridge: University Press, 1895); R. Macuch and E.Panoussi, *Neusyrische Chrestomathie* (Porta linguarum orientalium, ns 13; Wiesbaden: Harrassowitz, 1974); A. Merx, *Neusyrisches Lesebuch: Texte im Dialekte von Urmia* (Breslau/Tübingen, 1873); T. Nöldeke, *Grammatik der neusyrischen Sprache am Urmia-See und in Kurdistan* (Leipzig: T. O. Weigel, 1868); R. Hetzron, "The Morphology of the Verb in Modern Syriac (Christian Colloquial of Urmi)," *JAOS* 89 (1969) 112-27. On *Salamas:* J. Rhétoré, *Grammaire de la langue soureth ou chaldéen vulgaire selon le dialecte de la plaine de Mossoul et des pays adjacents* (Mosul: Dominican Press, 1912); R. Duval, *Les dialectes néo-araméens de Salamas: Textes sur l'état de la Perse et contes populaires publiés avec une traduction française* (Paris, 1883). On *Thumic:* H. Jacobi, *Grammatik des thumischen Neuaramäisch (Nordostsyrien)* (Abhandlungen für die Kunde des Morgenlandes, 40/3; Wiesbaden: DMG [F. Steiner], 1973). On *Zakho:* Y. Sabar, "The Hebrew Elements in the Neo-Aramaic Dialect of Zakho in Kurdistan," *Lĕšonénu* 38 (1974) 206-19; J. B. Segal, "Neo-Aramaic Proverbs of the Jews of Zakho," *JNES* 14 (1955) 251-70. On *Azerbaijan:* I. Garbell, *The Jewish Neo-Aramaic Dialect of Persian Azerbaijan: Linguistic Analysis and Folkloristic Texts* (The Hague: Mouton, 1965); E. Cerulli and F. A. Pennacchietti, *Testi neo-aramaici dell'Iran settentrionale* (Pubblicazioni del seminario di semitistica, ricerche 8; Naples: Istituto orientale di Napoli, 1971).

[42]See O. Schroeder, *Keilschrifttexte aus Assur historischen Inhalts* (Wissenschaftliche Veröffentlichungen der deutschen Orient-Gesellschaft, 37; Berlin/Leipzig: Deutsche Orient-Gesellschaft, 1922) §63. Cf. D. D. Luckenbill, *Ancient Records of Assyria and Babylonia* (Chicago: University of Chicago, 1926), 1. §286–87; J. B. Pritchard, *ANET,* 275. Here they are listed specifically as Arameans; even earlier they were probably included in the *Aḫlame.* See E. Fohrer, "Aramau," *Reallexikon für Assyriologie* 1 (1928) 130-39; R. T. O'Callaghan, *Aram Naharaim: A Contribution to the History of Upper Mesopotamia in the Second Millennium B.C.* (AnOr 26; Rome: Biblical Institute, 1948) 93-118; A. Dupont-Sommer, *Les Araméens* (L'orient ancien illustré; Paris: Maisonneuve, 1949) 15–19.

[43]See W. F. Albright, "Recent Progress in North-Canaanite Research," *BASOR* 70 (1938) 18-24, esp. p. 21.

[44]This is a widely-held opinion about the origin of the alphabet; if it is not correct, its origin would have to be sought in some Semitic people in an area adjacent to Phoenicia (see T. O. Lambdin, "Alphabet," *IDB,* 1. 89; cf. K. Beyer, "Die Problematik der semitischen Konsonantenschrift," *Ruperto-Carola* 42 (1967) 12-17). In any case, the immediate source of the alphabet used by the Arameans was that of the Phoenicians. The Aramean role in the spread of the alphabet may have been as important as that of the Phoenicians, since at the time that it was adopted by the Greeks, it was adopted with signs already being used for vocalic sounds. Indeed, S. Segert ("Altaramäische Schrift und Anfänge des griechischen Alphabets," *Klio* 41 [1963] 38-57) has argued: "Da eine direkte Bezeichnung von Vokalen bei den Phönikern nicht in Gebrauch war, ergibt sich die Schlussfolgerung, dass die Griechen die Vokalbuchstaben und die Buchstaben überhaupt von der Aramäern übernommen haben" (pp. 48-49). The names of most of the letters of the alphabet, however, seem to have been derived from Phoenician (because of their vocalization [e.g., *ἰῶτα* < *yod*] in Greek form). Whether the Greek names with the ending *-a* (such as *alpha, bēta, delta, zēta, ēta, thēta, iōta, kappa, lambda, sigma*) could be regarded as Aramaized forms of the Phoenician names might be debated. A case might be made out for *alpha, bēta,* and possibly for *kappa* (with the doubled *p*). But here one has to be cautious, because of an inner-Greek development: the adding of an *a*-sound to foreign words taken over that end in a consonant other than *n, r,* and *s.* See E. Schwyzer, *Griechische Grammatik* (Handbuch der Altertumswissenschaft, 2/1/1; 2d ed.; Munich: Beck, 1953), 1. 140. Cf. T. Nöldeke, "Die semitischen Buchstabennamen," *Beiträge zur semitischen Sprachwissenschaft* (Strassburg: Trübner, 1904)

124-36; S. Segert, "Aramäische Studien: IV. Die Rolle der Aramäer bei der Vermittlung des westsemitischen Alphabets an die Griechen," *ArOr* 26 (1958) 572-78. C. H. Gordon ("The Greek Unilinguals from Parisos and Dreros and Their Bearing on Eteocretan and Minoan," Πεπραγμένα τοῦ γ΄ διεθνοῦς Κρητηλογικοῦ συνεδρίου [Athens, 1973], 1. 97-103, esp. p. 102) lists the following letters as borrowed from "a people using the Aramaic forms with the postpositive article *ā*": *alpha, bēta, gamma, delta, ēta, zēta, thēta, iōta, kappa, lambda,* the old letter *koppa*, and perhaps *sigma.* Cf. J. Naveh, "Some Semitic Epigraphical Considerations on the Antiquity of the Greek Alphabet," *AJA* 77 (1973) 1-8.

[45]See J. Naveh, *The Development of the Aramaic Script* (n. 18 above). Cf. G. R. Driver, *Semitic Writing from Pictograph to Alphabet* (Schweich Lectures, 1944; London: British Academy, 1948) 119-23; F. M. Cross, Jr., "The Development of the Jewish Scripts," *The Bible and the Ancient Near East: Essays in Honor of William Foxwell Albright* (ed. G. E. Wright; Anchor Books; Garden City: Doubleday, 1965) 170-264; N. Avigad, "The Palaeography of the Dead Sea Scrolls and Related Documents," *Aspects of the Dead Sea Scrolls* (Scripta hiersolymitana, 4; Jerusalem: Magnes, 1958) 56-87.

[46]E.g., the voiced dental sibilant *(z)* was used to write the voiced dental spirant *(ḏ)*; the unvoiced dental sibilant *(š)* was used to write the unvoiced dental spirant *(ṯ).*

[47]How this sound was originally pronounced in Proto-Semitic is quite debatable. It is usually said to represent *ḏ̣*, but its Ugaritic counterpart(s) create(s) a problem. It is not easy to say why the Aramaic sound would have been represented in the script by a Phoenician *q*.

[48]See further my commentary on the Sefire Inscriptions (n. 29 above), 149-50; S. Moscati, *An Introduction to the Comparative Grammar of the Semitic Languages: Phonology and Morphology* (Porta linguarum orientalium, ns 6; Wiesbaden: Harrassowitz, 1964) §8.18.

[49]*Early Hebrew Orthography* (n. 10 above).

[50]Cross and Freedman failed to treat certain forms (*mlkh* in Hamath Graffito 1; *šwr*ᵓ in Zakir a 17) and wrongly analyzed other forms (*lḥzy* in Sujin Aa 13 [read now *lḥzyh*, a Pael infinitive, Sf I 13]; *klmh*, Sujin Ab 7 [understand it now as *kl mh*, Sf I A 26]). They were embarrassed by *tgltplysr* (Bar-Rakib 3, 6) for *Tukulti-apilešarra.* But such defects are now seen as minor; some of them indicate the *inceptive* use of vowel letters in a medial position—the adjustment that has to be made to their otherwise acceptable basic thesis.

[51]"Une inscription araméenne inédite de Sfiré," *BMB* 13 (1956, appeared in early 1958) 23-41; "Les inscriptions araméennes de Sfiré (Stèles I et II)," *MPAIBL* 15 (1960, appeared in 1958) 197-351 (+ 29 pls.). For the evidence that bears out the Cross and Freedman thesis, see my commentary on these inscriptions (n. 29 above), 139-49.

[52](Pubblicazioni del seminario di semitistica, Ricerche 5; Naples: Istituto orientale di Napoli, 1969).

[53]"Some Observations on Early Hebrew," *Bib* 53 (1972) 413-20.

[54](Munich: UNI-Druck, 1971). Cf. K. Beyer, *BZ* 18 (1974) 139-40.

[55]"L'aramaico antico" (n. 30 above), 245-47.

[56]Garbini states (p. 247): "Nelle iscrizioni di Suğīn l'enfatico appare generalmente in ה- al maschile e in א- al feminile: ארבה (A b,8), ארקה (A b,9), רחבה (A a,10), שעותה (A b,16)." But every instance cited here is questionable, if not wrong: ארבה almost certainly represents ᵓ*arbêh* (< ᵓ*arbay*; cf. Hebr. ᵓ*arbēh*; Ugar. *irby*; Akkad. *arbū*); ארקה is a suffixal form on a fem. noun, "its land" (= ᵓ*arqah*); שעותה is non-existent; read שעותא (just what one would expect!); and רחבה is undoubtedly a proper name, about which little can be said. Similarly, מלכה in Hamath Graffito 1 is not certainly the emphatic state in ה, but the suffixal form, "his king" *(malkēh).*

[57]"Studi aramaici—1-2," *AION* 29 (1969) 1-15, esp. pp. 8-15.

[58]See *PPG*² §67; Z. S. Harris, *A Grammar of the Phoenician Language* (AOS 8; New Haven: American Oriental Society, 1936) 11-19.

[59]See n. 51 above. Cf. F. Rosenthal, *Die aramaistische Forschung* (n. 2 above), 22.

[60]"A Chapter on Old West Semitic Orthography," *The Joshua Bloch Memorial Volume: Studies in Booklore and History* (eds. A. Berger et al.; New York: New York Public Library, 1960) 82-91.

[61]"Aramäische Studien: III. Zum Problem der altaramäischen Dialekte," *ArOr* 26 (1958) 561-72. See also his *Altaramäische Grammatik* (p. 23 above, n. 53), §2.4.1-7 (pp. 62-65), which does not really cope with the problem.

[62]M. Tsevat ("A Chapter," 85) claims that לא "occurs in the Sujin Stele (Ab 9)," but his claim was based on the older publication of Ronzevalle that is now obsolete; cf. Sf I A 28. Moreover, what bearing does its occurrence in the Lachish letters have on this Aramaic problem? E. Y. Kutscher ("Aramaic," *Current Trends* [p. 23 above, n. 39] 373) quotes Tsevat approvingly; but he never checked out the Sefire inscription itself! What he says there contradicts what he says on p. 354 about "the (originally) consonantal character of the [א]." The example of *nbʾ*, "Nabu" begs the question; why should it not be *nābūʾ*, like *hʾ* = *hūʾ* (Sf I B 24) or *hʾ* = *hīʾ* (Sf I A 37)? In all these cases, the only real explanation is the persistence of the consonantal writing of *aleph* as a consonant. Both of the latter forms are identical with their Phoenician counterparts; see *PPG*^{2} §110.

[63]In a 9th century Cyprus Tomb inscription, לקבר זא (*KAI* §30:2).

[64]In the Yehawmilk inscription 6, 12, 14 (*KAI* §10:6, 12, 14). See further *PPG*^{2} §113, 115.

[65]Could not one also appeal to the historical spelling preserved in Hebrew זאת, where the fem. -*t* has been added to the original form of the demonstrative (possibly after the quiescence of the *aleph*)?

[66]There is, to be sure, evidence of some of the phonetic shifts that characterize the later phases of the language (e.g., *yrt* [Sf I C 24]; possibly *btn* [Sf I A 32]; see further my commentary, p. 150); but this is so sporadic and debatable that it perhaps should not even be considered.

[67]Ibid., 156.

[68]*Early Hebrew Orthography* (n. 10 above), 33 n. 53.

[69]Ibid., 21-34.

[70]Ibid., 64.

[71]See his review of the first edition of my commentary on the *Genesis Apocryphon*, *JSS* 13 (1968) 281-82.

[72]*Altaramäische Grammatik* (n. 16 above), 4-5.

[73]Ibid., 2.

[74]G. Garbini expresses this wonder a little more strongly in his review of Degen's grammar, *AION* ns 20 (1970) 275-77, esp. pp. 275-76.

[75]Degen is not alone in this separation of the Nērab inscriptions from Old Aramaic; cf. J. J. Koopmans, *Aramäische Chrestomathie* (p. 23 above, n. 53), v; F. M. Cross and D. N. Freedman, *Early Hebrew Orthography* (n. 10 above); G. Garbini, "L'aramaico antico" (n. 30 above); J. C. L. Gibson, *Textbook of Syrian Semitic Inscriptions* (p. 24 above, n. 56), 93-98 (he also includes Bar-Rākib 1-3 under "Imperial or Official Aramaic"!). But A. Dupont-Sommer has included the Nērab inscriptions in his treatment of "Ancient Aramaic Monumental Inscriptions" in *An Aramaic Handbook* (ed. F. Rosenthal; Porta linguarum orientalium, ns 10; Wiesbaden: Harrassowitz, 1967), I/1, 1-9; this section precedes that on "Aramaic Texts from Achaemenid Times."

[76]"'Siʾgabbar, Priest of Sahr in Nerab,'" *JAOS* 90 (1970) 270-71. Cf. E. Y. Kutscher, "Aramaic," *Current Trends* (p. 23 above, n. 39), 353.

[77]Approximate dates are the only ones ever given for these inscriptions: "7. Jh. v. Chr." (*KAI*, 3. §274); "probably vii cent. B.C." (G. A. Cooke, *NSI*, 186, 189); "aus dem 7. Jahrh. v. Chr." (J. J. Koopmans, *AC*, 92).

[78]*Aramaic Inscriptions of Sefire*, 140.

[79]C. Brockelmann, "Das Aramäische, einschliesslich des Syrischen," *Handbuch der Orientalistik: III. Semitistik* (Leiden: Brill, 1954) 135-62, esp. p. 136; W. F. Albright, *Syria, the Philistines and Phoenicia* (Cambridge Ancient History, rev. ed., I-II/51; Cambridge: Cambridge University, 1966), 47; F. M. Cross and D. N. Freedman, *Early Hebrew Orthography*, 64; R. Stiehl, "Kanaanäisch und Aramäisch," *Die Araber in der alten Welt: I. Bis zum Beginn der Kaiserzeit* (Berlin: de Gruyter, 1964) 213-36, esp. p. 219 n. 21. I should not go so far as to say with R. A. Bowman that "the so-called 'Old Aramaic' of the region . . . is almost completely

Canaanite rather than Aramaic. . . ." (*JNES* 7 [1948] 71). Bowman includes the Kilamuwa inscription, which is completely Phoenician save for the word בר, "son."

[80]*Altaramäische Grammatik,* 1-3.

[81]"Studi aramaici—1-2," *AION* 29 (1969) 1-15, esp. p. 3.

[82]*Altaramäische Grammatik,* 2-3.

[83]See Aḥiram 2 (*KAI* §1:2); cf. W. F. Albright, "The Phoenician Inscriptions of the Tenth Century B.C. from Byblus," *JAOS* 67 (1947) 153-60, esp. p. 156 n. 24. (R. Degen [*Altaramäische Grammatik,* 3 n. 20, citing J. Friedrich, *PPG* §266] is apparently not convinced of this example.) An example of an imperfect with *waw* occurs in 1QapGen 20:26; but there is here no real consecution, since the form really expresses contemporaneity: "What have you done to me because of Sarai, in telling me . . ." (ותאמר); cf. 2:12; 19:19; Dan 4:31.

[84]The intensifying infinitive occurs in Sf II C 8; III 2, 6, 12, 13, 18; I B 30[?] and in Nērab 2:6. It is unknown in Official Aramaic and Middle Aramaic; yet it is frequent in Hebrew, Phoenician (*PPG*[2] §267), and Ugaritic (*UT* §9.27). It begins to turn up again in Late Aramaic texts (e.g., in Tg. Onqelos, Tg. Neofiti I [Exod 19:13], and in Syriac). G. Dalman (*GJPA*, 280) is almost certainly correct when he says, "ohne Zweifel infolge des Einflusses der hebräischen Vorlage," with reference to the targums. For its use in Syriac, see T. Nöldeke, *Compendious Syriac Grammar* (n. 39 above), §295-96. Its appearance in Syriac is undoubtedly owing to biblical influence (through the Peshitta or other Old Syriac versions); in neither of these instances in Late Aramaic is it possible to establish a connection with the Old Aramaic usage.

[85]E.g., Sf I B 32; III 12, 13; Hadad 10, 23, 13, 14, 34. Cf. Ezra 5:3, 13 (*lbnʾ*).

[86]See *KAI* §233:8; cf. *AP* 2:3; 5:3, 12; 6:4; 8:3; 9:3; 10:3 and passim.

[87]"New Aramaic Texts," *JAOS* 74 (1954) 233-48; he borrowed the phrase from U. Weinreich (Publications of the Linguistic Circle of New York, 1; New York: International Linguistic Association, 1953). For a related problem involving "Canaanite," see J. C. Greenfield, "Amurrite, Ugaritic and Canaanite," *Proceedings of the International Conference on Semitic Studies, Jerusalem, 1965* (Leiden: Brill, 1969) 1-10. As I am using "Canaanite," I mean it as a tag to bind "Amurrite, Ugaritic and Canaanite into a group" (to paraphrase Greenfield, p. 2).

[88]"Studi aramaici—1-2," *AION* 29 (1969) 5; cf. S. Moscati, "Il semitico di nord-ovest," *Studi orientalistici in onore di Giorgio Levi della Vida* (Roma: Istituto per l'Oriente, 1956), 2. 202-21; "Sulla posizione linguistica del semitico nord-occidentale," *RSO* 31 (1956) 229-34.

[89]*AION* 29 (1969) 5.

[90]Ibid., 7.

[91]As is proposed by many writers; see, e.g., A. F. Johns, *A Short Grammar of Biblical Aramaic* (n. 5 above), 1.

[92]See H. B. Huffmon, *Amorite Personal Names in the Mari Texts: A Structural and Lexical Study* (Baltimore: Johns Hopkins, 1965). Cf. I. J. Gelb, "La lingua degli Amoriti," *Atti dell'Accademia Nazionale dei Lincei,* Rendiconti, 8/13 (1958) 143-64; A. Caquot, "Remarques sur la langue et le panthéon des Amorites de Mari," *Les annales archéologiques de Syrie* 1 (1951) 206-25. See further the bibliography presented by G. Garbini, "Semitico nord-occidentale e aramaico," *Linguistica presente e futuro* (ed. G. Levi della Vida; Studi semitici, 4; Roma: Centro di studi semitici, 1961) 59-90, esp. pp. 64-65 n. 15.

[93]"L'aramaico antico" (see n. 30 above), 241.

[94]*AION* 29 (1969) 4. A language can have its own definite character or physiognomy and still be under the influence of another; compare the Gallicisms in English.

[95]The Old Aramaic ending *-wh* is puzzling and is obviously related to the later ending *-why* of Official Aramaic (as well as to *-ôhī* of Biblical Aramaic and *-awhī* [better, *-aw(hy)*] of Syriac). E. Y. Kutscher ("Aramaic," *Current Trends,* 350) took an easy way out, when he wrote: "The defective spelling of the personal suffix in the 3rd person masculine singular of a masculine plural noun, e.g., *mlkwh* 'his kings', which in Elephantine *(E)* is generally spelt *mlkwhy* (=[*mal*k*o:hi:] in Biblical Aramaic [BA]), does not indicate that there was no vowel after the [h]. The suffix had a final vowel in Proto-Semitic (PS). Of course, it might have disappeared in *OA*. But then, how are we to account for its (re)appearance, e.g., in *OfA* (*E* and *BA*)?" Kutscher was obviously striving

for exactness, and his last two sentences are a commentary on the preceding ones. It is clear that Old Aramaic מלכוה and Official Aramaic מלכוהי must be traced back to an original form like **malkay-hū*; with the loss of intervocalic *he*, the form became **malkayū*, and eventually **malkaw*. Since this was soon to be contracted to *malkô*, the real sign of the 3d sg. masc. suffix was obscured and the suffix *-hū* was again, secondarily, added. But how was it added? The Old Aramaic evidence would suggest that consonantal *he* was added—perhaps on an analogy with ה of the singular מלכה, "his king." In Official Aramaic the added *-hū* became -הי (= *hī*, generally regarded as a dissimilation of *-hū*, perhaps on the analogy of such verbal forms as נקטלנהי [*A* 61]). In any case, to invoke a "defective spelling" in Old Aramaic for this sole case of final *ī* is problematic, in view of all the other evidence pointing to the full writing of final *ī* with *yodh*. See my commentary on the Sefire Inscriptions, p. 142. Note too that the ending -וה is occasionally found in Official Aramaic texts (e.g., *BMAP* 3:4, where Kraeling's note suggests reading אגרוה[י], following Rosenthal and Albright). It may be a scribal error; but it may also be a case of an archaizing historical spelling. Cf. *BMAP* 6:9, הח[ו]מוה. See further Cross and Freedman's attempt to vocalize the Old Aramaic form, *Early Hebrew Orthography* (n. 10 above), 68-69.

[96]See D. O. Edzard, "Mari und Aramäer," *ZA* 56 (1964) 142-49.

[97]"Standard Literary Aramaic" (n. 34 above); "Dialect Traits in Early Aramaic" (n. 30 above).

[98]"Aramaic," *Current Trends* (see p. 23 above, n. 39), 361-66.

[99]Ibid.

[100]*Studies in the Aramaic Legal Papyri from Elephantine* (Studia et documenta ad iura orientis antiqui pertinentia, 8; Leiden: Brill, 1969).

[101]"Aramaic," *Current Trends*, 363.

[102]Ibid., 366.

[103]In his review of F. Rosenthal, *Die aramaistische Forschung* (1939), *JAOS* 62 (1942) 232.

[104]See p. 61 above.

[105]See n. 71 above.

[106]See *MPAT*.

[107]"Der Reichsaramäische Einschlag in der ältesten syrischen Literatur," *ZDMG* 116 (1966) 242-54.

[108]For a handy collection of these texts, see H. J. W. Drijvers, *Old Syriac* (*Edessean* [sic]) *Inscriptions, Edited with an Introduction, Indices and a Glossary* (SSS 3; Leiden: Brill, 1972). See further his articles, "Syrische Inscripties uit de eerste drie eeuwen A.D.," *Phoenix* 15 (1969) 197-205; "Some New Syriac Inscriptions and Archaeological Finds from Edessa and Sumatar Harabesi," *BSOAS* 36 (1973) 1-14 (+ pls. I-XII). Cf. E. Jenni, "Die altsyrischen Inschriften, 1.-3. Jahrhundert nach Christus," *TZ* 21 (1965) 371-85; F. Vattioni, "Appunti sulle iscrizioni siriache antiche," *Augustinianum* 11 (1971) 435-46; 13 (1973) 131-40; "Le iscrizioni siriache antiche," ibid., 279-338; J. B. Segal, *Edessa: 'The Blessed City'* (Oxford: Clarendon, 1970).

[109]*RB* 74 (1967) 102; see further his review of E. Vogt, *Lexicon linguae aramaicae Veteris Testamenti, RB* 79 (1972) 614-17, esp. p. 617; his review of J. T. Milik, *The Books of Enoch, RB* 83 (1976) 605-18, esp. p. 614. This opinion of Grelot has been blithely cited, and without any scrutiny, by A. Paul, "Bulletin de littérature intertestamentaire," *RSR* 60 (1972) 429-58, esp. p. 440. One would not expect much difference between Official Aramaic and such Qumran texts as 1QapGen, 4QprNab, 4QEnoch, 4QTLevi. As for the differences between this Aramaic of Qumran and that of Daniel, one has only to read E. Y. Kutscher, "The Language of the Genesis Apocryphon" (n. 4 above); cf. H. H. Rowley, "Notes on the Aramaic of the Genesis Apocryphon," *Hebrew and Semitic Studies Presented to Godfrey Rolles Driver* (ed. D. Winton Thomas and W. D. McHardy; Oxford: Clarendon, 1963) 116-29. Grelot (*RQ* 8 [1972-76] 114) bemoans the fact that we do not have a text of Daniel as old as that of 11QtgJob with which to compare the orthography of the two. Perhaps he has forgotten about the Daniel fragments in 1Q*71-72* (DJD, 1. 150-52); see J. C. Trever, "Completion of the Publication of Some Fragments from Qumran Cave I," *RQ* 5 (1964-66) 323-44; "1QDan[a], the Latest of the Qumran Manuscripts," *RQ* 7 (1969-71) 277-86.

[110]*El Targum: Introducción a las traducciones aramaicas de la Biblia* (Barcelona: Consejo superior de investigaciones científicas, 1972) 41-42.

[111]Ibid., 42.

[112]*Neophyti 1: Targum palestinense, MS de la Biblioteca Vaticana: Tomo I, Génesis: Edición príncipe, introducción general y versión castellana* (Madrid / Barcelona: Consejo superior de investigaciones científicas, 1968) 95* (". . . el Neofiti, en su conjunto partinece ya al la época neotestamentaria"); M. Black, *An Aramaic Approach* (p. 21 above, n. 13), 22 ("The language of the Palestinian Pentateuch Targum is, on the other hand, first-century Aramaic.").

[113]*CBQ* 32 (1970) 107-12.

[114]*RevScRel* 47 (1973) 196-231, esp. pp. 179-81; reprinted in *Exégèse biblique et judaïque* (ed. J.-E. Ménard; Strasbourg: Faculté de théologie catholique, 1973 [distributed by E. J. Brill, Leiden]) 15-77, esp. pp. 26-27. The substance of it has been repeated in the introduction to *Neophyti 1, Targum palestinense, MS de la Biblioteca Vaticana: Tomo IV, Números, Edición príncipe, introducción y versión castellana* (Madrid: Consejo superior de investigaciones científicas, 1974) 80*-86*.

[115]See p. 39 above; also *MPAT*, §1-149.

[116]See p. 168 below.

[117]See p. 37 above.

[118]See *MPAT*, App., §A1-A56.

[119]See E. Schwyzer, *Griechische Grammatik* (n. 44 above), 1. 159; T. Nöldeke, *Compendious Syriac Grammar* (n. 39 above), xxxii-xxxiii. Cf. A. Schall, *Studien über griechische Fremdwörter im Syrischen* (Darmstadt: Wissenschaftliche Buchgesellschaft, 1960).

[120]See E. Y. Kutscher, "Aramaic," *Encyclopaedia judaica* (Jerusalem: Keter; New York: Macmillan, 1971), 3. 259-87, esp. col. 271; J. C. Greenfield, Review of M. Black, *Aramaic Approach, JNES* 31 (1972) 58-61.

[121]Indeed, as M. D. Herr notes (*Encyclopaedia judaica* [Jerusalem: Keter; New York: Macmillan, 1971], 7. 399): ". . . *Genesis Rabbah* mentions the last group of Palestinian amoraim who flourished in the second half of the fourth century C.E. . . ." But he thinks that some of the material may have "originated close to the period of the Mishnah" (col. 400). The question, of course, is how much of it originated then or can be traced back to this period.

Chapter 4

The Contribution of Qumran Aramaic to the Study of the New Testament*

Our knowledge of the corpus of extra-biblical and extra-rabbinical Aramaic texts has largely been the acquisition of the last seventy-five to a hundred years. Through numerous discoveries in Egypt, Arabia, Palestine, Syria, Asia Minor, Armenia, Mesopotamia, Persia and the Indus Valley we have come to know what various phases of Aramaic were like from the tenth century B.C. until roughly the eighth century A.D.[1] This knowledge has enabled us to situate the biblical Aramaic of Ezra and Daniel in a matrix similar to that provided by extra-biblical Hebrew texts for biblical Hebrew. And the same can be said for the long-known rabbinical Aramaic texts, the classic targumim and midrashim, not to mention Syriac and related forms of Aramaic.[2] The discoveries of the last two decades, however, have revealed a corpus of Palestinian Aramaic texts, which for all sorts of reasons attract the attention of the biblical commentator.[3] A sizeable bulk of these Palestinian Aramaic texts comes from the first century B.C. or A.D., and a portion of them date from the beginning of the second century A.D. (roughly up to the time of the Second Palestinian Revolt against Rome under Simon ben Kosiba). Many of these texts come from the Qumran caves, and their titles are generally familiar—at least those that are already published. Some of the Qumran Aramaic texts have been studied in great detail, others less so. In some of the detailed studies many scattered items pertinent to the study of the NT have been singled out and commented on; some others are still to be revealed. To describe the contribution of Qumran Aramaic texts to the study of the NT I should like to bring together the more important items in this paper.

But before I turn to the topic proper, I should propose a few preliminary remarks about the general question of the study of Aramaic and the NT. Anyone who begins to be interested in this subject soon realizes in what a morass one finds oneself, for there are all sorts of things that are understood today when one hears the generic expression, "Aramaic and the NT." In a paper on methodology recently delivered at the *Journées Bibliques* of Louvain,[4] I sought to distinguish various aspects of the question—and I readily admit that I am not yet sure that I have them all rightly sorted out. At the moment eight aspects seem to be distinguishable: (1) Aramaic as a language of Jesus, or more broadly, as a language of first-century Palestine; (2) Aramaic words, names and phrases preserved as such in the writings of the NT, Josephus and the early rabbinic tradition (e.g. in the Mishnah, which is otherwise composed in Hebrew); (3) Aramaisms in NT Greek, usually of a lexical or syntactic nature—this is the question of Aramaic interference proper; (4) the problem of mistranslations from an alleged Aramaic substratum; (5) Aramaic literary forms in prose and poetry; (6) Aramaic and variant readings in the NT textual tradition; (7) Jewish literary traditions found in the NT and in known Aramaic literature; (8) Aramaic epistolography. A moment's reflection on these eight aspects of the Aramaic problem suffices to reveal their diversity and the need for a rigorous methodology in approaching them. In each instance one must be, moreover, rigorous in not taking refuge in evidence that is merely "Semitic," for that cannot be invoked as evidence for Aramaic without further ado. Furthermore, the discussion of the entire matter must initially and seriously reckon with all the firm data and admitted advances in the source-critical, form-critical, and redaction-critical study of the Greek NT; it cannot, as it were, go its own way in neglect of these forms of NT study. And consequently, because of such work no conclusion can be drawn from the study of the Aramaic substratum about the authenticity of the sayings of Jesus, John the Baptist, Peter, or any other Gospel figure. If the sayings of such figures prove to be authentic, that will be for reasons other than their mere Aramaic substratum. The discussion of details under each of these aspects has to be left for another occasion; but the mere listing of them here serves to stress the complexity of the problem of Aramaic and the NT.

My purpose now is rather to present some of the more important data which have emerged from Qumran Aramaic texts bearing on the study of the NT. The data cut across the aspects listed above; at a later date it may be possible to sort them out according to such categories, but at the moment my intention is different. I should like to cull from this body of Palestinian Aramaic material some of the things that bear on the study of the NT, even if they do cut across the various aspects just mentioned. The reason is that this form of Palestinian Aramaic—as well as that from other contemporary Palestinian sources—should be recognized for what it is: privileged data that take precedence over the material derived from the classic targumim and midrashim (the dates of which are far from certain and the language of which is suggestive of several centuries later than the NT writings themselves).[5]

What is meant by Qumran Aramaic can be seen from the list of texts provided in chart II—some of which are familiar as already published texts, others are only known to exist and as yet await publication.[6] These works, composed in Palestinian Aramaic, range in date from at least 150 B.C. to A.D. 70.[7] They are known to have been used by the Essene community of Qumran, a community that is often regarded as an esoteric sect in Palestinian Judaism.[8] At least two of the larger Aramaic works in the list, the *Genesis Apocryphon* of Cave I and the targum of Job of Cave XI,[9] display nothing that is clearly an Essene tenet or theologoumenon.[10] Because this is so, the question has been raised whether such texts might have been composed in Aramaic outside the community itself and might have merely been introduced into it for reading and study.[11] If this were so, then the language we find in them might represent a type of Aramaic that was spoken on a wider scale than in the small Essene community at Qumran, where post-biblical Hebrew was used for most of the sectarian writings. At the moment it is not easy to resolve this question with certainty, but J. T. Milik has recently published some fragments of Qumran Cave IV about the Visions of ᶜAmram,[12] in which one finds many of the features of Qumran dualism that have so far been known only from the Hebrew texts of the Manual of Discipline, the War Scroll, etc. Now, however, such expressions as "sons of light" or the the contrast of "light" and "darkness" have turned up in Aramaic, and they suggest that the language was used for active creative writing within the community itself.[13] It gives evidence of an active literary production in Aramaic at a time when it was hitherto unsuspected.[14]

My discussion of the contribution of Qumran Aramaic texts to the study of the NT will highlight what I consider important features of them; it obviously makes no pretence about exhausting the details. The discussion will fall into three sections: (I) lexical matters that supply a first-century Palestinian background to certain NT problems; (II) Jewish Palestinian practices or beliefs that emerge in these texts; and (III) literary parallels that have become known through them.

I. *Lexical Matters Supplying a First-Century Palestinian Background to Certain New Testament Problems*

We shall begin with the Qumran Aramaic material that bears on certain titles of Jesus used in the Greek NT: (ὁ) *κύριος*, *υἱὸς θεοῦ*, *ὁ λόγος*, and (ὁ) *υἱὸς* (*τοῦ*) *ἀνθρώπου*. It is obvious that my remarks will bear largely on the philological aspects of the use of such titles, and what I have to say about the Qumran data and their bearing on the use must presuppose some knowledge of the debates surrounding the titles. It is impossible to recapitulate them all here or to exploit all the aspects of the new material. I shall, therefore, limit myself to essentials.

There has recently come to light the absolute use of מָרֵא, "Lord," as a title for God in the Qumran targum of Job, and no one will fail to realize the pertinence of this evidence to the long-standing debate about the origin of the absolute use of (*ὁ*) *κύριος* for Jesus in the NT.

At least since the time of G. Dalman it has been repeated that "to speak of 'the Lord' with no suffix is contrary to Palestinian usage."[15] Dalman himself sought the origin of the Greek title for Jesus in Aramaic forms such as *mārī* or *māran*, which he said was the form of address for a teacher or a rabbi.[16] W. Bousset, who rejected this origin of "the specifically religious significance of κύριος," repeated that "in Aramaic usage the simple Mara (מרא) without a suffix is quite unusual, and only the form Mari or Maran (my lord, our lord) is found."[17] R. Bultmann proposed it again in his own way: "Judaism, at any rate, never entitled the Messiah 'Lord.' At the very outset the unmodified expression 'the Lord' is unthinkable in Jewish usage. 'Lord' used of God is always given some modifier; we read: 'the Lord of heaven and earth,' 'our Lord' and similar expressions."[18] Both Bousset and Bultmann championed the hellenistic origin of the NT title κύριος, regarding it as derived from the use of κύριος for earthly rulers or for gods in various hellenistic mystery cults. But scholars such as W. Foerster,[19] O. Cullmann,[20] E. Schweizer[21] and F. Hahn[22] in various ways argued to explain the Greek title as rooted in Palestinian tradition.

Over a decade ago, S. Schulz discussed the Aramaic data that bore on the problem, amassing evidence from the fifth-century Elephantine material onward.[23] He brought forward the Aramaic evidence for the title "Lord" in a construct-chain: e.g., ליהו מרא שמיא, "to Yahu, the Lord of Heaven" (*AP* 30:15); מרא מלכין, "Lord of kings" (Dan 2:47); מרא שמיא, "Lord of heaven" (Dan 5:23);[23a] also for the suffixal form used of God in a form of address: e.g., מרי, "my Lord" (1QapGen 20:12, 14, 15; 22:32).[24] Schulz saw in the use of this title by the Aramaic-speaking Christian community an affirmation of the *königliche Richterautorität* attributed to Jesus as the enthroned Son of Man who was awaited, and not an affirmation of divinity as in the hellenistic Kyrios-Homologie.[25] And this he sought to establish even though the Aramaic evidence that he adduced did not point incontrovertibly to the absolute usage that the Greek (ὁ) κύριος suggests.[26]

Against the background of such discussions—and I am aware that I have not done justice to the whole background—we should now consider the new Aramaic evidence from the targum of Job of Qumran Cave XI. But before we look at the Aramaic text itself, a comment is necessary about the various names for God in the Hebrew text of Job. In the prologue to the book, in Job's answer to God (42:1-6), and in the epilogue one finds the names of God as יהוה and אלהים; but in the long section of the book known as the dialogue—the debates of Job with his friends, and the speeches of God—the divine names are שדי, אלהים, אלוה, אל,[27] and the name יהוה scarcely appears. Now in the Qumran targum of Job the tetragrammaton in the Hebrew text of Job's answer to God and in the epilogue is translated by אלהא (11QtgJob 37:3 [= Hebr. 42:1]; 38:2bis [= Hebr. 42:9], 3 [Hebr. 42:10], 7 [= Hebr. 42:11]). But in the dialogue, where the tetragrammaton does not normally occur in the Hebrew text, the name שדי is twice rendered by מרא in the absolute state, in one case being partially restored (11QtgJob 24:[5], 7 [= Hebr. 34:10, 12]); it has also been plausibly restored in 26:8 (= Hebr. 35:13). In one instance it significantly stands in parallelism to אלהא.

The Hebrew text of Job 34:12 is part of Elihu's second poetic discourse, in which the just ways of God are extolled. It reads:

Of a truth, God will not act wickedly,	אף אמנם אל לא ירשיע
and the Almighty will not distort justice.	ושדי לא יעות משפט

The Qumran targum (24:6-7), in spite of its fragmentary state, renders this verse thus:

Now will God really do what is deceitful,	הכען צדא אלהא ישקר
and will the Lord [distort justice]?[28]	ומרא [יעות דינא]

Despite the fact that the name מרא occurs in a broken text here, the parallelism with אלהא assures it of its function in the verse as the name for God. Thus in this Palestinian Jewish document we have an instance of the missing link in the development from the construct and suffixal forms of מרא to the absolute usage of *κύριος* in the NT as a title for both Yahweh and Jesus. It is hard to say how often מרא was used in the whole targum, since only about fifteen percent of the Book of Job is preserved in it. In any case, it is a factor that has to be considered in future discussions of the NT title *κύριος*. Moreover, the parallelism with אלהא would seem to indicate that the meaning of the title is not to be restricted to a judicial, kingly authority, but that it is also suggestive of divine status.

Two further comments on the title מָרֵא must be made before we move on to others. The first is that in none of the Palestinian Aramaic material from the first centuries B.C. or A.D. does the absolute form מָר (*mār*) ever occur. Consequently, the fashion of speaking of a *mār*-christology is clearly dependent on obsolete studies and should be abandoned. To justify this, I shall have to explain the formation of the word and beg the reader's indulgence. Whether the Aramaic word for "lord" is ultimately derived from a *lamedh yodh* or a *lamedh aleph* root can be debated, for, as is well known, these classes of verbs fell together in Aramaic.[29] The absolute state of the word may be the **qātal* adjective, **māray*, which became **mārê* (written with a final *aleph* [as in 11QtgJob 24:7] or with a final *he* [as in 1QapGen 20:13, 15] as *matres lectionis*). The suffixal forms, such as מָרְאִי (*mārʾī* < **mārĕʾī* [or **mārĕyī*]) or מָרְאַן (*mārʾan* < *mārĕʾan*), are regularly attested from the eighth century B.C. on, and usually have the *aleph* written.[30] The *aleph*, following a shewa and followed by a full vowel, quiesced in time and produced the form מָרִי, such as we find in the *Genesis Apocryphon*, used not only of men (2:8, 13; 20:25), but also of God (20:12, 14, 15; 22:32), sometimes even in a context of prayer. The forms מָר or מָרָא represent a still later formation, when the original formation was lost sight of, and by the process of back-formation מר (*mār*) was produced from מרי (*mārī*), and the emphatic state was formed accordingly by the addition of final -*ā* (מרא, written with *aleph* as the *mater lectionis*).[31] The forms מָר and מָרָא are well known in Syriac and Palestinian Jewish

Aramaic of later centuries; but they are unattested in first-century Palestinian Aramaic.[32]

Secondly, the absolute usage of מרא may bear on the interpretation of Ps 110:1, as it is used in Mark 12:36 (Matt 22:44; Luke 20:42). The play on *κύριος* in "The Lord said to my lord," is not found in the Hebrew original, נאם יהוה לאדני שב לימיני. But it comes across perfectly in the Greek of both the so-called LXX and the NT: Εἶπεν Κύριος *τῷ κυρίῳ μου*. Leaving aside the question whether the Old Greek translation of the Psalter had already translated the tetragrammaton by *κύριος*,[33] the question is raised about the substitution of other names for it at this period in Palestine. F. Hahn has said, "We should . . . have to assume with Dalman that in Ps 110:1 just as יהוה had been replaced by אֲדֹנָי so אֲדֹנִי had been replaced by מָרִי, but this is an extremely problematic thesis."[34] It has been debated whether the substitution of אדני for יהוה in the reading of Hebrew texts in the synagogues had taken place in pre-Christian times—but there are good reasons for maintaining that it had.[35] Yet the question still remains about the role that the word מרא might have played in an Aramaic form of this verse of Psalm 110. Can one rule out the possibility that the pun in the Greek reflects an Aramaic form such as אֲמַר מָרֵא לְמָרְאִי תֵּב לִימִינִי, "the Lord said to my lord, Sit at my right hand?"[36] I am not so naïve as to wish to conclude from such a possible reconstruction to the authenticity of either the saying or the debate; but others have argued for the authenticity of the saying on other grounds.[37] The consideration that I have been proposing here simply makes arguments of that sort more plausible.

I am aware that I have not produced evidence for מרא as the translation of יהוה with the result that the Aramaic material being discussed is not parallel to the Old Greek translation (in certain manuscripts at least), *κύριος* for יהוה. 11QtgJob has translated שדי by מרא; and that is not exactly the same thing. My point is rather that the title, "the Lord," for God was *not* "unthinkable in Jewish usage" (Bultmann). Once that point is made, we can proceed. For in the Old Greek translations of the Book of Daniel (2:47) מרא is rendered by *κύριος*: מרא מלכין becomes *κύριος τῶν βασιλέων* in both Theodotion and the so-called LXX. Consequently, though one may wonder about the attempted retranslation of Ps 110:1 into Aramaic from the Greek of Mark, the Septuagintal use of *κύριος* as a translation for Aramaic מרא may have to be considered in the future. Admittedly, the evidence from Daniel is not that of the 'absolute usage' of which we spoke earlier; but the evidence, such as it is, cannot be lightly dismissed.[38]

Another Qumran Aramaic text that bears on the titles of Jesus in the NT is a Pseudo-Danielic text from Qumran Cave IV (4QpsDan A[a] [=4Q*246*]), in which the title "Son of God" turns up for the first time in a Qumran text. Acquired from Kando, the quondam Syrian cobbler of Bethlehem, on 9 July 1958, it has been in the care of J. T. Milik since that time. Cryptic references have been made to it in a number of writings from time to time,[39] and at length Milik made it public in a lecture at Harvard University in December 1972, at which he passed out a tentative English translation of the text and exposed the Aramaic text.[40] A full discussion of the text is impossible here and must await Milik's own publication of it. But what is known of it can be mentioned here, since it pertains to the topic of this paper.

What is preserved in this document is a two-columned fragment of nine lines, in which the first third of the lines of col. 1 is unfortunately missing (the text having been torn vertically). But it is a striking text, not only because it contains the titles, "Son of God" and "Son of the Most High" but because it has phrases parallel to Luke 1:32 and 35. These are attributed to someone in the text, but because of the torn condition of the fragment the subject of attribution is not clear. And herein the great debate will ensue. In any case, Milik dates the text on palaeographic grounds to the last third of the first century B.C., and in this lies the extreme importance of this text for our purposes.

Before presenting that part of the text which is pertinent, I should like to cull from it the firm data on which the restoration of the missing parts of the lines must depend. The language of the text makes it clear that it is apocalyptic in character. It speaks of distress that will come upon the earth, of the rule of enemies which will be short-lived, and lasting only "until there arises the people of God." But there are also references to a "king of Assyria" and to "Egypt," and one is consequently tempted to see in them allusions to historical figures or places. But are they?

The text begins with a fragmentary narrative sentence: When something happened, someone fell before the throne. The fallen person seems to address the enthroned person, a king, using the second singular independent personal pronoun and pronominal suffixes (*-k*). The enthroned king seems to be described as shaken by the evils that are to come (described in lines 4-6 of col. 1); among them are references to "the king of Assyria" and to "Egypt." This description could continue on to line 7 ("[ ] will be great upon the earth"); but line 7 could also be the beginning of a change that is promised to the enthroned king: "he / it will be great," will be served by all, will be given lofty titles (lines 8-9, and col. 2, line 1). In col. 2, which is completely preserved, the end of line 1 describes the short-lived duration of the enemy's rule (with plural suffix and third plural verbs). Their reign will continue (only) "until there arises the people of God" (line 4). Its / his rule is then extolled: respite from war, everlasting rule, paths of truth and peace with all cities in submission. For the Great God is / has been with it / him, and He will now subject all enemies to it / him.

The problem in interpreting the text is threefold. (*a*) Are the references to the "king of Assyria," to "Egypt," and the plurals being used as allusions to historical figures and situations, or are they of the sort that one finds in col. 1 of the War Scroll (1:2-4)? (*b*) If they are to be taken in an apocalyptic sense rather than a historical sense, to whom do they refer? (*c*) To whom does the third singular masculine refer? Is it "the people of God" (2:4)? Is it an individual person? Or is it a person representing a collectivity (in the manner of the "one like a son of man" in Dan 7:13 (representing the "holy ones of the Most High" in Dan 7:18)?

One further thing should be noted: the speech addressed to the king seems to be largely made up of compound sentences (two short paratactic clauses are connected by the copula *w-* and at times they betray some rhythm—a feature that has to be respected in the restoration of the lacunae of col. 1).

Milik has interpreted the text in a historical sense, identifying the subject of attribution as Alexander Balas, one of the Seleucid rulers of Syria and Palestine (150-145 B.C.), the son of Antiochus IV Epiphanes, successor to Demetrius I Soter, and the one who bestowed the high priesthood on Jonathan (Josephus, *Ant.* 13.1.1-2, §35-45). He explains the titles "Son of God" and "Son of the Most High" as applicable to Alexander Balas, because his coins identify him as *θεοπάτωρ* or *Deo patre natus*; and as an Alexander, he is "named" by the name of the great king (Alexander the Great). But to do this, he has to restore the last line of col. 1 in a most crucial way: וכלא ישמשון / [לה חלפת מלכא ר]בא יתקרא ובשמה יתכנה, ". . . and all of them will serve [him. Successor of the G]reat [King] he will be called and with his name will he name himself." Milik introduces thus the notion of the *Διάδοχοι* and the "Great King."[41]

The text will long be debated because of its fragmentary nature. Because it is broken in the most crucial spot, it is obviously open to another interpretation—at least one other. I prefer to see it throughout as properly apocalyptic. This would suggest that the enthroned king who is addressed in his worries is someone on the Jewish side rather than on the Seleucid side. Since אל רבא, "the Great God," is explicitly mentioned in 2:7, it is not impossible that that expression should be restored in 1:9, and that the subject of the attribution is a "son" or a descendant of the enthroned king who will be supported by the "Great God." In other words, I should prefer to substitute for Milik's "successor" a word for "son." For the crucial lines 7-9 of col. 1 and the beginning of col. 2, I should read:[42]

7 [ו]רב להוה על ארעא
8 [ברך מלכא כלא שלם י]עבדון וכלא ישמשון
9 [לה והוא בר אל ר]בא יתקרא ובשמה יתכנה

1 ברה די אל יתאמר ובר עליון יקרונה כזיקיא
2 די חזותא כן מלכותהן תהוה שני[ן] ימלכון על
3 ארעא וכלא ידשון עם לעם ידוש ומדינה למד[ינ]ה
4 *vacat* עד יקום עם אל וכלא ינוח מן חרב

[But your son] [7]shall be great upon the earth, [8][O King! All (men) shall] make [peace], and all shall serve [9][him. He shall be called the son of] the [G]reat [God], and by his name shall he be named. (Col. 2) [1]He shall be hailed (as) the Son of God, and they shall call him Son of the Most High. As comets (flash) [2]to the sight, so shall be their kingdom. (For some) year[s] they shall rule upon [3]the earth and shall trample everything (under foot); people shall trample upon people, city upon ci[t]y, [4](*vacat*) until there arises the people of God, and everyone rests from the sword.

No matter what interpretation of this text will eventually prove to be acceptable, there is no doubt that the Aramaic titles, בְּרֵה דִּי אֵל and בַּר עֶלְיוֹן, as applied to some human being in the apocalyptic setting of this Palestinian text of the last third of the first century B.C., will have to be taken into account for any future discussions of the title used of Jesus in the NT.

At this point I should simply point out four things to be considered. (*a*) These titles are not applied to anyone who is called a messiah or anointed one. If my apocalyptic interpretation proves to be right, then they would be applied to the son of some enthroned king, possibly an heir to the throne of David. What this would mean in the context of Hasmonean rule would have to be further investigated. (*b*) In the first title, ברה די אל, one should note the form of the divine name; it is אל, and not the usual Aramaic form, אלה or אלהא. Though the compound אל עליון turns up in the *Genesis Apocryphon* (12:17; 20:12, 16; 21:2, 20; 22:15, 16 bis, 21), the form אל has not, to my knowledge, been attested in Aramaic of this period heretofore. Even though we still do not have the suffixal form of it (אלי) such as the Greek of Matt 27:46 would call for (*ἠλὶ ἠλὶ λεμὰ σαβαχθάνι*), this form of the divine name should be recalled in discussions that bear on that verse (it has often been maintained that *ἠλί* is Hebraic). (*c*) The parallelism of a number of phrases in this text with Luke 1 is tantalizing. Compare:

οὗτος ἔσται μέγας (1:32)	(1:7) [ו]רב להוה על ארעא
υἱὸς ὑψίστου κληθήσεται (1:32)	(2:1) ובר עליון יקרונה
κληθήσεται υἱὸς θεοῦ (1:35)	(2:1) ברה די אל יתאמר
βασιλεύσει . . . εἰς τοὺς αἰῶνας (1:33)	(2:5) מלכותה מלכות עלם
ἐπελεύσεται ἐπὶ σέ (1:35)	(1:1)[43] [ע]לוהי שרת

(*d*) Since this is not the first time that an Aramaic parallel to an expression in the Lucan infancy narrative has turned up in Qumran literature, it raises a further question about the long-standing debate concerning the sources used by Luke in that part of the Third Gospel.[44] Did he compose the infancy narrative in dependence on some Hebrew source, or are the Semitisms in the text merely owing to Luke's imitation of Septuagintal style? In 1957, while working in the scrollery of the Palestine Archaeological Museum, I discovered a phrase in a fragmentary text of Starcky's lot which is related to Luke 2:14, *ἐν ἀνθρώποις εὐδοκίας*, "men of (his) good pleasure": שביעי באנוש רעות[ה וי]קרה "(he [probably Aaron] will be) seventh among men of [his] good will and his [hon]our."[45] In this case the phrase is attested in both

Hebrew and Aramaic.[46] Unfortunately, neither the Aramaic form in that instance nor the new Aramaic parallels in the text just discussed are of a nature to solve the question of Lucan sources in the infancy narrative one way or the other.

Still another title used of Jesus in the Greek NT on which the Qumran Aramaic texts have shed some light is that of מאמר for ὁ Λόγος. As is well known, מאמרא is often used in targumic texts either as a substitute for some anthropomorphism of the Hebrew Scriptures or as an addition to the text when the Hebrew original says that God did, said, commanded, or revealed something. Especially in the latter sense it expresses a certain mediation between Yahweh and the effects of his creative, sustaining or revealing activity and has been regarded as a sort of buffer for his transcendent status.[47] And especially in this sense has it been compared with the Johannine use of λόγος in the prologue of the Fourth Gospel.[48] The so-called Second Targum of Job abounds in instances of מימרא as a buffer. E. Dhorme described the use of it there as attempts "to avoid every kind of anthropomorphism or any expression concerning God that is deemed too realistic."[49] But that targum is clearly of a later date.[50] Now that a targum has been published that clearly dates from pre-Christian times, one naturally wonders whether this feature of the classic targumim is to be found in it. Does מאמר occur in the Qumran targum of Job? The word is used there and the usage has to be scrutinized before we can draw a conclusion about it.

מאמר occurs twice in the Qumran targum of Job, in each case in a suffixal form.[51] The first instance is found in 11QtgJob 28:9, a fragmentary line, which merely reads:

[ ]על מאמרה מן[ ], "at his order" (literally, "his word").

It is part of the Aramaic translation of Job 36:32, which in the Hebrew reads: על כפים כסה אור ויצו עליה במפגיע, 'He covers his hands with the lightning and commands it to strike the mark' (*RSV*). The editors of the Qumran targum think that על מאמרה might correspond to Hebrew על כפים and that the targumist might have sought to avoid the anthropomorphism of God's hands, but they are not sure of it. However, it seems obvious that the targum is not a literal translation of the Hebrew at this point. So one can ask whether על מאמרה is not possibly a paraphrase of Hebrew ויצו. The question would still remain whether the targumist sought to avoid the anthropomorphism of God's hands, especially since the targum does not otherwise eliminate anthropomorphisms. For example, the Hebrew of Job 40:9 reads: ואם זרוע כאל לך ובקול כמהו תרעם, "Have you an arm like God, and can you thunder with a voice like his?" (*RSV*). The Qumran targum renders this verse almost literally: או הא דרע כאלה איתי לך או בקל כותה תרעם, "Or do you have an arm like God, or do you thunder with a voice like his?" (11QtgJob 34:4-5).

The second instance of מאמר in the Qumran targum is better preserved. In fact, it is found in a translation of a verse that has always been problematic in Hebrew and that brings new evidence to support a solution that had been proposed earlier.[52] In Job 39:27 which is part of God's final speech to Job, God says:

"Is it at your command that the eagle mounts up,	אם פיך יגביה נשר
and makes his nest on high?" (*RSV*)	וכי ירים קנו

The Aramaic translation in the targum (11QtgJob 33:8-9) renders it thus:

"Or is it at your word that the eagle mounts up,	או על מאמרך יתגב[ה] נש[רא]
and the black eagle makes his nest on high?"	ועוזא ירים קנ[ה]

(In using עוזא, "the black eagle," the Qumran targum lends its support to the view that כי in the Hebrew text represents the name of a bird, or better is a corrupted form of the name of a bird.)[53] What interests us here is the Hebrew phrase על פיך, "at your command" (*RSV*, but literally "at your mouth[ing]"), which is translated as על מאמרך, "at your word." Here, at first sight, it may seem to be an instance of the substitution of מאמר for Hebrew פה, the substitute for an anthropomorphism. But these are God's words addressed to Job, and the instance is scarcely one of anthropomorphism. Beyond these instances, there is not one example of the buffer usage of מאמרא that is found in the Qumran targum. Since it is precisely the buffer usage which suggests the personification of the Word in the later targumic tradition that has been in question in discussions of the Jewish background of the Johannine λόγος, one still has to ask how early that usage really is in rabbinical writings. While the evidence from the Qumran texts in this matter is really negative, there is always the danger of exaggerating; but, on the other hand, it may suggest a difference between earlier and later targumic traditions. It seems to me that Qumran evidence puts the burden of proof on those who would maintain an early date for the buffer or personified usage of מאמרא in the discussion of the Johannine λόγος. In any case, it is noteworthy that in none of the places where the Second Targum of Job uses מימרא does one find it employed in the Qumran targum, when it has the passage preserved.

Lastly a few words about the Qumran Aramaic data bearing on the title *ὁ υἱὸς τοῦ ἀνθρώπου* as applied to Jesus in the Greek NT. I shall be discussing this matter elsewhere in some detail,[54] and shall only summarize here the bearing of it on the question of titles with which we are dealing. First of all, בר אנש (or in the slightly Hebraized form בר אנוש) is now clearly attested in Qumran Aramaic as a designation for the individual belonging to the collectivity (mankind), meaning generically "a human being" (so in 11QtgJob 26:3), or as a more indefinite designation, meaning "someone" (or with the negative לא, "no one"; so in 1QapGen 21:13). Secondly, there is no instance of its use either (*a*) as a form of address directed to some person, such as the Hebrew בן אדם used of the prophet Ezekiel; (*b*) as a title for an expected or apocalyptic figure, least of all for a messiah or an anointed one; or (*c*) as a surrogate for "I."[55] Thirdly, just as the fashion of speaking of a *mār*-christology is clearly dependent on obsolete philological studies of that title, so too the fashion of speaking about *bar nāš* or *bar nāšā*. The word for "man" is always written at this period with the initial *aleph*, and this should make us wary about citing evidence for the Aramaic background of the title from passages which have only the tell-tale later forms (either without the initial *aleph* or with the *aleph* but also with the fuller orthography of it, ᵓ*y*-, אינש).[56] Finally, if Milik's latest theory about the second part of Ethiopic Enoch, the so-called Similitudes, proves to be acceptable—that that is a Christian substitution for the Book of the Giants, which is attested in Qumran Aramaic texts[57]—then the whole question of the conflated titles in the second part of *1 Enoch,* including the "Son of Man," must be reworked in the discussions of the material regarding the title as used of Jesus.

Such is the evidence from Qumran Aramaic texts that bears on several titles used of Jesus in the Greek NT. Some of the evidence is positive, some of it is negative; but in all instances it makes its own contribution to the modern discussion and study of those titles. The evidence is such that it bears mainly on the philological aspects of the study; but these are basic, and no theological constructs can be proposed that do not at least reckon with this evidence.

II. *Jewish Practices or Beliefs That Have Emerged from Qumran Aramaic Texts*

I should now like to turn to evidence from the Qumran Aramaic texts that is of a different sort and bears on the interpretation of the NT in other ways, and first of all to Jewish practices and beliefs that have come to light in them. The most obvious example is, first of all, the laying-on of hands to exorcize an unclean spirit or to cure an illness. It is found in the *Genesis Apocryphon,* where Abram is begged by the Pharaoh Zoan and his courtier Hirqanos to lay his hands upon the Pharaoh and pray for him that the evil spirit might be exorcized from him and the plagues and afflictions cease. The passage in 1QapGen 20:21, 28-9 has been discussed by others such as D. Flusser and A. Dupont-Sommer.[58] While the prayer that Abram utters is an imitation of Gen 20:1, the cure is accomplished by the laying on of hands, a rite of healing that is not attested among Jews of the OT period and that is not found in rabbinic literature.[59] Consequently, the pertinence of this Aramaic passage for such NT verses as Mark 5:23; 6:5; 7:32; 8:32-35; 16:18, and especially Luke 4:40-41 (where the laying on of hands and the rebuke both occur); Luke 13:13; Acts 9:12, 17-18; 28:8 is especially obvious. In particular, I may cite 1QapGen 20:28-9:

וצלית על [מר]דפא/הו וסמכת ידי על רא[ישה] ואתפלי מנה מכתשא ואתגערת [מנה רוחא] באישתא וחי, "So I prayed for that [per]secutor, and I laid my hands upon his [he]ad. The plague was removed from him and the evil [spirit] was commanded (to depart) [*or*: was exorcized] [from him], and he was cured." Of importance here is the translation of the verbs סמך and גער in the Greek OT by *ἐπιτιθέναι* (e.g., Exod 29: 10, 15, 19; Lev 1:4, 3:2, 4:4) and *ἐπιτιμᾶν* (Gen 37:10; Ruth 2:16; Zech 3:3), by precisely those used in the pertinent NT passages. Though G. R. Driver was inclined to regard this rite in the *Genesis Apocryphon* as "an echo of a Christian passage,"[60] most commentators see the matter the other way round, even though there is still the further question as to how the rite got into the Palestinian Aramaic text in question and into the Qumran community. Its own background is still open to discussion.[61]

In the same passage two other minor parallels might be pointed out: (*a*) the belief in demon-sickness: when the secondary causality of an affliction is not recognized, a spirit is invoked to explain it; consequently, a cure is considered possible through prayer and a rite (of exorcism); (*b*) prayer for a persecutor (if my reconstruction of the text, as given above, is correct).[62] Possibly, this passage in the *Genesis Apocryphon* fills in the background for Matt 5:44, "Pray for those who persecute you," or Rom 12:17, "Bless those who persecute you."

Another instance of a Qumran tenet that has emerged from an Aramaic text confirms the notion of Melchizedek as a heavenly being. This seems to be the view of him that is presented in 11QMelchizedek, a Hebrew text, and the pertinence of this view to the understanding of the comparison of Christ the high priest with him in Hebrews 7 has been noted elsewhere. [63]But recently J. T. Milik published some fragments of an Aramaic text that presents Melchizedek's counterpart, Malki-reša^{c}, as an evil spirit in the heavenly court.[64] Most of the information about him comes from Hebrew texts, but he is mentioned in a fragment of 4Q^{c}Amram^{b} 2:3′.[65] Aside from the new light that is cast on the dualism in Qumran theology by these two spiritual adversaries, Melchizedek and Malki-reša^{c}, there is now some further Jewish background material for Jude 9 (the archangel Michael contending with the devil over the body of Moses).[66] For in Milik's explanation of the texts Melchizedek is merely another name for Michael.

Such are some of the items that have come to light in Qumran Aramaic texts that reveal Jewish beliefs or practices that have bearing on some NT passages.

III. *Qumran Aramaic Literary Parallels to the New Testament*

To terminate my discussion of the contribution of Qumran Aramaic texts to the study of the NT, I should like to gather together here a number of items that are less easily defined or grouped than those in the two preceding sections.

First of all, with reference to the infancy narratives it is surprising how little the first part of the *Genesis Apocryphon* has been exploited for the type of literature found there. There are certain elements in the story of the birth of Noah that give us clear Palestinian literary parallels to details in the Gospel stories of the childhood of Jesus. For instance, Joseph's doubts about Mary in Matt 1:18-23, and the heavenly reassurance given to him are not without parallel in Lamech's doubts about the conception of Noah (1QapGen 2:1-2). Lamech is not reassured by the angel of the Lord, but his father Methuselah does run to Enoch, whose lot is with the holy ones in paradise; he makes known everything to Methuselah (2:19-23; 5:3-25). The extraordinary character of the child born to Mary is better understood against the background of the doubts about the extraordinary Noah, whose conception Lamech feared might have been caused by the watchers, or the holy ones, or the Nephilim. This Qumran parallel does not solve the problem about the origin of the notion of the virginal conception of Jesus or its *religionsgeschichtliche* background; but it may warn us at least not to search too far afield for parallels about the origins of a child born of something other than human conception. In the broken and fragmentary section of the *Genesis Apocryphon* it is almost certain that Enoch reassures Methuselah that Noah is the child of Lamech (see col. 5), an ordinary human being. Yet the idea of another sort of conception is at least entertained in the *Genesis Apocryphon* itself.

In a similar way perhaps one should relate the dream of Joseph, in which he is warned about the machinations of Herod against the child (Matt 2:13-14) and because of which the child is delivered through the flight to Egypt, to the dream that Abram has on the night of his passing the border of Palestine into Egypt. In it Abram is warned about the covetousness of the Egyptians, especially of the Pharaoh, and he is told how he will be delivered through Sarai herself (1QapGen 19:14-24). The dream of deliverance differs, of course, in each story; and Abram's dream has an allegorical symbolism that none of the heavenly communications in the dreams of the Matthean infancy narrative have. In fact, in its symbolism it is more like the dream-vision in Peter's trance, as narrated in Acts 10:10-16. But the motif of the dream of deliverance is there, and its connection with Egypt is not to be missed.

Finally, literary parallels of another sort may be mentioned. These consist of a number of isolated phrases that are similar to NT expressions and are perhaps significant for the interpretation of the latter. Since they are isolated and somewhat disparate, it is impossible to draw any conclusion from them; but there may be some advantage in gathering them together (without any hope of exhausting the list of them).[67]

Matt 11:25	κύριε τοῦ οὐρανοῦ καὶ τῆς γῆς	מרה שמיא וארעא	1QapGen 22:16
Matt 22:16	ἐν ἀληθείᾳ	בקושט(א)	1QapGen 2:5
Luke 3:4	βίβλῳ λόγων Ἠσαΐου	ל[כתב] מלי חנוך	1QapGen 19:25

Luke 4:25	ἐπ᾽ ἀληθείας	בקושט(א)	1QapGen 2:5
Luke 6:7	ἵνα εὕρωσιν κατηγορεῖν αὐτοῦ	די לא ישכח... לממניה	1QapGen 21:13
Luke 7:21	νόσων καὶ μαστίγων καὶ πνευμάτων πονηρῶν	מכתשיא ונגדיא	1QapGen 20:18
Luke 10:21	κύριε τοῦ οὐρανοῦ καὶ τῆς γῆς	מרה שמיא וארעא	1QapGen 22:16
Luke 13:13	πνεῦμα ἀσθενείας	רוח שחלניא, רוח מכדש	1QapGen 20:26, 16
Luke 16:19	ἐνεδιδύσκετο πορφύραν καὶ βύσσον	לבוש סגי די בוץ וארגואן	1QapGen 20:31
Luke 22:15	ἐπιθυμίᾳ ἐπεθύμησα[68]	ובכית אנה אברם בכי תקיף	1QapGen 20:10-11
Acts 7:2	ὁ θεὸς...ὤφθη τῷ πατρὶ ἡμῶν Ἀβραάμ	אתחזי אלהא לאברם בחזוא	1QapGen 22:27
Acts 5:17, etc.	ἀναστάς + verb[69]	קום (asyndetically joined to a verb)	1QapGen 20:5, 29; 21:13
Acts 19:21	τὰ πνεύματα τὰ πονηρά	רוח באישא	1QapGen 20:16-17
Acts 20:3; 15:33; 18:23	ποιήσας τε μῆνας τρεῖς	תרתין עבדתה (understand שנין)	1QapGen 22:28
Gal 1:18	Κηφᾶς	(Hebrew סלע = כפא)	11QtgJob 32:1
2 Thes 2:7	τὸ μυστήριον...τῆς ἀνομίας	רז רשעא	1QapGen 1:3
Jude 9	ὁ δὲ Μιχαὴλ ὁ ἀρχάγγελος, ὅτε τῷ διαβόλῳ διελέγετο περὶ τοῦ Μωϋσέως σώματος	והא תרין דאנין עלי ואמרין	4Q῾Amram[b] 1:10
Matt 7:16; Luke 6:44	(indefinite 3rd pl. = passive verb; cf. BDF §130.2)	יתיבו נה לשרי וינדעון	1QapGen 20:25 1QapGen 20:15

This list will undoubtedly grow with more study and further publication of the Aramaic texts. In a number of the instances listed above one can find similar phraseology in the OT itself, and hence one may query which was really the source of the NT phrase. For instance, "purple and fine linen" may be derived from Prov 31:22 by both Luke and the author of the *Genesis Apocryphon*. The above listing is intended merely to call attention to parallels, without in this instance moving to the further step of trying to establish literary contacts.[70] The only point being made here is that for some NT expressions literary parallels do exist in Palestinian Aramaic texts of a more or less contemporary period and that these may have to be considered in the last analysis when one is debating the origins of NT traditions.

The data that have emerged from the Qumran Aramaic texts are of diverse nature and they bear on the study of NT problems in various ways. For many students of the NT these items will be of no little interest, as they have been for the present writer.

CHART 1[71]

PALESTINIAN ARAMAIC TEXTS

	Text	*Century*	*Editio princeps or preliminary report*
1	῾Ein Gev Jar Inscription	mid 9th	B. Mazar et al., *IEJ* 14 (1964) 27-29 (+pl. 13B)
2	Tel Dan bowl inscription	9th	N. Avigad, *Yediot* 30 (1966) 209-12; *PEQ* 100 (1968) 42-44 (+pl. XVIII)
3	Deir ῾Alla inscription	mid 8th	H. J. Franken, *VT* 17 (1967) 480-81; cf. J. Naveh, *IEJ* 17 (1967) 256-58
4	Amman inscription	9th-8th	R. D. Barnett, *ADAJ* 1 (1951) 34-36

5	Tell Zeror inscription	8th	M. Kochavi, *RB* 72 (1965) 549
6	Inscribed seals	9th on	F. Vattioni, *Augustinianum* 11 (1971) 47-87; cf. *Bib* 50 (1969) 357-87
7	Adon letter	c. 600	A. Dupont-Sommer, *Sem* 1 (1948) 43-68
8	Tell Siran bottle inscription	c. 600	H. O. Thompson and F. Zayadine, *BASOR* 212 (1973) 5-11
9	Elath ostraca	7th-5th	N. Glueck, *BASOR* 80 (1940) 3-10; 82 (1941) 3-11; cf. J. Naveh, *BASOR* 183 (1966) 27-30
10	Heshbon ostraca (?)	525-500	F. M. Cross, *AUSS* 7 (1969) 223-29; 11 (1973) 126-31; cf. J. Naveh, *BASOR* 203 (1971) 27-32
11	Samaria sherds	6th-4th	S. A. Birnbaum, *The Objects from Samaria* (ed. J. W. Crowfoot et al.; London: P.E.F., 1957) 9-34; G. A. Reisner et al., *Harvard Excavations at Samaria 1908-1910* (Cambridge, MA: Harvard, 1924), 1.247-48; 2, pl. 58*a-h*
12	Ashdod ostracon	mid-5th	J. Naveh, *Atiqot* 9-10 (1971) 200-1
13	ʿAraq el-Emir inscription	6th-5th	E. Littmann, *Greek and Latin Inscriptions* (Princeton University Arch. Expedition to Syria 1904-5; Leiden: Brill, 1907) 1-4
14	Lachish incense altar	5th-4th	A. Dupont-Sommer, *Lachish III: The Iron Age* (ed. O. Tufnell; London: Oxford, 1953) 358-59; cf. F. M. Cross, *BASOR* 193 (1969) 21-24
15	Tell Arad ostraca	5th-4th	Y. Aharoni and R. Amiran, *IEJ* 14 (1964) 141-42 (+pl. 38B), 280-83; 17 (1967) 233-49
16	Tell Abu Zeitun jar fragment	Persian P.	J. Kaplan, *Yediot* 22 (1958) 98-99
17	Beersheba ostraca	Persian P.	Y. Aharoni (cf. J. Naveh, *BASOR* 203 [1971] 31)
18	Gibeon jar inscription	Persian P.	J. Naveh, *BASOR* 203 (1971) 31
19	Horvat Dorban jar inscription	Persian P.	Y. Aharoni, *IEJ* 13 (1963) 337
20	Ezra (Aramaic parts)	Persian P.	
21	Wadi ed-Daliyeh papyri	c. 350	F. M. Cross, *BA* 26 (1963) 110-21
22	Yehud jar handles	Persian P.	
23	En-Gedi ostraca	400-350	B. Mazar and I. Dunayevsky, *IEJ* 14 (1964) 123; 15 (1965) 258-59; *Yediot* 27 (1963) pl. 26, fig. 3
24	Nebi Yunis ostracon	350-300	F. M. Cross, *IEJ* 14 (1964) 185-86 (+pl. 41H)
25	Kerak inscription	350-300	J. T. Milik, *SBFLA* 9 (1958-59) 331-41; 10 (1959-60) 147, 154
26	Tell el-Farʿah ostraca	c. 300	A. E. Cowley, *JRAS* (1929) 111-12; E. Macdonald et al., *Beth Pelet II: Prehistoric Fara* (London: British School of Archaeology in Egypt, 1932) 29 (+pl. LXI/3); J. Naveh, *BASOR* 203 (1971) 31
27	Khirbet el-Kom ostraca	277	L. T. Geraty, *BASOR* 220 (1975) 55-61
28	Daniel (Aramaic parts)		
29	Qumran Aramaic texts	150 B.C.-A.D. 70	See chart 2; also my commentary on 1QapGen (2d ed., 1971), p. 20 n. 55

	Text	*Century*	*Editio princeps or preliminary report*
30	Jerusalem ossuaries	100 B.C.-A.D. 100	See my commentary on 1QapGen (2d ed., 1971), pp. 21-22 nn. 58-9; see also pp. 39, 53 above and *MPAT*, ¶68-148
31	Uzziah inscription	1st century B.C./A.D.	E. L. Sukenik, *Tarbiz* 2 (1930-31) 288-92; cf. *CBQ* 32 (1970) 520 n. 68; see p. 53 above
32	Masada ostracon	A.D. 66-73	Y. Yadin, *IEJ* 15 (1965) 111
33	Murabbaʿat Texts	1st-2d centuries A.D.	See my commentary on 1QapGen (2d ed., 1971), p. 28 n. 67; see p. 54 above, n. 76
34	Synagogue inscriptions	3rd-6th centuries A.D.	See p. 54 above, n. 89; *MPAT*, A1-A56
35	Coins		E.g. see F. Vattioni, *Augustinianum* 11 (1971) 47-87; J. Naveh, *IEJ* 18 (1968) 20-25; *AION* 16 (1966) 33-34

CHART 2[72]

QUMRAN ARAMAIC TEXTS

	Siglum	*Brief Description*	*Editio princeps or preliminary report*
1	1QapGen	Book of the Patriarchs	N. Avigad and Y. Yadin, *A Genesis Apocryphon: A Scroll from the Wilderness of Judaea* (Jerusalem: Magnes, 1956)
2	1Q*20*	Part of 1	DJD, 1.86-87
3	1QTLevi	Testament of Levi (= 1Q*21*)	DJD, 1.87-91
4	1Q*23*	Book of the Giants	DJD, 1.97-98; cf. J. T. Milik, "Turfan et Qumran" (see p. above, n. 57), 120-21; *HTR* 64 (1971) 366-72
5	1Q*24*	Book of the Giants (?)	DJD, 1.99; cf. J. T. Milik, *HTR* 64 (1971) 366-72
6	1QNewJerus	New Jerusalem (= 1Q*32*)	DJD, 1.134-35
7	1Q*63-68*	Miscellaneous	DJD, 1.147
8	2QNewJerus	New Jerusalem (= 2Q*24*)	DJD, 3.84-89; M. Baillet, *RB* 62 (1955) 222-45
9	2Q*26*	Book of the Giants	DJD, 3.90-91; cf. J. T. Milik, *HTR* 64 (1971) 366
10	3Q*12*	Fragments	DJD, 3.102
11	3Q*13*	Fragments (Aramaic?)	DJD, 3.102
12	3Q*14*	Fragments	DJD, 3.103
13	4QTLevi[a,b,c]	Testament of Levi	(MS b) J. T. Milik, *RB* 62 (1955) 398-406; *Ten Years of Discovery in the Wilderness of Judaea* (SBT 26; London: SCM, 1959) 34
14	4QTQahat	Testament of Qahat	J. T. Milik, *RB* 79 (1972) 97
15	4QTBenj	Testament of Benjamin (?)	Starcky's lot
16	4QTestuz	'Precious Tablets'	M. Testuz, *Sem* 5 (1955) 37-38; cf. J. Starcky, *RB* 63 (1956) 66
17	4QșNab	Prayer of Nabonidus	J. T. Milik, *RB* 63 (1956) 407-11; *Ten Years*, 36-37
18	4QpsDan[a,b,c]	Pseudo-Daniel Texts	J. T. Milik, *RB* 63 (1956) 411-15
19	4QpsDan A[a]	Pseudo-Daniel ('Son of God')	J. T. Milik, See pp. 90-94 above
20	4QMess aram	Birth of Noah (end of the Book of Giants)	J. Starcky, *Mémorial du cinquantenaire 1914-1964: Ecole des langues orientales anciennes de l'Institut Catholique de Paris* (Paris: Bloud et Gay, 1964) 51-66; cf. J. T. Milik, *HTR* 64 (1971) 366
	Siglum	*Brief Description*	*Editio princeps or preliminary report*
21	4QTob aram[a]	Book of Tobit	J. T. Milik, *RB* 63 (1956) 60; *Congress Volume, Strasbourg 1956* (VTSup 4; Leiden: Brill, 1957) 23-24; *RB* 73 (1966) 522-30, esp. p. 522 n. 3
22	4QTob aram[b,c,d]	Book of Tobit	J. T. Milik, *RB* 63 (1956) 60; 73 (1966) 522 n. 3
23	4QAh A, C	Texts about Aaron	J. T. Milik, *Ten Years*, 36
24	4QBront	Brontologion (Zodiac)	J. T. Milik, *Ten Years*, 42
25	4QDCP	"Devin à la cour perse" (texte pseudo-historique)	J. Starcky, *RB* 63 (1956) 66
26	4Q'Amram[a]	Visions of Amram[a]	J. Starcky, *RB* 63 (1956) 66; J. T. Milik, *RB* 79 (1972) 77, 81, 84, 94; *Ten Years*, 36
27	4Q'Amram[b]	Visions of Amram[b]	J. T. Milik, *RB* 79 (1972) 78-84
28	4Q'Amram[c]	Visions of Amram[c]	J. T. Milik, *RB* 79 (1972) 77
29	4Q'Amram[d]	Visions of Amram[d]	J. T. Milik, *RB* 79 (1972) 83-84
30	4Q'Amram[e]	Visions of Amram[e]	J. T. Milik, *RB* 79 (1972) 90-92
31	4QḥYa'qob	Vision of Jacob (?)	J. Starcky, *RB* 63 (1956) 66
32	4QNewJerus	New Jerusalem	J. Starcky, *RB* 63 (1956) 66; cf. J. T. Milik, DJD, 3.184-93
33	4QkMika'el	Book of Michael (*Kĕtāb Mīkā'ēl*)	J. Starcky, *RB* 63 (1956) 66
34	4QmNoah	Birth of Noah (*Môlad Nōăḥ* [part of the Book of Giants?]	J. Starcky, *RB* 63 (1956) 66; J. T. Milik, *Ten Years*, 35; *HTR* 64 (1971) 366

35	4QHenAstr[a]	Calendar (related to 1 Enoch)	J. T. Milik, *RB* 63 (1956) 60; *HTR* 64 (1971) 336-37; *Ten Years*, 33-34
36	4QHenAstr[b]	Calendar + 1 Enoch 76:13-82:13	J. T. Milik, *HTR* 64 (1971) 338-39, 342; *RB* 65 (1958) 76
37	4QHenAstr[c]	Astronomical Part of 1 Enoch 76:3-78:8	J. T. Milik, *RB* 65 (1958) 76; *HTR* 64 (1971) 336-37
38	4QHenAstr[d]	Astronomical Part following on 1 Enoch 82:20	J. T. Milik, *HTR* 64 (1971) 336-37, 371
39	4QHen[a]	1 Enoch 1:1-9:3 (with gaps)	J. T. Milik, *HTR* 64 (1971) 336-37, 344-54, 374
40	4QHen[b]	1 Enoch 5:9-10:12 (with gaps)	J. T. Milik, *HTR* 64 (1971) 336-37, 344-54
41	4QHen[c]	1 Enoch 1:9-36:4; 84:2-89:37; 104:13-107:2 (with gaps)	J. T. Milik, *HTR* 64 (1971) 336-37, 344-65; *RB* 65 (1958) 70-77
42	4QHen[d]	1 Enoch 22:13-27:1; 89:11-44 (with gaps)	J. T. Milik, *HTR* 64 (1971) 336-37, 344-54
43	4QHen[e]	1 Enoch 18:15-34:1; 88:3-89:30 (with gaps)	J. T. Milik, *RB* 65 (1958) 70-77; *HTR* 64 (1971) 336-37, 344-54
44	4QHen[f]	1 Enoch 86:1-3 (with gaps)	J. T. Milik, *HTR* 64 (1971) 336-37, 354-60
45	4QHen[g]	1 Enoch 91:10-94:2 (with gaps)	J. T. Milik, *HTR* 64 (1971) 336-37, 360-65, 374
46	4QHenG[a]	Enoch, "Book of the Giants"	J. T. Milik, "Turfan et Qumran", 125-26; *HTR* 64 (1971) 366-72
47	4QHenG[b-f]	Enoch, "Book of the Giants"	J. T. Milik, "Turfan et Qumran", 121-25; *HTR* 64 (1971) 366-72
48	4QtgLev	Targum of Leviticus (16:12-15, 18-21)	J. T. Milik, DJD, 6.86-89; R. Le Déaut, *Introduction à la littérature targumique* (Rome: Biblical Institute, 1966) 64-65
49	4QtgJob	Targum of Job (3:4-5; 4:16-5:4)	J. T. Milik, DJD, 6.90
50	5QNewJerus	New Jerusalem (= 5Q*15*)	J. T. Milik, DJD, 3.184-93
51	5Q*24*	Fragment	DJD, 3.196
52	6Q*8*	Book of the Giants	DJD, 3.116-19; cf. J. T. Milik, "Turfan et Qumran", 119-20
53	6Q*14*	"Texte apocalyptique"	DJD, 3.127-28
54	6Q*19*	Genesiac text	DJD, 3.136
55	6Q*23*	Fragments	DJD, 3.138
56	6Q*26*	Fragments	DJD, 3.138-39
57	6Q*31*	Fragments	DJD, 3.141
58	11QtgJob	Targum of Job (= 1/6 of the Hebrew text)	J. P. M. van der Ploeg and A. S. van der Woude, *Le targum de Job de la grotte XI de Qumrân* (Leiden: Brill, 1971)
59	11QNewJerus	New Jerusalem	Cf. J. T. Milik, DJD, 3.184-93

IV. *Addendum: Implications of the 4Q "Son of God" Text*

Since the implications of the use of מרא for Yahweh in Palestinian Judaism of the period contemporary with the NT are spelled out in some detail in the following chapter, it might be well to reflect a little more on the implications of the titles "son of God" and "son of the Most High" which are found, now for the first time, in a Palestinian Aramaic text, discussed briefly above.

The designation of Jesus in the NT as the "Son of God" is widespread, and no other title of his can claim as much significance for later theological development than it. If the title *ὁ υἱὸς τοῦ ἀνθρώπου* outstrips it in enigma, it certainly does not in implication. Whether it is used in the anarthrous form *υἱὸς θεοῦ* or the arthrous form *ὁ υἱὸς τοῦ θεοῦ*, or is uttered by a heavenly voice as *υἱός μου*, or used as a description of Jesus by some NT writer as *υἱὸς αὐτοῦ* or υἱὸς ἑαυτοῦ, its implication is clear: it expresses the distinct relationship that NT writers understood was enjoyed by Jesus of Nazareth to Yahweh, the God of the OT, who is Father.

It is not restricted to the Synoptics (Mark 1:1, 11; 3:11; 5:7; 15:39; Matt 2:15; 3:17; 4:3, 6; 8:29; 14:33; 16:16; 17:5; 26:63; 27:40, 43, 54; Luke 1:32, 35; 3:22; 4:3, 9, 41; 8:28; 9:35; 22:70) and John (1:18, 34, 49; 3:18; 5:25; [9:35]; 10:36; 11:4, 27; 19:7; 20:31); but it is found also in Acts (8:37; 9:20; 13:33), Paul (Rom 1:3-4, 9; 5:10; 8:3, 29, 32; 1 Cor 1:9; 2 Cor 1:19; Gal 1:16; 2:20; 4:4, 6; Eph 4:13; 1 Thes 1:10), Hebrews (1:5; 4:14; 5:5; 6:6; 7:3; 10:29), 1 John (1:3, 7, 8; 3:23; 4:9, 10, 15; 5:5, 9, 10, 11, 12, 13, 20), 2 John (3), Apocalypse (2:18), and 2 Peter (1:17). Moreover, not only is it found in some Pauline passages that are often regarded as kerygmatic fragments (1 Thes 1:10; Rom 1:3-4), but it even develops within the NT itself to the point that it becomes an absolute title, "the Son," on the lips of Jesus himself (Mark 13:32; Matt 24:36), and is so used by Paul (1 Cor 15:28).

This immediately suggests a certain parallelism with the title κύριος, for the absolute (ὁ) κύριος is also found along with modified expressions. On the other hand, interpreters of the NT title ὁ υἱὸς τοῦ Θεοῦ, aware of the various OT uses of the word בן (or υἱός) to designate a relationship of someone to God, have often noted that it is "a long way" from such simple uses in the OT expressions to the solemn and lofty connotation of the title ὁ υἱὸς τοῦ Θεοῦ, as we find it in the NT. W. Bousset posed the question years ago: "May we, without further ado, assume that already the first community of Jesus' disciples had taken the daring step and had creatively formed the title 'the Son of God,' which the Old Testament and the messianic faith of late Judaism did not know, out of Old Testament beginnings (Ps. 2:7) and the tradition about Jesus' baptism and transfiguration? Or did this title ultimately develop first on Greek soil, in the Greek language?"[73]

Though Bousset himself expressed real hesitations about the connection of the NT title with what he called "Jewish messianology"[74] and thought that it came to undisputed dominance in "the area of popular conceptions in the Gentile Christian church and in that of the Pauline-Johannine Christology,"[75] he did not go so far as A. Deissmann had, in seeing its close "connection with the imperial cult and the well-known formula *Divi Filius* (Θεοῦ υἱός...)."[76] Thus, for Bousset, the NT title ὁ υἱὸς τοῦ Θεοῦ was not so clearly of Hellenistic and pagan origin as was κύριος. And yet, as is well known, several writers have sought blatantly to relate this NT title to such an origin; so with varying nuances G. P. Wetter,[77] and W. G. Kümmel.[78]

R. Bultmann hedged somewhat in this matter, for though he asserted that "Hellenistic-Jewish Christians had brought along the *title* "Son of God" embedded in their missionary message, "for the earliest Church had already called Jesus so,"[79] yet he frankly related the connotation of the title as indicative of "divine origin" or of being "filled with divine 'power'" (and not merely messiahship) to a Gentile setting.[80] For him it was a title related to the role of Jesus as θεῖος ἀνήρ[81] (a title that NT writers never gave him), and the real content-element of it was thus of Hellenistic imprint.

Now it would be foolhardy to deny that such Hellenistic notions as "demigods" or "heroes," born of gods or goddesses, or θεῖοι ἄνδρες (to whom the title θεοῦ υἱοί was on occasion given), influenced the early Christian use of it and the connotations that it bore, especially in the Pauline or Johannine writings. But the problem is really to trace that "long way" from the OT data, which many NT interpreters still think were at the root of the title, to the solemn use of the title itself. No little part of this aspect of the problem is the fact that the title "son of God" (in the singular) occurs as such only rarely in late books of the OT in spite of numerous allusions to figures in the OT who are called "son(s)"—scarcely with the connotations that the word or title sometimes has in the NT.

Hence it might be well to review the OT data that bear on the NT title "son of God." The plural expressions in Hebrew בני (ה)אלהים (Gen 6:2, 4; Job 1:6; 2:1; 38:7), בני אלים (Ps 29:1; 89:6), and בני עליון (Ps 82:6),[82] are found in the OT as names of angelic beings in the heavenly court of Yahweh. Again, the plural, either as בני אל חי (Hos 2:1) or simply some form of בנים (Deut 14:1; Isa 1:2; 30:1; Jer 3:22), is used by God of the Israelites. Indeed, on occasion collective Israel is even addressed in the singular as בני, "my son" (Exod 4:22; Hos 11:1). The closest one comes to the singular expression, resembling the NT title, is found not in Hebrew, but in Greek and Aramaic: thus Israel is referred to in the singular as θεοῦ υἱόν (Wis 18:13); and the figure who appears with Shadrach, Meshach, and Abednego walking about unfettered in the fiery furnace is described as דמה לבר אלהין, lit., "resembling a son of (the) god(s)" (Dan 3:25). None of these expressions imply a physical father-son relationship between Yahweh and the person(s) so designated. Hence, it is obvious that neither the descriptive title of the angel(s) nor the collective title for Israel provides an intelligible background to the NT title for Jesus.

On the other hand, the title "son" is given at times to other individuals in the OT tradition. Though he is never called explicitly "son of God," the king who sits on David's throne is three times related to Yahweh as "son": 2 Sam 7:14; Ps 2:7; 89:26-27. Although Ps 2:7 uses of the Davidic king the graphic expressions ילדתיך, "I have begotten you," nevertheless OT commentators are generally loathe to admit that this implies a sort of sacral kingship in the sense of a physical divine sonship of the king, such as could be the connotation of similar expressions in the ancient eastern Mediterranean world.[83] The father-son relationship in the OT rather guarantees divine support and assistance, possibly even divine designation, for the Davidic king, and by implication for his dynasty. This legal legitimation of the dynastic rule is described in poetic language in Ps 89:3-4, 19-37; according to some, it may even have been played out in the concrete in a coronation ritual.[84]

In the deuterocanonical writings of Ben Sira and Wisdom one also finds the name "son" used of the righteous individual Israelite. "Be like a father to the fatherless, help a widow as a husband would; and God will call you son, show you his favor, and save you from the pit" (Sir 4:10).[85] Again, "if the righteous man is God's son, he will help him" (Wis 2:18).[86]

In four instances then we find the singular expression "son of God" used in a titular sense in OT passages: once of an angel, once of collective Israel, and twice of an upright individual Israelite. The connotations vary, but they are all figurative and scarcely approach the nuance of the NT title.

Psalm 2 is the source of the tendency of some biblical interpreters to regard the OT expression as "messianic." Since this adjective properly denotes OT figures who were "anointed" agents of Yahweh in some way or other, the title "son of God" obviously does not express that idea *in se*. And yet, the question, whether the title "son of God" was used of an "anointed" agent—or of a "messiah"—in pre-Christian Judaism is constantly debated. The root of this problem is found in Ps 2:2, where the king on the Davidic throne is called "his [i.e., Yahweh's] anointed" (על יהוה ועל משיחו), whereas v. 7 of the same psalm says, "You are my son, today I have begotten you" (בני אתה אני היום ילדתיך). As has been pointed out many times before, the expression in v. 2 is used of an historical king, not of a future, ideal "David" (such as Jer 30:9 once spoke of: "they shall serve the Lord their God and David their king, whom I will raise up for them"). To cite Psalm 2 as if it were clear evidence in pre-Christian Judaism of a belief in a "messianic" figure (= a future, ideal anointed David) with the title "son of God" is to go beyond the evidence of the psalm (or other related OT passages).[87] The connection between divine sonship and an anointed agent of Yahweh is present in Psalm 2; but it is another question to ask whether the psalm is to be understood "messianically." Moreover, there is no evidence from pre-Christian Palestinian or Diaspora Judaism that Psalm 2 was ever understood or interpreted of a messiah (= a future, ideal anointed Davidic king) nor that the title "son of God" (as such) was applied to a messianic figure, i.e., to an expected "anointed" agent of Yahweh.[88]

It is over against such a background of OT data that we must consider the Qumran text discussed in section I above. In this Aramaic text the titles ברה די אל and בר עליון are applied to some figure or person. Coming from Palestine itself and from the last third of the first century B.C., as is to be judged on palaeographic grounds, it is significant, indeed, since it is the first attestation of such titles in a clearly Aramaic-speaking context. Even if Milik's interpretation of the text were to be correct and the titles were attributed to a Gentile ruler such as Alexander Balas, they were predicated of him by someone who has written in Aramaic but who has apparently borrowed from an OT background. Though Aramaic was also being used in Syria of the period (perhaps in a slightly different dialect), is it likely that it would represent some non-Jewish writing composed in Syria and brought to Qumran? The general thrust of the document and its apocalyptic cast, as well as certain Jewish or OT expressions that it contains (e.g., עם אל; cf. עמי, Jer

6:14, etc.) militate against such an interpretation. The best chances are that the text represents a Jewish composition and that the titles are predicated of some person of Jewish background, possibly historical, but more likely expected. He is not, however, called משיח, an anointed agent of Yahweh.

The implications of this Qumran text and especially of the titles, "son of God" and "son of the Most High," are numerous. First, the titles are clearly related to an *apocalyptic* setting; the trappings or the stage-props (coming distress, flashing comets) serve to enhance the future (eschatological) deliverance, "until there arises the people of God" (2:4).

Second, the *titular* use of the expressions is clear. No matter who the person is to whom the expressions are attributed, they are clearly meant in the titular sense. The verbs יתאמר, "he shall be hailed," and יקרונה, "they shall call him" (in the context of other expressions of naming, יתקרא, יתכנה) leave no doubt about the appellative sense in which the expressions are used. Used presumably of some human being, they raise the question of the precise figurative sense in which they are intended.

Third, unless the figure addressed with these titles was elsewhere called משיחא in the part of the text now lost, there is no indication that he was regarded as an anointed agent of Yahweh. Hence this text supplies no evidence for the alleged *messianic* use of the title "son of God" in pre-Christian Palestinian Judaism. If my thoroughly apocalyptic interpretation of the text were to prove correct, then the titles would be used of a son of some enthroned king, possibly an heir to the Davidic throne. What that would mean, in the context of Hasmonean rule or of opposition to it, would still have to be explored. But, as Bousset and others had maintained earlier, there is still no direct connection between the title "son of God" and "Jewish messianology."[89]

Fourth, if there is no connection of the titles with messianic expectations (in the strict sense) in Palestinian Judaism or even with the messianism of the Qumran community, then there is even less of a connection of the titles with a *θεῖος ἀνήρ* of a miracle-working setting or an association of them with gnostic redeemer myths.[90] The context of the fragmentary text deals with a political strife, in which the "son of God" figure is hailed as the harbinger of peace and everlasting dominion, as a bearer of those things associated with the restoration of Davidic kingship.

Fifth, the title בר עליון, "son of the Most High," supplies indirectly the Palestinian background for the title used by the demoniac of Gerasa, *υἱὲ τοῦ Θεοῦ τοῦ ὑψίστου* (Mark 5:7; Luke 8:28). Whereas Ps 82:6 (*υἱοὶ ὑψίστου*) could be taken as the OT background of Luke 6:35 (*υἱοὶ ὑψίστου*), where the plural phrase is used, "sons of the Most High," the singular phrase (as used in Mark 5:7) is attested only after a fashion in the OT (in LXX Sir 4:10); and the discovery of the Palestinian usage in this Aramaic text is consequently significant.

Sixth, the Palestinian attestation of the title "son of God" in a pre-

Christian text makes it at least possible that this title was part of the early Christian kerygma that was carried abroad from its Jerusalem matrix to the Hellenistic world, where it encountered the Graeco-Roman use of *divi filius* or *Θεοῦ υἱός* in the widespread emperor-worship. Whether or not "son of God" was already a kerygmatic title for Jesus will have to be judged on still further grounds, viz., according to the levels of tradition that can be sorted out in the NT passages where it occurs. But at least one cannot rule out the kerygmatic use of the title on the basis that it could only be the product of missionary activity among the Gentiles of the eastern Mediterranean world. Moreover, linked to this question is that about the nature of its traditional character. From the Qumran text it would seem that the titles are associated with someone who will rule, probably the son of a king. This, then, would call in question the suggestion made by W. Grundmann, that "son of God" was the title for the *priestly* messiahship of Jesus.[91]

Lastly, the title "son of God" in the Aramaic text scarcely expresses the divine begetting of the person to whom it is attributed. There is not the slightest hint that the titles are meant in this sense, nor in the sense of an incarnation of God. The connotations with which the NT title for Jesus is fraught and the connections made with it (the implication of pre-existence, adoptionism, miraculous conception, etc.) are left untouched by this Qumran text. But it was scarcely to be expected that a text which would mention a "son of God" in a Palestinian Jewish context would carry with it all the *impedimenta* associated with the NT title itself.

The study of the NT titles for Jesus of Nazareth will continue. The discovery of this Aramaic text with examples of an important title that is attributed to him by NT writers reopens many aspects of the discussion indulged in up to this point. What we have put together here only scratches the surface; and much still remains to be discussed.

NOTES TO CHAPTER 4

*A paper originally read at the Southampton meeting of the S.N.T.S., 31 August 1973, and published in *NTS* 20 (1973-74) 382-407.

[1]For the phases of Aramaic with which one has to deal in these discoveries, see pp. 57–84 above.

[2]For the new discoveries of Old Syriac inscriptions, see p. 83 above, n. 108.

[3]See chart 1 at the end of this chapter for a list of the more important texts from Palestine. "Palestine" is used here in a slightly broad geographical sense to include certain Transjordanian sites that have yielded material which is so similar to finds from Palestine proper that they have to be included in a survey such as this. The pertinence of such finds to the OT commentator is obvious in most cases. In some instances there is hesitation about one text or another because scholars question whether it may be Edomitc, Ammonite, Hebrew, or Phoenician, but written in

Aramaic scripts; see p. 77 above, n. 31; cf. J. Naveh, "Hebrew Texts in Aramaic Script in the Persian Period?" *BASOR* 203 (1971) 27-32. It should be noted also that in some instances the text is quite small (e.g., an inscription of a few words on a piece of pottery) and seemingly of little value; this is admitted, but even such small texts attest to the use of the language in Palestine over a long period.

[4]See chap. 1 above.

[5]I have touched upon this problem briefly in a number of places elsewhere: *CBQ* 30 (1968) 420-21; 32 (1970) 110-12, 524-25 (see pp. 40–42 above). Cf. also the statement of J. C. Greenfield, quoted above (p. 8); the review of M. McNamara, *Targum and Testament* (Grand Rapids: Eerdmans, 1972) by B. Z. Wacholder, *JBL* 93 (1974) 133; F. Rosenthal, *Die aramaistische Forschung* (p. 75 above, n. 2), 103-9.

[6]It is readily admitted that none of these texts is complete; all of them are fragmentary, but they do constitute a considerable bulk of material and cannot be dismissed as "miscellaneous 'bits and pieces.'" The list is as complete as I can make it at this time; references are either to the definitive publications or to the provisory and preliminary notices. See further my book, *The Dead Sea Scrolls: Major Publications and Tools for Study* (SBLSBS 8; Missoula: Scholars Press, 1975); cf. C. Burchard, *Bibliographie zu den Handschriften vom Toten Meer II* (BZAW 89; Berlin: Töpelmann, 1965) 321-44; continued in *ZDPV* 83 (1967) 95-101; J. A. Sanders, "Palestinian Manuscripts 1947-1967," *JBL* 86 (1967) 431-40; "Palestinian Manuscripts 1947-1972," *JJS* 23 (1973) 74-83 (also in F. M. Cross and S. Talmon [eds.], *Qumran and the History of the Biblical Text* [Cambridge: Harvard University, 1975] 401-13.

[7]The date of composition of one or other text might well be prior to 150 B.C. By and large, the dates given are based on palaeographical evidence, and one must consult the discussions of the individual texts.

[8]So the community of Qumran is often judged to have been, mainly because of its communal, ascetic, and secret practices. But one should recall that Josephus said of them that they "settled in large numbers in every town" (*JW* 2.8.4 §124). We still do not know how to specify the relation between such groups and those at the "mother-house" of Qumran. This bears on the question of Aramaic as a language used among them and precisely at the Qumran settlement itself. I am presently much taken by the hypothesis proposed by J. Murphy-O'Connor for the origin of the Essenes and the history of their beginnings; see "The Essenes and Their History," *RB* 81 (1974) 215-44.

[9]N. Avigad and Y. Yadin, *A Genesis Apocryphon* (p. 54 above, n. 72); for an extended bibliography on this text, see my commentary (p. 22 above, n. 27), 42-46; a few more recent things can be found in B. Jongeling, C. J. Labuschagne, and A. S. van der Woude (eds.), *Aramaic Texts from Qumran with Translations and Annotations* (SSS 4; Leiden: Brill, 1976) 80-81. J. P. M. van der Ploeg and A. S. van der Woude, *Le targum de Job de la grotte xi de Qumrân* (p. 22 above, n. 32); bibliography on this text is found on pp. 175–76 below.

[10]See further p. 9 above and p. 166 below.

[11]See pp. 8–9 above.

[12]"4Q Visions de ᶜAmram et une citation d'Origène," *RB* 79 (1972) 77-97.

[13]See J. T. Milik, "*Milkî-ṣedeq* et *Milkî-rešaᶜ* dans les anciens écrits juifs et chrétiens," *JJS* 23 (1972) 95-144, esp. pp. 126-29.

[14]Cf. W. F. Albright, *The Archaeology of Palestine* (5th ed.; Baltimore: Penguin, 1960) 201-2. See pp. 38–39 above.

[15]*The Words of Jesus* (p. 23 above, n. 53), 326.

[16]Ibid., 324-40. The reader will want to investigate his connection between Aramaic *mārêᵓ* and Hebrew *môreh*. Is there any?

[17]*Kyrios Christos: A History of the Belief in Christ from the Beginnings of Christianity to Irenaeus* (Nashville: Abingdon, 1970) 126-27.

[18]*Theology of the New Testament* (2 vols.; London: SCM, 1956), 1. 51.

[19]*Herr ist Jesus* (Gütersloh: Bertelsmann, 1924); W. Foerster and G. Quell, "Κύριος, etc." *TDNT* 3 (1965) 1046-95.

[20] *The Christology of the New Testament* (London: SCM, 1963) 195-237.

[21] "Discipleship and Belief in Jesus as Lord from Jesus to the Hellenistic Church," *NTS* 2 (1955-56) 87-99.

[22] *The Titles of Jesus in Christology: Their History in Early Christianity* (New York / Cleveland: World, 1969) 68-128.

[23] "Maranatha und Kyrios Jesus," *ZNW* 53 (1962) 125-44. Some of the data amassed there need slight correction today.

[23a] Other instances of the construct-chain usage can be found in Qumran texts: מרה עלמא, "the eternal Lord" (1Q*20* 2:5); מרה עלמיא, "the Lord of the ages" (1QapGen 31:2); במרה רבותא, "by the Great Lord" (lit., "by the Lord of Greatness [or Majesty]", 1QapGen 2:4); מרה שמיא, "the Lord of the heavens" (1QapGen 7:7; 12:17); מרה שמיא וארעא, "the Lord of heaven and earth" (1QapGen 22:16, 21).

[24] See also 4QTLevi 1:10, 18; 2:6. The example of מָרִי in 1QapGen 20:25, cited by Schulz (*ZNW* 53 [1962] 136) as "Gottesaussage," is actually addressed to the Pharaoh. In 4Q^{c}Amram^{b} 2:3 one also finds the form, but with the older spelling מראי (see J. T. Milik, *RB* 79 [1972] 79).

[25] *ZNW* 53 (1962) 138.

[26] Lest there be any misunderstanding in the subsequent discussion, it is to be noted that the word "absolute" in the *kyrios*-debate has normally been applied to the use of *the title* (with or without the definite Greek article) *alone*, when it has no possessive adjective (such as "my" or "our") or when it is not modified by a genitive or a prepositional phrase (e.g., *κύριος . . . τοῦ σαββάτου*, Matt 12:8; or Κ*ύριε τοῦ οὐρανοῦ καὶ τῆς γῆς*, Matt 11:25). This terminology, used of the Greek expression, should not be confused with the absolute *state* of an Aramaic noun. The Aramaic evidence underlying the Greek absolute usage could be in either the absolute state (strictly = "a lord") or the emphatic state ("the lord"). The Greek absolute usage is intended in the sense of *attributlos*. This has been confused by no less a scholar than G. Vermes, *Jesus the Jew: A Historian's Reading of the Gospels* (London: Collins, 1973) 112.

[27] See M. H. Pope, *Job: Introduction, Translation and Notes* (AB 15; 3d ed.; Garden City: Doubleday, 1973) xxiv. Cf., however, Job 12:9 (יד יהוה); but check the *apparatus criticus*.

[28] See J. P. M. van der Ploeg and A. S. van der Woude, *Le targum de Job de la grotte XI de Qumrân* (p. 22 above, n. 32) 58. The top of the *aleph* of מרא is barely visible in the photograph, and the editors have marked it as a probable reading. Even though the lacuna commences immediately after this broken letter, it is unlikely that the word had a suffix, either *ī* or *ān*. One could not, of course, exclude some form of the emphatic state ending (e.g., *-āh*, written with a final *he* instead of the *aleph* because of the preceding *aleph*; the more normative form would be *māryā*ʾ a form now attested in 4QEn^{b} 1 iv 5). Indeed, that would make a better parallel with the emphatic אלהא; but it would still mean "the Lord." That the reading מרא is not improbable here can be seen from the support to be had for it in a few other Qumran Aramaic phrases that I had pointed out earlier; one of them is a bit ambiguous, but it can still be cited to support the reading used here. In 1QapGen 20:12-13 Abram prays to God after Sarai has been taken away from him for the Pharaoh: בריך אנתה אל עליון מרי לכול עלמים די אנתה מרה ושליט על כולא "Blessed (are) you, O God Most High, my Lord, for all ages! For you are Lord and Master over all." The form מרה is in the absolute state (as predicate), but it is also *attributlos* (since it is otherwise unattested as construed with the preposition על; the phrase על כולא is dependent on שליט; cf. Dan 2:48 . . . על השלטה). It was the only example of the absolute usage of מרה that I had known in which the title was "close to the Palestinian absolute use" or "Lord" for God, when I wrote my brief sketch of *Pauline Theology* (Englewood Cliffs, NJ: Prentice-Hall, 1967) 36. Whether one hesitates about the coordination here or not, the absolute state is attested and would support the reading in 11QtgJob under discussion. Interestingly, G. Vermes (*Jesus the Jew* [n. 26 above] 112) cites the same instance in 1QapGen 20:12-13, saying that it "comes very close to a titular or absolute use" of "Lord." But he cites a second example, אנתה מרה לכול מלכי ארעא (1QapGen 20:15-16), "you are the Lord of all the kings of the earth." Though מרה occurs here again in the absolute *state*, the following prepositional phrase would preclude its being understood in the absolute sense intended in the discussion of the Greek title, since it is not *attributlos* (see p. 133 below, n. 18).

As for my restoration of line 7, the root עות, used in the Hebrew text, is also known in Aramaic, and so it is retained; the Hebrew noun משפט is translated by דין in 11QtgJob 34:4, and on the basis of that equivalence it is used here. The later targum of Job (see P. de Lagarde, *Hagiographa chaldaice* [Leipzig: Teubner, 1873; reprinted, Osnabrück: Zeller, 1967] 110) translates the verse thus:

ברם בקושטא אלהא לא יחייב ושדי לא יקלקל דינא,

"But truly God will not act in guilty fashion, and the Almighty will not make light of justice." This is a good instance of the difference in the two targums. Save for אלהא and the restored [דינא], the translation in the later targum is quite independent of the Qumran version—as is the case almost everywhere (see pp. 167–74 below).

[29]See F. R. Blake, "Studies in Semitic Grammar, V," *JAOS* 73 (1953) 7-16, esp. pp. 12-14. Cf. G. Widengren, "Aramaica et syriaca," *Hommages à André Dupont-Sommer* (Paris: A. Maisonneuve, 1971) 221-31, esp. pp. 228-31.

[30]*Bar Rākib* 1:5, 6, 9; *Panammu* 19; *AP* 16:8; 37:17; 38:[2]; 39:2; 54:10; 67:7; 68:[9]; 70:1, 2; 77:1; 80:9; *BMAP* 13:1, 9; *AD* 3:3, 5; 4:2; 10:1, 2; *Herm WP* 3:1; etc. The form מרי also turns up sporadically before the first century (*Aššur ostracon* 6; *APO* 86:10); but these texts are problematic. In any case, the evidence is not from Palestine.

[31]It should be obvious that מרא cannot be vocalized in the absolute state as *mārāʾ* or *mārāh*. The ending *-āʾ* would make an emphatic state of it; and the ending *-āh* would either be an alternate ending for the masculine emphatic state or the feminine absolute state. Compare G. Vermes, *Jesus the Jew*, 112.

[32]An isolated instance of מר at an earlier date is found on a seal impression from Khorsabad; see M. Sprengling, "An Aramaic Seal Impression from Khorsabad," *AJSL* 49 (1932) 53-55.

[33]Cf. P. E. Kahle, *The Cairo Geniza* (2d ed.; Oxford: Blackwell, 1959) 222; see further below, p. 120.

[34]*The Titles of Jesus* (n. 22 above), 105.

[35]See S. Schulz, "Maranatha und Kyrios," 133; also pp. 126–27 below.

[36]The targum on the Psalms is of no help at this point, since it has preserved two paraphrases of v. 1, and in neither of them is there the play on the words.

אמר יי במימריה לשואה יתי רבון על כל ישראל ברם אמר לי תוב
ואורך לשאול דמן שבטא דבנימן עד דימות ארום לית מלכותא מקרבא
אחברתא ובתר כן אשוי בעלי ,דבבך כביש לרגלך:

"Dixit Dns in verbo suo, se constituturum me dominum totius Israelis, sed dixit mihi denuo, operire vero Saulem, qui est de tribu Benjamin, donec moriatur, quia non convenit regno cum socio, et postea ponam inimicos tuos suppedaneum pedum tuorum." The second targumic paraphrase reads:

אמר יי במימריה למתן לי רבנותא חלף דיתבית לאולפן אוריתא
דימיני אורך עד דאשוי בעל דבבך כביש לרגלך

"Dixit Dns in verbo suo, se daturum mihi dominatione(m), eo quod incubuerim doctrinae Legis dexterae ejus; Expecta donec ponam inimicum tuum suppedaneum pedum tuorum." The text of these targumic paraphrases is taken from B. Walton, *S. S. Biblia polyglotta* (6 vols.; London: Thomas Roycroft, 1957), 3. 266; with slight variations they can be found in P. de Lagarde, *Hagiographa chaldaice*, 67.

[37]See David M. Hay, *Glory at the Right Hand: Psalm 110 in Early Christianity* (SBLMS 18; Nashville: Abingdon, 1973) 158-59.

[38]Further support for this evidence can be found in the remarks of M. Black, "The Christological Use of the Old Testament in the New Testament," *NTS* 18 (1971-72) 1-14, esp. pp. 9-11. For further discussion of the *kyrios*-problem, see pp. 115–42 below.

[39]See A. D. Nock, *Gnomon* 33 (1961) 584; A. J. B. Higgins, *CJT* 6 (1960) 202; J. A. Fitzmyer, *TS* 25 (1964) 429; R. E. Brown, *TS* 33 (1972) 32 n. 86. What is now clear from the text is that the titles used here are not linked with the title "messiah" or "anointed one" (contrast 11Q Melch 18), so that even if the regal figure with whom the text may deal has to be understood in an apocalyptic

sense rather than in a historical sense, this fragmentary text does not yet reveal the explicit conflation of titles such as one finds in the second part of Ethiopic *Enoch*. Hence one should beware of Nock's formulation about Qumran evidence "stating the Messiah's relationship to God in terms of sonship" in this text.

[40]It was reported that Milik was to publish the text shortly in *HTR*. One should recall that he had already published some fragments of a Pseudo-Danielic cycle from Qumran Cave IV; see "'Prière de Nabonide' et autres écrits d'un cycle de Daniel, fragments de Qumrân 4," *RB* 63 (1956) 407-15.

[41]Likewise gratuitous is the introduction of the mention of angels in 1:3. Milik translated אתור as "Syria," rather than as "Assyria" (see 1QM 1:2-4, where it occurs in collocation with מצרים in a Hebrew text of apocalyptic tenor). Again, in 1:4 [ר]ברבין must be masculine, and then it could hardly modify שנין, "years" (as restored by Milik), since this word is feminine. Moreover, in Aramaic רב normally means "great," and not "many" (for which the usual term is שגיא). Lastly, does the feminine form חלפת really mean "successor" in the sense intended?

[42]Details and full discussion of this text will have to await another occasion. For the restoration of 1:8 ("all men shall make peace"), I have simply borrowed an expression that occurs in 2:6 of the text, וכלא יעבד שלם.

[43]Milik supplies רוחה before this phrase, "[and His spirit] rested upon him."

[44]See, for instance, P. Winter, "Some Observations on the Language in the Birth and Infancy Stories of the Third Gospel," *NTS* 1 (1954-55) 111-21; N. Turner, "The Relation of Luke i and ii to Hebraic Sources and to the Rest of Luke-Acts," *NTS* 2 (1955-56) 100-9; P. Benoit, "L'Enfance de Jean-Baptiste selon Luc i," *NTS* 3 (1956-57) 169-94.

[45]"'Peace upon Earth among Men of His Good Will' (Lk 2:14)," *TS* 19 (1958) 225-27; reprinted in *ESBNT*, 101-4.

[46]Ibid., for bibliography on the Hebrew usage.

[47]See M. Ginsburger, "Die Anthropomorphismen in den Thargumim," *Jahrbücher für protestantische Theologie* 17 (1891) 262-80, 430-58; G. F. Moore, "Intermediaries in Jewish Theology: Memra, Shekinah, Metatron," *HTR* 15 (1922) 41-85; V. Hamp, *Der Begriff 'Wort' in den aramäischen Bibelübersetzungen* (Munich: Neuer-Filser-V., 1938).

[48]See, for instance, R. E. Brown, *The Gospel according to John (i-xii)* (AB 29; Garden City: Doubleday, 1966) 523-24. An attempt to remedy the "neglect of targumic evidence" concerning the מאמרא background for John's "choice of Logos as a designation for Christ" has recently been made by M. McNamara (*Targum and Testament: Aramaic Paraphrase of the Hebrew Bible: A Light on the New Testament* [Grand Rapids: Eerdmans, 1972] 102-3). He bases his argument on Tg. Neofiti 1 and its insertion into Exod 12:42 of "a song in honour of four nights" of deliverance in salvation history. He quotes approvingly A. Díez Macho's Aramaic version of John 1:14 (from "El Logos y el Espiritu Santo," *Atlantida* 1 [1963] 389-90), without ever asking himself whether such Aramaic surrogates as מאמרא or שכינתא (in the buffer sense) or such Aramaic words as חמא ("see"), היכמא (conjunction) are otherwise attested at this period in Palestinian Aramaic. See further M. McNamara, "*Logos* of the Fourth Gospel and *Memra* of the Palestinian Targum (Ex 12:42)," *ExpTim* 79 (1967-68) 115-17.

[49]*A Commentary on the Book of Job* (tr. H. Knight; London: Nelson, 1967) ccxviii-ccxix.

[50]This targum is said to be of Palestinian origin and to date from the fourth or fifth century A.D.; see P. Grelot, *RQ* 8 (1972-76) 105; "before the fall of Rome in 476 C.E." (*Encyclopaedia judaica* [Jerusalem: Keter; New York: Macmillan, 1971], 4. 848).

[51]It seems to occur also in 4Q^{c}Amram^{b} 2:6′ in the sense of "command"; but the text is damaged and little can be concluded from it. See J. T. Milik, "4Q Visions de ^{c}Amram" (n. 12 above), 79.

[52]See J. Reider, "Etymological Studies in Biblical Hebrew," *VT* 4 (1954) 276-95, esp. p. 294; G. R. Driver, "Job 39:27-28: the KY-bird," *PEQ* 104 (1972) 64-66.

[53]See further below, p. 174.

[54]See chap. 6 below.

[55]*Pace* G. Vermes, "Appendix E: The Use of בר נשא / בר נש in Jewish Aramaic," in M. Black, *Aramaic Approach* (3d ed., 1967), 310-28, it is never used as a circumlocution for "I" (p. 320), nor does it "mean 'I'" (p. 323). See the similar criticism levelled against him by J. Jeremias, cited above p. 25, n. 71. Vermes reiterates his position in *Jesus the Jew*, 188–91.

[56]See further *CBQ* 30 (1968) 426-27. To the data given there one should now add the following instances of אנש(א): 11QtgJob 2:8; 9:9; 11:2; 12:[9]; 19:[7]; 21:5; 22:6; 24:4, 5; 25:6; 26:3; 28:[1], 2bis; 31:4.

[57]See "Problèmes de la littérature hénochique à la lumière des fragments de Qumrân," *HTR* 64 (1971) 333–78; "Turfan et Qumran" (p. 24 above, n. 66), 117–27.

[58]D. Flusser, "Healing through the Laying-on of Hands in a Dead Sea Scroll," *IEJ* 7 (1957) 107-8; A. Dupont-Sommer, "Exorcismes et guérisons dans des écrits de Qoumrân," *Congress Volume, Oxford 1959* (VTSup 7; Leiden: Brill, 1960) 246-61; H. C. Kee, "The Terminology of Mark's Exorcism Stories," *NTS* 14 (1967-68) 323-46.

[59]The closest that one comes to it in the OT is 2 Kgs 5:11, there the Syrian Naaman expects that Elisha would "wave his hand over the place" (והניף ידו אל המקום); cf. the LXX. The text is problematic at best; see my comments on it, *CBQ* 22 (1960) 284 n. 27.

[60]*The Judaean Scrolls* (New York: Schocken, 1965) 461. This view, of course, depends on Driver's interpretation of the Qumran Scrolls in general, on which see R. de Vaux, *RB* 73 (1966) 212-35; *NTS* 13 (1966-67) 89-104; *New Blackfriars* 47 (1966) 396-411.

[61]Assyrian or Babylonian? (so A. Dupont-Sommer); Hellenistic? (see O. Weinreich, *Antike Heilungswunder: Untersuchungen zum Wunderglauben der Griechen und Römer* (Religionsgeschichtliche Versuche und Vorarbeiten, 8/1; Giessen: Töpelmann, 1909) 63-66.

[62]Reading [מר]דפא הו in 1QapGen 20:28-29; see my commentary, p. 139. Cf. Giv^{c}at Ha-Mivtar Tomb Inscription, lines 3-4 (*MPAT* § 68). Another possibility would be [מג]דפא הו, "that blasphemer," which really does not suit the context as well.

[63]"Further Light on Melchizedek from Qumran Cave 11," *JBL* 86 (1967) 25-41; reprinted in slightly revised form in *ESBNT*, 245-67.

[64]"Milkî-sedeq et Milkî-reša^{c}" (see n. 13 above).

[65]"4Q Visions de ^{c}Amram" (n. 12 above), 79.

[66]See K. Berger, "Der Streit des guten und des bösen Engels um die Seele: Beobachtungen zu 4Q Amr^{b} und Judas 9," *JSJ* 4 (1973) 1-18.

[67]For a similar list of non-Aramaic parallels, see R. E. Murphy, "The Dead Sea Scrolls and New Testament Comparisons," *CBQ* 18 (1956) 263-72.

[68]Contrast the remarks of G. Dalman, *The Words of Jesus* (p. 23 above, n. 53), 34; *Die Worte Jesu* (2d ed.; Leipzig: Hinrichs, 1930), 27; M. Black, *Aramaic Approach,* 238.

[69]See G. Dalman, *The Words of Jesus,* 23-24; *Die Worte Jesu,* 17-18.

[70]For the distinction between "parallel" and "contact" and its bearing on what S. Sandmel has called "parallelomania," see my remarks, *ESBNT,* 205 n. 1.

[71]The list in this chart is as complete as I can make it at this time. It may be that I have overlooked some texts. I should be grateful to anyone who would inform me of lacunae in it and of the neglected material. When this list first appeared in *NTS* 20 (1973-74) a number of errata were detected at the time of the proofreading of the galleys and were sent in for correction; but, alas, the corrections were not made in the press. We hope that we have remedied the situation here.

[72]Trying to keep track of the published Qumran texts is an arduous task. Aside from the fact that some of the preliminary publications appear in unexpected places, there is the further complication of the change of sigla for some of them. Milik has done this at times with some of the Enoch material. I have tried to sort out the details, and it is to be hoped that I have given them correctly in this chart. Milik has recently published *The Books of Enoch: Aramaic Fragments of Qumran Cave 4* (Oxford: Clarendon, 1976).

[73]*Kyrios Christos* (n. 17 above), 95-96. See further M. Hengel, *Der Sohn Gottes: Die Entstehung der Christologie und die jüdisch-hellenistische Religionsgeschichte* (Tübingen: Mohr [Siebeck], 1975).

[74]Ibid., 207.

[75]Ibid., 97.

[76]Ibid., 207 n. 142. Cf. A. Deissmann, *Bible Studies* (2d ed.; Edinburgh: Clark, 1909) 166-67; *Light from the Ancient East: The New Testament Illustrated by Recently Discovered Texts of the Graeco-Roman World* (New York: G. H. Doran, 1927) 346-47.

[77]*Der Sohn Gottes* (FRLANT 26; Göttingen: Vandenhoeck & Ruprecht, 1916).

[78]*The Theology of the New Testament according to Its Major Witnesses: Jesus—Paul—John* (Nashville: Abingdon, 1973) 76.

[79]*Theology of the New Testament* (n. 18 above), 1. 128.

[80]Ibid., 128.

[81]Ibid., 130.

[82]According to some OT commentators the phrase refers rather to "judges" in this psalm.

[83]See C. J. Gadd, *Ideas of Divine Rule in the Ancient East* (Schweich Lectures of the British Academy, 1945; London: Oxford University, 1948) 45-50.

[84]See G. von Rad, "Das jüdische Krönungsritual," *TLZ* 72 (1947) 211-16; K. H. Rengstorf, "Old and New Testament Traces of a Formula of the Judaean Royal Ritual," *NovT* 5 (1962) 229-44.

[85]The Hebrew text reads: ואל יקראך בן ויחנך ויצילך משחת; the Greek: *καὶ ἔσῃ ὡς υἱὸς ὑψίστου καὶ ἀγαπήσει σε μᾶλλον ἢ μήτηρ σου.*

[86]The Greek text reads: *εἰ γάρ ἐστιν ὁ δίκαιος υἱὸς θεοῦ, ἀντιλήμψεται αὐτοῦ.*

[87]See further my article, "The Son of David Tradition and Mt 22:41-46 and Parallels," *Concilium* (British ed.) 10/2 (1966) 40-46; in slightly revised form, *ESBNT*, 113-26, esp. pp. 115-19.

[88]Indirectly related to this problem is the question raised by one of the Qumran texts about God's begetting of the Messiah. The text concerned is 1QSa 2:11-12 (see D. Barthélemy and J. T. Milik, *Qumran Cave I* [DJD 1; Oxford: Clarendon, 1955] 108-18; see my comments on it in *ESBNT*, 153).

[89]*Kyrios Christos*, 207. One would now have to modify the way that he phrased the idea on p. 93, where he wrote: "The whole of later Jewish apocalypticism was unacquainted with the messianic title 'Son of God.'" It is now clear that Jewish apocalypticism was not unacquainted with the title "Son of God," but there is no evidence as yet that it associated it with a *messianic* figure, i.e., an anointed agent of Yahweh.

[90]Cf. R. Bultmann, *Theology of the New Testament* (n. 18 above), 1. 130.

[91]See "Sohn Gottes," *ZNW* 47 (1956) 113-33.

Chapter 5

The Semitic Background of the New Testament *Kyrios*-Title*

The title (ὁ) Κύριος is given to Jesus with various nuances by many NT writers, and the use of it has suggested to some commentators that this christological title originated in the kerygma of the early Christian community prior to the writing of the NT books themselves. To others it was not part of the kerygma, but a product of the missionary endeavor of early disciples among the Gentiles. Moreover, the varied use of the title has often been examined, and diverse hypotheses have been proposed to explain the genesis of the title and the development of its use. Part of the debate centers on the background of the title, e.g., whether it was of Palestinian, Hellenistic Jewish, or Hellenistic pagan origin; part of it concerns the original application of the title to a certain phase of Jesus' existence, e.g., whether it was originally predicated of the earthly Jesus, the risen Jesus, the exalted Jesus, the present Jesus, the parousiac Jesus; and part of it concerns the implications of the title, e.g., what did it mean or what does it mean to affirm that "Jesus is Lord." To take up each of these aspects of the *Kyrios*-title in detail would call for a monograph equalling former studies of the topic. But my main purpose is rather to call attention to some new data that bear directly on the background question of this title, and only secondarily to draw some inferences from it about the other subordinate aspects of the problem.[1]

I. *The Background of the* Kyrios-*Title*

Before we look at the new data, however, it might be wise to sketch briefly the four more or less current explanations of the background of the title that are in use.

(1) *A Palestinian Semitic Secular Background,* which sees the title ὁ Κύριος for Jesus as having developed out of the vocative or suffixal forms of either Hebrew אדון or Aramaic מרא, e.g., from אדני, "my lord" (or milord) or מראי, "my lord." Thus F. Hahn, for whom the absolute *(attributlos)* title[2] (ὁ) Κύριος developed from the "secular mode of address" in the course of the earthly life of Jesus and is preserved in the Greek κύριε, "sir" of Mark 7:28;

Matt 15:27; or in "Q" (Matt 8:8; Luke 7:6). This profane usage probably reflects the Aramaic form מראי.[3]

(2) *A Palestinian Semitic Religious Background,* which sees the absolute use of ὁ Κύριος as having originated in the post-Easter Jewish-Christian community of Palestine, in which Jesus would have been hailed as אדון or מרא. This would have been a title derived from one that Palestinian Jews already used for Yahweh. With varying nuances and reasons, this explanation has been proposed by G. Dalman,[4] W. Foerster,[5] O. Cullmann,[6] E. Schweizer,[7] R. H. Fuller,[8] and others. In most instances, these interpreters lean heavily on the Palestinian Jewish evidence of suffixal forms of מרא, such as מראן, "our Lord" or מראי, "my Lord" or on מרא in the construct chain of an Aramaic title for Yahweh such as מרא שמיא (Dan 5:23).

(3) *A Hellenistic Jewish Background,* which sees the absolute title ὁ Κύριος for Jesus as developed by Greek-speaking Jewish-Christians from the Greek equivalents of Semitic suffixal or genitival titles for Yahweh. In some instances, the translation of יהוה by *κύριος* in the so-called LXX has been invoked. In fact, this explanation has often been joined to the preceding one as a more direct explanation of the Greek absolute usage of the NT title. This is often said to represent a transition from the Palestinian Jewish-Christian community to a Hellenistic Jewish-Christian community, by which is meant a non-Palestinian Christian community in the Jewish diaspora. Thus, again with varying nuances, W. Foerster (and G. Quell),[9] O. Cullmann,[10] E. Schweizer,[11] and others can be mentioned.

(4) *A Hellenistic Pagan Background,* which sees the absolute title of Jesus as taken over from the use of *κύριος* as a title for gods or human rulers in the eastern Mediterranean Hellenistic world. This explanation has been proposed, with varying nuances, by W. Bousset,[12] R. Bultmann,[13] P. Vielhauer,[14] H. Conzelmann,[15] and others. Intricately bound up with this explanation is a shift in NT christology itself, influenced not merely by the geographical difference that is implied, but by a development in conception from the primitive Palestinian kerygma to the missionary preaching or evangelization of the Hellenistic world, as the kerygma came into contact with the title used there for gods and human rulers.

These are the four main positions that have been assumed in the present-day debate about the origin of the *Kyrios*-title. My remarks and the data that I should like to present will support the second of these positions. But before I turn to them positively, I should like to comment briefly on two of the other explanations in the light of recent developments.[16] I shall treat the matter then in the following order: (1) A Hellenistic Pagan Background? (2) A Hellenistic Jewish Background? (3) A Palestinian Jewish Religious Background? But by way of transition to the main discussion I should like to make two preliminary remarks.

(a) Attempts have been made to relate the Greek absolute title to the Aramaic form מראן or מראנא reflected in *μαραναθά* (1 Cor 16:22) or to the form of address מרי (attested in 1QapGen 2:9, 13, 24; 20:12, 14, 15, 25; 22:18, 22) or to other titles for Yahweh such as מרא שמיא (Dan 5:23) or מרא עלמיא (1QapGen 21:2). They have usually encountered the objection that such Aramaic forms are either suffixal or in the construct state of the noun and that they do not reflect the absolute usage of the NT Greek title.[17] To be valid evidence in the discussion of the Aramaic background of the Greek title, the form must be: (i) neither suffixal nor in the construct state (or its equivalent);[18] (ii) either in the absolute state or the emphatic state: מרא or מרה (= *mārê*ʾ / *h*), *κύριος*; מראה or מריא (= *mārĕʾāh* / *mārĕyāʾ*);[19] (iii) *attributlos* (without a modifier).[20]

(b) Sometimes a parallel is drawn between *κύριε* / *ὁ κύριος*, "lord!" / "the Lord" and *διδάσκαλε* / *ὁ διδάσκαλος*, "teacher!" / "the teacher." It is argued that the shift from a form of address to the absolute usage, from *διδάσκαλε* to *ὁ διδάσκαλος*, is supported by underlying Aramaic usage: behind *διδασκαλε* lies Aramaic רבי. This originally meant "my master, my teacher," but in the course of time it came to be simply a title, "Rabbi." The shift from a vocative or a form of address to the absolute title is thus possible, and one could assume a similar development in the case of *κύριος*.[21] Appeal is further made to the later forms of מר and רב as titles for a human lord or a scribe, both being non-suffixal. What is to be said of this sort of argument? Without getting involved in the questions of the antiquity of the title "Rabbi,"[22] or of the authenticity of the application of it to Jesus in the NT,[23] I should only stress that whereas the titular use of רבי (i.e., the suffixal form meaning simply "Master" or "Teacher" [as an absolute title]) is attested,[24] there is no known instance of the suffixal form מרי which came to be understood simply as "Lord." As far as I know, there is, further, no comparable Greek transliteration of this word in a title like *ῥαββί*. Consequently, for the parallel argument to be valid, one would have to show that מרי, which originally meant "my lord," came in time to mean simply "Lord," just as רבי, which originally meant "my master" came in time to mean "Master" or "Rabbi." Granted, רב did in time come into usage as an absolute form; but at least its suffixal form is attested as a title, which is not the case for מרא.[25]

With these preliminary methodological remarks we may now turn to the various explanations of the origin of the *Kyrios*-title for Jesus.

(1) *Does the Kyrios-title Have a Hellenistic Pagan Background?* Here my remarks will be brief. This solution has in large part been adopted because of the unsatisfactory evidence hitherto adduced for other solutions and because a Pauline passage such as 1 Cor 8:5-6 in the NT itself seemed to reflect it. It is well known that *κύριος* was used absolutely of gods and human rulers in the ancient world of the eastern Mediterranean; the Greek title is attested in this way from *at least* the beginning of the first century B.C. in texts from Egypt, Syria, and Asia Minor.[26] Indeed, it occurs once in the NT itself for Nero (Acts 25:26). So no one who works seriously with the NT title can ignore this

extrabiblical Greek material. However, I should like to call attention to three things.

First, I share the uneasiness of some commentators who do not think that this Greek title *κύριος* was used with a purely political connotation in contrast to the title *θεός*, with which it was sometimes associated for the same person.[27] Even O. Cullmann, who cares little for the Hellenistic origin of the *kyrios*-title for Jesus, has seen that the distinction of *κύριος* as a political title over against *θεός* in Hellenistic pagan usage has little to commend it.[28] Certainly, if it were admitted that the title came from this origin, its application to Jesus in this sense would seem deficient in the light of 1 Cor 8:5-6, where *εἷς κύριος Ἰησοῦς Χριστός* seems to involve precisely a religious connotation, which is not limited to *θεός* alone. The religious connotation of *κύριος* in the NT, when applied to Jesus, must have been *influenced* by this use of the Greek title in the contemporary Hellenistic pagan world.

Second, one must concede that the Hellenistic pagan usage has *influenced* the NT usage. But that still leaves open the question whether that usage is the sole origin or background for the NT use of it for Jesus. Similarly, it leaves open the question whether the missionary endeavors of early Christians in Hellenistic pagan areas were responsible for the adoption of the title and the consequent introduction of a new dimension into early Christian christology. To say that the Hellenistic pagan usage has been the sole origin leaves too many factors unexplained—factors to which I shall be returning below. But at the moment I shall mention only one such here: the pre-Pauline hymn to Christ Jesus in Phil 2:6-11, the background of which is debated.[29] But its climax is found precisely in the bestowal of the title *Κύριος* on Jesus "to the glory of God the Father." At least since the time of E. Lohmeyer, a strong case has been made for the origin of this passage in a Christian Aramaic setting: that it is not only pre-Pauline, but "wohl ursprünglich griechisch geschrieben ist, aber von einem Dichter, dessen Muttersprache semitisch war." Recently, P. Grelot has proposed a most convincing retroversion of the hymn into contemporary Palestinian Aramaic, which will have to be taken seriously into consideration in any future discussions of this passage.[30] But if there is any validity to his thesis, then it colors radically the contention that the absolute use of the *Kyrios*-title in the NT is drawn solely from the contemporary Hellenistic pagan use of *κύριος*. (I shall return to a detail of Grelot's translation below.)

Third, it might be well to recall that the pagan use of the title "lord" for gods in the period in which we are involved is not exclusively found in Greek material. The title אדן is well attested in Punic inscriptions, and this evidence would have to be classed as Semitic. For instance, it occurs time after time in dedicatory inscriptions from the Punic sanctuary of El-Hofra at Constantine (in modern Algeria).[31] Usually the votive text begins:

לאדן לבעל חמן אש נדר . . . שמע קלא ברכא

"To the Lord, to Baᶜal Ḥammon: (this is) what X son of Y vowed. He heard his voice; he blessed him." The absolute use of אדן in these texts seems unmistakable.[32] Lest it might seem that this is merely a defective spelling for a suffixal form, one can cite a Punic text from the same place written in Greek characters and vocalized:

ΛΑΔΟΥΝ ΛΥ ΒΑΛ ΑΜΟΥΝ ΟΥ
ΛΥ ΡΥΒΑΟΩΝ ΘΙΝΙΘ ΦΑΝΕ ΒΑΛ (read *ῥυβαθων*)
ΥΣ ΝΑΔΩΡ ΣΩΣΙΠΑΤΙΟΣ ΒΥΝ (read *Σωσιπατρος*)
ΖΩΠΥΡΟΣ ΣΑΜΩ ΚΟΥΛΩ ΒΑ
ΡΑΧΩ

Au Seigneur, à Ba^cal Hammon et
à notre Dame Tinit Phane Baal
ce qu'a voué Sosipatros fils
de Zopyros; il a entendu sa voix,
il l'a béni.[33]

This Punic evidence is certainly not the direct pagan background of the NT *Kyrios*-title, and it does not in any way exclude the more direct influence of the corresponding Hellenistic use of *κύριος*. But it at least shows that the absolute use of "the Lord" was also known in the *pagan Semitic* world, and that the interplay of Semitic and Hellenistic in that Mediterranean pagan world might also have something to say about the Jewish world of Palestine and its influence on the topic at hand to be discussed below.

(2) *Does the Kyrios-title Have a Hellenistic Jewish Background?* It is not easy to discuss this background of the absolute *kyrios*-title in an isolated fashion. For it is often proposed in conjunction with that of a Palestinian Semitic religious background. Consequently, if it is not a question of the Hellenistic Jewish *origin* of the title, then it is at least a question of the *influence* of Hellenistic Jewish custom at the time that the Greek title was adopted. For the sake of clarity I should like to restrict the discussion of this matter mainly to Palestine and to envisage it as a problem related to Greek-speaking Jewish Christians, not of the diaspora, but of Palestine itself. (I realize that the question about Jews and Jewish-Christians in the diaspora is closely related to it and will in time come into the discussion; but first it is wise to try to deal with the problem in Palestine.) For we must ask whether the absolute title *κύριος* could owe its origin to a distinction in the early Jewish-Christian community of Palestine between the "Hebrews" and the "Hellenists" (Acts 6:1-6). In other words, were the ᶜ*Ελληνισταί* responsible for translating a suffixal or genitival form of מרא simply by the absolute *κύριος*? E. Schweizer once wrote: "that an original 'our Lord' becomes in Greek the absolute 'the Lord' under the influence of Hellenistic usage is easily explainable."[34] But is there really a special reason why the shift to the absolute title must be associated with a shift to Hellenistic Greek? Could it not just as easily have taken place in a Semitic context? Moreover, the distinction involves the meaning of the terms

ᶜΕβραῖοι and ᶜἙλληνισταί in the early Palestinian Christian community, and to this I shall return below.

But first one of the arguments associated with the Hellenistic Jewish background of the *kyrios*-title has to be treated, viz., the translation of יהוה by κύριος in the so-called LXX. It has often been assumed that this Greek version of the OT had been in use in first-century Palestine, and it is cited as pre-Christian evidence for the absolute use of the Greek title κύριος for Yahweh. Indeed, this use is said to antedate the pagan use of κύριος for gods and human rulers.[35] But there are serious arguments against this alleged pre-Christian use in the LXX, and H. Conzelmann has succinctly summed them up in his attempt to relate the NT *kyrios*-title to a Hellenistic pagan background. He writes:

> 3. Outside the Septuagint, *Kyrios* is unusual in Judaism as a designation for God.
> 4. It has recently been disputed that the Septuagint in fact renders יהוה by *Kyrios*. *Kyrios* occurs only in Christian manuscripts of the LXX, and not in Jewish ones:
> (a) Papyrus Fouad 266 (second century B.C.): it has יהוה in the quotation from Deut. 31f.: cf. O. Paret, Die Bibel, *Ihre Überlieferung in Druck und Schrift* (1949), p. 75 and table 2.
> (b) 4Q Minor Prophets: also tetragrammaton.
> (c) 4Q fragments of Lev. 2-5 LXX: ΙΑΩ.
> (d) Aquila fragments from Cairo: tetragrammaton.
> (e) Fragments from the second column of the Hexapla; tetragrammaton (cf. Origen and Jerome).
> (f) Examples of ΠΙΠΙ in Hatch and Redpath, *A Concordance to the LXX, Supplement* (1906), p. 126.
> (g) Symmachus: cf. *TWNT* III 1082, lines 12f.
>
> Compare, too, the use of the Old Hebrew scripts in the tetragrammaton in the quotations of the Q *pesharim*: 1QpH; 4QpPs 37; אל: 1QH I 26. II 34. XV 25; 1Q35 I 5.
>
> Thus the Christian use of κύριος cannot be derived from the LXX. The reverse is in fact the case. Once the title began to be used, it was found again in the Bible.[36]

Such arguments may indeed invalidate the claim that early Greek-speaking Christians were influenced by the so-called Septuagintal use of κύριος for Yahweh (either in Palestine or the diaspora). But I am not sure that they close the question, whether Palestinian Jews called or could call Yahweh κύριος. P. Vielhauer, on whom H. Conzelmann largely depends, rapped the knuckles of F. Hahn for not having properly informed himself by consultation of the writings of P. Kahle before writing on LXX problems.[37] Yet it remains to be seen whether Kahle had said the last word on this subject. Moreover, even though the main point of my discussion of the *kyrios*-title does not hinge on the use of κύριος as a title for Yahweh among Greek-speaking Jews, it seems to me that it was a factor in the Palestinian development (among others); and so it must be looked into. Hence I should like to call attention to several points in connection with the possible use of κύριος for Yahweh by Palestinian Jews who spoke Greek.

(a) It is clear that in a number of Greek translations of the OT from pre-Christian or early Christian times, especially in those used by Jews, the Hebrew tetragrammaton was simply preserved,[38] or else it was transcribed as ΙΑΩ,[39] or was written in Greek as ΠΙΠΙ.[40] Moreover, it seems clear that the *widespread use* of κύριος in so-called LXX manuscripts dating from Christian times is to be attributed to the habits of Christian scribes.[41] Indeed, the *widespread use* may well have been influenced by the use of κύριος for Yahweh in the NT itself.[42] But the question arises, Where did the NT writers get the *kyrios*-title for God (Yahweh)? I have never heard it said that Christian scribes or copyists introduced it as well into NT writings, whereas the writers themselves had actually used some other word for God. For instance, if κύριος = יהוה is a device found only in Christian copies of the OT, where did Luke get it when he quoted Deut 6:5 in 10:27, *ἀγαπήσεις κύριον τὸν Θεόν σου*?[43] A facile answer to this question would be, From Christian copies of the Greek OT. But the Lucan verse chosen here as an illustration is found in the oldest copy of Luke, in the Bodmer Papyrus (P^{75}), dating from A.D. ± 200. As far as I know, there is no earlier dated manuscript of the so-called LXX which uses κύριος for Yahweh.[44] Hence, as stated above, the widespread use of κύριος for יהוה in Christian copies of the so-called LXX may well have been influenced by the use of κύριος for Yahweh in the NT, but the question still remains, Where did the NT writers get it?

(b) Though Josephus normally used δεσπότης as the Greek equivalent for the tetragrammaton, he does use a form of κύριος on two occasions, one of which is significantly in a quotation from the OT. In *Ant.* 20.4.2 §90 he wrote: *εἰ μὴ μάτην, ὦ δέσποτα κύριε, τῆς σῆς ἐγευόμην χρηστότητος, τῶν πάντων δὲ δικαίως μόνον καὶ πρῶτον ἥγημαι κύριον.* This is found in a prayer of King Izates, a convert to Judaism. Again, in *Ant.* 13.3.1 §68 he presents a quotation of Isa 19:9 in a letter from Onias the High Priest. Here Josephus quotes the OT in a form that does not agree with the so-called LXX, and one would have to do some manoeuvring to show that it depends on it. Moreover, Josephus realized that it was not right to make known to foreigners the divine name that God had revealed to Moses,[45] and this undoubtedly influenced his use of δεσπότης on various occasions.[46] Whereas it is significant that he did not use κύριος more frequently as a name for God, which, in fact, supports the rarity of it in pre-Christian Greek translations of the OT, the fact remains that it does occur at least twice in his writings.[47] One might argue, of course, that it has been introduced into the manuscripts of Josephus in these places in dependence on Christian usage or Christian manuscripts of the LXX. But is that really likely?[48] And why would it be restricted to these places alone? Most discussions of Josephus's use of κύριος compare his text with the LXX.[49] But more recent studies of the Greek OT stress the diversity of the versions even in the first century A.D. in Palestine and tend to relate the Greek text of the Scriptures that Josephus used to a Proto-Lucianic revision of the Old Greek made in Palestine itself, a revision of the Old Greek to make it conform to a

Hebrew text then current in Palestine.[50] Is it possible that these stray instances of *κύριος* in Josephus reflect such a revision of the Greek OT in Palestine, even though his composition may have reached its final form outside of that area? This may sound like a speculative question, but the form of the Greek text of the OT in first-century Palestine is an important aspect of the problem that we are discussing. One cannot simply dismiss the use of *κύριος* by an appeal to Christian copies of the so-called LXX. Recent studies of the LXX show us that the issue is much more complex.

Granted that the evidence from Josephus is not much and that he actually wrote in Greek outside of Palestine, the question still remains, How did these isolated examples of *κύριος* get into his Greek text? If they should reflect or be a vestige of an incipient practice among Greek-speaking Jews of Palestine to refer to Yahweh in this way, then that would be important for our discussion.[51]

(c) There is an instance of *κύριος* that is preserved in the Letter of Aristeas to Philocrates, and in this case it is a clear allusion to Deuteronomy, though not an exact quotation of it: "For the chewing of the cud is nothing else than recalling life and its subsistence, since life appears to subsist through taking food. And therefore does he admonish us through Scripture, when he says, 'Thou shalt well remember what great and marvelous things the Lord thy God did in thee'; when clearly understood they do indeed appear 'great and glorious'" (§155). The allusion to Deut 7:18-19 here reads: *μνείᾳ μνησθήσῃ κυρίου τοῦ ποιήσαντος ἔν σοι τὰ μεγάλα καὶ θαυμαστά*.[52] Again, are we to invoke the habits of Christian scribes in a text-tradition such as this? (Similarly, one could here appeal to further pseudepigraphical writings of this period.)

(d) Though the tetragrammaton is normally preserved in the fragments of Aquila's translation of 1 Kgs 20:13-14; 2 Kgs 23:21, 23 (from the Cairo Geniza palimpsest fragments),[53] and in other texts (of the same provenience), such as Ps 91:2, 9; 92:2, 5, 6, 9, 10; 96:7, 8, 9, 10, 13; 97:1, 5, 9, 12; 102:16, 17, 20; 103:2, 6, 8,[54] there is at least one instance (2 Kgs 23:24) where, because of a lack of space at the end of a line, the Hebrew tetragrammaton is replaced by the Greek abbreviation *κ̅υ̅*.[55] Was this a desperate solution to a problem of space borrowed from a Christian practice?[56] Or does it not represent a custom among Jews themselves to translate יהוה on occasion by *κύριος*, a custom that may not yet have become as widespread as it was to become in Christian copies of the so-called LXX? And could this Jewish custom be part at least of the origin of the Christian usage of *κύριος*?

(e) There are manuscripts of the Greek translation of the OT in which ΠΙΠΙ was used for יהוה. Here we may readily grant that the Greek-speaking scribes no longer understood the Jewish problem when they substituted ΠΙΠΙ for יהוה. But what did they say when they read such a text? In any case, I doubt that Jewish readers would normally have said *pee-pee*. What Christian readers made of it is another matter.[57] But here one must distinguish clearly between transcription, translation, and pronunciation. What did a Greek-speaking Jew say when he read his Scriptures and found in it either the tetragrammaton or the letters ΠΙΠΙ?

(f) This evidence for the use of *κύριος* among Jews in pre-Christian times or among Jews contemporary with early Christians in Palestine does not outweigh the evidence for the preservation of the tetragrammaton in most Jewish copies of the Greek OT. But it is evidence that must be considered in the background of the following data that are to be adduced from the Semitic area in the next section of this paper. Before turning to those data, however, there is one last remark to be made. It concerns the distinction between Hebrews and Hellenists in Palestine of the first century A.D., to which I alluded earlier. This is a distinction in the *Jewish Christian* community of Palestine, that we first learn about in Acts 6:1-6. Various explanations of the distinction have been proposed. The only plausible one, in my opinion, is that of C. F. D. Moule, who on the basis of the meagre evidence available proposed that "Hellenists" were "Jews who spoke only Greek," while "Hebrews" were "Jews who, while able to speak Greek, knew a Semitic language *also*."[58] However, this distinction between "Hebrews" and "Hellenists" existed not only within the Jewish Christian community of Palestine, but also among the Jews themselves, as Acts 9:29 intimates.[59] Now if this is so, it too bears on the entire question about the early formulation of the Palestinian Christian kerygma. Was it formulated solely in a Semitic language, as so much of the current argument presupposes? For instance, it has been said that the absolute title *κύριος* used of Jesus "offers a particularly clear reflection of the change from the primitive community to Hellenistic Christianity."[60] And by "Hellenistic Christianity" here is meant that of Greek-speaking communities in a pagan environment (such as Syria, Egypt, or Asia Minor). But can it be excluded that Palestinian Christian Hellenists had part in the formulation of the primitive kerygma? Is it not rather among these Jewish Christian ᶜΕλληνισταί that we should seek the emergence of the Greek *kyrios*-title for Jesus—especially if there is some evidence for an absolute usage of its Semitic counterpart for God among the Jewish ᶜΕβραῖοι of Palestine itself?

The foregoing consideration of the use of *κύριος* among Greek-speaking Palestinian Jews, meagre as the evidence for it is, is proposed here merely as a backdrop against which the main material now to be presented has to be viewed. The new Aramaic evidence, and the Hebrew evidence, take on a different hue, when seen in this way. Part of the problem with it all—and this is frankly admitted at the outset—is that we are arguing *from Palestinian Jewish* evidence, either Semitic or Greek, *to a Christian* usage. Would that we had some clear Semitic or Greek Palestinian texts used or composed by *Jewish Christian* Hellenists or Hebrews!

(3) *The Kyrios-title Has a Palestinian Jewish Religious Background.* For the Palestinian Semitic religious background of the *Kyrios*-title for Jesus in the

NT one has often invoked the Aramaic phrase μαραναθά, preserved for us in 1 Cor 16:22.[61] 1 Corinthians is the most Hellenistic letter of the Pauline corpus, and the phrase is transmitted to us by one who openly identified himself as ἑβραῖος (2 Cor 11:22; Phil 3:5). But the suffixal form of μαράνα / מראנא has always been seen as the difficulty, because it does not provide the basis for an explanation of the emergence of the absolute usage.[62] At least since the time of G. Dalman it has been repeated that Palestinian Jews did not refer to Yahweh in the absolute sense as "the Lord."[63] R. Bultmann maintained that the "un-modified expression 'the Lord' is unthinkable in Jewish usage."[64] Now it is precisely on this point that the evidence discussed in chap. 4 above has to be brought to bear.

In the recently published targum of Job from Qumran Cave XI we find the absolute usage of Aramaic מרא for God and standing in parallelism with אלהא. The text is fragmentary but clear, and I argue from the form of it that was published by the original editors, who did not suspect the impact of the title being used.[65]

In his poetic discourse, Elihu addresses Job and says to him:

> אף אמנם אל לא ירשיע ושדי לא יעות משפט (34:12)
> Of a truth, God will not do wickedly, and the Almighty will not pervert justice (*RSV*).

The Aramaic version of the targum (24:6-7) reads:

> הכען צדא אלהא / ישקר ומרא [יעות דינא]
> Now will God really prove faithless and [will] the Lord [distort judgment]?

Here God is clearly referred to as מרא, and the Aramaic noun is not only in the absolute state, but it is unmodified; moreover it stands in parallelism with the ordinary word for God, אלהא. See further 11QtgJob 24:[5]; 26:[8]. Two further instances of the absolute state of the title can be found in 1QapGen 20:12-13; 20:15.[66]

But the absolute usage of the title is also attested with the noun in the emphatic state. In the recently published Aramaic fragments of the Books of Enoch I 4QEn[b] 1 iv 5 reads:

> [ולגבריאל אמר מ]ריא אז[ל נא על ממזריא],
> [And to Gabriel] the [L]ord [said]: "G[o now to the bastards . . ."]

And the corresponding Greek text of the passage bears the abbreviated form, ὁ $\overline{κς}$.[66a]

What should be noted here is that the *absolute usage* of מרא (and not just the absolute state of the Aramaic noun) is attested in Qumran literature. However, it is not a translation of יהוה in the targum;[67] in 11QtgJob 24:6-7 it rather renders the OT title שדי, which the Old Greek usually translates as *παντοκράτωρ*.[68] Hence, though it is not a case of the tetragrammaton being rendered by מרא, for which we must still await attestation, it is at least scarcely "unthinkable" that the "un-modified expression 'the Lord'" has been in "Jewish usage." Though we do not yet have the equation יהוה = מרא = *κύριος*, we have at least the absolute usage of מרא, "the Lord," for God.

How מרא might have been translated into Greek, I have already discussed above.[69]

Consequently, the absolute use of מרא in 11QtgJob 24:7 becomes one of the missing-links between an OT title for God and the NT use of *κύριος* for God himself, first of all, and then for Jesus.

Here we may return to the hymn to Christ in Phil 2:6-11, which we have mentioned earlier, and especially to the recent retroversion of it into Palestinian Aramaic of the first century attempted by P. Grelot.[70] He translates the last verse of it as follows:

> וכל לשן יודא די מרא ישוע משיחא ליקרה די אלהא אבא
> *καὶ πᾶσα γλῶσσα ἐξομολογήσηται ὅτι κύριος Ἰησοῦς Χριστὸς εἰς δόξαν Θεοῦ πατρός.*
> "and every tongue confess that Jesus Christ is Lord, to the glory of God the Father" (*RSV*).

Interestingly enough, Grelot simply writes מרא, without so much as questioning the existence of such an absolute use of the word.[71] That usage is, of course, now attested in the targum of Job, in the *Genesis Apocryphon*, and in 4Q Enoch, making his suggestion quite valid.

Now if this Aramaic evidence were not enough, there is also some Hebrew evidence from Qumran literature that may support it. This is not the place to discuss the relative position of Hebrew and Aramaic as Semitic languages spoken or used in first-century Palestine, and I may be permitted to refer the reader to chap. 2 above,[72] where the pertinent material is reviewed. But as for the Semitic background of the *kyrios*-title, some Hebrew evidence also has to be considered.

Psalm 151 was known for a long time in Greek, being in the Greek psalter of the so-called LXX. It has turned up in Hebrew in a text from Qumran Cave XI.[73] Significantly enough for the matter under discussion, it contains an example of אדון being used absolutely of Yahweh in the sense of "the Lord," and stands in parallelism to אלוה, "God" (to give us a striking parallel to 11QtgJob 24:6-7). Moreover, it is found in a Hebrew text in which the tetragrammaton is otherwise written in the archaizing paleo-Hebrew script, otherwise known at Qumran. 11QPs[a] 28:7-8 reads:

> ומי ידבר ומי יספר את מעשי אדון הכול ראה אלוה הכול הוא שמע והוא האזין
> "and who can mention and who can recount the deeds of the Lord? Everything has God seen, everything has he heard, and he has heeded."[74]

There is no doubt here that "the Lord" refers to Yahweh, even though his name is otherwise written in paleo-Hebrew script as יהוה. J. A. Sanders, who prepared the scroll for publication, has assigned a date to it "in the first half of the first century A.D."[75] Apparently for those Jews who used or composed the scroll it was not "unthinkable" to refer to Yahweh as "the Lord."

Finally, one should not fail to mention the canonical psalter itself, where in the text of Ps 114:7 we read:

> מלפני אדון חולי ארץ מלפני אלוה יעקב
>
> "Tremble, O earth, at the presence of the Lord, at the presence of the God of Jacob" (*RSV*).

One could also compare Mal 3:1; Isa 1:24; 3:1; 10:33; 19:4.

Now when such Aramaic and Hebrew evidence is considered together with the use of *κύριος* in the Greek writings of Josephus, the Letter of Aristeas, and the isolated attestation of it in a text of even Aquila's translation of the OT, one can conclude to at least an incipient custom among Jews of Palestine of referring to Yahweh as "the Lord," a custom that would be supported by such diaspora references as those in Philo's writings and in the NT itself.[76] Granted, what I have presented here is not evidence so widespread for either מרא or אדון as that which was once thought to be available for *κύριος* in the ancient Greek translation of the OT that is now recognized to be preserved in Christian manuscripts. But the evidence does seem to suggest that Palestinian Jews, who were able to refer to God as מרא or אדון, could, on becoming the Ἑβραῖοι of the Palestinian Christian community, transfer the title to Jesus. The evidence also suggests that these Ἑβραῖοι, who also spoke Greek, may well have translated מרא or אדון by *κύριος* in their dealings with the Ἑλληνισταί of the primitive Palestinian community. Thus the absolute usage of "the Lord" as a NT christological title can be traced to the primitive Palestinian Christian community, either as מרא or אדון among the "Hebrews" or as *κύριος* among the "Hellenists" (and the "Hebrews"). A mutual influence of these two language groups in the early Palestinian Christian community was the real matrix of the primitive kerygma which was a-borning.

A final remark about the Palestinian Semitic religious background of the *kyrios*-title is in order. It concerns the reverence for the sacred name יהוה among Palestinian Jews, which is part of the background of the *kyrios*-title. There is not space to discuss this in detail. But if the reason for the substitution of *κύριος* for יהוה in manuscripts of the Greek translation must be recognized as mainly a practice of Christian scribes, the evidence is, nevertheless, abundant that the Jews themselves developed a special reverence for the divine name. In addition to the devices mentioned earlier, we need only recall the various ways of treating the tetragrammaton in Qumran literature: (a) the clear substitution of אדוני for יהוה (and vice versa!) in 1QIsa[a];[77] (b) the writing of the name in archaizing paleo-Hebrew characters,[78] (c) in ordinary square characters,[79] (d) in square characters, but in red ink.[80] Moreover, surrogates for it are found in (a) four dots;[81] (b) the use of אל;[82] (c) the use of אל in paleo-Hebrew script;[83] (d) the use of הואהא.[84] In one instance we even find לאל with the *aleph* written by what looks like an inverted Greek *alpha*.[85] Furthermore, there is the abundant use of אדוני as a title for God in the non-biblical texts of Qumran (such as 1QH 2:20, 31; 3:19, 37; 4:5; 5:5; 7:6, 34; 14:8, 23; etc.).[86] All of this evidence, which comes from roughly 100 B.C. to A.D. 68, provides simply a more generic Palestinian background against which the earlier material has to be judged.

II. *The Original Application of the* Kyrios-*Title to Jesus*

If the evidence available today supports the Palestinian Semitic and Greek religious matrix for the origin of the NT title *κύριος* for Jesus, the next question is, To what phase of Jesus' existence was it originally applied? Was it used as a title for him during his earthly ministry? Was it an expression of faith in him as risen? Was it a title expressive of his exaltation to the Father's right hand? Was it a title meant to convey his actual, ongoing influence exerted on those who put faith in him? Or was it originally a title related to his future coming, his parousia? In other words, was it originally a title for the earthly Jesus, the risen Jesus, the exalted Jesus, the ever-present Jesus, or the parousiac Jesus?

The gospels attest that various persons, disciples or pagans, addressed the earthly Jesus as *κύριε* (e.g., Mark 7:28 [the Syrophoenician woman] = Matt 15:27; Matt 8:6, 8 = Luke 7:6, "Q" [the Roman centurion]; Matt 8:2 = Luke 5:12 [a leper of Palestine]; Luke 5:8 [Peter at the miraculous catch of fish]; Matt 8:25 [disciples in the boat during the tempest]; John 4:11 [the Samaritan woman]; etc.). Three things have to be noted about this usage of *κύριε* in the gospels: (1) The vocative usage in many cases has nothing more than the secular sense, "Sir," which would tell us nothing about the application of the religious title, "Lord," to Jesus during his public ministry. That a pagan or even a disciple might have addressed him as "Sir" has little bearing on the titular sense which we are discussing. (2) In reading the gospels, we must remember that in passages such as Luke 5:8, where Peter exclaims after the miraculous catch of fish, "Depart from me, *κύριε*, for I am a sinful man," or Matt 14:30, where he cries out as he sinks in the waves, "*κύριε*, save me," these instances should rather be translated as "Lord." Here the evangelists have retrojected back into the public ministry narratives that almost certainly stem from post-Eastern appearances of the risen Jesus to Peter. But, the title, "Lord," for the risen Jesus, thus retrojected into the public ministry, tells us little about the use of such a religious title for him during his earthly ministry. (3) The same sort of retrojection of the title is found elsewhere in the gospel tradition, where there is no evidence of appearances of Jesus or of his miraculous powers, e.g., Luke 12:41-42, where Peter asks,

"Lord (κύριε), are you telling this parable for us or for all?" And Luke the evangelist comments, "And the Lord said. . . ." Here we find not only the vocative, but also the absolute title ὁ κύριος. In such cases the evangelist has simply used of the earthly Jesus a title that had already become stereotyped in the early Christian community of his own day and retrojected it into the account of the public ministry. In sum, there is no real evidence pointing to the application of the religious title ὁ κύριος to the earthly Jesus.

That κύριος was applied to the risen Jesus is reflected in various ways in the NT. In the saying of Paul already quoted, "Am I not an apostle? Have I not seen Jesus our Lord?" (1 Cor 9:1), he relates his claim to apostleship to his vision of the risen Jesus. And even though it uses the possessive form, "our Lord," it clearly relates "Lord" to the resurrected phase of Jesus' existence and reflects an affirmation of the post-Easter faith of the Christian community. Elsewhere in 1 Corinthians, Paul insists that "no one can say 'Jesus is Lord' except by the Holy Spirit" (12:3) and thereby clearly shows that the affirmation is one of faith and Spirit-prompted. Thus Paul's use of the title in 1 Cor 9:2 betrays its faith-origin and supports the data of the gospel passages such as we have already considered (Luke 5:8 or Matt 14:30), which imply the application of the title to the risen Jesus.

That the title κύριος was applied even earlier to the exalted Jesus emerges from the pre-Pauline Jewish Christian liturgical hymn in Phil 2:10-11. Paul took over an already existent hymn that climaxes in the confession of Jesus as κύριος. What is remarkable in this hymn is that, for all the phases of Jesus' existence that it details, it bypasses an explicit mention of the resurrection. The structure of the hymn is debated, but some analysts see it proposing six phases: Jesus' pre-existence, his *kenōsis*, his further humiliation in death, his heavenly exaltation, the adoration of him by the universe, and the application to him of the name κύριος. In this hymn κύριος is used of Jesus precisely as the super-exalted one who is worthy of the same adoration as Yahweh himself (as the allusion to Isa 45:23 in v. 10 suggests). This pre-Pauline, cultic usage, applying the absolute title to the exalted Jesus, i.e., to a status posterior to his resurrection as such, is significant.

In a similar way Paul at times uses the title, "the Lord," to express the actual, ever-continuing existence of Jesus on the Christian community or on individual Christians. This usage is found throughout his writings, when he employs the pregnant prepositional phrase, "in the Lord" (ἐν κυρίῳ). This is found especially in greetings, blessings, exhortations (often with imperatives), and in formulations of Paul's own apostolic activity and plans.[87] It denotes for him the influence of the risen or exalted Jesus on the ongoing course of Christian practical life or ethical conduct. These are to be lived out "in the Lord," who is clearly understood as the post-Easter, post-resurrected Jesus.

But there are a few places in his letters which reflect the application of the title to the parousiac Jesus or "the Lord" of future coming. Significantly, this is found in the earliest of Paul's letters, in the eschatological teaching of 1

Thessalonians. Here Paul consoles the young Christians of Thessalonica, concerned about their confrères who have died before the parousia; he assures them that those who have died ἐν Χριστῷ, "in Christ," will rise first, when "the Lord himself will descend from heaven," and "we who are alive, who are left, shall be caught up together with them, . . . and so we shall always be with the Lord (σὺν κυρίῳ, 4:16-17). In this, one of the earliest affirmations of Paul's *kyrios*-faith, he refers to the parousiac Jesus as κύριος four times over (4:15, 16, 17a, b). The destiny of the Christian is to be "with the Lord," with the parousiac Jesus at his coming.

This eschatological application of κύριος is likewise reflected in the Aramaic liturgical acclamation, to which we have referred earlier. By being preserved precisely in Aramaic, μαραναθά (of 1 Cor 16:22) reveals its early, pre-Pauline, and Jewish-Christian provenience. It probably stems from Palestine (though other parts of the early Jewish-Christian world cannot be completely excluded). Though the analysis of the phrase has been debated—does it mean, "Our Lord has come!" or "Our Lord, come!"?—the eschatological or future (imperatival) explanation is preferred today by most commentators, because the Aramaic expression seems to underlie the Greek imperatival acclamation found at the end of the Book of Revelation, ἔρχου, κύριε Ἰησοῦ, "Come, Lord Jesus" (22:20). In this sense, the Christian community applied precisely to the parousiac Jesus the title κύριος, and its early Aramaic form[88] betrays the primitive character of that application.

Moreover, the cultic use of *kyrios*, applied at first to the Jesus of the parousia and later extended to other, earlier phases or events of his existence, seems to be reflected in another passage in Paul, where he speaks of the Eucharist. In 1 Cor 11:23-26 Paul passes on to us a teaching of the early Christian community before him, citing with technical vocabulary the παράδοσις or tradition to which he was himself tributary. For he says that he passed on what he himself had received about the "Lord's supper," and then he quotes from some liturgical formula already in use the words of institution of the Eucharist, ending with the declaration: "For as often as you eat this bread and drink this cup, you proclaim the Lord's death until he comes" (1 Cor 11:26). For Paul the Christian's participation in the Lord's supper is a proclamation of the effects of the Christ-event by the Christian community that ever looks forward to the coming of its "Lord." Paul here speaks of the "death" of the parousiac "Lord," not in the sense that the Jesus of the parousia is expected to die, but that the title for the parousiac Jesus is now applied to the event of his death—again, by retrojection. In this we see the thrust of the process of application at work. At least it gives us the basis for an hypothesis. What evidence there is in the NT itself, and especially in its earliest layers, seems to indicate that the *kyrios*-title was first applied to Jesus of the parousia and that the general extension of it brought about the gradual retrojection of it to other phases or states of his existence, even to that of his earthly mission.

This process of the retrojection of the *kyrios*-title has its parallels in other christological titles. In fact, it can be said to be indicated by the various stages of NT christology in general. For example, there are indications that the title "Messiah" was at one time applied to the parousiac Jesus (see Acts 3:20), and from there it was retrojected to the public ministry. Both John and Paul have a three-staged christology (parousiac, resurrectional, pre-incarnational) which differs from the three-staged christology in Matthew and Luke (resurrectional, public ministry, infancy narrative). This reveals to us a process of the developing awareness in the early church, which accounts for the different uses of *κύριος* that we have been discussing.

If any confirmation of this were needed, it can be found in the late writing of 1 John, where the title *κύριος* is completely avoided. Why this is so we are not sure, but it is probably to be ascribed to the desire to avoid the association of Jesus with the "many 'gods' and many 'lords'" (1 Cor 8:6) of the contemporary Hellenistic-Roman religious world. By the time 1 John was written, it was realized that Jesus as *κύριος* stood on an infinitely higher plane than these empty figures.[89] A similar avoidance of it is noted in the Johannine gospel, where, however, it does occasionally occur (e.g., 4:1; 20:28).

III. *The Implication of the* Kyrios-*Title for Jesus*

Finally, it remains to ask what is implied in calling Jesus *κύριος*. Having asked the questions about the origin of the title and the phase of his existence to which it was originally applied, we should inquire further into its nuances. What did and what does it mean for a Christian to say "Jesus is Lord"?

In a sense, we have already answered this question in part. For if the evidence presented in section I supports the contention that the *kyrios*-title was kerygmatic and was part of the early Palestinian Jewish-Christian proclamation, then it at least implies that early Christians regarded Jesus as sharing in some sense in the transcendence of Yahweh, that he was somehow on a par with him. This, however, is meant in an egalitarian sense, not in an identifying sense, since Jesus was never hailed as אבא. It involved a *Gleichsetzung*, but not an *Identifizierung.*[90] By "transcendence" here is meant that Jesus was somehow regarded as other than a mere human being; but the otherness is not spelled out in the NT with the clarity that would emerge in the Councils of Nicaea or Chalcedon, when the NT data were not only reformulated, but even reconceived in terms of other modes of philosophical thinking. The *Gleichsetzung* can be seen in two ways that involve the title *κύριος*. First of all, the title מרא used of God in the targum of Job, which translated שדי of the Hebrew text, stood in parallelism with אלהא.[91] Even though the nuances of each title may be specifically different, the parallelism in itself is suggestive. The hymn to Christ in Phil 2:6-11 climaxes with the bestowal of the title, which was otherwise used of Yahweh (at least in an incipient way) by Palestinian Jews, on Jesus himself. This suggests that he was somehow regarded as worthy of the same title otherwise employed for Yahweh. Second, if there should be any hesitancy about the first suggestion, it would seem to be confirmed by the adoration that is said to be his in the immediately preceding verse of the hymn. It is widely admitted that Phil 2:10-11 allude to Isa 45:23; in the latter the adoration is directed to Yahweh. Here in Philippians 2 it is accorded to Jesus—and precisely as "Lord."

If this seems to be the implication of the title, it is nevertheless clear that *κύριος* does not simply mean *θεός*, "God." If so, we may ask, What is the further nuance connoted by *κύριος*? As is well known, the NT rarely calls Jesus *θεός*; and when it does turn up, it is found in the later writings (Heb 1:8; John 1:1; 20:28—to cite only the more or less uncontested occurrences).[92] This usage reflects the time that it took for the early Christian community to come to the realization of faith that the title *θεός*, otherwise restricted in the NT to Yahweh, could also be given to Jesus. The gradual awareness of him as *θεός*, as someone on a par with Yahweh, and yet not אבא himself, eventually led to the development of the Christian doctrine of the Trinity. But if in time a Christian writer in the NT period could put on the lips of a Thomas the acclamation addressed to the risen Jesus, "my Lord and my God," that very acclamation suggests a difference in nuance between the two titles.

S. Schulz has investigated the Aramaic background of the suffixal and genitival forms of the title מרא as applied to God in various extrabiblical documents.[93] From the use of it in such texts as Elephantine documents of the fifth century B.C. and literary texts from Qumran he has concluded that the title "lord" connoted the judicial authority of a king *(königliche Richterautorität)*. Hence for him, the Aramaic-speaking Christian community, in attributing to Jesus the title "Lord," was not so much affirming his divinity, as might be implied in the use of *kyrios* in the claim that it was a title derived from pagan Hellenistic usage of the eastern Mediterranean, as an assertion of his authority as judge associated with his regal condition. Schulz too was reacting against the exclusive derivation of the title from the pagan Hellenistic background. But his insistence on the judicial aspect of the title is not wholly convincing. Most of his evidence for it, however, comes not from the use of the title itself in the NT but from his association of it with the title "Son of Man." That the latter has judicial nuances in some of the contexts in which it is used (e.g., Mark 8:38 or 13:26 and parallels) goes without saying. But the two titles "Lord" and "Son of Man" should not be confused.[94] Their origins are distinct, their applications are distinct, and their implications should also be kept distinct.

That the *kyrios*-title has regal connotations can be clearly seen in one passage in the Synoptic tradition which depicts Jesus in debate with a temple audience (Mark 12:36), or Pharisees (Matt 22:41), or scribes (Luke 20:39): "How can the scribes say that the Messiah is the son of David? David himself, inspired by the Holy Spirit, declared, 'The Lord said to my Lord, Sit at my right hand, . . ." (Mark 12:36).[95] Here an association is suggested between Jesus as *κύριος* (or מרא) and a king of the Davidic dynasty; the regal implication of the title is clear.

Moreover, the entire tradition of the royal character of Yahweh in the OT would seem to be associated with the *kyrios*-title.[96]

But there is even more in the NT use of the title for Jesus. This is seen at times in the parallelism between κύριος and δοῦλος, between "lord" and "servant" (or "slave"). Indeed, in the hymn to Christ in Phil 2:6-11, there is an explicit contrast of these two conditions applied to Jesus himself. Despite the fact that he took up "the status of a slave" he was, nevertheless, eventually exalted as "Lord." Moreover, Paul often depicts either himself or the Christian disciple as δοῦλος. For all his proclaiming of the good news of Christian freedom, redemption, and emancipation in Christ Jesus, he insists that in another sense he or the Christian disciple is "the slave of Christ Jesus" (Phil 1:1; Rom 1:1; Gal 1:10; Col 4:12). Indeed, he sums up his entire role thus: "For what we preach is not ourselves, but Jesus Christ as Lord, with ourselves as your servants (*or* slaves) for Jesus' sake" (2 Cor 4:5). In effect, Paul says, "you were bought with a price" (1 Cor 6:20)—you *belong* to Christ, who is your "lord."

Involved in the affirmation that the Christian makes, Jesus is Lord, is the entire concept of Christian faith, as Paul sees it: "If you confess with your lips that Jesus is Lord and believe in your heart that God raised him from the dead, you will be saved" (Rom 10:9). Though that faith begins for Paul as a "hearing" (ἀκοή, "Faith comes from what is heard," Rom 10:17), it does not stop there. It involves the entire personal commitment of a man/woman to Christ Jesus as "Lord." It ends as ὑπακοὴ πίστεως, often mistakenly rendered simply as "the obedience of faith" (*RSV*, Rom 1:5; 16:26). It should rather be understood as "the commitment of faith." The word ὑπακοή implies the "*sub*mission" or total personal response of the believer to the risen Lord.[97]

Finally, it must be remembered that to acknowledge with lips and heart (i.e., with the total self) that "Jesus is Lord" is the essence of Christian faith. It means to acknowledge that one recognizes that "Jesus our Lord, who was put to death for our trespasses and raised for our justification" (Rom 4:25), still exerts an influence over the Christian disciple. The latter belongs to him, is committed to him and his service.[98]

NOTES TO CHAPTER 5

*Originally published as "Der semitische Hintergrund des neutestamentlichen Kyriostitels," *Jesus Christus in Historie und Theologie: Neutestamentliche Festschrift für Hans Conzelmann zum 60. Geburtstag* (ed. G. Strecker; Tübingen: Mohr [Siebeck], 1975) 267-98. This form in English has been somewhat revised and expanded.

[1]This chapter repeats in part some of the Aramaic material presented on pp. 87–90 above, but relates it to other material (Greek, Hebrew, and Punic) which bear on the topic.

[2]On the "absolute" usage of the Greek title, see p. 109 above, n. 26.

[3]*The Titles of Jesus* (p. 109 above, n. 22), 73-89.

[4]*The Words of Jesus* (p. 23 above, n. 53), 324-31.

[5]*Herr ist Jesus* (p. 108 above, n. 19), 201-8.

[6]*Christology* (p. 109 above, n. 20), 195-237.

[7]"Discipleship and Belief," (p. 109 above, n. 21), 87-99. Cf. *Erniedrigung und Erhöhung bei Jesus und seinen Nachfolgern* (ATANT 28; Zürich: Zwingli, 1962) 77-86.

[8]*The Foundations of New Testament Christology* (New York: Scribner, 1965) 50.

[9]"Κύριος, etc.," *TDNT* 3 (1965) 1039-98, esp. p. 1094.

[10]*Christology,* 201-15. "The non-Christian use of the *Kyrios* name in the Hellenistic world, its relation to emperor worship, and above all its use as the name of God in the Septuagint—all this certainly contributed to making *Kyrios* an actual *title* for Christ. But this development would not have been possible had not the original Church already called upon Christ as the Lord" (p. 215).

[11]"Discipleship and Belief," 93.

[12]*Kyrios Christos* (p. 108 above, n. 17), 119-52.

[13]*Theology of the New Testament* (p. 108 above, n. 18), 1. 124. "The Kyrios-cult originated on Hellenistic soil" (1. 51).

[14]"Ein Weg zur neutestamentlichen Christologie? Prüfung der Thesen Ferdinand Hahns," *Aufsätze zum Neuen Testament* (Theologische Bücherei, 31; Munich: C. Kaiser, 1965) 141-98 [leicht verändert vom Original, *EvT* 25 (1965) 24-72].

[15]*An Outline of the Theology of the New Testament* (New York: Harper & Row, 1969) 82-84.

[16]I shall not delay on F. Hahn's attempt (*The Titles of Jesus,* 73-89) to explain the title as a development from a Palestinian Semitic secular usage. The inadequacies of that explanation have already been dealt with by P. Vielhauer ("Ein Weg," 150-57). It amounts to an assertion without proof.

[17]See p. 124 below.

[18]By "its equivalent" I mean some circumlocution for the construct chain, such as the use of Aramaic די/ד with a following noun (absolute or emphatic) or a prepositional phrase.

[19]The various forms of the Aramaic word for "lord" call for some further comment. Throughout the centuries of its attestation the forms of it indicate that it was originally **māray* or **mārī*ʾ, a *qātal* or a *qātil* noun-type of either a Tertiae Infirmae or a Tertiae Aleph root. The earliest forms in Aramaic turn up with the *aleph,* and early cognates in Canaanite, Ugaritic, and Akkadian also have the *aleph* (see W. F. Albright, "The Early Alphabetic Inscriptions from Sinai and Their Decipherment," *BASOR* 110 [1948] 6-22, esp. p. 21 n. 78; *The Vocalization of the Egyptian Syllabic Orthography* [AOS 5; New Haven: American Oriental Society, 1934] 43, §VIII.A.2; C. H. Gordon, *UT,* 437 §1543; W. von Soden, *Akkadisches Handwörterbuch* [Wiesbaden: Harrassowitz, 1966] 615). It is not certain at what period the mixing of Aramaic verbal forms of Tertiae Aleph and Tertiae Infirmae began, but that they were mixed is certain (see p. 110 above, n. 29). The intervocalic position of the *aleph* or the *yodh* was undoubtedly the reason for the mixing.

The absolute/construct form מָרֵא, in Biblical Aramaic, is perhaps to be explained as a contraction of **māray* (*qātal*-type) › *mārê*, with the final *aleph* (or *he*; cf. 1QapGen 20:13, מרה) being understood as a vowel letter. Cf. בְּנֵין (Ezra 4:12); F. R. Blake [p. 110 above, n. 29], 13; P. Joüon, *Grammaire de l'hébreu biblique* (Rome: Biblical Institute, 1947) 159 n. 2 (listed as an alternate explanation). Older explanations tended to explain the form as a *qātil*-type: **mārī*ʾ › *mārē*ʾ › *mārê*. See G. Dalman, *Grammatik des jüdisch-palästinischen Aramäisch—Aramäische Dialektproben* (Darmstadt: Wissenschaftliche Buchgesellschaft, 1960) 152; H. Bauer and P. Leander, *Grammatik des Biblisch-Aramäischen* (Halle/S.: Niemeyer, 1927) §51y′′. Cf. L. F. Hartman, *CBQ* 28 (1966) 497.

In the suffixal form like מָרְאִי the sequence of *shewa/aleph/vowel* led in time to the quiescence of the *aleph* and to the eventual disappearance of it even in the orthography. Thus, מראי (= *mārĕ*ʾ*ī*, Aššur Ostracon 8; *AP* 16:8) › מרי *(mārī)*, both of which forms are attested in Qumran Aramaic texts: 1QapGen 2:9, 13, 24; 4Q^c^Amram^b^ 2:3 (see J. T. Milik, *RB* 79 [1972] 79).

Once the form מרי developed, the passage to an absolute or construct state in מר (= *mār*) by a back-formation was easy (see p. 89 above). But the form מר is as yet unattested in Palestinian Aramaic of the first century A.D. (*pace* O. Cullmann, *Christology,* 199). It is, however, attested in later Palestinian Jewish Aramaic and in Syriac, along with the further development of an emphatic state in מרא (= *mārāʾ*)—a vocalization that should not be foisted on first-century consonants, *pace* K. G. Kuhn, *TDNT* 4 (1967) 467; G. Vermes, *Jesus the Jew,* 111.

The emphatic state (מריא) is now attested in Palestinian Aramaic (4QEn^b 1 iv 5); see p. 124 below.

[20]The same must be said, *mutatis mutandis*, of any Hebrew evidence that might be used as part of the Semitic background of the *Kyrios*-title. See p. 125 below.

[21]See, e.g., F. Hahn, *The Titles of Jesus,* 73-81.

[22]See H. Shanks, "Is the Title 'Rabbi' Anachronistic in the Gospels?" *JQR* 53 (1962-63) 337-45; S. Zeitlin, "A Reply," ibid., 345-49. Cf. E. Schürer, *A History of the Jewish People in the Time of Jesus Christ* (Edinburgh: Clark), 2/1 (1890) 315.

It has been argued that an ossuary discovered on Mt. Olivet dating from the period before the destruction of the Temple and bearing on one side the name תדטיון and on the other the title ΔΙΔΑΣΚΑΛΟΥ in the genitive (published by E. L. Sukenik, "מערת קברים יהודית במורד הר הזיתים (ב)," *Tarbiz* 1 [1930] 137-43 [+ pls. א-ה], esp. pp. 139-41; see also *Jüdische Gräber Jerusalems um Christi Geburt* [Jerusalem: (Azriel Printing House), 1931] 17-18; J.-B. Frey, *CII*, 2. §1266; *SEG*, 9. §179) is evidence of the early use of ῥαββί as a title (so W. F. Albright, "Recent Discoveries in Palestine and the Gospel of St. John," *The Background of the New Testament and Its Eschatology: Studies in Honour of Charles Harold Dodd* [ed. W. D. Davies and D. Daube; Cambridge: Cambridge University, 1956] 153-71, esp. pp. 157-58; E. Lohse, "Ῥαββί, ῥαββουνί," *TDNT* 6 [1968] 961-65, esp. p. 963 n. 26). But though the Greek title is thus attested, the alleged extrabiblical evidence for the equivalent of διδάσκαλος and ῥαββί, supposedly supporting John 1:38, is strikingly absent. This ossuary lends no support to the antiquity of the Aramaic title *rabbī*.

[23]See J. Donaldson, "The Title Rabbi in the Gospels—Some Reflections on the Evidence of the Synoptics," *JQR* 63 (1973) 287-91.

[24]See E. Lohse, *TDNT* 6 (1968) 963.

[25]This difficult item also has a remote bearing on an analogous problem that is beginning to emerge in the scholarly debate about the relation of אבי to אבא. The former is attested as a form of address in 1QapGen 2:24, being preceded by an interjection, יא אבי ויא מרי, "O my father and my lord," addressed by Methuselah to Enoch. In three places in the NT we find the Aramaic vocative ἀββά literally translated as ὁ πατήρ (Gal 4:6; Rom 8:15; Mark 14:36); in the Synoptic parallels Matthew has πάτερ μου (26:39), whereas Luke has simply πάτερ (22:42). This matter has often been discussed (see G. Kittel, "ἀββά," *TDNT* 1 [1933] 4-6; G. Schrenk, "πατήρ . . . ," *TDNT* 5 (1967) 977-78, 989-90; J. Jeremias, *Abba: Studien zur neutestamentlichen Theologie und Zeitgeschichte* [Göttingen: Vandenhoeck & Ruprecht, 1966] 15-67). But recently M. McNamara, reviewing the second edition of my commentary on the *Genesis Apocryphon* (*ITQ* 40 [1973] 286), argues that the form אבי is the "earlier and literary Aramaic" vocative, whereas אבא represents the spoken "regular vocative in Palestinian targumic Aramaic," of an equally early period. This may be, but how does he know? Surely, the use of the emphatic state as the vocative is not without attestation in literary texts; I do not refer explicitly to an instance of אבא, but the phenomenon is found in Daniel: מלכא (2:4, 29, 37; 3:4, etc.). Moreover, is it certain that Matthew's πάτερ μου simply reflects Mark's ἀββά, which the Second Evangelist (or his source) literally translated as ὁ πατήρ? After all, πάτερ μου is a strict translation of אבי and could reflect Matthew's change to the other form of address, known perhaps in an independent tradition. On the other hand, Luke's simple πάτερ is a more correct Greek translation of the Marcan ἀββά. I personally would hesitate to say which form, אבי or אבא, was earlier in this instance. Moreover, אבא could be just as "literary" a form as אבי. I would cite precisely its occurrence in targumic Aramaic as the evidence for that. It still has to be shown that targumic Aramaic is nothing more than a "spoken" form of

the language. As far as I am concerned, it is as much a literary form of the language as that of the Qumran texts—but of a different period (see p. 72–73 above).

The reason for mentioning this here, however, is that in it we have an analogous use of a suffixal form and an emphatic state (which when used as a form of address approaches the "absolute usage" of *κύριος* of which we have been speaking). In this instance, both forms are attested, אבי (in Aramaic) and *ἀββά* (in Greek, with אבא parallels in later Aramaic texts). Even though the shift from אבי to אבא would not be the same as in רבי, where the shift occurs in different meanings of the same form, it does point up the inadequacey of the parallel argument between *κύριε* / *ὁ κύριος* on the one hand, and *διδάσκαλε* / *ὁ διδάσκαλος*, on the other.

G. S. Glanzman has called to my attention how complicated this question of suffixal and absolute forms can be, when one compares Hebrew and so-called Septuagintal usage. Compare 2 Kgs 13:14 in the MT (אבי אבי) and the LXX (*πάτερ, πάτερ*); Gen 22:7 (אבי and *πάτερ*); Gen 27:18 (אבי and *πάτερ μου* in cod. A). Similarly, Ps 22:2 (אלי אלי and *ὁ θεός, ὁ θεός μου*). Other examples could be cited.

There is, moreover, a related problem in the form אדני that is only remotely connected with this issue, but not wholly unrelated. It is usually said that the word originally meant "my lord" and was given the plural vocalization (with pausal lengthening) in "solemn pronunciation" *(Affektbetonung).* Yet H. Bauer and P. Leander (*Historische Grammatik der hebräischen Sprache des Alten Testaments* [Olms Paperbacks, 19; Hildesheim: G. Olms, 1965 (reprint of 1922 edition)] §2*h*, 29*t*, 68*i*) have explained the form as a non-Semitic loanword with an ending *āy*, which was only later taken to be the 1st pers. suffix. If their explanation were correct, and I am not sure that it is, then *ʾădōnāy* would have originally meant only "lord." Cf. O. Eissfeldt, "אדון," *TWAT* 1 (1970) 62-78, esp. pp. 67-68 (which N. Lohfink has called to my attention). Further L. Cerfaux, "Le nom divin 'Kyrios' dans la Bible grecque," *RSPT* 20 (1931) 27-51; "'Adonai' et 'Kyrios,'" *RSPT* 20 (1931) 417-52; J. Lust, "'Mon Seigneur Jahweh' dans le texte hébreu d'Ezéchiel," *ETL* 44 (1968) 482–88; G. H. Dalman, *Studien zur biblischen Theologie: Der Gottesname Adonaj und seine Geschichte* (Berlin: Reuther, 1889) 20-25.

[26]See, e.g., F. Cumont, *Les religions orientales dans le paganisme romain: Conférences faites au Collège de France en 1905* (4th ed.; Paris: P. Geuthner, 1929) 109, 257 n. 56; E. Williger, "*Κύριος*," *RE* (Pauly-Wissowa) 23 (1924) 176-83; A. Deissmann, *Light from the Ancient East* (2d ed.; London: Hodder & Stoughton, 1927) 348-57; P. Wendland, *Die hellenistisch-römische Kultur in ihren Beziehungen zu Judentum und Christentum* (HNT 1/2-3; 3d ed.; Tübingen: Mohr [Siebeck], 1912) 220-21; H. Lietzmann, *An die Römer* (HNT 8; 4th ed.; Tübingen: Mohr, 1933) 97–101; W. Bousset, *Kyrios Christos* (p. 108 above, n. 17), 138–48; L. Cerfaux and J. Tondriau, *Le culte des souverains dans la civilisation gréco-romaine: Un concurrent du christianisme* (Tournai: Desclée, 1957) with an extensive bibliography, pp. 9-73; W. Fauth, "Kyrios," *Der kleine Pauly* (ed. K. Ziegler and W. Sontheimer; Stuttgart: A. Druckenmüller) 3 (1969) 413-17; W. Foerster, "*Κύριος*, etc.," *TDNT* 3 (1965) 1046-58; W. W. Baudissin, *Kyrios als Gottesname im Judentum und seine Stelle in der Religionsgeschichte* (4 vols.; Giessen: Töpelmann) 3 (1929) 70-73.

[27]So W. Foerster, *TDNT* 3 (1965) 1056.

[28]*Christology* (p. 109 above, n. 20), 198. Similarly, H. Conzelmann, *Outline of the Theology of the New Testament* (n. 15 above), 84.

[29]See, e.g., E. Lohmeyer, *Kyrios Jesus: Eine Untersuchung zu Phil. 2,5-11* (Sitzungsberichte der Heidelberger Akademie der Wissenschaften, Phil-hist. Kl., 1927-28/4; Heidelberg: C. Winter, 1928; 2d ed., 1961); E. Käsemann, "Kritische Analyse von Phil. 2.5-11," *Exegetische Versuche und Besinnungen* (Göttingen: Vandenhoeck & Ruprecht) 1 (1960) 51-95; F. W. Beare, *A Commentary on the Epistle to the Philippians* (BNTC; London: A. & C. Black, 1956) 76; P. Bonnard, *L'épître de saint Paul aux Philippiens* (CNT 10; Neuchâtel: Delachaux et Niestlé, 1950) 47-48; R. P. Martin, *Carmen Christi: Philippians ii. 5-11 in Recent Interpretation and in the Setting of Early Christian Worship* (SNTSMS 4; Cambridge: Cambridge University, 1967) 38-41; D. Georgi, "Der vorpaulinische Hymnus Phil 2,6-11," *Zeit und Geschichte: Dankesgabe an*

Rudolf Bultmann zum 80. Geburtstag (ed. E. Dinkler; Tübingen: Mohr [Siebeck], 1964) 263-93; J. Jeremias, "Zu Phil 2,7," *NovT* 4 (1963) 182-88; G. Strecker, "Redaktion und Tradition des Christushymnus," *ZNW* 55 (1964) 63-78.

[30]The consideration of the hymn as derived from a Semitic or Aramaic background is derived mainly from E. Lohmeyer (*Kyrios Jesus,* 9). Though he himself never attempted a retroversion of the hymn, it was subsequently done by P. P. Levertoff in W. K. L. Clarke, *New Testament Problems: Essays—Reviews—Interpretations* (London: S.P.C.K.; New York: Macmillan, 1929) 148. Levertoff's translation is reproduced in R. P. Martin, *Carmen Christi,* 40-41. But that Aramaic retroversion is a hodge-podge of forms drawn from Aramaic of various periods and dialects. It has been rightly criticized by P. Grelot ("Deux notes critiques sur Philippiens 2,6-11," *Bib* 54 [1973] 169-86, esp. pp. 176-79). Grelot himself has undertaken a retroversion of the hymn (pp. 180-86). (I should prefer נפשה for גרמה in vv. 7, 8; and I am not happy about שמוע [*šāmōa*ᶜ] for *ὑπήκοος*, but I am unable to suggest a better form at the moment). For the early, pre-Pauline dating of this hymn, see I. H. Marshall, "Palestinian and Hellenistic Christianity: Some Critical Comments," *NTS* 19 (1972-73) 271-87, esp. p. 284 n. 1.

[31]See A. Berthier and R. Charlier, *Le sanctuaire punique d'El-Hofra à Constantine* (Paris: Arts et métiers graphiques, 1955). The earliest dated text is El-Hofra 58, which mentions the 46th year of Masinisan the Prince (= 163/62 B.C.). However, most of the inscriptions are undated. Punic evidence was cited by earlier scholars (see G. H. Dalman, *Studien* [n. 25 above] 13), but it is neglected in many modern discussions.

[32]In Phoenician and Punic texts the suffix of the 1st sg. is *-y* (see *PPG*² §112.1; Z. Harris, *GPL* §15.2). But *-y* is also used at times for the 3d sg. masc. suffix; and in Punic texts -ʾ (pronounced -*ō*) is used too, as in the examples cited here.

[33]*Le sanctuaire punique d'El-Hofra,* Inscriptions grecques, 1. 167-68. The Punic text that it represents would probably read as follows:

לאדן לבעל חמן ו/לרבתן תנת פן בעל / אש נדר ספפטרס בן / זפרס שמע קלא ב/רכא.

[34]"Discipleship and Belief" (p. 109 above, n. 21), 93.

[35]E.g., O. Cullmann, *Christology* (p. 109 above, n. 20), 201; F. Hahn, *The Titles of Jesus* (p. 109 above, n. 22), 71–73.

[36]*Outline of the Theology of the New Testament* (n. 15 above), 83-84. Less pertinent are Conzelmann's first two arguments: "1. In Paul, the title *Kyrios* in fact serves to distinguish Jesus and his position before God (I Cor. 8.6)." [1 Cor 8:6 would be a valid argument for Conzelmann only against those commentators who conclude from the LXX rendering of יהוה by *κύριος* "that the Christians identified Jesus with Yahweh." But how many NT commentators would conclude to such an *identification*? Suppose one only concludes that the title suggests that Jesus is somehow on a transcendent level with Yahweh? The end of the hymn in Phil 2:6-11 implies this sort of equality, which is not identification.] "2. There is no explanation of the fact that this title is used primarily in acclamations." [True, but so what? These arguments have to do with the use made of the title within the NT rather than with the *origin* of the title. More will be said below about the use of the title.]

[37]"Ein Weg" (n. 14 above), 149.

[38]The name is not preserved in any form in the oldest Greek (Proto-Lucianic!) manuscript, Pap. Ryl. Gk. 458 (from 2d century B.C. (?); see C. H. Roberts, *Two Biblical Papyri in the John Rylands Library, Manchester* [Manchester: Manchester University, 1936]). The most important evidence comes rather from a Palestinian (Proto-Theodotionic) translation of the Minor Prophets published by D. Barthélemy, *Les devanciers d'Aquila: Première publication intégrale du texte des fragments du Dodécaprophéton trouvés dans le Désert de Juda, précédée d'une étude sur les traductions et recensions grecques de la Bible réalisées au premier siècle de notre ère sous l'influence du rabbinat palestinien* (VTSup 10; Leiden: Brill, 1963) 163-78. Barthélemy has dated the fragments, written in two different hands, to "le milieu du premier siècle de notre ère" (p. 168). On this dating, see the opinion of C. H. Roberts and W. Schubart quoted by F. Dunand *Papyrus grecs bibliques (Papyrus F. Inv. 266): Volumina de la Genèse et du Deutéronome* (Recherches

d'archéologie, de philologie et d'histoire, 27; Cairo: L'Institut français d'archéologie orientale, 1966) 31: between 50 B.C. and A.D. 50; cf. P. Kahle, "Problems of the Septuagint," *Studia patristica I* (TU 63; Berlin: Akademie, 1957) 332. This is a modification of the date originally proposed by Barthélemy in *RB* 60 (1953) 19-20. The tetragrammaton, written in archaizing paleo-Hebrew script, is found in the Greek text of Jon 4:2; Mic 1:1, 3; 4:4; 5:3; Hab 2:14, 16, 20; 3:9; Zeph 1:3, 14; Zech 1:3; 3:5, 6, 7; 8:20; 9:1, 4. (On this text, see F. M. Cross, Jr., "The Contribution of the Qumran Discoveries to the Study of the Biblical Text," *IEJ* 16 [1966] 81-95, esp. pp. 84-85; "The History of the Biblical Text in the Light of the Discoveries in the Judean Desert," *HTR* 57 [1964] 282-99, esp. pp. 282-83; S. Jellicoe, *JAOS* 84 [1964] 178-82.)

But the tetragrammaton is also found still earlier in a Greek translation of Deut 32:3, 6, preserved in Papyrus Fuad 266 (of Egyptian provenience in the diaspora, from the 2d / 1st century B.C.). See W. G. Waddell, "The Tetragrammaton in the LXX," *JTS* 45 (1944) 158-61; O. Paret, *Die Bibel: Ihre Überlieferung in Druck und Schrift* (2d ed.; Stuttgart: Privilegierte Würtembergische Bibelanstalt, 1950) 76 and pl. 2. Further fragments of this papyrus were first published in the *New World Translation of the Christian Greek Scriptures* (Brooklyn, NY: Watchtower Bible and Tract Society, 1950) 11-16, esp. pp. 13-14. Cf. A. Vaccari, "Papiro Fuad, Inv. 266: Analisi critica dei frammenti pubblicati in 'New World Translation of the Christian Greek Scriptures,' Brooklyn (N.Y.) 1950, p. 13s.," Appendix to P. Kahle, "Problems of the Septuagint" (see above), pp. 328-41 [יהוה is preserved also in Deut 18:5; 31:27]. Cf. P. Kahle, *Die hebräischen Handschriften aus der Höhle: Franz Delitzsch-Vorlesungen* (Stuttgart: Kohlhammer, 1951) 7-8, 63-64, and pl. 11; *The Cairo Geniza* (2d ed.; Oxford: Blackwell, 1959) 218-28; H. H. Rowley, *The Old Testament and Modern Study* (Oxford: Clarendon, 1951) 249 n. 1; B. J. Roberts, *The Old Testament Texts and Versions* (Cardiff: University of Wales, 1951) 173; M. Noth, *Die Welt des Alten Testaments* (2d ed.; Berlin: Töpelmann, 1953) 254 n. 1; *The Old Testament World* (Philadelphia: Fortress, 1966) 322; E. Würthwein, *The Text of the Old Testament: An Introduction to Kittel-Kahle's Biblia hebraica* (tr. P. R. Ackroyd; New York: Macmillan, 1957) 132-33 (p. 25). Further fragments of this papyrus are now available in F. Dunand, *Papyrus grecs bibliques (Papyrus F. Inv. 266)* (see above), 26, 39-50. Also cf. *Etudes de papyrologie* 9 (1971) 81-150; G. D. Kilpatrick, "The Cairo Papyrus of Genesis and Deuteronomy (P. F. Inv. 266), ibid., 221-26; Z. Aly, "Addenda," ibid., 227-28 (+ pl. I). S. Schulz ("Maranatha und Kyrios Jesus," *ZNW* 53 [1962] 125-44, esp. p. 129) speaks of having had the opportunity to inspect the papyrus and of having counted 31 examples of יהוה in what is now known to be more than 100 fragments of Pap. Fuad 266. It seems that further fragments of this papyrus are still to be published.

The tetragrammaton is regularly preserved also in fragments of Aquila's translation of Kings from the Cairo Geniza (see p 122 below).

It has likewise been said to be preserved in 3d / 4th century fragments of Symmachus' translation of Ps 69:13, 31, 32 (see C. Wessely, "Un nouveau fragment de la version grecque du Vieux Testament par Aquila," *Mélanges offerts à M. Emile Chatelain (Paris: H. Champion, 1910) 224-29*. But cf. G. Mercati, *"Frammenti di Aquila o di Simmaco?" RB* 8 (1911) 266-72; P. Capelle, "Fragments du psautier d'Aquila?" *Revue bénédictine* 28 (1911) 64-68; D. Barthélemy, "Qui est Symmaque?" *CBQ* 36 (1974) 451-65, esp. p. 455.

Moreover, both Origen and Jerome knew about the practice of writing the name in Hebrew in Greek manuscripts. See Jerome, *Prologus galeatus* (*PL* 28. 594-95): "Nomen Domini tetragrammaton in quibusdam graecis voluminibus usque hodie antiquis expressum litteris invenimus." Again, "(Dei nomen est) tetragrammum, quod *ἀνεκφώνητον*, id est ineffabile, putauerunt et his litteris scribitur: *iod, he, uau, he.* Quod quidam non intellegentes propter elementorum similitudinem, cum in Graecis libris reppererint, IIIII legere consueuerunt" (Ep. 25, *Ad Marcellam*; CSEL 54. 219).

The tetragrammaton is written with two paleo-Hebrew *yodhs* in P. Oxy. 1007 verso 1:4 (= Gen 2:8) and 2:14 (= Gen 2:18), dated by the editor (A. S. Hunt) to "late third century." Compare P. Oxy. 1075 ("third century"), which has $\overline{\text{ΚΣ}}$ on line 12 (= Exod 40:35). A similar abbreviation is partially preserved in P. Oxy. 1166 ("third century"), lines 11 and 24 (= Gen 16:10, 11). Different forms of the abbreviation can also be found in *Papyrus Bodmer IX* ("du début du IV[e] siècle"), e.g., 1:1, 3, 5, 7 (= Ps 33:2-5), etc.

[39]This form is preserved in 4QLev[b] as a reading of Lev 4:27 (τῶν ἐντολῶν Ἰαώ), and probably also in 3:12; see P. W. Skehan, "The Qumran Manuscripts and Textual Criticism," *Volume du Congrès, Strasbourg 1956* (VTSup 4; Leiden: Brill, 1957) 148-60, esp. p. 157. See also Ezek 1:2 and 11:1 (according to the margin of the 6th century Codex Marchalianus (Vat. gr. 2125): Ἰαώ. Cf. Diodorus Siculus, 1.94: παρὰ δὲ τοῖς Ἰουδαίοις Μωυσῆν τὸν Ἰαὼ ἐπικαλούμενον θεόν; cf. Origen, *In Ps. 2:4* [*PG* 12.1104: Ἰαή]; *Comm. in Ioan.* 2:1 [*GCS* Origen, 4. 53]. See further A. Lukyn Williams, "The Tetragrammaton—Jahweh, Name or Surrogate?" *ZAW* 54 (1936) 262-69, esp. p. 266.

[40]See the end of n. 38 above. Cf. E. Hatch and R. A. Redpath, *A Concordance to the Septuagint and the Other Greek Versions of the Old Testament (Including the Apocryphal Books)* (2 vols. + suppl.; Graz: Akademische Druck- u. Verlagsanstalt, 1954), suppl., p. 126 for examples. Also C. Taylor, *Hebrew-Greek Cairo Genizah Palimpsests from the Taylor-Schechter Collection: Including a Fragment of the Twenty-Second Psalm according to Origen's Hexapla* (Cambridge: Cambridge University, 1900), folio B recto, pl. II (on Ps 22:20).

[41]This is more or less the opinion of P. Kahle (*The Cairo Geniza,* 222; "Problems of the Septuagint," 329); S. Schulz ("Maranatha und Kyrios Jesus," 128-29); P. Vielhauer ("Ein Weg," 149); et al.

[42]Κύριος as a name for Yahweh in the NT is found, for instance, in Mark 5:19; 13:20; Matt 5:33; Luke 1:6, 9, 28, 46; Rom 4:8; 9:28, 29; 11:34; 2 Thes 3:3; Eph 6:7. See L. Cerfaux, "'Kyrios' dans les citations pauliniennes de l'Ancien Testament," *Recueil Lucien Cerfaux* (BETL 6; Gembloux: Duculot, 1954), 1. 173-88, esp. pp. 174-77.

[43]This issue, of course, is complicated by the transmission of the NT text itself. In the verse cited, Codex Bezae reads θεός instead of κύριος. But the bulk of the good mss. are against that reading, and it may be there for another reason.

[44]However, Chester Beatty Papyrus VI is dated not "later than the second century" and probably not "after the middle of that century"; see F. G. Kenyon, *Chester Beatty Biblical Papyri . . . Fasciculus V: Numbers and Deuteronomy* (London: E. Walker) Text (1935), Pls. (1958), p. ix. E.g., it has $\overline{κς}$/$\overline{κυ}$ in Num 5:17, 18, 21; Deut 1:25, 27, 30, etc. Cf. Pap. Oxy. 656 ("carefully written in round upright uncials. . . , having in some respects more affinity with types of the second century than of the third"), *The Oxyrhynchus Papyri* (ed. B. P. Grenfell and A. S. Hunt; London: Egypt Exploration Fund) 4 (1904) 29. The editors mention "the absence of the usual contraction for θεὸς κύριος, &c." In line 17 "a blank space, sufficient for four letters, was left by the original scribe between τὰ and κατὰ, and in this κύριε was inserted by the second hand" (p. 33). See also lines 122, 166.

But, as R. A. Kraft has pointed out to me, how does one distinguish between Jewish and Christian copies of these Greek texts? Moreover, even P. Kahle ("Problems of the Septuagint," 333) admitted that "the ancient Christians used texts of the Greek Bible which had already been adapted to the Hebrew original by the Jews in pre-Christian times."

A still further question could be asked about the use of κύριος in such Greek writings as Judith, Wisdom, Maccabees, the additions to Esther, and 1 Esdras. But here the question is more complicated, because the text of many of these books is contained in the manuscripts of the so-called LXX, and whatever might finally be said about the *kyrios*-problem of the LXX might have to be said about these original Greek compositions as well.

[45]*Ant.* 2.12.4 §276.

[46]*Ant.* 1.3.1 §72; 1.18.6 §272; 2.12.2 §270; 4.3.2 §40, 46; 5.1.13 §41; 5.1.25 §93; 11.3.9 §64; 8.4.3 §111; 11.6.8 §230; *JW* 8.8.6 §323. Josephus also knows of κύριος as the Greek equivalent of Hebrew אדון; see *Ant.* 5.2.2 §121.

[47]For an interpretation of this phenomenon, see A. Schlatter, *Die Theologie des Judentums nach dem Bericht des Josefus* (BFCT 2/26; Gütersloh: C. Bertelsmann, 1932) 25-26; *Wie sprach*

Josephus von Gott? (BFCT 14/1; Gütersloh: C. Bertelsmann, 1910) 8-11. Cf. E. Nestle, "Miscellen: 6. Josephus über das Tetragrammaton," *ZAW* 25 (1905) 201-23, esp. p. 206; J. B. Fischer, "The Term ΔΕΣΠΟΤΗΣ in Josephus," *JQR* 49 (1958-59) 132-38. H. St. J. Thackeray, "Note on the Evidence of Josephus," *The Old Testament in Greek, II/1: I and II Samuel* (ed. A. E. Brooke, N. McLean, and H. St. J. Thackeray; Cambridge: Cambridge University, 1927) ix; A. Mez, *Die Bibel des Josephus untersucht für Buch V-VII* (Basel: Jaeger & Kober, 1895); P. Kahle, *The Cairo Geniza* (2d ed.; see p. 110 above, n. 33) 229-35; G. Howard, "*Kaige* Readings in Josephus," *Textus: Annual of the Hebrew University Bible Project* 8 (1973) 45-54.

48Even the variant in the margin of ms. A of Josephus' text contains κύριον; see LCL, 9. 434.

49E.g., by J. B. Fischer, *JQR* 49 (1958-59) 132-38.

50See F. M. Cross, Jr., "The Contribution of the Qumran Discoveries" (n. 38 above), 84-85; "The History of the Biblical Text," 281-99; P. W. Skehan, "The Biblical Scrolls from Qumran and the Text of the Old Testament," *BA* 28 (1965) 87-100, esp. pp. 90-95. Compare Kahle's comment in n. 44 above.

51One could also ask about Philo's references to Yahweh as κύριος in a diaspora situation. Commenting on Exod 3:14 in *De mutatione nominum* (2 §12), he says: "Yet that the human race should not totally lack a title to give to the supreme goodness He allows them to use by licence of language, as though it were His proper name, the title of Lord God of the three natural orders, teaching, perfection, practice, which are symbolized in the records as Abraham, Isaac, and Jacob" (δίδωσι καταχρῆσθαι ὡς ἂν ὀνόματι κυρίῳ τῷ "κύριος ὁ θεὸς" τῶν τριῶν φύσεων, διδασκαλίας, τελειότητος, ἀσκήσεως, ὧν σύμβολα Ἀβραάμ, Ἰσαάκ, Ἰακὼβ ἀναγράφεται). Cf. *Quis rerum divinarum heres* 6 §22-29. But Philo also uses the absolute form κύριος of God, ὤφθη κύριος τῷ Ἀβραάμ, and this precisely in a quotation of Gen 17:1. Where did he get κύριος? From Christian manuscripts of the LXX? Or did Christian scribes tamper with his text in its transmission too? It is clear, however, that Philo was aware that his Greek Bible gave Yahweh the title not only of θεός, but also of κύριος, since he explains the latter as a title betokening sovereignty and kingship (ἡ γὰρ κύριος πρόσρησις ἀρχῆς καὶ βασιλείας ἐστι), *De somniis*, 1.63. Cf. *De vita Mosis* 1.14 §75. See H. Wolfson, *Philo: Foundations of Religious Philosophy in Judaism, Christianity, and Islam* (2d ed.; Cambridge: Harvard University, 1948), 2. 120; P. Katz, *Philo's Bible: The Aberrant Text of Bible Quotations in Some Philonic Writings and Its Place in the Textual History of the Greek Bible* (Cambridge: Cambridge University, 1950) 47, 59-60. Cf. G. E. Howard, "The 'Aberrant' Text of Philo's Quotations Reconsidered," *HUCA* 44 (1973) 197-209.

52See M. Hadas, *Aristeas to Philocrates (Letter of Aristeas) Edited and Translated* (New York: Harper, 1951) 161; cf. H. St. J. Thackeray, "The Letter of Aristeas," in an appendix to H. B. Swete, *An Introduction to the Old Testament in Greek* (rev. R. R. Ottley; New York: Ktav, 1968) 578 (the *apparatus criticus* gives a variant recorded in Eusebius, which only adds τοῦ θεοῦ to κυρίου). Cf. E. Bickerman, "Zur Datierung des Pseudo-Aristeas," *Studies in Jewish and Christian History* (AGJU 9; Leiden: Brill, 1976) 109-36.

53See F. C. Burkitt, *Fragments of the Books of Kings According to the Translation of Aquila from a MS. Formerly in the Geniza at Cairo* (Cambridge: Cambridge University, 1897) 8, 15-16.

54See C. Taylor, *Hebrew-Greek Cairo Geniza Palimpsests* (n. 40 above), 53-65 (+ pls. III-VIII).

55See F. C. Burkitt, *Fragments of the Books of Kings* (n. 53 above), 16. Cf. H. B. Swete, *An Introduction* (n. 52 above), 39; F. Dunand, *Papyrus grecs bibliques* (n. 38 above), 51; J. Reider, "Prolegomena to a Greek-Hebrew and Hebrew-Greek Index to Aquila," *JQR* 7 (1916-17) 287-366.

56Aquila's concern for literalness in translation and his opposition to the use of the LXX by Christians are well known; see B. J. Roberts, *The Old Testament Texts and Versions* (n. 38 above), 123. Was the scribe who copied Aquila's text a Christian? If so, why was the abbreviation not used throughout (or at least κύριος)?

57It seems, however, that it was so read at times. See *j. Nedarim* 11:1; also the text of Jerome quoted above in n. 38. Cf. J. Halévy, "L'origine de la transcription du texte hébreu en caractères grecs dans les Hexaples d'Origène," *JA* 9/17 (1901) 335-41; J.-B. Chabot, ibid., 349-50; G.

Mercati, "Il problema della colonna II dell'Esaplo," *Bib* 28 (1947) 173-215, esp. pp. 189-90; "Note bibliche: 1. Sulla scrittura del tetragramma nelle antiche versioni greche del Vecchio Testamento," *Bib* 22 (1941) 339-54 (+ "Post Scriptum," 365-66); J. A. Emerton, "Were Greek Transliterations of the Hebrew Old Testament Used by Jews before the Time of Origen?" *JTS* ns 21 (1970) 17-31, esp. pp. 18-22; N. Fernandez Marcos, "Ἰαΐε, ἐσερεέ, ἀϊά y otros nombres de Dios entre los hebreos," *Sefarad* 35 (1975) 91-106.

One does not have to wonder what the Syriac scribes made of it, when translating or copying from Greek OT manuscripts; they wrote in Syriac *pypy*. See E. Nestle, "Jakob von Edessa über den Schem hammephorasch und andere Gottesnamen: Ein Beitrag zur Geschichte des Tetragrammaton," *ZDMG* 32 (1878) 465-508 (see Severus, *Hom.* 123 [*PO* 29/1.190-207]); "Berichtigungen und Nachträge zu dem Scholion des Jakob von Edessa über den Schem hammerphorasch," *ZDMG* 32 (1878) 735-36; G. Hoffmann, "Zu Nestle's Aufsatz S. 465," *ZDMG* 32 (1878) 736-37. (I am indebted to S. P. Brock of Oxford for some help in this matter.)

58 See p. 21 above, n. 15.

59 I do not agree with Moule that the "Hellenists" spoken of in Acts 9:29 were Christians. See E. Haenchen, *The Acts of the Apostles: A Commentary* (Philadelphia: Westminster, 1971) 333; M. Simon, *St Stephen and the Hellenists in the Primitive Church* (London: Longmans, Green and Co., 1958) 14-15.

60 H. Conzelmann, *Outline of the Theology of the New Testament,* 82. Conzelmann apparently understands the "Hellenists" and the "Hebrews" of Acts 6:1 pretty much as I do. He writes that it is "essential to differentiate between the two types (the primitive community and the Hellenistic community)" (p. 32), although by "the Hellenistic community" he means "the Hellenistic church in the wider sense," which came into being when the Hellenists who regarded "themselves as Jews" were expelled from Jerusalem and began the "mission to the Gentiles (Acts 11.19ff.)" (p. 31). He thus distinguishes between "Hebrews," "Hellenists," and the "Hellenistic community" (in the wider sense). I should only insist that the Jerusalem "Hellenists" were as much a part of the early Christian "primitive community" as were the "Hebrews." And this insistence allows for a conceptualization and a formulation of the primitive kerygma within that community that is both Semitic and Hellenistic in its modes and for a mutual influence of them, especially in the matter of the *kyrios*-title.

61 On this expression, see K. G. Kuhn, "Μαραναθά," *TDNT* 4 (1967) 466-72; S. Schulz, "Maranatha und Kyrios Jesus" (n. 38 above); C. F. D. Moule, "A Reconsideration of the Context of Maranatha," *NTS* 6 (1959-60) 307-10; J. Betz, "Die Eucharistie in der Didache," *Archiv für Liturgiewissenschaft* 11 (1969) 10-39; W. Dunphy, "Maranatha: Development in Early Christianity," *ITQ* 37 (1970) 294-308; M. Black, "The Maranatha Invocation and Jude 14, 15 (I Enoch 1:9)," *Christ and Spirit in the New Testament: In Honour of Charles Francis Digby Moule* (ed. B. Lindars and S. S. Smalley; Cambridge: Cambridge University, 1973) 189-96. It is not my intention to imply that מרנא played no role in the development of the absolute usage of the Greek title. It certainly had at the same time a great role as an acclamation-form in the cultic setting of early Palestinian Christianity; and that is reflected still in the Greek form (of the vocative) in Rev 22:20, ἔρχου κύριε Ἰησοῦ.

62 See p. 117 above. The suffixal form has recently turned up as a theophoric element in a proper name; see J. Naveh, "'פחלץ' באוסטרקון ארמי חדש" ['*Pḥlṣ*' in a New Aramaic Ostracon]," *Lĕšonénu* 37 (1972-73) 270-74. Line 2 of the fragmentary ostracon reads: [ ]קר בר עבדמראן, "[ ]qar bar ᶜAbedmarᵓan." Naveh thinks that the theophoric element is *Marna(s)*, a deity worshipped in Gaza from the Persian period onwards. Whether this is correct remains to be seen. If it were to refer to Yahweh, then we would have an interesting use of a suffixal form of מרא. Should the first name be restored as [ᵓ*Aḥī*]*qar*? The form מרנא has now turned up in 4QEn^b 1 iii 14; see J. T. Milik, *The Books of Enoch: Aramaic Fragments of Qumrân Cave 4* (Oxford: Clarendon, 1976) 146-47.

63 *The Words of Jesus* (p. 23 above, n. 53).

64 *Theology of the New Testament* (p. 108 above, n. 18), 1. 51. See other opinions cited above, pp. 87–88. Cf. H. Lietzmann, *An die Römer*, 99 "מרא 'der Herr' ist nie so verwendet worden."

65 See pp. 109 above, n. 28.

[66]Ibid. Cf. one of the passages in Josephus where *κύριος* is used, *Ant.* 20.4.2 §90, with 1QapGen 20:13.

[66a]See J. T. Milik, *The Books of Enoch,* 175.

[67]On the use of יהוה in the Book of Job, see p. 88 above.

[68]The title שדי is also translated by אלהא in 11QtgJob 6:1 (= Hebr. 22:3); 7:3 (= Hebr. 22:17). Cf. G. Bertram, "Zur Prägung der biblischen Gottesvorstellung in den griechischen Übersetzung des Alten Testaments: Die Wiedergabe von *schaddad* und *schaddaj* im Griechischen," *WO* 2 (1959) 502-13; H. Hommel, "Pantokrator," *Theologia viatorum* 5 (1953-54) 322-78.

[69]See p. 90 above. What is one to make of *κύριος* in the LXX and Theodotion translation of Dan 2:47? It is not a question of a translation of יהוה. Is this too to be attributed to Christian scribes? Recall that מרא מלכן turns up as a Pharaonic title in the Adon Letter (*KAI* §266); although it is not the same as *κύριος βασιλείων* of the Rosetta Stone, there is at least some relation here between מרא and *κύριος*. See my discussion in "The Aramaic Letter of King Adon to the Egyptian Pharaoh," *Bib* 46 (1965) 41-55; reproduced below, pp. 233–35.

[70]"Deux notes critiques," (n. 30 above), 184-86.

[71]Since מרא is the predicate here, it has to be in the absolute *state* in Aramaic; but what is to be noted is that it is used absolutely (as defined on p. 109 above, n. 26), i.e., *attributlos.* For an attempt to retrovert Ps 110:1 into contemporary Aramaic, see p. 90 above. What should be noted is that מרא is now attested as an absolute title for God and the suffixal form מרי is found for a human being in 1QapGen 2:9, 13, 24. The play on the words in Greek (*εἶπεν κύριος τῷ κυρίῳ μου*, Mark 12:36) can reflect an Aramaic form of Ps 110:1, if we may presume that Hebrew יהוה was translated by מרא.

[72]Pp. 44–46 above.

[73]See J. A. Sanders, *The Psalms Scroll of Qumrân Cave 11* (DJD 4; Oxford: Clarendon, 1965) 49, 55, 57 (28:7-8). See also his *The Dead Sea Psalms Scroll* (Ithaca: Cornell University, 1967) 88-89, 94-103 for further discussions of Psalm 151. Some commentators (I. Rabinowitz, J. Carmignac) have tried to interpret אדון as a construct state with the following הכול. But see P. W. Skehan, "The Apocryphal Psalm 151," *CBQ* 25 (1963) 407-9, for a defense of the absolute usage and the translation, "Who can recount the works of the Lord?" Cf. A. Hurvitz, "The Post-Biblical Epithet אדון הכול," *Tarbiz* 34 (1965) 224-27. The absolute use of אדון is also found in 1QH 10:8, but it is followed there by a prepositional expression (לכול רוח), which is the equivalent of a construct chain; it makes it similar to the use of מרה in 1QapGen 20:15 (see p. 109 above, n. 28). Cf. also Sir 10:7: שנואה לאדון, *μισητὴ ἔναντι κυρίου* (I am indebted to G. S. Glanzman for calling this instance to my attention). See further P. W. Skehan, *CBQ* 38 (1976) 147.

[74]The Greek version of Ps 151:3, though it twice contains *κύριος*, is not an exact rendering of the Qumran Hebrew texts: *καὶ τίς ἀναγγελεῖ τῷ κυρίῳ μου; αὐτὸς κύριος, αὐτὸς εἰσακούει.*

[75]*The Psalms Scroll*, 9; In *The Dead Sea Psalms Scroll*, 6, Sanders sets the date more precisely as "between A.D. 30 and 50."

[76]At this point one should really take time out to look at other Greek writings of the intertestamental period, such as those mentioned toward the end of n. 44 above. Κύριος is found, e.g., in the Greek text of *1 Enoch* 9:4; 10:9; 14:24; 25:3; 106:11, 13.

[77]See 1QIsa[a] 3:20-25 (= Isa 3:15-18). Cf. M. Burrows, "Variant Readings in the Isaiah Manuscript," *BASOR* 113 (1949) 24-32, esp. p. 31; M. Delcor, "Des diverses manières d'écrire le tetragramme sacré dans les anciens documents hébraïques," *RHR* 147 (1955) 145-73; J. P. Siegel, "The Employment of Palaeo-Hebrew Characters for the Divine Names at Qumran in the Light of Tannaitic Sources," *HUCA* 42 (1971) 159-72.

[78]E.g., 1QpHab 6:14 (= Hab 2:2); 10:7, 14 (= Hab 2:13-14); 1QpMic 1-5:1, 2 (= Mic 1:2-3); 11QPs 2:1, 4, 6, 11 (= Ps 146:9, 10; 148:1, 7); etc.

[79]4QFlorilegium (4Q*174*) 1-2 i 3; 1Q*29* 3-4:2.

[80]In fragments as yet unpublished from Qumran Caves IV and XI; see (in part) P. Benoit, "Le travail d'édition des fragments manuscrits de Qumrân," *RB* 63 (1956) 49-67, esp. p. 56.

[81]1QS 8:14 (quoting Isa 40:3); 4QTestimonia (4Q*175*) 1, 19 (quoting Deut 5:28 and 33:11); 4QTanḥumim (4Q*176*) 1-2 i 6, 7, 9; 1-2 ii 3; 8-11:6, 8, 10.

[82]1QM 15:12 (cf. 1 Sam 18:17).

[83]1QH 1:26; 2:34; 1Q*27* 1 ii 11; 1QpMic 12:3; 4Q*180* 1:1; 4Q*183* 1 ii 3.

[84]1QS 8:13.

[85]4QpPs^{b} 5:4 (= Ps 118:20).

[86]This usage stands in contrast to that of the Mishnah. Cf. S. T. Byington, "יהוה and אדני," *JBL* 76 (1957) 58-59.

[87]See further *Pauline Theology: A Brief Sketch* (p. 109 above, n. 28), 69.

[88]In this case, a suffixal form; see the end of n. 61 above.

[89]See F. C. Grant, *The Gospels: Their Origin and Their Growth* (London: Faber and Faber, 1957) 165; similarly, R. Bultmann, *The Theology of the New Testament* (p. 108 above, n. 18), 2. 36.

[90]H. Conzelmann, (*An Outline of the Theology of the New Testament* [n. 15 above], 83) rightly objects against this sort of terminology. He refers to O. Cullmann in this context. The word "identification" is used in the English translation of Cullmann's *Christology* (p. 109 above, n. 20), 218. But in the original German (*Die Christologie des Neuen Testaments* [Tübingen: Mohr (Siebeck), 1957] 224) Cullmann speaks of *Gleichsetzung*, which, as I understand it, is not the same thing as *Identifizierung*. See n. 36 above.

[91]Compare also the parallelism of אדון and אלוה in Psalm 151 cited above.

[92]See R. E. Brown, "Does the New Testament Call Jesus God?" *TS* 26 (1965) 545-73; reprinted in *Jesus God and Man: Modern Biblical Reflections* (Milwaukee: Bruce, 1967) 1-38.

[93]"Maranatha und Kyrios Jesus," *ZNW* 53 (1962) 125-44.

[94]See further my article, "The Son of David Tradition" (p. 113 above, n. 87).

[95]For a possible retroversion of this saying into Aramaic, see p. 90 above.

[96]See, e.g., L. Cerfaux, "Le titre Kyrios et la dignité royale de Jésus," *RSPT* 11 (1922) 40-71: "un titre du protocole des rois" (p. 42); E. Lipiński, *La royauté de Yahwé dans la poésie et le culte de l'ancien Israël* (Brussels: Paleis der Academiën, 1965).

[97]See further *Pauline Theology: A Brief Sketch* (p. 109 above, n. 28), 64-65.

[98]See further I. H. Marshall, "Palestinian and Hellenistic Christianity: Some Critical Comments," *NTS* 19 (1972-73) 271-87; M. Hengel, "Christologie und neutestamentliche Chronologie: Zu einer Aporie in der Geschichte des Urchristentums," *Neues Testament und Geschichte: Historisches Geschehen und Deutung im Neuen Testament: Oscar Cullmann zum 70. Geburtstag* (ed. H. Baltensweiler and B. Reicke; Zürich: Theologischer Verlag, 1972) 43-67, esp. 60-61. For a further specific interpretation of the implication of the *kyrios*-title in the Matthean Gospel, see J. D. Kingsbury, "The Title 'Kyrios' in Matthew's Gospel," *JBL* 94 (1975) 246-55.

Chapter 6

The New Testament Title "Son of Man" Philologically Considered*

Among the many titles given to Jesus in the NT none has been so contested and continuously debated as that of the "Son of Man." The debate has centered on the origin and background of the title, the occurrence of it on the lips of Jesus and of others in NT writings, and the connotations that it would carry. It is likewise controverted in its application to the various stages of his existence, and the question is raised whether he used it during his earthly ministry either of himself or of another person. These questions reveal that the title has been a complex problem in recent NT interpretation, and the sorting out of the various facets of the problem is not always easy. The philological aspect, being mainly concerned with the origin and background of the title and of the meaning(s) which the phrase might have had in Palestinian Judaism, is more or less propaedeutic to the theological discussion. Yet the latter cannot be seriously engaged in without due regard for the philological question. A disregard of the latter as *belanglos* would be tolerated only in a dialectical interpretation of the NT in which the consideration of new empirical data proves traumatic.

Aspects of the philological consideration of the title have often been rehearsed before this, and if I now address myself to them, it is with the hope that some of these observations may at least query some commonly accepted interpretations and bring some new material to bear upon the problem. Indirectly, my observations will also bear on the theological considerations involved in the title. Moreover, the philological data have to be related to the proper phases of Aramaic; for the disregard of this aspect has been responsible for the introduction of many extraneous and irrelevant notions into the debate.

The literature on the "Son of Man" is vast, and I make no pretense about covering it.[1] But I hope to cope at least with some of the more important recent discussions of the philological aspects of the title.

My remarks will fall under three headings: (1) A brief resume of the NT data and of some recent attempts to translate the phrase; (2) The Semitic data, Hebrew and Aramaic, that bear upon the title; and (3) The connotations of the title in a first-century Palestinian context.

I. *The New Testament Data and Attempts to Translate the Title*

A summary of the NT usage of the title is necessary initially so that a clear view of what is involved may be before us.

The title *ὁ υἱὸς τοῦ ἀνθρώπου* is used of Jesus by other persons in the NT in a few instances: the arthrous form is employed by Stephen in Acts 7:56, whereas the anarthrous form (*υἱὸς ἀνθρώπου*) is used by the author of Revelation (1:13; 14:14, in an allusion to Dan 7:13), and possibly also by the author of the Epistle to the Hebrews (2:6, quoting Ps 8:5).[2] Indirectly, John 12:34a,b implies the application of the arthrous form to him by others. In the passages that allude to or quote the OT, the phrase agrees with the form found in the LXX and Theodotionic versions of the OT books involved.

Within the Synoptic tradition the arthrous phrase is found only on the lips of Jesus. It is applied to him (a) *in his earthly ministry*: in the Marcan source and its parallels (2:10 [= Matt 9:6; Luke 5:24]; 2:28 [= Matt 12:8; Luke 6:51; *10:45 [= Matt 20:28; Luke 22:27 has "I"]; Matt 16:13 [Mark 8:27 and Luke 9:18 have "me"]); from "Q" (*Matt 8:20 = Luke 9:58; *Matt 11:19 = Luke 7:34; Matt 12:32 = Luke 12:10; *Luke 6:22 [Matt 5:11 has "my"]); in Matthew alone (13:37); in Luke alone (19:10; [9:56 in some MSS.]);[3] (b) *in his suffering*: in the Marcan source (8:31 [= Luke 9:22; Matt 16:21 has "he"]; 9:12 [= Matt 17:12]; 9:31 [= Matt 17:22; Luke 9:44]; 10:33 [= Matt 20:18; Luke 18:31]; 14:21bis [= Matt 26:24 bis; Luke 22:22 changes once to "he"]; 14:41 [= Matt 26:45]); in Matthew alone (26:2); in Luke alone (22:48; 24:7); (c) *in his exalted state, sometimes as Judge*: in the Marcan source (†8:38 [= Matt 16:27; Luke 9:26]; 9:9 [= Matt 17:9]; 13:26 [= Matt 24:30b; Luke 21:27]; 14:62 [= Matt 26:64; Luke 22:69]); from "Q" (Matt 12:40 = Luke 11:30; Matt 24:27 = Luke 17:24; Matt 24:37 = Luke 17:26; Matt 24:44 = Luke 12:40; †Luke 12:8 [Matt 10:32 has "I"]); in Matthew alone (10:23; 13:41; 16:28; 19:28; 24:30a; 24:39; 25:31); in Luke alone (17:22, 30; 18:8; 21:26).[4]

Moreover, in the Johannine Gospel the arthrous phrase is found on the lips of Jesus in the majority of instances (11 times in all): in three of them it is applied to his being "lifted up" (3:14; 8:28; 12:34a), and in the others it is used of the exalted "Son of Man" (1:51; 3:13; 6:27, 53, 62; 9:35 [with a *v. l.*]; 12:23; 13:31). The anarthrous phrase, however, is found in the latter sense in 5:27.[5]

Of the two forms of the phrase, the anarthrous *υἱὸς ἀνθρώπου* has proved to be the less objectionable since it can at least be explained as a Semitism, reflecting the construct chain in either Hebrew (בן אדם) or Aramaic (בר אנש). But the arthrous phrase *ὁ υἱὸς τοῦ ἀνθρώπου* has been regarded as a literary monstrosity,[6] and in normal classical or hellenistic Greek it would mean simply "the man's son" or "the son of the man." The tendency of modern biblical translators to render it as "(the) son of man" reflects the Semitic anarthrous phrase and the OT background to which it is judged to be related.

A few years ago J. B. Cortés and F. M. Gatti, in a lengthy discussion of the title, sought to interpret the Greek phrase as "meaning simply the Son of

Adam."[7] Their discussion has proved to be a tour de force. It has apparently made little impression on the modern debate. That Hebrew בן אדם could mean "son of Adam" is undeniable. That this possible meaning of the Hebrew phrase was what was intended by NT writers who used *ὁ υἱὸς τοῦ ἀνθρώπου* is another matter. Since Ἀδάμ is used as a name by NT writers—and, indeed, Luke even traced the genealogy of Jesus back to Ἀδάμ (3:38)—it seems that they would have written *ὁ υἱὸς τοῦ* Ἀδάμ, if they had meant that. Moreover, that "son of Adam" was admitted in late targumic translations of the Hebrew expression seems clear; but that such evidence has anything to do with the NT period is another matter (see p. 151 below).

A further question about the arthrous phrase *ὁ υἱὸς τοῦ ἀνθρώπου* has been raised by C. F. D Moule. He queries whether one should not translate it as "*the* Son of Man" or "*the* human figure," giving almost demonstrative force to the definite article.[8] He would then relate the phrase to Dan 7:13, suggesting that Jesus chose to take that figure of the Book of Daniel as a symbol for his own vocation—"the vocation to *be* God's true people, going to any lengths of suffering in loyalty to do his will, and ultimately to be vindicated in the heavenly court."

Such attempts to translate the peculiar Greek phrase differently have at least pointed up the philological problem. They make it clear that though the phrase functions plainly as a title in the NT, as it now stands, its background and historical usage have to be considered in any attempt to determine its theological overtones and the use that Jesus of Nazareth may have made of it, either in reference to himself or to someone else.

II. *The Semitic Data, Hebrew and Aramaic, That Bear upon the Title*

Because the peculiar Greek arthrous phrase *ὁ υἱὸς τοῦ ἀνθρώπου* is otherwise unattested in non-Christian writings prior to the NT and the Semitic-looking anarthrous phrase *υἱὸς ἀνθρώπου*,[9] is related to it, NT interpreters have looked to a Hebrew or Aramaic background for the expression. A figurative sense of *υἱὸς* is indeed attested in Greek, in the sense of a pupil, a follower, a helper, or an heir (e.g., of guild secrets).[10] But this usage scarcely seems to explain the NT phrase, "Son of Man." Moreover, there are other NT Greek phrases using *υἱὸς* that must be related to Semitic influence, such as *υἱοὶ φωτός* (1 Thes 5:5 [anarthrous]; Luke 16:8 [arthrous]; John 12:36 [anarthrous]),[11] or *υἱοὶ βροντῆς* (Mark 3:17), given as the explanation of the mysterious *βοανηργές*. But even such a consideration of the figurative use of Greek *υἱός* must ultimately yield to the historical attestation of the phrase in the Semitic realm.

In the areas of Hebrew and Aramaic the last thorough survey of the material was presented over twenty years ago by E. Sjöberg, and it need not be repeated here.[12] It will suffice to summarize from it what is pertinent for our purpose and add to it what new material has come to light since Sjöberg wrote. I shall not concern myself with either the singular nouns איש or אנש or the plural expressions בני אנשא or אנשים. Sjöberg also discussed these forms, for they were pertinent to his treatment. But they scarcely bear on the topic that interests us here, viz., the singular phrase that eventually became a title, save in a very indirect way.[13]

In the Hebrew Bible the singular phrase is found in two forms: בן אנוש (Ps 144:3) and בן אדם (93 times in Ezekiel as a form of address or quasi-vocative;[14] and 14 times elsewhere in the OT: Num 23:19; Jer 49:18, 33; 50:40; 51:43; Isa 51:12; 56:2; Ps 8:5; 80:18; 146:3; Job 16:21; 25:6; 35:8; Dan 8:17 [in the last instance like the quasi-vocative in Ezekiel]). As Sjöberg and others have already pointed out, none of these instances reflects ordinary day-to-day usage; they are found only in contexts composed in poetic or solemn diction and style.[15]

The Hebrew expression with the definite article, בן האדם, is unknown either in the OT or the Mishnah. G. Vermes not long ago called attention to the occurrence of it in 1QS 11:20, where the article has been added above the line:[16] "And what is the son of man himself amidst all Thy marvellous works?"[17] But just what nuance בן האדם is to carry here is debatable; when it is compared with לבן אדם of 1QH 4:30, parallel to לאנוש,[18] it is hard to detect any difference. In other words, what precisely is the connotation of the added Hebrew article in this isolated occurrence of it? Vermes may be right in calling it an Aramaism.[19] In any case, this isolated Hebrew instance of the definite expression is hardly likely to be the sort of thing that explains the peculiar Greek arthrous form of the NT expression.

In the postbiblical Hebrew of a still later period we find an isolated instance of בן אדם in rabbinical writings. It is found in the Palestinian Talmud, *Taᶜanit* II.1 (65b), which in its final form was redacted ca. A.D. 425.[20] The instance is found in a saying ascribed to R. Abbahu, of the third generation of Palestinian Amoraim:[21]

א״ר אבהו אם יאמר לך אדם אל אני מכזב הוא, בן אדם אני
סופו לתהות בו, שאני עולה לשמים ההוא אמר ולא יקימינה.

"R. Abbahu said, 'If someone says to you, "I am God," he (is) a liar; "I am the son of Adam (or: a son of Man)," his end will be a regret to him; "I am ascending to heaven," that man has said it (indeed), but he will not substantiate it.'" The passage is usually regarded as an allusion to Num 23:19, the oracle of Balaam in which one finds the sole use of בן אדם in the Pentateuch, and precisely in parallelism with איש: "God is not man, that he should lie, or a son of man, that he should repent. Has he said, and will he not do it? Or has he spoken, and will he not fulfil it?" (*RSV*). It is not easy to determine the thrust of R. Abbahu's statement or the exact meaning of בן אדם in it. The latter may have had titular force at that time, if one were to concede that R. Abbahu, otherwise known for his disputations with Christians,[22] were referring to the Christian use of the phrase for Jesus.[23] This is, however, the surprisingly sole instance of the expression in rabbinical Hebrew writings—

which stands in significant contrast to the frequent attestation of the Aramaic expression.

When one surveys, then, the Hebrew material that might bear on the background of the Greek expression, one sees that it is meagre, indeed, and realizes why the Aramaic material usually commands more attention.

When Sjöberg wrote over twenty years ago, the oldest Aramaic instance of the phrase to which he could point was בר אנש in Dan 7:13,[24] and this instance has been the subject of much debate, as is well known. P. Benoit, in reacting against interpretations of the NT Greek expression that tended to water down its meaning by an appeal to the Aramaic phrase and a claim that it meant no more than "man," once wrote that "Aramaic had other more simple terms to express the latter idea" and that "the formula 'son of man' was rare in Aramaic and was only used in the plural to designate members of the human race (cf. Mark 3:28; Eph 3:5)."[25] Indeed, H. Lietzmann is said to have gone so far as to affirm that "Jesus never applied to Himself the title 'Son of man,' for this term does not exist in Aramaic, and for linguistic reasons is an impossible term."[26] G. Dalman cited this view and labelled it a "grievous error, which careful observation of the biblical Aramaic alone would have rendered impossible."[27] Such assertions sound a little presumptuous today, when newer evidence makes possible a slightly different assessment. However, the instances of בר אנש in pre-Christian Aramaic are still not numerous, when judged against the growing corpus of Aramaic texts and inscriptions that have come to light in the last three quarters of a century.

The earliest occurrence of the phrase is now to be found in one of the treaty stipulations imposed by Bir-Gaʾyah, king of KTK, on Matiʿel, son of ʿAttarsamak, king of Arpad, in the third Sefire inscription (Sf III 16-17):

בכל מה זי ימות בר אנש שקרתם לכ/ל אלהי עדיא זי בספרא זנה

"In whatever way a man shall die,[28] you will have been false to all the gods of the treaty which is in this inscription."[29] Here the phrase בר אנש (absolute) means no more than "someone, anyone," i.e., "a man," a member of the human race (used indefinitely). It differs little from אש (= ʾ*īš*), which occurs in Sf II B 16 with a prefixed negative in the sense of "no one." The context in which בר אנש occurs in the Sefire inscription is scarcely poetic; engraved on stone as part of several treaty stipulations, it could undoubtedly be regarded as solemn. And yet, the way in which it is used suggests that it reflects the ordinary daily usage of the time.

This instance is isolated in the phase of Old Aramaic. In Official Aramaic there is not one instance of it outside of Dan 7:13. Neither in literary texts like ʾAḥiqar or the Bar Puneš story nor in the many letters and contracts from Egyptian provenience has an example of the phrase been found.[30] It is difficult to say why this is so. In the sole instance of it in Biblical Aramaic it occurs with a generic meaning in Dan 7:13:

וארו עם־ענני שמיא כבר אנש אתה הוה,

"and lo, with the clouds of heaven one like a human being was coming" (or, more literally, "one like a son of man"). The use of the phrase in Daniel has long been debated, and its contextual sense does not concern us now.[31] What does seem clear, however, is that the generic sense made use of in Daniel scarcely provides the immediate background to the titular use in the Greek phrase of the NT.[32]

The first instance of the expression in extrabiblical Aramaic after Sefire III is to be found in Qumran literature. Here again one finds it in the indefinite sense in the *Genesis Apocryphon* of Qumran Cave I:

ואשגה זרעך כעפר ארעא די לא ישכח כול בר אנוש לממניה

"I shall make your descendants as numerous *as the dust of the earth which no man can number"* (1QapGen 21:13, paraphrasing Gen 13:16: ושמתי את־זרעך כעפר הארץ אשר אם־יוכל איש למנות את־עפר הארץ גם־זרעך ימנה).[33] In this instance, the hebraized form בר אנוש translates איש of the Hebrew text of Genesis,[34] and it scarcely means anything more than "no one."

An instance of the generic sense, meaning "a human being" and designating an individual belonging to the collectivity of mankind, can further be found in the Targum of Job from Cave XI:

[לגבר כות]ך חטיך ולבר אנש צדקתך

"Your sin affects a man like yourself, and your righteousness (another) human being" (11QtgJob 26:2-3, translating Job 35:8, לאיש־כמוך רשעך / ולבן־אדם צדקתך).[35] This is said by Elihu, as he asks Job what his sinning against God would really accomplish. Implied is a contrast between "man" and "God." Significantly, בר אנש here translates one of the OT instances of בן אדם.[36] The text of col. 26 is fragmentary, and the editors have restored גבר as the translation of the Hebrew parallel word איש.[37] If the restoration be correct, then בר אנש functions here as a mere synonym for גבר; yet even if one should prefer to restore אנש, the generic sense of the phrase would still be clear. It would be a mere stylistic variant for "man."

Another instance of the generic sense seems to be found in 11QtgJob 9:9 (= Hebr. 25:6); the text is fragmentary and only [ב]ר אנש תולע[תא] is preserved, "[the s]on of man, (who is) a wor[m]." It too is a comparison of man with God in a speech of Bildad the Shuhite, and בר אנש again is a translation of Hebrew בן אדם.[38] From these instances we learn that in at least two of the three passages where the Hebrew of the Book of Job has בן אדם (16:21; 25:6; 35:8) the Qumran targum has rendered it by בר אנש. Since there is no instance of בר אנש being used in the rest of this fragmentary targum, it is hard to say to what extent the expression might have been a translation for other Hebrew words for "man." This must be recalled later, when mention is made of the frequent use of בר נש in later targums, even though we have in the Qumran targum only about one-sixth of the Book of Job preserved.

These few instances in Qumran literature reveal at least that the phrase was in use in the first century B.C. or A.D. in Palestine,[39] and, indeed, both in the indefinite sense of "someone" and the generic sense of "a human being."

Before considering the rabbinic and targumic material of a later period that may bear on this question, I should like to introduce an aspect of the philological argument on which the above judgment is based. I have treated this aspect briefly elsewhere;[40] but since it has been more recently challenged,[41] I should like to reconsider it here with the aid of some new data that affect it.

It is striking that in none of the evidence from the Aramaic texts known to us prior to the Second Revolt do we ever find the form בר נש or בר נשא. Whenever the phrase is found, it is always written with an initial *aleph* on אנש (Sf III 16; 1QapGen 21:13; 11QtgJob 9:9; 26:3). This, moreover, agrees with the numerous instances of the word אנש or אנוש found in various phases of Aramaic prior to the Second Revolt and in various dialects from geographically distinct areas. It is always written with initial *aleph*.[42] On the other hand, the form without *aleph* is well known in Palestinian Jewish and Christian Aramaic of a later date and in Syriac. In the latter dialect it is sometimes retained in the writing, but then fitted with the *linea occultans*, warning the reader not to pronounce it (in carefully pointed texts of the Late Phase). The absence of the initial *aleph* is telltale evidence, therefore, of the later date.[43] Hence, *if* certain senses of the phrase might be attested in expressions using בר נש and going beyond those of an earlier period, one must be careful not to apply the later senses to earlier periods without further ado.

Problematic here is the initial *aleph* with a reduced vowel. It is well known that in Aramaic the whole syllable disappeared eventually with the aphaeresis of the *aleph*. In some instances, in an effort to preserve the syllable the reduced vowel was secondarily given full pronunciation, e.g., in Syriac, *ᵓenā*, "I". The same process explains the full vowel in אֱינָשׁ which turns up especially in the Aramaic of the Babylonian Talmud. But this secondary lengthening of the vowel is as much a sign of lateness as the aphaeresis.

Now my argument for the late date of the phrase בר נש from the aphaeresis of the initial *aleph* has been found to be "curious."[44] Objection to it has been raised because the NT form of the Palestinian name *Lazar(us)* is written in Greek without the initial syllable, *Λάζαρος* (Luke 16:20). Its Semitic counterpart would be אלעזר, a form found in a Murabbaᶜat bill of divorce (Mur 19:29) and on a Jerusalem ossuary, and precisely with the initial *aleph*. Hence it is argued: "Now the form *Lazar* derives from Eleazar by omission of the initial *aleph* in the same way as *nash* is a shortened version of *ᵓenash*. But as is well known, this dropping of the opening guttural is a peculiarity of the Galilean Aramaic dialect, and characteristically the Palestinian—i.e., Galilean—Talmud often truncates the names of Eleazar and Eliezer to read Lazar or Liezer. Similarly, in the Galilean necropolis of Beth Sheᶜarim, Greek-Jewish inscriptions attest the abbreviated form Lazar and even Laze."[45]

Concerning this objection I should like to make several observations: (1) Evidence from proper names is extremely difficult to interpret and to apply to common nouns. It is well known that names develop colloquial abbreviations, nickname-forms, and formal abbreviations (or hypocoristica). Is it certain that Greek Λάζαρος or Λάζαρ (without the Greek ending), developed simply because of the aphaeresis of initial *aleph* at this period? How do we know that this is not a colloquial or formal abbreviation?[46] (2) In a recently discovered inscription from a tomb in the Givᶜat ha-Mivṭar region of Jerusalem, dated to the first century A.D.[47] or possibly to "the end of the first century B.C. or the first century A.D.,"[48] the very name cited above has turned up and is written in a way that runs counter to the stated objection. For the name is divided, part of it being written at the end of line 1 and part of it at the beginning of line 2. On line 1 the *aleph* alone appears! Here is the text, as I read it:

I, Abba, son of the priest E-	אנה אבה בר כהנה א
leaz‹ar›, son of Aaron the high (priest), I	לעז‹ר› בר אהרן רבה אנ
Abba, the oppressed and the persecuted,	ה אבה מעניה מרד
who was born in Jerusalem,	פה די יליד בירושלם
and went into exile to Babylonia and brought (back to Jerusalem) Mattathi-	וגלא לבבל ואסק למתת
ah, son of Jud(ah); and I buried him in the	י בר יהוד וקברתה במ
cave, which I acquired by the (*or* his?) writ.	ערתה דזבנת בגטה

Now, aside from other interesting features in this inscription, the initial *aleph* of the name אלעז‹ר›[49] is written separately on line 1. To me, it is inconceivable that it would have been so written, if it was not pronounced as a separate syllable. Compare the other divided words in the inscription (lines 2-3, 3-4, 5-6, 6-7). A form of the name is also written fully in 1QapGen 22:34: אליעזר (= ᵓ*Elīᶜēzer*), just as one would expect it at this period. Admittedly, part of the difficulty here is the unvocalized evidence with which we are dealing; but from the standpoint of the consonantal text there is no evidence of the aphaeresis of initial *aleph* at this period, either in the Aramaic/Hebrew forms of proper names or in common nouns. (3) In the Givᶜat ha-Mivṭar tomb inscription I restored the final consonant on the name, אלעז‹ר›, "Eleaz‹ar›." Now it may be that that syllable should not be restored and that it really represents the name *Eleaz*, another shortened form of Eleazar. This form has, in fact, been found in a Greek text from one of the Murabbaᶜat caves (Mur 94 a 7): Ἐλεαζ Βαρη. . .[ ]. The name is found in a list of names and a record of accounts, which P. Benoit, who published the text (DJD 2.224), regards as a "relevé récapitulatif de comptes." It is not dated, but it must have been written shortly before or about the time of the Bar Cochba revolt. What is significant for our discussion is not only the Greek attestation of the form of the name in the Aramaic inscription without the final syllable, but the presence of the first syllable, which supports my contention about the non-aphaeresis of *aleph* with a reduced vowel in such words at this time in Palestine. By the same token, if one consults the list of names in E. Testa, *Il simbolismo dei Giudeo-Cristiani* (Jerusalem: Franciscan Press, 1962) 479, one finds that the forms ליעזר, לזר, לעזר are listed only in inscriptions from the Diaspora, with no reference being given to Murabbaᶜat texts. Seeing that the name Lazarus is found in the canonical gospels—of final redaction in non-Palestinian areas—there may be some significance to this form of the name that is found here. (4) It is rightly asserted that the Palestinian Talmud often truncates the names of Eleazar and Eliezer to read *Lazar* and *Liezer*. But that is exactly what one would expect at the time of the Palestinian Talmud.[50] Implied here, however, is that the evidence of this Talmud is as old as the NT itself—which it is not. (5) The evidence of the Galilean names in the necropolis of Beth Sheᶜarim is scarcely pertinent. Proper account has not been taken of the dating of that necropolis. According to the archaeologists, these burials do not antedate the third century A.D.,[51] and some of the tombs come from even later centuries. Interesting as the inscriptions on these tombs may be, they all belong to the phase of Late Aramaic and are fine examples of Palestinian Jewish Aramaic of the classic, rabbinic period (between the Mishnah and the closing of the Talmud). If one is going to argue on the basis of archaeological material, then one must respect its date and its provenience. For these reasons, I shall continue to consider the forms of the phrase בר נש(א) without the initial *aleph* to be signs of Late Aramaic, until clear evidence from first-century Palestine emerges to the contrary. With this we may turn to the Aramaic evidence from the Late Phase.

In the material of the Late Phase of Aramaic that bears on the problem of the Son of Man, one has to distinguish what is found in the targums from the material in other rabbinical writings. The reason for this is twofold: (a) the translation process, in which some instances of the phrase reflect a Hebrew counterpart and thus give pause about the everyday character of the phrase; (b) the targumic usage may reflect older customs than the talmudic, midrashic, or other material.

In the targumic material, we may first consider those passages in which בן אדם or בן אנוש occur in the Hebrew text of the OT. The only instance of בן אדם in the Pentateuch is found in Num 23:19, in parallelism to איש; both are used in the generic (inclusive) sense of "man" in contrast to God. The verse is expanded in Targum Onqelos: איש is twice rendered by the plural בני אנשא, whereas בן אדם is translated as בני בסרא (literally, "sons of the flesh"). In each case the plural has been used instead of a generic singular. The plural is also found in the Fragmentary Targum of Num 23:19: three instances of בני אנש. Tg. Pseudo-Jonathan, however, used the singular בר נש twice to translate איש, and the plural בני ביסרא for Hebrew בן אדם. Neofiti 1 reads בני אנשא three times too. The verse is not found in the fragmentary texts of the Cairo Genizah.

In the Tg. Jonathan of the Prophets one finds בר אנש, in parallelism to אנש, as the translation of בן אדם (in parallelism to איש or אנוש), in Isa 56:2; Jer 49:18, 33; 50:40; 51:43; and in one instance (Isa 51:12), the emphatic form בר אנשא (in parallelism with אנשא).[52] In the late targums on the Writings one usually finds Hebrew בן אדם rendered as בר נש (Ps 8:5; 80:18; 146:3; Job 25:6;

35:8), and Hebrew בן אנוש (Ps 144:3) is likewise so translated. Sometimes בר נש is even introduced as the translation of parallel words such as אנוש (Ps 8:5; Job 25:6) or גבר (Job 16:21). In all of these instances the meaning is generic, "a human being," a stylistic variant of אנש, איש, or גבר. None of these instances differs significantly from the generic usage of 11QtgJob 9:9; 26:2-3.

By contrast, the בן אדם of Ezekiel and Dan 8:17 is consistently rendered as בר אדם, which G. Dalman and others have translated as "son of Adam."[53] In the case of this quasi-vocative usage, this translation seems to be a deliberate shift to avoid the ordinary בר אנש and to insure the solemnity of the phrase.

Beyond the instances in which a form of בר אנש renders Hebrew בן אדם in the targums, there are many instances in which it translates such simple Hebrew words as אדם or האדם (e.g., Gen 1:26 [Neof.], 27 [Neof.]; 2:18 [Neof.]; 8:21 [Neof.]; 9:5 [Neof., Ps.-J.]; Deut 5:21 [Ps.-J.]; 20:19 [Ps.-J.]; Ps 144:4; Job 34:29), or איש (Exod 19:13 [Cairo F]; Deut 34:6 [Cairo F]), or בני אדם (Mic 5:6), or even הנפש ההוא (Num 9:13 [Ps.-J.]). These instances serve merely as stylistic variants of "man" in the generic sense, or of "someone" in the indefinite sense. But this use of a form of בר נש spreads and becomes very frequent in the targums of the Late Phase, where, further, the distinction between the absolute state and the emphatic state is no longer observed.

G. Vermes has collected many examples of the indefinite use of בר נש and of its generic use from the Palestinian Talmud and the midrashim of this period, and there is no need to repeat his material here. Apropos of his treatment of this material in the appendix of the third edition of M. Black's *Aramaic Approach to the Gospels and Acts*, I should like to express the following observations: (1) I cannot agree that the material cited from either the Palestinian Talmud or the *Genesis Rabbah* reflects second century A.D. data;[54] and even if it could be shown at that time to be an older literary tradition, it would not necessarily mean that it was preserved in second-century Aramaic. (2) I cannot agree that the phrase ההוא גברא, which for the sake of the argument *(dato non concesso)* may be a circumlocution for either "I" or "thou,"[55] has anything to do with the alleged circumlocutional use of the phrase בר נש(א). J. Jeremias has already noted the essential difference between the two phrases:

> *Hāhū gabrā*, referring to the person who speaks, means 'I (and no other),' and thus is strictly limited to the speaker; *bar ᵓĕnāšā*, on the other hand, keeps its generic or indefinite significance, 'the (or a) man, and therefore also I,' 'the (or a) man like myself,' even where the speaker does include himself. . . .[56]

(3) I grant that the surrogate usage of בר נש for "I" is now found in two parallel targumic translations of Gen 4:14: in Neofiti 1 Cain says, "It is impossible for me to hide" (לית אפשר לי למטמרה), whereas in Cairo Targum B he says, "It is impossible for a man to hide" (לית אפשר לברנש למטמרה).[57] Here at length we are provided with a parallel that is similar to the Synoptic parallels which have

the pronoun in place of ὁ υἱὸς τοῦ ἀνθρώπου. Interesting though this parallel is, it remains to be shown that it represents a first-century Palestinian usage. (4) Many of the examples which are cited by Vermes from the Palestinian Talmud and *Genesis Rabbah* and said to mean "I" or "me" can just as easily be translated "a man" or "man" in an indefinite or generic sense.[58] (5) I could not agree more with Vermes when he states that he has found no evidence in any of the rabbinic material that "*bar nāsh(ā)* was ever employed as a messianic designation."[59] This use is non-existent in both Middle and Late Aramaic texts. The same would have to be said about the "apocalyptic" Son of Man.[60]

III. *The Connotations of the Title in a First-Century Palestinian Context*

From the foregoing survey of the Hebrew and Aramaic material it seems obvious that the Hebrew data have little to offer as an explanation of the NT title. Though the Aramaic phrase בר אנש is attested, at least in the indefinite sense, from the 8th century B.C., and three instances are now known in the extrabiblical Aramaic of Qumran, one in the indefinite sense and two in the generic sense, it is clear that we do not as yet have the abundant and frequent attestation of it such as is found in the rabbinic writings of the Late Period. The phrase is attested in Old Aramaic (Sf III 16), in Official Aramaic (Dan 7:13), in Middle Aramaic (1QapGen 31:13; 11QtgJob 9:9; 26:2-3); thus it is found in inscriptions and literary texts. It is still to be found in what might be called texts representing ordinary, daily usage (letters, contracts, bonds, such as are found in the material from Elephantine, Murrabbaᶜat, etc.). Though it is now no longer as "rare" as it was once thought to be, it is still not as abundantly attested as in the targums and rabbinic writings.

What should above all be noted is that there is no example of any of the following senses in the Aramaic material prior to the composition of the NT— and hence prior to the titular use of ὁ υἱὸς τοῦ ἀνθρώπου: (a) *As a form of address* directed to a person, such as the Hebrew בן אדם, used of Ezekiel or Daniel. Given this biblical use of it, one might expect to find it in the parabiblical literature of the last two pre-Christian centuries. In any case, this quasi-vocative use is scarcely the background for the NT Greek phrase.[61] (b) *As a title for an expected or apocalyptic figure*, least of all for a messiah or an anointed one. The phrase does occur indeed in the apocalyptic chapter of Daniel (7:13), but it is used there in the generic sense, not as a title. It has been regarded as a "messianic" title, mainly because of its association with the title Messiah in Ethiopic Enoch (e.g., 48:2, 10), whereas it in no way suggests an anointed figure *per se*. But if J. T. Milik's latest theory about the second part of the Book of Enoch, the so-called Similitudes, were to prove acceptable, then the entire question of the conflated titles for the mysterious figure in that part of the book would have to be scrutinized again and precisely for the roots of this conflation in pre-Christian Palestinian Judaism. For Milik maintains that the Similitudes represent a Christian substitution. It replaced the Book of the Giants which was part of the Book of Enoch at Qumran and which he has now discovered among some published and unpublished material from Qumran.[62] We cannot go into the problems of that identification now. But it obviously bears on the Palestinian background of the Aramaic phrase בר אנש being used as a title for an individual person. (c) *As a surrogate for "I."*[63] Though this usage can now be documented in the Aramaic translation of Gen 4:14 in the targums Neofiti 1 and Pseudo-Jonathan, it is still problematic for first-century Palestinian usage, unless one is willing to admit such a dating for these targums—which I am not. Indeed, one may well ask whether this usage would ever have been queried or sought for, if it were not for the NT parallels such as Mark 10:45 = Matt 20:28 = Luke 22:27; Mark 8:27 = Matt 16:13 = Luke 9:18; Matt 5:11 = Luke 6:22; Matt 10:32 = Luke 12:8. Even in these NT instances one has to ask whether the phrase "son of Man" has not really been secondarily introduced.[64] If so, is the surrogate usage then a real one for first-century Palestinian Aramaic?

In the Aramaic material from the Late Phase one finds בר נש(א) not only used in the indefinite sense and in the generic sense, as in the earlier phases, but also the surrogate use. But what is significant is the abundant attestation of בר נש(א) as a substitute for the simple words for "man" like איש, גבר, and אנש.

When one views the NT Greek phrase *ὁ υἱὸς τοῦ ἀνθρώπου* over against this background, one sees that the NT usage is special. As it now appears in the Gospels, the arthrous form must be understood as a title for Jesus. Whether it stems from an Aramaic phrase that he himself used, either of himself or of someone else, may be and will continue to be debated, because it is a question to which in the long run only a speculative answer can be given. Certainly, there is nothing in the indefinite or generic Aramaic usage to prove it impossible. That either of these attested uses could be the springboard for the development of the titular usage is not immediately obvious, and the missing-link still has to be found.

It is not at all certain that the Aramaic emphatic state was as moribund in first-century Palestine as it is sometimes supposed to have been. There are clear instances of the emphatic state in Qumran literature.[65] But in any case, the arthrous Greek phrase could be an attempt to translate the emphatic state of the Aramaic; but it may be something more. I suspect that it was deliberately fashioned to carry the nuance of a title.

Aramaic-speaking Christians of later periods certainly understood it in that sense: *ὁ υἱὸς τοῦ ἀνθρώπου* was translated into Syriac and Christian Palestinian Aramaic as *bĕreh dĕ(ʾ)nāšā* (Pešitta, Mark 2:10) or *ʾebreh dĕ-gabrā* (CPA, Luke 6:5). Here we are dealing with a stage of the Aramaic language in which there was no longer a difference of meaning between בר נש and בר נשא, and in order to express the determination of the arthrous Greek phrase the prospective pronominal suffix with the following *dĕ*-phrase was employed. For even if they had used ברא דאנשא, it would not necessarily have carried the definite nuance of *ὁ υἱὸς τοῦ ἀνθρώπου.*

These philological considerations of the Semitic background of the NT phrase "Son of Man" are not uncomplicated. They limit in their own way the further discussion of the theological import of the christological title.

For my part, I think that in analyzing the theological or christological use of the title in the gospels, one has to reckon with several factors: (a) the secondary intrusion of the title into passages where it is lacking in parallels; (b) the evidence for the phrase as a *title* for a "supernatural, apocalyptic figure" as quite questionable, since if there is any validity to this sort of extension of the phrase which describes a being resembling a human in Dan 7:13, it is still not clear that this extension predates Jesus himself or even the NT writings; (c) there is no other or more plausible starting-point for the titular use of the phrase for Jesus in the NT than Dan 7:13, even though the phrase is not used in a titular sense there. But the reason for seeing a reference to Daniel in the NT use comes from other phrases and explicit allusions to that passage in some parts of the NT; yet they also seem to suggest a development of the phrase beyond what one finds there. Finally, the NT phrase must be so interpreted as to fit the varied uses made of it in differing situations.

NOTES TO CHAPTER 6

*This essay appears here for the first time. It was originally delivered as one of the Speaker's Lectures at Oxford University, May 1974.

[1]A survey of literature on the title up to 1966 can be found in R. Marlow, "The Son of Man in Recent Journal Literature," *CBQ* 28 (1966) 20-30. More recent surveys can be found in the following discussions: J. Coppens, *De Mensenzoon-Logia in het Markus-Evangelie* (Mededelingen van de koninklijke Academie voor Wetenschappen, Letteren en schone Kunsten van België, Kl. der Letteren, 35/3; Brussels: Paleis der Academiën, 1973); I. H. Marshall, "The Synoptic Son of Man Sayings in Recent Discussion," *NTS* 12 (1966) 327-51; "The Son of Man in Contemporary Debate," *EvQ* 42 (1970) 67-87; R. Maddox, "The Quest for Valid Methods in 'Son of Man' Research," *Australian Biblical Review* 19 (1971) 36-51; C. Colpe, "Der Begriff 'Menschensohn' und die Methode der Erforschung messianischer Prototypen," *Kairos* 11 (1969) 241-63; 12 (1970) 81-112; 13 (1971) 1-17; 14 (1972) 241-57; R. N. Longenecker, "'Son of Man' Imagery: Some Implications for Theology and Discipleship," *Journal of the Evangelical Theological Society* 18 (1975) 3-16; F. J. Moloney, *The Johannine Son of Man* (Biblioteca di scienze religiose, 14; Rome: Libreria ateneo salesiano, 1976); J. Coppens, "Le Fils de l'Homme dans l'évangile johannique," *ETL* 52 (1976) 28-81 (with extensive bibliography in note 3).

[2]It may be debated whether the author intends this phrase of Psalm 8 to refer to Jesus, since the OT quotation is really introduced for another reason.

[3]References with an asterisk (*) indicate passages in which the title expresses service or lowliness; the others, dignity.

[4]References with a dagger (†) may be instances in which Jesus refers to someone other than himself as the coming "Son of Man."

[5]See R. Schnackenburg, "Der Menschensohn im Johannesevangelium," *NTS* 11 (1964-65) 123-37; S. Schulz, *Untersuchungen zur Menschensohn-Christologie im Johannesevangelium* (Göttingen: Vandenhoeck & Ruprecht, 1957); R. E. Brown, *The Gospel According to John (i-xii)* (AB 29; Garden City: Doubleday, 1966) 84; B. Lindars, "The Son of Man in the Johannine Christology," *Christ and Spirit in the New Testament: In Honour of Charles Francis Digby Moule* (ed. B. Lindars and S. S. Smalley; Cambridge: Cambridge University, 1973) 43-60. See also the Moloney entry mentioned in n. 1 above.

[6]G. Dupont, *Le fils d'homme: Essai historique et critique* (Paris: Presses universitaires, 1924) 25: "cet étrange vocable."

[7]"The Son of Man or the Son of Adam," *Bib* 49 (1968) 457-502, esp. p. 486.

[8]"Neglected Features in the Problem of 'the Son of Man,'" *Neues Testament und Kirche: Für Rudolf Schnackenburg* (Freiburg im B.: Herder, 1974) 413-28.

[9]NT grammarians have often so regarded the anarthrous form; see M. Zerwick, *Biblical Greek* (Rome: Biblical Institute, 1963) §183; BDF §259; C. F. D. Moule, *An Idiom Book of New Testament Greek* (2d ed.; Cambridge: Cambridge University, 1959) 177; A. T. Robertson, *A Grammar of the Greek New Testament in the Light of Historical Research* (4th ed.; New York: Hodder and Stoughton, 1914) 651.

[10]See Maximus of Tyre 4.2c; W. Dittenberger, *Sylloge inscriptionum graecarum* (3d ed.; 4 vols.; Leipzig: S. Hirzel, 1915-24), 3. §1169:12. Cf. N. Turner, *Syntax* in J. H. Moulton, *A Grammar of New Testament Greek*, III (Edinburgh: Clark, 1963) 208.

[11]The Semitic counterpart is now well attested in Qumran literature; both in the Hebrew form בני אור (1QS 1:9; 2:16; 3:13, 24, 25; 1QM 1:1, 3, 9, 11, 13) and in an Aramaic form בני נהורא (see J. T. Milik, "4Q Visions de ᶜAmram" [p. 108 above, n. 12], 90). Since this expression occurs neither in the OT nor in rabbinic literature, its use in Qumran literature, along with its counterpart, "sons of darkness," as a designation for two great classes of humanity, is significant for the understanding of the NT phrase. See further *ESBNT*, 208-10; J. Jeremias, *New Testament Theology* (p. 112 above, n. 55), 260.

[12]"בן אדם und בר אנש im Hebräischen und Aramäischen," *AcOr* 21 (1950-53) 57-65, 91-107. Earlier treatments can be found in G. Dalman, *The Words of Jesus* (p. 23 above, n. 53), 234-67; P. Fiebig, *Der Menschensohn: Jesu Selbstbezeichnung mit besonderer Berücksichtigung des aramäischen Sprachgebrauches für "Mensch"* (Tübingen / Leipzig: Mohr, 1901). Cf. C. Colpe, "ὁ υἱὸς τοῦ ἀνθρώπου," *TDNT* 8 (1972) 401-5.

[13]See below pp. 147, 151.

[14]E.g., Ezek 2:1, 3; 3:1, 3, 4, 10. Cf. W. Zimmerli, *Ezechiel* (BKAT 13/1; Neukirchen: Neukirchener Verlag, 1969) 70-71; F. Maass, "אדם," *TWAT* 1 (1970) 81-94, esp. col. 87.

[15]E. Sjöberg, "בן אדם und בר אנש," 57-59.

[16]"The Use of בר נש / בר נשא in Jewish Aramaic," in M. Black, *An Aramaic Approach* (p. 23 above, n. 43), 310-30, esp. p. 327.

[17]A. Dupont-Sommer, *The Essene Writings from Qumran* (tr. G. Vermes; Oxford: Blackwell, 1961) 103. Cf. M. Burrows (ed.), *The Dead Sea Scrolls of St. Mark's Monastery, Volume II, Fascicle 2: Plates and Transcription of the Manual of Discipline* (New Haven: American Schools of Oriental Research, 1951), pl. XI; F. M. Cross et al., *Scrolls from Qumran Cave I: The Great Isaiah Scroll, The Order of the Community, The* Pesher *to Habakkuk, from Photographs by John C. Trever* (Jerusalem: Albright Institute of Archaeological Research and the Shrine of the Book, 1972) 146-47.

[18]Cf. 1QH 10:28 (partly restored).

[19]"The Use of בר נש / בר נשא," 327.

[20]H. L. Strack, *Introduction to the Talmud and Midrash* (Temple Books; New York: Atheneum, 1969) 65 ("at the beginning of the fifth century"). Cf. L. I. Rabinowitz, "Talmud, Jerusalem," *Encyclopaedia judaica* (Jerusalem: Keter; New York: Macmillan, 1971), 15. 773: ". . . many *amoraim* who were active until the middle of the fourth century are quoted in it." Col. 775: "The Jerusalem Talmud was completed about a century before the compilation of the Babylonian Talmud in c. 500."

21H. L. Strack, *Introduction to the Talmud and Midrash,* 125.

22Ibid.

23It is so interpreted by E. Sjöberg, "בן אדם und בר אנש," 59. Cf. C. Colpe, "ὁ υἱὸς τοῦ ἀνθρώπου," *TDNT* 8 (1972) 404 n. 24.

24"בן אדם und בר אנש," 60.

25"La divinité de Jésus," *Lumière et vie* 9 (1953) 64; reprinted in *Exégèse et théologie* (Paris: Cerf, 1961), 1. 134; cf. "The Divinity of Christ in the Synoptic Gospels," *Son and Saviour: The Divinity of Jesus Christ in the Scriptures* (ed. A. Gelin; Baltimore: Helicon, 1965) 81; reprinted in *Jesus and the Gospel: Volume 1* (tr. B. Weatherhead; New York: Herder and Herder, 1973) 63.

26So at least G. Dalman (*The Words of Jesus* [p. 23 above, n. 53], 239) quotes him. Lietzmann actually wrote: "Jesus hat sich selbst nie den Titel 'Menschensohn' beigelegt, weil derselbe im Aramäischen nicht existierte und aus sprachlichen Gründen nicht existieren kann" (*Der Menschensohn: Ein Beitrag zur neutestamentlichen Theologie* [Freiburg im B./Leipzig: Mohr, 1896], 85). Was Lietzmann referring merely to the titular sense of the phrase?

27*The Words of Jesus,* 239.

28In the context this verb must refer to death by treachery or assassination. L. A. Bange (*A Study of the Use of Vowel-Letters in Alphabetic Consonantal Writing* [see p. 64 above], 91) prefers to understand *ymwt* as a pual form (*yĕmuwwat*, "is slain" [?]). Cf. R. Degen, *Altaramäische Grammatik* [p. 75 above, n. 16], 28, 75.

29See A. Dupont-Sommer and J. Starcky, "Une inscription araméenne de Sfiré," *BMB* 13 (1956 [appeared 1958]) 23-41, esp. pp. 27, 34; cf. my commentary, *The Aramaic Inscriptions of Sefire* (p. 77 above, n. 30), 98, 115. See further G. Garbini, "Nuovo materiale per la grammatica dell'aramaico antico," *RSO* 34 (1959) 41-54, esp. p. 47; F. Vattioni, "La prima menzione aramaica di 'figlio dell'uomo,'" *Biblos-Press* 6/1 (1965) 6-7.

30See A. Cowley, *Aramaic Papyri of the Fifth Century B.C. Edited, with Translation and Notes* (Oxford: Clarendon, 1923; reprinted, Osnabrück: Zeller, 1967) 204-48 (= *A*), 179-82 (= *AP* 71). Cf. C.-F. Jean and J. Hoftijzer, *Dictionnaire des inscriptions sémitiques de l'ouest* (Leiden: Brill, 1965) 19; E. Vogt, *Lexicon linguae aramaicae Veteris Testamenti* [p. 23 above, n. 41], 13; I. N. Vinnikov, "Dictionary of the Aramaic Inscriptions," *Palestinkii sbornik* 3 (66, 1958) 205-6, 218.

31G. Dalman (*The Words of Jesus,* 237-38) thought that the Danielic phrase was uncongenial to poetry, regarded it as a parallel to עתיק יומיא, and gave it a more solemn, poetic meaning than was necessary. In this he was corrected by P. Fiebig (*Der Menschensohn* [n. 12 above], 53-60), who stressed that the phrase scarcely differed from כאנש in Dan 7:4. For a recent and interesting discussion of the contextual meaning of the phrase, see J. J. Collins, "The Son of Man and the Saints of the Most High in the Book of Daniel," *JBL* 93 (1974) 50-66, esp. pp. 61-62.

32Perhaps one should further distinguish the generic sense of this phrase into a collective and an inclusive sense, as is sometimes done elsewhere: the former would be the use of the singular to designate the collectivity, mankind; the latter would be the use of the singular to designate an individual belonging to the collectivity, a human being. In this way 11QtgJob would be an instance of the inclusive sense. It is, however, not always easy to detect this difference, and so I prefer to refer to both of them as the generic sense of the phrase. It is thus a stylistic variant for "man." As such it is clearly to be distinguished from the indefinite usage ("anyone, someone"), the quasi-vocative usage (though this could also be "inclusive" in the sense just defined, but it is used as a form of address), the use for a definite individual, the titular usage (of the NT), and the surrogate usage (on which see below, p. 154).

33See N. Avigad and Y. Yadin, *A Genesis Apocryphon* (p. 54 above, n. 72) 45 (+ pl. XXI); on p. לח it is translated into Modern Hebrew as כל איש. See my commentary, *The Genesis Apocryphon of Qumran Cave I* (p. 22 above, n. 27) 68-69, 151. Italics in the translation used above indicate the words that are literally translated into Aramaic from the Hebrew.

34It is interesting to compare the translation of Gen 13:16 in the various later targums: Onqelos has

כמא דלית אפשר לגבר דימני ית עפרא דארעא

Pseudo-Jonathan reads

דהיכמא דאית איפשר לגבר למימני ית עפרא דארעא

and Neofiti I has

ארום היך מה דלית אפשר די כל גבר למימני ית עפרא דארעא

The verse is not preserved in the Fragmentary Targum or the targumic texts of the Cairo Genizah.

35See *Le targum de Job de la grotte XI de Qumrân* (p. 22 above, n. 32), 62.

36The later Targum II translates the Hebrew text thus:

לגבר דרשיעא דיכמך חיובך ולבר נש דכיא צדקתך

"a man of wickedness like yourself your guilt (affects), and an innocent human being, your righteousness." Noteworthy is the orthography of the phrase in this case; see below p. 171.

37The Aramaic word גבר is used to translate איש in 11QtgJob 38:7-8 (= Hebr. 42:11), but there it is used in a distributive sense of "each." Elsewhere in the extant passages איש is translated by Aramaic אנש (see 11QtgJob 31:4; 24:5; 21:[5]), save for 11QtgJob 36:2, where it is rendered by אנתה, "woman." The editors were possibly influenced in their restoration by Targum II (see note 36). When גבר occurs elsewhere in the extant parts of the Qumran targum, it usually translates Hebrew גבר (see 24:3; 23:7; 25:10; 30:1; 34:3), save for 15:3, where it renders אשר.

38Targum II renders Job 25:6 thus:

אף כל דכן בר נש דהחיוי ריחשא ובר נש דבמותוי מורני

39On the dating of the *Genesis Apocryphon,* see my commentary, *The Genesis Apocryphon of Qumran Cave I* (2d ed.) 14-19; on the dating of the Targum of Job, see J. P. M. van der Ploeg and A. S. van der Woude, *Le targum de Job,* 3-4. The editors tend to place the targum between the Book of Daniel and the Genesis Apocryphon. See further S. A. Kaufman, "The Job Targum from Qumran," *JAOS* 93 (1973) 317-27, esp. pp. 325-27; cf. P. Grelot, review of the *editio princeps, RQ* 8 (1972-76) 104-14, esp. pp. 113-14.

40See my review of M. Black, *Aramaic Approach* (3d ed.), *CBQ* 30 (1968) 426-27.

41By G. Vermes, *Jesus the Jew* (p. 23 above, n. 44), 188-91 ("Excursus II: Debate on the Circumlocutional Use of the Son of Man").

42See 1QapGen 20:16, 17, 18, 19; 21:19, 21; 22:15; 1Q*21* 8:2; 5/6Ḥev 14:2 (*Lĕšonénu* 25 [1961] 127); 11QtgJob 2:8; 9:9; 11:3; 12:[9]; 19:[7]; 21:5; 22:6; 24:4, 5; 25:6; 26:3; 28:[1], 2bis; 31:4. Cf. I. N. Vinnikov, *Palestinskii sbornik* 3 (66, 1958) 205-6; 11 (74, 1964) 213; C-F. Jean and J. Hoftijzer, *Dictionnaire*, 19, 186-87; J. Cantineau, *Le Nabatéen* (Paris: E. Leroux), 2 (1932) 65; E. Vogt. *Lexicon*, 12-13.

43E. Sjöberg, ("בן אדם und בר אנש," p. 102) hints at the same explanation.

44G. Vermes, *Jesus the Jew*, 189.

45Ibid., 190-91.

46G. S. Glanzman has called to my attention the names אחירם (Num 26:38) and חירם (2 Sam 5:11, etc.); the latter is known in a Phoenician inscription as אחרם (*KAI* §1:1), and it turns up in Akkadian as *Ḫi-ru-um-mu*, but in Ugaritic as *aḫrm*. And the short form is almost certainly a hypocoristicon. See F. L. Benz, *Personal Names in the Phoenician and Punic Inscriptions* (Studia Pohl, 8; Rome: Biblical Institute, 1972) 263-64. See C. Taylor's note on the names Laᶜzar and Liᶜezer in *Pirqe Aboth* 2:10 (*Sayings of the Jewish Fathers Comprising Pirqe Aboth in Hebrew and English with Notes and Excursuses* [New York, Ktav, 1969] 33 n. 23; also "Notes on the Text," 143). Cf. R. Travers Herford, *Pirke Aboth: The Ethics of the Talmud: Sayings of the Fathers* (New York: Schocken, 1962) 51.

47See E. S. Rosenthal, "The Givᶜat ha-Mivtar Inscription," *IEJ* 23 (1973) 72-91, esp. p. 81 for the date. See *MPAT* §68.

48The inscription was also studied by J. Naveh, "An Aramaic Tomb Inscription Written in Paleo-Hebrew Script," *IEJ* 23 (1973) 82-91; see esp. p. 90.

49If one would prefer not to restore the final *reš*, אלעז would possibly reflect another nickname-form (similar to those of Beth Sheᶜarim below).

50See the date for this writing quoted above in n. 20.

51See Moshe Schwabe and Baruch Lifshitz, *Beth Sheᶜarim, Volume Two: The Greek Inscriptions* (Jerusalem: Israel Exploration Society, 1967), §177 (Λαζαρ, p. 73); §93 (Λαζε, p. 34).

However, on p. vii we read: "[Beth Sheᶜarim] était la résidence du patriarche vénéré Rabbi Juda, qui fut inhumé dans cette ville (premier quart du IIIe siècle de l'ère chrétienne). C'est précisément après la mort de Rabbi Juda que Beth Sheᶜarim s'est transformée en une nécropole centrale, parce que les Juifs pieux désiraient être enterrés près de la tombe du patriarche. Nous connaissons la période de la nécropole—la ville a été détruite en 352 par l'armée de Gallus qui a supprimé la révolte juive." Moreover, 1200 coins minted in the first half of the fourth century under Constantine (307-37) and Constantius II (337-62) were found there—and none from the second half of it. Cf. B. Mazar, *Beth Sheᶜarim, Volume One: The Catacombs I-IV* (Jerusalem: Israel Exploration Society, 1957) 21-26.

[52]The emphatic form is also used as the parallel in Isa 56:2.

[53]*The Words of Jesus* (p. 23, n. 53), 237; G. Vermes, "The Use of בר נשא/בר נש," 328.

[54]See H. L. Strack, *Introduction to the Talmud and Midrash*, 65 (for the Palestinian or Jerusalem Talmud). On p. 217 Strack uses the usual date for *Genesis Rabbah*, the first generation of the Amoraim; but this has been contested because it mentions the last group of Palestinian Amoraim of about 150 years later. See M. D. Herr, "Genesis Rabbah," *Encyclopaedia judaica*, 7. 399-400; he dates the final redaction of the work to about "425 C.E."

[55]See P. Haupt, "The Son of Man = hic homo = ego," *JBL* 40 (1921) 183; "Hidalgo and Filius Hominis," ibid., 167-70; C. Colpe, "*ὁ υἱὸς τοῦ ἀνθρώπου*," *TDNT* 8. 403.

[56]*New Testament Theology* (p. 112 above, n. 55), 261; see also C. Colpe, *TDNT* 8. 403.

[57]See A. Díez Macho, *Neophyti 1: Targum palestinense . . . Génesis* (p. 84 above, n. 112), 25; P. Kahle, *Masoreten des Westens* (BWANT 3/14; Stuttgart: Kohlhammer) 2 (1930) 7. Note the form ברנש, even written here as one word; also the pael infinitive with initial *mem*, which is unknown in first-century Palestinian Aramaic, but characteristic of that of the Late Phase (where it has been levelled through from the peal to all conjugations); compare מטמיא (1QapGen 20:15); אסיותה (1QapGen 20:19)—and the haphel infinitives in 11QtgJob, להש[היה] (9:5); להנחתה (31:3); להסבעה (31:4); להנפקה (31:5).

[58]E.g., the instance from *Genesis Rabbah* 7:2 (cited by Vermes on p. 321) could just as easily be translated, "Should a man be scourged who proclaims the word of Scripture?" And even though "you" parallels בר נש in *Numbers Rabbah* 19:3 ("Should a man be scourged who proclaims the word of Scripture?" R. Haggai said, "Yes, because you did not give the right ruling" [cited on p. 321]), the distinction between the question generically put and the answer specifically given may have to be respected. Similarly *j. Ber.* 5c (". . . that a man cannot eat a pound of meat until he has been given a lash!"); *j. Ber.* 5b (cited on p. 323: "A man's disciple is as dear to him as his son"), where the emphatic state in this Late Aramaic is simply indefinite. As for *Genesis Rabbah* 38:13, see the obvious interpretation of it provided by E. Sjöberg, "בן אדם und בר אנש," 94-95.

[59]"The Use of בר נשא/בר נש," 327.

[60]This means that I am fundamentally in agreement with the thesis of R. Leivestad, "Exit the Apocalyptic Son of Man," *NTS* 18 (1971-72) 243-67, although I should want to nuance some of the details in his treatment a little differently. On the other hand, I am not sure that the apocalyptic Son of Man has re-entered; see B. Lindars, "Re-enter the Apocalyptic Son of Man," *NTS* 22 (1975-76) 52-72. The interpretation that Lindars gives is most congenial to me in many respects. But he is too cavalier with philological material and swallows hook-line-and-sinker what G. Vermes says without any personal scrutiny. In this Son-of-Man discussion—perhaps above all others—one simply has to begin with the philological material before one erects theological theories that may prove to be only sand castles.

[61]The quasi-vocative use is apparently reflected in *1 Enoch* 60:10 (addressed to Noah).

[62]See "Problèmes de la littérature hénochique" (p. 112, n. 57), 333-78; "Turfan et Qumran" (see ibid.), 117-27; *The Books of Enoch: Aramaic Fragments of Qumrân Cave 4* (Oxford: Clarendon, 1976) 89-107, 298-317. It, of course, remains to be seen whether Milik's explanation of the presence of the Book of Similitudes in Ethiopic Enoch will be finally accepted. He may be right that the Enoch literature in pre-Christian times was mainly a pentateuch and was so used by the Qumran community. He may also be right in maintaining that the Book of Similitudes was substituted for the Book of Giants in certain circles in the Christian era. But it still remains a

question whether the Book of Similitudes stems from a Christian author. For, though the titles, "anointed One," "righteous One," "elect One," and "Son of Man" are conflated and applied to one individual in the Similitudes, as they are applied to Jesus in the NT, the Similitudes otherwise lack specific "Christian differentia" (to use a phrase of R. H. Fuller [*The Foundations of New Testament Christology* (New York: Scribner, 1965) 38] in a sense a little more widely than he did). Indeed, it still has to be shown that this part of Ethiopic Enoch could not have stemmed from a Jewish author. See further E. Sjöberg, *Der Menschensohn im äthiopischen Henochbuch* (Lund: Gleerup, 1946); J. C. Greenfield, "Prolegomenon," in H. Odeberg, *3 Enoch or The Hebrew Book of Enoch* (New York: Ktav, 1973) xvii-xviii. If, indeed, it could be shown that the Book of Similitudes was an original pre-Christian Jewish writing (that was subsequently substituted for the Books of Giants in the form of the book known from the Ethiopic), then one would have to reckon with an apocalyptic Son of Man in the pre-Christian Jewish tradition, against my skepticism (see n. 60 above). But the evidence for arriving at that origin of the Book of Similitudes is not yet apparent.

[63]See G. Vermes, "The Use of בר נש / בר נשא," 320, 323. He not only calls it a circumlocution for "I" (p. 320), but even says that it "means I" (p. 323). Similarly R. Bultmann, *Theology of the New Testament* (p. 108 above, n. 18), 1. 30: ". . . meant 'man' or 'I.'"

[64]Cf. J. Jeremias, "Die älteste Schicht der Menschensohn-Logien," *ZNW* 58 (1967) 159-72.

[65]See my commentary on the *Genesis Apocryphon of Qumran Cave I* (2d ed., 1971) 221, 217. Despite the attempt of T. Muraoka ("Notes on the Aramaic of the Genesis Apocryphon," *RQ* 8 [1972-76] 7-51, esp. pp. 12-14) to explain all the instances of the emphatic state that I once questioned as definite, I still remain skeptical. I am not at all sure that the waning of the emphatic state is something that can be identified solely with the eastern branch of Aramaic dialects.

Chapter 7

The First-Century Targum of Job from Qumran Cave XI*

Ever since the discovery of Qumran Cave XI in 1956 and the announcement that a targum of Job figured among the texts discovered in that cave,[1] the scholarly world for many reasons patiently awaited the definitive publication of that important Aramaic text.[2] Preliminary reports from the editors, J. P. M. van der Ploeg and A. S. van der Woude, had whetted scholarly appetites in many ways.[3] Since the publication of the *editio princeps* in 1971, reviews and brief articles have commented on the text and pointed out features of it beyond those noted by the editors themselves.[4] It is obvious that the targum of Job from Qumran Cave XI is not only an important text but one that will demand years of study before its secrets are fully divulged. Anyone acquainted with the difficulties of the Hebrew text of Job and of its relationship to extant ancient versions will readily realize what it means to gain access suddenly to another previously unknown ancient version that a priori has the possibility of putting all earlier theories regarding those relationships into a new light. The study of the Qumran targum has only begun, and I should like to record here some preliminary observations about it.

These observations were originally made as a contribution to a volume honoring an American Catholic biblical scholar, Msgr. Patrick W. Skehan, Professor at the Catholic University of America, who has long been noted for his own studies of the problems of the Book of Job. His knowledge of the intricacies of the Hebrew text contributed much to the English translation of that book in the *New American Bible*, and I am sure that it would also have improved many paragraphs among the observations that follow, had he had the opportunity to see them in advance. In any case, they are offered as a token of gratitude, friendship, and esteem.

My observations will be grouped about three points: (1) Job in the Qumran community; (2) the Qumran targum of Job; and (3) the Qumran targum and the Second Targum of Job.

I. *Job in the Qumran Community*

When the word of the Lord came to the prophet Ezekiel about the land that was acting faithlessly toward him, three paragons of righteousness were singled out. But it was made clear to the prophet that not even their righteousness would save such a land: "Even if these three men, Noah, Daniel, and Job, were in it, they would deliver but their own lives by their righteousness" (Ezek 14:14). Though the "Daniel" or "Danʾel" who is mentioned among them was undoubtedly a more ancient figure than the better-known biblical character and was probably even of Canaanite background, the ancient Danʾel and the biblical Daniel were eventually conflated in Jewish tradition of a later date.[5] Similarly, the figure of Job in the Ezekiel passage may refer to a more ancient character who also appears in the substratum of parts of the canonical Book of Job and with whom the poetic dialogues of that book were eventually associated.[6] In any case, the three paragons of righteousness mentioned in Ezekiel eventually took on the shapes of the biblical characters whom we know as Noah, Job, and Daniel.

Now it is not surprising that the three of them turn up as figures who fed the piety of the Qumran community, given its well-known emphasis on the pursuit of righteousness.[7] In one way or another all three of these paragons appear in Qumran literature.

Noah appears in the paraphrase of the biblical story in the *Genesis Apocryphon* of Qumran Cave I;[8] and he figured in this "Book of the Patriarchs," as it undoubtedly should be more properly called,[9] more largely than we can imagine, since much of the story pertaining to him in that scroll has unfortunately been lost. Other as yet unpublished fragments from Qumran Cave IV seem to belong to an Infancy Narrative of Noah.[10] In the *Genesis Apocryphon* itself, one fragmentary sentence, paraphrasing Gen 6:9, makes Noah say, "During all my days I practiced truth" (קושטא, 1QapGen 6:2), a Qumran virtue related to "righteousness."

The esteem for Daniel in Qumran literature is also well attested. He is hailed as a "prophet" in 4Q*174* 1-3 ii 3,[11] and the end of the canonical book ascribed to him has served as the springboard for the introductory columns of the Qumran War Scroll.[12] A cycle of writings, which is only published so far in part, but which is clearly related to that biblical book, exists among the fragments of Qumran Cave IV. J. T. Milik has referred to them as "Pseudo-Danielic," and they seem to include the well-known Prayer of Nabonidus,[13] as well as the Aramaic text that mentions the Son of God and the Son of the Most High in phrases reminiscent of Luke 1:32, 35.[14] Just what the relation of all these fragments actually is to the canonical Book of Daniel will only be made clear when they are all finally published.

Job, the third paragon of righteousness, is now known to us in the targum from Qumran Cave XI, and through it we get a glimpse of the way in which the Qumran community used the biblical book that was ascribed to him. The significance of the targum, however, lies not so much in its recasting of steadfast Job as in the interpretation of the biblical book attributed to him in Palestinian Jewish tradition, as well as in the light that it sheds on targumic origins, and the new evidence that it brings to our understanding of Palestinian Aramaic at the beginning of the Christian era. And yet, we may be sure that one of the reasons why the targum of Job was preserved in Qumran caves was precisely the esteem that the community had for this ancient paragon of righteousness.

Before we turn to the targum itself and the picture of Job that is in it, it might be well to recall that his righteousness was also known outside of Qumran confines. He was singled out from the mass of OT worthies by Ben Sira, as is now clear from the Hebrew text of that book. He has, moreover, recently entered into the English Bible tradition in the *New American Bible*'s version of that book and its "Praise of Famous Men," which makes an explicit reference to Ezekiel's mention of Job: "Ezekiel beheld the vision and described the different creatures of the chariot; he also referred to Job who always persevered in the right path" וגם הזכיר את איוב המכלכל כל דר[כי צ]דק, Sir 49:9.[15] Again, the tradition of Job's righteousness is remembered.

And a Christian writer a few centuries later would sum up Job's career in a way in which he has usually been remembered: *τὴν ὑπομονὴν Ἰὼβ ἠκούσατε, καὶ τὸ τέλος κυρίου εἴδετε, ὅτι πολύσπλαγχνός ἐστιν ὁ κύριος καὶ οἰκτίρμων*, "You have heard of the steadfastness of Job and have seen what the Lord, who is compassionate and merciful, did in the end" (Jas 5:11 *NAB*).[16]

It is against this developing Jewish and Christian picture of the righteous and steadfast Job that we must view the Qumran targum that has come to light. In general, it presents a picture of Job that agrees with that of the Hebrew text. E. W. Tuinstra, who has made a study of the hermeneutical tendencies of the Aramaic version, has pointed out certain shifts of emphasis that appear in the targum. According to him, Job "is not only a righteous sufferer, but also a man upon whom 'knowledge' is bestowed," and he "seems to be a special assignee of God."[17] Tuinstra also thinks that there is in the targum the tendency to depict Job as the Teacher of Righteousness in the Qumran community,[18] a notion to which I shall return later, and that the "tendency to tone down and suppress the defiance-motif, which is a characteristic of the LXX portrayal of Job, is less clear in the targum."[19] If these few distinct traits prove right, then there is a slightly different picture of Job in the targum. But I should hesitate to say with Tuinstra that "the figure of Job in 11QtgJob differs significantly from that of the masoretic text."[20] In any case, the emphasis on Job's wisdom in the targum is interesting, since it fills out in its own way the Wisdom teaching found in other Qumran texts.

II. *The Qumran Targum of Job*

The Aramaic version of Job that has come to light in this targum is unfortunately fragmentary. It contains less than a sixth of the canonical book;

the editors estimate that only about 15 per cent of the text is preserved. Though the fragments range from Job 17:14 to 42:11, it is only from 37:10 on that the text is substantially intact. In the latter section one finds an Aramaic translation of Yahweh's speech following the discourses of Elihu—the section that is often called the "theophany" or "the Voice from the Whirlwind"[21] (38:1–41:34)—then Job's answer (42:1–6), and finally part of the epilogue (42:9-11). The most important part of the book is thus extant in this targum. What is contained in the fragmentary columns that precede this better-preserved portion of the targum is the last part of the second cycle of debates in the dialogue (15:1-21:24, beginning with 17:14), parts of the allegedly disordered third cycle of debates (22:1-31:40), and significantly enough, in the same order as the MT, with even portions of the Hymn to the Inaccessibility of Wisdom (28:1-28). And then considerable parts of the poetic discourses of Elihu (32:1-37:24). Thus this targum of Job gives us an ancient form of the Book of Job that agrees in large part with the structure and build-up of the Hebrew text, as we know it in the MT. There are, of course, verses and parts of verses that are missing in the Aramaic, and this not because of the fragmentary character of the targum, but because of a different recensional activity. Yet such differences do not modify the judgment about the build-up of the book as a whole in this version.

The text ends with Job 42:11 in the middle of a line with a *vacat* following. This indicates the end of a paragraph, as in 11QtgJob 10:6. Conceivably, there could have been a few further lines at the bottom of col. 38, which is now lost. But the space is insufficient for vss. 12-17 of the Hebrew; and the skin on which a following column could have been written is preserved, and it is blank. So the chances are that the targum lacked 42:12-17, verses which are in the present-day Hebrew text of Job, as well as the expanded epilogue of the book found in the LXX.[22]

By and large the targum is a rather literal translation of the Hebrew; at times one finds added phrases or paraphrastic renderings.[23] When the Aramaic does depart from the Hebrew, it is often enough at those spots where the Hebrew text itself has been suspect or scarcely intelligible and where other ancient versions had different renderings.

On the basis of the paleography of the fragments, the editors have suggested a date in the late Herodian period for this copy of the targum.[24] In this they are dependent on the work of W. F. Albright, F. M. Cross, and others, and their suggested date seems to be beyond cavil. That would mean an early first-century A.D. date for the Qumran Cave XI copy.

As for the composition of the targum, the editors have proposed a date somewhere between the final redaction of Daniel and the composition of the *Genesis Apocryphon*, and they list a whole series of details to support their dating.[25] At the moment, I am inclined to go along with their proposal, even though some others have expressed some misgivings about it and the full assessment of the problem will take considerable time yet. This will not be possible until all the linguistic features of the text are completely sorted out and compared with other Qumran Aramaic texts, many of which are still to be published.[26] There is, however, nothing in this material that would militate against a pre-Christian dating of the composition of this targum.

Since the copy from Qumran Cave XI is to be dated early in the first Christian century, and since it is almost certainly not the autograph, and since the language in which it is written could reflect Palestinian usage of at least a century earlier, we are confronted with a targum that for the first time can be truly said to date from a pre-Christian period. Significantly, it is not a version of the Pentateuch, but of one of the books of the *Kĕtûbîm*. Moreover, this targum may even antedate the time when the Book of Job came to be regarded as canonical, though its status as such does not seem to have been much contested.[27]

11QtgJob is not the only targum of Job that is extant from Qumran. Another small fragmentary copy of a targum of this book is reported from Qumran Cave IV, and contains only a few words from Job 3:4-5 and 4:16-5:4.[28] Indeed, it may well be part of the same Aramaic version as that in 11QtgJob. In any case, this situation suggests that the targum of Job existed among the Essenes of Qumran in multiple copies.

Targumic texts at Qumran are represented also by two fragments containing Lev 16:12-15, 18-21, a part of the ritual for the Day of Atonement.[29] This fragmentary text, however, raises a tantalizing problem. Is it part of a full targum of the Pentateuch or a fragment of some other Aramaic work that just happened to quote or use Leviticus 16 for some purpose? The question is not idle, given the interest of the Qumran Essenes in the ritual of the Day of Atonement that is found in other Qumran texts.[30] Milik, who has published these fragments, is convinced that they belong to a full targum; if he is correct, then the existence of a *written pre-Christian targum of the Pentateuch* is also attested. However, if the fragments should only be part of some larger Aramaic text that is really different, then it at least supplies a version of an important pentateuchal passage, either derived from an existing written targum or reduced to writing from some oral version.

All of this material now reveals that written Aramaic translations of OT texts were in use in Palestine of the first century A.D. and undoubtedly also in the first century B.C. as well. This has to be emphasized as the importance of the Qumran discoveries because of the exaggerated claims for the pre-Christian origins of other known targums. Such claims have been legion in recent years and have been more supported by extrapolated conclusions than direct evidence.[31] Milik may well be right in ascribing the paucity of Aramaic translations of biblical books within the Qumran community itself to the "highly educated" character of that community.[32] After all, most of their *sectarian* literature was composed, not in Aramaic, but in Hebrew, and this would seem to indicate that they did not have need of Aramaic translations of biblical books. Indeed, in some instances we even have the Hebrew commentaries *(pěšārîm)* that they had composed on the texts of the prophets and psalms. But was the Hebrew text of Job so difficult even for this community of Jews that it had to have recourse to it in an Aramaic version? Such a question is not easily answered.

It is further complicated by the issue raised by S. Segert, who thinks that the Aramaic texts found at Qumran were really non-Essene compositions, produced elsewhere and brought into the community, in which they were merely read or used by members who otherwise spoke and wrote in Hebrew.[33] If he were correct in this view, then the Qumran Aramaic texts would be witnesses to a form of Aramaic used by Jews in an even wider scope or area than this esoteric community. In my study of the *Genesis Apocryphon*, I came to the conclusion that there was nothing in it that directly or positively betrayed an Essene origin.[34] And I feel the same way about the targum of Job at this point. E. W. Tuinstra, however, is convinced that the Qumran Targum of Job is indeed an Essene composition, as I mentioned earlier.[35] The main reasons which he gives for this view are the remodelling of the figure of Job in the targum after the pattern of the Teacher of Righteousness, and the omission of the mention of Job's "sisters" at the meal that Job finally takes with "his friends, brothers, and acquaintances" (11QtgJob 38:5; contrast Hebr. 42:11)—a reflection of their celibate character. Now such reasons are tantalizing, but the evidence cited in support of them is so slight that it is not convincing. Why the targumist omitted the "sisters" in Job 42:11 is puzzling; it *might* reflect a celibate concern, but that is at best a remote possibility and one that raises the entire question about how celibate the Qumran Essenes really were. In this regard I prefer to remain with the judgment that J. van der Ploeg originally set forth about the targum: nothing, apart from its discovery in Qumran Cave XI, suggests that it had an origin in the Qumran community.[36] It was read there and bears witness to the use of Aramaic in the community, as well as to a literary creativity in Aramaic in Palestine of the first century B.C.

This consideration, however, evokes a further comment. Whereas the targum gives still further evidence of literary activity in Aramaic, that does not necessarily mean that the targum was composed in "the literary Aramaic of the intertestamental period," i.e., "an artificial, literary Aramaic, colored, to be sure, by the local spoken dialect" and "a conscious attempt to imitate a 'classical' language generally similar to Official Aramaic."[37] So to regard the language of the targum is to take refuge in what cannot be substantiated—that the Aramaic of the targum represents an "artificial, literary" type of the language that was clearly different from, albeit influenced by, the spoken form of the language.

Two further aspects of the language of the targum should be considered. First, though it seems to come from a stage between the Book of Daniel and the *Genesis Apocryphon*, and thus otherwise belongs to the phase of Middle Aramaic, it nevertheless contains some Persian words, four—possibly five—of them: פתגם, "word, thing" (9:2; 30:1; 34:3; 29:4; 22:7); דחשת, "desert" (32:5;

15:[7]); נזך, "spear, javelin" (33:5); חרתך, "thorn" (35:5);[38] and possibly דת, "law, religion" (30:8). The appearance of Persian words in Qumran Hebrew or Aramaic texts is not new.[39] The abundance of them in earlier Official (or Imperial) Aramaic is well known,[40] and this undoubtedly accounts for the persistence of them or even the emergence of hitherto unknown forms even in a Qumran targum. Secondly, by way of contrast, the targum is notably lacking in Greek words. To date only one word has been possibly so identified, סיף, "sword" (11QtgJob 33:5), said to be a borrowing of Greek *ξίφος*.[41] Though it appears here for the first time in Qumran Aramaic, it is attested otherwise in earlier Official Aramaic and in Palestinian Aramaic (Strasbourg Ostracon 6; 5/6Ḥev 1 ar: 4).[42] The absence of Greek words in this targum is to be noted in conjunction with the data that I have tried to collect on this question elsewhere.[43] And the absence of them in the Aramaic of the Qumran targum of Job is striking by contrast with the many Greek words that appear in the targums from the period of Late Aramaic, and in Syriac.

So much for the observations on the Qumran targum of Job in itself.

III. *The Qumran Targum and the Second Targum of Job*

It had been known for a long time that versions of the Book of Job in Aramaic were extant in antiquity. The fourth/fifth century MSS of the Greek OT (א,B,A,C) contain an expanded form of the book's epilogue. Whereas the last verse of the Hebrew text reads, "And Job died, an old man, full of days" (42:17), and this is literally rendered in the Old Greek version as *καὶ ἐτελεύτησεν Ἰὼβ πρεσβύτερος καὶ πλήρης ἡμερῶν*, it continues, *γέγραπται δὲ αὐτὸν πάλιν ἀναστήσεσθαι μεθ' ὧν ὁ κύριος ἀνίστησιν· οὗτος ἑρμηνεύεται ἐκ τῆς συριακῆς βίβλου*, "it is written that he will rise again with those whom the Lord raises up; it (or he?) is translated (*or* interpreted?) from the Syrian book" (LXX, 42:17a-b).[44] It further continues with biographical details about Job. The reference to *ἡ συριακὴ βίβλος* has often been understood as an Aramaic version of Job,[45] and it possibly seeks to express some dependence of the Greek version on an Aramaic targum. One might like to argue from this notice to the existence of an Aramaic version of Job that existed prior to the earliest attempt to render Job into Greek; but is that precisely what is meant? The expansion of the epilogue in Greek is problematic in that it is not certain from what period it really dates. Does it come from the same pre-Christian period as the bulk of the Greek translation of Job? Does it further imply that an Aramaic version of Job was known one or two centuries earlier than the Qumran translation that we now have from Cave XI (and Cave IV)?[46] The least one can say is that by the time the Greek epilogue acquired its expansion, an Aramaic version of Job was known, and that possibly the expansion did exist earlier in some Aramaic form. But, in any case, that expansion of the Greek epilogue is neither found in nor derived from 11QtgJob;[47] thus it would seem to refer to some other Aramaic version of Job.

Reference to another Aramaic version of Job is made in rabbinical literature. In the Babylonian Talmud, *Shabbat* 16:1 (fol. 115a), we read:

> Said R. Jose: It once happened that my father Halafta visited R. Gamaliel Berabbi at Tiberias and found him sitting at the table of Johanan b. Nizuf with the Targum of the book of Job in his hand which he was reading. Said he to him: "I remember that R. Gamaliel, your grandfather, was standing on a high eminence of the Temple Mount, when the Book of Job in a Targumic version was brought to him, whereupon he said to the builder, 'Bury it under the bricks.'" He [R. Gamaliel II] too gave orders, and they hid it. R. Jose, son of R. Judah, said: They overturned a tub of mortar upon it. . . .[48]

This rabbinic text thus knows of an Aramaic version of Job that existed toward the end of the first century A.D. (being read by Rabbi Gamaliel II) and of another that had been immured somewhere in the Temple area roughly a half-century earlier (at the order of R. Gamaliel I—who, according to Acts 22:3, was the teacher of Paul of Tarsus in Jerusalem). This text has usually been taken as testimony to the prohibition of written Aramaic versions of the biblical writings.[49] In any case, the question arises whether this rabbinic reference to the targum ordered immured by R. Gamaliel I could be to the targum of Job now known to us from Qumran Cave XI (or from Cave IV). The editors of 11QtgJob are inclined so to regard it.[50] Though there is no certainty about the identification, there is nothing that is against it. E. W. Tuinstra, who, as we have already mentioned, regards the targum as an Essene composition, even goes so far as to say that it was ordered to be immured "because of its heretical, i.e., Essene origin."[51] There is, however, not a shred of evidence for this speculative reason.

Still another Aramaic version of Job has been known for a long time, being found in various polyglot Bibles, and published as part of *Hagiographa chaldaice* by P. de Lagarde.[52] We shall hereafter refer to it as "Targum II." It is said to be of Palestinian origin and to come from the 5th century A.D.[53] The purpose for which it was made is unknown, but it is usually regarded as having had nothing to do with synagogal service, because the Book of Job does not usually figure in synagogal lectionary cycles. The editors of 11QtgJob have already noted that, save for a few common exegetical traditions, the Qumran targum is wholly unrelated to Targum II.[54]

A detailed comparison of 11QtgJob with Targum II is needed for various reasons, not the least to make clear the amount of independence of the latter from the former, but also to highlight the difference in exegetical and translation techniques between a datable early targum and one of clearly later provenience.[55] I have undertaken such a study, and I should like to present a summary of the results. Chart I, which accompanies this paper, reveals that of the 1437 Aramaic words preserved in this Qumran targum,[56] only 295 are identical in Targum II, 133 are the same word but with a later (usually fuller) writing, and 255 words in Targum II are formed of the same root but with either phonological or morphological differences. The total of words that might be said to be *similar* in Targum II is 683 or about 47%, whereas only 428 words or about 30% could be said to be the *same*.[57] While some of the differences might be accounted for by postulating a different Hebrew recension for the Targum II, the significant thing is that the targums are so different. Two things are particularly striking: (a) the choice of entirely different Aramaic synonyms in Targum II to render the Hebrew words; (b) the number of clearly isolable words or phrases that reflect early and late translations. In so many of the latter instances the Qumran Targum has the form or the word that one would expect in the first century B.C. or A.D., whereas the Targum II has forms and words that are easily paralleled in later Jewish Palestinian Aramaic of the classic targumim, midrashim, and the talmud.

As examples of the latter type of differences, the following are to be noted. First of all, in 11QtgJob 25:5 the targumist has preserved the anthropomorphism of the Hebrew text, translating ויסתר פנים ומי ישורנו, "if he hides his face, who then can behold him?" (34:29 *NAB*), by [ויסת]ר אנפוהי מן יתיבנה, "and (if) he hides his face, who will bring him back?" But Targum II translates, ויסלק שכינתא ומן יסכיניה, "and (if) he removes the presence (Shekinah), who will bring him into danger?"[58] This is the only place in Targum II where the surrogate שכינתא is found in a passage corresponding to those extant in 11QtgJob. But the situation is somewhat the same for another such surrogate, מימרא, "the Word."[59] It is never found in the sense of a buffer, a means to safeguard the transcendence of Yahweh, when some creative, sustaining, or revelatory activity of his is described. The difference in treatment between 11QtgJob and Targum II is clearly seen in this regard in the following passage:

MT	*11QtgJob*	*Targum II*
9 וילכו אליפז התימני ובלדד השוחי צפר הנעמתי ויעשו כאשר דבר אליהם יהוה וישא יהוה את פני איוב: 10 ויהוה שב את שבית איוב בהתפללו בעד רעהו ויסף יהוה את כל אשר לאיוב למשנה	] אלהא] ושמע א[ל]הא בקלה די איוב ושבק להון חטאיהון בדילה ותב אלהא לאיוב ברחמין ויהב לה חד תרין בכל די הוא לה	9 ואזלו אליפז דמן תימן ובלדד דמן שוח צופר דמן נעמה ועבדו היך דמליל להום מימרא דיהוה ונסיב מימרא דיהוה ית אפי איוב: 10 ומימרא דיהוה אתיב ית גלוות איוב בצלאותיה מטול דחברוי ואוסיף מימרא דיהוה ית כל די לאיוב בכופלא
(42:9-10)	(38:2-4)	(42:9-10)
Then Eliphaz, the Temanite, and Bildad the Shuhite, and Zophar the Naamathite, went and did as the Lord had commanded them.	[as] God [had commanded them].	Then Eliphaz who was from Tema, and Bildad who was from Shuh, and Zophar who was from Naamah went and did as the Word of Yahweh had spoken to them.
And the Lord accepted the intercession of Job.[60]	And God listened to the voice of Job, and he forgave them their sins because of him.	And the Word of Yahweh accepted the inter- cession of Job.[60]
Also, the Lord restored the prosperity of Job, after he had prayed for his friends; the Lord even gave to Job twice as much as he had before.	And God returned to Job in mercy and gave him twice as much as all that he had had.	10 And the Word of Yahweh restored the captivity[61] of Job because of his prayer on behalf of his companions; and the Word of Yahweh increased twofold all that belonged to Job.

Though there are other differences in the two targums that might be called to attention, the main item to be noticed here is the absence of מימרא in the Qumran targum and the fourfold use of it in Targum II within two verses. This, of course, raises the real question about the antiquity of such surrogates in the targumic tradition. Admittedly, the evidence from the Qumran targum is negative, but it does have a bearing on the whole question of whether such ideas as שכינתא or מימרא were current among Jews of first-century Palestine and whether they really may be invoked for the explanation of NT passages.[62]

Second, the Qumran targum time after time attests the typically early forms of nouns in contrast to those found in Targum II: for example, ידיכון, "your hands" (11QtgJob 4:4), in contrast to the form with the prosthetic *aleph*, אידא, in Targum II (21:5); or דרע, "arm" (11QtgJob 34:5), in contrast to אדרע (Targum II 40:9);[63] or סגיא, "abundance" (11QtgJob 26:1, 3) in contrast to a form of the same word with *ᶜayin*, סוגעי (Targum II 35:6, 9). Similarly, 11QtgJob consistently has אנש(א) (with initial *aleph*), whereas Targum II has simply נש or בר נש (contrast 11QtgJob 9:9; 22:6; 24:5; 25:6; 26:3; 28:2 with Targum II 25:6; 33:12; 34:11; 34:30; 35:8; 36:25). Again 11QtgJob consistently writes the word for "bad, evil" as באיש (with the medial *aleph*: 19:4; 27:4) in contrast to the form ביש (Targum II 31:29; 36:10).[64]

Third, the verb "to see" in the Qumran targum is consistently a form of חזא (11QtgJob 11:2; 14:2, [5]; 23:4, 7; 28:2bis; 34:7; 37:8). In all the corresponding passages of Targum II one finds instead the verb חמא (27:12; 29:8, 11; 33:26, 28; 36:25; 40:11; 42:5). The use of חזא not only agrees with the biblical Aramaic usage (e.g., Ezra 4:14; Dan 2:41) and that of earlier Aramaic in general,[65] but it is found elsewhere in Qumran Aramaic (e.g., 1QapGen 2:12; 19:14, 23; 20:9, 14, [22]; 21:8, 9bis, 10, 14, 15; 22:27, 29). By contrast, the verb חמא, "see," is never found in the Aramaic of Qumran or earlier. Yet it is often said to be Palestinian.[66] Is it really? Its earliest attestation seems to be in a Palmyrene text, that is still unpublished,[67] and it is used further in the Babylonian Talmud in addition to the so-called Palestinian targums.[68] The instances of חמא in Targum II thus fit in with the evidence of other late texts, where this verb is used abundantly, and stand in contrast to the earlier Palestinian usage.

Fourth, there is the consistent spelling of the third personal pronominal suffix on masculine plural nouns and prepositions, which in 11QtgJob is always written as -והי (with the medial *he*: 5:3; 8:4; 23:4; 25:5; 33:4; 35:3; 36:4), in contrast to the form in Targum II, which is consistently written as -וי (without the medial *he*: 21:21, 24; 24:13; 33:26; 39:23; 40:24; 41:10). There is no instance of -וי in the Aramaic of Qumran, *pace* A. Díez Macho,[69] in the case of the masculine plural nouns of which we are speaking.

Fifth, one can further cite the forms of such a word as איתי, "there is" (11QtgJob 9:5; 23:[1]; 31:5; 34:5, 10), or in the negative form לא איתי (11QtgJob 6:4; 21:3), which agree with the consistent older form of the particle,[70] and stand in contrast to the later form in Targum II, אית, and especially to the contracted negative לית (= *lêt*, 25:3; 33:32; 38:28; negative, 22:5; 32:12). These forms are abundantly attested in Aramaic of the Late Period.

Sixth, whereas the construct chain is still a live feature in 11QtgJob (e.g., צפרי שמיא, "the birds of heaven" [13:12]; [בפ]ום ארמלה, "in a widow's mouth" [14:8]; בגבורת אלהא, "God's power" [29:5]), the substitution of a *dĕ*-clause for it is frequent in Targum II (e.g., in the passages corresponding to those just cited: ומעופא דשמיא, 28:21; ולבא דארמלתא, 29:13; פרישותא דאלהא, 37:14). The construct chain has not wholly disappeared from Targum II, to be sure, but it is not as abundant as it is in 11QtgJob (see further: 5:5; 7:4; 11:1; 13:1, 5; 14:1, 8; 15:3, 5, 7; 20:7; 22:9; 23:3, 4-5; 24:2; 26:1, 7-8; 27:1; 29:1, 3; 30:5, 6; etc.). On the other hand, there is one instance of the genitive expression with די in 11QtgJob 38:2, בקלה די איוב, "to the voice of Job" (= 42:9).[71]

Seventh, the Qumran targum makes use of the conjunction על דברת די, "in order that" (11QtgJob 34:4 [restored too in 1:7]), as a translation of Hebrew למען. This phrase is known in Biblical Aramaic (Dan 2:30; 4:14) and is related to the extrabiblical phrases in Elephantine (*AP* 6:6, 8; 40:3; 45:3; 28:8, 10, 11; 62:5; 71:30; *BMAP* 4:13; 13:2, 6; *A* 202; *RES* 1792A 3), על דברת זי, על דברה, על דבר, so that there is no doubt about its antiquity. This conjunction, however, is apparently unattested in later Jewish Palestinian Aramaic, and Targum II renders the Hebrew expression as אמטול (in Job 18:4) and as בגלל ד (in Job 40:8). Both of these forms are characteristically late and stand in contrast to על דברת די of the Qumran targum.[72]

Eighth, the Qumran targum uses לעבע, "quickly" (11QtgJob 3:7), which is the same word as לעובע (1QapGen 20:9 [see my commentary, 127]) and an intermediary form between עבק (found in Official Aramaic [*AP* 26:6, 22]) and Late Aramaic אבע. Targum II uses a paraphrase, בעגל.

Lastly, whereas the Qumran targum frequently introduces a question with the prefixed particle -ה(e.g., 33:7; 35:4, 5, 6, 7), Targum II often employs the phrase אפשר ד, lit., "Is it possible that . . . ?" (e.g., 39:26; 40:26, 27, 28, 29).

Still other features could be added to this list.[73] However, these examples suffice to illustrate the difference between an early and a late targum *of the same biblical book*. At the moment, this is important, since this is the only instance in which we can make such a comparison between a clearly pre-Christian targum and one from the Late Period. Now admittedly, the so-called Palestinian targums of the Pentateuch are not in all respects identical with Targum II of Job, and there is always the danger of extrapolating from the evidence given here to pentateuchal targums of the same period. And yet, anyone who has worked with the so-called Palestinian targums of the Pentateuch and with these two targums of Job will easily recognize that the features of Targum II are the ones that one meets mostly in the pentateuchal targums, not those of the Qumran targum. What is presented here is merely the beginning of a comparison that must be carried out on a still greater scale.

Finally, when the fragments of 4QtgLev are published, we shall be in a position to institute a similar comparison of them with the other known targums of the Pentateuch. Unfortunately, in that case the fragments of the Qumran targum are so small and so few that little will be able to be concluded from them.[73a]

CHART 1

11QtgJob COMPARED WITH THE SECOND TARGUM

11QtgJob Column	*Number of Aramaic Words Preserved in 11QtgJob*	*Number of Words Identical in Tg. 11*	*Number of Same Words with Later Orthography*	*Number of Words with Other Forms of Same Root*	*Total Number with Some Similarity*
1(17:14-18:4)	18	3	1	2	6
2(19:11-19)	23	9	3	3	15
3(19:19-20:6)	18	3	2	4	9
4(21:2-10)	24	5	0	3	8
5(21:10-27)	26	9	6	2	17
6(22:3-9)	14	2	1	5	8
7(22:16-22)	13	3	1	0	4
8(24:12-17)	14	3	1	1	5
9(24:24-26:2)	34	10	1	5	16
10(26:10-27:4)	29	4	1	5	10
11(27:11-20)	30	6	2	6	14
12(28:4-13)	8	1	1	0	2
13(28:20-28)	23	7	1	5	13
14(29:7-16)	45	3	2	18	23
15(29:24-30:4)	38	8	4	4	16
16(30:13-20)	33	6	1	4	11
17(30:25-31:1)	10	1	0	1	2
18(31:8-16)	27	9	0	9	18
19(31:26-32)	23	8	4	2	14
20(31:40-32:3)	16	1	3	2	6
21(32:10-17)	38	9	6	4	19
22(33:6-16)	46	11	8	9	28
23(33:24-32)	41	5	5	11	21
24(34:6-17)	45	14	2	6	22
25(34:24-34)	41	8	2	7	17
26(35:6-15)	56	12	9	10	31
27(36:7-16)	51	10	2	11	23
28(36:23-33)	57	9	1	11	21
29(37:10-19)	68	12	2	15	29
30(38:3-13)	69	21	3	13	37
31(38:23-34)	64	18	5	16	39
32(39:1-11)	66	13	6	17	36
33(39:20-29)	63	12	7	5	24
34(40:5-14)	63	9	4	11	24
35(40:23-31)	51	5	11	5	21
36(41:7-17)	52	4	9	9	22
37(41:25-42:6)	47	12	7	5	24
38(42:9-11)	53	10	9	9	28
Totals	1437	295	133	255	683

Given the differences between the two targums of Job that we have pointed out, and still other features—e.g., the greater amount of paraphrasis in Targum II, the occasional introduction into it of a secondary version of certain verses,[74] its use of Greek words in Aramaized forms—it is obvious that only rarely can the version of Targum II be used for the restoration of a lacuna in 11QtgJob. And the editors have normally restrained themselves from this. In attempts to restore the Aramaic text of the lacunae in the Qumran targum the principle should be this: One should look to see whether the Hebrew word to be translated is found elsewhere in the Book of Job and whether that passage is preserved in the extant parts of the Qumran targum; if it is, then the Aramaic counterpart of the Hebrew word found there should be given preference over other possible synonyms such as are often found in Targum II.

There is, of course, at least one other Aramaic translation of Job, with which one should ideally make the same sort of comparison as has been done here with Targum II. That is the version of Job that is found in the Peshitta. It would, of course, be wise to await the critical text of Syriac Job in *Vetus Testamentum syriace.*[75] But that brings up another aspect of the problem to which I have addressed myself above. My use of Targum II has depended solely on the edition of P. de Lagarde, which may not be perfect. It is now time to turn attention to a better edition of Targum II, a critical edition of which is now an obvious desideratum.

My remarks on the Qumran targum have concentrated on the text as an Aramaic version and its relation to another Aramaic rendering of the Book of Job. I noted earlier that the Qumran targum is by and large a literal translation of the Hebrew text, with only rare additions or paraphrastic renderings and no effort made to eliminate the anthropomorphisms of the original. Such a judgment, of course, presupposes a comparison with the present-day Hebrew text—and such comparisons have already been undertaken by others.[76] But it might be well in conclusion to recall that the Hebrew text of the Book of Job at Qumran or elsewhere in contemporary Palestine might not have been in all respects identical with the so-called Masoretic text. The editors of 11QtgJob admit that the targum presupposes a text that "se rapproche de celui des massorètes,"[77] but they also admit that sometimes the targumist seems to have had before him a slightly different Hebrew text. Now a few Hebrew fragments of Job have indeed been found in Qumran caves, and the editors of 11QtgJob have made no allusion to them. There is, for example, a Hebrew fragment of Job 33:28-30, which has been published as 2Q*15*.[78] M. Baillet, who published it, describes it as a fragment that presupposes "un texte du type massorétique."[79] Its tiny text agrees with the MT of Job and is part of Elihu's first poetic discourse. It bears on 11QtgJob 23, which seems, however, to bear witness to a different Hebrew *Vorlage.* Unfortunately, 2Q*15* is so small that it does not help to solve the problem of what might have been the Hebrew text being translated there. Several other fragmentary texts of Hebrew Job are known from Cave IV. Two of them are to be published by F. M. Cross, 4QJob[a, b] and are said to contain part of Job 36.[80] Another fragmentary text is represented by at least three small fragments in paleo-Hebrew script, 4QpaleoJob[c].[81] It is to be published by P. W. Skehan, but it will not affect the study of this targum, since the latter unfortunately lacks chaps. 13-14, which are found in these fragments. Chap. 36, however, has substantial verses preserved in 11QtgJob (cols. 27-28), and so one awaits anxiously Cross' publication of the Hebrew fragments to study this aspect of the targum. An intriguing question, however, is raised by

Skehan's fragments, written in the paleo-Hebrew archaizing script of Qumran: Why should a book such as Job have been copied in such a script? Is it perhaps a further indication of the esteem in which the Book of Job was held in the Qumran community?

My remarks on the Qumran targum of Job have been restricted to only a few aspects of the study of it. Though there is little in it that advances our knowledge of the Aramaic background of the NT, it does make its own contribution to the study of the language of that period in Palestine and thus bears indirectly on this area of investigation as well.[82]

NOTES TO CHAPTER 7

*Originally published as "Some Observations on the Targum of Job from Qumran Cave 11," *CBQ* 36 (1974) 503-24 (in the issue published as the Patrick W. Skehan Festschrift).

[1]See, among others, G. L. Harding, "Recent Discoveries in Jordan," *PEQ* 90 (1958) 7-18, esp. p. 17.

[2]The *editio princeps* was published by J. P. M. van der Ploeg and A. S. van der Woude, *Le targum de Job de la grotte XI de Qumrân* (p. 22 above, n. 32).

[3]See J. van der Ploeg, "Le targum de Job de la grotte 11 de Qumran (11QtgJob), première communication," *Mededelingen der koninklijke nederlandse Akademie van Wetenschappen,* Afd. Letterkunde, Nieuwe Reeks, Deel 25, No. 9 (Amsterdam: N. V. Noord-Hollandsche Uitgevers Maatschappij, 1962) 543-57. Cf. idem, "Een targum van het boek Job: Een nieuwe vondst in de Woestijn van Juda," *Het heilig Land* 15/11 (1962) 145-49; A. S. van der Woude, "Das Hiobtargum aus Qumran Höhle XI," *Congress Volume, Bonn 1962* (VTSup 9; Leiden: Brill, 1963) 322-31; J. P. M. van der Ploeg, "Un targum du livre de Job: Nouvelle découverte dans le désert de Juda," *BVC* 58 (1964) 79-87; A. S. van der Woude, "The Targum of Job from Qumran Cave Eleven," *AJBA* 1 (1969) 19-29 (a translation of VTSup 9 [1963] 322-31).

For secondary literature, based mainly on van der Ploeg's preliminary communication, see G. Fohrer, "4QOrNab, 11QtgJob, und die Hioblegende," *ZAW* 75 (1963) 93-97; A. Dupont-Sommer, "Notes qoumraniennes," *Sem* 15 (1965) 71-78, esp. pp. 71-74; S. Segert, "Sprachliche Bemerkungen zu einigen aramäischen Texten von Qumran," *ArOr* 33 (1965) 190-206, esp. pp. 193, 198; R. Le Déaut, "Le substrat araméen des évangiles: Scolies en marge de l'*Aramaic Approach* de Matthew Black," *Bib* 49 (1968) 388-99, esp. p. 391.

[4]Reviews of the *editio princeps*: B. Z. Wacholder, *JBL* 91 (1972) 414-15; P. Grelot, *RQ* 8 (1972-76) 105-14; D. Lys, *ETR* 47 (1972) 365-66; S. Kaufman, "The Job Targum from Qumran," *JAOS* 93 (1973) 317-27; J. Coppens, *ETL* 48 (1972) 221-22; P. M. Bogaert, *RTL* 3 (1972) 86-90; (G. Fohrer), *ZAW* 84 (1972) 128; M. Dahood, *Bib* 54 (1973) 283-86; G. R. Driver, *Book List 1973* (Durham: SOTS, 1973) 56; E. Cortes, *Estudios franciscanos* 48 (1972) 124–25; S. Medala and Z. J. Kapera, *Folia orientalia* 14 (1972–73) 320–23; C. T. Fritsch, *TToday* 30 (1973–74) 442–43; H. Bardtke, *OLZ* 70 (1975) 468–72.

Other studies based on the *editio princeps*: B. Jongeling, "Een belangrijke Dode-zeerol: Job in het Aramees," *Rondom het Woord* 13 (1971) 282-93; E. 4. Tuinstra, *Hermeneutische Aspecten van de Targum van Job uit Grot XI van Qumrân* (Groningen: Dissertation, 1971 [available from Hendrik Kraemer Instituut, Leidsestraatweg 11 (Postbus 12), Oegstgeest 2407, Holland]); P. Grelot, "Note de critique textuelle sur Job xxxix 27," *VT* 22 (1972) 487-89; J. C. Greenfield and S. Shaked, "Three Iranian Words in the Targum of Job from Qumran," *ZDMG* 122 (1972) 37-45;

M. Dahood, "Is the Emendation of *yādîn* to *yāzîn* Necessary in Job 36,31?" *Bib* 53 (1972) 539-41; H. Bardtke, "Literaturbericht über Qumrān VI. Teil III: Das Hiobtargum aus Höhle XI von Qumrān (11Qtg Job)," *TRu* 37 (1972) 205-19; M. Delcor, "Le targum de Job et l'araméen du temps de Jésus," *Exégèse biblique et judaïsme* (ed. J.-E. Ménard; Strasbourg: Faculté de théologie catholique [distributed by Brill, Leiden], 1973) 78-107; B. Jongeling, "Contributions of the Qumran Job Targum to the Aramaic Vocabulary," *JSS* 17 (1972) 191-97; F. J. Morrow, Jr., "11 Q Targum Job and the Massoretic Text," *RQ* 8 (1972-76) 253-56; A. D. York, "*Zrᶜ rwmʾh* as an Indication of the Date of 11QtgJob?" *JBL* 93 (1974) 445-46; R. Weiss, "Further Notes on the Qumran Targum to Job," *JSS* 19 (1974) 13–18. See further *MPAT*, pp. 195–97.

A more complete study of the targum has now appeared: M. Sokoloff, *The Targum to Job from Qumran Cave XI* (Bar-Ilan Studies in Near Eastern Languages and Culture; Ramat-Gan, Israel: Bar-Ilan University, 1974). See further B. Jongeling, C. J. Labuschagne, and A. S. van der Woude (eds.), *Aramaic Texts from Qumran* (p. 108 above, n. 9).

5See S. Spiegel, "Noah, Danel, and Job," *Louis Ginzberg Jubilee Volume* (New York: Jewish Theological Seminary, 1945) 305-55; M. Noth, "Noah, Daniel und Hiob in Ezechiel XIV," *VT* 1 (1951) 251-60.

6See N. M. Sarna, "Epic Substratum in the Prose of Job," *JBL* 76 (1957) 13-25; A. Alt, "Zur Vorgeschichte des Buches Hiob," *ZAW* 55 (1937) 265-68.

7See H. Ringgren, *The Faith of Qumran: Theology of the Dead Sea Scrolls* (Philadelphia: Fortress, 1963) 63-67, 108-9; F. Nötscher, *Zur theologischen Terminologie der Qumran-Texte* (BBB 10; Bonn: Hanstein, 1956) 161, 183-87; S. Schulz, "Die Rechtfertigung aus Gnaden in Qumran und bei Paulus," *ZTK* 56 (1959) 155-85; P. Stuhlmacher, *Gerechtigkeit Gottes bei Paulus* (FRLANT 87; Göttingen: Vandenhoeck & Ruprecht, 1965) 148-66; K. Kertelge, *"Rechtfertigung" bei Paulus: Studien zur Struktur und zum Bedeutungsgehalt des paulinischen Rechtfertigungsbegriffs* (NTAbh ns 3; 2d ed.; Münster: Aschendorff, 1967) 28-33; P. Wernberg-Møller, "*Ṣdq, ṣdyq* and *ṣdwq* in the Zadokite Fragments (CDC), the Manual of Discipline (DSD) and the Habakkuk-Commentary (DSH)," *VT* 3 (1953) 310-15.

8N. Avigad and Y. Yadin, *A Genesis Apocryphon* (p. 108 above, n. 9), 16–22, 40 (+pl. 11). Cf. my commentary on *The Genesis Apocryphon* (p. 22 above, n. 27), 50–59, 78–104.

9Ibid., 5.

10See J. T. Milik, *Ten Years* (p. 22 above, n. 31), 35; "'Prière de Nabonide' et autres écrits d'un cycle de Daniel: Fragments araméens de Qumran 4," *RB* 63 (1956) 407-15, esp. p. 412. Cf. C. Burchard, *Bibliographie zu den Handschriften vom Toten Meer II (Nr. 1557-4459)* (BZAW 89; Berlin: Töpelmann, 1965) 333.

11See J. M. Allegro (with the collaboration of A. A. Anderson), *Qumrân Cave 4: I (4Q*158-*4Q*186) (DJD 5; Oxford: Clarendon, 1968) 54 *(bspr Dnyʾl hnbyʾ)*. Cf. my article, "David, 'Being Therefore a Prophet . . .' (Acts 2:30)," *CBQ* 34 (1972) 332-39; Josephus, *Ant.* 10.11.7 §266-68; also "Further Light on Melchizedek from Qumran Cave 11," *ESBNT*, 245-67, esp. pp. 248, 250, 265-66.

12Cf., e.g., 1QM 1:4-6 and Dan 11:41-44.

13"'Prière de Nabonide' et autres écrits d'un cycle de Daniel" (see n. 10 above), 411-15.

14See pp. 90–94 above.

15*The New American Bible* (Paterson: St. Anthony Guild, 1970) 820. By contrast, the *RSV*, which has a translation of Ben Sira from the Greek (Sirach), reads: "It was Ezekiel who saw the vision of glory which God showed him above the chariot of the cherubim. For God remembered his enemies with storm, and did good to those who directed their ways aright." See F. Vattioni, *Ecclesiastico: Testo ebraico con apparato critico e versioni greca, latina e siriaca* (Pubblicazioni del seminario di semitistica, Testi 1; Naples: Istituto orientale di Napoli, 1968) 266-67; cf. R. Smend, *Die Weisheit des Jesus Sirach hebräisch und deutsch* (Berlin: Reimer, 1906) 57 (Hebr.), 89 (Germ.).

16The text of Jas 5:11 has always been problematic. The last six words are an OT allusion (see Exod 34:6; Ps 103:8; 111:4). The problematic phrase is καὶ τὸ τέλος κυρίου εἴδετε, which is sometimes translated as above, or (with the *RSV*) as, "you have seen the purpose of the Lord."

The latter meaning of τέλος is explained by BAG (p. 819) as "*the outcome which the Lord brought about* in the case of Job's trials." But the same *Lexicon* offers still another interpretation, "the end = *the death . . . of the* Lord Jesus," which shows how problematic the verse is; cf. A. Bischoff, "Tò τέλος κυρίου," *ZNW* 7 (1906) 274-79. However, the *apparatus criticus* in E. Nestle, *Novum Testamentum graece* (24th ed.; Stuttgart: Priv. Württembergische Bibelanstalt, 1960) 252, notes the variant ἔλεος for τέλος in the minuscle ms. 1739* and a few other witnesses. This is interesting, for the allusion in Jas 5:11 is often said to be also to Job 42:10ff. (see the margin in Nestle). In the Aramaic version of Job 42:11, the Qumran targum significantly adds a phrase (38:3): "And God returned to Job *in mercy* (ותב אלהא לאיוב ברחמין) and gave him twice as much as all that he had had." Contrast the *RSV* of the Hebrew text: "And the Lord restored the fortunes of Job, when he had prayed for his friends; and the Lord gave Job twice as much as he had before." Is it possible that Jas 5:11 should preferably be read as τὸ ἔλεος κυρίου εἴδετε, "you have seen the mercy of the Lord"? Or have ms. 1739* and other witnesses possibly been tributary to a Job-tradition represented in 11QtgJob? This is only a question; more evidence would have to be forthcoming before the reading τὸ ἔλεος would prove convincing.

[17]See *Hermeneutische Aspecten* (n. 4 above), 55-57 (extended discussion); 108 (English summary). Tuinstra contrasts the shift from Job's "speaking" (Hebr. Job 21:3) to his "knowledge" (11QtgJob 4:2) with the reverse in the case of Elihu, whose "knowledge" (Hebr. 32:10, 17) becomes his "words" (11QtgJob 21:1, 9). He also finds Job's qualities stressed (Hebr. 29:25 = 11QtgJob 15:1, 2; Hebr. 29:13 = 11QtgJob 14:1, 6; Hebr. 30:15 = 11QtgJob 16:1, 4; Hebr. 34:31 = 11QtgJob 25:1, 7). Furthermore, the translation of Job 40:10-11 is for him "very striking" because "God's ironic reproach of Job is turned into an assignment for Job to punish the godless. The last words of Job are interpreted in a most remarkable way: instead of repentance there is only a complaint: 'Therefore I am poured out and dissolved and I have become dust and ashes' (42:6; col. XXXVIII, 1.8f; cf. Ps 22:15a)" (p. 108).

[18]Ibid., 66, 109. Some writers had earlier discussed Job as an "Essene model," basing their remarks on the attitude toward suffering and confidence in God that is displayed in the *Hôdāyôt*. See H. Kosmala, *Hebräer—Essener—Christen: Studien zur Vorgeschichte der frühchristlichen Verkündigung* (Studia post-biblica, 1; Leiden: Brill, 1959) 292; J. Carmignac, "La théologie de la souffrance dans les Hymnes de Qumrân," *RQ* 3 (1961-62) 365-86, esp. p. 386. If there is any validity to these claims, they would rather support the understanding of Job in the Qumran community, as discussed above in this part of the paper.

[19]*Hermeneutische Aspecten,* 108.

[20]Ibid.

[21]See M. Burrows, "The Voice from the Whirlwind," *JBL* 47 (1928) 117-32.

[22]Cf. L. W. Batten "The Epilogue of the Book of Job," *ATR* 15 (1933) 125-28; A. Alt, "Zur Vorgeschichte" (n. 6 above).

[23]See *Le targum de Job* (p. 22 above, n. 32), 7. The variants have been discussed in detail by E. W. Tuinstra, *Hermeneutische Aspecten,* chap. 1. Cf. F. J. Morrow, Jr., "11 Q Targum Job and the Massoretic Text," *RQ* 8 (1972-76) 253-56.

[24]*Le targum de Job*, 2-3.

[25]Ibid., 3-5. "Appartiendrait-il à la deuxième partie du deuxième siècle av. J.-C.? Ce n'est qu'une suggestion, ou plutôt une question" (p. 4). The editors use as chief criteria the following details: (1) the use of *dī* (never *dĕ*) as the relative or determinative pronoun; (2) the predominance of the haphel as causative (in 1QapGen it is always ᵓaphel); (3) the reflexive in *hit-* (instead of ᵓ*it*); (4) the conditional conjunction as *hen* (never ᵓ*in*); (5) the interrogative *kĕmā*ᵓ (never *kĕmān*); (6) the adverb *tmh* (never *tmn*). See further S. A. Kaufman, "The Job Targum from Qumran" (n. 4 above), 325-27; J. T. Milik in DJD 3. 184-85; P. Grelot, Review of the *editio princeps, RQ* 8 (1972-76) 113; M. Delcor, "Le targum de Job" (n. 4 above), 83-86.

[26]For a list of Qumran Aramaic texts, see pp. 101–2 above.

[27]See M. H. Pope, *Job* (AB 15; Garden City: Doubleday, 1965) xxxviii-xxxix; 3d ed. (1973) xlii-xliii.

[28]Private communication from J. Strugnell. Cf. R. Le Déaut, *Introduction à la littérature targumique: Première partie* (Rome: Biblical Institute, 1966) 68. Le Déaut speaks of "two small fragments," which use a final *aleph* or *he* (but in what connection?), *ḥzʾ* ("see") "instead of the Palestinian *ḥamaʾ*" (?), and the suffix *-why*. See now R. de Vaux and J. T. Milik, *Qumrân Grotte 4, II* (DJD 6; Oxford: Clarendon, 1977) 90.

[29]Preliminary notice of this targum has been given by J. T. Milik, *Ten Years* (p. 22 above, n. 31), 31. A. Díez Macho ("La lengua hablada por Jesucristo," *OrAnt* 2 [1963] 96-132, esp. p. 107) records an oral communication made to him by Milik about the text: "two fragments of Leviticus in a literal Aramaic version like that of Onqelos, and in Imperial Aramaic. The fragments come from Qumran Cave IV and seem to be from the 1st century B.C." However, in his article, "Targum" (*Enciclopedia de la Biblia* [Barcelona: Ediciones Garriga, 1965], 6. 867), he speaks of them as "Preonqelos." See further R. Le Déaut, *Introduction,* 64-65. The latter is of the opinion that the literal translation of Leviticus, as well as that of Job in 11QtgJob, indicate that the oldest written targums were actually guides which closely followed the Hebrew text (and which permitted oral improvisation with haggadic embellishments that the translator would draw from a fund of oral tradition; only later on did the more paraphrastic targums come to be written down).

Having seen the fragments of the Leviticus passages in the "scrollery" of the Palestine Archaeological Museum some years ago, I hesitate to characterize the language in them simply as "Imperial Aramaic" (see pp. 71–73 above). It does not differ from that of other Qumran Aramaic texts, which has to be regarded as one of the several developments of Imperial Aramaic between 200 B.C. and A.D. 200. It does not use *kzy*, but rather *kd*[*y*]; the suffix of the 3d plur. masc. is not *-hm*, but *-hwn*. On the other hand, it does not yet have the forms that become frequent in later targums; it has *dm*, "blood," as in 1QapGen 11:17, and not *ʾdmʾ* with the later prosthetic *aleph*; *shwr*, "around" (cf. 1QapGen 21:15-18), instead of *ḥzwr*, which is found in Neofiti 1 and Ps.-Jonathan); the 3d sg. masc. suffix in *-h*, not in *-yh*. See now *Maarav* 1 (1978) 5–23.

[30]See M. R. Lehmann, "'Yom Kippur' in Qumran," *RQ* 3 (1961-62) 117-24. Cf. 11QMelchizedek 7, 25; 1Q*34bis* 2+1:6; 1QpHab 11:7. See further my article, "Further Light on Melchizedek," *ESBNT,* 247, 249, 251, 259.

[31]See M. Black, *Aramaic Approach* (p. 23 above, n. 43), 22; A. Díez Macho, *Neophyti 1, Targum palestinense . . . Génesis* (p. 84 above, n. 112), 95*.

[32]*Ten Years* (p. 22 above, n. 31), 31.

[33]"Sprachliche Bemerkungen zu einigen aramäischen Texten von Qumran," *ArOr* 33 (1965) 190-206, esp. pp. 205-6; "Die Sprachenfragen in der Qumrāngemeinschaft," *Qumran-Probleme* (ed. H. Bardtke; Berlin: Akademie-Verlag, 1963) 313-39, esp. pp. 325-30; and his review of my commentary, *JSS* 13 (1968) 281-82. Similarly, A. G. Lamadrid, *EstBíb* 28 (1969) 169.

[34]*The Genesis Apocryphon of Qumran Cave I* (2d ed.) 11-14.

[35]*Hermeneutische Aspecten* (n. 4 above), 65-70, 108-9.

[36]"Première communication" (n. 3 above), 553. See also P. Grelot, *RQ* 8 (1972-76) 113.

[37]S. A. Kaufman, "The Job Targum from Qumran" (n. 4 above), 325.

[38]See now J. C. Greenfield and S. Shaked, "Three Iranian Words in the Targum of Job from Qumran," *ZDMG* 122 (1972) 37-45; J. van der Ploeg, "Première communication," 549.

[39]Recall *raz*, "secret" (1QapGen 1:2, 3; 1Q*27* 1:2; 1QH 5:36; fr. 50:5; 1QM 14:9; 1QS 3:23; 4:6, 18, etc.); *naḥšîr*, "carnage" (1QM 1:9, 10, 13; 4Q*243* 1:5).

[40]See H. H. Schaeder, *Iranische Beiträge* (see p. 50 above, n. 27), 199–296.

[41]See C. Brockelmann, *Lexicon syriacum* (2d ed.; Halle / S.: Niemeyer, 1928) 472.

[42]The Strasbourg Ostracon is probably of Egyptian provenience; see M. Lidzbarski, *Ephemeris* 3 (1915) 25-26. For 5 / 6Ḥev 1 ar: 4, see E. Y. Kutscher,"The Languages of the Hebrew and Aramaic Letters of Bar Cocheba and His Contemporaries," *Lĕšonénu* 25 (1961) 117-33, esp. p. 119. Neither G. Dalman (*ANHW*, 289) nor M. Jastrow (*A Dictionary of the Targumim, the Talmud Babli and Yerushalmi, and the Midrashic Literature* [New York / Berlin: Choreb, 1926], 978) identify the word as Greek. It is probably nothing more than a **qatl*-type of a hollow root,

swp, "cut off." So it is listed by M. H. Segal, *A Grammar of Mishnaic Hebrew* (Oxford: Clarendon, 1927) 100.

[43]See pp. 40–41 above. Cf. J. C. Greenfield, *JNES* 31 (1972) 59: ". . . The Qumrān Scrolls have very interesting Iranian loan words but one would not use these to date the scrolls in the Persian period."

[44]See A. Rahlfs, *Septuaginta* (2 vols.; Stuttgart: Privil. Württembergische Bibelanstalt, 1949), 2. 344; H. B. Swete, *The Old Testament in Greek according to the Septuagint* (Cambridge: Cambridge University, 1922), 2. 602.

[45]L. Zunz, *Die gottesdienstlichen Vorträge der Juden historisch entwickelt* (rev. ed.; Hildesheim: Olms, 1966) 64, 84; A. Berliner, *Targum Onqelos herausgegeben und erläutert* (2 vols.; Berlin: Gorzelanczyk, 1884), 2. 91.

[46]See A. T. Olmstead, "Could an Aramaic Gospel Be Written?" *JNES* 1 (1942) 41-75, esp. p. 59. Cf. P. Kahle, *The Cairo Geniza: Schweich Lectures, 1941* (London: British Academy, 1947), p. 124; but Kahle omitted this view in the second edition (Oxford: Blackwell, 1959). H. Birkeland (*The Language of Jesus* [p. 22 above, n. 35], 35) argues: "That the Targum of Job was found in Palestine in the time of Rabbi Gamaliel (about 50 A.D.) does not necessarily mean that it was written for Palestinian Jews. Since it seems to be quoted already in the Greek translation of Job (see Kahle, p. 124 [first edition], with reference to Olmstead), it was obviously known in the Hellenized world outside Palestine." But does all that necessarily follow?

The Greek of the expanded epilogue is not easily translated. The version given above is very literal and allows for variant interpretations. It has been translated thus: "This (man) is referred to in the Syriac book as dwelling in Ausis. . . ," or "This man is described in the Syriac book as living in the land of Ausis" (*The Septuagint Version of the Old Testament and Apocrypha with an English Translation* [Grand Rapids: Zondervan, 1972] 698). But this does violence to the verb *ἑρμηνεύεται* and to the preposition *ἐκ*. On the other hand, the "Syrian book" has been understood as a reference to "some Aramaic apocryphal work" by M. McNamara, *Targum and Testament* (p. 26 above, n. 94), 66.

See further P. Winter, "Lc 2 49 and Targum Yerushalmi," *ZNW* 45 (1954) 145-79, esp. pp. 155-58; M. Delcor, "Le Testament de Job, la prière de Nabonide et les traditions targoumiques," *Bibel und Qumran: Beiträge zur Erforschung der Beziehungen zwischen Bibel- und Qumranwissenschaft: Hans Bardtke zum 22. 9. 1966* (Berlin: Evangelische Haupt-Bibelgesellschaft, 1968) 57-74, esp. pp. 68-69; M. H. Pope, *Job* (3d ed.; n. 27 above), 354; G. Gerleman, "Date of the Greek Book of Job," *Studies in the Septuagint: I. Book of Job* (Lunds Universitets Arsskrift, N.F. Avd. 1, Bd. 43, Nr. 2; Lund: Gleerup, 1946) 73-75.

[47]Indeed, the text of Job at this point in the Qumran targum is even shorter than the Hebrew; see above p. 164. F. M. Cross (*The Ancient Library of Qumran and Modern Biblical Studies* [The Haskell Lectures 1956-57; Garden City: Doubleday, 1958) 26 n. 48; rev. ed. [1961] 34 n. 48; *Die antike Bibliothek von Qumran und die moderne biblischen Wissenschaft* [Neukirchen: Neukirchener Verlag, 1967] 48 n. 56) once speculated that the addition at "the end of the Septuagint to Job may be quoted from this Targum," but this has not proved to be the case.

[48]I. Epstein (ed.), *The Babylonian Talmud: Seder Moᶜed* (London: Soncino, 1938) 564-65. The text itself reads:

אמר רבי יוסי: מעשה באבא חלפתא שהלך אצל רבן גמליאל בריבי לטבריא ומצאו שהיה יושב על שלחנו של יוחנן הנזוף ובידו ספר איוב תרגום והוא קורא בו אמר לו זכור אני ברבן גמליאל אבי אביך שהיה עומד על גב מעלה בהר הבית והביאו לפניו ספר איוב תרגום ואמר לבנאי שקעהי תחת הנדבך אף הוא צוה עליו וגנזו רבי יוסי בר יהודה אומר עריבה של טיט כפו עליו.

(L. Goldschmidt, *Der babylonische Talmud* [Berlin: Calvary, 1897], 1. 595).

Slightly different forms of the same story are found in the Jerusalem Talmud, *Shabbat* 16:1 (16a; ed. M. Schwab, *Le Talmud de Jérusalem* [Paris: G.-P. Maisonneuve, 1960], 3. 160-61); the Tosephta, *Shabbat* 13:2 (ed. S. Liebermann [New York: Jewish Theological Seminary, 1962] 57).

[49]R. Le Déaut (*Introduction* [n. 28 above], 70) thinks that such versions were forbidden only in synagogue services. But R. Gamaliel's reaction undoubtedly comes from some other reason. It

probably should rather be explained as part of the general early prohibition of "writing down" what was normally transmitted by oral tradition; see H. L. Strack, *Introduction to the Talmud and Midrash* (New York: Meridian, 1959) 12-13; B. J. Roberts, *The Old Testament Texts and Versions* (p. 137 above, n. 38), 197–98. R. Gamaliel thus probably treated the Aramaic version of Job as comparable to written *haggadah* or *halakah*, i.e., under interdict. The Mishnah (*Yadaim* 4:5) states that "if [Scripture that is in] Hebrew was written in an [Aramaic] translation *ᶜbryt šktbw trgwm),* or in Hebrew script [i.e., what we often call "paleo-Hebrew" script), it does not render the hands unclean" [i.e., it was not considered *kitbê haqqōdeš*]. See H. Danby, *The Mishnah* (London: Oxford, 1933) 784; G. Lisowsky, *Jadajim* (Die Mischna 6/11; Berlin: Töpelmann, 1956) 71-73. Thus 11QtgJob, 4QtgJob, and even 4QpaleoJob[c] would not have been *kitbê haqqōdeš.*

[50]*Le targum de Job*, 8. See further J. van der Ploeg, "Première communication" (n. 3 above), 552, 556; F. M. Cross, *The Ancient Library of Qumran (1961* [see n. 47 above]*) 34.*

[51]*Hermeneutische Aspecten* (n. 4 above) 109; see also pp. 69–70. Cf. A. Dupont-Sommer, *The Essene Writings from Qumran* (p. 156 above, n. 17), 306.

[52]Leipzig: Teubner, 1973 (reprinted; Osnabrück: Zeller, 1967) 85-118. E. Dhorme (*A Commentary on the Book of Job* [London: Nelson, 1967] ccxviii) says that Targum II was written by the same author as that of the Psalms and before the year A.D. 476. He refers to E. Nestle, "Jüdisch-aramäische Übersetzungen (Targumim)," *Realencyclopädie für protestantische Theologie und Kirche* (3d ed.; Leipzig: Hinrichs, 1897), 3. 103-10. Nestle in turn depends on W. Bacher, "Das Targum zu Hiob," *MGWJ* 20 (1871) 208-23, 283-84. Cf. E. Mangenot, "Targums," *Dictionnaire de la Bible* (Paris: Letouzey et Ané) 5 (1912) 2005-6; A. Weiss, *De libri Jobi paraphrasi chaldaica* (Breslau: H. Lindner, 1873).

[53]P. Grelot (*RQ* 8 [1972-76] 105) would date it to the 4th-5th century, but gives no reason for pushing it back to the fourth century. See W. Bacher, "Das Targum zu Hiob," 216-17. He finds an allusion to the division of the Roman Empire into East and West in the version of 4:10.

[54]*Le targum de Job,* 6.

[55]Cf. A. D. York, "The Dating of Targumic Literature," *JSJ* 5 (1974) 49-62.

[56]I have disregarded in the count the presence or absence of a *waw* as the prefixed conjunction; this varies in the two targums. Similarly, the fluctuation between final *aleph* and *he* on words such as *māᵓ* or *māh*, a phenomenon that is frequently attested in Middle Aramaic as well as in Late Aramaic. Again, I have not counted separately the prefixed prepositions; in one or other instance, this might make a slight difference, but overall it is so minor as to be negligible. (The only instance that one might query in this regard would be the use of *m-* for *min*; but again, both are attested in the Qumran targum.)

[57]The "same" means here the sum of the figures in cols. 3 and 4 ("Identical" plus "Same").

[58]The Qumran targumist must have taken *yĕšûrennû* as a form of *šwb*, confusing the *reš* with a *beth*. On the other hand, the sense of the Aramaic in Targum II is not clear. M. Jastrow (*A Dictionary*, 996) gives as the meaning of *slp*, "twist, pervert," and notes that *wyslp* in Targum II should be read here as *wyslq*, from *sĕleq*. The meaning of the verb in the second half of the line is not clear either; it seems to be a deliberate pun, playing on *škyntᵓ*, as G. S. Glanzman has called to my attention.

[59]See pp. 94–95 above.

[60]Lit., "lifted up the countenance of Job."

[61]Targum II seems to have understood *šbyt* of the MT as *šĕbît*, whereas *šĕbût* is more probably to be understood.

[62]See, e.g., R. E. Brown, *The Gospel according to John (i–xii)* (p. 111 above, n. 48), 33, 523–24. See p. 95 above.

[63]The MT of Ezra 4:23 also has *ᵓedrāᶜ*, and the question arises when and how that form got into the text. Similarly, in Hebrew (Jer 32:21), *ᵓezrōaᶜ*. Even if it were to prove to be from the time of Ezra, the emphasis should rather be put on the frequency with which such forms turn up in Targum II. Obviously, the usage had to begin somewhere, and early isolated examples do not weigh against the otherwise abundant attestation of forms without the prosthetic *aleph.*

[64]The same would have to be said about *byš* as was said about the prosthetic *aleph* in the preceding note. The form without the *aleph* is found in 1Q*20* 1 ii 8; and in the Kesećek Köyü inscription from Cilicia (*KAI* §258:3). Here, however, the argument is built on the number of such cases over against isolated early instances.

[65]For references, see E. Vogt, *Lexicon linguae aramaicae Veteris Testamenti* (p. 23 above, n. 41) 61-62.

[66]See R. Le Déaut, quoted in n. 28 above.

[67]See C.-F. Jean and J. Hoftijzer, *Dictionnaire des inscriptions sémitiques de l'ouest* (Leiden: Brill, 1965) 90; J. Cantineau, *Grammaire du Palmyrénien épigraphique* (Publications de l'institut d'études orientales de la faculté des lettres d'Alger, 4; Cairo: Institut français d'archéologie orientale, 1935) 91.

[68]See M. L. Margolis, *A Manual of the Aramaic Language of the Babylonian Talmud* (Clavis linguarum semiticarum, 3; Munich: Beck, 1910) 114*; G. J. Cowling, *Concordance to the Geniza Fragments of the Palestinian Targum* (based on P. Kahle, Masoreten des Westens II, Texts A-F) (London: privately mimeographed, 1969) 23; R. Le Déaut and J. Robert, *Targum des Chroniques* (AnBibl 51; Rome: Biblical Institute, 1971), 2. 180.

[69]See "Le targum palestinien," *Exégèse biblique et judaïsme* (p. 84 above, n. 114) 31. This article is a masterpiece of twisting evidence to fit a preconceived thesis. I shall cite only one instance: the early and later writing of the 3d masc. sg. suffix on a plural noun or a preposition. In Official Aramaic it regularly appears as *-why*. Following the lead of Biblical Aramaic vocalization, most scholars would vocalize it *-ôhī* (for an explanation of the form, see p. 82 above, n. 95). It is well known that in the Aramaic of the Late Period this ending becomes *-wy* in most cases; this is abundantly attested in the classic targumim. The vocalization is undoubtedly *-ôï* (with the loss of the intervocalic *he*). Díez Macho groups all this together and says that "le suffixe pronominal *why*/*wy-why* est régulier dans l'araméen d'Empire, à Qumrân (4 Qtg Lev, *Apocryphe*, etc.), dans l'Onqelos, dans le Talmud de Babylone, syriaque." Now just where in Imperial Aramaic does one find *-wy* (unless one agrees with Díez Macho that this sort of Aramaic is found beyond 200 B.C.)? The ending *-wy* for this suffix does not occur in Qumran Aramaic texts. Díez Macho cites an example from 1QapGen 21:34, but that is אחוי, which he does read correctly, but vocalizes wrongly (at least by implication). For that is a 3d sg. masc. suffix on a *singular* noun—on a noun, indeed, which has (like a few others) a special formation. "His brother" is in Official Aramaic *ʾăḥūhī* (a dissimilation of **ʾaḥū-hū*); the full writing of the form is found in 1QapGen 22:3, 5, 11 (אחוהי). The form אחוי has, then, nothing to do with the suffix *-why* (= *-ôhī*) for all its consonantal similarity. It does, indeed, represent a similar loss of intervocalic *he*; and this isolated instance is to be expected, because the pronunciation reflected in the later targums, the Talmud, and Syriac had to begin somewhere. The argument, however, is from the abundance of these forms later on. And it still has to be shown that the intervocalic *he*, which is written in the majority of instances in the Aramaic of the Middle Phase, represents historical spelling and nothing more. To take refuge in "contamination" from "spoken Aramaic" is a *petitio principii* at this period.

[70]I do not deny that sporadically one finds *ʾyt* even in Official Aramaic texts (*AP* 46:3[?]; 54:4; 67:7[?]; *BMAP* 7:31 [with lacuna immediately following]; B-M 15). But again it is the frequent incidence of the form *ʾyt* in the targums and the absence of it in the Qumran material. How early is the first attestation of the contracted negative?

[71]This isolated instance is paralleled by a number of instances in 1QapGen (see my commentary [2d ed.], 217). Even A. Díez Macho ("Le targum palestinien," 28) admits the difference of incidence, when he cites 36 examples of the construct chain in *Mĕgillat Taʿănīt* over against 2 of *d* + the noun there.

[72]On the expression *ʿal dibrat dī*, see F. Rosenthal, *Die aramaistische Forschung* (p. 75 above, n. 2), 51; H. Bauer and P. Leander, *Grammatik des Biblisch-Aramäischen* (Halle / S.: Niemeyer, 1927) §69*z*. I am indebted to G. S. Glanzman for calling this seventh item to my attention.

[73]For the time being, see the list of the items to be considered that A. Díez Macho has drawn up ("Le targum palestinien," 27-31).

[73a]See now my article, "The Targum of Leviticus from Qumran Cave 4," *Maarav* 1 (1978) 5–23.

[74]W. Bacher ("Das Targum zu Hiob" [n. 52 above], 218-19) mentions 46 verses which have "another Targum," a second version of the same Hebrew verse, and in at least four instances a third version (24:19; 28:17; 36:33; 38:25; in the Breslau Codex also 12:5; 13:4). It is usually introduced by תא (= *targūm* ᵓ*āḥēr*).

[75]Being published by the Peshiṭta Institute of the University of Leiden (Leiden: Brill). Cf. L. J. Rignell, "Notes on the Peshitta of the Book of Job," *ASTI* 9 (1973) 98-106.

[76]See n. 23 above.

[77]*Le targum de Job*, p. 7.

[78]See M. Baillet, J. T. Milik, and R. de Vaux, *Les 'petites grottes' de Qumrân: Exploration de la falaise, Les grottes 2Q, 3Q, 5Q, 6Q, 7Q à 10Q, Le rouleau de cuivre* (DJD 3; Oxford: Clarendon, 1962) 71.

[79]Ibid.

[80]See C. Burchard, *Bibliographie II* (n. 10 above), 327; cf. "Le travail d'édition des fragments manuscrits de Qumrân," *RB* 63 (1956) 49-67, esp. p. 57; P. Benoit et al., "Editing the Manuscripts Fragments from Qumran," *BA* 19 (1956) 75-96, esp. p. 85 (where Cross then spoke of only "one MS of Job").

[81]See C. Burchard, *Bibliographie II*, 327; "Le travail d'édition," 58; P. Benoit et al., "Editing," 86.

[82]For one important item in 11QtgJob that does affect NT study (the absolute use of מרא as a title for Yahweh and its bearing on the background of the Greek title *κύριος* for Jesus), see pp. 88–90, 124 above.

Chapter 8

Aramaic Epistolography*

Though other areas of Aramaic studies have had a more or less adequate treatment, that of Aramaic epistolograhy has not yet been so blessed. The number of letters and messages preserved in ancient Aramaic is not negligible, but it cannot compare with that in other ancient languages such as Sumerian, Akkadian, Greek, or Latin. Hebrew epistolography is not much better off than Aramaic, and a survey of it might be as useful as this one. In any case, but little interest in this form of Aramaic composition has hitherto been manifested.[1] Even in the present survey the starting-point has been Greek or Hellenistic epistolography, or more specifically NT epistolography; and thus the incentive to look at Aramaic letter-writing has come from an extrinsic concern.[2]

In a sense this inquiry forms but another aspect of the generic problem of the Aramaic background of NT writings, or more properly of Aramaic interference in NT Greek. This may indeed stimulate the comparative study of the two bodies of correspondence; but Aramaic epistolography deserves a full study in and of itself.[3] On the other hand, it should be obvious at the outset that the contribution of Aramaic epistolography to the study of the NT letters cannot be as significant as the Aramaic background of other areas of NT study (e.g., the Aramaic substratum of the sayings of Jesus, or the possible Aramaic sources of various NT writings).[4] For most of the NT letters or epistles come from areas outside of Palestine or Syria, where Aramaic was not spoken. True, we are faced with the anomaly that Paul has preserved for us two clearly Aramaic words, אבא (Gal 4:6) and מראנא תא (1 Cor 16:22), and commentators have discussed at times other possible Aramaisms in his writings or Aramaic sources that he may have used.[5] But the Greek of his letters does not reveal Aramaic interference, or even Semitic interference in general, to the same extent as that of the Gospels and Acts. Furthermore, J. N. Sevenster has raised a question about the Palestinian origin of James and 1 Peter in a new way,[6] and in the light of it one could further ask about the influence of Aramaic epistolography on such letters. It might also be the proper question to ask if one were to consider seriously the proposal that the Captivity Letters in the Pauline corpus were composed in Caesarea Maritima.[7] While there may be initial doubts, therefore, about the validity of the inquiry into the Aramaic background of such NT writings as the epistles, still the inquiry may have a legitimacy, at least in a limited way. But even aside from such considerations there is still the likelihood that the study of the corpus of Aramaic letters and messages would cast some light on the NT epistles, at least from the comparative standpoint, since they represent a form of ancient epistolography from the eastern Mediterranean area.

Obviously a study of Aramaic letter-writing bears also, and more immediately, on certain OT passages, because some examples of ancient Aramaic epistolography have been preserved in the OT itself. Passages in Ezra have often been treated in the light of Aramaic letters discovered only toward the beginning of this century. Save for these biblical examples, an isolated fragment (such as *AP* 77), and letters preserved in rabbinic writings (e.g., of the Gaonic period), the rest of ancient Aramaic letters known today have come to light only since about 1902. About a dozen or so of them have been discovered only in the last quarter of a century.

The earliest phase of the Aramaic language, so-called Old Aramaic, dating roughly from 925 to 700 B.C., is represented entirely by inscriptions; no letters come to us from this period of the language. In the subsequent phase, so-called Official or Imperial Aramaic, dating roughly from 700 to 200 B.C., one finds a considerable number of letters and messages which begin a long list of texts that continues down into the phases of Middle Aramaic, roughly 200 B.C. to A.D. 200, and Late Aramaic, roughly A.D. 200 to 700.[8]

Epistolary correspondence in Aramaic has turned up in texts written on skin, papyrus, and potsherds or ostraca; some of it is also preserved in the Bible and in rabbinic literature. The correspondence which was written on skin or papyrus is, by and large, better known; but the number of messages written on ostraca is not small, and they have their own contributions to make to the study of Aramaic epistolography because of the mundane, everyday character of the messages transmitted in them. Since they were written on ostraca, they are usually brief,[9] and the message is more like a note, often cryptic and difficult to decipher or interpret. Consequently, I shall concentrate for the most part on the letters proper and bring in evidence from the ostraca when it is pertinent for comparison or contrast. My purpose here is to survey in a general way the corpus of Aramaic letters, highlighting those elements that may be of interest to the study of the NT and OT letters; the study of specific details will have to be left to others.[10]

I. *The Types, Provenience, and Contents of Aramaic Letters*

Among the many texts that have been preserved in the corpus of Aramaic epistolography, there is none that could really be called an "epistle" in the sense in which A. Deissmann once defined it: ". . . an artistic literary form, a species of literature, just like the dialogue, the oration, or the drama. It has nothing in common with the letter except its form; apart from that one might venture the paradox that the epistle is the opposite of a real letter. The contents of an epistle are intended for publicity—they aim at interesting 'the public.'"[11] By contrast, Deissmann described a "letter" as "a means of communication between persons who are separated from each other."[12] While there are all sorts of difficulties which modern students of epistolography have with Deissmann's definitions—and especially with the application of them to NT writings[13]—his definitions are being used here merely to indicate that the Aramaic corpus is made up solely of "letters" in Deissmann's broad category. Even though they may deal with official or business matters and be reports sent to or by persons in authority, they can only be described as "letters," for they deal with concrete, *ad hoc* problems, request aid, propose solutions, seek advice, express concern, and so on; and they were hardly intended for publication. The sole departures—and this is problematic—are found in Dan 3:31-33, depending on how one relates that quasi-epistolary introduction to the rest of the story in chap. 4,[14] and Dan 6:25-27, which is a decree in epistolary form. It is, of course, significant that the only possible exceptions are in biblical writings. Aside from these instances there are in the limited Aramaic corpus no examples of epistles or literary letters (either of the philosophical, hortatory, or imaginative types); nor do we know of any spurious or pseudepigraphical letters. Those that have survived are all either private letters or official letters, treating matters either of concern, news, or business.

For the most part the Aramaic letters come from Egypt. The main source of them has been the excavations on the island of Yeb or Elephantine in the Nile opposite the town of Aswan; but a number of them has also come from elsewhere in Egypt, especially from Lower Egypt (Memphis, Saqqarah, and Hermopolis West). The letters preserved in the Book of Ezra, which now have striking parallels in extrabiblical examples, have always been known as instances of Aramaic correspondence between Palestine and the Persian king.[15] A small batch of letters, often referred to as the Arsames correspondence, was found in Egypt but came originally from either Mesopotamia or Persia.[16] A further small group of letters, from either Šimᶜon bar Kosibah or his colleagues, reveals the use of Aramaic for correspondence within Palestine of the early second century A.D.[17] This diverse geographical provenience of the letters merely reflects the status of the language itself, which for a considerable period served as a *lingua franca* in the ancient Near East.

Among the Aramaic letters found in Egypt, some have brought to light interesting international affairs. For instance, one was a papyrus letter, unfortunately not completely preserved, found at Saqqarah in Lower Egypt, that has been dated ca. 604 B.C.[18] Written by ᵓAdon, the ruler of a Philistine(?) town in Palestine(?), and addressed "to the Lord of Kings, the Pharaoh," it informs the Egyptian ruler of the advance of the troops of the Babylonian king and asks for military support against them. Though the date of the letter is not certain, it seems to be related to the advance of Nebuchadrezzar ca. 600 B.C. It is clear testimony to the use of Aramaic for official correspondence on an international level between rulers.

Another example of international correspondence in Aramaic is the letter of the leaders of the Jewish community at Elephantine, Yedaniah and his associates, priests in the fortress Yeb (*AP* 30).[19] It was addressed to Bagohi, the governor of Judah in 408 B.C. (dated precisely: 20 Marḥešwan, 17th year of Darius [II]). It complains about the problems that have faced the Jewish community in Yeb since the departure of Arsames on a visit to the Persian king. Egyptian priests of the god Khnub have plotted with Widarang, the Persian satrap, to bring about the destruction of the sanctuary of Yahu which has been in Yeb and which had been built by the Jews "in the days of the Kings of Egypt," well before "Cambyses entered Egypt." The letter tells how the Jews have sat in sackcloth, prayed, and fasted that Widarang might be requited—which eventually happened. The Jewish leaders recall that they have written previously to Bagohi to enlist his aid, and also to Yoḥanan, the high priest, and his colleagues, the priests in Jerusalem. Now they seek from Bagohi the permission to rebuild the sanctuary in Yeb, in which they promise to offer sacrifice and to pray to Yahu on his behalf. They mention that they have also written about this matter to Delaiah and Shelemiah, sons of Sanballat, the governor of Samaria (probably Sanballat I, known from Neh 2:10, 19; 3:33; 4:1; 6:1, 2, 5, 12, 14; 13:28, grandfather of the Sanballat of the Samaria papyri found in the cave of the Wadi ed-Daliyeh[20]). This is obviously a first-class example of an official letter concerning a matter of moment and importance to the Jews of Elephantine. What is noteworthy about it is that the letter was found at Elephantine itself; it probably represents a copy of the letter that was sent to Bagohi and, what is more, a duplicate of it (*AP* 31) was also found with a version of the letter that is slightly different. Was it an alternate version prepared by a scribe and eventually rejected in favor of the other? Was it a preliminary draft that was emended? Which version was actually sent? Or were both versions slightly different from the letter that Bagohi actually received? We have no way of answering such questions. In any case, it is certain that at least a similar letter was sent, since there is a reply, or better a "memorandum" (זכרן), sent about the matter (*AP* 32), and still further correspondence on the subject (*AP* 27, 33).[21] This gives a brief idea of the most important letters from Elephantine. There are many others that deal with other subjects: the celebration of the Passover (*AP* 21),[22] an appeal to a higher court (*AP* 16), an order to repair a government boat (*AP* 26), etc.

From Egypt, but outside of Elephantine, comes another group of papyri known today as the letters from Hermopolis West.[23] In seven of the eight letters the place of origin seems to have been Memphis, for the addressees are blessed by the sender(s) in the name of the god Ptaḥ, who had a temple in Memphis. They deal with family matters, handle business transactions, or simply express concern for persons who are absent. The place of destination in four of the letters is סון, Syene (modern Aswan), and in three of them אפי,

Luxor. One of the editors of these letters, E. Bresciani, insists on the pagan character of them because of the destination and of the gods whose temples are mentioned in them. Yahu does not appear; the proper names are sometimes Semitic, sometimes Egyptian, sometimes as yet unanalyzed.[24] If their destination was Syene and Luxor, the puzzle is why they were found, folded up, sealed, and for the most part preserved intact in a jar stored in an underground gallery of an Ibieion, dedicated to Thot, at Hermopolis West in the Delta region.

The letters of Bar Cochba from the Cave of Letters in the Wadi Ḥabra (Naḥal Ḥever) are for the most part as yet unpublished. What is presently available is often fragmentary; but the letters reveal the diverse matters of concern to Simon bar Kosibah and his officers at the time of the Second Revolt against Rome (A.D. 132-35). Perhaps the most striking one expresses his concern to have the "palm-branches and citrons," the "myrtle and willow twigs" delivered for the feast of Succoth or Tabernacles.[25] The topic of the letter is of interest because it is the subject not only of an Aramaic letter, but also of a Greek one written about the same time by one who calls himself Σουμαῖος. He writes about the same individuals, Yehonathan bar Baᶜyan and Masabbalah (יהונתן בר בעין, מסבלה), to whom the Greek letter is addressed: Ἰωναθῆι Βαιανοῦ καὶ Μα[σ]άβαλα (in the dative case).[26] In the Greek letter, instructions are given for the furnishing of σ[τε]λεοὺς καὶ κίτρια . . . ἰς [κ]ιτρειαβολὴν Ἰουδαίων, "beams and citrons for the Citron-celebration of the Jews." These two letters come from the same general Palestinian situation, and aside from attesting to the use of the two languages to send messages about rather ordinary affairs and needs, they reveal that Aramaic was not simply a literary language of the period.

Finally, from what has been said it should be obvious that some of the Aramaic correspondence comes from other than Jewish writers. Here one touches on the problem of the identification of the "Jews" and the "Arameans" in the Elephantine texts, a problem that is larger than that of the letters alone.[27] But it is also related to the international character of the language to which we have already alluded.

II. *Some Features of Aramaic Epistolography*

What follows is an attempt to organize briefly under various headings some of the obvious formal elements in Aramaic letters. As I have already indicated, most of the data is drawn from the letters proper, those preserved on skin or papyrus; occasionally formal elements from the ostraca are also used. In a sense, some of these elements may prove to be distinctive of Aramaic epistolography, but a judgment about their distinctive character would imply a comparative study which has not yet been undertaken. Attention is rather being centered here on the features themselves in a descriptive way, without any attempt to compare them or to explain their origin or what might have influenced them. No attempt is being made to analyze all of the features, e.g., the stock phrases that one often finds in letters in other languages expressing rebuke, surprise, etc. My remarks will fall rather under eight headings: (a) the names for the Aramaic letters; (b) the *praescriptio*; (c) the initial greeting; (d) the secondary greetings; (e) the concluding formulae; (f) the mention of a scribe or secretary; (g) the date; and (h) the final or exterior address. Such features, which are found in many of the letters, are easily detected; but it will still remain a question of how many of them actually structure the Aramaic letter. The answer to that question must await a further discussion.

(a) *The Names for the Aramaic Letter.* At least three different terms are found in this type of writing for the "letter": אגרה (אגרתא), ספר (ספרא), and נשתון (נשתונא). The most common term is אגרה, a borrowed Akkadian word, *egertu*, which is also found in biblical Aramaic (Ezra 4:8, 11; 5:6). It is often used with the verb שלח, "send." Thus, e.g.. אגרה חדה בשלמך לא שלחת עלי, "you did not send me a letter about your well-being" (*AP* 41:5). Similarly: *AP* 30:7, 18, 19, 24, 29; 31:6, 17, 18, 28; 38:10; 40:3; *AD* 10:2. Indeed, the frequency of this idiom eventually seems to have given the verb שלח the nuance of "sending a message" (*AD* 12:1; 4:1; 7:5; *Herm WP* 3:6; 5:7; *AP* 16:8; 38:9; etc.), whereas a verb whose meaning was long misunderstood, הושר, became the more normal term for sending other objects (see *BMAP* 13:4; *AD* 13:2, 3), though it too was occasionally used with a message as its object. Other verbs, of course, were used too with אגרה; thus, יהבת, "was delivered" (*AD* 12:1); תמטא, "will arrive" (*AP* 42:6); כתבו, "they wrote" (Ezra 4:8). In one instance, the document itself is explicitly labelled as אגרת שמעון בר כוסבה, "a letter of Simon bar Kosibah" (*5/6Ḥev* 4:1).

The second term is ספר and strictly means a "writing" (often a "book"); but in this type of literature it is used explicitly of the letter. Thus, לשלמכי שלחת ספרא זנה, "I am sending this letter to greet you" (literally, "for your peace [of mind?]"), *Herm WP* 1:12-13; 6:[10]; cf. 2:17; 3:13; 4:12-13; 5:9; 7:4; *Pad* II v 4-5. Cf. *Herm WP* 1:5; 5:4 (with הושר!).

The third term, נשתון, is derived from the Persian **ništavāna*, and probably still carries the nuance of a "written document, decree" (see *AP* 17:3), even in such biblical passages as Ezra 4:18, 23; 5:5.

One further term should be mentioned here, for it is the "label," as it were, given to a document: זכרן, "a memorandum" (*AP* 32:1: זכרן זי בגוהי ודליה), "a memorandum of Bagohi and Delaiah."[28] It is an interesting parallel to Ezra 6:2 (דכרונה).

(b) *The Praescriptio.* The term *praescriptio* is often taken to mean a phrase in a letter like Ἰάκωβος . . . ταῖς δώδεκα φυλαῖς ταῖς ἐν τῇ διασπορᾷ χαίρειν (Jas 1:1), expressing the name of the sender, that of the addressee, and the greeting. But I am limiting the sense of it to indicate solely the names of the sender and the addressee, because the greeting is sometimes absent in the extant Aramaic letters or else is formulated in various elaborate ways that call for a distinct discussion of the initial greeting. However, when the initial greeting is used, it is closely related to the *praescriptio* and this must be recognized, even though they are separated here for the convenience of discussion.

The *praescriptio*, when it is not simply implied,[29] is usually expressed in one of five ways: (i) "To X, your servant / brother / son, (greeting)"; (ii) "To X, from Y, (greeting)"; (iii) "From X, to Y, (greeting)"; (iv) "X to Y, (greeting)"; (v) "To X, (greeting)".

As examples of (i), the following may be singled out: [אל א]חי פרור . . . אחוך בלטר, "[To] my [br]other Pirawur, your brother Beletir . . ." (*AšOst* 1). Similarly (with some form of אח): *AP* 21:1-2; 40:1; 41:[1]; 42:1; Shunnar 1; *Cl-G Ost* 277:1-2; *Bodl Aram Inscr* 3 A 1; *Strasbourg Ost* 1-2; possibly *Pad* III. Or אל מרא מלכן פרעה עבדך אדן מלך [אשקלון], "To the Lord of Kings, the Pharaoh, your servant ᵓAdon, King of [Ashkelon] . . ." (*AdonL* 1).[30] Similarly (with some form of עבד): *AP* 17:1; 30:1; 31:1; 37:1; 38:1-2; 39:1; 70:1; *HermWP* 3:1; *BMAP* 13:1;[31] Ezra 4:11; *ClG Ost* 70 A -2. Or again, אל אמ[י] יה[ו]י[ש]מע ברך שלום בר פטמ[ון], "To [my] mother, Yah[u]yi[sh]ma^{c}, your son, Shallum bar Peṭam[on]" (*Pad* II v 1).[32] Similarly (with a form of בר): *Cambr Ost* 131-133:1.

As examples of form (ii) the following may be cited: אל אחתי רעיה מן אחכי מכבנה, "To my sister Ra^{c}yah, from your brother Makkabanit" (*HermWP* 1:1). Similarly: *HermWP* 2:1; 3:5; 4:1-2; 5:1; 6:1; 7:1; *Pad* I v 1.

As examples of form (iii) we may cite: מן ארשם על וחפרעמחי, "From Arsames, to Waḥpri^{c}maḥi" (*AP* 26:1). In this case no greeting follows. Similarly (with a greeting): *AD* 1:1; 2:1; 3:1; 5:1; (without a greeting): *AD* 4:1; 8:1; 9:1; 10:1; 11:1; 12:1; Letter of R. Judah the Prince; *papMird* A 1-4.[33]

As examples of form (iv) we cite the following: ארתחשסתא מלך מלכיא לעזרא כהנא ספר דתא די אלה שמיא גמיר, "Artaxerxes, the King of Kings, to Ezra the priest, scribe of the religion of the God of Heaven, . . ." (Ezra 7:12).[34] Similarly: Dan 3:31; *5/6Ḥev* 1:1; *5/6Ḥev* 8:1-3; *5/6Ḥev* 10:1; *5/6Ḥev* 11:1; *5/6Ḥev* 14:1-2; *5/6Ḥev* 15:1.

As examples of form (v) the following may be mentioned: לאחנא בני דרומא, "To our brothers, inhabitants of the South, . . . (*Gamaliel*, 1). Similarly: *Bodl Libr Ost* 1 (with אל); *Cairo Ost* 35468a 1 (with על); *Gamaliel* 2 and 3 (both with ל).

Such are the various forms of the *praescriptio* in the Aramaic letters. The difference is at times characteristic of a certain group of letters; thus the form "From X to Y" is preferred in the texts of the so-called Arsames correspondence (letters found in Egypt but written in Mesopotamia or Persia). Yet that form also turns up elsewhere too; and it is not easy to say to what extent local variations or chancery practices are operative.

Three further remarks should be made about the *praescriptio* in an Aramaic letter. First of all, in some of the Hermopolis letters and in one of the Padua papyri there is a peculiar greeting which precedes the *praescriptio*, and it is not to be confused with the "initial greeting," which is also present. It is a greeting addressed to a temple *before* the mention of the sender and the addressee; it begins the letter. Thus, שלם בית נבו, "Greetings to the Temple of Nabu" (*Herm WP* 1:1), or שלם בית בנת בסון, "Greetings to the Temple of Banit in Syene" (*Herm WP* 2:1; 3:1), or שלם בית ביתאל ובית מלכת שמין, "Greetings to the Temple of Bethel and the Temple of the Queen of Heaven" (*Herm WP* 4:1). The fragmentary text of *Herm WP* 8:1 may have had a similar formula. This greeting, however, is not solely addressed to the temples of pagan gods, for one instance salutes the "Temple of Yahu in Elephantine" (שלם ב]ית יהו ביב], *Pad* I v 1). These letters seem to begin with an invocation of the deity honored in the place where the addressee is found. The greeting is peculiar, and its implications have not yet been fully explored, as far as I know.[35] As far as epistolographic style is concerned, it is a salutation distinct from the initial greeting expressed to the addressee and indicative of the piety of the writer of the letter.

Secondly, one should note the preposition used for "to" in these *praescriptiones.* Though אל was used as an ordinary preposition in Old Aramaic to express motion toward or direction (Sefire I B [29]; II B 13?; III 1ter, [8], 8, 19, 20), it gradually disappeared in Aramaic and was supplanted by על. However, the preposition אל did persist as a stereotype in the *praescriptiones* of letters long after it was supplanted elsewhere. Thus, אל פרעה מרא מלכן, *AdonL* 1; cf. *Herm WP* 1:1; 2:1; 3:5; 4:1; 5:1; 6:1; 7:1; *AP* 17:[1]; 21:[1]; 30:1; 31:1; 37:1; 38:1; 39:1; 40:1; 41:1; 42:[1]; 70:1; Shunnar 1; *Pad* I v 1; *Pad* II v 1; *Pad* III; *Cl-G Ost* 277:1; *Cl-G Ost* 70:1; *BMAP* 13:[1].[36] But the preposition על began to invade the *praescriptio* as well, especially in the Arsames correspondence. Thus, על מראי פסמי, *Herm WP* 3:1; cf. *AP* 26:1; *AD* 1:[1]; 2:1; 3:1; 4:1; 5:1; 6:1; 7:1; 8:1; 9:1; 10:1; 11:1; 12:1; 13:1; Ezra 4:11, 17. Yet even this preposition in time gave way to the simple ל. Thus, לדריוש מלכא, "to Darius, the King" (Ezra 5:7b); cf. Ezra 7:12; Dan 3:31; *5/6Ḥev* 1:1; *5/6Ḥev* 4:1; *5/6Ḥev* 8:2-3; *5/6Ḥev* 10:1; *5/6Ḥev* 11:1; *5/6Ḥev* 14:1-2; *5/6Ḥev* 15:1; *Gamaliel* 1, 2, 3; *R. Judah the Prince; papMird* A 1-3.

Thirdly, note should be made of the titles used in the *praescriptio* to designate the addressee and the sender. The contrast of מרא and עבד causes no problem, since they designate a difference of social rank or persons of varying authority; "servant" and "lord" obviously do not imply slavery, but are used as polite customary expressions among persons of differing rank or status. Among persons of equal rank it seems that the term אח, "brother," was used. That it may sometimes designate a blood-brother is clear; but what is striking is the use of it as a title with a more generic connotation. Thus a father, Osea bar Peṭ[ ], writes to his son, Shelomam, who is away on a caravan, and twice refers to himself as "brother": "To my son, Shelomam; from your 'brother,' Osea." In the exterior address of the letter: "To my 'brother,' Shelomam bar Osea, your 'brother,' Osea bar Peṭ[ ]" (*Pad* I v 1; 1 r 7). In the course of the letter the father refers to אמך, "your mother" (I v 2; I r 5). Such a use of אח was at one time misunderstood, but it is now clear.[37] Moreover, it is confirmed by the related use of אחת, "sister," in what must be a similar polite form of address among men and women of equal standing. In *HermWP* 7:1 the addressee is given as אל אחתי תבי, "to my sister, TBY," but in the exterior address one reads: [ ] אל אמי, "To my mother [ ]." Similarly in *HermWP* 7:1 the letter is addressed: אל אמי עתררמרי, "To my mother, ᶜAttar-RMRY," but the exterior address rather has אל אחתי עתררי, "To my sister, ᶜAttar-RY" (with a different [erroneous?] spelling of the name, *HermWP* 7:5). And to complicate the usage, *HermWP* 3:1, which is addressed, "My lord PSMY, your servant Makkabanit," has the exterior address, "To my father PSMY, from Makkabanit bar PSMY" (*HermWP* 3:14). If further examples of such letters were to be discovered, it is possible that this usage would be further clarified.

On the ostraca one finds, undoubtedly because of the brevity of the messages, an opening that mixes greeting and *praescriptio* (שלם אוריה); we shall comment on this below.

(c) *The Initial Greeting.* Though the initial greeting of an addressee was sometimes omitted in Aramaic letters, especially in those which had an official or quasi-official character (e.g., *AD* 4:2; 7:1; 8:1; 9:1; 10:1; 11:1 [the so-called Arsames correspondence]; *AP* 26:1; Ezra 4:11-12), in the vast majority of instances some expression involving שלם, "peace, well-being," or the verb ברך, "bless," has been used. In a few cases שלם was used alone and probably had only the stereotyped meaning of "greetings," functioning like the Greek *χαίρειν*. Thus, על רחום בעל טעם ושמשי ספרא . . . שלם, "To Rehum, the governor, Shimshai, the scribe, . . . greetings" (Ezra 4:17); see further *AšOst* 1(?); *5/6Ḥev* 1 (spelled סלם!); *5/6Ḥev* 4:1; *5/6Ḥev* 10:2. In Ezra 5:7b one finds שלמא כלא.[38] To this brief, formulaic usage one should probably relate the short greeting, mentioned above, that is often found on ostraca: שלם אוריה, "Greetings, Uriah" (*APE* 76/1:1); see further *AP* 77:1(?); *APE* 78/2:1; *Bodl Aram Inscr* 2:1; *Cl-G Ost* 69 A 1; *Munich* 898 A 1; *Cl-G Ost* 44 A 1; *Cl-G* 70 A 1. Likewise the short formula such as שלם אחי בכל עדן, "Peace (*or* greetings), my brother, at all times" (*Strasbourg Ost* 3).

Such brief formulae, including the name of a person, are undoubtedly stereotyped abridgements of longer greetings. But it is not easy to say from which of the several longer formulae, to be cited below, they would have been abbreviated. In the use of longer formulae one can detect a pattern with variants; I shall list about nine different forms, but one should remember that it may be questionable to regard them as distinct varieties. They fall into two main classes, those using a שלם formula, and those using a ברך formula.

(i) The most commonly attested greeting makes use of this formula: שלם מראי אלהיא כלא [ישאלו] שגיא בכל עדן, "May all the gods be much [concerned] for the well-being of my lord at all times" (*BMAP* 13:1; *AP* 41:1;

Shunnar 1).[39] Sometimes the adjective "all" may be omitted (e.g., *AP* 56:1), and sometimes the deity may be specifically named ("the God of Heaven," *AP* 30:2; 31:2; 38:[1]; 40:[1]; "Yahu Ṣebaoth," *Cl-G Ost* 167:1-2; *Cl-G Ost* 186 A 1; "Bel and Nabu, Shamash and Nergal," *Cl-G Ost* 277:1-2). The mention of the gods seems to characterize this formula as a religious wish; in one form or another it can be found in *AP* 17:1-2; 21:2; 37:1-2; 39:1; 40:1; 41:1; 56:1; *BMAP* 13:1; Shunnar 1.

(ii) An extended form of the preceding formula is found in a few instances: שלם מראן אלה שמיא ישאל שגיא בכל עדן ולרחמן ישימנך קדם דריוהוש מלכא ובני ביתא יתיר מן חד אלף וחין אריכין ינתן לך וחדה ושריר הוי בכל עדן, "May the God of Heaven be much concerned for the well-being of our lord (Bagohi) at all times, and may he show you favor[40] before Darius the King and the princes of the palace a thousand times more than now, and may he grant you a long life, and may you be[41] happy and prosperous at all times" (*AP* 30:1-3). Compare *AP* 31:1-3; *AP* 38:2-3 (expansion: "And may you have favor before the God of Heaven").

(iii) A less pious form of greeting is found in the following formula: שלם וחין שלחת לך, "Peace and life I send you" (*Herm WP* 3:5; 7:1; *Bodl Aram Inscr* 3 A 1-2; *Cambr Ost* 131-133 A 1-2). In one instance this formula is expanded with a ברך formula: שלם וחין שלחת לך ברכתך ליהה ולחנ׳, "Peace and life I send you; I bless you by Yahu and by Khnub" (*Cl-G Ost* 70 A 2-3). Not only is this formula a mixture of the secular and the religious, but it is syncretistic to boot.

(iv) Another form of a secular greeting is found in the following שלם ושררת [שגיא הושרת לך], "[I send you] greetings and prosperity[42] [in abundance]" (*Pad* I v 1). See further *AD* 2:1; 3:1; 5:1; 13:1. In one instance this is expanded by the addition of [אף] שלם תמה קדמיך [יהוי], "[moreover may there be] peace there in your presence" (*AD* 1:1). The fragmentary nature of *AP* 70:1-2 makes it difficult to determine whether the greeting used there belongs in this category or not; possibly it does.

(v) The last form of a שלם greeting is found in biblical and rabbinical texts (in the latter probably in imitation of the biblical formula): שלמכון ישגא, "and may your well-being be increased" (Dan 3:31; 6:26; *Gamaliel* 1; *Gamaliel* 2; *Gamaliel* 3).[43]

In all of these שלם formulae one may wonder whether the word means simply "greetings" or whether it is at times pregnant with further nuances, such as I have tried to bring out in some of the above translations. It is not easy for the twentieth-century reader of these texts to discern accurately the nuance intended in what seem to be stereotyped formulae.

There are two forms of the ברך formula. In the first the verb is used in a finite form: ברכתכי לפתח זי יחזני אפיכי בשלם, "I bless you by Ptaḥ, who may grant me to see your face[44] (again) in peace" (*Herm WP* 2:2). Similarly: *Herm WP* 3:1-2; 4:2; 5:1-2; 6:1-2; 8:1-2. The other form is only found once, in a sort of secondary greeting; but it is related to the first, even though the verb-form is participial: ברך אנת [ליהו אלהא]/[זי יח]וני אנפיך בשלם, "(May) you (be) blessed [by Yahu, the God, who may sh]ow me your face (again) in peace" (*Pad* I v 2-3).[45]

Such are the main features of the initial greetings in the extant Aramaic letters. One last comment should be made about them. The initial greeting is often followed by כענת, וכעת, כעת, וכען, כען, "and now," a word that either introduces the body of the message or is repeated in the course of it as a sort of message divider; it marks logical breaks in the letter and has often been compared to English "stop" in telegrams. The word was often misunderstood in the past, being taken to mean "et cetera,"[46] and was wrongly linked to the preceding greeting (see Ezra 4:10, 11b, 17; 7:12 [following גמיר!]). But now its usage is clear from extrabiblical evidence (see *AP* 30:4; *AD* 4:1; 5:1; 7:1, 3, 5; *HermWP* 1:6-11).

(d) *The Secondary Greetings.* In some letters after the initial greeting that is closely linked to the *praescriptio* there follows a series of secondary greetings, either of the type, "Say hello to . . . ," or "X sends greetings." In these formulae שלם is again used, but it is found in a cryptic expression which is not always clear; the Aramaic construct chain, which literally means "the peace of X," is used to convey the sense of both "greetings to" and "greetings from." I shall try to sort them out, but opinions may differ about them. Sometimes other words in the phrase or the immediate context help to determine the sense of the construct chain. Thus, שלם בנתסרל וארג ואסרשת ושרדר הרוץ שאל שלמהן וכעת שלם {ל}לחרוץ תנה "Greetings to Banit-SRL and ᵓRG and ᵓSRŠT and Śardur; Ḥorwaṣ asks about their well-being. Now Ḥorwaṣ is well here. . . ." Or, שלם אמי ממה שלם אחי בתי ואנשתה ובנוהי שלם רעיה "Greetings to my mother MMH, greetings to my brother BTY and his wife and children, greetings to Raᶜyah" (*HermWP* 3:2-3). Similarly: *HermWP* 4:3, 10-12, 13-14; 7:2, 3-4; *AP* 39:1-3; 40:1; 57:1(?). Two other cases are relatively clear: [אנה ומכ]בנת שאלן שלמכי ושלם תרו[ ], "[I and Makka]banit inquire about your well-being and the well-being of TRW[ ]" (*HermWP* 6:7-8). וכעת בזנה קדמי שלם אף תמה קדמ[י]ך שלם יהוי, "Now all goes well with me here;[47] and (hopefully) it goes well with you too there" (*AD* 5:1-2).

The problematic greeting is the following: [ ] לך שלם גלגל תנם שלם ינקיה, which I once translated as "To you greetings from Galgul TNM, greetings from the children![ ]."[48] The letters *TNM* should be read as תנה; compare שלם נבושה תנה, "Nabusheh is well here" (*HermWP* 2:2-3).[49] But then what is to become of לך at the beginning of the line? Moreover, the following phrase also becomes problematic, because שלם must be singular and the following word is plural. Could it mean rather "to you (comes) the greeting of Galgul here, (and) the greeting of the children"? In this case Galgul would be with the writer and would be sending his greetings; hence "greetings from . . ." would be the force of שלם. See further *Pad* I r 5 (שלם אמך וינקיא, "greetings from your mother and the children").

These secondary greetings do not always follow on the heels of the initial greeting; in one instance or other they are found further along in the body of the letter (see *HermWP* 4:10-12, 13-14). In one case the greeting is expressed toward the end of the letter, and one hesitates to include it here because it may rather be part of a concluding formula. There is so far only one example of it and no way of being sure that it is actually formulaic. Hence I include it here: שלם ביתך ובניך עד אלהיא יחוו[נ]א בהן, "Peace be to your house and your children till the gods let *us* see (our desire) *upon them*" (Cowley's translation, *AP* 34:7).[50]

(e) *The Concluding Formulae.* Only two phrases have appeared so far in a formulaic way that permits them to be described as conclusions to a message. Both of them again make use of שלם, but in different ways. The more common is of this sort: לשלמכי שלחת ספרא זנה, "I have sent this letter for your peace (of mind)" (*HermWP* 1:12-13; 6:[10]). Similarly *HermWP* 2:17; 3:13; 4:12-13; 5:9; 7:4; *Pad* II v 4-5; *Cl-G Ost* 70 B 2. The other formula is shorter and somewhat harder to explain: הוא שלם, "Be (at) peace!" (*5/6Ḥev* 4:5; *5/6Ḥev* 15:5) or in the plural, הוו שלם, "Be (at) peace!" (*5/6Ḥev* 11:3).[51]

(f) *The Mention of a Scribe or Secretary.* Toward the end of a letter one finds at times the mention of a secretary who seems to have drafted the letter and of a scribe who copied it or took the dictation for it. This is found in more or less official letters, usually in the so-called Arsames correspondence. Thus, ענני ספרא בעל [טע]ם נבועקב כתב, "ʿAnani, the secretary, drafted the order; Nabuʿaḳab wrote (it)" (*AP* 26:23, Cowley's translation).[52] And on the exterior, just before the date one reads: נבועקב ספרא, "Nabuʿaqab (was) the scribe."[53] Again, another official is sometimes introduced: בגסרו ידע טעמא זנה אחפפי ספרא, "Bagasraw is cognizant of this order; ʿAḥpipi (was) the scribe" (*AD* 4:4). Similarly: *AD* 6:6; 7:10; 8:6; 9:3; 10:5. A slightly different formula is found in one of the letters of Simon bar Kosibah: שמעון בר יהודה כתבה, "Šimʿon bar Yehudah wrote it" (*5/6Ḥev* 8:7).

(g) *The Date.* In a few instances the letter is dated. This is usually done toward the end, but once it follows the initial greeting (*AP* 21:3). In this case the date is more or less part of the message: וכעת שנתא זא שנת 5 דריווהוש מלכא, "Now this year is the 5th year of Darius, the King." Aside from that instance the date normally occurs in a prepositional phrase: ב19 למרחשון שנת 37 ארתחשס[ש], "on the 19th of Marḥešwan, the 37th year of Artaxerxes" (*AP* 17:7).[54] Or again, ב20 למרחשון שנת 17 דריהוש מלכא, "On the 20th of Marḥešwan, the 17th year of Darius, the King" (*AP* 30:30; 31:[29]). Similarly *AP* 26:28. In one instance the name of the month is given with both Egyptian and Babylonian names: ב27 לתעבי ה[ו נים]ן [ש]נת, "On the 27th of Tybi, th[at is Nis]an, [the ?th] year of [ ]" (*AP* 42:14).[55] A fuller form is sometimes used: [ב?] למחיר כתבת אגרתא זא, "[On the ?th] of Meḥir I have written this letter" (*Pad* I r 6).[56]

(h) *The Final or Exterior Address.* When the papyrus or skin letter was completed, it was usually folded up carefully and sealed. On the outside a line was written which indicated the name of the sender and the addressee. In many instances this address was similar to the *praescriptio*, or abbreviated it, or simply repeated it. Two basic forms can be detected: those that begin with the preposition "to" and those that begin with "from."

(i) *The "To" Form.* Usually the same preposition that was employed in the *praescriptio* is found in the exterior address. Thus, [אל] אחי ידניה וכנותה חילא יהודיא אחוכם חנני[ה], '[To] my brothers, Yedaniah and his colleagues, the Jewish garrison, your brother, Hanani[ah]" (*AP* 21:11). In this instance the exterior address is identical with the *praescriptio.* Similarly, to the extent that the address is preserved: *AP* 37:17; 39:5; *Pad* II r 1. Occasionally, the difference is simply a case of the titles (אח, אחת) being omitted in the exterior address (*Herm WP* 2:18) or of full names being used in it (*AP* 40:5; 41:[9?]; 42:[15?]; Shunnar 9). But often enough it is a little more complicated. Thus, the titles are changed, as we have noted above (p. 190): *Herm WP* 3:15; 6:11; 7:5. Or the titles are omitted, and the full name of the sender alone is given (*Herm WP* 4:15). Or the letter is addressed to only one person, though two are named in the *praescriptio*, and the full name of the sender is given (*Herm WP* 5:10). Or the titles are changed and full names are used (*Pad* I v 7); or some names and titles used in the *praescriptio* are omitted, but the full name of the sender is given (*AP* 38:12). In one instance the letter is addressed to a different person in the exterior address: אל אבי פסמי בר נבונתן מן מכבנת, "To my father, PSMY bar Nabunathan, from Makkabanit"; but the *praescriptio* reads: אל אחתי רעיה מן אחכי מכבנת, "To my sister, Ra^c^yah, from your brother, Makkabanit" (*Herm WP* 1:1).[57]

In the letters from Hermopolis West a further element appears, a directive for the carrier indicating the destination of the letter, usually given at the end of the line and separated a bit from the address proper. Thus, סון יבל, "(To) be carried (to) Syene" (*Herm WP* 1:14; 2:18; 3:14); אפי יבל, "(To) be carried (to) Luxor" (*Herm WP* 5:10; 6:11; 7:5); or simply סון, "(To) Syene" (*Herm WP* 4:15).[58]

(ii) *The "From" Form.* The exterior address that begins with מן instead of "to" is almost exclusively confined to the so-called Arsames correspondence, and it is not easy to say whether it represents the style of a locality or of an official letter. In many instances there is a little fuller identification of the sender or of the addressee(s), sometimes including the directive, "who are in Egypt." Thus, [מן] אר[שם בר ביתא ע]ל אר[תונת זי במצ]רי[ן], "[From] Ar[sames, the palace prince, t]o Ar[tawont who is in Eg]yp[t]" (*AD* 1).[59] In this case the address adds the identification of Arsames as "the palace prince" and the directive, "who are in Egypt." Similarly: *AD* 2, 3, 5. The simple addition of the directive is found in *AD* 4. In *AD* 7 the address identified the addressee as "the officer who is in Lower Egypt," an addition to the *praescriptio*-formula;

similarly: *AD* 8, 9, 10, 12, 13. Note the form in *AD* 11: מן ורוהי על נחתחור וחנ[ד]סירם ו[כנותה המרכריא זי במצרין], "From Warohi to Neḥtiḥur and the comptroller(?) and his col[leagues, the accountants, who are in Egypt]." Here there are an additional title and an indication of the destination. To this group belongs *AP* 26:27, which is fragmentary.

The Arsames correspondence in *AD* is also distinctive in having a docket written on the outside along with the address; it explains in brief the contents of the letter. For example, על דשנא זי אחחפי פקידא זי [במצ]רין, "Concerning the grant of ᶜAḥḥapi, the officer who is in Egypt" (*AD* 2). This item is often very difficult to read. Traces of it can be found in *AD* 1, 3, 4, 5, 7, 9, 10, 12.

There is one letter in the Arsames correspondence that completely lacks an address, but the nature of the letter explains the reason for the absence of it. It is a sort of passport, a letter to be carried and showed to various subordinate officials along the way to Egypt, who are instructed by it to provide rations and (presumably) lodging for the bearer and his travelling companions (*AD* 6). It is obviously an official letter, addressed to several persons in different places.

III. *Conclusion*

Having come to the end of the enumeration of the items that are formulaic or somewhat stereotyped in Aramaic letters, we may ask now to what extent one can detect a structure in them. This is not easy to answer, but the majority of the letters normally have the following schema: (1) the *praescriptio*, (2) the initial greeting, either religious or secular, (3) secondary greetings, (4) the body of the letter, and (5) a concluding statement. Whether one should include the exterior address is debatable. Many of these features have a similarity with counterparts in other corpora of letters from the ancient eastern Mediterranean world, which a comparative study would illustrate in abundance. As for the biblical letters, those in Ezra supply the closest parallels to the extrabiblical material; those in Daniel less so—and there is a real question whether the latter should even be considered. Certain items in NT epistolography find illustration in some elements of the Aramaic letters discussed above, but a more detailed study of the bearing of Aramaic letters on them remains to be done.

Lastly, it should be noted that because Aramaic was used as a sort of international language over a wide area and for several centuries, some of the different formulae and features may have to be accounted for in this way. There is no certainty that the various features which we have sorted out were all being used simultaneously. At times some of the features were obviously confined to one group of letters or other; hence one has to be careful about extrapolating and predicating such features of Aramaic epistolography as a whole.

CHART 1

ARAMAIC LETTERS ON SKIN OR PAPYRUS

	Name and Provenience	*Museum No.*	*Easy Access*	*Editio Princeps*
1	ʾAdon Letter (Saqqarah)	Cairo 86984	*KAI* 266	A. Dupont-Sommer, *Sem* 1 (1948) 43-68
2	Hermopolis West Papyrus I			E. Bresciani and M. Kamil, *Le lettere aramaiche di Hermopoli* (AdANdL, Memorie VIII/xii/5; Rome: Accademia Nazionale dei Lincei, 1966) 372-82
3	HermWP II			Ibid., 384-90
4	HermWP III			Ibid., 392-96
5	HermWP IV			Ibid., 398-403
6	HermWP V			Ibid., 404-7
7	HermWP VI			Ibid., 408-10
8	HermWP VII			Ibid., 412-15
9	HermWP VIII			Ibid., 416-18
10	Barley(?) Letter (Elephantine, 484 B.C.)	Berlin 13455	*AP* 4	E. Sachau, *Aramäische Papyrus und Ostraka* (Leipzig: Hinrichs, 1911), pl. 36, pap. 41, p. 136
11	Letter to Higher Court (Elephantine, 435 B.C.)	Berlin 13478	*AP* 16	*APO*, pl. 7, pap. 7, pp. 41-43
12	Letter to Arsames (Elephantine, 428 B.C.)	Berlin 13480	*AP* 17	*APO*, pl. 5, pap. 4, pp. 34-35
13	Passover Letter (Elephantine, 419 B.C.)	Berlin 13464	*AP* 21	*APO*, pl. 6, pap. 6, pp. 36-40
14	Letter of Boat Repairs (Elephantine, 412 B.C.)	Berlin 13492	*AP* 26	*APO*, pls. 8-9, pap. 8, pp. 44-49
15	Petition to Satrap (Elephantine, 410 B.C.)	Strasbourg	*AP* 27	J. Euting, *MPAIBL* 11/2 (1903) 297-311
16	Petition to Bagohi (Elephantine, 408 B.C.)	Berlin 13495	*AP* 30	*APO*, pls. 1-2, pap. 1, pp. 3-22
17	Duplicate of §16 (Elephantine, 408 B.C.)	Berlin 13496	*AP* 31	*APO*, pl. 3, pap. 2, pp. 23-26
18	Memo from Bagohi to Jews (Elephantine, 408 B.C.)	Berlin 13497	*AP* 32	*APO*, pl. 4, pap. 3, pp. 28-30
19	Letter to Satrap (Elephantine, 407 B.C.)	Berlin 13472	*AP* 33	*APO*, pl. 4, pap. 5, pp. 31-33
20	Letter to Satrap (Elephantine, 407 B.C.)	Berlin 13471	*AP* 34	*APO*, pl. 15, pap. 15, pp. 63-65
21	Letter from Shewa b. Z. (Elephantine, 399 B.C.)	Brooklyn 47.218.151	*BMAP* 13	E. G. Kraeling, *BMAP*, pp. 281-90
22	Letter to Yedaniah (Elephantine, 5th c.)	Berlin 13468	*AP* 37	*APO*, pl. 11, pap. 10, pp. 51-54
23	Letter to Yedaniah (Elephantine, 5th c.)	Berlin 13494	*AP* 38	*APO*, pl. 12, pap. 11, pp. 55-57
24	Letter to Lady Shelwah (Elephantine, 5/4 c.)	Berlin 13462	*AP* 39	*APO*, pl. 13, pap. 12, pp. 58-59
25	Letter of Hosea to Palṭi (Elephantine, 5/4 c.)	Berlin 13473	*AP* 40	*APO*, pl. 13, pap. 14, pp. 59-60
26	L. to Seḥo, my brother (Elephantine, 5/4 c.)	Berlin 13463	*AP* 41	*APO*, pl. 14, pap. 13, pp. 60-61
27	Business Letter (Elephantine, 5/4 c.)	Berlin 13490	*AP* 42	*APO*, pl. 16, pap. 16, pp. 66-68
28	Fragmentary Letters (Elephantine, 5/4 c.)	Berlin 13457	*AP* 54	*APO*, pl. 36, pap. 39, pp. 133-34
29	Letter Fragment (Elephantine, 5/4 c.)	Berlin 13460	*AP* 55	*APO*, pl. 36, pap. 40, p. 135
30	Letter Fragment (Elephantine, 4th c.)	Berlin 13456	*AP* 56	*APO*, pl. 37, pap. 43, p. 138
31	Letter Fragment (Elephantine, 4th c.)	Berlin 13450	*AP* 57	*APO*, pl. 38, pap. 45, p. 140
32	Address of Letter (Elephantine, 4th c.)	Berlin 13454	*AP* 58	*APO*, pl. 37, pap. 42, pp. 137-38
33	L. to Mithravahisht (Egypt, ?)		*AP* 70	*CIS* 2.144 + pl. XV
34	Garrison Letter (Elephantine, 5/4 c.)		*AP* 80	M. de Vogüé, *CRAIBL* 1902, p. 49
35	Letter Fragments (Elephantine, 5/4 c.)		*RES* 248	M. de Vogüé, *CRAIBL* 1902, 49

	Name and Provenience	*Museum No.*	*Easy Access*	*Editio Princeps*
36	Letter about a Boat (Elephantine, 5/4 c.)	Berlin 23000		Z. Shunnar, in *Geschichte Mittelasiens im Altertum* (eds. F. Altheim and R. Stiehl; Berlin, 1970) 111-17 (+pls. 1-2)
37	Mariette Fragment (Memphis, 4th c.)		*AP* 77	J. Euting, *SPAW* 23 (1887) 670; *CIS* 2. 152, pl. XX
38	Padua Pap. Letter I (Egypt, 5th c.)			E. Bresciani, *RSO* 35 (1960) 11-24 (+pls. 1-5), esp. pp. 18-22
39	Padua Pap. Letter II			Ibid., 22-24
40	Padua Pap. Letter III			Ibid., 24
41	Arsames Letter I (found in Egypt; 5th c.)	Bodleian Library, pellis aramaica VI	*AD* 1	G. R. Driver, *AD*, pp. 10-12
42	Arsames Letter II	Bodl. L. p. a. XII	*AD* 2	Ibid., 12-13
43	Arsames Letter III	Bodl. L. p. a. VII	*AD* 3	Ibid., 13-15
44	Arsames Letter IV	Bodl. L. p. a. II	*AD* 4	Ibid., 16-17
45	Arsames Letter V	Bodl. L. p. a. IV	*AD* 5	Ibid., 17-20
46	Arsames Letter VI	Bodl. L. p. a. VIII	*AD* 6	Ibid., 20-23
47	Arsames Letter VII	Bodl. L. p. a. I	*AD* 7	Ibid., 23-25
48	Arsames Letter VIII	Bodl. L. p. a. XIII	*AD* 8	Ibid., 25-28
49	Arsames Letter IX	Bodl. L. p. a. III	*AD* 9	Ibid., 28-29
50	Arsames Letter X	Bodl. L. p. a. IX	*AD* 10	Ibid., 29-31
51	Warohi Letter (found in Egypt, 5th c.)	Bodl. L. p. a. V	*AD* 11	Ibid., 31-33
52	Warphish Letter (found in Egypt, 5th c.)	Bodl. L. p. a. XIV	*AD* 12	Ibid., 33-35
53	Artahay Letter (found in Egypt, 5th c.)	Bodl. L. p. a. X	*AD* 13	Ibid., 35-36
54	Letter to King Artaxerxes (5th c.)		Ezra 4:11-16	
55	Letter to Rehum and Shimshai (5th c.)		Ezra 4:17-22	
56	Letter to King Darius		Ezra 5:7b-17	
57	Letter(?) to Tattenai		Ezra 6:6-12	
58	Letter to Ezra		Ezra 7:12-26	
59	Nebuchadrezzar's Encyclical(?)		Dan 3:31-33 (98-100)	Cf. LXX 4:37b
60	Darius' Letter to All Peoples		Dan 6:26-28	
61	Letter of Šim'on bar Kosibah I		*5/6Ḥev* 1	E. Y. Kutscher, *Lěš* 25 (1961) 119-21
62	L. of Š. b. Kosibah II		*5/6Ḥev* 2	Ibid., 122
63	L. of Š. b. Kosibah III		*5/6Ḥev* 4	Ibid., 122-24
64	L. of Š. b. Kosibah IV		*5/6Ḥev* 8	Ibid., 124-25
65	L. of Š. b. Kosibah V		*5/6Ḥev* 10	Ibid., 125-26
66	L. of Š. b. Kosibah VI		*5/6Ḥev* 11	Ibid., 126-27
67	L. of Š. b. Kosibah VII		*5/6Ḥev* 14	Ibid., 127-29
68	L. of Š. b. Kosibah VIII		*5/6Ḥev* 15	Ibid., 129
69	Letter of R. Gamaliel I		*ArDial* p. 3	jSanhedrin 18d
70	Letter of R. Gamaliel II		*ArDial* p. 3	jSanhedrin 18d
71	Letter of R. Gamaliel III		*ArDial* p. 3	jSanhedrin 18d
72	L. of R. Judah the Prince to Emperor Antoninus		*AAH* I/1, p. 64	*Běrēšît Rabbāh* 75
73	Christian Palestinian Aramaic Letter (8th-10th c. A.D.)		papMird A	J. T. Milik, *RB* 60 (1953) 533-39; *Bib* 42 (1961) 21-27

CHART 2

ARAMAIC MESSAGES ON OSTRACA

	Name and Provenience	*Museum No.*	*Easy Access*	*Editio Princeps*
1	Asshur Ostracon (650 B.C.)	Berlin 8384	*KAI* 233	M. Lidzbarski, *ZA* 31 (1917-18) 193-202
2	Murabba at Letter(?) (100-50 B.C.)	Ecole Biblique	*Mur* 72	J. T. Milik, *Les grottes de Murabba'at* (DJD 2; Oxford: Clarendon, 1961) 172-74
3	Yarḥaw Ostracon (Elephantine, 5/4 c.)	Cl-G Ost 277		A. Dupont-Sommer, *RHR* 128 (1944) 28-39
4	Double Message to Uriah and Ahitab (Elephantine, 5/4 c.)	Berlin 11383	*APE* 76/1	E. Sachau, *APO*, no. 76/1, pl. 63/1, pp. 233-34
5	Ostracon to ḤWNY (Elephantine, 5/4 c.)	Berlin 11364	*APE* 76/2	*APO*, 76/2, pl. 63/2, pp. 234-35
6	Fragmentary Ostracon (Elephantine, 5/4 c.)	Berlin 11369	*APE* 76/3	*APO*, 76/3, pl. 63/3, p. 235
7	Fragmentary Ostracon (Elephantine, 5/4 c.)	Berlin 11384	*APE* 76/4	*APO*, 76/4, pl. 63/4, pp. 235-36
8	Fragmentary Ostracon (Elephantine, 5/4 c.)	Berlin 11377	*APE* 76/5	*APO*, 76/5, pl. 63/5, p. 236
9	Fragmentary Ostracon (Elephantine, 5/4 c.)	Berlin 8763	*RES* 496, 1804	A. Cowley, *PSBA* 25 (1903) 314
10	Passover Ostracon (Elephantine, 5/4 c.)	Berlin 10679	*APE* 77/2	M. Lidzbarski, *Ephemeris*, 2.229-34
11	Hosha'yah Ostracon (Elephantine 5/4 c.)	Bodleian Libr. Ost.	*RES* 1793	A. H. Sayce, *PSBA* 33 (1911) 183-84
12	Fragmentary Ostracon (Elephantine, 5/4 c.)	Berlin 11380	*APE* 78/1	*APO*, 78/1, pl. 65/1, pp. 238-39
13	Aḥutab Ostracon (Elephantine, 5/4 c.)	Berlin 10680	*APE* 78/2	M. Lidzbarski, *Ephemeris*, 2.234-36; 3.257, n. 1
14	Dream Ostracon (Elephantine, 5/4 c.)	Berlin 1137	*KAI* 270	A. Dupont-Sommer, *ASAE* 48 (1948) 117-30 (+pl. II)
15	Salt Ostracon (Elephantine, 5/4 c.)	Cl-G Ost 16		A. Dupont-Sommer, *ASAE* 48 (1948) 109-16 (+pl. I)
16	Fragmentary Ostracon (Elephantine, 5/4 c.)	Berlin 11367		*APO*, 80/6, pl. 67/6, p. 242
17	Uriah Ostracon (Elephantine, 5/4 c.)	Ashmolean Mus. (lost)	*APE* 91	A. Cowley, *PSBA* 25 (1903) 259-66
18	Cucumber Ostracon (Elephantine, 5/4 c.)	Bodleian, Aram Inscr 2	*RES* 493, 1801	A. Cowley, *PSBA* 25 (1903) 311-12
19	Fragmentary Ostracon (Elephantine, 5/4 c.)	Bodleian, Aram Inscr 3	*RES* 494, 1802	A. Cowley, *PSBA* 25 (1903) 312
20	Fragmentary Ostracon (Elephantine, 5/4 c.)	British Mus. 14220	*APE* 95	*CIS* 2.139 (+pl. XII)
21	Haggai Ostracon (Elephantine, 5/4 c.)	Cairo Ost 35468a	*RES* 1295	A. H. Sayce, *PSBA* 31 (1909) 154-55
22	Barley Ostracon (Elephantine, 5/4 c.)	Cairo Ost 35468b	*RES* 1296	M. Lidzbarski, *Ephemeris*, 3.121-22; N. Aimé-Giron, *Textes araméens d'Egypte* (Cairo: Institut français, 1931), No. 3
23	Nabudalah Ostracon (Elephantine, 5/4 c.)	Cairo Ost 49635		N. Aimé-Giron, *ASAE* 26 (1926) 23-27
24	Shallu'ah Ostracon (Elephantine, 5/4 c.)	Cairo Ost 48624		N. Aimé-Giron, *ASAE* 26 (1926) 27-29
25	Fragmentary Ostracon (Elephantine, 5/4 c.)	Cairo Ost 49625		N. Aimé-Giron, *ASAE* 26 (1926) 29-31
26	Yirpeyah Ostracon (Elephantine, 5/4 c.)	Munich 898	*RES* 1298	M. Lidzbarski, *Ephemeris*, 3.21-22
27	Fragmentary Ostracon (Elephantine, 5/4 c.)	Munich 899	*RES* 1299	M. Lidzbarski, *Ephemeris*, 3.20-21
28	Yedaniah Ostracon (Elephantine, 5/4 c.)	Cl-G Ost 44		A. Dupont-Sommer, *Hebrew and Semitic Studies: Presented to G. R. Driver* (eds. D. W. Thomas and W. D. McHardy; Oxford: Clarendon, 1963) 53-58
29	Michiah Ostracon (Elephantine, 5/4 c.)	Cl-G Ost 70	*ANET* 491	A. Dupont-Sommer, *RHR* 130 (1945) 17-28

	Name and Provenience	Museum No.	Easy Access	Editio Princeps
30	Yislaḥ Ostracon (Elephantine, 5/4 c.)	Cl-G Ost 152	*AC* 33A	A. Dupont-Sommer, *Sem* 2 (1949) 29-39
31	Yahu-Ṣeba'oth Ostracon (Elephantine, 5/4 c.)	Cl-G Ost 167		A. Dupont-Sommer, *CRAIBL* 1947, pp. 179-81
32	Aḥutab Ostracon (Elephantine, 5/4 c.)	Cl-G Ost 169		A. Dupont-Sommer, *RevEtSém* 1941-45, pp. 65-75
33	Fragmentary Ostracon (Elephantine, 5/4 c.)	Cl-G Ost 186	*AC* 33B	A. Dupont-Sommer, *Scritti in onore di Giuseppe Furlani* (= *RSO* 32 [1957]; Rome: Bardi, 1957) 403-9
34	Parasceve Ostracon (Elephantine, 5/4 c.)	Cl-G Ost 204		A. Dupont-Sommer, *MPAIBL* 15 (1950) 67-88
35	Qawwiliah Ostracon (Elephantine, 5/4 c.)	Cambridge 131-33		A. Cowley, *JRAS* 61 (1929) 107-11
36	Meshullak Ostracon (Elephantine, 5/4 c.)	Berlin 11379		*APO*, 84/7, pl. 71/7, p. 250
37	Yashib Ostracon (bought at Edfu; probably from 2d c. B.C.)	Berlin 10964	*APE* 81/1	*APO*, 81/1, pl. 68/1, p. 243
38	Leptines Ostracon (found in Egypt; Hellenistic period)	Strasbourg Libr.	*RES* 1300	M. Lidzbarski, *Ephemeris*, 3.23-25

NOTES TO CHAPTER 8

*Originally published as "Some Notes on Aramaic Epistolography," *JBL* 93 (1974) 201-25.

[1]A cursory treatment of it can be found in G. Beer, "Zur israelitisch-jüdischen Briefliteratur," *Alttestamentliche Studien Rudolf Kittel zum 60. Geburtstag dargebracht* (ed. A. Alt et al.; Leipzig: Hinrichs, 1913) 20-41. See also the article by J. Marty in n. 46 below.

[2]This paper grew out of a consultation on ancient letter-writing held at the SBL annual meeting in Chicago, 1973.

[3]A study of Aramaic epistolography is being undertaken by John David Whitehead.

[4]For instance, the theories of C. C. Torrey about Aramaic Gospels, the Aramaic source(s) of Acts, R. Bultmann's Aramaic Revelatory Discourse source in John, the question of Papias' *logia* underlying Matthew, etc. See my methodological remarks in chap. 1 above (pp. 1–27).

[5]See, e.g., the writings of W. C. van Unnik, W. F. Albright and C. S. Mann, and P. Grelot referred to above, p. 21, end of n. 15.

[6]*Do You Know Greek? How Much Greek Could the First Jewish Christians Have Known?* (p. 50 above, n. 32).

[7]This proposal has been put forth, for instance, for Philippians by H. E. G. Paulus, J. Schmid, E. Lohmeyer, L. Johnson; for Colossians, by M. Goguel, E. Lohmeyer, J. de Zwaan, M. Dibelius, L. Johnson.

[8]For further details on these phases of the Aramaic language, see pp. 57–84 above.

[9]The notable exception is the Aššur Ostracon, which does not come from Egypt, but was sent (ca. 650 B.C.) from Babylon to Assyria and contains a military report (about fugitive prisoners to be returned) from Beletir, a captain of the Assyrian cavalry, to Pirawur; and another message as well to Nabuzerušabši (whom he tries to appease). The text is written on six fragments of the ostracon, is incomplete, and difficult to interpret. See M. Lidzbarski, *Altaramäische Urkunden aus Assur* (Wissenschaftliche Veröffentlichung der deutschen Orient-Gesellschaft, 38; Leipzig: Hinrichs, 1921) 5-15. See further *Ephemeris* 2. 1-23; *AC* 14; *KAI* §233; also M. Lidzbarski, "Ein aramäischer Brief aus der Zeit Ašurbanipals," *MDOG* 58 (1917) 50-52 [preliminary report]; *ZA*

31 (1917-18) 193-202; D. H. Baneth, "Zu dem aramäischen Brief aus der Zeit Assurbanipals," *OLZ* 22 (1919) 55-58; (Anonymous), "Zeitschriftenschau," *ZAW* 47 (1929) 150-51; R. A. Bowman, "An Interpretation of the Assur Ostracon," *Royal Correspondence of the Assyrian Empire* (ed. L. Waterman; University of Michigan Studies, Humanistic Series, 20; Ann Arbor: University of Michigan) 4 (1936) 273-82; A. Dupont-Sommer, "Séance du 22 octobre," *CRAIBL* 1943, 465-66; "L'ostracon araméen d'Assour," *Syria* 24 (1944-45) 24-61; *Les Araméens* (L'orient ancien illustré; Paris: Maisonneuve, 1949) 85.

[10]As an aid to the reader, two charts listing the known Aramaic letters and ostraca are appended to this article. The author would be grateful to readers who might detect omissions or errors in them and send them on to him; obviously no claim is made for the exhaustive character of these lists. See now D. Pardee, *JBL* 97 (1978) 323 n. 9.

[11]*Light from the Ancient East* (London: Hodder and Stoughton, 1927) 229.

[12]Ibid., 228.

[13]See, e.g., O. Roller, *Das Formular der paulinischen Briefe: Ein Beitrag zur Lehre vom antiken Briefe* (Stuttgart: Kohlhammer, 1933) 23-29 (and Anm. 144-52); J. Sykutris, "Epistolographie," *RE* Suppl. 5 (1931) 187; W. G. Doty, *Letters in Primitive Christianity* (Philadelphia: Fortress, 1973) 24-27; "The Classification of Epistolary Literature," *CBQ* 31 (1969) 183-99.

[14]Engl. 4:1-4. This is the introduction to the story of Nebuchadrezzar's madness. Verse 31 (Engl. 4:1) reads like the *praescriptio* of an ancient Aramaic letter: "King Nebuchadrezzar to all peoples, nations, and languages that dwell in all the earth: Peace be multiplied to you!" The epistolary character of this introduction was recognized in some MSS of the so-called LXX version of Daniel; 3:31(98) reads: *ἀρχὴ τῆς ἐπιστολῆς*. At the end of the story the same version records: *ἔγραψε δὲ ὁ βασιλεὺς Ναβουχοδόνοσορ ἐπιστολὴν ἐγκύκλιον πᾶσι τοῖς κατὰ τόπον ἔθνεσι καὶ χώραις καὶ γλώσσαις πάσαις ταῖς οἰκούσαις ἐν πάσαις ταῖς χώραις* . . . (4:37b). But the rest of the introduction (3:32-33 [Engl. 4:2-3]) immediately alerts the reader to a change of literary form, and 4:1 (Engl. 4:4) begins the narrative proper. In the general setting of the stories in Daniel 1-6 one may hesitate about the function of that introduction, and hence about the quasi-epistolary character of this section in Daniel.

[15]The letter of Rehum, the commander, and Shimshai, the scribe, et al., "settled in the cities of Samaria and in the rest of the province Beyond the River," to King Artaxerxes II about the Jews who were rebuilding "that rebellious and wicked city" (Ezra 4:11-16); Artaxerxes' reply to Rehum, Shimshai, and their associates in Jerusalem to stop the rebuilding of the city (Ezra 4:17-22); the letter of Tattenai, governor of the province Beyond the River, and Shethar-bozenai, and their associates to King Darius I about the Jews in the province of Judah who were rebuilding the "house of God which is in Jerusalem" (Ezra 5:7b-17); Darius' reply (lacking a *praescriptio*) to Tattenai, Shethar-bozenai, and their associates, instructing them to "let the work on this house of God alone; let the . . . Jews rebuild this house of God on its site" (Ezra 6:6-12); Letter of Artaxerxes II to Ezra, the priest and scribe, conveying to him the king's decree (permission to go to Jerusalem, to make inquiries about Judah and Jerusalem, to convey the silver and gold which the king and his counsellors offer to the God of Israel), as well as the free-will offerings, money intended for temple sacrifices and other needs, and to take back the temple vessels (Ezra 7:12-26).

[16]See G. R. Driver, *Aramaic Documents* (p. 76 above, n. 21).

[17]Only a few of these letters have seen preliminary publication: see Y. Yadin, "Expedition D," *IEJ* 11 (1961) 36-52; "מחנא ד," *Yediot* 25 (1961) 49-64. Cf. E. Y. Kutscher, "לשונן של האיגרות העבריות והארמיות של בר־כוסבא ובני דורו" [The Languages of the Hebrew and Aramaic Letters of Bar Cocheba and His Contemporaries], *Lĕšonénu* 25 (1961) 117-23; 26 (1962) 7-23; Y. Yadin, "New Discoveries in the Judaean Desert," *BA* 24 (1961) 34-50; "More on the Letters of Bar Cocheba," *BA* 24 (1961) 86-95; "Expedition D—The Cave of Letters," *IEJ* 12 (1962) 227-57; "מחנא ד׳—מערת האיגרות," *Yediot* 26 (1962) 204-36; המִמצאים ממי בר־כוכבא במערת האיגרות: *The Finds from the Bar-Kokhba Period in the "Cave of Letters"* (Judean Desert Studies; Jerusalem: Israel Exploration Society and the Bialik Foundation, 1963). Cf. Y. Aharoni, "The Caves of Naḥal Ḥever," *ᶜAtiqot* 3 (1961) 148-62; M. C. Salzmann, "Ricerche in Israele," *BeO* 3 (1961) 23-25.

[18]A. Dupont-Sommer, "Un papyrus araméen d'époque saïte découvert à Saqqarah," *Semitica* 1 (1948) 43–68; see pp. 231–42 below.

[19]This letter was first published by E. Sachau, *Aramäische Papyrus und Ostraka* (see p. 76 above, n. 21), §1, pls. 1-2. The subsequent literature on this letter is vast and cannot be included here.

[20]See F. M. Cross, Jr., "The Discovery of the Samaria Papyri," *BA* 26 (1963) 110-21.

[21]For recent discussions of these texts, see B. Porten, *Archives from Elephantine: The Life of an Ancient Jewish Military Colony* (Berkeley / Los Angeles: University of California, 1968) 105-22; P. Grelot, *Documents araméens d'Egypte* (p. 26 above, n. 89), 386–419.

[22]The so-called Passover Letter (*AP* 21) has been the subject of considerable recent discussion: W. R. Arnold, "The Passover Papyrus from Elephantine," *JBL* 31 (1912) 1-33; J. Barth, "Zu den Papyri von Elephantine (ed. Sachau)," *OLZ* 15 (1912) 10-11; B. Couroyer, "L'origine égyptienne du mot 'Pâque,'" *RB* 62 (1952) 381-96; A. Dupont-Sommer, "La Pâque dans les documents araméens d'Eléphantine," *CRAIBL* 1945, pp. 174-76; "Sur la fête de la Pâque dans les documents arameéns d'Eléphantine," *REJ* 107 (1946–47) 39–51; H. J. Elhorst, "The Passover Papyrus from Elephantine," *JBL* 31 (1912) 147–49; P. Grelot, "Etudes sur le 'Papyrus Pascal' d'Eléphantine," *VT* 4 (1954) 349-84; "Le papyrus pascal d'Eléphantine et le problème du Pentateuque," *VT* 5 (1955) 250-65; "Le papyrus pascal d'Eléphantine: Nouvel examen," *VT* 17 (1967) 114-17; "Le papyrus pascal d'Eléphantine: Essai de restauration," *VT* 17 (1967) 201-7; "Le papyrus pascal d'Eléphantine et les lettres d'Hermopolis," *VT* 17 (1967) 481-83; *Documents araméens d'Egypte,* 373-85; J. Halévy, "La Pâque à Eléphantine," *JA* 19 (1912) 622-23; E. G. Kraeling, *BMAP*, 93 (translation); E. Meyer, "Zu den aramäischen Papyri von Elephantine," *SPAW* 47 (1911) 1026-53; C. Steuernagel, "Die jüdisch-aramäischen Papyri und Ostraka aus Elephantine und ihre Bedeutung für die Kenntnis palästinensischer Verhältnisse," *ZDPV* 35 (1912) 85-105, esp. pp. 101-4; "Zum Passa-Massothfest," *ZAW* 31 (1911) 310; C. C. Torrey, "The Letters Prefixed to Second Maccabees," *JAOS* 60 (1950) 120-50; A. Vincent, *La religion des Judéo-Araméens d'Eléphantine* (Paris: Geuthner, 1937) 237-311; B. Porten, *Archives from Elephantine,* 130-33; S. Talmon, "Divergences in Calendar-Reckoning in Ephraim and Judah," *VT* 8 (1958) 48-74, esp. pp. 72-73. See further my commentary on the *Genesis Apocryphon of Qumran Cave I* (2d ed.) 219.

[23]E. Bresciani and M. Kamil, *Le lettere aramaiche di Hermopoli* (p. 76 above, n. 21), 357–428 (+ pls. I-X). See further M. Dahood, "La regina del cielo in Geremia," *RivB* 8 (1960) 166-68; E. Bresciani, "Nouveaux papyrus araméens d'époque perse provenant d'Hermopolis," *CRAIBL* 1967, pp. 301-2; A. Dupont-Sommer, "Observations sur les papyrus araméens d'époque perse provenant d'Hermopolis," *CRAIBL* 1967, pp. 302-4; P. Grelot, "Le papyrus pascal d'Eléphantine et les lettres d'Hermopolis," *VT* 17 (1967) 481-83; review of the *editio princeps, RB* 74 (1967) 432-37; R. Yaron, "'כסף זוז' בתעודות יב," *Lĕšonénu* 31 (1967) 287-88; J. T. Milik, "Les papyrus araméens d'Hermoupolis et les cultes syro-phéniciens en Egypte perse," *Bib* 48 (1967) 546-622; B. Porten and J. C. Greenfield, "The Aramaic Papyri from Hermopolis," *ZAW* 80 (1968) 216-31; B. Porten, *Archives from Elephantine,* 164-77; E. Hammershaimb, "Some Remarks on the Aramaic Letters from Hermopolis," *VT* 18 (1968) 265-67; J. P. Hayes and J. Hoftijzer, "Notae hermopolitanae," *VT* 20 (1970) 98-106; R. du Mesnil du Buisson, *Etudes sur les dieux phéniciens hérités par l'empire romain* (Etudes préliminaires aux religions orientales dans l'empire romain, 14; Leiden: Brill, 1970) 81-104; E. Hammershaimb, "De aramaiske papyri frå Hermopolis," *DTT* 34 (1971) 81-104; H. Donner, "Bemerkungen zum Verständnis zweier aramäischer Briefe aus Hermopolis," *Near Eastern Studies in Honor of William Foxwell Albright* (ed. H. Goedicke; London / Baltimore: The Johns Hopkins University, 1971) 75-85; E. Y. Kutscher, "The Hermopolis Papyri," *Israel Oriental Studies* 1 (1971) 103-19; J. Naveh, "The Palaeography of the Hermopolis Papyri," *Israel Oriental Studies* 1 (1971) 120-22; P. Grelot, *Documents araméens d'Egypte,* §25-31; J. C. L. Gibson, *Textbook of Syrian Semitic Inscriptions: Vol. II, Aramaic Inscriptions* (Oxford: Clarendon, 1975) 125-43. The numerous preliminary notices of the discovery of these letters are omitted here.

[24]See P. Grelot, "Les données de l'onomastique," *Documents araméens d'Egypte,* 455-502; "Notes d'onomastique sur les textes araméens d'Egypte," *Sem* 21 (1971) 95-117; M. H. Silverman, "Aramean Name-Types in the Elephantine Documents," *JAOS* 89 (1969) 691-709.

[25]5/6Ḥev 15 aram (see E. Y. Kutscher, *Lĕšonénu* 25 [1961] 129). See my discussion of it, *ESBNT*, 336-38.

[26]The Greek letter apparently comes from the same cave (5/6 Ḥev); see pp. 35–36 above.

[27]See B. Porten, *Archives from Elephantine* (n. 21 above), 3–27.

[28]See further *AP* 32:2; 63:10; cf. Sefire I C 2-3.

[29]As may be the case in Dan 6:26, a literary context that could tolerate the omission of it. Cf. Ezra 6:6.

[30]For an explanation of this translation of the *praescriptio*, see pp. 233–35 below.

[31]Because of the fragmentary nature of this letter, one cannot be certain about the form of the *praescriptio*; it may rather belong to form (ii).

[32]For a discussion of these letters, see pp. 219–30 below.

[33]Possibly one should include here *AP* 54:10 ([מן ע]קבנבו שלם מראי). For a discussion of whether ancient Aramaic letters began with מן or not, see S. Zeitlin, "The Fiction of the Recent Discoveries near the Dead Sea," *JQR* 44 (1953-54) 85-115; S. Yeivin, "Some Notes on the Documents from Wadi Murabba^cat Dating from the Days of Bar-Kokh^ɔba," *Atiqot* 1 (1955) 95-108.

[34]The translation of גמיר is problematic. H. L. Ginsberg (in *AAH*, 1/2, p. 21) takes it as "et cetera (i.e., 'and the rest of the customary salutation')." E. Vogt (*Lexicon linguae aramaicae Veteris Testamenti* [p. 23 above, n. 41], 35) prefers to supply ‹שלם› before גמיר: "‹salutem› perfectam (precor)."

[35]See E. Bresciani and M. Kamil, *Le lettere aramaiche,* 365-66.

[36]*BMAP* 13:[1] is problematic; Kraeling restores line 1 on the basis of the exterior address, where the *aleph* is far from certain. The preposition also occurs in the final or exterior addresses.

[37]See further *AP* 21:2, 11; 40:1, 5; 41:1, 9; *Cl-G Ost* 227:1-2. Cf. 1QapGen 2:9. See my remarks on this question on p. 221 below.

[38]For further discussion of this phrase, see pp. 210–11 below.

[39]The verb ישאלו is restored with certainty, given the many other instances of its use; literally, "may they seek after."

[40]Literally, "and may he set you for favor before Darius."

[41]Literally, "be happy and prosperous" (הוי is the impv.).

[42]The meaning of שררת is not certain; it is usually translated "prosperity," but it may rather mean "stability" or "security."

[43]This formula probably underlies the greeting in 1 Pet 1:2, which may be influenced, of course, more directly by the Greek of Dan 4:1 (Theodotion).

[44]The verb here is the haphel of חזי, "may he cause me to see." A variant is found in *HermWP* 4:2; 6:2; *Pad* I v 3: יחוני, "may he show me."

[45]"Yahu, the God" is restored on the basis of the temple of Yahu that is greeted in line 1; see pp. 219–22 below.

[46]See J. Marty, "Contribution à l'étude de fragments epistolaires antiques, conservés principalement dans la Bible hébraïque: Les formules de salutation," *Mélanges syriens offerts à Monsieur René Dussaud* (Paris: Geuthner, 1939), 2. 845-55, esp. p. 849.

[47]Literally, "and now in this (place?) before me (there is) peace; moreover there before you may there be peace."

[48]See p. 228 below.

[49]In this case שלם is probably not the noun, but the adjective *šĕlim*; this would fit with Galgul. But how can one construe it with the following ינקיה? Here שלם seems to be a noun in the construct state, as it does also in *Pad* I r 5.

[50]For the restoration and translation of the end of this line, see *AP* 30:16; 31:15.

[51]My translation is literal; the phrase may mean simply something like "goodbye" or "farewell." For the construction, see E. Y. Kutscher, *Lĕšonénu* 25 (1961) 123-24.

[52]Literally, "^{c}Anani, the clerk, (is) the issuer of the order; Nabu^{c}aqab, the scribe."

[53]Cowley's translation is wrong at this point.

[54]A peculiar word follows this date, לותהם. It seems to mean "to them," but no adequate explanation of it has yet been proposed.

[55]The double dating, first with an Egyptian name and then with a Babylonian equivalent, is otherwise found in many documents of the Elephantine corpus which are non-epistolary: e.g., *AP* 5:1; 6:1; 8:1; 10:1; *BMAP* 1:1; 3:1; 4:1.

[56]In this case a further note was appended, a sort of postscript.

[57]There is also one instance in which the *praescriptio* is missing so that one cannot tell whether the preserved address conforms to it or not (*AP* 56:4).

[58]The exact construction of this additional element is not clear. There is no difficulty in the lack of a preposition before the place name; this is common in other texts with verbs expressing motion toward a place (see p. 224 below). But how should one explain יבל, since in *Herm WP* 7:5 it is written fully as יובל? Is it the 3d sg. masc. impf. causative passive, "Let it (viz., ספרא זנה) be carried"? This seems to be the best explanation.

[59]G. R. Driver chose not to number the addresses in relation to other lines in this correspondence. The address and the docket usually precede the text of the letter in his edition. The restoration of this address is certain, being based on details in other letters of the same group.

Chapter 9

The Syntax of כל, כלא, "All" in Aramaic Texts from Egypt and in Biblical Aramaic*

The new Aramaic documents published by Kraeling and Driver have considerably augmented the *corpus* of Official Aramaic.[1] The number of texts now available permits a more detailed study of the grammar of this dialect of Aramaic than was previously possible. While most of the grammatical analyses of P. Leander[2] have been confirmed by the new texts and hence are still valid, a few additions and minor corrections, however, must be made. In any case, his work still remains an indispensable aid to the study of what he called "Egyptian" Aramaic.

But the syntax of Official Aramaic was never worked out by Leander on the same scale as his treatment of the phonology and morphology. Though scattered syntactical remarks are occasionally found in the morphological section of his grammar, a thorough treatment of the syntax of this phase of Aramaic remains to be done.[3]

Moreover, the value of the Official Aramaic texts for the study of Biblical Aramaic has been remarked upon ever since they were first discovered. The excellent *Grammatik des Biblisch-Aramäischen* of Bauer and Leander frequently illustrates the Biblical Aramaic usage with examples of Official Aramaic.[4] The newly published texts shed further light on the Aramaic of the Bible. Consequently, we are in a position to begin an inductive study of the syntax of Official Aramaic and compare it in detail with that of Biblical Aramaic.

The present essay attempts to present a detailed treatment of an important pronoun used both in the texts found in Egypt and in the Bible. The various forms and uses of כל that occur in the Aramaic texts from Egypt will be classified and discussed, and the corresponding phenomena of Biblical Aramaic will be related to them. Our study of this pronoun will incorporate the partial treatments of Leander (*L* §18e-0) and of Joüon (*J* §48-50).

In the Official Aramaic texts found in Egypt the pronoun כל occurs in three forms, כל, כלא and כלה, aside from the questionably restored form in *A*

166, [כל[ך]. The form כל can be either construct or absolute; scholars disagree on the interpretation of כלא, some maintaining it is the emphatic state, others holding it to be an adverbial form of כל; the form כלה is usually interpreted as a suffixal form. In Biblical Aramaic we find כל as construct, כלא (whose function is likewise disputed) and כלהון (once as a *kĕtīb* for כלהין), the suffixal form.

I. כל *in the Absolute State*

Though it may seem at first difficult to decide whether the form כל is absolute or construct in a given case, there are a few instances in the Egyptian documents that offer a clue to the interpretation. Leander (*L* §18g-f) has already distinguished the two uses of the absolute state of כל in these texts. In this respect we follow him with a few slight modifications.

(1) *The Absolute* כל *with Numbers.* כל is used before a number to express a sum or total and is usually found at the end of an enumeration. According to Joüon (*J* §48), "Ils emploient constamment l'indéterminé *kl* devant un nombre (presque toujours écrit en chiffres) indiquant compatibilité." In such a case he translates it, "total x" or "en tout." The latter translation seems to fit the sense better, because the phrase is obviously a *parenthetical addition*, making a technical document more precise. Since it most likely originated in lists, it cannot be accounted for easily within the ordinary syntactical framework of a simple sentence.

והבו פתף לגברן חלכין תרין אמן חד כל תלתה עלימן זילי,
"and give a ration to two Cilicians, one craftsman—in all, three of my servants" (*AD* 6:4).

אנת ואנתתך וברך כל 3,
"you and your wife and your son, in all three" (*AP* 6:4-5).
Similarly: *AP* [2:6];[5] 17:6; 46:15; *Bowm* A6, B7(?).

Special mention should be made here of 2 כל, which is often translated "both." Joüon (*J* §48) objects to such a rendering of this phrase. He is probably right, for in all instances where it occurs it can be interpreted simply as the expression of a total after an enumeration.

אמר מחסיה בר נתן 1 ידניה בר נתן 1 כל 2,
"Maḥsiyah, son of Nathan, 1, Yedanyah, son of Nathan, 1, in all 2, said . . ." (*AP* 28:2).[6]
Similarly: *AP* 20:[2], 3, 16, [19], 20; 25:8, 21; 26:8; *BMAP* 3:10; 4:18; 12:3, 11, 33; *NSI* 71:1.[7]

In the foregoing cases כל is followed by a numeral. There are, however, instances in which כל is followed by a noun modified by a number. At first sight, such a phrase might seem to be a construct chain, but its similarity with the foregoing construction is obvious. It is basically the same type of phrase. Hence כל is in the absolute state and means "in all."

כל גברן 5,
"in all, five men" (*AP* 33:5 [at the end of a list of five proper names]).[8]

כל גברן 8,
"in all, 8 men" (*AD* 3:5).
Similarly: *AP* 24:27, [28], [29], [30]; 26:16; 73:17; *AD* 5:5; 12:2; *BMAP* 7:13.

That the form כל in such an expression is absolute and not construct is shown by the following examples:

אמר בגזשת . . . ונשן אובל . . . כל גבר 1 נשן 1,
"Said Bagazust . . . and the woman ʾUbil . . . , in all, one man, one woman" (*BMAP* 3:3 [in this case כל cannot be construct]).[9]

בכל רעי 10,
"in all, 10 re'i" (*AP* 73:6 [cf. 73:17]).

בכל 5 ת[ ],
"in all, 5 t[. . .]" (*BMAP* 7:19).

The last two examples admittedly come from corrupt texts. Nevertheless, the readings are clear enough and show that כל cannot be taken as the construct.

(2) *Absolute* כל *in Apposition.* There are a few cases where כל follows either a noun in the emphatic state or a definite construct chain and means "all," in the sense of "the entirety of them (it)." In such a case it can only be explained as an absolute form used as an appositive.

אלהיא כל ישאלו שלמכי,
"May the gods all seek your welfare" (Cowley's translation; *AP* 39:1).[10]

כען עבדיך ידניה וכנותה ויהודיא כל בעלי יב כן אמרין,
"Now your servants Yedanyah and his colleagues and the Jews, all (of them), inhabitants of Yeb, say as follows . . ." (*AP* 30:22).

Cowley has rightly translated this sentence, for the sense does not seem to be: "and the Jews, all the inhabitants of Yeb." That would imply that the Jews were the only inhabitants of Yeb. The sense is rather, "and all the Jews, inhabitants of Yeb."

Were it not for the first example, one might be tempted to label the second case as a "faute de grammaire," as does Joüon (*J* §49). His reason for doing so is that all the other examples of this construction are found in *AP* 30 (lines 14, 17, 22, 27), a document usually judged inferior to the other version found in *AP* 31. In the latter version the corresponding passages read כלא, a form frequently found in apposition. Consequently, Joüon suggests that כל in *AP* 30 be vocalized as *kullāʾ*, regarding כל as *scriptio defectiva* for the emphatic state. This solution is hardly convincing, especially since Joüon himself, strangely enough, offers a parallel construction found in Syriac, where the absolute state of *kl* is used in apposition to an emphatic plural: *ṭĕlayê kol* (Matt 2:16S, for πάντας τοὺς παῖδας of the Greek).

Neither of these uses of the absolute state of כל is found in Biblical Aramaic.

II. כל *in the Construct State*

As might be expected, the most common use of the pronoun כל is that of its construct state. In this state it means "every" with a singular noun, and "all" with a plural or collective noun. An adequate treatment of the uses of כל in the construct state must account for the various types of words (and their states) that are found with it as *nomina recta.* We shall give, first of all, the uses of כל found in the Aramaic documents from Egypt, indicating whether or not the individual type of construct chain is also found in the Bible. Then we shall list types that are found only in Biblical Aramaic. The headings in the following classification indicate the type of *nomina recta* used with the construct *kl.*

(1) *The Compound Relative* זי.

מפטחיה הי שליטה בביתה . . . וכל זי איתי לה,
"Mipṭaḥiah is entitled to his house . . . and all that he has" (*AP* 15:9).[11]

וכל זי הנעלת בידה תהנפק,
"and all that she brought with her, she shall take away" (*BMAP* 2:8). Similarly: *AP* 2:[16]; 15:24, 27; 40:3; 43:[10]; 49:4; *A* [132]; *AD* 13:[4]; *BMAP* 2:10; 7:22, 31, 35; *B-M* 9. The same construction (with די) is found in Dan 2:38; 6:8 (כל די יבעא בעו, "everyone who offers a petition"); Ezra 7:21, 23, 26.

(2) *The Absolute Singular.*

מן כל דין,
"from every court-action" (*AP* 6:16; 14:11).
Similarly: *AP* 10:9, 10, 17; 11:6; 37:2b; *A* [96], 97, 98, 127a,b;[12] *Dup* 175 conc 4; *AP* 78:5, 6.

בכל עדן,
"at all times" (*AP* 17:2; 30:2, 3, 26; 31:2, 3; 37:2a; 38:[2]; 39:1; 40:1; 41:[1]; 42:[1]; 56:1; *BMAP* 13:1; *Dup* 186 conc 2.

כל מנדעם זי,
"anything at all which" (*AP* 21:7; 49:3).

The following passages in Biblical Aramaic can be compared with these examples: Dan 2:10(bis), 35; 3:10, 28, 29; 4:6; 5:7; 6:5(bis), 6, 8, 13(bis), 16, 24; Ezra 6:11, 12; 7:16.[13] In Ezra 7:13 the absolute singular is a participle.

(3) *The Emphatic Singular.*

כל כספא,
"all the money" (*AP* 15:13; 42:[4]; 48:2; *BMAP* 2:6).
Similarly: *AP* 2:[13]; 17:2; 24:31; [33]; perhaps also *A* [36].

In Biblical Aramaic this usage is frequent. כל ארעא, "all the earth" (Dan 2:35).

Likewise Dan 2:39; 3:31; 4:8, 9, 17; 6:2, 4, 26; 7:23; Ezra 7:25. With a proper name: Ezra 6:17.

(4) *A Construct Chain.*

כל מאת שנזן,
"all the company of Siniddin" (*AP* 22:19).
Similarly: *AP* 78:5, 6; *BMAP* 7:[15]; 13:6.

This construction is found in Dan 2:12: לכל חכימי בבל, "all the wise men of Babylon" (direct object). Likewise in Dan 2:48(bis); 3:2, 3, 5, 7, 10, 15; 4:3, 15, 32; 5:8; 6:8, 27; Ezra 4:20; 7:16, 25 (participle).

(5) *A Singular Noun with a Suffix.*

כל כספך,
"all your money" (*AP* 11:7). No parallel is found in the Bible.

(6) *A Plural Noun with a Suffix.*

לכל עבדיך,
"for all your servants" (*A* 83).
Similarly: *AP* 45:6.

In Biblical Aramaic: Dan 4:34 (כל מעבדוהי, "all his works"); 5:23; 6:25.

(7) *The Absolute Plural.*

כל שערן וטלפחן,
"all the barley and lentils" (*AP* 2:5; 3:6).

כל נכסן,
"all the goods" (*AP* 14:4; 30:16a; *BMAP* 2:11, 12).
Similarly: *AP* 30:16b; 45:8; 75:[9]; *BMAP* 3:23 (perhaps singular).

The construct כל with an absolute plural *nomen rectum* is not found in the Bible.

(8) *A Participle with a Suffix.*

כל נטחוהי,
"all who meet him" (*A* 167).[14]

This usage is without parallel in Biblical Aramaic.

The preceding eight categories exhaust the usage of the construct of כל in the Aramaic documents of Egypt.[15] A few other combinations are found in the Bible that have not yet appeared in extrabiblical texts from Egypt.

(9) *A Noun in the Emphatic Plural.*

מן כל חייא,
"different from all (other) living beings" (Dan 2:30). Likewise Dan 2:44; 3:7, 31; 5:19; 6:26; 7:7, 14, 23, 27(bis); Ezra 7:21, 24.

(10) *A Demonstrative Pronoun.*

כל אלין תדק,
"it will break all these to pieces" (Dan 2:40). Likewise 5:22; 7:16.

It would be rash to try to draw any conclusion from the foregoing classes regarding the differences between Biblical and non-Biblical Aramaic. The fact that certain constructions appear only in the Bible and others only in the texts from Egypt is almost certainly due to the limited material on which our study is based.

III. *The Emphatic State* כלא

The form כלא has been the subject of some discussion. The dictionary of Gesenius-Buhl listed it as the emphatic state of כל.[16] This was certainly the common interpretation of כלא in Biblical Aramaic until 1923, when James A. Montgomery published an article on "Adverbial *kúlla* in Biblical Aramaic and Hebrew."[17] Instead of accepting the final *aleph* as the emphatic ending *(-āʾ)*, he proposed to regard it as the adverbial ending which is found on a few other words (see *L* §47b; *BLA* §55b). "As an adverb the form is to be explained as a survival of the ancient accusative in *-a,* sc. *kúlla,* not *kullâ.*"[18] Consequently, he suggested that the greeting in Ezra 5:7, שלמא כלא, should be translated, "Peace wholly (be yours)," instead of the usual "all peace." The same interpretation was applied likewise to Dan 2:40, חשל כלא, "smashing wholly," and to 4:25, כלא מטא, "wholly it came upon."

In 1927 Bauer and Leander hesitatingly approved of Montgomery's suggestion.[19] In the following year Leander, discussing כל and כלא in "Egyptian" Aramaic, regarded כל as construct or absolute, but refused to call כלא the emphatic form.[20] In 1932, G. R. Driver, apparently unaware of Montgomery's suggestion, gave the same adverbial interpretation to כלא in *A* 61, a passage already treated by the latter. In his publication, *Aramaic Documents of the Fifth Century, B.C.,* Driver translates כלא as the adverb, "altogether" (*AD* 8:2; 12:6, 7). This interpretation is also accepted by St. Segert in his study of these Aramaic documents.[21]

But P. Joüon objected to this adverbial interpretation of כלא both in Ezra 5:7 and in the Aramaic texts from Egypt (*J* §49). His study has been overlooked at times. Using the texts published by Cowley, he showed that כלא

should be interpreted always as a pronoun in the emphatic state: "est toujours substantif: 'la totalité, le tout'" (*J* §49). Applying this to Ezra 5:7, Joüon translates שלמא כלא, "'le salut, la totalité,' *sous-entendu* 'de lui.'"[22] After examining the texts, both biblical and extrabiblical, I think that Joüon was on the right track. It is necessary, however, to examine the arguments advanced by Montgomery, Driver, and Leander to see how valid they are for the adverbial interpretation of כלא.

Montgomery argued, first of all, that כלא is *milʿel* in Ezra 5:7, "contrary to the universal rule of the Massora that the emphatic ending *-â* has the tone."[23] Hence, the form must come from *kúlla*, not *kullā́*. But the greeting is obviously an abbreviated formula,[24] and as such could easily bear a pausal accent.[25] It might be objected that כלא in Dan 4:25 is *milʿel* and not in pause. True, but then כלא in Dan 4:9, 18 is also *milʿel* and cannot possibly be an adverb *(ûmāzôn lĕkóllâʾ-bēh).* If it is necessary to justify the Masoretic accent of *kóllâʾ*, the explanation of Bauer and Leander seems sufficient (*BLA* §25h). At any rate, the Masoretic accentuation should not be given preponderance over the syntactical evidence of documents which are fairly contemporaneous with the consonantal text of the Bible.

Secondly, Montgomery suggested that for the meaning, "all peace," we should rather expect כל שלמא or כלה שלמא (like Hebrew *kullô*). Perhaps we should, but as Joüon pointed out, we have extrabiblical evidence for שלמא כלא in the sense, "all peace." From the evidence to be offered below it will be seen that שלמא כלא means the same as the suffixal form would.

Thirdly, Driver remarks, "The use of *klʾ* now with a masc. sing. noun (*DL* 12:6, 7) and now with a fem. plur. noun as here [*AD* 8:2] (s. Cowley, *AP*, 292) shows that the final ʾ is adverbial, being probably the accusative termination. . . ."[26] But if כלא is understood as the emphatic state of the pronoun, it could be used as an appositive or as a resumptive to either a masculine or a feminine noun, singular or plural. Hence we must say that Driver's reason for maintaining that כלא is an adverb is not sufficient or convincing.

Fourthly, Montgomery appealed to the use of כלא in the Elephantine Papyri. When he wrote, he did not have Cowley's excellent edition of them and used only the following 12 examples from Sachau's edition: *AP* 30:11, 12a,b, 29, 30; 31:10, 22, 26, 29; 41:1; *A* 43, 61. Though the adverbial translation, "wholly," might conceivably be suitable in a few cases, it is certainly forced in the majority of the examples that Montgomery used. Moreover, there are now 23 instances of כלא in the Aramaic texts from Egypt on which to base one's judgment.

We shall divide the various occurrences of כלא in the Aramaic texts into five classes, according to the functions it has.

(1) *Independent Usage* (i.e., not as an appositive or resumptive pronoun).

כלא זי עביד לן ארשם לא ידע,

"of all that was done to us Arsames was ignorant" (*AP* 31:29; compare 30:30). The most natural explanation is to take כלא as a pronoun, the antecedent of זי. If כלא followed ידע, then we might have reason to construe it as an adverb; but it does not.

עקי ארז לובר חסין תמים אמן עשרן כלא יהיתה חליפתהם . . . על גנזא,
"planks of cedar, seasoned (?), strong, TMYS, 20 cubits—let relays of them bring it all to the treasury" (*AP* 26:13). This text is very difficult to interpret, since many of the words are not certain. It may be that כלא is a resumptive pronoun following the list of objects that precedes.

In Biblical Aramaic כלא is also used independently in Dan 2:40 ("and smashes everything"); 4:9, 18 ("and there was food for all on it"); 4:25 ("and all [this] befell N.").

(2) *Preceding a Noun.* In one case כלא is found preceding the noun that it qualifies:
אף כלא מליא באגרת חדה שלחן בשמן על דליה ושלמיה,
"We have also sent all the details in a letter in our name to Delaiah and Shelemiah" (*AP* 30:29). Compare Montgomery's translation: "Moreover, wholly we have sent a message in a letter . . ."![27] To take כלא as an adverb here is impossible, for it makes no sense. It qualifies מליא and means the same as כל מליא. Contamination has obviously taken place here, resulting from a confusion of two otherwise frequently used constructions: כל מליא and מליא כלא.[28] The two preceding uses are more or less isolated cases; the more normal constructions with כלא are the following.

(3) *As an Appositive Following a Definite Noun.*

[וע]ל עטתה ומלוהי הות אתור כלא,
"and on whose advice and words all Assyria (depended)" (*A* 43).

[ ]ויהודיא כלא בעלי יב כן אמרן,
"and all the Jews, citizens of Yeb, say as follows" (*AP* 31:22). Montgomery did not attempt to translate this sentence, using כלא as an adverb. The fuller context of the sentence can be found in *AP* 30:22. It is difficult to understand how כלא could be an adverb between a noun and its appositive (בעלי יב). Cowley translated the phrase well: "and the Jews, all of them, citizens of Yeb."

ונצ[לה . . .]ויהודיא כלא זי תנה,
"and we shall pr[ay . . .] and all the Jews who are here" (*AP* 31:26; compare 30:26 for the full context).

[שלם אחי אלה]יא כלא ישא[לו]שגי בכ[ל עדן],
"may all the gods seek the welfare of my brother abundantly at all times" (*AP* 41:1). Montgomery used this case as his chief example to illustrate Ezra 5:7; he remarked, "Here again not *klhn* nor *kl* ᵓ*lhy*ᵓ; the form is not grammatically related, but is evidently adverbial, 'altogether.'"[29] But what Montgomery

failed to note was the peculiar resumptive character of כלא, which enables it to be used either as an appositive immediately following a noun or a construct chain or as a pronoun separated from the word it qualifies and placed immediately before the verb. The position of the verb in many of the sentences of the Aramaic texts from Egypt is peculiar; it is often found near the end of the sentence. Hence it is not strange that כלא would be used to resume a subject placed at the beginning of the sentence. In *AP* 41:1 we have the verb following the subject and כלא immediately; compare the other examples below.

שלם מראי אלהיא כלא [ישאלו] שגי בכל עדן,
"May all the gods seek the welfare of my lord abundantly at all times" (*BMAP* 13:1).

Appositive כלא has been restored by Cowley in *AP* 6:[5]. In the obscure passage of *AP* 26:17 כלא may be an appositive or it may be a resumptive. From the foregoing examples it should be clear that שלמא כלא of Ezra 5:7 is the same type of construction and means "all peace"—an abbreviated formula similar to those of *AP* 41:1 and *BMAP* 13:1.

שלם אמך וינקיא כלא,
"Greetings from your mother and all the children" (*Pad* I r 5).

(4) *As an Appositive to a Construct Chain or Its Equivalent.*

ועל עטתה ומלוהי חיל [אתו]ר כלא הוו,
"and by his counsel and words all the army of Assyria were (guided)" (*A* 60-61 [Cowley's translation]; cf. *A* [55-56]).[30]

כזי נשי ביתן כלא א[בדו],
"when all the women of our house perished" (*AD* 8:2). G. R. Driver translates: "when the women of our house perished altogether." This translation is, of course, possible in this case; but judged over against the other instances, it loses its plausibility.

חמר לם זי בפפרם ועבור ארקתא כלא נחתחור לקח עבד לנפשה,
"Now the wine which was in Papremis and the grain from the fields Nehtihûr has taken it all (and) made it over to himself" (*AD* 12:6). (Or possibly: "N. has taken the wine that was in P. and all the grain from the fields . . .").

ואגורי אלה[י] מצריא [כ]ל[א מגרו],
"And they overthrew all the temples of the gods of the Egyptians" (*AP* 31:[13]). Cf. *AP* 30:14.

[ ]אלך נחש ומטלל אגורא זך כלא,
"those . . . , of bronze, and the roof of the temple, all of it" (*AP* 31:10).

ומטלל עקהן זי ארז כלא עם שירית אשרנא ואחרן זי תמה הוה כלא באשה שרפו,
"and all the roof-beams of cedar which were with the rest of the furnishings and other things which were there, all of it, they burned with fire" (*AP* 30:11-

12). Here the first כלא is an appositive following a זי-clause which is an equivalent of a construct chain. The second כלא really belongs in the following category.

(5) *As a Resumptive Pronoun, Separated from the Phrase It Resumes.*

בזנה זי עביד לן כלא ארשם לא ידע,
"of all this which was done to us Arsames was ignorant" (*AP* 30:30).

ומזרקיא זי זהבא וכספא ומנדעמתא זי הוה באגורא זך כלא לקחו ולפשיהון עבדו,
"and the basons [sic] of gold and silver and everything that was in that temple, all of it, they took and made their own" (*AP* 30:12b [Cowley's translation]).

[ ]בעה באיש לאגורא זך כלא קטילו,
". . . sought to do evil to that temple, all of them, were killed" (*AP* 31:16; cf. *AP* 30:16-17 for the complete context).

כעת חמרא עבורא ומנדע[ם] אחרן זי לקחת כלא התבה,
"now restore all the wine, grain, and anything else that you have taken" (*AD* 12:7).

If Cowley's restoration in *AP* 27:18 is correct, we have another instance of this construction.

From the foregoing examples it can be seen why we prefer to regard כלא as the emphatic state of כל. Moreover, if כל is used in these texts as a construct and an absolute, is it not natural to regard כלא as the emphatic state of the same word, a pronoun?[31]

IV. *The Form* כלה

Aside from *A* 166, where Cowley has restored כל[ך], the only form of כל that occurs with what looks like a suffix in the Aramaic texts from Egypt is כלה. Leander (*L* §18e) and Joüon (*J* §49) regard כלה as the suffixal form. The suffixal form כלה is found in Old Aramaic (Panammu 17, 19) and in Biblical Aramaic (כלהון, Dan 2:38; כלהון [K for כלהין Q], Dan 7:19), not to mention later types of Aramaic. Now in the Aramaic texts from Egypt כלה is found at least four times and is restored in three other places by Cowley. Although the emphatic ending in these texts is normally *aleph*, as noted by Leander and Baumgartner,[32] *he* is also used at times as the emphatic ending. Is it not possible, then, that כלה is just another spelling for כלא? The syntax is the same in both cases. Consequently, it is impossible to state categorically that כלה is not the suffixal form. If כל[ך] in *A* 166 were not a restoration, it could be cited as evidence that the suffixal form is used in these texts. However, כל[א] could be restored just as easily, with the same meaning: "Thou art all thorns to him who touches thee" (Cowley's translation).

In five cases we find אתור כלה in the same sense as אתור כלא, "all Assyria"; but three of them are restorations of the editor (*A* 12, 55, [2], [18], [28]). It would have been just as easy to restore כלא.

Other instances:

מפתחיה הי שליטה בביתה . . . וכל זי איתי לה על אנפי ארעא כלה,
"Miptahiah shall be entitled to his house . . . and all that he possesses on the face of the whole earth" (*AP* 15:20, or perhaps: "on the face of the earth, all of it"—taking כלה as a resumptive pronoun, referring to all that precedes).

אנה ענני גבר אחרן אמי ואבי אח ואחה ואיש אחרן לא ישלט בביתה כלה,
"I, Anani, or another man, my mother or my father, my brother or my sister, or another person, shall not be entitled to this house—any (part) of it" (*BMAP* 4:20). Note also that in this example the emphatic state of בית is written with *ḥe*.[33]

[פ]רסכן זי כלי כלה,
"Your pay which is withheld, all of it"(*Pad* I v 6). Cf. also *Pad* II v 2 and *Pad* I r 5 (p. 224 below).

The foregoing study of the syntax of כל in the Aramaic texts found in Egypt sheds light on the Biblical Aramaic usage of the same word.[34] Further aspects of it in other areas remain to be studied.[35]

NOTES TO CHAPTER 9

*Originally published in *Bib* 38 (1957) 170-84 under the title, "The Syntax of *kl, klʾ* in the Aramaic Texts from Egypt and in Biblical Aramaic."

[1]See p. 75 n. 3 and p. 76 n. 21 above.

[2]*Laut- und Formenlehre des Ägyptisch-Aramäischen* (Hildesheim: G. Olms, 1966); originally published in *Göteborgs högskolas årsskrift* 34/4 (1928) 1-135. Leander's study was based almost wholly on the edition of the Elephantine material published by A. E. Cowley, *Aramaic Papyri of the Fifth Century B.C.* (p. 76 above, n. 21).

[3]The major part of this treatment was undertaken by me in a doctoral dissertation presented to the Johns Hopkins University in 1956. Written under the direction of Profs. W. F. Albright and T. O. Lambdin, it was entitled, *The Syntax of Imperial Aramaic Based on the Documents Found in Egypt* (Baltimore, 1956 [unpublished]). The present essay is an expansion of a small section of chap. 1, "The Syntax of the Pronoun." The syntax of these texts had been treated only in a very skimpy way in earlier publications. Less than one page of Sayce and Cowley's folio publication, *Aramaic Papyri Discovered at Assuan* (p. 76 above, n. 21), was devoted to a few points of syntax. When E. Sachau published *Aramäische Papyrus und Ostraka* (p. 76 above, n. 21) in 1911, he discussed a few syntactical problems in a section of his "Grammatischer Anhang," entitled "Zur Syntax und Wortfolge" (2 pages). Cowley promised a grammatical study of the Aramaic papyri in 1923, but this study has never appeared. Leander brought out his excellent monograph in 1928, but it was devoted exclusively to phonology and morphology. A few syntactical features of the papyri were studied by P. Joüon ("Notes grammaticales, lexicographiques et philologiques sur les papyrus araméens d'Egypte," *MUSJ* 18 [1934] 1-90). As a result, F. Rosenthal was able to point out the lack of a comprehensive study of the syntax of the Aramaic of this period (*Die aramaistische Forschung* [p. 75 above, n. 2] 48) that would compare with that of Bauer and Leander's treatment of the syntax of Biblical Aramaic. My own dissertation sought to remedy

that lack in part at least; it has not been published because it was not conceived along the lines of modern studies in syntax. It followed the method used by Bauer and Leander in their study of Biblical Aramaic. What is really needed is a study of these Official Aramaic texts, conducted along the lines that R. Degen used for his study of the Old Aramaic texts in *Altaramäische Grammatik* (p. 75 above, n. 16). The grammar recently published by S. Segert, *Altaramäische Grammatik* (p. 23 above, n. 53) has an entire section devoted to "Funktion der Wörter im Satz" (pp. 318-445); but it is not a study restricted to Official Aramaic, since Segert understands "Old Aramaic" in the sense that F. Rosenthal used the expression (see p. 58 above). It mixes the syntax, therefore, of texts from the periods that I should call Old, Official, and Middle Aramaic.

[4](Halle/S.: M. Niemeyer, 1927; reprinted, Hildesheim: Olms, 1962). Their remarks on the syntax of "Egyptian" Aramaic can be found in numbers 72b,c, 73b, 81v, 84b, 85d, 87e,f,i, 88j,k,l,m, 91g, 95j,n,o, 96f, 98p, 99o, 100u, 101h, 103g, 104e, 106c, 107j, 108q,t, 109x, 111c.

[5]In this essay the text is cited with the restorations of the editor, but the reference to a text containing a restoration is always bracketed. This policy has been adopted, since some of the restorations are certain and obvious, while others are only probable and vary greatly in degree. Hence each bracketed reference must be judged individually and not simply dismissed as a restored example. The bracket merely indicates that some part of the text is restored; despite the restoration the syntax is often clear.

[6]Joüon (*J* §48) remarks: "Autre exemple avec ce total minimum: 20,2sq. 'Ont dit Menaḥem et ᶜAnaniyah, total 2, fils de Mešullam fils de Selomen à Yadenyah et à Maḥseyah, total 2, fils de Asḥor. . .'. Les sens n'est pas 'both sons of . . .' (Cowley), qui se dirait *kltryn* (26,8)." Though I agree with Joüon's interpretation of *AP* 20:2, it seems far from certain that *kltryn* would have to be used to express the idea of "both."

[7]Leander, after having mentioned that כל is used in the absolute state with numerals (*L* §18f-g), subsequently lists the examples, כל תרין and 2 כל, under כל as a construct (with the dual—*L* §18i). This seems illogical. Certainly the sole instance of the number written out in full as one word with כל (*AP* 26:8 כלתרין) does not prove that כל is a construct in this case.

[8]Bauer and Leander (*BLA* §88k, n. 2) cite this instance together with *AP* 30:16 as an example of the construct of כל. But the construction here is not the same as in 30:16, where no numeral is present.

[9]Objection may be made that in *BMAP* 3:3 1 גבר is written above the line as an afterthought, and hence is not valid as evidence. However, it seems quite certain that the addition was made to remedy a scribal omission, when the writer reread the document. No change in thought is the result of the addition; it is clear that 1 גבר should have been written with the rest from the start. For a parallel to the construction discussed in the text in Biblical Hebrew, see Jos 21:39 (*kōl ᶜārîm ᵓarbaᶜ*).

[10]In this example כל cannot possibly be the construct, and there is no reason to construe it with שלמכי. One cannot exclude the possibility, however, of a scribal error in this instance; see p. 213 below (III, 3).

[11]For a full treatment of this text, see pp. 243–71 below.

[12]The letters a, b, c in a reference are used to indicate the first, second, and third occurrences of the word in the line.

[13]See the remarks in *BLA* §88k on this particular construction.

[14]On this form, see *BLA* §38b; P. Joüon, *Bib* 22 (1941) 268.

[15]כל also occurs in the following places, too corrupt to permit analysis: *AP* 22:5, 31; 31:15; 73:2.

[16](17th ed.; Berlin: Springer, 1949) 910. See also E. Kautzsch, *Grammatik des Biblisch-Aramäischen* (Leipzig: F. C. W. Vogel, 1884) 150 ("das Heil die Gesamtheit = alles Heil" in Ezra 5:7); H. L. Strack, *Grammatik des Biblisch-Aramäischen* (Munich: C. H. Beck, 1911) 50*; K. Marti, *Kurzgefasste Grammatik der Biblisch-Aramäischen Sprache* (3d ed.; Berlin: Reuther und Reichard, 1925) 74*; L. Palacios, *Grammatica aramaico-biblica* (Rome: Desclée, 1933) 63.

[17]*JAOS* 43 (1923) 391-95.

[18]Ibid., 394.

[19]*BLA* §25h.

[20]*L* §18n.

[21]"Aramäische Studien: I. Die neuen Editionen von Brooklyn Papyri und Aršāms Briefe in ihrer Bedeutung für die Bibelwissenschaft," *ArOr* 24 (1956) 395.

[22]"Notes de grammaire et de lexicographie araméenne," *Bib* 22 (1941) 265.

[23]*JAOS* 43 (1923) 391.

[24]Kraeling (*BMAP*, 296) asks whether the שלמא כלא of Ezra 5:7 could be an abridgement of the "paganizing phraseology" found in the greeting often used in the Aramaic letters. This is hardly likely, even though it may be an abbreviation of a longer formula. See p. 191 above.

[25]So E. Kautzsch, *Grammatik* (n. 16 above), 39.

[26]*AD*, 27.

[27]*JAOS* 43 (1923) 393.

[28]Leander remarks (*L* §18n): "Dass *klʾ* auch v o r dem Nomen stehen kann (30,29 . . .), spricht für die These Montgomerys, dass es kein St. det., sondern vielmehr ein erstarrter ursem. Akkusativ auf *-ā* ist." Does it really? "Il est même fort douteux que 'totalement' puisse s'exprimer par l'accusatif de *kl*. En arabe, où l'accusatif adverbial est très développé, 'totalement' ne s'exprime pas par *kullā*" (*J* 49 n. 4).

[29]*JAOS* 43 (1923) 392.

[30]Cf. Zenjirli, *Panammu* 17.

[31]Montgomery himself admitted, "In Syriac *klʾ* is found, apparently, as the emphatic" (*JAOS* 43 [1923] 393).

[32]*L* §15c; W. Baumgartner, "Das Aramäische im Buche Daniel," *ZAW* 45 (1927) 91.

[33]ביתה כלה is also found in Zenjirli, *Panammu* 19.

[34]In the Hermopolis West Papyri the construct state כל occurs three times (1:12; 2:15; 3:7). The form כלה seems to be an appositive in *Herm WP* 4:12, but the meaning of the noun to which it is in apposition (סחתח) is unknown. The editors translate the phrase thus: "Saluti a tutto il vicinato(?)" (p. 399). Similarly, the instance of כלה in *Herm WP* 4:4.

[35]In 1QapGen the construct state כל is found with a variety of *nomina recta* (nouns and pronouns): 2:4, 7, 16ter; 6:2; 7:1; 10:13; 11:17; 12:10; 16:11; 19:19, 20, 23; 20:3, 4, 5bis, 6bis, 7, 9, 12, 13, 15bis, 16, 17, 18, 19ter, 20bis, 24, 28; 21:1, 3, 5, 9, 10, 11bis, 12bis, 13, 14, 19, 21, 25, 26, 27, 33; 22:1, 3, 10, 11quater, 12, 13, 15, 17, 22bis, 24bis, 25, 29, 30, 33. The form is probably construct in 1Q*20* 1 i 8; 1 ii 4. The emphatic state כולא is used in apposition in 1QapGen 19:10, בארעא דא כולא, "in all this land." The non-appositional use of כולא (= "everything, all") is found in 1QapGen 2:5, [10], 19, 20, 21, 22; 20:13. In a number of instances the suffixal forms of כול emerge in this text; they are used both in apposition and in a non-appositional construction. Thus, in apposition: כולהון (12:10, 13; 20:19-20); כולהא (10:13; 16:13); non-appositional: ולנשי כולנא, "and the wives of all of us" (12:16); ארי הוא רוחא כתש לכולהון, "for the spirit afflicted all of them" (20:20); cf. 20:13; 22:9, 26; לעלא מן כולהן, "high above all of them" (20:7).

In 11QtgJob the construct state כל is found in 2:8; 25:3; 28:2; 29:3; 30:5; 32:7; 34:7b; 37:2; 38:4, 5ter, 6, 7 (and probably in 22:[5], 7a). The emphatic state כלא is used in a non-appositional sense in 37:3, whereas the suffixal form כלכון is found once (11:[2]).

Chapter 10

The Padua Aramaic Papyrus Letters*

The Museo Civico of Padua acquired some time ago fragments of three papyrus letters, which are written in Aramaic and are apparently related to similar Aramaic documents of fifth-century Egypt already known to the scholarly world. Their provenience in Egypt is unfortunately not certain,[1] a fact which complicates the interpretation of the texts. Edda Bresciani has published a study of these letters and has supplied excellent photographs of the papyri.[2] Her study is well done, but there is always room for further comments on the interpretation of such documents. We propose to give an English translation of the texts, suggest some restorations of the lacunae and add several remarks about the language and contents of the letters, thus treating certain points which the original editor has passed over.

The letter, of which the beginning and the end of the lines are unfortunately lost, was written by a father (Osea bar Pet. . .) to his son (Shelomam bar Osea), who had gone off on a caravan. We gather that the son had written to his parents and mentioned something about clothes; the father who resides with the family in Migdol in Lower Egypt writes to inform his son that some salary which is due to him has not been paid and takes up the question of the clothes. If the greeting of the first line of the *verso* is correctly interpreted by the editor, it would seem that the son has gone with the caravan to Upper Egypt, to the vicinity of Elephantine. That seems to be the reason why the father begins the letter with a greeting or blessing invoked in the name of the god of the area where the son is.

Padua Papyrus I (= *Pad* I)

Text[3]

Verso

1 [שלם ב]ית יהו ביב אל ברי שלמם [מ]ן אחוך אושע שלם ושררת [שגיא הושרת לך]
2 [כעת מ]ן יום זי אזלת בארחא זך בר[י] לי טיב אף אמך כעת ברך אנת [ליהו אלהא]
3 [זי יח]וני אנפיך בשלם כעת מן יום [ז]י נפקתם מן מצרין פרס לא י[היב לכן]
4 [וכזי] קבלן לפחותא על פרסכן תנה ב[מ]גדל כן אמיר לן לאמר על זנה[ ]
5 [קבל ל]ספריא ויתיהב לכן כעת כזי תאתון מצרין על[ ]

6] פ]רסכן זי כלי כלה כעת איך ביתא עביד ואיך נפקת הן יהו[ה [
7] ש]לם ומחבל לא איתי גבר הוי אל תתאשד עד תאתה [מנפי [

Recto

1] [
2] כתבת]באגרתא זילך על כתון ולבש כתונך ולבשך עבידן[[
3]]לאמך עבדת אל תמלי לבת בזי לא איתית המו מנפי כזי ת[תוב [
4 [תנה איתי] המו קדמתך כעת זבנת לי אנה [כ]תן 1 זי כתן כעת[[
5]]דן ולבש עד תאתה שלם אמך וינקיא כלא כעת תנה הוין[[
6] ב ?]למחר כתבת אגרתא זא כע[ת] כן שמיע לן לאמר תתפטרן[[

Address

7] [אל אחי שלמם בר [או]שע אחוך אושע בר פט[[

Translation

Verso

[1][Greetings to the temp]le of Yahu in Elephantine! To my son, Shelomam; from your "brother," Osea. [I send you] greetings and prosperity [in abundance!] [2][Sin]ce the day when you went on that caravan, my son, all goes well with me and your mother too. May you be blessed [by Yahu, the God, [3]who may gr]ant me to see your face (again) in peace! Since the day when you left Lower Egypt, the salary has not been gi[ven to you. [4]And when] we lodged a complaint with the governors about your salary here in [Mig]dol, we were told thus: "About this (matter) [5][complain to] the clerks and it will be given to you." When you come (back) to Lower Egypt, about [[6]] your [sa]lary, which has been withheld, all of it. As the house has been made, and as you have departed, so (?) there is [[7] pe]ace, and there is no one who (tries to) seize (it) in pledge (?). Be a man; do not dissipate; until you come (back) [to Memphis]

Recto

[1][ ] [2][You wrote] in your letter about a tunic and clothing. Your tunic and clothing have been made [[3]] for your mother I have done. Do not be angry, because I have not brought them to Memphis. When you [return [4]here, I shall bring] them (there) before you. I have bought for myself a tunic of linen. Now [[5]] . . . and clothing until you come. Greetings from your mother and all the children! Here we have been [[6] On the ? (day)] of Meḥir I have written this letter. We have (just) heard a rumor to the effect that you will be released [ ]

Address

To my "brother" Shelomam bar Osea; your "brother" Osea bar Peṭ[ ].

Notes

Verso

1. שלם ב]ית יהו ביב]: This is Bresciani's restoration, based on similar beginnings of the papyrus letters from Hermopolis (see p. 190 above). The

other Hermopolis letters mention greetings sent to the temples of Nabu, *Bnt* (= Banit, "creatrix"), Bethel, Malkat-sĕmayin. This suggests that letters were begun with a greeting or blessing invoked in the name of the deity of the place in which the addressee was found. The expression בית יהה is found on an ostracon studied by A. Dupont-Sommer, "La maison de Yahvé et vêtements sacrés à Eléphantine," *JA* 235 (1946-47) 79-87, esp. p. 86.

יהו ביב: The veneration of Yahu in Yeb (= Elephantine) is most clearly expressed in *BMAP* 12:2, יהו אלהא שכן יב ברתא, "Yahu, the God, who dwells in Elephantine, the fortress." The simpler formula used here, יהו ביב, occurs in *BMAP* 1:2; 9:2. Cf. יהו אלהא זי ביב ברתא (*BMAP* 2:2; 4:2; 10:2); see further *BMAP* 3:3; 4:10; *AP* 6:4; 25:6; 30:6, 24-26; 31:7, 24-25; 34:8-9.

ברי: This address, which is used again in line 2, indicates the real relationship between the writer and the addressees. It is confirmed by אמך (I v 2; I v 5). See p. 190 above.

אל: The preposition, "to," is used at this period almost exclusively in the addresses of letters; see *AP* 30:1; 31:1; 37:1, 17; 38:1, 12; 39:1, 5; 40:1, 5; 41:1, 9; 63:6(?); 67:8; 70:1; *RES* 3.1300; *Cl-G Ost* 277:1 (*RHR* 128 [1944] 29); *Cl-G Ost* 70: conc. 1 (*CRAIBL,* 1947, 177); *BMAP* 13:[1], 9; *Pad* II v 1, r 1; *Pad* III.1; *RES* §1300. Contrast the addresses in *AD* 1:1; 2:1; 3:1, etc., where the more common preposition of this period, *ᶜl*, is found; likewise in *RES,* 3.1295.

שלמם: This name occurs in *AP* 49:1 with the same spelling. The full spelling, *šlwmm*, is found elsewhere (*AP* 1:2, 10; 20:2, 6, 12, 13, 17, 19; 46:2, [8], 11, 16. M. Noth, *IPN*, p. 165, regards it as a form of *šālôm* + *-ām*; but he is inclined to separate *šlmm* and *šlwmm* for a reason which is not apparent.

אחוך: See I r 7, where the writer again calls himself אחוך. It may seem that אח is used here merely in the sense of "kinsman." Indeed, in *AP* 40:1, 5 E. Sachau had been confronted with a similar problem and understood אח as "step-brother." But A. E. Cowley corrected this, pointing out that אח was used rather as a polite form of address to an equal, comparing *AP* 21:2, 11. This usage is now confirmed by the clear example in this letter, for it is obvious that it is a father who writes to his son, and uses אח both of himself and of his son in the address. See further *AP* 41:1, 9 and *Cl-G Ost* 277:1-2 (אל אחי חגי אחוך ירחו, which H. L. Ginsberg [*ANET*, p. 491] interprets as a "Greeting from a pagan to a Jew"). Compare also the use of אח in 1QapGen 2:9, where Bit-enosh employs it in addressing her husband, Lamech.

אושע: Osea, shortened form of אושעיה (*AP* 20:18), "Yahu has saved, helped." See M. Noth, *IPN*, p. 176. The shortened form occurs also in *AP* 12:2; 13:14; 22:90, etc. Note that whereas Osea's name is Semitic, his father's name is Egyptian—a phenomenon already well attested in the Elephantine texts.

שלם ושררת [שגיא הושרת לך]: Restored by Bresciani on the basis of *AD* 3:1; 5:1; 13:1; to be read also in *AP* 42:1.

2. [כעת]: Supplied on the basis of further examples which occur regularly at the beginning of sentences; see I v 2, 3, 5, 6; I r 4, 5, 6. It marks the beginning

of a sentence (something like the English "stop"), and meant originally "now." However, for the sake of the smoothness of the English translation we have omitted it.

[מ]ן יום זי: See line 3. The emphatic state of יום might have been expected here, but this and similar uses of the absolute state before a rel. pron. are fairly frequent in Aramaic: . . . ביום זי אלהן (Sf I B 31); ביום זי יעבד כן (Sf I C 20); ביום זי אמות (*Cl-G Ost* 175: conc. 1 [*CRAIBL* 1947, 181]); עד יום זי אשלמנהי (*AP* 11:3, 10); אתר די אנתה יתב (1QapGen 21:9); מן יום די נפקתה (1QapGen 22:28). See also Ezra 7:15; *BLA* §88m.

אזלת: 2d sg. masc. pf. peal. The 2d sg. is used here, as in the suffixal forms (אחוך [I v 1; I r 7]; אמך [I v 2; I r 5]; אנפיך [I v 3]; זילך, כתונך, לבשך [I r 2]; קדמתך [I r 4]); the verbal forms (נפקת [I v 6]; תתאשד [I v 7]; תאתה [I v 7; I r 5]; תמלי [I r 3]); and the independent personal pronoun (אנת [I v 2]). But it is to be noted that the father also addresses his son with the 2d pl. form, apparently without any distinction of meaning. Thus we find נפקתם (I v 3 [which might at first sight seem to refer to the caravan as a whole; cf. line 6]); תאתון (I v 5); תתפטרן (I r 6). There are also plural suffixal forms: פרסכן. As Bresciani rightly points out, כן- is not the 2d pl. fem. suffix, but the masc. with the so-called later spelling.

בארחא זך: "On that caravan." Cf. Hebr. ארחה, "travelling company, caravan" (Gen 37:25; Isa 21:13; Job 6:18-19), a meaning connected with the Hebr. and Aram. word ארח, "road, way."

לי טיב: We have here not the adjective *ṭāb*, but the impersonal use of the 3d sg. masc. pf. peal, as in *BMAP* 1:[4]; 3:6; 12:6, 14, 26; etc. *A* 67 (כנותה ועטתא זא טיבת על) shows that the form is verbal. Cf. *L* §39b.

ברך אנת: Bresciani completes the line with ליהו אלהא, understanding *brk* as defective spelling for *bryk* and comparing the Hebrew expression in 1 Sam for *bryk* and comparing the Hebrew expression in 1 Sam 15:13; 23:21, etc. She admits that קדם יהו אלהא would also be possible, comparing the Carpentras stele (*CIS*, 2. 141; Cooke, *NSI*, §75), line 3. In fact, both *l* and *qdm* are well attested in Aramaic blessing formulas found in graffiti, so that either can be restored here. Bresciani admits that they are equivalent but thinks that the form with *l* "è yahvista ed ebraica, mentre la seconda è tipicamente aramaica" (pp. 20-21). But ל precedes the name חנם (= Khnum) in *Cl-G Ost* 70: conc. 3 (cited by her) and is also found with the names of other Egyptian gods (לחר [*RES* 960, 961]; לאסרי [*RES* 1366]; לוסרי [*RES* 1788]). See further the Ammonite seal published by N. Avigad, חתם מנגאנרת ברך למלכם, "Seal of Mannu-ki-Inurta, blessed by Milkom" (*IEJ* 15 [1965] 222-28). ברך קדם is found also in *RES* 607, 1364, 1368, 1370, 1376, 1377, 1817. In most of these cases the defective spelling *brk* is found, agreeing with the usage here.

3. [זי יח]וני אנפיך בשלם: Lit: "who may make your face known to me in peace." To support this restoration, Bresciani cites similar formulas from the letters of Hermopolis with either the verb חוא or חזא. She points out that this

formula should be read also in *BMAP* 13:3-4. It should preferably be restored also in *AP* 34:7, [עד אלהיא יחווננ]י אנפיך בשלם. Similarly in *AP* 41:8.

נפקתם: 2d pl. masc. pf. peal; see the note on אנלת, line 2.

מצרין: "Lower Egypt," as in Isa 11:11; Jer 1:15; Ezek 30:16, since the context suggests that מגדל and מנפי are in the area, and the greetings in the first line suggest the contrast with Elephantine in Upper Egypt. However, מצרין is often found in the Elephantine texts as the name for Egypt in general (*AP* 30:13, 14, 24; 31:12; 32:2; 38:7; 64:20; 66:6; 71:8, 26; 72:2, 4; cf. *AD* 7:2, 4. See Bresciani's remarks on the identification of מגדל.

פרס: "Salary." The word is found with this meaning in *AP* 11:6; 2:16. Is it a *qatl*-type (like *parsīn*, Dan 5:25) or a *qatāl*-type (like the later Aramaic פְּרָס; cf. G. Dalman, *ANHW*, 350)?

לא י[היב לכן]: "Has not been given to you." Or possibly לא י[הבו לכן], "they (indefinite) have not given (it) to you." I prefer the passive participle because of *AP* 24:42; [י]היב פתף לחיל, "a ration has been given to the army." Bresciani notes the similar use of פרס and פתף in the Elephantine texts, and in *BMAP* 11:5 the פתפא is a ration apparently paid regularly to members of the military דגל stationed in Elephantine; it is doled out from the אוצר מלכא, "the royal storehouse" (11:4), which may be the same as בית פרסא (*BMAP* 9:4, which Kraeling merely transliterates as "beth parsa"). Cf. *AP* 11:6; 2:16. The passive participle of peal is otherwise found in this letter (אמיר [I v 4]; עביד [I v 6; I r 2]; שמיע [I r 6]).

4. קבלן: "We lodged a complaint." This meaning of קבל is well attested in the Elephantine texts. Four formulas are found:

קבל על (object of complaint) קדם (authorities): *AP* 6:5, 16; 10:12, 18; 47:7.

קבל על (object of complaint) ל (authorities): *BMAP* 9:19; 12:28; so here.

קבל על (object of complaint) + direct object (= authorities): *AP* 8:13; *BMAP* 1:5; 1QapGen 20:14.

קבל על (person complained against) בגו (object of complaint): *BMAP* 1:4, 5, 6.

Note that the 1 pl. ending is only *-n*, which is usual for this period; cf. *L* §25a, 12f.

לפחותא: Bresciani has simply transliterated this form, "ai *pḥwtʾ*," comparing פחה, "governatore," but she is apparently reluctant to use this meaning here. The meaning is clear, however, from *AP* 30:29 (פחת שמרין); 30:1 (פחת יהוד); *B* 18, 38 ([פ]חתא); Dan 3:2, 3, 27 (פחותא). The latter is precisely the form which we have here; it is, furthermore, found there in a list of other rulers like satraps, etc. It is related to the Akkadian *pi/aḫatu*. Hence, the meaning "governor" is to be preferred to that which Bresciani uses in her note, "funzionari (evidentemente collegiali) del 'tesoro'." Moreover, whenever קבל is used in the papyri of lodging a complaint, we find that it is lodged before either דין, סגן, or מרא, names which suggest some person of judicial or executive function in the colony. So too here; the parents lodged the complaint with the "governors," who referred them to the ספריא, the treasury "clerks."—See P. Nober, *VD* 39 (1961) 110-11; E. Y. Kutscher, "פחוא and Its Cognates." *Tarbiẓ* 30 (1960-61) 112-19; G. Garbini, "The Dating of Post-Exilic Stamps," *Excavations at Ramat Raḥel: Seasons 1959 and 1960* (Rome: *Centro di studi semitici*, 1962) 61-68, esp. p. 68 n. 42; *BA* 24 (1961) 110-11.

פרסכן: "Your salary." The suffix is 2d pl. masc., כן- being written with a *nun* instead of the *mem* of the older form, which is otherwise more frequent at this period. Cf. *L* §12m, x, ב׳. This is apparently the earliest known occurrence of כן- as 2d pl. masc. suffix, but the 3d pl. masc. ending הן- is well attested: להן (*AP* 34:7; 37:4, 14 [to be compared with *BMAP* 4:21]; בהן (*AP* 34:6; 82:11 [to be compared with *AP* 31:6]); ביניהן (*BMAP* 12:19, 21 [to be compared with *BMAP* 3:8, 10; 6:6, 11; *AP* 13:14; 25:7]).

ב[מ]גדל: "In Migdol." Identified with Migdol (Jer 44:1; 46:14) in מצרין (see line 3) by Bresciani. It is located most probably at Tell el-Heir in the east delta about 18 kms. southwest of Pelusium.

לאמר: The stereotyped formula which preserves the old peal inf. without preformative *mem*; see *AP* 2:3; 5:3; 6:4; etc. Contrast *AP* 32:2; 43:2; *A* 115.

5. ספריא: "The clerks" of the treasury, as in *AP* 2:12, 14 (ספרי אוצרא). Cf. *AP* 17:1, 6. Both documents deal with the supplying of grain to a garrison and the ספריא are probably recorders engaged in the work.

לכן: See note on פרסכן in line 4 above. Here, however, the plural may really be meant; but it is not certain, for the father uses the 1 pl. of himself (apparently) in line 4, קבלן.

מצרין: Used with a verb of motion toward it, but without a preposition. Such a construction is found elsewhere in Aramaic: see Sf III 5 (יהכן חלב); *Pad* I r 3 (איתית המו מנפי); *BMAP* 13:3 (יהיתון מנפי); *AP* 42:7 (חת מנפי [contrast 42:11, הן נחת אנת למנפי]); *AP* 83:2 (מטא צחא מנפי); *AD* 6:2, 4, 5. Contrast *AP* 37:11. See further p. 252 below.

6. כלי: "Has been withheld." This specific sense of the verb also occurs in *AP* 37:13, 14, 15.

כלה: Is this the suffixal form of כל or the emph. state written with *he* instead of *aleph*? Cf. *AP* 15:20; *BMAP* 4:20; *A* 12, 55, [2, 18, 28]. So far no clear case of a suffixal form of כל in the Aramaic texts from Egypt has turned up, but there is no reason why it should not. See p. 214 above. Even here the issue is not certain, for the emphatic state with *he* is found in *Pad* II v 2 (ינקיה = ינקיא), II v 5 (ספרה = ספרא). Hence כלה may be merely another spelling of כלא, used as a resumptive pronoun, as in *Pad* I r 5 (שלם אמך וינקיא כלא).

איך ביתא עביד: Bresciani understands this puzzling phrase as a question, "come la casa è fatta e come sei partito?" But this hardly fits the context of a father at home writing to a son on a caravan. It seems better, therefore, to take איך in the sense of "as"; but we cannot be certain because of the broken and fragmentary context. If correct, it would stand for the fuller איך די (זי); cf. Sf I A 35, 38, 39; Syriac *ʾak dĕ*.

הן: This may well be the conjunction, "if," as interpreted by Bresciani. However, since the context is broken, there is another possibility which must be reckoned with: the emphatic adverb הן, which appears in *AD* 6:2; 12:3; *Cl-G Ost* 152, conc. 3, 7 [*Sem* 2 (1949) 31]. See my discussion of this adverb in Sf I B 36; III 4 (*Aramaic Inscriptions of Sefire* [p. 76 above, n. 29] 70–71). It seems to mean something like "so," a meaning which could correspond to איך.

7. מחבל: Bresciani understands this as a noun, meaning "destruction." This is not impossible, even though no noun forms of the root חבל with preformative *mem* are otherwise attested. The word מחבל in *AP* 27:2, to which she refers, is interpreted by Leander as a pael pass. ptc. (*L* §32d). G. S. Glanzman has suggested to me the possibility that the root may rather be חבל, "to take something as a pledge." The form would then be a pael act. ptc. In the broken context in which a house is mentioned, this is not impossible. The root is well known in Hebr., but found also in the targums in a nominal form, חבולא or חבוליא, "interest." See G. Dalman, *ANHW*, 134.

אל תתאשד: "Do not dissipate," lit., do not pour yourself out. In Syriac the root *ʾšd* occurs in a figurative sense; *zabnan ʾašīdā*, "tempus nostrum dissolutum, mollitie diffluens" (*Act. Mart.* i. 166; R. Payne Smith, *Thesaurus syriacus,* 1. 404).

מנפי: Restored according to I r 3; מגדל would also be possible.

Recto

2. כתון: "Tunic," also spelled כתן in line 4. In the same sense the word also occurs in *A* 41 (where it is rent); *AP* 42:8(?), 9, 10, 13; *AD* 13:3; *Cl-G Ost* 16, conv. 2 (*ASAE* 48 [1948] 110); *Cl-G Ost* 49:1 (*JA* 235 [1946-47] 79-87). See G. R. Driver's note on *AD* 13:3.

לבש: Is this the defective spelling for לבוש or was it pronounced *lĕbāš*, as in later Aramaic and Syriac? לבוש is found in Biblical Aramaic (Dan 3:21; 7:9), in Qumran Aramaic (1QapGen 20:31), and also in some of the Elephantine texts themselves (*AP* 14:14; *BMAP* 11:11). Hence, though לבש occurs here and elsewhere (*AP* 15:7, 10; 20:5; *BMAP* 2:4; 7:6, 8, [10], 13, 17, 23; *Cl-G Ost* 70: conc. 4 [*CRAIBL* 1947, 177; *RHR* 130 (1945) 20]), it should be regarded as a defective writing for לבוש, the earlier form.

3. אל תמלי לבת: "Do not be angry," lit., do not be filled with anger. Cf. *AP* 37:11; 41:4; Aššur Ostr. 19-20 (M. Lidzbarski, *Altaramäische Urkunden aus Assur* [Leipzig: Hinrichs, 1921] 8). A. E. Cowley, following D. H. Baneth, related the expression to the Akkadian plural noun *libbātu* and suggested its adoption in Ezek 16:30. This was taken up by G. R. Driver (*JTS* 29 [1927-28] 393; 32 [1930-31] 366); see further my note, "A Note on Ez 16,30," *CBQ* 23 (1961) 460-62. If there were any hesitation about the meaning of the Aramaic phrase before this, because of damaged contexts, we need hesitate no longer, for the sense of the expression is now clear. תמלי is 2d sg. masc. impf. peal. See further *Herm WP* 1:6 (זי מלתי לבתי), as recognized also by B. Porten and J. C.

Greenfield, "The Aramaic Papyri from Hermopolis," *ZAW* 80 (1968) 216-31, esp. pp. 226, 228. Contrast J. T. Milik, *Bib* 48 (1967) 581.

בזי: A causal conjunction, as in *AP* 30:23; 37:4, 7.

מנפי: See note above on I v 5 (מצרין).

4. קדמתך: "Before you," preferably to be understood in a temporal sense, since קדמת- usually has this nuance, whereas קדם is used for the local idea. See Dan 6:11; Ezra 5:11; *AP* 30:17; 71:3; *A* 2; *B* 54(?); but in *A* 101 the sense is apparently local.

זי כתן: "Of linen." This meaning for כתן is also found in *AP* 20:5; 26:14, 20; *BMAP* 7:11, 12(?), 13. See note on line 2 above.

5. [ ]דן: Bresciani suggests רן- as also possible. Could it not even be כן-?

שלם אמך וינקיא כלא: "Greetings from your mother and all the children!" The phrase is actually a construct chain, "The peace of your mother and all the children." This has been taken by Bresciani as if it were the equivalent of שלם ל- (like *AP* 57:1?): "Saluti a tua madre e a tutti i bambini." Yet the mother seems to be in Migdol with the father according to I v 2. In *BMAP* 13:6, toward the end of the letter again, we find a broken expression akin to the one here, שלם ענני בר נריה שלם כל בני [ ]. Kraeling (*BMAP*, 289) discussed the possibility of its meaning that greetings were sent from persons with the writer, but rejected it on "the analogy of other letters, notably those from Hermopolis," which suggest that שלם is "a noun and that greetings to people in Elephantine are meant (cf. *AP* 39:2f.)." However, this is not clear. Perhaps even *AP* 39:2-3, as well as 40:1-2, should now be interpreted in the sense of "greetings from. . . ." The evidence is such that שלם is used in these Aramaic texts both in the sense of "greetings to" and "greetings from." Certainly, in the very frequent formula, שלם מראן אלה שמיא שגיא בכל עדן (*AP* 30:2; 31:2; [38:2]; 40:1; 56:1; 18:2; 37:2), the "peace" is the property or quality of the person to whom the greeting is sent. This is even more evident in the case of suffixal forms (*AP* 41:2, 3, 5, 7; 56:1; 39:1; 57:4). However, "peace" can also be sent, as the restored formula in I v 1 shows; see note there for the basis of the restoration. See also *RES* 493:1 ([ש]לם מן . . .). Moreover, *Pad* II v 2, לך שלם גלגל תנה שלם ינקיא , would seem to confirm this interpretation, for לך expresses the person greeted. Hence, when we have a construct chain involving שלם, we must have recourse to the context to determine the sense, whether it means "greetings to" or "greetings from." Cf. *AP* 68:1; 66:9.

6. למחר: "Of Meḥir," the name of an Egyptian month, as rightly interpreted by Bresciani, comparing *BMAP* 13:8 (בל 5 לאפף כתיב אגרתי). מחיר appears to be the name of a month in *AP* 24:[34, 35], 44; *RES*, 1801:8(?). See further references in Bresciani's article.

תתפטרן: "You will be released." Cf. *BMAP* 13:7. Could this possibly refer to service in the caravan, a member of which the son is? Is the withholding of the salary somehow connected with this?

Padua Papyrus II (= *Pad* II)

Text

Verso

1 אל אמ[י] יה[ו]י[ש]מע ברך שלום בר פטמ[ון [
2 לך שלם גלגל תנה שלם ינקיה . . . זכ. [. [
3 בלא הבה לפחנום בר נבודלה ויעב[ד [
4 יגרוהי והן איתי כסף הבי על פמי ע[ל [שלמך
אמי
5 שלחת ספרה זנה שלם מנחמת שלם[[
6 יהוישמע [

Recto

1 [א]ל אמי יה[וי]שמע . . .[[

Translation

Verso

[1]To my mother, Yahuyishma^{c}; your son, Shallum bar Peṭam[un.] [2]Greetings to you from Galgul here, greetings from the children! [ ] [3]BL$^{\supset}$ give it to Pakhnum bar Nabudalah and let him d[o] [4]they will prosecute him, and if there is money, give (it) according to my instruction .[For your welfare] [5]I send this note. Greetings from Menaḥemet, my mother (?); greetings [ ] [6]Yahuyishma$^{\supset}$.

Recto

(Address) [T]o my mother, Yahuyishma$^{\supset}$ . . .[ ]

Notes

Verso

1. ברך: If אמי is correctly restored here and in the address (in both places Bresciani puts dots under the letters read without brackets), and if Yahuyishma^{c} is the correct reading, then בר with the suffix *-k* is peculiar, because we would expect ברכי, with a fem. suffix. As a fem. name, יהוישמע occurs frequently in *BMAP* (6:8; 7:3, 4, etc.). The same problem is met in לך (line 2), the impv. הבה (line 3), where we should expect הביה, and the restored לשלמך (line 4). On the other hand, the fem. form of the impv. הבי in line 4 favors the interpretation that the letter is written to a woman. What we have here, then, is simply the use of masc. forms in addressing a woman—a phenomenon which is otherwise attested in the Aramaic texts from Elephantine (e.g., אנת [instead of אנתי], *BMAP* 6:8, 10[?]; 9:14; דילך [instead of דילכי], *BMAP* 9:14; זילך [instead of זילכי], *BMAP* 9:11, 12, 14; לך [instead of לכי], *BMAP* 6:14; 9:12; יגרנך [instead of יגרנכי], *BMAP* 4:16). Note that in *BMAP* 6:3 Anani bar Azariah even calls his daughter, Yahuyishma^{c}, ברי! In this case, however, we may have to regard this as a scribal omission for בר‹ת›י;

cf. 6:8, 17, 19. Note the absence of מן here before the writer's name; cf. *Pad* I v 1.

שלום: Shallum, a name which occurs in *BMAP* 11:13; *AP* 23:6; 25:18; [35:2]; 63:10.

פטמ[ון]: Peṭamun, "the one given by Amon." Cf. *RES* 1364 (פטמון). Bresciani notes that the name occurs also in the Hermopolis letters (4:3); she suggests the possibility also of reading פטמ[ת], as in *AP* 24:1, but that form is by no means a certain reading. See *B-M* 17.

2. לך: See note on ברך, line 1 above.

שלם: See note on *Pad* I r 5.

גלגל תנה: Bresciani reads this all as one word and as the form גלגלתנם. In my original study of this text, I too hesitatingly read the last letter as a *mem*. However, the last three letters are now to be read as תנה, "here." This is certain from *Herm WP* 2:2-3 (שלם נבושה תנה); 6:8 (שלם בנתסר תנה); and possibly 8:11 ([שלם . . . נ]בושה תנה). The proper name גלגל (and גלגול) appears in *AP* 49:1; 10:21; *RES* 907; Mur 42:2; 43:2; 44:1; 51:1; 115:4, 5 (vocalized in Greek as Γαλγουλᾶ). M. Noth (*IPN*, 223) related it to the Arabic *juljulun*, "Schelle, Klingel."

ינקיה: Emphatic state written with *he* instead of *aleph*; cf. *sprh* (II v 5).

3. בלא: Owing to the lacuna at the end of line 2 it is impossible to interpret this word with certainty. בלא is found as a proper name in *AP* 28:5, but this hardly fits the context here. Bresciani suggests a connection with the root בלא, "be worn out," used in *AP* 26:1 of a boat. Could it possibly be another spelling of *bĕlô*, "tribute, tax (paid in kind)," which occurs in Ezra 4:13; 7:24?

הבה: Apparently the masc. sg. impv. with a suffix; for *hbyh*, as Bresciani notes.

פחנום: Pakhnum, "the one belonging to Khnum." The name also occurs in *AP* 23:5, spelled פחנם⁾ *and in BMAP* 11:2, 10, 15.

נבודלה: Nabudalah, "Nabu has drawn up (from the depths, rescued)." Bresciani states that the name is Babylonian; but both H. V. Hilprecht (*The Babylonian Expedition of the University of Pennsylvania* [Philadelphia: University of Pennsylvania, 1898], IX, 64) and K. Tallqvist (*Assyrian Personal Names*, p. 279) regard *Nabû-da-la*⁾ as an Aramaean name. Moreover, Nabu was apparently venerated at Elephantine; see A. Dupont-Sommer, "'Bēl et Nabû, Šamaš et Nergal' sur un ostracon araméen inédit d'Eléphantine," *RHR* 128 (1944) 29-30 (translated by H. L. Ginsberg, *ANET*, 491). Cf. *AD* 6:1 (*Nbwdl*⁾, but corrected in abridged edition to *Nbwdlny*).

4. יגרוהי: "They will prosecute him." The verb גרא is frequently used in this sense with the suffix in the Elephantine texts; see Kraeling, *BMAP*, 310.

5. שלחת ספרא זנה: Cf. *Cl-G Ost* 70: conv. 2 (לשלמך שלחת ספרא), which supports the restoration of the original editor on line 4.

אמי: This word is written above the line and creates a problem. If it is intended to be an appositive to מנחמת, then it cannot mean the same thing as אמי in line 1; the same is true, if it is the *nomen rectum* and מנחמת is the appositive. In such a case אם would have to be a title of address, similar to אח in *Pad* I v 1. But is אם ever found in that sense? We know of no parallels for it. Is אמי then a vocative? At any rate, it was added later as an afterthought and it seems to upset the sense of the greeting.

מנחמת: Menaḥemet, "the Consoler," a fem. form of Menaḥem. It is also found in *AP* 22:81, [95], 108.

Padua Papyrus III (= *Pad* III)

Text

אל אחתי יהושמע[

]באגורא שלם אושע בר זכ[

Translation

a: To my sister, Yahushemaᶜ [

b: [ ] in the temple. Greetings from Osea bar Zak[

Notes

a: אחתי: Bresciani understands this word also as a term of address similar to אח. But what is the evidence for this?

יהושמע: Yahushemaᶜ, "Yahu has heard." The name also occurs in *AP* 22:84, 87, 98, 99, 117. Cf. M. Noth, *IPN*, 185.

b: באגורא: "In the temple"; the word (< Accad. *ekurru*) is used in the Elephantine texts either of the temple of Yahu (*BMAP* 12:18; *AP* 30:6), or of that of other gods (*AP* 30:14).

[ ]זכר: Possibly Zakkur (*AP* 10:3) or Zekaryah (*AP* 5:5). It is also possible, of course, that the greetings are sent *to* Osea bar Zak. . . .

It is hoped that the above remarks will contribute to the further understanding of these papyrus letters.

NOTES TO CHAPTER 10

*Originally published under the same title in *JNES* 21 (1962) 15-24.

[1] J. C. L. Gibson (*Textbook of Syrian Semitic Inscriptions* [p. 76 above, n. 29], 2. 143–47) regards *Pad* I as coming from Migdol in Egypt. That seems to be the place from which the letter was written; but it is another question as to where it was found.

[2]"Papiri aramaici egiziani di epoca persiana presso il Museo Civico di Padova," *RSO* 35 (1960) 11-24 (+ 5 pls.). For further literature on these texts, see E. Bresciani, "Postilla a RSO, XXV, 11-24," *RSO* 35 (1960) 211; F. Díaz Estaban, "Una formula de cortesia epistolar de Ugarit, repetida en una carta judeo-aramea del siglo V a. C.," *Sefarad* 22 (1962) 101-2; J. Naveh, "Old Aramaic Inscriptions (1960-64)," *AION* 16 (1966) 19-36, esp. pp. 25-29; J. T. Milik, "Les papyrus araméens d'Hermoupolis et les cultes syro-phéniciens en Egypte perse," *Bib* 48 (1967) 546-621, esp. p. 549.

[3]The transcription of the *editio princeps* should be consulted concerning letters which are doubtful in the text. No attempt is made here to mark them or to describe the physical state of the papyri.

Chapter 11

The Aramaic Letter of King Adon to the Egyptian Pharaoh*

The Aramaic letter sent by the king of a small territory in Palestine or Phoenicia, informing the contemporary Egyptian Pharaoh of the advance of the troops of the Babylonian king and asking for the Pharaoh's military support against them, is well known. It was first published in 1948 by A. Dupont-Sommer,[1] and its historical significance has been discussed by several writers since then.[2] It sheds precious light on the period just before the destruction of Jerusalem by Nebuchadrezzar II and the great experience in Israel's history known as the Babylonian Captivity. Though several writers have attempted to bring out further aspects of the letter, either philological or historical, its full message is not yet entirely clear. The main reason is that the letter is fragmentary, since the ends of the nine extant lines are lost. There is no way of telling just how much is lost at the end of the lines. The estimate of one-third, which has been suggested, may be correct, but then it may be that we have only about a half of the lines, since the attempt to fill in the lacunae and establish a plausible coherence between the lines demands a considerable restoration. We are attempting a re-study of the letter, hoping to bring out a few more details and offer some observations on previous interpretations of different phrases which call for some reconsideration.

From the standpoint of the Aramaic language the letter is significant in that a kinglet of Canaanite background writes for aid to his Egyptian overlord in this language. It is a very early example of Official Aramaic, and important in that it is the earliest sample of it to come from Palestine or Phoenicia. Even though the fragment was found at Saqqârah in Egypt, it is important to keep this in mind, as it bears on the interpretation of certain phrases.

The date of the letter is not established with certainty. It is generally agreed—and rightly—that the letter belongs to the period of the contest for power between the 26th (Saite) Dynasty of Egypt and the Neo-Babylonian (Chaldean) Kingdom of Mesopotamia. With the destruction of Nineveh in 612 B.C. and the eventual ejection of the Assyrians from Harran in 610, Egypt and Babylonia strove to dominate Palestine and Syria. The Pharaoh Necho II (609-593) marched to the aid of the Assyrian Asshur-uballiṭ II, hoping to retake Harran from the Babylonians and set up again a center of Assyrian influence. King Josiah of Judah, who tried for some reason to stop Necho, was killed at Megiddo in 609. The Pharaoh was eventually defeated by the Babylonians at Carchemish in 605. But he had already tried to consolidate his holdings in Palestine. After Jehoahaz had reigned for three months as the heir of Josiah, he was summoned to the Pharaoh's headquarters in Riblah (central Syria), deposed, and deported to Egypt (2 Kgs 23:31-35; Jer 22:10-12). Jehoahaz' brother, Eliakim, was put on the throne as an Egyptian vassal, and was given the throne-name of Jehoiakim. The Pharaoh must have attempted to dominate other kings in the area too, for King Adon, who writes this Aramaic letter, seems to have been another such vassal of the Egyptian Pharaoh. The advance of the Babylonians which he mentions in the letter is generally associated—and again rightly—with the campaigns of Nebuchadrezzar II, because it was under the latter that the campaigns against Palestine and Syria took place. It is, however, a matter of dispute as to the year in which the letter was written. D. Winton Thomas' view that it was written in 587 has won scarcely any support, since it is unconvincing. A. Malamat at first preferred to relate the letter to the events of 598, the Babylonian campaign in which Jehoiachin surrendered to the invader and was deported (2 Kgs 24:10-12). Similarly, R. Meyer. However, since the publication of the Chronicles of Nebuchadrezzar, in which the fall of Ashkelon is explicitly mentioned for December 604 B.C.,[3] a date for the writing of this letter has been proposed somewhere in the immediately preceding period, 605-4. In substance, this is the date of W. F. Albright, A. Dupont-Sommer, E. Vogt, A. Malamat, etc.[4]

If the almost contemporary Lachish letters have shed light on such a passage as Jer 34:1-7, esp. 34:7, it is not impossible that the Aramaic letter of King Adon does the same for Jer 36:9-32, the burning of the scroll. This incident has been related to the capture of Ashkelon by Nebuchadrezzar II, as both E. Vogt and A. Malamat have suggested. But more recently (*IEJ* 18 [1968] 142-43) Malamat has preferred "the king of Gaza" as the "most likely" candidate for restoration.

Text

1 אל מרא מלכן פרעה עבדך אדן מלך .[שלם מראי עשתרת בעלת]
2 שמיא וארקא ובעלשמין אלה[א רבא ישאלו בבל עדן וישימו כרסא]
3 פרעה כיומי שמין אמין זי[חילא]
4 זי מלך בבל אתו מטאו אפק וש[ראו]
5 [ ] אחזו . ל . . לו . ל[ ]
6 כי מרא מלכן פרעה ידע כי עבד[ך לא יכל למקם קדמוה ירקה מראי]
7 למשלח חיל לחצלתי אל ישבקנ[י מרא מלכן פרעה כי מומאה]
8 וטבתה עבדך נצר ונגדא זנה[ ]
9 פחה במתא וספר שניוי ספ[ ]

Translation

[1]To the Lord of Kings, the Pharaoh, your servant ᵓAdon, the king of [May Astarte, the Mistress] [2]of the heavens and the earth, and Baᶜalshamayn, [the great] god, [seek the welfare of my lord at all times and make the throne] [3]of Pharaoh (as) enduring as the days of heaven. Since [the troops] [4]of the king of Babylon have come (and) have arrived (at) Aphek, and have enca[mped] [5][. . . .] and have taken .L. .LW .L [ ] [6]for the Lord of Kings, the Pharaoh, knows that [your] servant [cannot withstand him. May my lord be pleased] [7]to send an army to rescue me. May [the Lord of Kings, the Pharaoh], not forsake m[e, for] [8]your servant has kept [his oath] and his good relations. And this commander [has set up] [9] a governor in the land and has recorded his changes (?) [ ]

Notes

1. אל: The preposition ᵓ*el* was used in Old Aramaic inscriptions (Sf III 1, 19, 20). Though it was normally replaced by על in Official Aramaic, it was retained in the addresses of letters as here. See the note on *Pad* I 1.

מרא מלכן: "The Lord of Kings." At this period of Aramaic מרא can only be cst. sg.; excluded, therefore, is any such meaning as "the lord, our king," which might be theoretically possible in later Aramaic. The title is the same as that found in Dan 2:47, where it is applied to Yahweh by the Babylonian king Nebuchadrezzar. Dupont-Sommer rightly stressed that the title מרא מלכן is not found in Egyptian documents, and that it should not be confused with the Akkad. *šar šarrāni*, or with the Achaemenid title, "King of Kings," used of Nebuchadrezzar in Ezek 26:7 (מלך מלכים, or the Aram. form, מלך מלכיא, Dan 2:37; Ezra 7:12). For מרא מלכן is rather the equivalent of the Phoen. אדן מלכם (Ešmunᶜazor 18), and of the Akkad. *bēl šarrāni* (*ABL* 256.1, 2; 281.3, 16-17, 32; 992.2). The Phoen. expression became more current in the time of the Ptolemies (*NSI* 10:5; 27:1; 28:2; 29:4; cf. also 9:5 [used of Alexander the Great]). Dupont-Sommer compared it to the Greek title *κύριος βασιλέων*, but gave no references to the occurrence of this phrase. H. L. Ginsberg maintained that the title was rather *κύριος βασιλειῶν*. The latter occurs in the Rosetta Stone, line 1 (cf. W. Dittenberger, *OGIS* 1.90,1). This was translated by Ginsberg as "Lord of Kingdoms," and he insisted that מרא מלכן should be translated in the same way (similarly J. Bright, R. Meyer). מלכן would be *molkîn*. He compared Dan 2:47, Arab. *mulk*, and appealed to Phoen. and Ugar. instances of *mlk* equalling *mulk*, "kingdom," "kingship." See C. H. Gordon, *Ugaritic Manual*, 49:V:5; VI:28. —However, even granting that *mlk* in Arab., Phoen. and Ugar. has the meaning "kingdom," it is still not certain that מרא מלכן means anything more than "Lord of Kings." First of all, this Aram. phrase is a reflection of both the Phoen. and Akkad. expressions. In the latter case, *bēl šarrāni* cannot mean anything but "Lord of Kings." Secondly, the connection between מרא מלכן and the Gk. expression is quite tenuous. Ginsberg understood *κύριος βασιλειῶν*, "lord of Kingdoms," to refer to the kingdoms of Upper and Lower Egypt. But this is far from certain, in the Gk. text of the Rosetta stone at least. A spot-check of several translations of that text shows that the meaning normally accepted for *κύριος βασιλείων* is "the Lord of Crowns." So, for instance, E. A. Wallis Budge, *The Rosetta Stone in the British Museum* (London: British Museum, 1929) 51; J. P. Mahaffy, *A History of Egypt Under the Ptolemaic Dynasty* (London: Methuen, 1899) 152; E. Bevan, *A History of Egypt,* vol. 4; London: Methuen, 1927) 263; M. Letronne, "Inscription grecque de Rosette," in C. and T. Müller (ed.), *Fragmenta historicorum graecorum* (Paris: Didot, 1874) App. pp. 1 and 7 [This celebrated translation gives "maître des couronnes," but the commentary admits that one cannot entirely exclude the meaning "royaume"]. In this Gk. expression the reference is to the ten gold crowns of the Ptolemaic king, which were symbolic of power enjoyed (at least at some time) over Egypt, Libya, Syria, Phoenicia, Cyprus, Lycia, Caria, Cyclades, Arabia, Aethiopia (see W. Dittenberger, *OGIS*, 1.90,43). Part of the problem is the uncertainty whether *βασιλείων* is to be taken as the gen. pl. of *βασιλεία* ("kingdom") or of *τὸ βασίλειον* ("diadem, crown"). Given this uncertainty about the meaning of the Gk. expression, one cannot assert apodictically that it shows that Ptolemaic kings were called "Lord of Kingdoms." Further evidence must be adduced to establish the connection between the Aram. מרא מלכן and the Phoen. אדן מלכם, on the one hand, and the Gk. expression *κύριος βασιλείων*, on the other. Does the expression turn up anywhere else in Gk.? We have been unable to discover it. —Moreover, as both Koopmans and Donner-Röllig point out, the normal word for "kingdom" in Aram. is מלכו, which could easily have been used if one wanted to say "Lord of Kingdoms." H. L. Ginsberg objected to Dupont-Sommer's translation, "Au Seigneur des rois," on the grounds that it would demand the emphatic state. This, however, is not the problem that it seems to be at first sight, because it is a title (cf. Dan 2:47). —This note was already written when K. Galling's article arrived, "Eschmunazar und der Herr der Könige," *ZDPV* 79 (1963) 140-51. In it the reader will find further references to Akkad. literature which is contemporary and is probably the source of the Aram. and later Phoen. expression. Galling also explains *βασιλείων* as having nothing to do with *βασιλεία*, which for him is a "Singulare tantum," but as the gen. pl. of *τὸ βασίλειον*. Galling's article is the latest contribution to a discussion on the date of the Ešmunᶜazor inscription, which he carried on earlier with H. L. Ginsberg (see "'King of Kings' and 'Lord of Kingdoms,'" *AJSL* 57 [1940] 71-74; *JBL* 56 [1937] 142-43; K. Galling, "Denkmäler zur Geschichte Syriens und Palästinas unter der Herrschaft der Perser," *PJB* 34 [1938] 59-79, esp. pp. 71-73.) —The upshot of all this is that King Adon, writing to the Egyptian Pharaoh predicates of him an Akkad. or possibly a Phoen. title. There is no evidence so far that it is an Egyptian title, and its relation to the Ptolemaic Greek title is tenuous at best. Cf. J. Friedrich, "Griechisches und römisches in phönizischem und punischem Gewand," *Festschrift Otto Eissfeldt* (Halle/S.: Niemeyer, 1947) 109-24, esp. p. 112.

פרעה: "The Pharaoh." The title, apparently first used in the time of Amenophis IV (ca. 1370 B.C.), became rather common in the Saite dynasty, to which this letter is dated. It is a title meaning, "Great House," and as in many texts in the OT and Akkad. the Pharaoh is not further identified; Sargon II refers in his annals merely to *Pirʾu*. The Pharaoh in question is almost certainly Necho II (609-593 B.C.), to whom King Adon writes. Cf. 2 Kgs 23:29, 33-35; Jer 46:2; 2 Chr 35:20, 22; 36:4. See S. H. Horn, "Where and When" (n. 2 above), 32.

עבדך: "Your servant," an expression relatively common in letters sent to superiors: *AP* 30:4; 38:2; 54:9; 70:1; *BMAP* 13:9, etc.; Ezra 4:11. See p. 190 above. Cf. also the use of *waradka* in Akkad. texts.

אדן A Canaanite proper name, probably a shortened form of some name like *ʾAdonîṣedeq* (Jos 10:1, 3), *ʾAdōnîqām* (Ezra 2:13), *ʾAdōnîrām* (1 Kgs 4:6), *ʾdnbʿl* (*CIS*, 1.138), etc. As a hypocoristicon, it occurs in Akkad. as *A-du-na* (cf. Tallqvist, *APN*, 13), the name of a Phoenician king of ʿArqa; possibly a genuine Akkad. occurrence is found in ^I^*A-du-ni-i* (ND 5447: 12). As a common noun, it means the same as Aram. מרא, "lord." See p. 125 above. But it is a proper name here, as can be seen from the fact that it follows עבדך and precedes מלך. Since this cannot be the name of any king of Judah in this period, it must be the name of a king in one of the Philistine coastal cities (or countries), Gaza, Ashkelon, Ashdod, Ekron, or Gath. —A. Malamat (*IEJ* 18 [1968] 143 n. 11) considers the name *ʾAdonimelek* a possibility here.

מלך: "King of. . . ." The combination of the name (Adon) and the situation described in the letter call for a restoration of the name of some Philistine or Phoenician town. In Philistia only two are possible, when all is said and done: either Ashkelon or Gaza. W. F. Albright was apparently the first to suggest Ashkelon, and many have found his suggestion plausible. R. Meyer calls it "höchst unsicher," without giving any reasons. What is certain is that Ashkelon had a king about this time, for the mention of "two sons of Agaʾ, the king of Ashkelon," is found in the Weidner Tablets. See E. F. Weidner, "Jojachin, König von Juda, in babylonischen Keilschrifttexten," *Mélanges syriens offerts à M. René Dussaud* (Paris: Geuthner, 1939) 2. 923-35, esp. p. 928: *2 mārē^meš^ šá^I^ A-ga-ʾ, šarri ša ^māt^Iš-qil-lu-nu.* It has been suggested that Nebuchadrezzar had deposed Adon after the capture of Ashkelon and set up in his stead Agaʾ as a Babylonian vassal. Albright sees the two sons of Agaʾ as hostages; they would have been taken to Babylonia, and the tablets would record rations doled out to them. However, E. Vogt has found some difficulty in this, because the Wiseman Chronicles of Nebuchadrezzar, in recording the capture of Ashkelon, note that he "marched to the city of Ashkelon and captured it in the month of Kislev. He captured its king and plundered it and carried off [spoil from it . . .]. He turned the city into a mound and heaps of ruins, and then in the month of Šebat he marched back to Babylon" (B. M. 21946 obv. 18-20). The destruction of Ashkelon is recorded with the same expressions as that of Nineveh and is quite different from the mention of the appointment of a king "in the city of Judah" (B. M. 21946 rev. 13). Vogt, therefore, concludes that Nebuchadrezzar did not set up a king in Ashkelon and that Agaᵓ must have been the last king of Ashkelon—the one whom Nebuchadrezzar besieged and defeated. He and his sons would have been deported; he is not otherwise mentioned in the Weidner Tablets, because he had probably died meanwhile in captivity. Though Vogt's objection is real, it is not serious enough to outweigh the other evidence which points toward Ashkelon as the most likely town over which Adon would have ruled. For one thing, we do not know how long Adon lived after he wrote to the Pharaoh. It is not impossible that Agaᵓ had already succeeded Adon before the troops of Nebuchadrezzar arrived at the town. After all, Adon wrote and sent the letter to the Pharaoh in Egypt; there must have been some time which elapsed between the arrival of the Babylonian army at Aphek and its coming to Adon's town; otherwise there would have been little point in writing. —If the objection of E. Vogt is considered a real obstacle to the identification of the town of Adon with Ashkelon, then there remains Gaza, as the Philistine coastal town even closer to Egypt, which would be a possibility. In either case Nebuchadrezzar is presumably advancing from the north (from the area already conquered). Adon's kingdom is to the south of Nebuchadrezzar's position and to the south of Aphek.

But there is no certainty that the city over which Adon ruled was situated in Philistia. H. Donner and W. Röllig consider the possibility of its localization in Phoenicia (*KAI*, 313). J. T. Milik thinks that this is more probable too. Having examined the photograph again, he finds the trace of a letter following מלך, which cannot be an *aleph*. This rules out the possibility of Ashkelon. Nor can it be an ᶜ*ayin*, ruling out the possibility of Gaza. Milik thinks that the only two possibilities are a *daleth* or a *ṣadhe*; he reads either צ[ידון] or preferably צ[ור], since Tyre was the home of the cult of Melqart, Astarte, and Baᶜalshamayn (*Bib* 48 [1967] 561). Cf. H. Seyrig, "Antiquités syriennes," *Syria* 40 (1963) 19-28.

Since no certainty can be gained in this matter, I have chosen to leave the lacuna blank in this case; but I do think that Milik was right in returning to the suggestion of Dupont-Sommer about the names of the deities to be restored.

[שלם מראי עשתרת בעלת] שמיא וארקא . . . [ישאלו בכל עדן]: "May Astarte, the Mistress of the heavens and the earth . . . seek the welfare of my lord at all times." The greeting is restored according to the usual one found in Aramaic letters from Egypt (*AP* 30:1–2; 21:2; 39:1). See further pp. 191–92 above.

[עשתרת בעלת] שמיא וארקא: "Astarte, the Mistress of the heavens and earth." This was Dupont-Sommer's original restoration, appealing to Akkad. *Ištar bēlit šamē ū irṣitim* (*Hymn to Ishtar*, 27: *ANET*, 383) and comparing Jer 7:18; 44:17–19, 25. Istar and Ba-al-samēmē are also invoked in a treaty between Esarhaddon and Baal, king of Tyre (cf. R. Borger, *Die Inschriften*

Asarhaddons Königs von Assyrien [Beiheft AfO 9; Graz: Private publication, 1956] 69 IV 10 and 18 [p. 109]). This now seems more plausible to me than the suggestion of H. L. Ginsberg to read [מרא], which I originally followed. It would be a reference to the god El (see Sf I A 11; Gen 14:19; 1QapGen 22:16, 21).

2. בעלשמין: "Baʿalshmayn," or more correctly *baʿlšamayn*. He is identical with Hadad, the Syrian storm-god. See Zakir A 3. Cf. O. Eissfeldt, "Baʿalšamēm und Jahwe," *ZAW* 57 (1939) 1-31; M. H. Pope, *El in the Ugaritic Texts* (Leiden: Brill, 1955) 57.

[אלה]א רבא: "The great god." Some epithet seems to have followed the name Baʿalshamayn. We have adopted Ginsberg's suggestion of רבא.

[וישימו כרסא] פרעה כיומי שמין אמין: "May they make the throne of Pharaoh (as) firm as the days of heaven." Or, if there would be space enough, one could add with Dupont-Sommer מרא מלכן at the end of line 2. The restoration is based on Ps 89:30 (שמתי לעד זרעו וכסאו כימי שמים); cf. v. 37; Deut 11:21; Sir 45:15. J. J. Koopmans regards אמין as the pass. ptc. of אמן; it may rather be the normal *qattīl* adjectival type in Aramaic (ʾ*ammīn*).

זי: A space precedes this word, and so it is probably to be taken as the beginning of a sentence. It is probably a conjunction. See S. H. Horn, *AUSS* 6 (1968) 31.

4. מלך בבל: "The king of Babylon." This is not the subject of the following verbs, since they are plural. The restoration of חילא is not unlikely; it would have to be understood in a collective sense. Cf. חילא with the plur. adj. אחרנן in *AP* 30:8, with the plur. verb קטלו in B 5, [48]. However, if one were to take a cue from 2 Kgs 24:10 (MT: עבדי נבוכדנאצר מלך בבל), perhaps we should restore עבדיא (= ʿ*abdayyā*ʾ), "the servants of the king of Babylon." This would yield a plural with which the verbs would easily agree. —The king is not named. Theoretically, he could be either Nabopolassar or the crown-prince who became king, Nebuchadrezzar II. Since the publication of the Wiseman Chronicles, it is almost certain that Nebuchadrezzar is meant. The title מלך בבל is given to him explicitly in the Louvre Tablet A 6-7 (see J. Starcky, *Syria* 37 [1960] 99-115, esp. p. 100), as well as in Jer 21:2, 7; 2 Kgs 24:1, 7, 11, 12; etc. However, the same title is borne also by Merodach-Baladan (2 Kgs 20:12), Evil-Merodach (2 Kgs 25:27; Jer 52:31), and Artaxerxes I (Neh 13:6). But there can be no question of these three kings here.

אתו: "Have come." See *AP* 30:8.

מטאו: "Have arrived." The two verbs are joined asyndetically. The second verb governs the name of a place directly without a prep., as frequently in earlier and later Aramaic (Sf III 5, *yhkn Ḥlb*; Pad I v 5, *tʾtwn Mṣryn*: I r 3 ʾ*ytyt hmw Mnpy*: *BMAP* 13:3; *AP* 42:7; 83:2; *AD* 6.2, 4, 5). Contrast *AP* 37:11; 42:11. —Note the orthography in the two verbs. Both are *tertiae infirmae*. verbs; but in אתו the final *aleph* (already quiescent) is not even written. Hence אתו must = ʾ*atô* or possibly ʾ*ătô*. But in the case of מטאו the *aleph* is written. Most likely it was no longer pronounced; hence *maṭô* (or even *mĕṭô*). There is as yet no evidence for the reduction of pretonic short vowels in an open syllable at this date.

J. T. Milik (*Bib* 48 [1967] 562) would read instead of מטאו the word מעב[ר]ת and would translate, "[une armée] du roi de Babylone est arrivé à la passe d'Afeq et de Š[. . .]." The last word he understands as *š*[*r*ᶜ*yt*], modern *Ser*ᶜ*îtā*, on the route from Baalbek to Byblos or Beirut (cf. Aramaic *šĕra*ᶜ*tā*ᵓ, "slope").

אפק: "Aphek." The identification of this place is problematic, since there are at least four towns so named in the OT. (1) Aphek, originally a Canaanite town on the plain of Sharon, at Ras el-ᶜAin, the Antipatris of NT times; cf. Jos 12:18; 1 Sam 4:1; 29:1. It lay E of Jaffa and about 10 mi. N of Lydda, on the upper course of the ᶜAujā River. It served as the base of Philistine operations against Israel and was mentioned in the list of Thutmose III (No. 66) as *Ipḳ*. It was also noted in the Annals of Esarhaddon for 671 B.C. as "Apqu which is in the region of Sama[ria?]" (uru*Ap-qu ša pa-ṭi KUR Sa-me-n*[*a?-x*], cf. R. Borger, *Die Inschriften Asarhaddons*, §76: Vs 16 [p. 112]; cf. *ANET*, 292). See W. F. Albright, *BASOR* 11 (1923) 6-7; *JPOS* 3 (1923) 50-53; A. Alt, *PJB* 28 (1932) 19-20; 22 (1926) 69; the results of soundings there are described by A. Eitan, *IEJ* 12 (1962) 151-52; *RB* 69 (1962) 407-8. (2) Aphek in Asher, i.e., Tell Kerdâne in the plain of Akko, at the source of the Naᶜmên River; cf. Jos 19:30; Judg 1:31. See A. Alt, *PJB* 24 (1928) 59-60; 25 (1929) 41 n. 1. (3) Aphek, to the east of the Lake of Tiberias, i.e., Fiq or Afiq in Jaulan, on the road from Damascus to Beisan; cf. 1 Kgs 20:26, 30; 2 Kgs 13:17. (4) Aphek in Phoenicia, near Byblos, i.e., modern Afqa in the Lebanon Mts. on the upper course of Nahr Ibrāhîm, the Adonis of antiquity; cf. Jos 13:4. —In general, see F.-M. Abel, *Géographie de la Palestine* (2 vols.; Paris: Gabalda, 1933-38), 2. 246-47; R. Dussaud, *Topographie historique de la Syrie antique et mediévale* (Paris: Geuthner, 1927) 13-14; M. du Buit, *Géographie de la terre sainte* (Paris: Cerf, 1958) 182. E. Vogt has discussed the likelihood of these sites in detail; only Aphek in Sharon enjoys any probability as the place named in this letter, if the city of King Adon lay in Philistia. However, if it was situated in Phoenicia, then modern Afqa is the more logical place. But see S. H. Horn, *AUSS* 6 (1968) 34–38, for a fifth possibility in southern Judah, Apheka (Josh 15:53), perhaps Khirbet eḍ-Ḍarrâme, SW of Hebron (so *KAI*, 314).

וש[ראו]: "And have encamped." One cannot entirely exclude the suggestion of Dupont-Sommer that *wš*[is the beginning of another proper name, coordinated with ᵓ*pq*. Milik follows this suggestion. But it is not impossible that it is a verb, as H. L. Ginsberg suggested. He restored it as the pael *šarrîw*, "they have begun" (cf. Ezra 5:2). It is not, however, impossible that it is the peal form of *šr*ᵓ, "and they have encamped" *(wa-šar*ᵓ*ô* < *wa-šar*ᵓ*aw).* See 1QapGen 20:34-21:1.

6. כי: For the use of this conjunction in Aramaic texts, see Sf III 22; Zakir A 13; Aššur Ostracon 8(?); *A* 95, 98, 99.

[עבד[ך: Restored as in line 1. This line expresses the vassal's condition and the reason why he is requesting aid in coping with it.

[לא יכל למקם קדמוהי]: "Cannot withstand him," i.e., the king of Babylon; lit., "is not able to stand before him." Cf. *A* 107 (מן הו זי יקום קדמוהי). It is impossible to decide whether one should write קדמוה (as in the earlier inscriptions and *BMAP* 3:4; *AP* 25:3), or קדמוהי (as in *Aḥiqar*).

[ירקה מראי]: "May my lord be pleased." Some such verb is needed to introduce the inf. in line 7. ירקה is 3 sg. m. peal short impf. (= jussive) of רקה, the early form of רעה (related to Hebr. *rṣh*). The pael of רקה occurs in Sf III 6, 18, 19. The form with the *qoph* is used because of ארקא (line 2).

7. למשלח: "To send" (peal inf.). The peal inf. has the preformative *mem* here, as in Sf I B 34; early infinitives peal often occur without it (Sf I B 32 [שגב]; III 12, 13 [נכה]).

לחצלתי: "To rescue me." Dupont-Sommer reads להצלתי (with *he*), but admits that *ḥeth* is also possible. Ginsberg, Donner-Röllig also read *he*. With Koopmans we prefer to read *ḥeth*, not only because it is the *lectio difficilior*, but because the left shaft is longer than that of *he* in the rest of the letter. Either form is grammatically possible. חצלתי is the pael inf. cst. with a suffix; its root is *ḥlṣ*, "draw off; rescue, deliver." It preserves the same metathesis as in Zakir A 14 (cf. T. Nöldeke, *ZA* 21 [1908] 382). The form with *he* would be the Haph. inf. cst. with a suffix; its root would be נצל, "deliver, set free." —J. J. Koopmans calls the suffix "strange" and expects rather -*ūtánī*. However, this is the form of the suffix on the inf. of derived conjugations in Old Aramaic; cf. Sf III 11, 15 (המתתי, haph. inf. of מות; = *hamītūtī*, "to kill me"). —Cf. Isa 30:3; 31:3.

[אל ישבקנ[י: "Let the Lord of Kings, the Pharaoh, not forsake me." Dupont-Sommer read at first [אל שבקנ[י, a negatived impv., which is unlikely, if not impossible. Later he changed it to a 2nd sg. form, [תשבקנ[י. Ginsberg preferred to read the 3d sg., which seems better according to the photo. It is also a polite form, more in keeping with the tone of the rest of the letter. Would the vassal who calls himself עבדך address the Pharaoh so bluntly? —Apparently the help from Egypt was not forthcoming; cf. 2 Kgs 24:7.

[כי מומאה] וטבתה עבדך נצר: "Has kept his oath and his good relations." It is this expression more than any of the others in the letter which makes it clear that King Adon was a vassal of the Egyptian Pharaoh. He uses covenant terminology here and emphasizes that he has been faithful to the Pharaoh, and implies thereby that he deserves to be aided by him. Dupont-Sommer translated טבתה simply as "ses biens (= les biens du Pharaon) ton serviteur a sauve-gardé." But he did not explain what he meant by "biens"; it sounds as though King Adon were protesting that he has watched out for the Pharaoh's possessions in his territory. Given the fragmentary state of the papyrus, one could not really exclude this meaning. But once it is realized that נצר טבתה is a treaty expression, then the last few lines of the letter take on a different nuance. H. L. Ginsberg translated, "Thy servant remembers his kindness," giving נצר another possible meaning, and taking the form not as the pf. but as a ptc. J. Bright simply followed Ginsberg, while Donner-Röllig followed Dupont-Sommer ("und seine Güter hat dein Sklave bewahrt"). But the suffix (apparently 3d sg. m.) on טבתה creates a problem. How can it refer to the Pharaoh when the suffix on the subject (עבדך) is in the 2d sg. m.? True, the Pharaoh is referred to in the 3d sg. in ידע (line 6), as well as in line 7, if the reading [ישבקנ[י be admitted. But with the subject עבדך would not one expect טבתה, if either of the above interpretations were correct? Furthermore, טבתה most likely has the meaning which it has in the Sefîre inscriptions, as has recently been pointed out by W. L. Moran ("A Note on the Treaty Terminology of the Sefîre Stelas," *JNES* 22 [1963] 173-76). He showed that טבתא there means "good relations," or the "friendship" demanded by the pact between the suzerain and the vassal. Cf. Sf II B 2; I C 19-20, 4-5. The likelihood that this meaning is required here is increased by the fact that in certain Akkad. texts the word *ṭabtu* (now shown to have a treaty connotation of "good relations") is used with *naṣāru*, "preserve, guard, keep." Cf. Annals of Asshurbanipal (Rassam Cylinder): *ina a-di-ia iḫ-ṭu-ú ṭabat e-pu-šu-uš lā iṣ-ṣur-ú-ma*, "he has sinned against my treaty; he has not preserved the good relations I made with him" (M. Streck, *Assurbanipal*, Cyl A 7.86 [VAB 7/2.64]). Again, *ina a-di-ia iḫ-ṭu-ú lā iṣ-ṣu-ru ma-mit ilāni rabuti MUN* (= *ṭabat*) *e-pu-us-su-nu-ti im-šū-ma* (Cyl A 1.119 [*VAB* 7/2. 12]). Cf. also Cyl A 9.72-73; Cyl B 7.91-95 [*VAB* 7/2.132]; Asshurbanipal No. CXCI. rs 1-4 (*VAB* 7/1 = Klauber 105 = K 159). The expression also occurs in an Akkadian text of a "brother-king" written to the king of Ugarit (RŠ 10.046: "Now in like manner preserve this friendship for me [*uṣ-ṣú-ur ṭābutta*]," reading the text as C. Virolleaud does in *RA* 38 (1941) 2, and correcting J. Nougayrol, *PRU* 3.10, accordingly. Cf. also D. C. Lyon, *Sargonidentexte,* 4.23. Though the more common expression is to "guard the oaths" and to "be mindful of the treaty," the expressions are often interchanged. Cf. Esarhaddon's Vassal Treaty, col. V. 292-92; *a-de-e an-nu-te uṣ-ra*, "guard this treaty" (Wiseman, p. 51). See also Ps 119:2, 22; 25:10. Such evidence makes our interpretation of the Aram. phrase plausible. Should there be any syntactical difficulty about the word order (Object Subject-Verb), which is admittedly not usual, one could point to Dan 2:27 and to the common greeting in letters, שלם מראן אלה שמיא ישאל (*AP* 17:1; 30:1-2). —Note that נצר is still written with *ṣ*, and not with the later *ṭ*; cf. Nêrab I. 12-13.—טבתה is probably plur., *ṭābāteh.*[5] (I am indebted to W. L. Moran for help in checking the examples in Akkadian literature and in supplying me with further references. The responsibility for the formulation of the note is mine.)

ונגדא זנה: Dupont-Sommer wrongly read the last word as זכם, and Ginsberg, Donner-Röllig, Koopmans, Malamat repeat it unquestioningly.

But the word is זנה, as F. Rosenthal saw quite independently (*BASOR* 111 [1948] 25 n. 4). R. Meyer calls Rosenthal's reading a "Konjektur" which he regards as unnecessary. But it is not a question of a conjecture. The last letter is quite different from any other clearly written *mem* in the letter (compare מרא [line 1]; למשלח [line 7]). Moreover, there is a vertical shaft on the left side, and the head of the letter slants in the wrong direction for a *mem*. Further, there is a syntactical problem in that זכם, which is an attested demonstrative, normally precedes its noun (cf. *AP* 9:2; 20:4; 65:3; *BMAP* 7:2). Finally, the second last letter is clearly a *nun* (compare מלכן [line 1]). As for the word which precedes *znh*, the reading and meaning of it are anybody's guess. Dupont-Sommer originally read נגדא, which would mean "commander, leader," as in Sf III 10. But to whom does it refer? Could it refer to the vassal king himself? Though this is unlikely, it would explain the use of the proximate demonstrative ("this"). If we may suppose that King Adon has mentioned some official of the Babylonian king's army in the lacuna, then possibly Adon is giving a further report about what he has been doing through the parts of Palestine and Syria already conquered. Dupont-Sommer's other alternative (נגרא), related to Accad. *nāgiru* is less likely. Ginsberg would read נגוא, "this region," i.e., the Philistine coastland; he compares Isa 20:6. There is a difficulty here, in that *nĕgāwātā* in later Aram. is usually fem. Strangely enough, S. H. Horn (*AUSS* 6 [1968] 31) follows Ginsberg in this interpretation despite the masculine demonstrative.

9. פחה: "A governor," see *Panammu* 12; *AP* 30:1, 29; *B* 18,[38]; Dan 3:2, 3, 27; *Pad* I r 4 (see note on p. 223 above).

במתא: "In the land." Though theoretically this word could mean "in / by death," yet the most natural meaning seems to be "in the land," as H. L. Ginsberg suggested. The word is *mātā*, already attested in Aššur Ostracon 2; *A* 36; *CIS* 2. 31; 1QapGen 2:33. Cf. Akkad. *mātu*.

וספר שניוי ספ[ ]: The meaning of this difficult phrase is sheer guesswork. The first word could be a noun: "and an inscription" (cf. Sf I B 8, 28, 33; etc.), or "and a scribe." It could also be a verb, "and he recorded." Could שניוי be related to Hebr. *šinnûy*, later Aram. *šinnûyā*, "change, alteration"? R. Meyer interpreted the words as *waspar šannīwē*, "und die Grenze—verändern wird man sie." Even if ספר could mean "Grenze" and *šannīw* is correctly understood as a verb, how could it have a future meaning? The form would be perfect, and the meaning would be past. This interpretation is quite inadequate. But we are not able to suggest anything more convincing.

It is hoped at least, however, that the above study of the letter of King Adon throws some light on the nature of the letter and the place it had in the treaty relations existing between him and the Egyptian Pharaoh. It is not a military document (*pace* A. Malamat, *JNES* 9 [1950] 222), but rather a political document, in which the Phoenician / Philistine (?) king is using the technical terminology of treaty relations. It is also a letter in which the vassal expresses his plight and reflects the panic that must have seized the Palestinian/Syrian rulers at the news of the advance of Nebuchadrezzar's army. If this line of interpretation is pursued further, perhaps someone will be able to unravel the mysteries of the phrases that still baffle us.

NOTES TO CHAPTER 11

*Originally published in *Bib* 46 (1965) 41-55 under the same title.

[1]"Un papyrus araméen d'époque saïte découvert à Saqqarah," *Sem* 1 (1948) 43-68.

[2]See Zaki Saad Effendi, "Saqqarah: Fouilles royales (1942)," *Chronique d'Egypte* 20 (1945) 80-81; H. L. Ginsberg, "An Aramaic Contemporary of the Lachish Letters," *BASOR* 111 (1948) 24-27; J. Bright, "A New Letter in Aramaic Written to a Pharaoh of Egypt," *BA* 12 (1949) 46-52; A. Dupont-Sommer, *Les Araméens* (Paris: Maisonneuve, 1949) 89; A. Bea, "Epistula aramaica saec. VII exeunte ad Pharaonem scripta," *Bib* 30 (1949) 514–16; A. Malamat, "מכתב ארמי חדש לפרעה מימי ירמיהו," *BJPES* 15 (1949) 34–39; R. Dussaud, *Syria* 26 (1949) 152–53; A. Malamat, "The Last Wars of the Kingdom of Judah," *JNES* 9 (1950) 218–27, esp. pp. 222–23; D. W. Thomas, "The Age of Jeremiah in the Light of Recent Archaeological Discovery," *PEQ* 82 (1950) 1–15, esp. pp. 8–13; R. Meyer, "Ein aramäischer Papyrus aus den ersten Jahren Nebukadnezars II.," *Festschrift für Friedrich Zucker zum 70. Geburtstage* (ed. W. Müller; Berlin: Akademie-Verlag, 1954) 251–62; A. Malamat, "A New Record of Nebuchadrezzar's Palestinian Campaigns," *IEJ* 6 (1956) 246–56, esp. p. 252; E. Vogt, "Die neu-babylonische Chronik über die Schlacht bei Karkemisch und die Einnahme von Jerusalem," *Volume du Congrès, Strasbourg 1956* (VTSup 4; Leiden: Brill, 1957) 67–96, esp. pp. 85–89; J. Bright, *A History of Israel* (Philadelphia: Westminster, 1959) 305; W. D. McHardy, "A Letter from Saqqarah," *Documents of Old Testament Times* (ed. D. W. Thomas; London/New York: Nelson, 1958) 251–55; J. D. Quinn, "Alcaeus 48 (B 16) and the Fall of Ascalon, (604 B.C.)," *BASOR* 16 (1961) 19–20; J. J. Koopmans, *AC* §16; H. Donner and W. Röllig, *KAI* §266; K. Galling, "Eschmunazar und der Herr der Könige," *ZDPV* 79 (1963) 140–51; F. Vattioni, "Il papiro di Saqqarah," *SPap* 5 (1966) 101–17; S. H. Horn, "Where and When Was the Aramaic Saqqara Papyrus Written?" *AUSS* 6 (1968) 29–45; A. Malamat, "The Last Kings of Judah and the Fall of Jerusalem," *IEJ* 18 (1968) 137–56; J. T. Milik, "Les papyrus araméens d'Hermoupolis" (p. 202 above, n. 23), 561–63; A. Malamat, "The Twilight of Judah: In the Egyptian-Babylonian Maelstrom," *Congress Volume, Edinburgh 1974* (VTSup 28; Leiden: Brill, 1975) 123–45.

[3]See D. J. Wiseman, *Chronicles of Chaldaean Kings (626-556 B.C.) in the British Museum* (London: British Museum, 1956) 68 (B.M. 21946 obv. 18-20). Cf. E. Vogt, "Die neu-babylonische Chronik" (n. 2 above), 85-89; A. Malamat, *IEJ* 6 (1956) 246-56; D. N. Freedman, "The Babylonian Chronicle," *BA* 19 (1956) 50-60.

[4]Albright's dating and comments on the text are found in the notes to Ginsberg's article (see n. 2 above), *BASOR* 111 (1948) 24-27. For Malamat's opinion, see *IEJ* 6 (1956) 252; cf. S. H. Horn, *AUSS* 6 (1968) 29-45.

[5]C.-F. Jean and J. Hoftijzer (*DISO*, 99) offer an interpretation which is similar to the one proposed here: "votre serviteur a gardé sa loyauté."

Chapter 12

A Re-Study of an Elephantine Aramaic Marriage Contract (*AP* 15)*

It was to be expected that E. G. Kraeling's publication of the *Brooklyn Museum Aramaic Papyri* would shed new light on some of the problems of older, well-known Elephantine texts. This article is a reconsideration of an Elephantine marriage contract which is often quoted in A. E. Cowley's version, but which needs a new, comprehensive presentation, because data from Kraeling's publication support certain interpretations of details in it that others have proposed, but which were strangely neglected by Cowley and others who treated the text. The foreword of Kraeling's volume acknowledges its indebtedness to Professor William F. Albright, in whose honor the present volume is being published. His interest in things Aramaic has been manifested in many ways during his scholarly career, and it is a privilege to include here a study of this Elephantine text as a tribute to a revered teacher. In it I hope to bring together items from many of the studies and discussions of the text to improve the understanding of the text as a whole. Recent studies of the legal aspects of the Elephantine contracts have also added to our understanding of this document.

The text of the marriage contract was first published by A. H. Sayce and A. E. Cowley in 1906 as papyrus G in the collection, *Aramaic Papyri Discovered at Assuan.*[1] This contract has been difficult to understand, partly because the papyrus is fragmentary and partly because its terminology and phraseology were often ambiguous. When it is studied today against the background of other marriage contracts from Elephantine, especially two in the Kraeling collection, some of the ambiguity can be resolved. In Cowley's publication at least three other texts belong to this genre, although they are rather fragmentary.[2] Among the Brooklyn Museum papyri there are three further contracts that can be used for comparative purposes.[3]

The papyrus in which we are interested contains the contract of a marriage, apparently the third one, of Miphṭaḥiah, the daughter of Maḥsiah, with Esḥor, the son of Ṣeḥo. It sets forth the terms of the marriage agreement: the date (line 1), the identification of the contracting parties (lines 2-3), the formal agreement of marriage (4), the record of the payment of the bride-price (4-6), of the dowry money brought by the bride (6-7), and of the valuable possessions brought with her (7-13). There follows the sum total of the amounts involved in the contract (13-15) and a record of the husband's acknowledgment of all this (15). Then a further list catalogues objects brought by the bride, the value of which is not determined (15-16). Certain stipulations begin in line 17: the bride's right to her husband's property should he die childless (17-20); his inheritance of his wife's property should she die childless (20-22). In case the bride divorces her husband she must pay the divorce fee, but she will be free and have the right to take what is hers (22-26). In case the husband divorces his wife he forfeits the bride-price, and she will be free and have the right to take what she brought to the marriage (26-29). The wife is further protected against a third party who might seek to drive her away from her husband's house and possessions (29-31). The husband is to be fined if he claims that he has another wife or other children (31-34); he is also to be fined if he tries to withdraw his property from his wife (35-36). Witnesses to the contract (37-39).

The Aramaic text of the marriage contract should be read as follows:[4]

1 ב[5]2 [ל]תשרי [הו יום] 6 לירח אפף [שנת. . .ארתחשס]ש מלכ[א]
2 אמר אסחור בר [צחא] ארדכל זי מלכא למח[סיה א]רמי זי סון לדגל
3 וריזת לאמר אנה [א]תית ביתך למנתן לי [ל]ברתך מפט‹ח›יה לאנתו
4 הי אנתתי ואנה בעלה מן יומא זנה ועד עלם יהבת לך מהר
5 ברתך מפטחיה [כסף] שקלן 5 באבני מלכ[א] על עליך וטב לבבך
6 בגו הנעלת לב[יתי] מפטחיה בידה כס[ף] תכונה כרש 1 שקלן 2 באבני
7 מלכא כסף ר 2 ל10 הנעלת לי בידה לבש 1 זי עמר חדת חטב
8 צבע ידין הוה ארך אמן 8 ב5 [ש]וה כסף כרשן 2 שקלן 8
9 באבני מלכא שביט 1 חדת הוה ארך אמן 8 ב5 שוה
10 כסף שקלן 8 באבני מלכא לבש אחרן זי עמר נשחט הוה
11 ארך אמן 6 ב4 שוה כסף שקלן 7 מחזי 1 זי נחש שוה
12 כסף שקל 1 ר 2 תמ[סא] 1 זי נחש שויה כסף שקל 1 ר 2 כסן זי נחש 2
13 שוין כסף שקלן [2] זלוע 1 זי נחש שוה כסף ר 2 כל כספא
14 ודמי נכסיא כסף כרשן 6 שקל‹ן› 5 חלר[ן] 20 כסף ר 2 ל10 באבני
15 מלכא על עלי [וט]יב לבבי בגו שוי 1 זי גמא בה נעבצן
16 זי אבן 4 פק 1 זי סלק כפן 2 פרכס 1 זי חצן חדת תקם חפנן 5 שנן משאן 1
17 מחר או יום א[חר]ן ימות אסחור ובר דכר ונקבה לא
18 איתי לה מן מפ[טח]יה אנתתה מפטחיה הי שליטה בביתה
19 זי אסחור ונכס[והי] וקנינה וכל זי איתי [ל]ה על אנפי ארעא
20 כלה מחר או יום ‹אחרן› תמות מפטחיה ובר דכר ונקבה לא
21 איתי לה מן אסחור בעלה אסחור הו ירתנה בנכסיה
22 וקנינה מחר [או י]ום אחרן תקום [מפ]טחיה בעדה
23 ותאמר שנאת לאסחור בעלי כסף שנאה בראשה תתב על
24 מוזנא ותתקל ל[אס]חור כסף שקלן 7 ר 2 וכל זי הנעלת
25 בידה תהנפק מן חם עד חוט ותהך [ל]האן זי צבית ולא
26 {י}דין ולא דבב מחר או יום אחרן יקום אסחור בעדה
27 ויאמר שנאת [לאנ]תתי מפטחיה מהרה [י]אבד וכל זי הנעלת

28 בידה תהנפק מן חם עד חוט ביום חד בכף חדה ותהך
29 לה אן זי צבית ולא דין ולא דבב ו[זי] יקום על מפטחיה
30 לתרכותה מן ביתה זי אסחור ונכסוהי וקנינה ינתן לה
31 כסף כרשן 20 ויע[בד] לה דין ספרא זנה ולא אכל אמר
32 איתי לי אנתה אחרה להן מפט‹ח›יה ובנן אחרנן להן בנן זי
33 תלד לי מפטחיה הן אמר איתי לי ב[נן] ואנתה אחר‹נ›ן להן
34 מפטחיה ובניה אנתן למפטחיה כס[ף] כרשן 20 באבני
35 מלכא ולא אכל [אהנ]תר נכסי וקניני מן מפ[טח]יה והן העדת המו
36 מנה {{קבל ס[פר אחר]ן}} אנתן למפטחיה [כסף] כרשן 20 באבני מל[כא]
37 כתב נתן בר ענניה [ספרא זנה כפם אסחור] ושהדיא בגו
38 פנוליה בר יזניה [. . .]יה בר אוריה מנחם בר [ז]כור
39 שהד רעיבל ב[ר]

Translation

[1]On the 2[5th of] Tishri, [that is, the] 6th [day] of the month of Epiph, [the 25th year of Artaxerx]es, [the] king, [2]Esḥor bar [Ṣeḥo], a royal architect, said to Maḥ[siah], an [A]ramean of Syene, of the [3]Varyazāt garrison: I have [co]me (to) your house (to ask you) to give me your daughter Miphṭa‹ḥ›iah in marriage. [4]She is my wife and I am her husband from this day forward. I have given you the bride-price for [5]your daughter Miphṭaḥiah, 5 [silver] shekels by roya[l] weight; you have received it and you are satisfied [6]with it. Miphṭaḥiah has brought into [my] hou[se] with her a dowry su[m] of 1 karsh, 2 shekels by royal [7]weight, (in) silver (of) 2 qu(arters) to the ten-piece. She has (also) brought with her to me: 1 new garment of wool, striped [8]with dye on both edges, measuring 8 cubits by 5, worth (in) cash 2 karshin and 8 shekels [9]by royal weight; 1 new shawl, measuring 8 cubits by 5, [wo]rth [10](in) cash 8 shekels by royal weight; another garment of wool, finely woven, [11]measuring 6 cubits by 4, worth (in) cash 7 shekels; 1 bronze mirror, worth [12](in) cash 1 shekel, 2 qu(arters); 1 bronze bo[wl], worth (in) cash 1 shekel, 2 qu(arters); 2 bronze cups, [13]worth (in) cash [2] shekels; 1 bronze pitcher, worth (in) cash 2 qu(arters). All the money and [14]the value of the possessions are 6 silver karshin, 5 shekel‹s›, 20 hallur[in], (in) silver (of) 2 qu(arters) to the ten-piece by royal [15]weight. I have received it [and] I am [sa]tisfied with it. (Also) 1 reed couch, on which there are [16]4 stone inlays; 1 *pq* of *slq*; 2 ladles; 1 new *prks* of palm-leaves; 5 handfuls of castor oil; 1 (pair of) leather (?) sandals. [17]Should Esḥor die tomorrow or some o[the]r day, having no child, (either) male or female, [18]by his wife Miph[ṭaḥ]iah, Miphṭaḥiah is entitled to the house [19]of Esḥor, [his] possessions and property, and all that he has on the face of the earth, [20]all of it. Should Miphṭaḥiah die tomorrow or ‹some other› day, having no child, (either) male or female, [21]by her husband Esḥor, Esḥor shall inherit her possessions [22]and her property. Should Miphṭaḥiah rise up in an assembly tomorrow [or] some other [da]y [23]and say, "I divorce my husband Esḥor," the divorce fee is on her head; she shall sit by the [24]scale and weigh out

to Esḥor 7 silver shekels, 2 qu(arters); and all that she brought [25]with her, she shall take out, from straw to string, and go [wh]erever she pleases, without [26]suit or process. Should Esḥor rise up in an assembly tomorrow or some other day [27]and say, "I divorce my [wife] Miphṭaḥiah," his bride-price shall go forfeit; and all that she brought [28]with her, she will take out, from straw to string, on one day (and) at one time, and she may go [29]wherever she pleases, without suit or process. [Whoever] rises up against Miphṭaḥiah [30]to drive her out of Esḥor's house or his possessions or his property, shall pay her [31]20 silver karshin and shall carry out in her regard the stipulation of this document. I shall not be able to say, [32]"I have another wife, other than Miphṭa‹ḥ›iah, and other children, other than those that [33]Miphṭaḥiah will bear to me." If I do say, "I have other chi[ldren] and a wife, other than [34]Miphṭaḥiah and her children," I shall pay Miphṭaḥiah 20 sil[ver] karshin by royal [35]weight. Nor shall I be able to [with]draw my possessions and my property from Miph[ṭaḥ]iah. If I do remove them [36]from her (according to [some ot]her doc[ument]), I shall pay Miphṭaḥiah 20 silver karshin by royal weight. [37]Nathan bar ᶜAnaniah wrote [this document at the behest of Esḥor]. The witnesses to it are [38]Penuliah bar Yezaniah, [ ]iah bar Uriah, Menaḥem bar [Z]akkur. [39]Witness: Reᶜibel ba[r].

General Remarks

The text is an example of what the Arameans and Jews at Elephantine in the fifth century B.C. called *sĕpar ᵓintū*, "a document of marriage" (or, more strictly, "of wifehood"); see *AP* 14:4; 35:4-5; *BMAP* 10:7, 9; 12:18. The difference between it and the later *kĕtûbāh* among the Jews has often been noted. How old the custom is that is represented by this text is hard to say. The reference to a written contract in Tob 7:14 seems to be the oldest. In any case, the marriage contracts from Elephantine have a set form that enables one to compare them and use them for interpretation.[5]

When Sayce and Cowley originally published this text they did not correctly understand the verb הנעלת in line 6 and their attempt to explain the total of the objects mentioned in lines 6-13 did not succeed. Though other suggestions were made for the interpretation of these lines,[6] Cowley's subsequent smaller edition repeated the original understanding of the text found in the *editio princeps*, at least on this point.[7] A more recent translation of the text was provided by H. L. Ginsberg, in two slightly differing forms,[8] but he made no attempt to render lines 6-16. Since the identification of some of the objects in the list was problematic—and still is, in fact—he prudently did not try to translate them in such a collection of texts as that for which his version was prepared. However, a notation he gives in the first edition highlights the problem; he writes: "Lines 6-16, Ashor's [or Mahseiah's] gifts to Miphtahiah and—perhaps—hers to him."[9] For the problem was, first, to determine whether the verb הנעלת was a first singular form (referring to Esḥor, who had the contract written), or a second singular masculine form (referring to Maḥsiah, the father of the bride), or a third singular feminine form (referring to Miphṭaḥiah, the bride). Cowley noted the lack of distinction between such forms in the bare consonantal text.

Several writers had seen clearly that הנעלת must be understood as the third singular feminine wherever it occurs in this papyrus,[10] and Kraeling confirmed this, noting that the Brooklyn Museum contracts had the same expression.[11] In *BMAP* 7:5 we read, הנעלת לי יהוישמע אחתך לביתי תכונה זי כסף כרשן ש[קל]ן 2 חלרן 5 "Yahuyishma^c, your sister, has brought to me, into my house, the dowry of 2 silver karshin, 2 shekels, 5 ḥallurin. . . ." Similarly in *BMAP* 2:4, הנעלת לי תמת בידה לבש 1 זי עמר שוה כסף שקלן 7, "Tamut has brought with her to me 1 garment of wool, worth in cash 7 shekels." These texts make it clear that the bride's dowry and possessions are indicated in the contract by the phrase הנעלת לי X לביתי or הנעלת לי X בידה, in which *X* stands for the proper name of the woman. Lidzbarski wanted to restore הנעלת לי [ברתך] in line 6 and הנעלת לי in line 7. Kraeling suggested the restoration of *ly* twice in lines 6 and 7. The restoration is correct for line 7, but a glance at the photo of the papyrus reveals that לי alone is not sufficient in line 6, since the lacuna is too long. Moreover, the head of the letter that follows *lamedh* is not clearly that of a *yodh*, but is possibly that of a *beth*, since this letter is written with different stances in the papyrus. If *yodh* is correct, then one should read לי[לביתי], as in *BMAP* 7:5. But if it is a *beth* that follows *lamedh*, then perhaps one should read simply לב[יתי], "to my house." This would be less crowded. Note too that Cowley read *lb*[.

The same understanding of הנעלת is to be given to the word in lines 24 and 27, "all that she brought with her," as Lidzbarski suggested earlier, but which Cowley did not accept. This suggestion is now confirmed by *BMAP* 7:22, כל זי הנעלת בביתה ינתן לה תכונתה ולבשיה, "all that she brought into his house he shall give to her, her dowry and her garments." Cf. *BMAP* 2:10.

One reason why Cowley did not accept the suggestion of Freund and Jampel, who wanted to understand הנעלת as the second singular masculine, referring to Miphṭaḥiah's father, Maḥsiah, was that for him "the sum total in l. 14 shows that the presents were given by the same person who paid the 5 shekels."[12] But since he did not correctly understand several other expressions in the text, he insisted that Esḥor, not Miphṭaḥiah, was the subject of the verb הנעלת. The five shekels in line 5 represent the מהר, "the bride-price," paid by the groom to the bride's father, Maḥsiah. This is not the "dowry," and though Cowley obviously used this English term for מהר in a loose sense, it is indicative of his basic misunderstanding of the contract as a whole. He understood the difference between "bride-price" and "dowry," as is obvious from his reference to Gen 34:12. However, he misunderstood the term כסף תכונה in line 6, translating it as "the cost of furniture." It is now clear that this is "dowry money," whatever may be the etymological explanation of the phrase. In any case, Cowley was right in saying that the מהר of 5 shekels was included in the sum given in lines 13-14.

To arrive at the sum of 6 karshin, 5 shekels, and 20 ḥallurin, one must total up the dowry (כסף תכונה), the value of the objects brought by Miphṭaḥiah, and the bride-price (מהר) that Esḥor paid. Thus:

Line	Object		Value		
5	Esḥor's *mhr*			5 shekels	
6	Miphṭaḥiah's	*ksp tkwnh*	1 karsh	2 shekels	
7-8	"	*lbš 1 zy ʿmr*	2 karshin	8 shekels	
9-10	"	*šbyt 1*		8 shekels	
10-11	"	*lbš ʾḥrn zy ʿmr*		7 shekels	
11-12	"	*mḥzy 1 zy nḥš*		1 shekel	2 R
12	"	*tmsʾ 1*		1 shekel	2 R
12-13	"	*ksn 2*		2 shekels[13]	
13	"	*zlwʿ 1*			2 R
			3 karshin	34 shekels	6 R

Cowley had shown that a כרש equalled a ten-shekel piece and that ר, probably standing for רבעא, "quarter," i.e., a quarter of a shekel, equalled ten ḥallurin.[14] Hence the above total is easily converted to 6 karshin, 5 shekels, and 20 ḥallurin, the sum formulated in lines 13-14. Cowley was, then, right in maintaining that the bride-price was included in the sum so formulated.

But does it mean that all that is included in the total came from one and the same person? This was Cowley's conclusion and the reason why he insisted that הנעלת was the first singular form, referring to Esḥor's presents. It is, however, clear from *BMAP* 7 that this conclusion is erroneous. Though *BMAP* 7:15 is fragmentary at one point, enough is preserved to show that the dowry and the bride-price were both included in the total, even though these sums come from different persons: [כ]ל [מ]אנ[י . . . נ]חש ותכ[ו]נתא ומהרא כסף כרשן שבעה ה[ו 7 ש]ק[ל]ן תמניה הו 8 חלרן 5 באבני מלכא כסף 2 ר לעשרתא, "all the vessels of [and br]onze, and the dowry, and the bride-price (equal) seven, that is 7, silver karshin, eight, that is 8, shekels, 5 ḥallurin by royal weight, (in) silver of 2 qu(arters) to the ten-piece."[15]

The reason for the inclusion of the מהר in the sum total has been explained in various ways. What seems to be clear is that the מהר was no longer a "bride-price" in the strict sense, i.e., a price paid to the father (or guardian) of the bride. Evidence from Alalakh, Babylonia, and Egypt indicates that the father at least turned it over to the daughter.[16] S. Greengus thinks that it was not paid at all, but represents merely "a penalty which would be forfeited by the divorcing party."[17] H. L. Ginsberg thinks rather that the מהר becomes the divorce fee.[18] The reason for the dispute in the last instance involves *BMAP* 2, where no מהר is mentioned and the sum written on the outside of the papyrus differs considerably from that written within. I shall leave this question aside, since it does not concern the contract now under study. The important thing to realize is that the מהר is included in the sum total and is regarded as something that belongs to the bride.[19]

After these general remarks we may proceed to the analysis of the text of the contract itself.

Notes

1. ב[25 ל]תשרי: "On the 25th of Tishri." This is the first part of the dating of the contract, which is also done according to the Egyptian calendar in the following phrase. The correspondence of Tishri and Epiph is also found in *BMAP* 4:1 and 7:1. See S. H. Horn and L. H. Wood, "The Fifth Century Jewish Calendar at Elephantine," *JNES* 13 (1954) 1-20. The preposition ב is common in such dates and probably is an abbreviation for ביום; it is usually followed by the cardinal number written in a cipher. In *AP* 26:16 one can find the number written out (and preceded by four hundred). The preposition ל has been restored on the basis of its frequent usage (see *BMAP* 1:1; 3:1; 4:1; 8:l; 9:1; 10:l; 10:1, 10), when the name of the month is not preceded by בירח or לירח. Kraeling omitted it in *BMAP* 6:1, but see plate VI; it is to be restored also in *BMAP* 2:1 (before [תמוז]). It is omitted, however, in *BMAP* 5:1.

[הו יום] 6 לירח אפף: "That is, the 6th day of the month of Epiph." This double dating is found in all the marriage contracts from Elephantine, but not in all other documents. See R. Yaron, "The Schema," p. 34; E. G. Kraeling, *BMAP*, 51-52. The restored form הו, without a final *aleph*, is normal in the Elephantine texts; see I. N. Vinnikov, *Slovar*, p. 194. Judging from the commonly used שנת, which is the construct state, the word יום should also be so regarded. Since the name of the Egyptian month is always written in these texts simply as אפף, I vocalize it as Epiph, not Epiphi. The latter is derived from Greek transcriptions of the name in papyri, but it is not universal in Greek by any means. Alongside of it one finds rather frequently *Epip, Epeip, Epeiph*, and in Coptic also *Epēp* or *Epep*. See F. Preisigke, *Wörterbuch der griechischen Papyrusurkunden*, 3 / 1 (1929) 86. There is no evidence that the Aramaic form would have been pronounced with a final *i*-vowel. Cf. J. Černý, *ASAE* 43 (1943) 173-81; *BIFAO* 57 (1958) 207.

[שנת] 25 ארתחשסש מלכ[א]: "The 25th year of Artaxerxes, the king." The restoration of the year depends on the usually admitted relation of this contract to *AP* 14, which is clearly dated to this year of Artaxerxes. The latter document is the settlement of a claim connected with the divorce of Miphṭaḥiah from her second husband in 440 B.C. The new third marriage, of which the present text is a record, probably took place a short time afterward. In any case, if it is wrong the date is off only by a year or so. But Horn and Wood (*JNES* 13 [1954] 13) prefer to date this text in 435 B.C. (?), with some hesitation.

The king is almost certainly Artaxerxes I Longimanus (464-24). The name is written in the official Aramaic transcription used in many of these texts, ארתחשסש (*AP* 6:2; 7:1; 10:1; 13:1; *BMAP* 1:1; 3:1; 4:1; etc.). In *BMAP* 2:1 it is written simply as ארתחש, which Kraeling rightly considers to be "a scribal error." In *KAI* 274:1; 275:1 we find the name ארתחשסי מלכא בר זי זריתר,

but is it the same? According to H. H. Schaeder (*Iranische Beiträge I* [Schriften der Königsberger Gelehrten Gesellschaft, Geisteswissenschaftliche Kl., 6/5; Halle: M. Niemeyer, 1930] p. 268) the Aramaic form found in the Elephantine texts represents the Persian *Artaxšassa* (< Old Persian *Artaxšathra*), whereas the forms in biblical Aramaic (ᵓ*Artaḥšaśt*ᵓ [Ezra 4:7], ᵓ*Artaḥšaśtā*ᵓ [Ezra 4:7], or ᵓ*Artaḥšastā*ᵓ [Ezra 7:1]) are attempts to come even closer to the Persian form with the final *-a*.

2. [אסחור בר [צחא: "Esḥor bar Ṣeḥo." The groom's father's name is supplied from *AP* 20:3, 20. The groom's name here is Egyptian, equalling *nś-Ḥr*, "Belonging to (the god) Horus," a form of name that is often transcribed into Greek with initial *Es-* or simply *s-* (see H. Ranke, *Die ägyptischen Personennamen* [Glückstadt: Augustin], I [1935] 178, 7). But in three other Elephantine documents the children born of the marriage recorded in this contract are listed thus: "Yedaniah and Maḥsiah, 2 in all, sons of Esḥor bar Ṣeḥo by Miphṭaḥiah, daughter of Maḥsiah" (*AP* 20:3); "Yedaniah bar Nathan and Maḥsiah bar Nathan, his brother, their mother being Mibṭaḥiah, daughter of Maḥsiah bar Yedaniah" (*AP* 25:3); "Maḥsiah bar Nathan 1, Yedaniah bar Nathan I, in all 2, . . . we have divided between us the slaves of Mibṭaḥiah, our mother" (*AP* 28:2-3). There is little doubt that the same children and parents are meant, though this has been contested (see E. Volterra, "*'Yhwdy' e 'ᵓrmy'* nei papiri aramaici del V secolo provenienti dall'Egitto," *ANL*, Rendiconti, Sc. mor. 8/18 [1963] 131-73; cf. R. Yaron, "Who is Who at Elephantine," *Iura* 15 [1964] 167-72; and Volterra's reply, ibid., 173-80). And yet Esḥor's name subsequently appears as Nathan in *AP* 25 and 28. Cowley speculated: Did Esḥor become a proselyte and take a Jewish name, Nathan (*AP*, p. 47)?

The patronymic *bar Ṣeḥo* is given here in its conventional vocalization. The father's name *Ṣḥ*ᵓ is Egyptian and represents *Ḏd-ḥr*, "Horus has spoken," or possibly "The face of X (a god) has spoken," because of the disappearance of final *r*. The name is apparently transcribed into Akkadian as *Ṣi-ḫa-a* and into Greek as *Teōs* or *Tachōs* (see H. Ranke, *Ägyptische Personennamen*, I. 411, 12; G. Fecht, *Wortakzent und Silbenstruktur: Untersuchungen zur Geschichte der ägyptischen Sprache* (ÄF 21; Glückstadt: Augustin, 1960], 84, § 151, n. 254).

ארדכל זי מלכא: "A royal architect," or "a builder to the king" (Ginsberg), i.e., some sort of government-hired builder. The name of the profession is found in *AP* 14:2, spelled ᵓ*rdykl*; it occurs in later Aramaic as ᵓ*ardīkĕlā* or ᵓ*ardēkĕlā*. This is basically an Akkadian word, reflecting the Babylonian *(w)arad ekalli*, "palace slave." The meaning of the word, however, developed within the Mesopotamian area and came to denote not a social class but a profession, specifically a workman in the building trade. See further, A. L. Oppenheim, "AKK. arad ekalli = 'Builder,'" *ArOr* 17 (1949) 227-35. In this sense it is used in these texts.

למח[סיה]: "To Maḥsiah," the father of Miphṭaḥiah. He is the son of Yedaniah (*AP* 25:3) and appears again in *AP* 5:2, 9, 12, 20; 6:3, 22; 8:1, 18, 28, 35; 9:1, 5, 16; 11:14; 13:1, 17bis, 21; 14:2; 25:3, 7; *BMAP* 1:13. The name is undoubtedly Hebrew, *Maḥsi-yāh,* "Yahu is my refuge." It occurs also in Jer 32:12; 51:59; but its Masoretic vocalization is questionable. The root of it is *ḥsy*, and one can understand how the Masoretic pointing *Maḥsēyāh* developed (as a *maqtal*-type); but one may ask whether it is accurate for the fifth century B.C. In any case, the vocalization *Meḥasiah* (S. Greengus, *Aramaic Marriage Contracts*, 122) is wrong.

[א]רמי זי סון: "An Aramean of Syene." This same identification is given to Maḥsiah in *AP* 5:2; 13:2; 14:3. But in *AP* 6:3 he is called יהודי בבירת יב, "a Jew in the fortress of Yeb," and identified in *AP* 8:2 as יהוד[י] מהחסן ביב בירתא, "a Jew owning property in Yeb, the fortress." Again in *AP* 9:2 he seems to be called a י[הודי זי ב]יב, but the text is very fragmentary here. On the problem of one and the same person being called a "Jew" and an "Aramean" in the Elephantine papyri, see E. Volterra, *ANL*, Rendiconti, Sc. mor. 8/18 (1963) 131-73. He seeks to distinguish such persons. But R. Yaron (*Iura* 15 [1964] 167-72) suggests that the terms יהודי and ארמי were used to designate the same persons, but from different points of view. He thinks that יהודי was used "especially in documents in which some non-Jewish factor is involved," and thus serves to identify the persons as such. But the Jews of Elephantine used the term ארמי "amongst themselves." This issue is far from settled, and there seems to be little at present in the text to allow of a solution.

The word ארמי is an appositive to a proper name, and yet occurs in the absolute state (see T. Nöldeke, *ZA* 20 [1907] 142; P. Joüon, "Notes grammaticales, lexicographiques et philologiques sur les papyrus araméens d'Egypte," *MUSJ* 18 [1934] 1-90, esp. pp. 10-11). This is true when the absolute is followed by some determination, as here.

The name סון, Syene, is usually vocalized after the Greek *Syēnē* or the Hebrew *Sĕwēnēh* (Ezek 29:10). Cf. the Coptic *Souan* and Arabic *ʾAswân*.

לדגל וריזת: "Of the Varyazāt garrison." The same identification is given for Maḥsiah in *AP* 5:3; 6:4; 13:2; 14:3; but in *AP* 8:2; 9:2 he seems to be said to belong to the דגל הומדת, "the Hawmadāt garrison." On the Persian names used here, see H. H. Schaeder, *Iranische Beiträge I* (Schriften der Königsberger Gelehrten Gesellschaft, Geisteswissenschaftliche Kl., 6/5; Halle: M. Niemeyer, 1930; reprinted, Darmstadt: Wissenschaftliche Buchgesellschaft, 1972) 269. The exact meaning of דגל is obscure. It is often said that it means basically a "standard" or "banner," but this is far from clear (see Y. Yadin, *The Scroll of the War of the Sons of Light against the Sons of Darkness* [New York: Oxford, 1962] 39). In these texts it seems to denote a military unit or detachment of undetermined size; cf. Num 1:52; 2:2-3, 10, 17-18, 25, 31, 34. To identify it as a military unit is not to deny a social organization that may also be involved in it. The shift from the Varyazāt garrison to the Hawmadāt may represent a real transfer. The proper name of the garrison is not easily explained; it is almost certainly Persian. In *BMAP* 8:11 it occurs as a personal name. Was the name of the garrison derived from the name of some chief or official in it? In any case it is interesting to note that the majority of names of such garrisons at Yeb or Syene are either Persian or Akkadian (e.g., *Hawmadāt, AP* 8:2; 9:2; *Bagapat, TA* 5:7, 9; *ʾAtroparan, AP* 6:9; *ʾArtabanu, AP* 6:3; *ʾIddinnabū, AP* 20:2; *BMAP* 14:2; *Nabūkudurr*[*i*], *AP* 7:3; *ʾArpaḥu, BMAP* 5:2; *Nmsw, BMAP* 3:2). B. Porten (*Archives from Elephantine*, 30) takes this as evidence that the דגלן were named after their "respective non-Jewish commanders."

3. לאמר: "Saying," a stereotyped, fossilized peal infinitive of אמר, which has persisted in such syntactical contexts, introducing direct statements. It is obviously akin to the Hebrew *lēʾmōr*; see T. Nöldeke, *ZA* 20 (1907) 137. Peal infinitives without the initial *mem* are found in early Aramaic texts; see above, p. 239. On the other hand, the real Aramaic form, מאמר, is found in *AP* 32:2 and *A* 115.

אנה [א]תית ביתך: "I have come to your house." This seems like a useless detail in the otherwise closely worded contract. It may represent an historical detail that is preserved here, but it may also be stereotyped language. It is peculiar in Aramaic and may involve a scribal error. For though there are many instances of verbs expressing motion toward a place with an object and no preposition (see p. 224 above), this is apparently a lone instance of such an expression with a common noun as object (at least in this period of Aramaic; cf. 1QapGen 10:12). Cf. *BMAP* 14:3 (אנה אתית עליך בבית[ך]); 7:3 (אנה אתית על [בי]תך); 2:3 (אנה אתית עליך). These examples make one suspect that the phrase in this text is a scribal error.

למנתן לי [ל]ברתך: "(To ask you) to give me your daughter." The cumbersome infinitival construction (where the infinitive's subject is different from that of the main verb on which it depends) is perhaps explained by *BMAP* 7:3, אנה אתית על [בי]תך ושאלת מנך לנשן יהוישמע, "I have come to your house and asked of you the woman Yahuyishmaᶜ." But the expression found in this text had apparently become stereotyped, since it is also found in *BMAP* 2:3. Cf. *AP* 2:13 (למובל); *HermWP* 2:12-13; Ezra 7:20; Dan 2:24; 4:23.

מפט‹ח›יה: "Miphṭaḥiah." The same scribal omission of *ḥ* occurs in line 32. The name is a dissimilated form of the more original *Mibṭaḥiāh*, "Yahu is my security," *Mibṭaḥi-yah*, found in *AP* 8:2; 9:3, 7, 10, 12; 14:2, 14; 20:3; 25:3, 7; 28:3, 5, 6. The dissimilation of the voiced bilabial occurs also in *AP* 13:2, 4. The shift from *p* › *b* is found in earlier Aramaic texts: נבש, Sf I A 37; בתן, Sf I A 32; אלב, Hadad 34. But the opposite shift is more rarely attested.

This is apparently Miphṭaḥiah's third marriage. From *AP* 14 (dated ca. 440 B.C.) it seems that her second marriage ended in divorce from an Egyptian named Piʾ. From *AP* 8:6 it is clear that Miphṭaḥiah was earlier married to Yezan bar Uriah (ca. 460 B.C.). Miphṭaḥiah thus appears to be an adult divorcee, but she is still given in marriage to Esḥor by her father.

לאנתו: "In marriage," or more strictly "for wifehood." This expression occurs again in *AP* 48:3; *BMAP* 2:3; 7:3. It states the purpose of the agreement that is recorded in this contract. Lidzbarski (*Ephemeris,* 3.80) called attention to the use of this phrase in official Jewish marriage contracts of a later date and compared the Mishnah, *Ketuboth*, 4:7ff. He also noted that Targum Onqelos on Gen 16:3 translated the Hebrew phrase *lĕʾiššāh* by *lĕʾintū*. Kraeling (*BMAP*, 146) further compared the expression to the Assyrian *nadānu ana aššūti*.

4. הי אנתתי ואנה בעלה מן יומא זנה ועד עלם: "She is my wife and I am her husband from this day forward," lit., "from this day and forever." The same formula is found in *BMAP* 2:3-4; 7:4 (but with the omission of *w*- before *ʿd* in the latter text). These words actually record the formal agreement that constitutes the marriage; Esḥor acknowledges his relationship to Miphṭaḥiah. The acknowledgment is formulated solely from the standpoint of the groom. The bride's consent is undoubtedly presupposed, but not recorded, if expressed at all. The omission of this undoubtedly reflects the attitude toward women in the ancient Near East. A few isolated texts record the bride's consent, but they are so isolated as to preclude any generalizations (see Gen 24:8, 58; C. H. Gordon, "The Status of Women in Nuzi Texts," *ZA* 43 [1936] 149). Even in the case of an adult marriage, such as Miphṭaḥiah's third, the consent is not recorded. This raises the question whether בעלה is too weakly translated merely as "her husband."

The last part of the agreement, מן יומא זנה ועד עלם, is also found in documents other than marriage contracts (e.g., *AP* 8:9; 14:6-7; 20:9-10; *BMAP* 4:4-5; 10:8). It in no way guarantees the indissolubility of the marriage, because a provision is made in the contract itself for divorce. Contrast the formula in Mur 20 i 3-4. Cf. S. Loewenstamm, "From This Time and Forevermore," *Tarbiẓ* 32 (1963) 313-16.

In Hos 2:4 one finds the Hebrew counterpart of this agreement negatively expressed, הי לא אשתי ואנכי לא אישה. Though this is scarcely a formal divorce formula, it undoubtedly reflects the ancient marriage formula that we find in this Aramaic text.

יהבת לך מהר ברתך מפטחיה: "I have given you the bride-price for your daughter Miphṭaḥiah." The noun is related to the Hebrew *mōhar* (Gen 34:12; Exod 22:16; 1 Sam 18:25). The construct is to be vocalized *mĕhar*, and the emphatic is either *muhrāʾ* or *mohŏrāʾ*; *pace* R. Yaron, *Introduction*, 45 n. 1, the Aramaic vocalization is not uncertain. No מהר is mentioned in the contract *BMAP* 2, and this has been variously interpreted (see H. L. Ginsberg, *JAOS* 74 [1954] 156; R. Yaron, *Introduction*, 57; S. Greengus, "Aramaic Marriage Contracts," 41-64). The מהר is in reality the same as the Akkad. *terḫatu*; the bride-price was an institution at Ugarit (see *UT* 77:19-20 *watn mhrh labh*) and also in ancient Egypt. But by Saite and Persian times it had lost the implication of a purchase of the bride; though nominally paid to the father or guardian, it apparently became the property of the bride. This usage is reflected in the Elephantine texts too.

5. 5 שקלן [כסף]: "5 silver shekels," or possibly "a sum of 5 shekels." At times—even in this text—כסף seems to be used generically in the sense of "money" or "cash," and it is not easy to tell to what extent it retains the nuance of "silver." My translation shifts back and forth between these two senses, depending on which seems more appropriate. Note the expression in *BMAP* 2:6 ודמי נכסיא כסף כסף שקלן 7, etc. where the double *ksp* may be dittographical; but it may also be an attempt to formulate the two nuances mentioned. The form שקלן is vocalized with the ending *-īn* by T. Nöldeke (*ZA* 20 [1907] 139) and P. Leander (*L* §45a). This vocalization of the masculine plural absolute has been questioned by H. L. Ginsberg, "Aramaic Dialect Problems," *AJSL* 52 (1936) 99-101. He prefers to vocalize it as *-ān* because of the defective spelling.

באבני מלכ[א]: "By royal weight," lit., "by (*or* according to) the stones of the king." This expression occurs again in lines 6-7, 9, 10, 14-15, 34-35, 36, and frequently in other Elephantine texts. The reference is to a standard of silver conforming to governmental stone-weights, which were apparently carried in small pouches and officially used. A similar expression is found in 2 Sam 14:26. Another standard was apparently also used at Elephantine, for in *AP* 11:2 we learn of "stones of Ptaḥ," [בא]בני פתח; cf. *AP* 26:21, תקלת פרס, *prs*, "the Persian weight." See further B. Porten, *Archives from Elephantine*, 63-64.

על עליך וטב לבבך בגו: "You have received it and you are satisfied with it," lit., "it has entered into you and your heart is content therewith." The expression occurs again in line 15. The verb על is the 3d sg. masc. pf. peal of *ᶜll*, "enter," and טב, which is sometimes written as טיב (see *AP* 2:9; 15:15; 20:9; *BMAP* 3:6; 12:6, 14, 26; etc.), is to be understood as a stative 3d sg. masc. pf. peal of *ṭyb* (a form like *myt* in *AP* 5:8 or *rim* in Dan 5:20). The adverb בגו is in reality a prepositional phrase, *b* + *gaww* ("interior"), simplified and contracted to *bĕgô*; for similar uses of it, see *AP* 2:9; 8:28; 9:6; *BMAP* 1:4, 10; etc. The implications of this formula in Aramaic business law and its relation to the long recognized analogues in Old Babylonian (*libbašu ṭāb*, "his [the seller's] heart is satisfied") and in Demotic (*dj.k-mtj hȝtj(.i)*, "you [the buyer] have satisfied my heart") have been extensively investigated in the recent book of Y. Muffs, *Studies in the Aramaic Legal Papyri from Elephantine* (Studia et documenta ad iura orientis antiqui pertinentia, 8; Leiden: Brill, 1969). On pages 53-56 he discusses the implications of the phrase in the clause regarding the מהר.

6. הנעלת לב[יתי] מפטחיה בידה: "Miphṭaḥiah has brought into my house with her," lit., "has caused to enter my house in her (own) hand." See the general remarks above (p. 246) for the reasons for understanding הנעלת as the 3d sg. fem. and for the reading לי [לביתי] or לב[יתי]. The *n* in the form represents the resolution of the secondary doubling of the first radical of the

Double ᶜAyin root *ᶜll*. It is not simply a substitution of nasalization for germination (which is true in this case); but sometimes liquids are used (e.g., *Dammeśeq* ⟩ *Darmeśeq*; *kussēʾāʾ* ⟩ *kuršēʾāʾ*). The phrase used here should be compared with *BMAP* 7:5; 2:4.

2 כס[ף] תכונה כרש 1 שקלן 2: "A dowry sum of 1 karsh, 2 shekels." The meaning of כסף תכונה has not always been correctly understood; indeed, R. Yaron (*Introduction*, 50) seems to think that its "exact meaning . . . is not clear" at all. Sayce and Cowley translated it hesitatingly, "money for an outfit," and Cowley subsequently used "the cost of furniture." W. Staerk rendered it "als (bar-)wert ihrer Ausstattung" (*Alte und neue aramäische Papyri*, 44). Kraeling (*BMAP*, 209) related it to Nah 2:10 and translated it "substance of silver." The amount designated by כסף תכונה certainly does not include the value of the items subsequently listed, as the list of them and its total reveal (see above, p. 248). It almost certainly represents a sum of money or an amount of silver distinct from the other items and from the *mhr*; it was the dowry sum in the strict sense. The only thing that may be uncertain about it is the etymology, since תכונה seems to be derived from the root *kwn* with a preformative *t*. See P. Leander (*L* §43j''''), who also translated it "Ausstattung." It is the money which has been put up by the bride for the marriage.

The כרש is equal in these texts to ten (heavy) silver shekels, or to the עשרתא, "ten-piece," which is often written in a cipher, as in the following line. The name כרש that is being used in these Aramaic texts from Egypt is undoubtedly derived from the Persian monetary system, but the weight is not exactly the same in Egypt as in Persia. Ten Elephantine shekels weigh 87.6 grams, whereas the karsh-weights found at Persepolis and outside of Egypt weigh between 83.33-83.36 grams. This is roughly 4.3 grams less than the Egyptian ten shekels, or a half shekel less. See further below, on line 7.

The שקל used at Elephantine seems to have weighed 8.76 grams. This calculation is based mainly on *AP* 35:3, כסף ש 2 הו [כס]ף סתתרי 1, "the sum of 2 shekels, that is the sum of one stater," and *BMAP* 12:5, כסף כרש חד הו 1 שקלן תלתה הו 3 כסף יון סתתרי 6 שקל 1 חד, "the sum of one karsh, that is 1, three shekels, that is 3, (in) the money of Greece, 6 staters, one, ‹that is› 1, shekel." See also *BMAP* 12:14. This shows that the Elephantine shekel was equivalent to a half of a stater, or the Athenian tetradrachm, which weighed at this time 17.52 grams. See B. Porten, *Archives from Elephantine*, 64-65.

7. כסף ר 2 ל10: "(In) silver (of) 2 qu(arters) to the 10-piece." This expression occurs again in line 14, and in other texts (*BMAP* 7:32). Often the word is written out, עשרתא (*AP* 6:15; 8:14, 21; 9:15; *BMAP* 3:16), but the abbreviation *r* is widespread. Its meaning as רבעא (*ribᶜāʾ* or *rubᶜāʾ*), "quarter," is widely admitted today, and almost certainly has nothing to do with the word רעי, found in *AP* 73:6, 13, 15, 17, *pace* S. Greengus, *Aramaic Marriage Contracts*, 51. Other phrases that are similar to this one in these texts make the identification of ר as a quarter shekel almost certain, for

one also finds 1 כסף ר2 לכרש (*AP* 20:15; 25:15–16; *BMAP* 4:15) and כסף זוז 10ל or לעשרתא (*BMAP* 3:15, 18; 7:17; 8:8), and 1 כסף זוז לכרש (*BAMP* 3:6). In these phrases the *r 2* is equivalent to the *zûz*, or half shekel, indicating that *r 2* is to be understood as *rib*ᶜ*īn 2* or *rub*ᶜ*īn 2*. The "quarter" is the equivalent also of 10 ḥallurin. See R. Yaron, "*Ksp zwz*," *Lešonénu* 31 (1966-67) 287-88; B. Porten, *Archives from Elephantine*, 62-67, 305-7. The phrase probably does not indicate an alloyed kind of silver, but rather an adjustment of the lighter Persian weight to the standard used in Egypt. This is the plausible explanation well worked out by B. Porten. There is only one slight difficulty in it, and that is to explain the constant appearance of כסף at the beginning of this phrase; perhaps one should rather translate "(with) 2 silver qu(arters) to the tenpiece (*or* karsh)."

לבש 1 זי עמר חדת חטב צבע ידין: "1 new garment of wool, striped with dye on both edges." This phrase begins the list of the items other than money that Miphṭaḥiah brought with her to the marriage; the first is an expensive woolen garment. The word for "wool," עמר, occurs in this text, written ca. 440 B.C., with an initial ᶜ*ayin*. But in a text dated ca. 420 B.C. we find the word written with an initial *qoph* (*BMAP* 7:6, 7, 13). The form עמר also appears in the still earlier text of *BMAP* 2:4 (dated ca. 449 B.C.). The shift from *q* > ᶜ is also attested in Jer 10:11 (both ᵓ*arqā*ᵓ and ᵓ*ar*ᶜ*ā*ᵓ). The *qoph* is certainly older, and its persistence in *BMAP* 7, after the shift to ᶜ*ayin* has taken place, is noteworthy. Cf. *AP* 20:5 (*qmr*, ca. 420 B.C.); 36:3 (*qmr*, undated); 42:9 (*qmr*, undated).

The word חטב is found with the full spelling חטיב in *BMAP* 7:7, confirming the participial explanation proposed by Cowley, who compared it to *ḥṭbwt* in Prov 7:16, "striped cloths."

The form צבע, which also occurs in *BMAP* 7:8; 14a; *AP* 42:9, has been understood by Cowley, Leander (*L* §34a), and Kraeling (*BMAP*, 317), as a participle, "dyed." The latter, however, gives a more plausible explanation in his commentary (*BMAP*, 210), where he takes it as a noun *(ṣb*ᶜᵓ*)*, related to Akkad. *ṣību*, *ṣīpu* (see *CAD*, 16. 205). Hence, "striped with dye." The form צבע has not yet turned up with the full spelling which might support the participial interpretation.

Both Cowley and Kraeling understood *ydyn* to mean "on both sides." G. R. Driver (*PEQ* 87 [1955] 93) sensed the difficulty in this interpretation, maintaining that "no material can be dyed only on one side." He preferred to understand the word to mean "twice dyed," to make the color fast. He compared the biblical phrase עשר ידות (Dan 1:20; Gen 43:34), and called attention to the twice-dyed Tyrian purple garments called *dibapha* (Pliny, *NH* 9.63,137). This is certainly a preferable interpretation, but is there not another possibility? Cannot ידין mean on "two edges"? Cowley had compared the Babylonian use of *idu* for his interpretation, but this would just as well support the idea of "edges" (*CAD*, 7.12). Moreover *BMAP* 7:8, 10 seems to express this idea in a more specific fashion in giving the measurements of the stripes, "1 handbreadth on each border" and "2 fingerbreadths to each border." ידין would in this interpretation be taken adverbially, and as a dual.

8. הוה ארך אמן 8 ב 5: "Measuring 8 cubits by 5," lit., "being (in) length 8 cubits by 5." The same expression occurs again in lines 9, 10-11. The word ארך has the same adverbial function that ידין has in the preceding expression.

[ש]וה כסף כרשן 2 שקלן 8: "Worth (in) cash 2 karshin and 8 shekels," or "worth 2 silver karshin, 8 shekels." It is this sort of phrase that suggests that כסף may no longer have the strict meaning of "silver," and that it is an attempt merely to record the monetary value of the goods. The form שוה is either the peal active participle *(šāwêh)*, "equalling," or (less likely) the passive participle *(šĕwêh)* with active force, "being worth." Cf. the examples of the latter in biblical Aramaic: דחיל (Dan 2:31); מהימן (Dan 2:45). Expressions similar to this phrase occur again in lines 9–10, 11, 11-12, 12, 13(bis). The value of this expensive woolen garment can be realized by comparing it to the price of a piece of property sold in *BMAP* 3:4-6, which is just half of the value given here.

9. שביט 1 חדת: "1 new shawl." The meaning of שביט is not certain. Cowley explained it as "closely-woven" stuff, adding that from its size it could only have been some kind of shawl. Kraeling (*BMAP* 7:9) accepted this meaning too; Staerk used simply "Gewebe" (*Alte und neue aramäische Papyri*, 45). Kutscher (*JAOS* 74 [1954] 236) related the word to Syriac *šbṭ*ʾ, "a smooth cloth."

10. לבש אחרן זי עמר נשחט: "Another garment of wool, finely woven." The only enigmatic word here is נשחט, which Cowley related to the Hebrew *šāḥûṭ* in Jer 9:7, which is explained by commentators as the equivalent of *nmšk*, "drawn out," and in 2 Chr 9:15, of "gold drawn out," i.e., beaten thin. Lidzbarski (*Ephemeris*, 3. 80) followed him in this and noted that the form may be a niphal, a technical trade-term, possibly borrowed from the Phoenician. Cf. P. Leander, *L* §21b. A related word is said to have been found in a Punic text (see J. Solá-Solé, *Sefarad* 20 [1960] 277-79); but even if it is correctly read there it does not seem to have any pertinence to this text. Another form with the initial *n-* is found in line 15, נעבצן; but its meaning is not fully understood either.

11. מחזי 1 זי נחש: "1 bronze mirror." The word מחזי is normally considered fem. (see P. Leander, *L* §43ś), but it is treated here, perhaps erroneously, as masc., being modified by the masc. ptc. שוה. Cf. the later Aramaic *miḥzīta*ʾ, and *BMAP* 2:5, מחזי 1 שויה כסף חלרן 7 פלג, in which שויה is fem.

12. כסף שקל 1 ר 2: "(In) cash 1 shekel, 2 qu(arters)." See the comment above on line 7.

תמ[סא] 1 זי נחש: "1 bronze bowl." Cowley had restored the lacuna as תמ[חי], "tray"; Lidzbarski (*Ephemeris*, 3. 131) preferred to read תמ[ני], but he did not attempt to translate it. The word תמסא is now clearly read in *BMAP* 7:13 in a very similar context of dowry items, and Kraeling rightly suggested that it be read here too. The meaning of it, however, is not clear; Kraeling compared it to an Assyr. noun, *nemsētu*, "bowl." This is, of course, possible, but it does not explain all the problems in the word. It is apparently feminine, since שויה follows as a modifier. This would suggest that the final -ᵓ here stands for the fem. sg. abs.; in the rest of the list the item usually stands before the cardinal in the absolute state.

כסן זי נחש 2: "2 bronze cups." A similar expressions occurs in *BMAP* 7:14; cf. *AP* 61:1, 3, 4, 13, 14. Kraeling (*BMAP*, p. 212) quotes Herodotus (2:37), who records that Egyptians drank from bronze cups.

13. זלוע 1 זי נחש: "1 bronze pitcher." The same expression occurs in *BMAP* 7:15; *AP* 36:4; cf. *BMAP* 7:18. The item mentioned here is undoubtedly not a "bowl" (so Cowley and Kraeling understood it), but a spouted jug or pitcher.

כל כספא ודמי נכסיא כסף כרשן 6 שקל‹ן› 5 חלר[ן] 20: "All the money and the value of the possessions are 6 silver karshin, 5 shekels, 20 ḥallurin." Cowley was certainly correct in regarding שקל as a scribal error for שקלן. Lidzbarski's explanation (see *Ephemeris*, 3. 80, 130), which seeks to retain the singular שקל, is too ingenious and strained to be convincing; see the general remarks above, p. 248, n. 13. The sum total given here represents not only the dowry money and the value of the items just enumerated but also includes the bride-price (see above, p. 247). Cf. *BMAP* 7:15 for the justification of this view. It is now clear that this total does not merely represent Esḥor's "own gifts," the value of which is stated because the deed is written in his name and he wants "to make the most of them" (so Cowley). Nor is the lack of a price in the list of items that follows this total due to Esḥor's judgment that it was unnecessary "to state the value of what he receives." All the objects belong to Miphṭaḥiah's dowry. What is not valued must have been considered of little value; but a couch with stone inlays (?) is hard to understand in this category. In any case, the מהר has been included in the sum total, probably for the reason already given above (see p. 247).

חלר[ן] 20: "20 ḥallurin," or a half shekel. The word *ḫalluru* meant in Akkadian a "chickpea" and became the name of a small weight. In the Babylonian scale, it represents one tenth of a shekel. See *CAD*, 6.47-48; A. Ungnad, "Aus den neubabylonischen Privaturkunden," *OLZ* 11 (1908), Beiheft, 26-28. However, according to the scale used in these papyri 40 ḥallurin = 1 shekel, as Cowley rightly established (*AP*, xxxi). Though פלג is used to indicate a half of a ḥallur, it apparently was not used after שקל. On the other hand, זוז could have been used, or else the phrase we have here, 20 ḥallurin. However, Kraeling (*BMAP*, 146) sought to regard the *ḥallur* as a tenth of the shekel, as in the Babylonian system. But this cannot be right. In totals the lower figures are always converted to the next higher weight, when they equal a unit or units of it. There would be no reason to write "20 ḥallurin," if ten of them equalled a shekel; this would have appeared as two shekels more. Moreover, the phrase in *BMAP* 7:14 would be meaningless, 10 ח 1 שקל, "one shekel, 10 ḥ(allurin)."

15. שוי 1 זי גמא: "1 reed couch." The form שוי is probably the same as the later Aramaic word *šiwwāy*, "couch" (see G. H. Dalman, *ANHW*, 417).

גמא: This word must be understood as the Aramaic equivalent of the Hebrew *gōmeʾ*, "papyrus (nilotica)." It is known in Coptic as *kam* and in later Aramaic as *gamyāʾ*. For its Egyptian origin, see T. O. Lambdin, "Egyptian Loanwords in the Old Testament," *JAOS* 73 (1953) 144-55, esp. p. 149.

בה נעבצן זי אבן 4: "On which there are 4 stone inlays," lit., "on it (there are) 4 inlays (?) of stone." No relative pronoun occurs in the similar phrase in *BMAP* 7:17. The expression should be compared with the relative clause in Dan 3:1, without a conjunction (see H. Bauer and P. Leander, *GBA* §108a). The meaning of נעבצן is unknown. The following number 4 suggests that the ending *-n* is plural. Sayce and Cowley wondered whether it might denote the stone feet of the reed couch; F. Peiser (*OLZ* 11 [1908] 28) sought an Assyrian cognate in *ḫabāṣu*, "swell up." Kraeling (*BMAP*, 213) related it to the Jewish Aramaic root, *ᶜbṣ*, "grow pale," and to the noun *ᶜbṣᶜ*, "tin," suggesting that it might mean "inlays." Possibly it is another technical trade-expression, a borrowed niphal form; see comment on *nšḥṭ* (line 10 above). The אבן is specified as שש, "alabaster," in *BMAP* 7:18 (see E. Y. Kutscher, *JAOS* 74 [1954] 236; H. L. Ginsberg, ibid., 159). Cf. Amos 6:4.

16. פק 1 זי סלק: "*1 pq* of *slq*." The meaning of this phrase is still unknown. J. N. Epstein (*JJLG* 6 [1908] 366 n. 3 suggested that פק might be another form of בק, related to *baqbūq*, "Krüglein." G. R. Driver compared it with the Akkad. *paqqu*, "bowl," and Scheftelowitz with Old Persian *pāka*, "cooking pot." But all these attempts seem to be difficult because the word has turned up as פיק (*BMAP* 2:6). In the latter passage one might be tempted to think that it is a measure smaller than חפן; but this meaning suits neither this passage nor *BMAP* 7:18. J. Reider (*JQR* 44 [1953-54] 340) translates the phrase as "a bottle of herbs," maintaining that both words occur in the Talmud, though with slightly different meanings; סלקא is a "beet" or "well-boiled vegetable." Is it possible that פיק is related to the Hebrew *pīqāh*, "spindle whorl"? Note that a different phrase using *slq* occurs in *BMAP* 7:18, דמן זי סלק 1, which Kraeling translates as "value of 1 *slq*," concluding that סלק must refer to some metal or coin (p. 147).

כפן 2: "Two ladles," or "2 bowls." In *BMAP* 7:19 the כפן are specified for "the carrying of ointment."

פרכס 1 זי חצן חדת: "1 new *prks* of palm-leaves." The meaning of חצן is now clear, "palm leaves," written חוצן in *AP* 20:6; *BMAP* 7:17. In the former passage the phrase מאני עק וחוצן, "vessels of wood and palm-leaves," would suggest that *prks* is a receptacle of some sort. Jean-Hoftijzer (*DISO*, 235) think that it is a "boite à cosmétiques," and T. Nöldeke (*ZA* 20 [1907] 148) suggested that it might be a tray or a small basket.

5 תקם חפנן: "5 handfuls of castor oil." This phrase and the following one are written above line 16, and it is not certain where one should insert them in the line. It makes little difference in the long run. The meaning of תקם was not understood for a long time. Cowley (*AP*, 49, 308) regarded it as a form of *qwm*, and suggested the meaning "containing," without explaining its morphology. M. Kamil and E. G. Kraeling used the meaning, "jar." But it is now certain that it means "castor oil" (see P. Grelot, "L'huile de ricin à Eléphantine," *Sem* 14 [1964] 63-70; see further H. Farzat, "Encore sur le mot *tqm* dans les documents araméens d'Eléphantine," *Sem* 17 [1967] 77-80; A. Dupont-Sommer, "Note sur le mot *tqm* dans les ostraca araméens d'Eléphantine," *Sem* 14 [1964] 71-72). The word also occurs in *AP* 37:10; *BMAP* 2:6; 7:20; *HermWP* 2:13; 3:12; 4:7; 5:5. The context of the two *BMAP* passages relates *tqm* to other oils or ointments. Grelot related the word to Demotic *tgm* (sometimes spelled *tkm*), and to older Egyptian *dgm*, "castor (oil)." He cited its use in lamps, and B. Porten (*Archives from Elephantine*, 92-93) has pointed out its use in anointing.

Cowley read the phrase as 8 תקם ח, taking *ḥ* as an abbreviation for a measure, as in *AP* 24:38 (and 41). This may be correct in the latter place, but it is to be noted that *ḥ* otherwise occurs as an abbreviation for *ḥlr* (*BMAP* 7:14, 15, 27). Lidzbarski (*Ephemeris*, 3.131) hesitatingly suggested the reading 5 חפנן, which is now almost certain, given its clear full writing in *BMAP* 2:6; 7:20, 21; *HermWP* 2:13; 3:12; *AD* 6:3, 4, 5. The difficulty is that the head of *p* is not clearly made, though the shaft is slightly curved; the two following strokes (for *nn*) are barely distinguishable from the unit strokes in the number that follows.

Aramaic חפנא is the cognate of Hebrew *ḥōpen* and Akkad. *upnu*, "hollow of the hand, handful." Used as a measure of oil it presents a difficult image, but the word was used to designate a commonly used amount, and its original meaning was undoubtedly forgotten. Its amount for this period is unknown. G. R. Driver (*AD*, p. 60) gives an approximation of 500 gr. and cites a third century A.D. inscription of Shapur I where *ḥwpn 5* is given as half a Greek *μόδιος* (see M. Sprengling, "Shahpuhr I, the Great on the Kaabah of Zoroaster (KZ)," *AJSL* 57 [1940] 387, 390).

1 שנן משאן: "1 (pair of) leather sandals." This same expression, the meaning of which is really unknown, occurs in *BMAP* 2:5. משאן probably is the same as the later Aramaic word, "shoe, sandal," see 1QapGen 22:21; cf. J. N. Epstein, *ZAW* 33 [1913] 225. The real difficulty is the meaning of שנן, which seems to be a construct state with משאן. In *BMAP* 7:20 it occurs before זי צל, which almost certainly means "of leather" (compare Jewish Aramaic *ṣallā*; and *AP* 37:10). This again relates the word to an item like sandals. Kutscher (*JAOS* 74 [1954] 234 n. 6) queried whether שאן could reflect the Old Assyrian *šēnān*, "two shoes." J. Reider (*JQR* 44 [1953-54] 339) understands the phrase to refer to a "leather bag." Whatever the meaning of it is, it is almost

certain that שנן is not a measure continuing the preceding phrase, as T. Nöldeke once thought (*ZA* 20 [1907] 147).

This brings us to the end of the dowry items in the contract. From this point on, various stipulations regarding the marriage agreement are recorded.

17. מחר או יום ׳[חר]ן: "Tomorrow or some other day," a stereotyped phrase that denotes some vague time in the future. It occurs again in lines 20, 22, 26; and in other Elephantine papyrus texts (e.g., *AP* 5:6, 8; 9:8, 13; *BMAP* 2:7, 9, 10, 12, 13; 7:21). J. J. Rabinowitz ("Meaning of the Phrase *mḥr* ᵓ*w ywm* ᵓ*ḥrn* in the Aramaic Papyri," *JNES* 14 [1955] 59-60); *Jewish Law*, 159-63) has compared the phrase to the Hebrew תמול שלשום, "yesterday and the day before yesterday," i.e., "in the past." He would accordingly translate the Aramaic phrase, "tomorrow or the day after (tomorrow)." He further cites kindred expressions from an Akkadian text of Ras Shamra (*urram šēram*, "demain, après-demain" [Thureau-Dangin's translation]), of Boghazkoi, and a Demotic text of the seventh century B.C. Y. Muffs (*Studies*, 206) notes that the Aramaic phrase is merely the last in a long line of idioms which express the idea of "(if), some time in the future," and that no idiom is a literal translation of any other. He cites also Ugar. *śḥr* ᶜ*lmt* and Neo-Assyrian *ina šērtu ina lidiš*. In this he is almost certainly correct, for although Rabinowitz' parallels, especially the one to Hebrew, might suggest that אחרן implies "after" (like ᵓ*ḥr*), it is to be noted that in all other cases where אחרן occurs, it means "other" (= ᵓ*oḥŏrān*). Kraeling (*BMAP*, 147) asked whether יום אחרן means "another day" or "the next day," and compared *b. Baba Mezia* 17a, *lmḥr wlywm*ᵓ ᵓ*ḥr*ᵓ. This is a later expression and may possibly mean "the next day." But it should be noted that it is in the emphatic state, and it is not quite the same thing. For this reason I prefer to remain with the translation given above, basically the same as that used by Cowley. The omission of או in *AP* 1:4 is undoubtedly a scribal error.

ימות אסחור: "Should Esḥor die." The same form of the conditional sentence, with the protasis in the imperfect and without the conjunction *hn*, is also found in lines 20, 22, 26, and in *BMAP* 2:7, 9, 11, 12; 7:21, 34. It is to be contrasted with *BMAP* 7:24 (. . . והן יה[וי]ש[מע] תשנא) and also with *AP* 15:35 (והן העדת המו, "If I do remove them") or *BMAP* 2:14 (והן הנצלתה מנך, "and if I take him away from you"). They are all future conditions. E. Y. Kutscher (*JAOS* 74 [1954] 234) explains the differences between them, by pointing out that הן usually takes the perfect (as in Arabic with ᵓ*in*), but only if the verb follows immediately after הן; the further it is removed from the conjunction the more it tends to occur in the imperfect. Sometimes the imperfect is used when the verb follows immediately, but the converse is not true. It never appears in the perfect if it is removed from הן. Hence in a clause without הן the verb will be in the imperfect. Kutscher's explanation is generally valid; one case, however, may be problematical: in *BMAP* 3:22a one finds ולא כהלן פצלן לה יתה, "and (if) we are not able to recover it for him." It seems to be a conditional use of the perfect without הן. In the preceding sentence הן was used with the perfect, and possibly the *w*- before the verb is to be understood as resuming it.

ובר דכר ונקבה לא איתי לה: "Having no child, male or female," lit., "and there is not to him, a child, male or female." The same expression occurs again in lines 20–21.

18. מפטחיה הי שליטה בביתה זי אסחור: "Miphṭaḥiah is entitled to the house of Esḥor," lit., "has power (*or* authority) over Esḥor's house." The problem in this clause is to determine the sense of *šlyṭ b*, since it undoubtedly expresses a legal situation different from that of Esḥor in the event of Miphṭaḥiah's death. According to line 21 he will inherit her property *(yrtnh)*. The same inheritance is expressed in *BMAP* 7:35. Unfortunately, the papyrus is broken in *BMAP* 7:29 and the phrase that is used of the bride there is not clear (see *BMAP*, 206; cf. J. T. Milik, *RB* 61 [1954] 250; R. Yaron, *JSS* 3 [1958] 8-9 [Yaron is convinced that *yrt* was not used of the woman]). L. Freund (*WZKM* 21 [1907] 177) has pointed out the different legal terms used here and suggests that whereas the husband would inherit his wife's property in the case of her death without children, the wife would be entitled only to the usufruct *(Nutzniessungsrecht)* of Esḥor's house and property, which would revert to her husband's family at her death. Yaron (*JSS* 3 [1958] 9-10), while not rejecting Freund's interpretation, has an alternate explanation. The husband's right was laid down by law and is thus referred to as inheritance *(yrt)*; the provision in the contract concerning him is merely declarative, not constitutive. But Miphṭaḥiah's right is created by the contract. There is really no evidence to support one or other of these interpretations, and so either is plausible. In *BMAP* 2:11, 12 שליט is used of both the husband and the wife; but since this document records the marriage of a slave, there is probably a different legal situation here.

19. וכל זי איתי [ל]ה על אנפי ארעא כלה: "And all that he has on the face of the earth, all of it." The last word כלה is either suffixal or an alternate form of the emphatic state of כל (with a final *he* instead of final *aleph*). If it be suffixal, its vocalization would differ depending on the noun that it resumes: *kulleh*, resuming כל זי, or *kullah*, resuming ארעא. For one could also translate, "and all that he has on the face of the whole earth." On the other hand, if it be emphatic, it could still be resumptive to either of these expressions. See p. 215 above. The resumptive use of כלה after כל זי is also paralleled in 1QapGen 10:13; 12:10; 16:11; see my commentary (p. 22 above, n. 27) 198, §4.

21. אסחור הו ירתנה בנכסיה וקנינה: "Esḥor shall inherit her possessions and her property." For the significance of this clause, see the comment on line 18 above. The use of הו may be emphatic; but it may also be merely influenced by the corresponding feminine in line 18, even though the expression differs. Instances of the emphatic use can be found in *AP* 6:4, 12-13; 10:15; 13:10; 20:9; *A* 24, 84; *BMAP* 3:10; 5:14; 7:35.

22. תקום מפטחיה בעדה ותאמר: "Should Miphṭaḥiah rise up in an assembly and say." The phrase is clear except for the problematic word בעדה. Sayce and Cowley rendered it, "in the congregation," as did Cowley later in his small edition; he was followed by S. Greengus, *Aramaic Marriage Contracts*, 72-73; R. Yaron, *JSS* 3 (1958) 14-16; Y. Muffs, *Studies*, 59. Kraeling (*BMAP*, 147), believing that the preposition בעד occurred in *BMAP* 11:10, sought to translate the word as a preposition here: "on account of her / him," or "on his own (or her) behalf." G. R. Driver (*PEQ* 87 [1955] 92) sought rather to understand בעדה as "behind her," an expression meaning "to find fault with." But neither Kraeling's interpretation nor Driver's have proved acceptable. H. L. Ginsberg (*JNES* 18 [1959] 148-49) disposed of the alleged preposition in *BMAP* 11:10, by showing that the text really reads בערבני "over my security (or pledge)." In his translation of this text he returned to the meaning "congregation," but correctly interpreted it as indefinite, "in a congregation." P. Leander (*L* §55b) and E. Y. Kutscher (*JAOS* 74 [1954] 234) also supported the absolute sense of "congregation," and the latter regarded the noun as a Hebraism, found also in Syriac. He compared Job 30:28, *qamtî baqqāhāl* (an interesting material parallel which has nothing to do formally with marriage or divorce).

The importance of the phrase lies in the need of a public declaration in the case of divorce. The further question about whether this was a court that would examine the reasons for the divorce, or whether *ᶜēdāh* refers to a specific number of persons before whom the declaration had to be made before it was considered valid is one that cannot be resolved on the basis of the data now available. See S. Funk, "Die Papyri von Assuan als älteste Quelle einer Halacha," *JJLG* 7 (1909) 378-79; R. Yaron, *Introduction*, 53-56; B. Porten, *Archives of Elephantine*, 210.

Another more basic consideration that this document manifests is the possibility that a Jewish woman at Elephantine could divorce her husband. In this matter she was the equal of her husband, her *bᶜl*. For the implications of this, see R. Yaron, *Introduction*, 53; and my article, "The Matthean Divorce Texts and Some New Palestinian Evidence," *TS* 37 (1976) 197–226, esp. pp. 204–5.

23. שנאת לאסחור בעלי: "I divorce Esḥor my husband," lit., "I have come to hate (*or* simply) I hate Esḥor." This formula for the declaration of divorce is found again in line 27, and in *BMAP* 2:7, 9; 7:21; for a slightly different formulation, see *BMAP* 7:25. It had already become stereotyped, whereas it undoubtedly expressed originally the motive for the divorce. On the problem of the origin of this term for "divorce," see J. J. Rabinowitz, *Jewish Law*, 40; R. Yaron, *JSS* 3 (1958) 32-34.

כסף שנאה בראשה: "The divorce fee is on her head," i.e., she will be held responsible for the payment of the divorce fee, the amount of which is set forth in the next phrase in the contract. For the idiom בראשה, denoting responsibility, see my note in *TS* 26 (1965) 669 n. 10, apropos of Matt 27:25.

J. J. Rabinowitz ("Demotic Papyri of the Ptolemaic Period and Jewish Sources," *VT* 7 [1957] 398-400) compares a phrase in P. Dem. Leiden 376, lines 28-29, to the Aramaic and NT phrase; but it is not parallel at all, since it lacks the phrase "on the head of."

תתב על מוזנא ותתקל ל[אס]חור כסף שקלן 7 ר 2: "She shall sit by the scale and weigh out to Esḥor 7 silver shekels, 2 qu(arters)." This clause is clear, except for the meaning of תתב, which also occurs in *BMAP* 7:26 but is omitted in *BMAP* 2:9-10. Sayce and Cowley understood it as a form of תוב, "she shall return," and in this they were followed by Cowley (*AP*, 46), Leander (*L* §39b), Verger (*Ricerche*, 117, 119). However, T. Nöldeke (*ZA* 20 [1907] 148) interpreted it rather as the impf. peal of יתב, and was followed in this by L. Freund (*WZKM* 21 [1907] 174), E. G. Kraeling (*BMAP*, 207, 215), H. L. Ginsberg (*ANET*², 223). Still another possibility was suggested by S. Jampel (*MGWJ* 51 [1907] 622), seeking to interpret it transitively, as if it were תיתב, "Sie soll als Hauptsumme das Scheidungsgeld auf die Wage legen." Similarly, R. Yaron, *JSS* 3 (1958) 13; *Introduction*, 54 ("she shall put on the scales"); J. J. Rabinowitz (*VT* 7 [1957] 398-400) understood it rather as the aphel of תוב, "she shall pay according to the scales." However, Cowley's peal impf. of תוב would be defectively written and the only other example of such defective spelling in Leander (*L* §39b) is תקם, a form that is now seen to have nothing to do with קום (see comment above on line 16). The defective spelling of the aphel of תוב (Rabinowitz' suggestion) is likewise unparalleled; and the same must be said about Jampel's תיתב. In the long run, then, the best solution is that of Nöldeke, תתב as the 3d sg. fem. peal impf. of יתב, "she shall sit." There are other figurative expressions in this text which would parallel this interpretation.

The כסף שנאה is given here as seven and one-half shekels. While it is one and one-half times the bride-price paid in line 5, as Ginsberg has pointed out (*ANET*², 223), it is to be noted that the divorce fee is always seven and one-half shekels in these texts, when it is explicitly mentioned. See *BMAP* 2:8, 10; 7:26. The penalties, however, for divorce are not always the same; sometimes it involves the payment of the divorce fee, which may have been this fixed sum; sometimes it involves the loss of the bride-price. In this case, the woman divorcing her husband must pay the divorce fee. In *BMAP* 2 the מהר was of the same sum as the divorce fee; but that was probably coincidental.

24. וכל זי הנעלת בידה תהנפק: "And all that she brought with her, she shall take out," lit., "all that she brought in her hand." See the general remarks above, p. 246.

25. מן חם עד חוט: "From straw to string." This is Y. Muff's happy translation of an alliterative phrase, expressing figuratively a totality by the use of extremely small samples. It occurs again in line 28, and in *BMAP* 2:8, 10. The second element in it was always clear, חוט, "a thread." The first was long a problem. Cowley (*AP*, 46) took it as "both shred (?) and thread." G. R.

Driver (*JRAS* [1932] 78) suggested, "both broom and thread," as the humblest symbols of a woman's work in the house. But E. A. Speiser ("A Figurative Equivalent for Totality in Akkadian and West-Semitic," *JAOS* [1934] 200-203; see also p. 299) pointed out a convincing Akkadian parallel and suggested the translation "straw" for *ḥam*. In the treaty between Suppiluliumma and Mattiwaza one finds *ḫāma u ḫuṣāba . . . ul ilqi*, "he did not take away (even) a straw or a splinter" (see *CAD*, 6:259). Though the expression is not the same, several commentators have called attention to Gen 14:23, *miḥūt weᶜad śerōk-naᶜal*, "from a thread to a sandal-strap," rendered in Aramaic in 1QapGen 22:21 as מן חוט עד ערקא דמסאן.

ותהך [ל]האן זי צבית: "And she shall go wherever she pleases," lit., "wherever she has pleased." The phrase occurs again in line 28. The form תהך is probably the impf. of הוך; cf. Sf III 5, 6; Sf I A 24; T. Nöldeke, *ZA* 20 (1907) 142. This clause stands in contrast to *BMAP* 7:28, ותהך לבית אבוך, "and she shall go to her father's house." The difference is that Miphṭaḥiah has been married before. See Y. Muffs, *Studies*, 55 n. 5.

ולא {י}דין ולא דבב: "Without suit or process." The expression occurs again in line 29, and often in the Elephantine texts (e.g., *AP* 6:12; *BMAP* 3:12, 13, 14; 9:18, 19—note the defective spelling of דן in *BMAP* 1:5 and the hypercorrection of זין וזבב in *BMAP* 3:17). An Akkadian expression underlies it: *tuāru dīni ū dabābi laššu*, "a re-opening of the case and the litigation is not to be" (see *CAD*, 3.153); compare the Greek formula in later papyrus texts: *ἄνευ δίκης καὶ κρίσεως*. E. Y. Kutscher (*JAOS* 74 [1954] 239-40) notes that the Aramaic formula is undoubtedly the link between the Akkadian and the Greek examples.

27. מהרה [י]אבד: "His bride-price goes forfeit," lit., "he shall lose his bride-price *(muhreh)*," or possibly "he shall lose her bride-price *(muhrah)*," i.e., the bride-price he paid for her. This is one of the most contested phrases in the Elephantine marriage contracts. Whose is it and loses it? Part of the problem is the determination of the meaning of the suffix (*-eh* or *-ah*?); part of it is the meaning of the verb יאבד. It was also complicated for a long time by the misunderstanding I have already mentioned several times about the inclusion of the מהר in the sum total of lines 13-15. It is, however, realized today that the penalties for divorce in these Elephantine contracts are not always the same. The verbal form יאבד could also be intransitive, "his bride-price is lost." No מהר is mentioned in *BMAP* 2, and hence none is lost. In *BMAP* 7:25 the loss of the מהר is included in the woman's penalty for divorce (in addition to the payment of the divorce fee). H. L. Ginsberg (*JAOS* 74 [1954] 159) has discussed the problems of *BMAP* 7 and thinks that the phrase is misplaced there. Whatever the solution to the problem of *BMAP* 7 is—and it is hotly debated—the understanding of *AP* 15 is less problematic. The loss of the מהר is clearly the penalty imposed on Esḥor; hence, either "he shall lose his bride-price" or "his bride-price is lost."

28. ביום חד בכף חדה: "On one day (and) at one time." The phrase seems to mean that there cannot be any partial or temporary withholding of her property. The same expression occurs in *BMAP* 7:28.

29. ו[זי] יקום על מפטחיה: "Whoever rises up against Miphṭaḥiah." Cowley had restored the lacuna with ו[הן], translating, "But if he should rise up." Many commentators followed him; and the clause, thus interpreted of an act of the husband, led to the theory of divorce by illegal expulsion in these texts. There was always a difficulty in this understanding, in that Esḥor was made to speak of himself in the third person (מן ביתה זי אסחור, line 30). In *BMAP* 7:30-32, part of the formula occurs again, but the context is unfortunately broken, the formula, however, is found in *BMAP* 6:16, which is not a marriage contract but a deed recording a gift of a house to a daughter by her father. He makes sure by the formula that she will not be driven out of it by some outsider without legal consequences: זי יקום עליך לתרכתכי מן בתיא, "Who rises up against you to drive you out of the houses. . . ." This sense must be introduced into the marriage contracts. Esḥor is thus making sure that Miphṭaḥiah will have the right to his house and property. The phrase is undoubtedly aimed at relatives of his. See also *AP* 46:8. This interpretation has been confirmed by a similar clause in a Demotic marriage contract from Elephantine, which begins with "Anyone in the world who . . ." (P. Dem. Berlin 13593, dated 198 B.C.; W. Erichsen, *AbhPAW*, Philos.-hist. Kl., 1939, Nr. 8, p. 10). See R. Yaron, "Aramaic Marriage Contracts: Corrigenda and Addenda," *JSS* 5 (1960) 66-70, esp. pp. 66-69. As a result of this interpretation, this clause is not concerned with a form of divorce at all. But compare A. Verger, *Ricerche*, 125-30.

30. לתרכותה מן ביתה זי אסחור ונכסוהי וקנינה: "To drive her out of Esḥor's house and his possessions and his property." Cowley was embarrassed by the phrase ביתה זי אסחור, which contains nothing more than the prospective suffix and means only "Esḥor's house," or "the house of Esḥor." There is no need of the cumbersome translation, "from his, Esḥor's house." Once this is seen, it is possible also to restore *BMAP* 7:30 differently. Instead of simply [י]קום [. . . ע]נניה, one should read, ומן י]קום ע]ל יהוישמע] לתרכותה . . ., "And whoever rises up against Yahuyishma^{c} to drive her away . . ." Instead of מן, one could also restore זי. The expression *qwm ^{c}l*, in the sense of violent or illegal activity against a person, is also found in the Bible; see Deut 28:7; Jdgs 9:18; 20:5. On the nature of this *clausula salvatoria*, see J. J. Rabinowitz, *Jewish Law*, 48-64.

ינתן לה כסף כרשן 20 ויע[בד] לה דין ספרא זנה: "He shall pay her 20 silver karshin and shall carry out in her regard the stipulation of this document." The stipulation is the prescription set forth in lines 29-31, *w*[*zy*] *yqwm . . . znh*. The stipulation thus sets a stiff penalty, since the sum of 20 karshin is very high, as can be seen by comparing it with the total dowry sum in lines 13-15; see also the comment on the woolen garment in line 8 (p. 257 above). Sayce and Cowley had restored ויע[מד], translating it, "and (the terms of) this deed shall hold good for her." Cowley later changed the restoration to ויע[די] and translated, "and the provisions of this deed shall be an*nulled*, as far as he is concerned." H. L. Ginsberg (*ANET*[2], 223) left the lacuna blank: "and the law of this deed shall [ ] for her." The phrase, however, has turned up in *BMAP* 7:32: ויעבד [לה] דין ספרא זנה, whence the reading adopted here. See also *AP* 14:3; *BMAP* 7:40; Ezra 7:26 for related expressions. The penalty כסף כרשן 20, is imposed again in lines 34, 36, and seems to be a fixed penalty in marital offenses.

31. ולא אכל אמר איתי לי אנתה אחרה להן מפט‹ח›יה: "I shall not be able to say, 'I have another wife, other than Miphṭaḥiah.'" The clause insures the unicity of the marital agreement. The formula used here is slightly different from that in *BMAP* 7:36, where it is stated that "[Anani shall no]t [be able to ta]ke [another] wife," i.e., another wife in the future. It is a protection against future polygamy. Here the formula assures Miphṭaḥiah that Esḥor has no other wife or children who can lay claim to his house or property. For the children born of Miphṭaḥiah and Esḥor, see *AP* 20:3; 25:3. Cf. B. Porten, *Archives of Elephantine*, 254.

33. הן אמר: "If I do say." See the comments on the syntax of the conditional sentence above, on line 17.

איתי לי ב[נן] ואנתה אחר‹נ›ן להן מפטחיה ובניה: "I have other children and a wife, other than Miphṭaḥiah and her children." The clause is not smoothly constructed here, and the form אחרן is undoubtedly a scribal error, as T. Nöldeke suggests (*ZA* 20 [1907] 136).

34. אנתן למפטחיה כס[ף] כרשן 20: "I shall pay Miphṭaḥiah 20 silver karshin." The penalty is the same as in line 31.

35. ולא אכל [אהנ]תר נכסי וקניני: "Nor shall I be able to withdraw my possessions and my property." Sayce and Cowley restored [אהנ]תר, the haphel impf., "take away," admitting that the *resh* was doubtful. The root is attested in Dan 4:11 and occurs possibly in an uncertain Nabatean text, *CIS*, 2. 224. When it occurs later, the causative stem has the nuance of "loose, throw off." The clause prohibits the withdrawal of Esḥor's property from Miphṭaḥiah as long as the marriage persists. As R. Yaron puts it, "the wife had to concur in the alienation of property by her husband. Her dissent could not indeed invalidate the transaction, but the penalty-clause would be a sufficient safeguard" (*JSS* 3 [1958] 25).

והן העדת המו מנה: "And if I do remove them from her." See the comments on line 17 above.

36. קבל ס[פר אחר]ן: "According to some other document." The whole phrase is set in double braces to indicate the scribal erasure of this clause. It is impossible to say what was behind the attempt to erase; it certainly leads one

to suspect that de facto there existed some other document to which Esḥor may have been in some way still obligated.

37. [ספרא זנה כפם אסחור] כתב נתן בר ענניה: "Nathan bar ᶜAnaniah wrote [this document at the behest of Esḥor]." The scribe, Nathan bar ᶜAnaniah, appears also in *AP* 10:20; 13:17; *BMAP* 2:14 in the same capacity. He signs his name as a witness in *AP* 8:32; 9:20, and he was apparently the father of several sons (*AP* 18:3; 22:128; *BMAP* 7:42). The lacuna which occurs here is restored as in *AP* 5:15; 6:17; *BMAP* 7:43. The phrase כפם means literally "according to the mouth of," i.e., at the dictation of (someone). Cf. *AP* 2:18; 11:16 (על פם). The scribe's name is recorded before that of the witnesses to the document, as in many other of these Elephantine texts. This seems to conform to contemporary Egyptian practice; see E. Seidl, *Ägyptische Rechtsgeschichte der Saiten- und Perserzeit* (Ägyptische Forschungen, 20; Glückstadt: Augustin, 1956) 71.

ושהדיא בגו: "The witnesses to it," lit., "thereto," or possibly "within," since בגו clearly functions here as an adverb. Cowley and Kraeling understood בגו in the first sense, "thereto." R. Yaron (*JSS* 2 [1957] 45-46) thinks that the word has a more technical sense, explained in part by a Mishnaic prescription (*Baba Bathra* 10:1: "A plain document has its witnesses within [on the recto]; a tied up document has its witnesses on its back [the verso]"), and in part by a phrase in a Judean deed of sale: כ[ת]בה דנה פשיט וחתמו בגוה (line 14), "this document is simple and they have signed (it) on the inside" (see J. T. Milik, *RB* 61 [1954] 182-90). Yaron is correct in pointing out the striking similarity in phrasing in the last instance. He also notes that the Elephantine practice of signing the contract on the inside differed from the contemporary Egyptian practice. He does not think that the Elephantine practice differed from the Jewish custom, disagreeing with J. J. Rabinowitz (see *BASOR* 136 [1954] 16), who cited Jer 32:10. If the Elephantine expression בגו has the technical meaning that Yaron suggests, then it is very cryptic and stereotyped. On the other hand, the equally stereotyped adverb בגו occurs many times in these texts (see comment on line 5 above). The full formula for the introduction of the names of the witnesses who signed the contract can also be found in many texts (e.g., *AP* 1:8; 2:19; 3:22; 5:15; 8:28; *BMAP* 2:14; 7:43; 8:10; etc.).

38. פנוליה בר יזניה: "Penuliah bar Yezaniah." This witness appears only here in the Elephantine texts, but he may be the father of several children (see *AP* 13:13; 18:5; 22:110; 25:19). The first name, פנוליה, means "Turn to Yahu," as T. Nöldeke (*ZA* 20 [1907] 134) pointed out, comparing the plural element in it to a name like הודויה (*AP* 20:18; Ezra 2:40; 1 Chr 5:24; 9:7). For the sense of it, see Isa 45:22. The other name, יזניה, is not easy to explain. It occurs several times in these texts from Elephantine (*AP* 6:9; 9:2; 19:8; 25:4; 66:10) and is undoubtedly related to ידניה. In the comment on דין ודבב (in line 26) I called attention to the hypercorrection in זין ודבב, found in *BMAP* 3:17. Though one might be tempted to think in terms of this root דין in these names, the form is

unlikely as an impf. of דין. It is probable that יזניה represents an older spelling of ידניה and that we have to do with a root ʾzn/ʾdn with the initial *aleph* completely quiesced. The vocalization would then be *Yēzanyāh* (< *yiʾzanyāh*), "May Yahu listen." Cf. 2 Kgs 25:23 *(Yaʾăzanyāhû)*. Similarly M. Noth, *IPN*, 198.

[ ]יה בר אוריה: "[ ]iah bar Uriah." There are several possible restorations for the first name: *Reᶜūyāh* (*AP* 22:118), *Hôšaᶜyāh* (*AP* 25:2), *Yēzanyāh* (*AP* 6:9; 9:2, etc.).

מנחם בר [ז]כור: "Menaḥem bar Zakkur," who also appears in *BMAP* 2:15 as a witness.

39. [ ]שהד רעיבל ב: "Witness: Reᶜibel ba[r]." One might at first hesitate about the function of *śhd* in such a line-up of witnesses, especially after the introductory formula in line 37. Does it follow the preceding name or precede the following? In some instances elsewhere it is also difficult to tell (*BMAP* 3:23b, 24; 5:17; 8:10), but in others it clearly precedes the name (*AP* 18:4; *BMAP* 10:18-20; 11:13-14; 12:33-34; cf. *BMAP* 2:15; 9:23, 25, 26). This should be taken, then, as the norm and applied even to the cases about which one might hesitate at first. Moreover, it is sometimes clear even from the handwriting. The form שהד is a participle, and may actually have so functioned originally (i.e., So-and-so is witnessing). But it is clearly a stereotyped formula in these texts and has been so understood in my translation.

With the name *Rĕᶜībel* ("Bel is my friend"), compare *Bytʾlrᶜy* (*BMAP* 8:11), "Bethel is my friend," and *Rᶜyh* (*HermWP* 1:1; 2:16; 3:3), "Yahu is my friend."[20]

NOTES TO CHAPTER 12

*Originally published under the same title in *Near Eastern Studies in Honor of William Foxwell Albright* (ed. H. Goedicke; Baltimore/London: The Johns Hopkins University, 1971) 137-68.

[1](London: A. Moring, 1906) 43-44 (with plates); Cairo Museum No. 37110.

[2]See *AP* 18, 36, 48 (Cowley, pp. 54-56, 131-32, 153).

[3]See *BMAP* 2, 7, 14 (Kraeling, pp. 139-50, 199-222, 291-96).

[4]In the transcription of the text, square brackets [ ] denote words or letters that have been editorially restored in a lacuna, angular brackets ‹ › my editorial additions, and braces { } my editorial deletions. In the translation that follows parentheses ( ) are used to spell out an abbreviated word or to indicate English words added for the sake of style, or (in line 36) to indicate an erasure that can still be read.

[5]For the historical questions involved in this matter, see J. J. Rabinowitz, *Jewish Law: Its Influence on the Development of Legal Institutions* (New York: Bloch, 1956) 39-100; R. Yaron, *Introduction to the Law of the Aramaic Papyri* (Oxford: Clarendon, 1961) 44-53; A. Verger, *Ricerche giuridiche sui papiri aramaici di Elefantina* (Studi semitici, 16; Rome: Centro di studi semitici, 1965) 105-30; S. Greengus, "The Aramaic Marriage Contracts in the Light of the Ancient Near East and the Later Jewish Materials" (Master's thesis, University of Chicago, 1959). For the

stereotyped character of the text, see R. Yaron, "The Schema of Aramaic Legal Documents," *JSS* 2 (1957) 33-61.

[6]For instance, L. Freund, "Bemerkungen zu Papyrus G. des Fundes von Assuan.," *WZKM* 21 (1907) 169-77; S. Jampel, "Der Papyrusfund von Assuan," *MGWJ* 51 (1907) 617-34, esp. pp. 621-22; M. Lidzbarski, *Ephemeris,* 3. 129-31.

[7]See *AP*, 46-47. In this he was followed by C. Clermont-Ganneau, Review of *APA, RCHL* 62 (1906) 341-54, esp. p. 349; W. Staerk, *Die jüdisch-aramaeischen Papyri von Assuan* (KIT 22/23; Berlin: de Gruyter, 1907) 28; P. Leander, *L* §41g.

[8]See *ANET*, 222-23; compare the first and second editions (1950, 1955).

[9]Ibid., 223.

[10]For example, W. Staerk, *Alte und neue aramäische Papyri übersetzt und erklärt* (KIT 94; Berlin: de Gruyter, 1912) 44; M. Lidzbarski, *Ephemeris*, 3. 129; B. Cohen, "Dowry in Jewish and Roman Law," *AIPHOS* 13 (1953) 57-85, esp. p. 61.

[11]See *BMAP*, 146. In this he was followed by S. Greengus, "Aramaic Marriage Contracts," 59; R. Yaron, "Aramaic Marriage Contracts from Elephantine," *JSS* 3 (1958) 1-39, esp. p. 6.

[12]See *AP*, 47; also Cowley's note on line 14, p. 48.

[13]There is a lacuna at this point in the papyrus and one stroke of the number following the plural *šqln* remains. In the *editio princeps*, Sayce and Cowley restored the number as [3], without justifying it. But Cowley later restored it more accurately as [2], while still admitting the possibility of [3]. Lidzbarski (*Ephemeris*, 3. 130) also read the number 3. His interpretation of the sum in lines 13-14, however, was erroneous. It was based on his insistence that *šql*, a singular, in line 14 was originally followed only by one stroke, i.e., 6 karshin, 1 shekel, 20 ḥallurin. This represented only Miphṭaḥiah's money and possessions. It did not include the 5 shekels of the *mhr* but did include the extra shekel restored in line 13. Then he suggested that four extra strokes were later added in line 14 to represent the value of the objects listed (without prices) in lines 15-16. It is, however, clear that the latter objects were not included in the sum and there is no evidence of a later addition of four strokes.

[14]Kraeling (*BMAP*, 39, 146) maintains that the *ḥallūr* represents a tenth of the silver shekel. This may be right for the Babylonian scale, but it cannot be correct in these Elephantine texts. See S. Greengus, "Aramaic Marriage Contracts," 44-51; his discussion strangely hesitates in this matter.

[15]A similar detailed list can be constructed for *BMAP* 7 to total up to this sum. However, the text is broken in places and the following list represents only my own way of restoring the individual values:

Line	Object	Value		
5	*mhr*	1 karsh		
5-6	*tkwnh zy ksp*	2 karshin	2 shekels	5 ḥallurin
6-7	*lbš 1 zy qmr*	1 karsh	2 shekels	
7	*gmydh 1 zy qmr*	1 karsh		
8-9	*lbš 1 mʿdr*		7 shekels	
9-10	*šbyṭ 1*		8 shekels	
10	*lbš 1*		[1 shekel	20 ḥallurin]
11	*šnṭʾ 1*		[1 shekel	10 ḥallurin]
11-12	*?*		[1 shekel]	
12	*? 1 ktn blyh*		1 shekel	
13	*mḥzy 1*		1 shekel	
13-14	*tmsʾ 1*		1 shekel	10 ḥallurin
14	*ks 1*		[1] shekel	
14	*ks 1*			20 ḥallurin
15	*zlwʿ 1*			20 ḥallurin
		5 karshin	26 shekels	85 ḥallurin
	or	7 karshin	8 shekels	5 ḥallurin

[16]See R. Yaron, *Introduction*, 48; "Aramaic Marriage Contracts," 6.

[17]"Aramaic Marriage Contracts," 57; see also idem, *Introduction*, 48; A. Verger, *Ricerche*, 112.

[18]"The Brooklyn Museum Aramaic Papyri," *JAOS* 74 (1954) 153-62, esp. pp. 156, 159.

[19]The issue is further complicated by the occurrence of the forfeiture phrase as a penalty for the bride in *BMAP* 7:24.

[20]See further B. Porten, "The Restoration of Fragmentary Aramaic Marriage Contracts," *Gratz College Anniversary Volume: On the Seventy-fifth Anniversary of the Founding of the College 1895–1970* (ed. I. D. Passow and S. T. Lachs; Philadelphia: Gratz College, 1971) 243–61.

I. INDEX OF SUBJECTS

(The subjects are those of the main text; the reader should check the notes that accompany the passages indicated by the following page numbers.)

Abram, 96, 98
Absolute State (of Aramaic Noun), 117, 206–8
Acco (Akko), 32, 238
Achaemenids, 59, 70
Acts of the Apostles, 4, 5, 183
Adam, 145, 152
Adonis, 238
Address (of a letter), 195–96
Adiabene, 34
Adon, King, 185, 231–42
Aethiopia, 234
Afiq, 238
Afqa, 238
Agaʾ, King, 235–36
Aḥiqar, 70, 147
Aḥiram, 67
Akkadian, 66, 183, 223, 225, 233, 234, 235, 240, 241, 256, 261
Alexander Balas, 92, 105
Alexander the Great, 32, 33, 92
"All" (*kl, klʾ*), 205–17
Alphabet, 60, 63
Amorite, 68, 69
Amoritization, 68
ʿAmram, 87
Anthropomorphism, 94, 95, 169
Antiochus III the Great, 32, 33
Antiochus IV Epiphanes, 33, 42, 92
Antipatris, 32, 238
Antonia, Fortress, 32
Aphek, 238
Apheka, 238
Apocalyptic, 91, 92, 106
Aquila, 120, 122, 126
Arabia, 40, 41, 61, 85, 234
Arabic, 62, 233
Aramaic, Kinds of
  Babylonian Talmudic, 58, 59, 62
  Biblical, 59, 205–17, 257
  Chancery, 59
  Eastern, 58, 60, 70, 72
  Edessene (Early), 62, 63, 71
  Egyptian, 60
  Galilean, 59, 149
  Hatran, 62, 63, 71
  Hebraized, 43
  Imperial (*Reichsaramäisch*), 59, 60, 61, 72, 184
  Late, 62, 63, 69, 151, 152, 153, 154, 167, 172, 184
  Literary vs. spoken, 39, 42, 72, 73, 166
  Mandaic, 58, 62
  Middle, 57, 60, 61, 62, 63, 69, 71, 153, 166, 184
  Modern, 58, 62, 69
  Murabbaʿat, 61, 71
  Nabatean, 40, 43, 58, 59, 60, 61, 63, 71
  Official (= Imperial), 59, 61, 62, 63, 68, 70–71, 72, 73, 153, 167, 184, 205, 231
  Old, 57, 58, 59, 60, 63–70, 147, 153, 184
  Palestinian, 5, 9, 38–43, 61, 63, 71, 73, 85, 86, 90, 99–100, 118, 163, 166, 167, 171
    Palestinian Christian, 9, 58, 59, 62, 154
    Palestinian Jewish, 58, 62, 89, 149, 151
  Palmyrene, 58, 59, 60, 61–62, 63, 71, 171
  Qumran, 60, 61, 71, 72, 85–113, 148, 165, 171
  Samaritan, 58, 59, 62
  Standard (= Official), 59, 61
  Syriac, 58, 62 (see further under "Syriac")
  Targumic, 59 (see further under "Targum(s)")
  Western, 58, 59, 60, 62, 70, 72
Aramaic Problems,
  Background of the New Testament, 1–27, 85–113, 183
  Epistolography, 19–20, 86, 183–204
  Interference, 7, 12–14, 39, 86, 183

Language of Jesus, 1, 2, 3, 6–10, 38–43, 45–46, 86
Literary forms, 15–17, 86
Mistranslations, 14–15, 86
Phases of the language, 57–84, 85, 184
Poetry, 16, 86
Substratum of the New Testament, 1, 2, 5, 85–113, 183
Words in Josephus, 39, 61, 86
Words in the New Testament, 10–12, 39, 61, 86
Arameans, 63
Aristeas, Letter of, 122, 126
Armenia, 61
Arsames, Correspondence of, 60, 185, 191, 196, 198, 212, 214
Artaxerxes I, 237, 249
Article, Postpositive, 66, 69
Ashdod, 234
Ashkelon, 232, 234, 235, 236
Asia Minor, 61, 85, 117
Asshurbanipal, 240
Asshur-uballit II, 231
Aššur Ostracon, 68, 70, 199, 241
Assyria, 59, 61, 91, 213
Astarte, 236
Aswan (Syene), 61, 185
Augustine, 12
Augustus, Edict of, 35
ᶜAuja River, 238

Baalbek, 238
Baᶜalshamayn, 236, 237
Babatha, 40, 41
Babylon(ia), 61, 62, 235, 239
Babylonian Captivity, 231
Babylonians, 232
Bagohi, 186, 192
Baḫᶜa, 62
Banit (goddess), 190, 221
Bar Cochba (*Simōn/Šiměᶜōn bar/ben Kōsibāh*), 5, 35, 36, 43, 71, 73, 85, 150, 185, 187, 198
Bar Hebraeus, 62
Bar Puneš, 147
Bar Rakib, 61, 66
Behistun, 70
Beirut, 238
Bel (god), 192, 228
Běnê Ḥězîr Tomb, 44
Bethel (god), 190, 221
Beth-Shan, 32
Beth-Sheᶜarim, 37, 149, 151
Bible, London Polyglot, 3, 110
Bildad, 148
Bir Gaʾyah, 147
Bir Hadad, 61, 66
Birth Story, 98
Bodmer Papyrus, 121
Bride-price, 244–48, 253, 265
"Brother," 190, 220, 221
Byblos, 238

Caesarea Maritima, 31, 32, 183
Caesarea Philippi, 32
Calah, 61
Cambyses, King, 186
Canaanite, 29, 44, 63, 66, 67, 68, 69, 162, 231, 234, 238
Capernaum, 35
Caria, 234
Carchemish, 232
Carpentras stele, 16, 222
Catilius Severus, L., 41
Cave of Letters, 40, 187
Chalcedon, Council of, 130
Chaldaic, 3
Chaldean Kingdom, 231
Christology, 1, 102–7, 127–32
Clement of Alexandria, 33
Codex Bezae, 17
Concluding Formulae (of letters), 194
Constantine (Algeria), 118
Construct Chain, 172, 193, 208–10
Corinth, 4
Corpus Hellenisticum, 5
Cyclades, 234
Cyprus, 234

Daliyeh, Wadi ed-, 186
Damascus, 238
Dan, Tell, 6, 61
Daniel, Book of, 39, 43, 59, 61, 72, 85, 90, 145, 147, 148, 153, 162, 164, 166
Darius, 190, 192
Darius II, 186
Daroma, 43
David, King, 104, 105, 106, 131
Ḍarrâme, Khirbet eḍ-, 238
Decapolis, 32
Delaiah, 186
Demetrius I Soter, 92
Dion, 32
Divorce, 263–64
Dowry, 247–48, 255
Dreams, 98
Dualism, 87
Dura Europos, 71

Edessa, 62, 71
Egypt, 85, 91, 117, 185, 186, 196, 205–17, 219, 223, 232, 234, 255, 256
ᶜEin Gev (ᶜEn Gev), 6, 61, 66
Ekron, 234
Elect of God Text, 39
Elephantine, 61, 68, 70, 131, 153, 185, 186, 187, 190, 197, 199, 200, 219, 223, 227, 243–71
Eliakim, 232
Elihu, 88, 124, 148, 164, 174
Emphatic State (of Aramaic Noun), 117, 210–14
Enoch, 14, 72, 98, 124
Enoch, Book(s) of, 39, 96, 153, 154
Ephesus, 4, 5
Epiphanius, 2
"Epistle," 184
Epistolography, 19–20, 183–204
Esarhaddon, 238, 240
Eshmunazor, 234
Esḥor, 243–71
Essenes, 86, 87, 166, 168
Eusebius of Caesarea, 2, 33
Evil-Merodach, 237
Ezekiel, 96, 146, 152, 153, 162, 163
Ezra, 43, 59, 61, 85, 184, 185, 196

Fiq, 238
Form Criticism, 10
Fuad, Papyrus, 120

Galilee, 37
Gamaliel I, R., 73, 168
Gamaliel II, R., 168
Gaonim, 62, 184
Gath, 234
Gaza, 32, 232, 234, 236
Genesis Apocryphon, 39, 43, 57, 60, 72, 86, 89, 93, 97, 98, 99, 148, 162, 164, 166
Genesis Rabbah, 74, 152
Gennesareth, Lake, 32
Gerasa, 106
Givᶜat ha-Mivtar, 150
Gospels, 4, 183
Greece, 5
Greek, 5, 29, 32–38, 39, 40, 183, 234
  Inscriptions, 35
  Sayings of Jesus (?), 37
  Words in Aramaic, 40–42, 62, 74, 167, 173
Greetings in Letters, 188, 191–94

Ḫabra, Wadi (= Naḥal Ḥever), 6, 39, 42, 43, 187
Hadad Inscription, 61, 65, 66, 69
Halaf, Tell, 61,66
Hama, 6
Hamath, 61
Hands, Laying-on of, 96–97
Hasmonean(s), 106
Hatra, 62
Haza'el, 61
Hazor, 61
Hebraisti, 36, 43
Hebrew, 6, 7, 29, 30, 44–46, 67, 183
  Aramaisms in, 7, 46
  Language of Jesus, 44–46
  Mishnaic, 6, 45
  Postbiblical, 12
  Proto-Mishnaic, 45
  Qumran, 167
Hebrews (NT *Hebraioi*), 36, 37, 119, 120, 123, 126
Hellenism in Palestine, 5, 32, 37, 38, 44–46, 74
Hellenistic Background of the New Testament, 5
Hellenists (NT *Hellēnistai*), 36, 37, 46, 119, 120, 123, 126
Hermopolis West, 61, 185, 186, 187, 197, 225, 226
Herod the Great, 98
Herodotus, 258
Hofra, El- (= Constantine), 118

Idumea, 43
Indus Valley, 61, 85
Iraq (Modern), 62
Italy, 5
Izates, King, 121

Jaffa, 238
James, Epistle of, 183
Jehoahaz, 232
Jehoiachin, 232
Jericho, 32
Jerome, 2, 120
Jerusalem, 32, 71
  New, Description of, 39
  Temple, 168
Jesus of Nazareth,
  Language of, 38, 44, 46, 86
  Person of, 1, 98, 154, 155
  Phases of his existence, 127
  Sayings or words, 8
Jewish Christians, 5, 37, 123
Job, 162–63, 167
  Book of, 148, 161–82
  Targums of, 39, 42, 72, 87–90, 94, 95, 124, 148, 161–82

John the Baptist, 86
John, Gospel of, 94, 95
Jonathan bar Ba^{c}yan, 36, 187
Joppa, 32, 37
Joseph, Husband of Mary, 98
Josephus, 2, 31, 33, 34, 61, 92, 121, 122, 126
Josiah, King, 232
Jubb^{c}adîn, 62
Judah the Prince, R., 71
Julius Africanus, 2
Jupiter Sarapis, 32
Justus of Tiberias, 33

Kando, 90
Karsh, 255
Kerdane, Tell, 238
Kerygma, 126, 130
Khnum/Khnub (god), 186, 192, 222
Kom, Khirbet el, 33
Kurdish, 62
Kyrios, 87–90, 115–42

Lagide(s), 32
Lamech, 98
Latin, 30–32, 183
Lazarus, 149, 150
Legions, Roman, 30–32
"Letter," 185–88
Levi, Testament of, 39, 72
Leviticus, Targum of, 39, 42, 165, 173
Libya, 233
Lingua franca, 6, 29, 32, 35, 185
Lithostrotos, 43
Logia (of Jesus), 45
Logos, 87, 94–95
Luristan, 61, 66
Luxor, 187
Lycia, 234
Lydda, 238

Maccabees, 30
Macedonia, 4
Maḥoz ^{c}Eglatain, 40, 43
Makkahanit, 191, 193, 195
Ma^{c}lula, 62
Mammon, 11–12
Marisa, 35
Marriage Contract, 243–71
Mary, Mother of Jesus, 98
Masabbalah, 36, 187
Masada, 39
Masoretic Text, 174
Mati^{c}el, 147
Megiddo, 232
Mĕgillat Ta^{c}ănît, 15, 38, 39

Melchireša^{c}, 9, 97
Melchizedek, 9, 97
Melqart, 236
Memphis, 185, 186, 198, 220
Mēmrā$^{\supset}$, 94–95, 169–71
Merodach-Baladan, 237
Mesopotamia, 60, 61, 85
Messiah, 93, 105, 106, 131, 153
Methuselah, 98
Michael, 97
Midrash, 86
Migdol, 219, 220, 224
Mipṭaḥiah, 243–71
Mishnah, 2, 71, 151
Mistranslations, 14–15
Moabite, 67
Morphology, 171
Mosaic Law, 41
Moses, 97, 121
Mossul, 62
Muhammadan Conquest, 62
Murabba^{c}at, 6, 35, 39, 42, 43, 45, 150, 151, 153, 199

Nabonidus, Prayer of, 39, 72, 162
Nabopolassar, 237
Nabu (god), 190, 192, 221, 228
Nahr Ibrahîm, 238
Na^{c}men River, 238
Nazareth, 32, 45
Nebuchadrezzar, 185, 231, 232, 233, 235, 236, 237, 242
Necho II, Pharoah, 231, 232, 234
Nephilim, 98
Nērab, 61, 66, 67
Nergal (god), 192, 228
Nero, Emperor, 7, 39
Nicaea, Council of, 130
Nicholas of Lyra, 2
Nineveh, 61
Noah, 98, 162
Numbers, 206

Onias, High Priest, 121
Ördek Burnu, 61
Origen, 120
Ossuaries, 35, 44
Ostraca, 184, 199–200

Padua Papyri, 198, 219–30
Pahlevi, 58
Palestine, 5, 29–46, 61–62, 74, 85, 92, 115, 116, 118, 119, 121–22, 126, 143, 148, 154, 171, 183, 185, 231, 241, 242
Palmyra, 62

Panammu, 61, 65, 66, 69
Passover, 186
Papias, 10–11, 45
Parallels, Literary, 97–99
Paul of Tarsus, 4, 168, 183
Pella, 32
Persia, 59, 85, 185, 255
Peshitta, 174
Peter, 86, 98
Pharaoh, 96, 98, 185, 231–42, 235, 239, 240, 241
Phasaelis, 32
Philadelphia, 32
Philistia, 234, 235, 236, 238
Philoteria, 32
Phoenicia, 234, 238
Phoenician(s), 60, 63, 65, 67, 231, 233, 234, 257
Pilate, Pontius, 31
Pompey, 30
Praefectus, 31
Praescriptio, 188–91
Proto-Aramaic, 69, 70
Proto-Lucianic Version of Greek Old Testament, 121
Ptaḥ (god), 186, 192
Ptolemais, 32
Ptolemies, 233, 234
Ptolemy II Philadelphus, 33
Ptolemy IV Philopator, 33
Punic, 12, 118, 119, 257
Purple, Tyrian, 99, 256

Qorban, 11, 39
Queen of Heaven, 190
Qumran, 39, 85–113
  Copper Roll of Cave III, 6, 45
  Hodayot, 44
  Manual of Discipline, 87
  Pěšārîm, 44, 166
  War Scroll, 44, 87, 91, 162
  (see also "Targum(s)")

Rabbat-Ammon, 32
Rabbi (title), 117
Rakib, Bar, 61, 66
Ras el-ᶜAin, 238
Ras Shamra, 261
Redaction Criticism, 10
Rehum, 191
Reichsaramäisch (see also "Official Aramaic," "Imperial Aramaic"), 59, 60, 61, 72
Riblah, 232
Rome, 34
Rosetta Stone, 233–34

Saite Dynasty (Egypt), 231
Samaria, 32, 186
Sanballat, 186
Saqqarah, 61, 185
Sarai (Sarah), 98
Scribe (of a letter), 194, 268
Script,
  Herodian, 164
  Paleo-Hebrew, 126, 127, 174, 175
Sebaste, 32
Second Revolt, 149, 187
Sefire, 61, 64, 65, 147, 148, 240
Seiyal, Wadi, 39, 71
Seleucid(s), 32, 92
Semitism, 2, 5
Septuagint, 90, 93, 120–23, 167
Shamash (god), 192, 228
Shekel, 248, 254, 255
Shekinah, 169
Shelemiah, 186
Shelomam bar Peṭ[ ], 190, 220, 221
Shimshai, the Scribe, 191
Simon ben Kosiba, see "Bar Cochba"
Son of God (title), 87, 90–94, 102–7
Son of Man (title), 87, 92, 95–96, 102, 131, 143–60
Source Criticism, 10
Succoth, 36, 187
Sujin, see "Sefire"
Sumerian, 183
Syene (see also "Aswan"), 186, 187, 190, 251, 252
Symmachus, 120
Synagogue(s), 35, 42
Syria, 5, 58, 60, 61, 85, 92, 105, 117, 183, 232, 234, 241, 242
Syriac, 2, 3, 9, 12, 42, 62, 89, 154, 167
  Jacobite, 62
  Modern, 58, 59
  Nestorian, 62
Syriacisms, 2

Tacitus, 31
Talmud,
  Babylonian, 149, 168, 171
  Palestinian, 151, 152
Targum(s), 3, 18, 86
  Non-Qumran Targums, 6, 73, 74
    Cairo Genizah Targums, 152
    Fragmentary Targum, 3, 151
    Targum Jonathan, 3, 4, 151
    Neofiti I, 152, 154
    Onqelos, 3, 4, 151

Palestinian, 18, 42, 72, 74, 172
Pseudo-Jonathan, 151, 154
Second Targum of Job, 94, 95, 167–74
Writings, 151, 165
Qumran Targums,
4QtgLev, 39, 42, 165, 173
4QtgJob, 38, 42
11QtgJob, 39, 42, 72, 87–90, 94–95, 124, 148, 161–82
Testimonia, 46
Tetragrammaton, 88, 90, 120–27
Textual Criticism, 17
Theios anēr, 104, 106
Theodotos Vettenos, 35
Thot (god), 187
Thutmose III, 238
Tiberias, Lake, 32, 238
Tiberieum, 31
Tiglath-Pileser I, 63
Titles (of Jesus), 87–96, 106, 107, 115–42, 143–60
Titus, Emperor, 34
Tobit, 39
Transcendence, 130–31
Ṭur ᶜAbdin, 62
Turkish, 62
Tyre, 236

Ugaritic, 65, 233, 240, 261
Uzziah, 39

Vespasian, Emperor, 31
Vowel-Letters, 64

Waw-Consecutive, 67
Witnesses (to documents), 268–69

Yaᵓdi, 61
Yahu, Yahweh, 88–90, 120–27, 186, 187, 190, 192, 193, 221
Yeb, 185, 186, 207, 252
Yedaniah, 186
Yoḥanan, High Priest, 186

Zākir, 61, 66, 67, 239
Zenjirli, 65

II. INDEX OF MODERN SCHOLARS

Aalen, S., 22
Abel, F.-M., 238
Ackroyd, P. R., 137
Aharoni, Y., 100, 201
Aimé-Giron, N., 76, 199
Albright, W. F., 12, 21, 24, 38, 49, 53, 56, 67, 79, 80, 81, 82, 83, 108, 133, 134, 164, 200, 215, 232, 235, 238, 242, 243, 269
Allegro, J. M., 176
Alon, G., 53
Alt, A., 176, 177, 238
Altheim, F., 22, 55, 198
Aly, Z., 137
Amiran, R., 100
Anderson, A. A., 176
Anschütz, H., 78
Argyle, A. W., 52
Arndt, W. F., 13
Arnold, W. R., 202
Auscher, D., 49
Avi-Yonah, M., 47, 55
Avigad, N., 6, 22, 47, 54, 55, 56, 80, 99, 101, 108, 157, 176, 222

Bacher, W., 180, 182
Bahat, D., 48
Baillet, M., 47, 101, 174, 182
Baltensweiler, H., 142
Baneth, D. H., 201
Bange, L. A., 64, 157
Barag, D., 47, 49
Bardtke, H., 175, 176, 178, 179
Barnett, R. D., 99
Barr, J., 22
Barrett, C. K., 51
Barth, J., 202
Barthélemy, D., 113, 136, 137
Barthélemy, J. J., 25
Batten, L. W., 177
Baudissin, W. W., 135
Bauer, H., 55, 133, 135, 181, 205, 210, 211, 215, 216, 259
Bauer, W., 13
Baumgartner, W., 58, 59, 75, 78, 214, 217
Bea, A., 242
Beare, F. W., 135
Beer, G., 200
Benoit, P., 25, 49, 51, 111, 141, 147, 150, 182
Benz, F. L., 158
Berger, K., 112
Bergsträsser, G., 58, 78
Berliner, A., 179

Berthier, A., 136
Bertram, G., 141
Betz, J., 140
Bevan, E., 234
Beyer, K., 12, 58, 71, 72, 73, 79, 80
Bickerman, E., 139
Birkeland, H., 7, 22, 45, 51, 55, 56
Birnbaum, S. A., 100
Bischoff, A., 177
Black, M., 4, 11, 13, 16, 19, 22, 23, 24, 25, 26, 27, 42, 84, 112, 140, 152, 156, 158, 175, 178
Blake, F. R., 78, 110, 133
Bligh, J., 53
Bliss, F. J., 49
Bogaert, P. M., 175
Boismard, M.-E., 17, 26
Bonnard, P., 135
Borger, R., 236, 238
Bousset, W., 87, 88, 103, 116, 135
Bowman, R. A., 58, 76, 81, 82, 201
Bresciani, E., 76, 77, 187, 197, 202, 203, 219, 220, 221, 222, 223, 224, 225, 226, 228, 229, 230
Bright, J., 233, 240, 242
Brock, S. P., 26, 140
Brockelmann, C., 67, 81, 178
Brooke, A. E., 139
Brown, R. E., 110, 111, 142, 156, 180
Brusa Gerra, C., 48
Büchsel, F., 51
Buhl, F., 210
Buit, M. du, 238
Bultmann, R., 88, 90, 103, 113, 116, 124, 136, 142, 160, 200
Burchard, C., 108, 176, 182
Burkitt, F. C., 139
Burney, C. F., 16
Burrows, M., 141, 156, 177
Buxtorf, J., 3, 21
Byington, S. T., 142

Cadbury, H. J., 52
Calderini, A., 48
Cantarino, V., 78
Cantineau, J., 7, 22, 158, 181
Capelle, P., 137
Caquot, A., 82
Carmignac, J., 141, 177
Cerfaux, L., 135, 138, 142
Černy, J., 249
Cerulli, E., 79
Chabot, J.-B., 139
Champion, L., 19, 26
Charlier, R., 136
Chase, F. H., 26
Chatelain, E., 137
Chomsky, W., 22
Clarke, W. K. L., 136
Clermont-Ganneau, C., 25, 55, 270
Cohen, B., 270
Collins, J. J., 157
Colpe, C., 50, 155, 156, 157, 159
Conzelmann, H., 116, 120, 132, 135, 136, 140, 142
Cook, S. A., 55
Cooke, G. A., 81
Coppens, J., 155, 175
Correll, C., 78
Cortes, E., 175
Cortés, J., 144
Couroyer, B., 25, 202
Cowley, A. E., 55, 76, 100, 157, 194, 199, 200, 204, 206, 207, 210, 211, 212, 213, 214, 215, 216, 221, 225, 243, 246, 247, 248, 255, 256, 257, 258, 259, 260, 261, 263, 264, 266, 267, 268, 269, 270
Cowling, C. J., 181
Cross, F. M., 58, 64, 65, 66, 67, 69, 75, 77, 80, 81, 83, 100, 108, 137, 139, 156, 164, 174, 179, 180, 182, 202
Crowfoot, J. W., 55, 100
Cullmann, O., 88, 116, 134, 136, 142
Cumont, F., 51, 135
Cymbermannus (Zimmermann), M., 21

Dahood, M., 175, 176, 202
Dalman, G., 4, 11, 13, 23, 55, 82, 87, 112, 116, 133, 135, 136, 147, 152, 157, 178, 223, 225, 259
Danby, H., 180
Daube, D., 134
Davies, W. D., 134
Degen, R., 58, 66, 67, 72, 75, 77, 81, 82, 157, 216
Degrassi, A., 48
Deissmann, A., 19, 26, 103, 113, 135, 184, 185
Delcor, M., 141, 176, 177, 179
Derenbourg, J., 25
Descamps, A., 22
Dhorme, E., 94, 180
Díaz Estaban, F., 230
Dibelius, M., 200
Díez Macho, A., 9, 22, 42, 72, 73, 111, 159, 171, 178, 181
Dinkler, E., 136
Diodati, D., 52
Dittenberger, W., 156, 233, 234
Dodd, C. H., 134

Donaldson, J., 134
Donner, H., 24, 202, 234, 236, 239, 240
Dothan, M., 55
Doty, W. G., 19, 26, 201
Draper, H. M., 52
Drijvers, H. J. W., 83
Driver, G. R., 76, 80, 97, 111, 112, 175, 198, 201, 204, 205, 210, 211, 213, 225, 256, 259, 260, 263, 265
Driver, S. R., 25
Dunayevsky, I., 100
Dunphy, W., 140
Dupont, G., 156
Dupont, J., 21
Dupont-Sommer, A., 22, 24, 55, 64, 79, 81, 96, 100, 110, 112, 156, 157, 175, 180, 197, 199, 200, 201, 202, 221, 228, 231, 232, 233, 234, 236, 237, 238, 239, 240, 241, 242, 260
Dussaud, R., 56, 203, 235, 238
Duval, R., 79

Edzard, D. O., 83
Eiss, W., 22
Eissfeldt, O., 135, 235, 237
Eitan, A., 238
Elhorst, H. J., 202
Emerton, J. A., 22, 140
Epstein, J. N., 53, 179, 259, 260
Erichsen, W., 266
Eschlimann, J.-A., 19, 26
Euting, J., 197
Exler, F. X. J., 19, 26

Falk, W., 53
Farzat, H., 260
Fascher, E., 19, 26
Fauth, W., 135
Fecht, G., 250
Ferguson, E., 26
Fernandez Marcos, N., 140
Fiebig, P., 156
Fischer, J. B., 139
Fitzmyer, J. A., 22, 26, 110
Fleisch, H., 78
Fletcher, B., 21
Flusser, D., 96, 112
Foerster, W., 88, 108, 116, 135
Fohrer, G., 79, 175
Franken, H. J., 77, 99
Frankfort, T., 49
Freedman, D. N., 58, 64, 65, 66, 67, 69, 80, 81, 83, 242
Freund, L., 247, 262, 264, 270
Frey, J.-B., 51, 134

Friedrich, J., 77, 78, 82, 234
Fritsch, C. T., 175
Frova, A., 48
Fuller, R. H., 116, 160
Funk, S., 263
Furlani, G., 200

Gabba, E., 49, 51
Gadd, C. J., 113
Galling, K., 234, 242
Garbell, I., 79
Garbini, G., 64, 67, 68, 69, 77, 80, 81, 157, 224
Garrod, H. W., 51
Gatti, F. M., 144
Gauze, J. H., 48
Gelb, I. J., 82
Georgi, D., 135
Geraty, L. T., 47, 100
Gesenius, W., 210
Gibson, J. C. L., 24, 76, 81, 202, 229
Gichon, M., 48
Gingrich, F. W., 13
Ginsberg, H. L., 8, 59, 70, 77, 203, 221, 228, 233, 234, 237, 238, 239, 240, 241, 242, 246, 248, 250, 253, 254, 263, 264, 265, 267
Ginsburger, M., 111
Ginzberg, L., 176
Glanzman, G. S., 135, 141, 158, 181, 225
Glueck, N., 100
Goedicke, H., 269
Goguel, M., 200
Goodspeed, E. J., 15, 25, 39, 50, 53
Goodwin, D. W., 64
Gordon, C. H., 80, 133, 233, 253
Grant, F. C., 142
Grant, R. M., 15
Greenfield, J. C., 8, 24, 70, 74, 76, 77, 82, 84, 108, 160, 175, 178, 179, 202, 225, 226
Greengus, S., 248, 251, 253, 255, 263, 269, 270
Greijdanus, S., 52
Grelot, P., 17, 21, 25, 26, 71, 72, 73, 75, 83, 111, 118, 125, 136, 158, 175, 177, 178, 180, 200, 202, 203, 260
Grenfell, B. P., 138
Grintz, J. M., 22
Grundmann, W., 107
Gutbrod, W., 23

Hadas, M., 139
Haenchen, E., 140
Hahn, F., 88, 90, 115, 120, 133, 134
Halévy, J., 139, 202
Halleux, A. de, 22
Hamilton, R. W., 55

Hammershaimb, E., 202
Hamp, V., 111
Harding, G. L., 175
Harrington, D. J., 22, 55
Harris, Z. S., 80, 136
Hartman, L. F., 133
Hatch, E., 138
Haupt, P., 159
Hay, D. M., 110
Hayes, J. P., 202
Hengel, M., 49, 112, 142
Herr, M. D., 84, 159
Hestrin, R., 54
Hetzron, R., 79
Higgins, A. J. B., 110
Hill, D., 12
Hilprecht, H. V., 228
Hirschfeld, O., 49
Hoffmann, G., 140
Hoftijzer, J., 77, 157, 158, 181, 202, 242, 259
Hommel, H., 141
Horn, S. H., 77, 235, 237, 238, 241, 242, 249
Howard, G., 52, 139
Huffmon, H. B., 82
Hunt, A. S., 137, 138
Hurvitz, A., 22, 141

Isaac, B. H., 48

Jacobi, H., 79
Jacoby, F., 50
James, J. C., 47
Jampel, S., 247, 264, 270
Jastrow, M., 178, 180
Jastrow, O., 78
Jean, C.-F., 157, 158, 181, 242, 259
Jeffery, G., 49
Jellicoe, S., 137
Jenni, E., 83
Jeremias, J., 11, 13, 23, 25, 112, 134, 152, 156, 160
Johns, A. F., 58, 77, 82
Johnson, L., 200
Jones, A. H. M., 49
Jongeling, B., 108, 175, 176
Joüon, P., 133, 205, 206, 207, 208, 210, 211, 214, 215, 216, 251
Joyce, R., 50

Kadman, L., 47
Käsemann, E., 135
Kahle, P., 12, 18, 110, 120, 137, 138, 139, 159, 179, 181
Kamil, M., 76, 77, 197, 202, 203, 260
Kapera, Z. J., 175
Kaplan, J., 100
Katz, P., 139
Kaufman, S., 66, 158, 175, 177, 178
Kautzsch, E. F., 11, 22, 23, 216, 217
Keck, L. E., 23, 52
Kee, H. C., 112
Kenyon, F. G., 138
Kertelge, K., 176
Kilpatrick, G. D., 137
Kim, C.-H., 19, 26
Kingsbury, J. D., 142
Kitchen, K. A., 47, 49, 54, 58
Kittel, G., 134
Kittel, R., 200
Kochavi, M., 100
Koehler, L., 75
Koffmahn, E., 54
Kooij, G. van der, 77
Koopmans, J. J., 11, 23, 75, 81, 234, 237, 239, 240, 242
Koskenniemi, H., 19, 26
Kosmala, H., 177
Kraeling, E. G., 58, 59, 83, 197, 202, 203, 205, 217, 226, 228, 243, 247, 249, 253, 255, 256, 257, 258, 259, 260, 261, 264, 268, 269
Kraft, R. A., 138
Krauss, S., 37, 42, 50, 53
Kropat, A., 47
Kümmel, W. G., 52, 103
Kuhn, K. G., 24, 134, 140
Kutscher, E. Y., 8, 54, 55, 58, 59, 60, 68, 70, 71, 74, 76, 77, 78, 81, 82, 83, 84, 178, 198, 201, 202, 203, 224, 257, 259, 260, 261, 263, 265

Labuschagne, C. J., 108, 176
Lagarde, P. de, 25, 110, 168, 174
Lamadrid, A. G., 178
Lambdin, T. O., 79, 215, 259
Lamer, H., 51
Lanci, M., 25
Landau, Y. H., 50
Landsberger, B., 77
Lapide, P., 22
Lauth, J., 25
Leander, P., 55, 133, 135, 181, 205, 206, 210, 211, 214, 215, 216, 217, 225, 254, 255, 256, 257, 259, 263, 270
Leclant, J., 77
Le Déaut, R., 17, 22, 26, 47, 102, 175, 178, 179, 181
Ledrain, E., 25
Lehmann, M. R., 178

Leivestad, R., 159
Leon, H. J., 35
Letronne, M., 234
Levertoff, P. P., 136
Levi della Vida, G., 82
Levine, L. I., 48
Levy, J., 11
Lidzbarski, M., 178, 199, 200, 225, 247, 253, 257, 258, 260, 270
Liebermann, S., 37, 42
Lietzmann, H., 135, 140, 147, 157
Lifshitz, B., 35, 37, 47, 48, 51, 52, 53, 55, 158
Lightfoot, J., 11
Lindars, B., 140, 156, 159
Lisowsky, G., 180
Littmann, E., 78, 100
Lösch, S., 51
Loewenstamm, S., 253
Lohfink, N., 135
Lohmeyer, E., 118, 135, 136, 200
Lohse, E., 134
Longenecker, R. N., 155
Luckenbill, D. D., 79
Lukyn Williams, A., 138
Lust, J., 135
Lyon, D. C., 240

Macdonald, E., 100
McHardy, W. D., 83, 199, 242
McKenzie, J. L., 51
MacLean, A. J., 79
McLean, N., 139
McNamara, M., 17, 18, 26, 108, 111, 134, 179
Maass, F., 156
Macuch, R., 79
Maddox, R., 155
Mahaffy, J. P., 234
Maier, P. L., 48
Malamat, A., 232, 235, 240, 241, 242
Malina, B., 17, 26
Mangenot, E., 180
Mann, C. S., 21, 24, 52, 200
Marcus, R., 49
Margolis, M. L., 181
Markwart, J., 59
Marlow, R., 155
Marshall, I. H., 136, 142, 155
Marti, K., 216
Martin, R. P., 135, 136
Marty, J., 203
Martyn, J. L., 52
Mazar, B., 6, 11, 22, 47, 99, 100, 159
Medala, S., 175
Ménard, J.-E., 84, 176
Mercati, G., 137, 140
Merx, A., 25, 79
Meshorer, Y., 50
Mesnil du Buisson, R. du, 202
Meyer, A., 2, 11, 21, 23
Meyer, E., 202
Meyer, R., 22, 232, 233, 235, 241, 242
Mez, A., 139
Milik, J. T., 7, 9, 11, 13, 14, 22, 24, 42, 45, 47, 49, 54, 56, 83, 87, 90, 91, 92, 96, 97, 100, 101, 102, 105, 108, 109, 111, 112, 113, 133, 140, 141, 153, 156, 159, 162, 165, 176, 177, 178, 182, 198, 199, 202, 226, 230, 236, 238, 242, 262, 268
Mitchell, T. C., 50
Moloney, F. J., 155
Montgomery, J. A., 210, 211, 212, 217
Moore, G. F., 111
Morag, S., 22
Moran, W. L., 240
Morison, F. (= A. H. Ross), 48
Morrow, F. J., Jr., 176, 177
Moscati, S., 58, 68, 80, 82
Moule, C. F. D., 21, 36, 37, 123, 140, 145, 156
Mueller, C., 50
Müller, C. and T., 234
Müller, H., 78
Müller, W., 242
Muffs, Y., 70, 254, 261, 263, 264, 265
Munck, J., 52
Muraoka, T., 160
Murphy, R. E., 112
Murphy-O'Connor, J., 108

Naveh, J., 76, 77, 80, 99, 100, 108, 140, 158, 202, 230
Negev, A., 48, 49
Nestle, E., 4, 139, 140, 177, 180
Neubauer, A., 23
Nickels, P., 26
Nober, P., 224
Nock, A. D., 110
Nöldeke, T., 78, 79, 82, 239, 251, 252, 254, 259, 261, 264, 265, 267, 268
Nötscher, F., 176
Noth, M., 137, 176, 221, 228, 229, 269
Nougayrol, J., 240

O'Callaghan, J., 47
O'Callaghan, R. T., 79
Odeberg, H., 160
Olami, J., 48
Olmstead, A. T., 15, 25, 53, 179
Oppenheim, A. L., 250

Oren, E., 49
Orfali, G., 51, 55
Ory, J., 55

Palacios, L., 216
Pannacchietti, F. A., 79
Panoussi, E., 79
Pardee, D., 201
Paret, O., 120, 137
Patterson, S. M., 52
Paul, A., 83
Paulus, A., 52
Paulus, H. E. G., 200
Payne, J. B., 50
Payne Smith, R., 225
Peiser, F., 259
Pflaum, H. G., 49
Ploeg, J. van der, 22, 42, 53, 54, 102, 108, 109, 158, 161, 166, 175, 178, 180
Polotsky, H. J., 40, 41, 54, 78
Pope, M. H., 109, 177, 179, 237
Porten, B., 76, 202, 203, 225, 252, 254, 255, 256, 260, 263, 267, 271
Powell, H. H., 78
Preisigke, F., 249
Pritchard, J. B., 79

Quell, G., 108, 116
Quinn, J. D., 242

Rabinowitz, I., 7, 22, 141
Rabinowitz, J. J., 261, 263, 264, 266, 268, 269
Rabinowitz, L. I., 156
Rabinowitz, L. M., 54
Rad, G. von, 113
Rahlfs, A., 179
Ranke, H., 250
Redpath, R. A., 138
Reich, S., 78
Reicke, B., 142
Reider, J., 111, 139, 259, 260
Reisner, G. A., 100
Rengstorf, K., 113
Rhétoré, J., 79
Riccobono, S., 51
Rigaux, B., 22
Rignell, L. J., 182
Ringel, J., 48
Ringgren, H., 176
Ritter, H., 78
Robert, J., 181
Roberts, A., 52
Roberts, B. J., 137, 139, 180
Roberts, C. H., 47, 136
Robertson, A. T., 156
Röllig, W., 24, 77, 234, 236, 239, 240
Roller, O., 19, 26, 201
Rood, L., 52
Rosenthal, E. S., 158
Rosenthal, F., 24, 55, 58, 59, 75, 78, 80, 81, 83, 108, 181, 215, 216, 241
Rowley, H. H., 54, 83, 137
Russel, J. K., 52

Saad, Z., 242
Sabar, Y., 79
Sachau, E., 76, 197, 199, 202, 211, 215, 221
Saller, S. J., 42
Salzmann, M. C., 201
Sanders, J. A., 108, 126, 141
Sandmel, S., 112
Sarfatti, G. B., 48
Sarna, N. M., 176
Saul, D. J., 55
Sayce, A. H., 76, 199, 215, 243, 246, 255, 259, 264, 266, 267, 270
Scaliger, J. J., 3
Schaeder, H. H., 50, 178, 250, 251
Schall, A., 84
Schlatter, A., 138
Schlottmann, K., 25
Schmid, J., 200
Schmitt, J., 51
Schnackenburg, R., 156
Schrenk, G., 134
Schroeder, O., 79
Schubart, W., 136
Schubert, P., 52
Schürer, E., 48, 49, 134
Schulz, S., 88, 109, 110, 131, 137, 138, 140, 176
Schwabe, M., 37, 53, 158, 179
Schwartz, J., 50
Schweizer, E., 88, 116, 119
Schwyzer, E., 79, 84
Segal, J. B., 79, 83
Segal, M. H., 56, 179
Segert, S., 7, 8, 9, 22, 23, 54, 55, 56, 58, 66, 71, 75, 79, 80, 166, 175, 216
Seidl, E., 268
Sevenster, J. N., 5, 19, 34, 37, 38, 50, 52, 183
Seyrig, H., 236
Shaked, S., 175, 178
Shanks, H., 134
Shelton, J. C., 52
Sherwin-White, A. N., 48, 49
Shunnar, Z., 198
Siegel, A., 78
Siegel, J. P., 141
Silverman, M. H., 203

Simon, M., 140
Sjöberg, E., 145, 146, 147, 156, 157, 158, 160
Skehan, P. W., 47, 138, 139, 141, 161, 174, 175
Smalley, S. S., 140
Smend, R., 176
Smith, M., 16, 23, 38, 51, 53
Soden, W. von, 133
Sokoloff, M., 176
Sola-Solé, J., 257
Speiser, E. A., 265
Spitaler, A., 78
Sprengling, M., 260
Staerk, W., 255, 270
Starcky, J., 54, 64, 101, 237
Stauffer, E., 48
Steuernagel, C., 202
Stirewalt, L., 19
Stiehl, R., 22, 55, 81, 198
Strack, H. L., 156, 157, 159, 180, 216
Streck, M., 240
Stecker, G., 132, 136
Strugnell, J., 178
Stuhlmacher, P., 176
Sukenik, E. L., 47, 53, 54, 55, 100, 134
Swete, H. B., 139, 179
Sykutris, J., 201

Tadmor, H., 77
Tallqvist, K., 228, 235
Talmon, S., 108, 202
Taylor, C., 138, 158
Taylor, R. O. P., 52
Taylor, W. R., 51
Tcherikover, V., 49, 53
Telegdi, S., 50
Testa, E., 150
Testuz, M., 101
Thackeray, H. S. J., 51, 139
Thomas, D. W., 83, 199, 232, 242
Thompson, H. O., 100
Thomsen, P., 49, 51
Tondriau, J., 135
Torrey, C. C., 4, 10, 22, 25, 200, 202
Towner, W. S., 25
Toy, C. H., 23
Travers Herford, R., 158
Treu, K., 50
Trever, J. C., 83, 156
Tsevat, M., 65, 81
Tuinstra, E. W., 23, 163, 166, 168, 175, 177
Turner, N., 111, 156

Ungnad, A., 76, 258
Unnik, W. C. van, 21, 200

Vaccari, A., 137
Vardaman, J., 48
Vattioni, F., 83, 100, 157, 176, 242
Vaux, R. de, 23, 49, 112, 178, 182
Verger, A., 266, 269, 271
Vermes, G., 23, 25, 109, 110, 112, 134, 146, 152, 153, 158, 159, 160
Vielhauer, P., 116, 120, 133
Vilnay, Z., 49
Vincent, A., 202
Vinnikov, I. N., 157, 158, 249
Virolleaud, C., 240
Vogt, E., 8, 83, 157, 158, 181, 203, 232, 235, 236, 238, 242
Vogüé, M. de, 197
Volkmann, H., 48
Volterra, E., 250, 251
Voss, I., 49

Wacholder, Z., 108, 175
Waddell, W. G., 137
Wagner, M., 22
Wallis Budge, E. A., 234
Walton, B., 3, 110
Waterman, L., 201
Weber, E., 48
Weber, R., 24
Weidner, E. F., 235, 236
Weill, R., 51
Weinreich, O., 112
Weinreich, U., 82
Weiss, A., 180
Weiss, R., 176
Wellhausen, J., 4
Wendland, P., 135
Wernberg-Møller, P., 176
Wessely, C., 137
Wetter, G. P., 103
White, J. L., 19, 26
Whitehead, J. D., 200
Widengren, G., 110
Widmanstadt, J. A. von, 2
Williger, E., 135
Wilson, R. M., 52
Windisch, H., 52
Winter, P., 111, 179
Wiseman, D. J., 237, 240, 242
Wolfson, H., 139
Wood, L. H., 249
Woude, A. S. van der, 22, 54, 102, 108, 109, 158, 161, 175, 176
Würthwein, E., 137

Yadin, Y., 40, 49, 51, 52, 54, 100, 101, 108, 157, 176, 201, 251
Yamauchi, E. M., 50
Yaron, R., 202, 249, 250, 251, 253, 256, 262, 263, 264, 266, 267, 268, 269, 270, 271
Yeivin, S., 203
Yelnitzky, L. A., 48
York, A. D., 176, 180
Zangmeister, K., 48
Zayadine, F., 100
Zeitlin, S., 53, 134, 203
Zerwick, M., 21, 156
Zimmerli, W., 156
Zucker, F., 242
Zunz, L., 179
Zwaan, J. de, 200

III. INDEX OF SCRIPTURE REFERENCES

Genesis

1:26 152
1:27 152
2:8 137
2:18 137, 152
4:14 152
6:2 104
6:9 162
8:21 152
9:5 152
13:16 157
14:23 265
16:10 138
16:11 138
17:1 139
20:1 96
22:7 135
24:8 253
24:41 24
24:58 253
27:18 135
31:47 6
34:12 247, 253
34:23 11
37:10 97
37:25 222
43:34 256

Exodus

4:22 104
12:42 111
19:13 152
22:16 253
28:4–7 47
29:10 97
29:15 97
29:19 97
34:6 176
40:35 137

Leviticus

1:4 97
3:2 97
3:12 138
4:4 97
4:27 138
16:12–15 165
16:18–21 165
26:2–16 47

Numbers

1:52 251
2:2–3 251
2:10 251
2:17–18 251
2:25 251
2:31 251
2:34 251
3:40–42 47
4:6–9 47
5:17–18 138
5:21 138
9:13 24
23:19 146, 151
26:38 158

Deuteronomy

1:25 138
1:27 138
1:30 138
5:21 152
5:28 141
6:5 121
7:18–19 122
11:21 237
14:1 104
18:5 137
20:19 152
26:5 44
28:7 266
29:19 24
31:27 137
32:3 137
32:6 137
33:11 141
34:6 152

Joshua

10:1 235
10:3 235
12:18 238
13:4 238
15:53 238
19:30 238

Judges

1:31 238
9:18 266
20:5 266

Ruth

2:16 97

1 Samuel

4:1 238
15:13 222
18:17 142
18:25 253
23:21 222
29:1 238

2 Samuel

5:11 158
7:14 104
14:26 254

1 Kings

4:6 235
20:13–14 122
20:26 238
20:30 238

2 Kings

5:11 112
13:14 135
13:17 238
18:26 29, 55, 59
18:28 29, 59
20:12 237
23:21 122
23:23 122
23:24 122
23:29 235
23:31–35 232, 235
24:1 237
24:7 237, 239
24:10–12 232, 237
25:23 269
25:27 237

1 Chronicles

5:24 268
9:7 268

2 Chronicles

9:15 257
35:20 235
35:22 235
36:4 235

Ezra

2:13 235
2:40 268
4:7 47, 55, 250
4:8 188
4:10 193
4:11 188, 189, 190, 191, 193, 198, 235
4:14 171
4:17 190, 191, 193, 198
4:18 47, 188
4:20 209
4:23 180, 188
5:2 238
5:5 188
5:6 188
5:7 190, 198, 210, 211, 213
5:11 226
6:2 188
6:6–12 198, 208
6:17 209
7:1 250
7:12 190, 193, 233
7:12–16 189, 198, 208
7:15 222
7:16 208, 209
7:20 252
7:21 208, 210
7:23 208
7:24 210
7:25 209
7:26 208, 267

Nehemiah

2:10 186
2:19 186
3:3 186
4:1 186
6:1–5 186
6:12 186
6:14 186
8:8 47
13:6 237
13:28 186

Tobit

7:14 246
8:5–6 16
8:15–17 16
13:1–8 16

1 Maccabees

1:11–15 49
13:43 49
13:48 49

Job

1:6 104
2:1 104
3:4–5 165
4:16–5:4 165
6:18–19 222
12:5 182
12:9 109
13:4 182
15:1–21:24 164
16:21 146, 148, 152
17:14 164
21:3 177
22:1–31:40 164
24:19 182
25:6 146, 148, 151, 152, 158
28:1–28 164
28:17 182
29:13 177
29:25 177
30:15 177
30:28 263
32:1–37:24 164
32:10 177
32:17 177
33:28–30 174
34:10 88
34:12 88, 124
34:29 152, 169
34:31 177
35:8 146, 148, 152
35:13 88
36 174
36:32 94
36:33 182
38:1–41:34 164
38:7 104
38:25 182
39:27 95
40:9 94
40:10–11 177
42:1–6 88, 164, 177
42:9–11 88, 164, 166, 170, 177
42:12–17 55, 164, 167

Psalms

2:2 105
2:7 103, 104, 105
8:5 144, 146, 151, 152
22 138
22:2 135
22:15 177
29:1 104

33:2–5 138
69:13 137
69:31–32 137
80:18 146, 151
82:6 104, 106
89:3–4 104
89:6 104
89:26–27 104
89:30 237
89:37 237
91:2 122
91:9 122
92:2 122
92:5–6 122
92:9–10 122
96:7–10 122
96:13 122
97:1 122
97:5 122
97:9 122
97:12 122
102:16–17 122
102:20 122
103:2 122
103:6 122
103:8 122, 176
110:1 90, 141
111:4 176
114:7 126
118:20 142
144:3 152
144:4 152
146:3 146, 151
146:9–10 141
148:1 141
148:7 141
151 125, 141, 142

Proverbs

7:16 256
30:1 22
31:22 99

Wisdom

2:18 105
18:13 104

Sirach

4:10 105
10:7 141
31:8 12
45:15 237
49:9 163
50:27 47

Isaiah

1:2 104
1:24 126
3:1 126
10:33 126
11:11 223
19:4 126
19:9 121
19:18 6, 29
20:6 241
21:13 222
30:1 104
30:3 239
31:3 239
36:11 6, 29, 55, 59
36:13 6, 29, 59
40:3 141
45:23 128, 131
51:12 146, 151
56:2 146, 151

Jeremiah

1:15 223
3:22 104
9:7 257
10:11 6, 256
21:2 237
21:7 237
22:10–12 232
30:9 105
32:12 251
32:21 180
34:1–7 232
36:9–32 232
44:1 224
46:2 237
46:14 224
49:18 146, 151
49:33 146, 151
50:40 146, 151
51:43 146, 151
51:59 251
52:31 237

Jeremy, Epistle of

43–44 47

Ezekiel

1:2 138
2:1 156
2:3 156
3:1 156
3:3–4 156
3:10 156
11:1 138
14 176
14:14 162
16:13 225
26:7 233
29:10 251
30:16 223

Daniel

1:20 256
2:4 43, 134
2:10 208
2:12 209
2:20–23 16
2:24 252
2:26 55
2:29 134
2:30 172, 210
2:31 257
2:35 208
2:37 134, 233
2:38 208, 214
2:39 209
2:40 210, 212
2:41 171
2:44 210
2:45 257
2:47 88, 90, 141, 233, 234
2:48 109, 209
3:1 259
3:2–3 209, 223, 241
3:4 134
3:5 33, 40, 209
3:7 209, 210
3:15 209
3:21 225
3:25 104
3:27 223, 241
3:28–29 208
3:31–33 16, 19, 185, 189, 190, 192, 198, 209, 210
4:1 203
4:3 209

4:6 208
4:7–13 16
4:8–9 209
4:9 211, 212
4:11 267
4:14 172
4:15 209
4:17 209
4:18 211, 212
4:23 252
4:25 210, 211, 212
4:31–32 16, 209
4:34 209
5:7 208
5:8 209
5:19 210
5:20 254
5:22 210
5:23 88, 117, 209
5:25 223
6:2 209
6:4 209
6:5–6 208
6:8 208, 209
6:11 226
6:13 208
6:16 208
6:24 208
6:25–28 16, 185, 192, 198, 203, 209
6:26 210
6:27 209
7:4 157
7:7 210
7:9–10 16, 225
7:13 14, 92, 144, 145, 147, 153, 155
7:13–14 16
7:14 210
7:16 210
7:18 14, 92
7:23–27 16, 209, 210
7:27 210
8:17 146, 152
11:41–44 176

Hosea

2:1 104
2:4 253
11:1 104

Amos

6:4 259

Jonah

4:2 137

Micah

1:1 137
1:2–3 141
1:3 137
4:4 137
5:3 137
5:6 152

Habakkuk

2:2 141
2:13–14 141
2:14 137
2:16 137
2:20 137
3:9 137

Zephaniah

1:3 137
1:14 137

Zechariah

1:3 137
3:3 97
3:5–7 137
8:20 137
9:1 137
9:4 137

Matthew

1:18–23 98
2:15 103
2:16 208
3:17 103
4:3 103
4:6 103
4:15 37
5:11 144, 154
5:33 138
5:44 97
7:6 14
7:16 99
8:2 127
8:6 127
8:8 127
8:20 144
8:25 127
8:29 103
9:6 144
10:23 144
10:32 144, 154
11:19 144
11:25 98, 109
12:8 109, 144
12:32 144
12:40 144
13:37 144
13:41 144
14:30 127, 128
14:33 103
15:5 11, 24
15:27 116, 127
16:13 144, 154
16:16 103
16:21 144
16:27 144
16:28 144
17:5 103
17:9 144
17:12 144
17:22 144
17:24 22
19:28 144
20:18 144
20:28 144, 154
22:16 98
22:41–46 90, 113, 131
24:27 144
24:37 144
24:39 144
24:44 144
25:31 144
26:18 22
26:24 144
26:39 134
26:63 103
26:64 144
27:2–65 48
27:25 263
27:40 103
27:43 103
27:46 93
27:54 103

Mark

1:1 103

1:11 103
2:10 144, 154
2:28 144
3:11 103
3:17 145
3:28 147
5:7 103, 106
5:19 138
5:23 96
6:5 96
7:11 11, 24, 39
7:25 5
7:28 115, 127
7:32 96
7:34 22
8:27 144, 154
8:31 144
8:32–35 96
8:38 131, 144
9:9 144
9:12 144
9:31 144
10:33 144
10:45 144, 154
12:36 90, 131, 141
13:6 21
13:26 131, 144
14:21 144
14:36 134
14:62 144
15:1–44 48
15:39 103
16:18 96

Luke

1:6 138
1:9 138
1:28 138
1:32 39, 91, 103, 162
1:35 39, 91, 103, 162
1:46 138
2:14 93, 111
2:49 179
3:1 48
3:4 98
3:16 21
3:22 103
4:3 103
4:16–30 7, 45
4:25 99
4:40–41 96, 103
5:8 127, 128
5:12 127
5:24 144
6:5 154
6:7 12, 13, 99
6:22 144
6:35 106
6:44 99
6:51 144
7:6 116, 127
7:21 99
7:34 144
8:28 103, 106
9:18 144, 154
9:22 144
9:26 144
9:35 103
9:44 144
9:56 144
9:58 144
10:21 99
10:27 121
11:30 144
12:8 144, 154
12:10 144
12:40 144
13:1 48
13:13 96, 99
16:1–13 24
16:8 145
16:19 99
16:20 149
17:22 144
17:24 144
17:26 144
17:30 144
18:8 144
18:31 144
19:10 144
20:39 131
20:42 90
21:26 144
21:27 144
22:15 99
22:27 144, 154
22:42 134
22:48 144
22:69 144
22:70 103
23:1–52 48
23:38 49
24:7 144

John

1:1 131
1:14 111
1:18 103
1:34 103
1:38 134
1:49 103
1:51 144
3:13 144
3:14 144
3:18 103
4:1 130
4:11 127
5:25 103
5:27 13, 144
6:27 144
6:53 144
6:62 144
7:38 26
8:28 144
9:35 103, 144
10:36 103
11:4 103
11:27 103
12 37
12:23 144
12:34 144
12:36 145
13:31 144
18:29–38 48
19:1–38 48
19:7 103
19:13 31, 43
20:28 130, 131
20:31 103

Acts of the Apostles

2:30 176
3:13 48
3:20 130
4:27 48
5:17 99
6:1 21, 36, 140
6:1–6 119, 123
7:2 99
7:56 144
8:37 103
9:12 96
9:17–18 96
9:20 103
9:29 123, 140

10:10–16 98
11:19 140
13:28 48
13:33 103
15:38 99
18:23 99
19:21 99
20:3 99
22:3 168
25:26 117
26:14 45
28:8 96

Romans

1:1 132
1:3–4 103
1:5 132
1:9 103
4:8 138
4:25 132
5:10 103
8:3 103
8:15 4, 134
8:29 103
8:32 103
9:28–29 138
10:6–8 18
10:9 132
11:34 138
12:17 97
16:14 52
16:26 132

1 Corinthians

1:9 103
6:20 132
8:5–6 117, 118, 130, 136
9:1–2 128
11:23–26 129
12:3 128
16:22 4, 116, 124, 129, 183

2 Corinthians

1:19 103
4:5 132
11:22 4, 21, 124

Galatians

1:10 132
1:16 103
1:18 99
2:20 103
4:4 103
4:6 4, 134, 103, 183

Ephesians

3:5 147
4:13 103
6:7 138

Philippians

1:1 132
2:6–11 118, 125, 128, 130, 131, 132, 135, 136
2:7 136
3:5 4, 21, 37, 124

Colossians

4:12 132

1 Thessalonians

1:10 103
4:15–17 129
5:5 145

2 Thessalonians

2:7 99
3:3 138

1 Timothy

6:13 48

Hebrews

1:5 103
1:8 131
2:6 144
4:14 103
5:5 103
6:6 103
7:3 103
10:29 103

James

1:1 188
5:11 163, 176, 177

1 Peter

1:2 19, 203

2 Peter

1:17 103

1 John

1:3 103
1:7–8 103
3:23 103
4:9–10 103
4:15 103
5:5 103
5:9–13 103
5:20 103

2 John

3 103

Jude

9 99
14 140
15 140

Revelation

1:13 13, 144
2:18 103
3:8 21
7:29 21
12:6 21
13:8 21
14:14 13, 144
20:8 21
22:20 129
